AN INTRODUCTION TO COUNSELLING

Third Edition

AN INTRODUCTION TO COUNSELLING

Third Edition

John McLeod

Open University Press

Open University Press
McGraw-Hill Education
McGraw-Hill House
Shoppenhangers Road
Maidenhead
Berkshire
SL6 2QL

email: enquiries@openup.co.uk
world wide web: www.openup.co.uk

and

Two Penn Plaza
New York, NY 10121-2289, USA

First Published 1993
Reprinted 1994 (twice), 1996 (twice), 1997

Second Edition published 1998
Reprinted 1999, 2000, 2001

First published in this third edition 2003
Reprinted 2003, 2004, 2005 (twice), 2006, 2007, 2008 (twice)

A catalogue record of this book is available from the British Library

ISBN-10   0 335 21189 5 (pb)   0 335 21190 9 (hb)
ISBN-13   978 0 335 21189 0 (pb)   978 0 335 21190 6 (hb)

Library of Congress Cataloging-in-Publication Data
McLeod, John, 1951–
    An introduction to counselling / John McLeod.—3rd ed.
      p. cm.
    Includes bibliographical references (p.) and index.
    ISBN 0-335-21190-9 – ISBN 0-335-21189-5 (pbk.)
    1. Counseling. 1. Title.

  BF637.C6 M379 2003
  361'.06–dc21

                      2002072276

Typeset by Graphicraft Limited, Hong Kong
Printed in Finland by WS Bookwell

For Julia

Contents

2   The cultural and historical origins of counselling   20

3   Counselling theories: diversity and convergence   41

4 Themes and issues in the psychodynamic approach to counselling   78

5 From behaviourism to constructivism: the cognitive–behavioural approach to counselling   122

8   Feminist approaches: the radicalization of counselling   205

9   Narrative approaches to counselling: working with stories   225

16   The organizational context of counselling   416

17   Alternative modes of delivery   434

18   The role of research in counselling and therapy   456

19   The skills and qualities of the effective counsellor   478

Preface

Counselling is an activity that is at the same time simple yet also vastly complicated. What can be simpler than talking to a concerned and interested listener about your problems? But it is what is involved in the telling and listening, knowing and being known, reflecting and acting, that can be so complex. In counselling, people talk about anything and everything. The relationship between the counsellor and the person seeking counsel is simultaneously taking place at a physical, bodily level, and through language, and in the thoughts, feelings and memories of each participant. This is what makes it so complicated, and this is what makes counselling a big topic. Counselling is an interdisciplinary activity, which contains different traditions and schools of thought, and spreads itself across the discourses of theory, research and practice. Counselling has generated a rich and fascinating literature, and a range of powerful theories and research studies. I believe that it is vital for counsellors to be able to find their way around this literature, to tap into all these different knowledges.

Reading a book like this is somewhat similar to looking through a window into a room. In the room there are people doing something, but their world is always on the other side of the glass. Counselling is a practical activity, and can only be grasped through the experience of doing it, as client and counsellor. Real knowledge about counselling can never be gained through reading a book. It requires immersion in an oral tradition, physically being there and doing it and – crucially – *feeling* what is happening, rather than merely looking at words on a page.

Any author knows that what he or she writes does not come freshly minted from their own personal and private thoughts about things, but is in fact an assemblage of words and ideas borrowed from other people. I have been fortunate to be in a position to learn from many people. Among those I would particularly like to thank are a number of generous friends and colleagues who have helped me in many ways: Lynne Angus, Joe Armstrong, Sophia Balamoutsou, Mike Beaney, Tim Bond, Sue Cowan, Robert Elliott, Kim Etherington, Stephen Goss,

Soti Grafanaki, Robin Ion, Janet Johnson, Kate Kirk, Colin Kirkwood, Gordon Lynch, Linda Machin, Moza Al-Malki, Dave Mearns, John Mellor-Clark, Marylou Reid, David Rennie, John Sherry, William West, Sue Wheeler and Val Wosket.

I also thank, in a different way, my wife Julia, who has provided unfailing support and encouragement, and my daughters Kate, Emma and Hannah, who have constantly reminded me of how much else there is to life. I owe them more than I can say.

An introduction to counselling

Introduction

Counselling is a wonderful twentieth-century invention. We live in a complex, busy, changing world. In this world, there are many different types of experience that are difficult for people to cope with. Most of the time, we get on with life, but sometimes we are stopped in our tracks by an event or situation that we do not, at that moment, have the resources to sort out. Most of the time, we find ways of dealing with such problems in living by talking to family, friends, neighbours, priests or our family doctor. But occasionally their advice is not sufficient, or we are too embarrassed or ashamed to tell them what is bothering us, or we just don't have an appropriate person to turn to. Counselling is a really useful option at these moments. In most places, counselling is available fairly quickly, and costs little or nothing. The counsellor does not diagnose or label you, but does his or her best to listen to you and work with you to find the best ways to understand and resolve your problem. For the majority of people, between one and six meetings with a counsellor are sufficient to make a real difference to what was bothering them. These can be precious hours. Where else in our society is there the opportunity to be heard, taken seriously, understood, to have the focused attention of a caring other for hours at a time without being asked to give anything in return?

Being a counsellor is also a satisfying and rewarding work role. There are times when, as a counsellor, you *know* that you have made a profound difference to the life of another human being. It is always a great privilege to be allowed to be a witness and companion to someone who is facing their own worst fears and dilemmas. Being a counsellor is endlessly challenging. There is always more to learn. The role of counsellor lends itself to flexible work arrangements. There are excellent counsellors who are full-time paid staff; others who work for free in the evenings for voluntary agencies; and some who are able sensitively to offer a counselling relationship within other work roles, such as nurse, doctor, clergy, social worker or teacher.

This book is about counselling. It is a book that celebrates the creative simplicity of counselling as a cultural invention which has made a huge contribution to the quality of life of millions of people. But the ordinary elegance of this special type of helping relationship has been transformed into competing 'schools' of therapy, dissected by researchers, and packaged for profit. There is, now, a clutter and clamour of voices making claims for the validity of their own special approach to counselling, or concretizing counselling practice in bureaucratic regulations. The aim of this book is to provide a framework for making sense of all the different aspects of counselling as it exists in contemporary society, while not losing sight of its ordinary simplicity and direct human value.

The focus of this introductory chapter is on describing the different forms that counselling can take. We begin with some stories of people who have used counselling.

Stories of counselling

Paula's story: coming to terms with trauma

Paula had been driving her car. Her friend, Marian, was a passenger. Without any warning they were hit by another vehicle, the car spun down the road, and Paula thought 'this is it'. Following this frightening event, Paula experienced intense flashbacks to the incident. She had nightmares which disturbed her sleep. She became irritable and hypervigilant, always on the alert. She became increasingly detached from her family and friends, and stopped using her car. Paula worked hard at trying to forget the accident, but without success. When she went to see a counsellor, Paula was given some questionnaires to fill in, and he gave her a homework sheet that asked her to write about the incident for ten minutes each day at a fixed time. In the next counselling session, she was asked to dictate an account of the event into a tape recorder, speaking in the first person as if it was happening now. She was told to play the trauma tape over and over again, at home, until she got bored with it. In session 3, the counsellor suggested a way of dealing with her bad dreams, by turning the accident into an imaginary game between two cartoon characters. In session 4 she was invited to remember her positive, pre-accident memories. She was given advice on starting to drive her car again, beginning with a short five-minute drive, then gradually increasing the time behind the wheel. Throughout all this, her counsellor listened carefully to what she had to say, treated her with great respect and was very positive about her prospects for improvement. After nine sessions her symptoms of post-traumatic stress had almost entirely disappeared, and she was able to live her life as before. A fuller account of this case can be found in Scott (1997).

Myra's story: being depressed

Myra Grierson has written a moving and honest account of a time in her life when she was trapped in a deep depression:

> all I knew in that far-off time was a need to go back to some forgotten safe place which I sensed had once existed but had no tangible existence that I could identify. At first I tried to reach it by withdrawing from the world phy-sically and emotionally. I gave up speech and nourishment. I shadowed on the edge of the deep pit of black despair which threatened to swallow me. I flirted with that dark place which vibrated with message, promises of oblivion and an ending to my pain . . . my life was a nightmare of numbness, occasionally punc-tuated by personal loss, depression, hospitalisation and a deep sense of being lost and isolation. I fitted in nowhere and found it hard to live in the world.
>
> (Grierson 1990: 28–9)

She describes a counsellor who met with her over many sessions, and how her relationship with this person enabled her to have a sense of being accepted and to believe that she was a powerful, worthwhile person in her own right.

Matthew's story: everything is getting on top of me

Matthew had a management position in the Health Service. He was 36, had been successful and popular throughout his career and was happily married. He felt trapped in his job, but could not find any way out. He felt depressed, was sleeping badly and reported that his thinking was becoming increasingly muddled. He felt he was spending too much time at work, and felt guilty about putting work ahead of his family. He had started to use drinking and gambling as coping mechanisms. When he completed a set of standardized measures of stress, anxiety and depression at the beginning of counselling, his scores indicated a level of distress usually associated with individuals receiving inpatient treatment for severe mental health problems. Over the course of 16 sessions of psychodynamic counselling, Matthew developed a much fuller understanding of how some of the themes in his own life (for example, his sense of never having been wanted as a child) were linked to his relationships both at work and at home. He became better able to express his needs and emotions, and found ways of delegating and receiving support at work. He reported an enhanced sense of satisfaction and commitment at work, and an improvement in his relationship with his wife. Counselling had not transformed Matthew, or the highly pressurized environment in which he worked, but it had allowed him to stand back from what has happening, look at himself and how he related to others, and find ways of restoring a degree of balance to his life. A complete account of this case can be found in Firth-Cozens (1992).

Laura's story: finding the right counsellor

Laura Allen consulted two counsellors. The first counsellor was a man who sat on a chair that was higher than the one she was directed to ('he would always be the superior one who had to be "looked up to"'). He was 'Dr Parker', and refused to disclose his first name. Throughout their sessions, he made little or no response to her distress and pain. Eventually, he suggested that she might be admitted to a psychiatric hospital. She swore at him and stormed out of the office. Her second counsellor was a woman who was warm, reassuring and motherly, but who avoided any difficult feelings or tears. After a couple of sessions, Laura found that she had started to protect her counsellor by not saying anything that might embarrass her. This counsellor was kind and gentle, but 'nothing much really happened'. These experiences are recounted in Allen (1990).

These are just some of the stories of people who have made use of counselling. They are all true stories, and can be followed up in more detail in the original case reports.

What is counselling?

The case vignettes presented above give some brief examples of what can happen when someone goes to see a counsellor. But what is counselling? What are the ideas and principles that link together the very different experiences of these counselling clients? How can we understand and define counselling?

Counselling is not just something that happens between two people. It is also a social institution that is embedded in the culture of modern industrialized societies.

It is an occupation, discipline or profession of relatively recent origins. In Britain, the Standing Council for the Advancement of Counselling (SCAC) was formed in 1971, and became the British Association for Counselling (BAC) in 1976. The membership of the BAC grew from 1,000 in 1977 to 8,556 in 1992 (BAC 1977, 1992). Renamed the British Association for Counselling and Psychotherapy in 2001, this organization entered the new millennium with over 18,000 members. In the USA the more specialized Division 17 (Counselling Psychology) of the American Psychological Association expanded from 645 members in 1951 to 2695 in 1978 (Whiteley 1984). These figures indicate only the extent of the growth in numbers of more highly trained or professionalized counsellors in these countries. There are, in addition, many people active in voluntary organizations who provide non-professional counselling and who are not represented in these statistics. And the majority of people now working in the 'human service' professions, including nursing, teaching, the clergy, the police and many others, would consider counselling to be part of their work role. Counselling has been a relatively recent addition to the range of 'human service' professions, and its meaning and place within contemporary culture are still evolving.

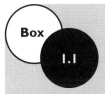

Box 1.1

What is the demand for counselling?

Has the expansion of counselling, in the past 50 years, been sufficient to meet the potential *demand* for counselling? It is very difficult to answer this question, for a variety of reasons. It is hard to measure the amount of counselling that is available within society, and it is probably even harder to estimate the potential demand for counselling. In addition, it seems clear that, as the number of counsellors has expanded, those practitioners with entrepreneurial skills and creativity have been effective in opening up new markets for their services. Thus, the demand for counselling can be seen to expand (to some extent) in line with supply.

There have been several attempts in the USA to estimate the proportion of the population using counselling. Although these studies have tended to use the term 'psychotherapy' to describe the kind of activity that is being surveyed, their definition of psychotherapy encompasses most professional forms of counselling. For example, Olfson and Pincus (1999) carried out an analysis of the National Medical Expenditure Survey of 1987, in terms of psychotherapy use within different sectors of the population. This survey was based on data from 38,000 individuals across the USA, reflecting a representative sample of the population as a whole. Participants in the survey were asked about their use of counselling and psychotherapy in the previous 12 months. It was found that, overall, 3.1 per cent of the sample had made use of therapy in that time period. This average figure concealed important differences between sub-groups, in terms of gender (female 3.6 per cent; male 2.5 per cent), education (those with university degrees 5.4 per cent; those with minimal educational qualifications 1.4 per cent), race (whites 3.4 per cent; blacks 1.4 per cent) and marital status (separated or divorced 6.8 per cent; married 2.7 per cent). However, the rate of psychotherapy use did not vary appreciably across different income levels. These figures probably underestimate the overall use of counselling, because the structure of the interview would have been likely to have predisposed participants to answer largely in terms of counselling/psychotherapy provided in health clinics, therefore omitting counselling delivered in Churches, schools and colleges etc.

It seems likely that the use of counselling is influenced by its accessibility and cost. For example, in workplace counselling services and employee assistance programs (EAPs), where free counselling services are made specifically available for employees of a company or organization, there is an average level of use each year of around 7 per cent (McLeod 2001). In their analysis of uptake of psychotherapy in the USA, Lueger *et al.* (1999) found that fewer than 10 per cent of clients whose therapy was being paid for by insurance cover did not show up for their first session. By contrast, the no-show rate of self-paying clients was 35 per cent. Self-paying clients also used fewer sessions of therapy, compared to those receiving insurance reimbursement.

If the definition of counselling is broadened to include informal counselling by advice workers and health professionals, the estimated proportion of the population receiving counselling increases markedly. The study carried out by Kirkwood (2000) of an island community in Scotland attempted to survey the application of both formal counselling and counselling skills within any kind of recognizable 'counselling' agency. Kirkwood (2000) found that, in one year, 2.15 per cent of the population had received formal counselling, while 23.1 per cent had received help through the use of counselling skills by an advice worker, social worker or health professional. It should be noted that the community studied by Kirkwood (2000) was one in which counselling services had only recently been developed.

How large is the potential demand for counselling? Research carried out by Goldberg and Huxley (1992) in Britain suggests that around 10 per cent of the population are known to their GP as suffering from a recognized mental health problem, with around 28 per cent of the general population in the community experiencing significant levels of mental health distress. Of course, not all the cases identified in the Goldberg and Huxley (1992) research would necessarily have problems that would be suitable for counselling, and among those who did have problems that could be helped through counselling, many might not perceive it as credible or valid for them individually.

Another means of estimating the demand for counselling and other psychological therapies is to monitor waiting times. It is hard to find published studies of waiting times for therapy in Britain. However, it is not uncommon for NHS specialist psychotherapy services to have waiting times of over 12 months, or for voluntary sector counselling agencies to decide to close their waiting lists as a means of controlling demand.

It seems reasonable to conclude, therefore, that the annual uptake of counselling and psychotherapy, narrowly defined, in Western industrialized societies is in the region of 4 per cent of the adult population per annum, with an unknown additional percentage wishing to use counselling but unable to gain access to services because of cost, waiting times and other obstacles.

Defining counselling

These are some definitions of 'counselling' formulated by professional bodies and leading figures in the field:

> The term 'counselling' includes work with individuals and with relationships which may be developmental, crisis support, psychotherapeutic, guiding or problem solving . . . The task of counselling is to give the 'client' an opportunity to explore, discover and clarify ways of living more satisfyingly and resourcefully.
>
> (BAC 1984)

> Counselling denotes a professional relationship between a trained counsellor and a client. This relationship is usually person-to-person, although it may sometimes involve more than two people. It is designed to help clients to understand and clarify their views of their lifespace, and to learn to reach their self-determined goals through meaningful, well-informed choices and through resolution of problems of an emotional or interpersonal nature.
>
> (Burks and Stefflre 1979: 14)

> a principled relationship characterised by the application of one or more psychological theories and a recognised set of communication skills, modified by experience, intuition and other interpersonal factors, to clients' intimate concerns, problems or aspirations. Its predominant ethos is one of facilitation rather than of advice-giving or coercion. It may be of very brief or long duration, take place in an organisational or private practice setting and may or may not overlap with practical, medical and other matters of personal welfare. It is both a distinctive activity undertaken by people agreeing to occupy the roles of counsellor and client . . . and an emerging profession . . . It is a service sought by people in distress or in some degree of confusion who wish to discuss and resolve these in a relationship which is more disciplined and confidential than friendship, and perhaps less stigmatising than helping relationships offered in traditional medical or psychiatric settings.
>
> (Feltham and Dryden 1993: 6)

It can be seen from these definitions that counselling can have different meanings. For example, Burks and Stefflre (1979) stress the idea of the 'professional' relationship, and the importance of 'self-determined' goals. The BAC definition places emphasis on exploration and understanding rather than action. Feltham and Dryden (1993) highlight the areas of overlap between counselling and other forms of helping, such as nursing, social work and even everyday friendship. The existence of such contrasting interpretations and definitions arises from the process by which counselling has emerged within modern society. Counselling evolved and changed rapidly during the twentieth century, and contains within it a variety of different themes, emphases, practices and schools of thought. In Chapter 2, the cultural and historical context that lies behind these definitions is examined in detail. It is important to be aware that the definitions of counselling listed here share one important feature in common: they are framed from the point of view of the *counsellor*. What this means is that they largely reflect the aim of professional bodies to establish counselling as a professional specialism within contemporary society. It can be argued that 'counselling' is a term in everyday use, and as such carries meanings that transcend such 'professionalized' definitions. At the conclusion of this chapter, an 'everyday' or 'user-oriented' definition of counselling is offered.

The relationship between counselling and psychotherapy

Counselling is provided under a variety of different labels. To employ a metaphor from the world of business, there are a range of competing products that offer the consumer or client more or less the same service. The upmarket version of the product is sold as 'psychotherapy', which is provided by practitioners who are usually very highly trained specialist professionals, often with a background in medicine. Psychotherapy can be a lengthy process. Although there is an increasing interest in forms of 'brief' psychotherapy, which may consist of a series of ten or twelve sessions, it is probably fair to say that most psychotherapists would consider it necessary for clients to be in treatment for a year or more for beneficial results to occur. The most expensive and exclusive version of psychotherapy remains classical Freudian psychoanalysis.

There has been considerable debate over the difference between counselling and psychotherapy. Some would claim that a clear distinction can be made between the two, with psychotherapy representing a deeper, more fundamental or involved process of change with more disturbed clients. Others maintain that counsellors and psychotherapists are basically doing the same kind of work, using identical approaches and techniques, but are required to use different titles in response to the demands of the agencies that employ them. For example, traditionally psychotherapy has been the term used in medical settings such as psychiatric units, and counselling the designation for people working in educational settings such as student counselling centres. One significant difference between counselling and psychotherapy is that much counselling is conducted by non-professional volunteer workers, whereas psychotherapy is an exclusively professional occupation. However, both counselling and psychotherapy can be viewed as activities distinct from advice-giving, caring and teaching.

Counselling and other helping professions

There are several other occupational titles that refer to people who are practising counselling. A term that is widely used is *counselling psychologist*. This refers to a counsellor who has initial training in psychology, and who uses psychological methods and models in his or her approach. This label explicitly imports the language of science into counselling, by associating it with a specific scientific discipline. There are also several labels that refer to counsellors who work with particular client groups: for example, *mental health counsellor, marriage counsellor* or *student counsellor*. The distinctive feature of these practitioners is that they will possess specialist training and expertise in their particular field in addition to a general counselling training.

There are also many instances where counselling is offered in the context of a relationship that is primarily focused on other, non-counselling concerns. For example, a student may use a teacher as a person with whom it is safe to share worries and anxieties. A community nurse may visit a home to give medical care to a patient who is terminally ill, but finds herself giving emotional support to the spouse. In these situations it seems appropriate to see what is happening as being a teacher or nurse using counselling skills rather than engaging in an actual counselling relationship. They are counselling, but not being counsellors. This is a useful distinction to make, because it reserves 'counselling' (or 'psychotherapy') for situations where there is a formal counselling contract and the counsellor has no other role in relation to the client. However, there are many situations where it can become difficult to draw a line between counselling and the use of counselling skills. The nurse in the example above, for instance, might be able to work with the spouse in a counselling mode over a fairly lengthy period, and anyone listening to a tape recording of their sessions might be unable to tell the difference between what the nurse was doing and what a trained bereavement counsellor would have done. From the point of view of the client or patient, what he or she is looking for, and receives, is a counselling relationship, which for them serves exactly the same function as going to see a professional therapist in a consulting room.

It is probably not helpful to draw rigid lines of professional demarcation which deny that teachers, nurses, probation officers or social workers can ever be counsellors to their clients. Nevertheless, it is also important to recognize that clients can become confused, or damaged, when the people who are trying to help them become enmeshed in role conflicts through attempting to be counsellor as well as, for instance, teacher or nurse. This issue is discussed further in Chapter 10. It can also be damaging for both client and worker if the counselling process moves into areas beyond the training or competence of the helper. The difficulties involved in making clear distinctions between counselling proper and the use of counselling skills have been a matter of much debate (see Bond 1989).

Even more difficult to define, as varieties of counselling and psychotherapy, are hypnotherapy and a whole range of activities in the area of healing. The use of hypnosis as a means of helping people with emotional or behavioural difficulties can be traced back to the eighteenth century. For a variety of reasons, however, hypnosis has never been accepted as part of the mainstream of psychotherapeutic or counselling thinking. Certainly, the training that most people who call themselves 'hypnotherapists' have had would tend not to be recognized or accepted by the main professional bodies in counselling or psychotherapy. Similarly, healing approaches, which may involve techniques such as meditation, prayer and the use of massage and herbal remedies, have generally been regarded as outside mainstream counselling. The theoretical basis and practical techniques associated with both hypnotherapy and healing do not, currently, fit readily into the ways that most counsellors and psychotherapists think and work, although many counsellors are interested in these perspectives and there have been many attempts to bridge this gap (Sheikh and Sheikh 1989; Graham 1990; Sollod 1993).

To summarize, it can be seen that it is no easy matter to define counselling. In some respects this can be frustrating for people seeking counselling, because it means that there are many situations in which it can be hard for them to know exactly what is on offer when they consult someone who labels himself or herself as a 'counsellor'. On the other hand, the fact that counselling has been, and continues to be, influenced and shaped by so many different traditions and helping approaches gives it a great deal of its vitality and energy. The whole question of 'what is counselling?' is discussed very fully by Feltham (1995).

The diversity of theory and practice in counselling

Karasu (1986) reported having come across more than 400 distinct models of counselling and psychotherapy. The fact that this whole field of study is of relatively recent origin means that there has not yet been time for the explosion of new ideas that appeared between 1950 and 1970 to have become integrated into a unified approach. There is some evidence of the emergence of a strong trend towards integration and unification of approaches in the 1980s (see Chapter 6). However, despite the movement in favour of theoretical unification and integration, it is widely recognized that the three 'core' approaches of psychodynamic, cognitive–behavioural and humanistic (see Chapters 3, 4 and 5) represent fundamentally different ways of viewing human beings and their emotional and behavioural problems.

There also exists a wide diversity in counselling practice, with counselling being delivered through one-to-one contact, in groups, with couples and families, over the telephone and even through written materials such as books and self-help manuals.

The mix of cultural, economic and social forces that contributed to the emergence of a multiplicity of counselling theories has also given rise to a wide diversity of settings where counselling is practised and client groups at whom it is targeted. There are, for example, many counselling agencies that are funded by, or attached to, organizations that have a primary task of providing medical and health care. These range from mental health/psychiatric settings, which typically deal with highly disturbed or damaged clients, through to counselling available in primary care settings, such as GP surgeries, and from community nurses. There has been a growth in specialist counselling directed towards people with particular medical conditions such as AIDS, cancer and various genetic disorders. Counselling has also played an important role in many centres and clinics offering alternative or complementary health approaches. One of the primary cultural locations for counselling and psychotherapy can therefore be seen to be alongside medicine. Even when counsellors and counselling agencies work independently of medical organizations, they will frequently establish some form of liaison with medical and psychiatric services, to enable referral of clients who may require medical or nursing care.

Counselling also has a place in the world of work. A variety of counselling agencies exist for the purpose of helping people through difficulties, dilemmas or anxieties concerning their work role. These agencies include vocational guidance, student counselling services and employee assistance programmes or workplace counselling provided by large organizations in industry and the public sector. Whether the work role is that of executive, postal worker or college student, counsellors are able to offer help with stress and anxiety arising from the work, coping with change and making career decisions.

There is yet another whole section of counselling practice that is not primarily focused on arriving at solutions to problems, but is instead directed towards the exploration of meaning and the expansion of awareness. This kind of counselling is strongly represented in private practice and 'growth centres'.

A number of counselling agencies have evolved to meet the needs of people who experience traumatic or sudden interruptions to their life development and social roles. Prominent among these are agencies and organizations offering counselling in such areas as marital breakdown, rape and bereavement. The work of the counsellor in these agencies can very clearly be seen as arising from social problems. For example, changing social perceptions of marriage, redefinitions of male and female roles, new patterns of marriage and family life, and legislation making divorce more available represent major social and cultural changes of the past century. Counselling provides a way of helping individuals to negotiate this changing social landscape.

A further field of counselling activity lies in the area of addictions. There exists a range of counselling approaches developed to help people with problems related to drug and alcohol abuse, food addiction and smoking cessation. The social role of the counsellor can be seen particularly clearly in this type of work. In some areas of addiction counselling, such as with hard drug users, counsellors operate alongside a set of powerful legal constraints and moral judgements. The possession and use of heroin, for example, is seen by most people as morally wrong, and has been made a criminal offence. The counsellor working with a heroin addict, therefore, is not merely exploring 'ways of living more satisfyingly and resourcefully' (BAC 1984), but is mediating between competing social definitions of what an acceptable 'way of living' entails. In other fields of addiction counselling, such as food, alcohol and cigarette abuse, the behaviour in question is heavily reinforced by advertising paid for by the slimming, drink and tobacco industries. The incidence of alcohol- and smoking-related diseases would be more effectively reduced by tax increases than by increases in the number of counsellors, an insight that raises questions about the role of counselling in relation to other means of control of behaviour.

The range and diversity of counselling settings is explored in more detail in Woolfe *et al.* (2002) and Palmer and McMahon (2000). It is important to acknowledge that counselling is not merely a process of individual learning. It is also a social activity that has a social meaning, Often, people turn to counselling at a point of transition, such as the transition from child to adult, married to divorced, addict to straight. Counselling is also a culturally sanctioned means of enabling adaptation to social institutions. Counsellors are rarely managers or executives who hold power in colleges, businesses or communities. Counsellors, instead, have a more 'liminal' role, being employed at the edge of these institutions to deal with those in danger of falling off or falling out.

The aims of counselling

Underpinning the diversity of theoretical models and social purposes discussed above are a variety of ideas about the aims of counselling and therapy. Some of the different aims that are espoused either explicitly or implicitly by counsellors are listed:

- *Insight.* The acquisition of an understanding of the origins and development of emotional difficulties, leading to an increased capacity to take rational control over feelings and actions (Freud: 'where id was, shall ego be').
- *Relating with others.* Becoming better able to form and maintain meaningful and satisfying relationships with other people: for example, within the family or workplace.
- *Self-awareness.* Becoming more aware of thoughts and feelings that had been blocked off or denied, or developing a more accurate sense of how self is perceived by others.
- *Self-acceptance.* The development of a positive attitude towards self, marked by an ability to acknowledge areas of experience that had been the subject of self-criticism and rejection.
- *Self-actualization or individuation.* Moving in the direction of fulfilling potential or achieving an integration of previously conflicting parts of self.
- *Enlightenment.* Assisting the client to arrive at a higher state of spiritual awakening.
- *Problem-solving.* Finding a solution to a specific problem that the client had not been able to resolve alone. Acquiring a general competence in problem-solving.
- *Psychological education.* Enabling the client to acquire ideas and techniques with which to understand and control behaviour.
- *Acquisition of social skills.* Learning and mastering social and interpersonal skills such as maintenance of eye contact, turn-taking in conversations, assertiveness or anger control.

- *Cognitive change*. The modification or replacement of irrational beliefs or maladaptive thought patterns associated with self-destructive behaviour.
- *Behaviour change*. The modification or replacement of maladaptive or self-destructive patterns of behaviour.
- *Systemic change*. Introducing change into the way in that social systems (e.g. families) operate.
- *Empowerment*. Working on skills, awareness and knowledge that will enable the client to take control of his or her own life.
- *Restitution*. Helping the client to make amends for previous destructive behaviour.
- *Generativity and social action*. Inspiring in the person a desire and capacity to care for others and pass on knowledge (generativity) and to contribute to the collective good through political engagement and community work.

It is unlikely that any one counsellor or counselling agency would attempt to achieve the objectives underlying all the aims in this list. On the whole, psychodynamic counsellors have focused primarily on insight, humanistic practitioners have aimed to promote self-acceptance and personal freedom, and cognitive–behavioural therapists have been mainly concerned with the management and control of behaviour. However, any valid counselling approach should be flexible enough to make it possible for the client to use the therapeutic relationship as an arena for exploring whatever dimension of life is most relevant to their well-being at that point in time.

Counselling as an interdisciplinary area of study

Although counselling and psychotherapy initially emerged from within the discipline of psychiatry, in more recent times they have come to be regarded as applied sub-branches of the academic discipline of psychology. In some European countries, holding a psychology degree is necessary to enter training in psychotherapy. In the USA, and increasingly in Britain, the term counselling psychology is widely used. Psychology textbooks give substantial coverage to the work of psychotherapists like Freud, Rogers and Wolpe. Being located in psychiatry and psychology has given counselling and psychotherapy the status of an applied science. However, despite the enormous value of psychological perspectives within counselling practice, it is essential to acknowledge that other academic disciplines are also actively involved.

Some of the most important ideas in counselling and psychotherapy have originated in philosophy. The concept of the 'unconscious' had been used in nineteenth-century philosophy (Ellenberger 1970) some time before Freud began to use it in his theory. The concepts of phenomenology and authenticity had been developed by existential philosophers such as Heidegger and Husserl long before they influenced Rogers, Perls and other humanistic therapists. The field of moral

> Philosophical approaches to counselling are discussed in detail in Chapter 11

philosophy also makes an input into counselling, by offering a framework for making sense of ethical issues (see Chapter 15).

Another field of study that has a strong influence on counselling theory and practice is religion. Several counselling agencies have either begun their life as branches of the church or been helped into existence by founders with a religious calling. Many of the key figures in the history of counselling and psychotherapy have had strong religious backgrounds, and have attempted to integrate the work of the counsellor with the search for spiritual meaning. Jung has made the most significant contribution in this area. Although the field of counselling is permeated with Judaeo-Christian thought and belief, there is increasing interest among some counsellors in the relevance of ideas and practices from other religions, such as Zen Buddhism (Suzuki *et al.* 1970; Ramaswami and Sheikh 1989).

A third sphere of intellectual activity that continues to exert a strong influence on counselling is the arts. There is a strong tradition in counselling and psychotherapy of using methods and techniques from drama, sculpture, dance and the visual arts to enable clients to give expression to their feelings and relationship patterns. In recent years psychodrama and art therapy have become well established specialist counselling approaches, with their own distinctive theoretical models, training courses and professional journals. There has similarly been valuable contact between counselling and literature, primarily through an appreciation that language is the main vehicle for therapeutic work, and that poets, novelists and literary critics have a great deal to say about the use of language. Specific literature-based techniques have also been employed in counselling, such as autobiography, journal writing, poetry writing and bibliotherapy.

Counselling is in many respects an unusual area of practice in that it encompasses a set of strongly competing theoretical perspectives, a wide range of practical applications and meaningful inputs from a number of contributing disciplines. Thorne and Dryden (1993) have edited a collection of biographical essays written by counsellors on the ways in which they have used early training in disciplines such as ecology, theology and social anthropology to inform their counselling practice. The field of counselling and psychotherapy represents a synthesis of ideas from science, philosophy, religion and the arts. It is an interdisciplinary area that cannot appropriately be incorporated or subsumed into any one of its constituent disciplines. An approach to counselling that was, for example, purely scientific or purely religious in nature would soon be seen not to be counselling at all, in its denial of key areas of client and practitioner experience.

A user-centred definition of counselling

Previous sections of this chapter have introduced some of the more widely adopted definitions of counselling, and have highlighted the complex ways in which counselling is located within contemporary society. However, while it is important to be able to appreciate the diversity that exists within counselling theory and practice, and the various ideas, values and traditions that have been emphasized within the literature on counselling, there is also a danger in getting lost in complexity, and losing sight of the essential simplicity of counselling. This book seeks to offer an introduction to counselling that will allow those who read it to appreciate not only what is common to all approaches to counselling, but also the value of specific approaches.

One of the essential common features of all counselling is that it can only happen if the person seeking help, the client, wants it to happen. Counselling takes place when someone who is troubled invites and allows another person to enter into a particular kind of relationship with them. If a person is not ready to extend this invitation, they may be exposed to the best efforts of expert counsellors for long periods of time, but what will happen will not be counselling.

Counselling must also be understood within its social and cultural context: 'counsellor' and 'client' are social roles, and the ways in which participants make sense of the aims and work of counselling are shaped by the culture within which they live. How many of us have grandparents who were counsellors or psycho-therapists, or who would even have known what a counsellor or therapist did? In many ways, counselling is a product of late twentieth-century modernity (see Chapter 2).

The remaining chapters of this book are informed by a user-centred, socially oriented understanding of counselling. This way of making sense of counselling begins with the wish or intention of the 'client', and can be summarized in the following terms:

- Counselling is an activity that takes place when someone who is troubled invites and allows another person to enter into a particular kind of relationship with them.
- A person seeks such a relationship when they encounter a 'problem in living' that they have not been able to resolve through their everyday resources, and that has resulted in their exclusion from some aspect of full participation in social life.
- The person seeking counselling invites another person to provide him or her with time and space characterized by the presence of a number of features that are not readily available in everyday life: permission to speak, respect for differ-ence, confidentiality and affirmation.
- *Permission to speak.* This is a place where the person can tell their story, where they are given every encouragement to give voice to aspects of their experience that have previously been silenced, in their own time and their own way, including the expression of feeling and emotion.
- *Respect for difference.* The counsellor sets aside, as far as they are able, their own position on the issues brought by the client, and his or her needs in the moment, in order to focus as completely as possible on helping the client to articulate and act on his or her personal values and desires.
- *Confidentiality.* Whatever is discussed is confidential: the counsellor undertakes to refrain from passing on what they have learned from the person to any others in the person's life world.

- *Affirmation.* The counsellor enacts a relationship that is an expression of a set of core values: honesty, integrity, care, belief in the worth and value of individual persons, commitment to dialogue and collaboration, reflexivity, the interdependence of persons, a sense of the common good.

These are simple principles, but taken together represent an arena for support, reflection and renewal that is distinctive within modern societies. Within this arena, the client and counsellor make use of whatever cultural resources come to hand (conversation, ideas, theories, rituals, altered states of consciousness, problem-solving algorithms, discourses, technologies) to achieve a satisfactory resolution of the initial problem in living that initiated the decision to engage in counselling.

The potential outcomes of counselling can be understood as falling into three broad categories:

1 *Resolution* of the original problem in living. Resolution can include: achieving an understanding or perspective on the problem, arriving at a personal acceptance of the problem or dilemma and taking action to change the situation in which the problem arose.
2 *Learning.* Engagement with counselling may enable the person to acquire new understandings, skills and strategies that make them better able to handle similar problems in future.
3 *Social inclusion.* Counselling stimulates the energy and capacity of the person as someone who can contribute to the well-being of others and the social good.

Conclusions

The aim of this chapter has been to provide an image of the complex mosaic of contemporary counselling practice. It is a depiction of counselling at a particular point in time, and there is no doubt that a similar survey carried out 20 or 30 years in the future would be quite different. The current picture may, on the surface, look fragmented and confused. Nevertheless, there is a unifying theme behind the multiplicity of theories and areas of application. Counselling is an activity that emerged within Western industrial society in the twentieth century as a means of buffering and protecting the individual in the face of the demands of large bureaucratic institutions. Counselling has for many people largely taken over the role in society once filled by religion and community life. In a mass urban society, counselling offers a way of being known and being heard.

The origins of counselling in a set of cultural and historical processes are the topic of the next chapter. In later chapters, some approaches to counselling – feminist, multicultural, systemic, narrative – are introduced that are edging beyond individualism, and moving in the direction of locating the person much more as a member of a culture.

Chapter summary

- Counselling is a form of helping that is focused on the needs and goals of the person.

- The popularity of counselling reflects the strain and fragmentation of life in contemporary society.

- There exist many definitions of counselling, each of which emphasizes different aspects of the counselling role and process.

- Counselling is similar to, and also different from, other forms of helping, such as psychotherapy, social work and psychiatric nursing.

- There are many competing theories of counselling, and a variety of settings for counselling practice.

- The diversity of counselling is also reflected in its roots in disciplines such as philosophy, religion and the arts, as well as psychology and psychiatry.

- The diversity and heterogeneity of counselling can be seen as a strength, reflecting the sensitivity of counselling to the enormous variations in human experience.

- The common elements within the great diversity of counselling provision can best be understood by defining counselling from a socially oriented, user-focused perspective.

Topics for reflection and discussion

1 Read through the definitions of counselling presented in this chapter. Do they capture the meaning of counselling, as you understand it? What might you wish to add to these definitions, or delete? How might these definitions come across to you if you were someone in extreme need of emotional help and support? How might they come across if you were a member of an ethnic minority group, were gay or lesbian, or disabled (in other words, not part of the dominant cultural way of looking at things)?

2 Feltham (1995: 163) has suggested that: 'a sharp distinction needs to be made . . . between counselling and therapy as a kind of personal growth hobby ('recreational therapeutics'), a substitute religious confessional, and counselling as a state-funded or state-regulated health profession which responds to

urgent mental health problems. There may well be a legitimate place for forms of freely chosen personal growth therapies, but it is difficult to see how the state could (or whether it should) fund these.' Do you agree? How clear is the distinction between 'recreational therapeutics' and counselling as a health profession?

3 Most writing and theorizing about counselling is from a psychological perspective. To gain an appreciation of the extent to which other disciplines can illuminate counselling, take a knowledge discipline that you are familar with, and apply it to counselling. For example, think through what might be involved in an economic, architectural, sociological, biological or management perspective on counselling.

4 Make a list of all the different settings in which counselling is applied. Can you categorize these into different types of setting? Are there any potential areas of application of counselling that are not included? If you have read later chapters on different counselling approaches, think about which theoretical approaches are best suited to each specific setting.

5 Generate a list of all the different forms of 'counselling', defined as widely as possible, that are available in the city or community where you live. Identify the groups of people who are most likely to use each service. What does this tell you about the links between counselling and social class, age, gender and ethnicity?

6 Imagine that you are someone seeking help for an emotional or psychological difficulty in your life. You look up a directory of health providers, or consult the Yellow Pages, and discover that there are several different types of help on offer: counselling, counselling psychology, psychotherapy, spiritual healing, a personal growth centre and so on. What are the contrasting images and expectations that each of these labels evokes in you?

Key terms and concepts

addiction	humanistic approach
art therapy	hypnotherapy
authenticity	phenomenology
cognitive-behavioural approach	private practice
counselling	psychodrama
counselling agencies	psychodynamic approach
counselling psychologist	psychotherapy
counselling skills	spirituality
healing	unconscious
human services professions	

Suggested further reading

This chapter is intended to introduce the general issues and topics that weave through subsequent chapters, so in a sense the further reading is the remainder of the book. However, many of the specific issues raised in this chapter are discussed in more depth and with great insight in *What Is Counselling?* by Colin Feltham (1995).

The writer who has perhaps been most successful in capturing what counselling or psychotherapy feels like (at least from the perspective of the practitioner) is Irving Yalom. His book *Love's Executioner and Other Tales of Psychotherapy* (Yalom 1989) is an international best-seller and contains a series of sensitive portraits of his encounters with clients. Howe (1993) offers a unique overview of the actual experience of being a client.

A central theme of this chapter has been the great diversity of current counselling theory and practice. Some of the flavour of this (sometimes almost overwhelming) diversity is captured in journals such as *Counselling and Psychotherapy Journal* and the *Journal of Counseling and Development*. The former is a British publication, while the latter is American. Useful collections of papers from the *Counselling and Psychotherapy Journal* have been compiled by Milner and Palmer (2001) and Palmer (2001).

2 The cultural and historical origins of counselling

Introduction

To understand the diversity of contemporary counselling, and to appreciate the significance of the current patterns of practice described in the previous chapter, it is necessary to look at the ways in which counselling has developed and evolved over the past 200 years. The differences and contradictions that exist within present-day counselling have their origins in the social and historical forces that have shaped modern culture as a whole.

People in all societies, at all times, have experienced emotional or psychological distress and behavioural problems. In each culture there have been well established indigenous ways of helping people to deal with these difficulties. The Iroquois Indians, for example, believed that one of the causes of ill-health was the existence of unfulfilled wishes, some of which were only revealed in dreams

(Wallace 1958). When someone became ill and no other cause could be determined, diviners would discover what his or her unconscious wishes were, and arrange a 'festival of dreams' at which other members of the community would give these objects to the sick person. There seems little reason to suppose that modern-day counselling is any more valid, or effective, than the Iroquois festival of dreams. The most that can be said is that it is seen as valid, relevant or effective by people in this culture at this time.

The emergence of the 'trade in lunacy'

Although counselling and psychotherapy only become widely available to people during the second half of the twentieth century, their origins can be traced back to the beginning of the eighteenth century, which represents a turning point in the way that society responded to the needs of people who had problems in their lives. Before this, the problems in living that people encountered were primarily dealt with from a religious perspective, implemented at the level of the local community (McNeill 1951; Neugebauer 1978, 1979). In Europe the vast majority of people lived in small rural communities and were employed on the land. Within this way of life, anyone who was seriously disturbed or insane was tolerated as part of the community. Less extreme forms of emotional or interpersonal problems were dealt with by the local priest: for example, through the Catholic confessional. McNeill (1951) refers to this ancient tradition of religious healing as 'the cure of souls'. An important element in the cure of souls was confession of sins followed by repentance. McNeill (1951) points out that in earlier times confession of sins took place in public, and was often accompanied by communal admonishment, prayer and even excommunication. The earlier Christian rituals for helping troubled souls were, like the Iroquois festival of dreams, communal affairs. Only later did individual private confession become established. McNeill (1951) gives many examples of clergy in the sixteenth and seventeenth centuries acting in a counselling role to their parishioners.

As writers such as Foucault (1967), Rothman (1971), Scull (1979, 1981b, 1989) and Porter (1985) have pointed out, all this began to change as the Industrial Revolution took effect, as capitalism began to dominate economic and political life, and as the values of science began to replace those of religion. The fundamental changes in social structure and in social and economic life that took place at this point in history were accompanied by basic changes in relationships and in the ways people defined and dealt with emotional and psychological needs. Albee (1977: 154) has written that:

> Capitalism required the development of a high level of rationality accompanied by repression and control of pleasure seeking. This meant the strict control of impulses and the development of a work ethic in which a majority of persons derived a high degree of satisfaction from hard work. Capitalism also demanded

personal efforts to achieve long-range goals, an increase in personal autonomy and independence . . . The system depended on a heavy emphasis on thrift and ingenuity and, above all else, on the strong control and repression of sexuality.

The key psychological shift that occurred, according to Albee (1977), was from a 'tradition-centred' (Riesman *et al.* 1950) society to one in which 'inner direction' was emphasized. In traditional cultures, people live in relatively small communities in which everyone knows everyone else, and behaviour is monitored and controlled by others. There is direct observation of what people do, and direct action taken to deal with social deviance through scorn or exclusion. The basis for social control is the induction of feelings of shame. In urban, industrial societies, on the other hand, life is much more anonymous, and social control must be implemented through internalized norms and regulations, which result in guilt if defied. From this analysis, it is possible to see how the central elements of urban, industrial, capitalist culture create the conditions for the development of a means of help, guidance and support that addresses confusions and dilemmas experienced in the personal, individual, inner life of the person. The form which that help took, however, was shaped by other events and processes.

The historical account pieced together by Scull (1979) indicates that during the years 1800–90 the proportion of the population of England and Wales living in towns larger than 20,000 inhabitants increased from 17 to 54 per cent. People were leaving the land to come to the city to work in the new factories. Even on the land, the work became more mechanized and profit-oriented. These large-scale economic and social changes had profound implications for all disadvantaged or handicapped members of society. Previously there had been the slow pace of rural life, the availability of family members working at home and the existence of tasks that could be performed by even the least able. Now there was the discipline of the machine, long hours in the factory and the fragmentation of the communities and family networks that had taken care of the old, sick, poor and insane. There very quickly grew up, from necessity, a system of state provision for these non-productive members of the population, known as the workhouse system. Inmates of workhouses were made to work, under conditions of strict discipline. It soon became apparent that the insane were difficult to control and disruptive of the workhouse regime. As one workhouse report from 1750 put it,

> The law has made no particular provision for lunaticks and it must be allowed that the common parish workhouse (the inhabitants of which are mostly aged and infirm people) are very unfit places for the reception of such ungovernable and mischievous persons, who necessarily require separate apartments.
>
> (Cited in Scull 1979: 41)

Gradually these separate apartments, the asylums, began to be built, beginning slowly in the middle of the eighteenth century and given further encouragement by the 1845 Asylums Act, which compelled local justices to set up publicly run asylums. This development marked the first systematic involvement of the state in the care and control of the insane in European society. At first, the asylums were seen as places where lunatics could be contained, and attempts at therapeutic intervention were rare. In a few asylums run by Quakers – for example, Tuke at the York Asylums – there evolved what was known as 'moral treatment' (Scull 1981a). In most institutions, however, lunatics were treated like animals and kept in appalling conditions. The Bethlem Hospital in London, for instance, was open to the public, who could enter to watch the lunatics for a penny a time. During this early period of the growth of the asylums movement, at the beginning of the nineteenth century, the medical profession had relatively little interest in the insane. From the historical investigations carried out by Scull (1975), it can be seen that the medical profession gradually came to recognize that there were profits to be made from the 'trade in lunacy', not only from having control of the state asylums, which were publicly funded, but also from running asylums for the insane members of the upper classes. The political power of the medical profession allowed them, in Britain, to influence the contents of Acts of Parliament that gave the medical profession control over asylums. The defeat of moral treatment can be seen as a key moment in the history of psychotherapy: science replaced religion as the dominant ideology underlying the treatment of the insane.

During the remainder of the nineteenth century the medical profession consolidated its control over the 'trade in lunacy'. Part of the process of consolidation involved rewriting the history of madness. Religious forms of care of the insane were characterized as 'demonology', and the persecution of witches was portrayed, erroneously, as a major strand in the pre-scientific or pre-medical approach to madness (Szasz 1971; Kirsch 1978; Spanos 1978). Medical and biological explanations for insanity were formulated, such as phrenology (Cooter 1981) and sexual indulgence or masturbation (Hare 1962). Different types of physical treatment were experimented with:

> hypodermic injections of morphia, the administration of the bromides, chloral hydrate, hypocymine, physotigma, caanabis indicta, amyl nitrate, conium, digitalis, ergot, pilocarpine, the application of electricity, the use of the Turkish bath and the wet pack, and other remedies too numerous to mention, have had their strenuous advocates.
>
> (Tuke 1882, *History of the Insane*, cited in Scull 1979)

An important theme throughout this era was the use of the asylum to oppress women, who constituted the majority of inmates (Showalter 1985). Towards the end of the century, the medical specialism of psychiatry had taken its place alongside other areas of medicine, backed by the system of classification of psychiatric disorders devised by Kraepelin, Bleuler and others. Many of these developments were controversial at the time. For example, there was considerable debate over the wisdom of locking up lunatics in institutions, since contact with other disturbed people was unlikely to aid their rehabilitation. Several critics of psychiatry during the nineteenth century argued that care in the community was much better than institutionalization. There was also a certain amount of public outcry over the cruelty with which inmates were treated, and scepticism over the efficacy of medical approaches.

The issues and debates over the care of the insane in the nineteenth century may seem very familiar to us from our vantage point over a century later. We are still arguing about the same things. But an appreciation of how these issues originally came into being can help us by bringing into focus a number of very clear conclusions about the nature of care offered to emotionally troubled people in modern industrial society. When we look at the birth of the psychiatric profession, and compare it with what was happening before the beginning of the nineteenth century, we can see that:

1 Emotional and behavioural 'problems in living' became medicalized.
2 There emerged a 'trade in lunacy', an involvement of market forces in the development of services.
3 There was an increased amount of rejection and cruelty in the way the insane were treated, and much greater social control.
4 The services that were available were controlled by men and used to oppress women.
5 Science replaced religion as the main framework for understanding madness.

None of these factors was evident to any extent before the Industrial Revolution and all are still with us today. They can be seen as fundamental to the way that any industrialized, urbanized, secularized society responds to the question of madness. The French social philosopher Foucault (1967) has pointed out that one of the central values of the new social order that emerged in the nineteenth century was reason or rationality. For a society in which a rational, scientific perspective on life was all-important, the irrational lunatic, who had lost his reason, would readily become a scapegoat, a source of threat to be banished to an asylum somewhere outside the city. Foucault (1967) describes this era as an age of 'confinement', in which society developed means of repressing or imprisoning representatives of unreason or sexuality.

The invention of psychotherapy

By the end of the nineteenth century psychiatry had achieved a dominant position in the care of the insane, now recategorized as 'mentally ill'. From within medicine and psychiatry, there now evolved a new specialism of psychotherapy. The earliest physicians to call themselves psychotherapists had been Van Renterghem and Van Eeden, who opened a Clinic of Suggestive Psychotherapy in Amsterdam in 1887 (Ellenberger 1970). Van Eeden defined psychotherapy as 'the cure of the body by the mind, aided by the impulse of one mind to another'

(Ellenberger 1970: 765). Hypnosis was a phenomenon of great interest to the European medical profession in the nineteenth century. Originally discovered by the pioneers of 'animal magnetism', Johann Joseph Gassner (1727–79) and Franz Anton Mesmer (1734–1815), hypnotism came to be widely used as an anaesthetic in surgical operations before the invention of chemical anaesthetics. During the 1880s, the influential French psychiatrists Charcot and Janet began to experiment with hypnosis as a means of treating 'hysterical' patients. There were two aspects of their hypnotic technique that have persisted to this day as key concepts in contemporary counselling and psychotherapy. First, they emphasized the import- ance of the relationship between doctor and patient. They knew that hypnosis would not be effective in the absence of what they called 'rapport'. Second, they argued that the reason why hypnosis was helpful to patients was that it gave access to an area of the mind that was not accessible during normal waking consciousness. In other words, the notion of the 'unconscious' mind was part of the apparatus of nineteenth-century hypnotism just as much as it is part of twentieth- and twenty-first-century psychotherapy.

The part played by hypnosis in the emergence of psychotherapy is of great significance. Bourguignon (1979), Prince (1980) and many others have observed that primitive cultures employ healing rituals which rely on trance states or altered states of consciousness. The appearance of Mesmerism and hypnosis through the eighteenth and nineteenth centuries in Europe, and their transformation into psychotherapy, can be viewed as representing the assimilation of a traditional cultural form into modern scientific medicine. Cushman (1995: 119) has written about the huge popularity of mesmerism in the USA in the mid-nineteenth cen- tury: 'in certain ways, mesmerism was the first secular psychotherapy in America, a way of ministering psychologically to the great American unchurched.'

The key figure in the process of transition from hypnosis to psychotherapy was, of course, Sigmund Freud. Having spent four months with Charcot in Paris during 1886–7, Freud went back to Vienna to set up in private practice as a psychiatrist. He soon turned his back on the specific techniques of hypnosis, choosing instead to develop his own technique of psychoanalysis based on free association and the interpretation of dreams. Freud became, eventually, an enormously powerful figure not only in medicine and psychotherapy, but in European cultural history as a whole. Without denying the genius and creativity of Freud, it is valuable to reflect on some of the ways in which his approach reflected the intellectual fashions and social practices of his time. For example:

1 Individual sessions with an analyst were an extension of the normal practice of one-to-one doctor–patient consultations prevalent at that time.
2 Freud's idea of a unitary life-force (libido) was derived from nineteenth- century biological theories.
3 The idea that emotional problems had a sexual cause was widely accepted in the nineteenth century.
4 The idea of the unconscious had been employed not only by the hypnotists, but also by other nineteenth-century writers and philosophers.

The distinctive contribution of Freud can probably be regarded as his capacity to assimilate all of these ideas into a coherent theoretical model that has proved of great value in many fields of work. The cultural significance of Freudian ideas can be seen to lie in the implicit assumption that we are all neurotic, that behind the facade of even the most apparently rational and successful person there lie inner conflicts and instinctual drives. The message of Freud was that psychiatry is relevant not just for the mad man or woman in the asylum, but for everyone. The set of ideas contained in psychoanalysis also reflected the challenges faced by members of the European middle classes making the transition from traditional to modern forms of relationship. Sollod (1982: 51–2) writes that in Victorian society

> it was quite appropriate to view elders as father figures and experience oneself as a respectful child in relationship to them. In the [modern] secular world, impersonal economic and employment arrangements rather than traditional ties bind one to authority, so such transferential relationships to authority figures could be inappropriate and maladaptive rather than functional.

Freudian ideas had a somewhat limited impact in Britain and Europe during his lifetime, where up until quite recently psychoanalysis was acceptable and accessible only to middle-class intellectuals and artists. In Britain, for example, the early development of psychoanalysis was associated with the literary elite of the 'Bloomsbury group' (Kohon 1986). It was not until psychoanalysis emigrated to the USA that psychotherapy, and then counselling, became more widely available.

The growth of psychotherapy in the USA

Freud had a great loathing of American society. He visited there in 1909 with Jung and Ferenczi, to give some lectures and receive an honorary degree at Clark University, and was later to write that America was a 'gigantic mistake' (Gay 1988). But American culture resonated to the ideas of psychoanalysis, and when the rise of fascism in Europe led to prominent analysts like Ferenezi, Rank and Erikson moving to New York and Boston, they found a willing clientele. Compared to Europe, American society demonstrated a much greater degree of social mobility, with people being very likely to live, work and marry outside their original neighbourhood, town, social class or ethnic group. There were therefore many individuals who had problems in forming satisfactory relationships, or having a secure sense of personal identity. Moreover, the 'American Dream' insisted that everyone could better themselves, and emphasized the pursuit of happiness of the individual as a legitimate aim in life. Psychotherapy offered a fundamental, radical method of self-improvement. The psychoanalysts arriving in the USA in the 1930s found that there was already a strong popular interest in psychology, as indicated by the self-help books of Samuel Smiles and the writings of the behaviourist J. B. Watson. There was also a strong tradition of applied psychology, which had been given impetus by the involvement of academic psychologists in the US Army in the First World War. Psychological tests were widely used in education, job selection and vocational guidance, which meant that the notion of using psychology to help ordinary people was generally taken for granted.

The idea of psychoanalysis held a great attraction for Americans, but for it to become assimilated into the culture required an Americanization of Freud's thinking. Freud had lived in a hierarchically organized, class-dominated society, and had written from a world-view immersed in classical scholarship and biological science, informed by a pessimism arising from being a Jew at a time of violent anti-Semitism. There were, therefore, themes in his writing that did not sit well with the experience of people in the USA. As a result there emerged in the 1950s a whole series of writers who reinterpreted Freud in terms of their own cultural values. Foremost among these were Carl Rogers, Eric Berne, Albert Ellis, Aaron Beck and Abraham Maslow. Many of the European analysts who went to the USA, such as Erikson and Fromm, were also prominent in reframing psychoanalysis from a wider social and cultural perspective, thus making it more acceptable to an American clientele.

One of the strongest sources of resistance to psychoanalysis in American culture lay in academic psychology. Although William James (1890), who had been one of the first scholars to make psychology academically respectable in American universities, had given close attention to Freudian ideas, American academic psychologists had become deeply committed to a behaviourist approach from about 1918. The behaviourist perspective emphasized the use of scientific methods such as measurement and laboratory experiments, and was primarily oriented to the study of observable behaviour rather than obscure internal processes, such as dreams, fantasies and impulses. The behaviourist academic establishment was consequently fiercely opposed to psychoanalysis, and refused to acknowledge it as worthy of serious study. Although some academic departments of psychiatry did show some limited interest in psychoanalysis, most practitioners and writers were forced to work in private practice or within the hospital system, rather than having an academic base. When Rogers, Berne and Ellis developed distinctive American brands of therapy in the 1950s and 1960s there was initially only very limited academic discussion of their work and ideas. One of the distinctive contributions of Rogers was to invent systematic methods of carrying out research into the processes and outcomes of therapy. The effect of this innovation was to reinforce the legitimacy of therapy as a socially acceptable enterprise by giving it the respectability and status of an applied science. In 1947 Rogers became the first therapist to be made President of the American Psychological Association (Whiteley 1984). The confirmation of therapy as an applied science was given further impetus by the entry into the therapy arena of cognitive–behavioural approaches in the 1960s, bringing with them the language and assumptions of behavioural psychology, and the image of the 'scientist-practitioner' (see Chapter 5).

The development of psychotherapy in the USA represented an enormous expansion of the 'trade in lunacy'. The weakness of the public health system in that country meant that most counselling and therapy was dominated by theories and approaches developed in private practice. The influence and prestige of the private-practice model has been such that even counselling agencies which emerged in the voluntary sector, or in educational settings, have followed its lead. In the field of social work the casework approach has been heavily influenced by psychotherapeutic practice.

The secularization of society

The relationship between organized religion and the historical development of counselling and psychotherapy is also worth noting at this point. Halmos (1965) has documented the correspondence in the twentieth century in Britain between the decline in numbers of clerical personnel and the rise in numbers of counsellors. He argues that religious faith is being replaced by a set of beliefs and values that he calls the 'faith of the counsellors'. Nelson and Torrey (1973) have described some of the ways in which therapy has taken over from religion in such areas of life as offering explanations for events that are difficult to understand, offering answers to the existential question 'what am I here for?', defining social values and supplying ritual ways of meeting other people. Holifield (1983) has documented the process through which some of the first 'psychotherapists' were in fact part of the Church in the USA, but gradually became transformed into a separate profession.

The origins of counselling and psychotherapy in the religious 'cure of souls' were discussed at the beginning of this chapter. The parallels between therapy and, for example, the use of the confessional in the Catholic Church are striking. It is also clear that in traditional, non-industrialized societies, emotional and psychological healing is largely carried out within a religious framework. However, until recently, few therapists would acknowledge that religion and spirituality had any relevance for counselling and psychotherapy. It was as if the pressure to establish therapy as a separate, independent profession meant that therapists had to make a clear-cut boundary between what they were doing and what a priest or minister might do. Of course, there are important differences. Yet there are also significant areas of convergence. In order to locate itself as a product in the twentieth-century market place, in order to build up a mental health 'industry' (Kovel 1981), therapy differentiated itself from religion. In general, mainstream theories of counselling and psychotherapy have little to say about religious or spiritual dimensions of life. Therapy is embedded in a scientific world-view, even if, as Halmos (1965) has argued, theories of therapy can be seen as a form of 'faith'. The tension between religion and science in the evolution of counselling is exemplified in the life and work of Carl Rogers.

The role of Carl Rogers

The story of the early life of Carl Rogers (1902–87), founder of the client-centred or person-centred approach to counselling and therapy (see Chapter 6), contains many of the themes already mentioned. The early background of Rogers (Rogers 1961; Kirschenbaum 1979) was that he was brought up in a rural community in the American Midwest, a member of a strictly religious Protestant family in which there was active disapproval of leisure activities such as gambling or theatre-going. As a substitute for forbidden leisure pursuits, Rogers displayed a strong interest in scientific agriculture, by the age of 14 conducting his own experiments on crops and plants. He decided to become a minister, and at the age of 20 in preparation for this vocation was a delegate to the World Student Christian Federation Conference in China. This exposure to other cultures and beliefs influenced him to break away from the rigid religious orientation of his parents, and when he entered theological college he chose one of the most liberal seminaries, the Union Theological Seminary. However, following exploration of his faith in the equivalent of a student-led 'encounter group', Rogers decided to change career and began training as a psychologist at Columbia University, where he was exposed to the ideas of the progressive education movement, which emphasized a trust in the freedom to learn and grow inherent in each child or student.

This account of Rogers's early life shows how the dual influences of religion and science came together in a career as a therapist. The respect for scientific rigour was expressed in his involvement in research, where he was one of the first to make recordings of therapy sessions, and developed a wide range of methods to investigate aspects of the therapy process. The influence of Protestant thought on client-centred theory is apparent in the emphasis on the capacity of each individual to arrive at a personal understanding of his or her destiny, using feelings and intuition rather than being guided by doctrine or reason. The client-centred approach is also focused on behaviour in the present, rather than on what has happened in the past. Sollod (1978: 96) argues that the Protestantism of client-centred therapy can be compared with psychoanalysis, where 'the trust is in the trained reason of the therapist (rabbi) and in his Talmudic interpretations of complex phenomena.'

Following his qualification as a clinical psychologist, Rogers worked mainly with disturbed children and adolescents, and their families, in a child study department of the Society for the Prevention of Cruelty to Children in Rochester, New York. Although he received further training in psychodynamically oriented therapy from Jessie Taft, a follower of Otto Rank (Sollod 1978), and was also influenced by the ideas of Alfred Adler (Watts 1998), he did not identify himself as a student of any particular approach. During his time at Rochester (1928 to 1940) he largely evolved his own distinctive approach, guided by his sense of what seemed to help his clients. Rogers was, in his clinical work, and earlier in his experience at Columbia, immersed in the values of American culture, and his theory contains many elements of that cultural context. Meadow (1964), for example, has suggested that client-centred therapy has adopted 'basic American cultural norms', such as distrust of experts and authority figures, emphasis on method rather than theory, emphasis on individuals' needs rather than shared social goals, lack of interest in the past and a valuing of independence and autonomy. Barrett-Lennard (1998) has drawn attention to the similarities between Rogers' approach and the philosophy of the 'New Deal' political movement in the USA in the 1930s.

Therapy as a response to the 'empty self'

One of the most influential writers on the history of psychotherapy has been Philip Cushman (1990, 1992, 1995). His approach has been to examine the underlying cultural factors in the nineteenth and twentieth centuries, particularly in the USA, that have led to the emergence and expansion of therapy. His thesis is that America was a new nation in which in the nineteenth century people were subjected to massive social change and transformation, and that the early precursors of psychotherapy, such as mesmerism or the revivalist movement, were attempts to find meaning and stability at a time of enormous social uncertainty. At the same time, the capitalist system, much more dominant in America than in European countries, demanded that individuals mould themselves to the requirements of particular niches in the economic system. People had to learn how to sell not only goods and services, but them*selves*. Self-improvement books and pamphlets were very popular, but psychotherapy offered a more effective way of achieving the right kind of personality.

The extent of social mobility in America meant that traditional social structures, such as family and community, became eroded and the sense of purpose and belonging associated with these structures was lost. A core experience of many Americans, Cushman (1990) has argued, has been that of the 'empty self':

> our terrain has shaped a self that experiences a significant absence of community, tradition and shared meaning. It experiences these social absences . . . as a lack of personal conviction and worth, and it embodies the absences as a chronic, undifferentiated emotional hunger. The post-World War II self thus yearns to acquire and consume as an unconscious way of compensating for what has been lost. It is empty.
>
> (Cushman 1990: 600)

The two major cultural responses to the empty self, according to Cushman, have been psychotherapy and consumerism/advertising. In order to assuage that 'undifferentiated emotional hunger', the citizen of an advanced capitalist economy has the choice of making an appointment with a therapist, or, perhaps, buying a new car.

The expansion of counselling in the late twentieth century

Up to now, the discussion has centred on the development of psychotherapy as a profession during the nineteenth and early twentieth centuries. Counselling, as a distinct profession, came of age only in the 1950s, and so an understanding of the history of psychotherapy is necessary to make the link between counselling and earlier forms of healing and care. Although in many respects counselling can be seen as an extension of psychotherapy, a way of 'marketing' psychotherapy to new groups of consumers, there are also at least two important historical strands that differentiate counselling from psychotherapy: involvement in the educational system and the role of the voluntary sector.

Counselling of various kinds came to be offered within the school and college systems in the 1920s and 1930s, as careers guidance and also as a service for young people who were having difficulties adjusting to the demands of school or college life. Psychological testing and assessment was bound up with these activities, but there was always an element of discussion or interpretation of the student's problems or test results (Whiteley 1984).

Counselling also has very strong roots in the voluntary sector. For example, the largest single counselling agency in Britain, the National Marriage Guidance Council (RELATE), was created in the 1940s by a group of people who were concerned about the threat to marriage caused by the war (Lewis *et al.* 1992). Similarly, other groups of volunteers have set up counselling services in areas such as rape, bereavement, gay and lesbian issues and child abuse.

The existence of educational and voluntary sector traditions, alongside strong psychotherapeutic and somewhat diffuse religious traditions, has meant that there has always been a face of counselling that has kept its gaze on current social problems. Further, counselling has a life outside of the medical establishment, whereas psychotherapy is closely identified with health care provision through psychiatry, and with professions allied to medicine, such as clinical psychology and psychiatric social work. And, finally, counselling has had a thriving non-professional sector, which has drawn it in to local communities as a means of securing volunteer workers and funding. So although counsellors and psychotherapists possess much the same skills, and tend to see similar groups of clients, they are culturally positioned in somewhat different territories. Unfortunately, a comprehensive cultural history of counselling remains to be written.

Why has counselling grown so rapidly in the past 25 years? Certainly in Britain and the USA, the number of counsellors and general availability of counselling have shown a significant increase since the 1970s. There would appear to be a number of converging factors responsible for this growth:

• In a postmodern world, individuals are reflexively aware of choices open to them around identity; the self has a 'project'; counselling is a way of reflexively choosing an identity (Giddens 1991).

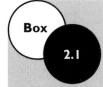

Box 2.1

From psychotherapy to psychotechnology: the reshaping of therapy by 'managed care'

Counselling and psychotherapy can be viewed as undergoing a continuous process of reconstruction in response to social, political and technological change. One of the most important dimensions of social change in the past 30 years has been the demand on health budgets resulting from an ageing population, increasingly expensive medical treatments associated with advances in technology and the general public expectation for improvement in health care standards and quality. These factors have led to pressure to control or 'ration' the amount of health care that is provided in a number of areas. In the USA, this policy is known as 'managed care'. For example, in relation to the provision of counselling and psychotherapy, health insurance companies rigidly control the number of sessions of therapy that are available, closely monitor the performance of therapists and only reimburse therapists where clients have specific diagnosed disorders that have been shown in research studies to be effectively treatable by the approach to therapy adopted by the practitioner. Many writers within the American counselling and psychotherapy professions have been highly critical of what they regard as a significant shift away from professional autonomy, and an ethical 'client-centred' approach, towards a style of therapy that could be described as the application of *psychotechnology* (techniques and measures) rather than the development of a healing relationship. Cushman and Gilford (1999: 25) have argued that:

> the therapist in managed care comes to light as an impersonal, somewhat computer-like person, stripped of individual characteristics . . . therapists seem like preprogrammed computers, which are adjusted by superiors during 'review' sessions in order to fine-tune their results . . . In complementary fashion, the patient comes to light as a compliant recipient of expert knowledge and technique. Patients seem to be plagued by problems that can be easily understood, categorized and treated by strangers.

For Cushman and Gilford, the acceptance of managed care on the part of the public reflects the next stage in the evolution of the 'empty self', into a series of shallow 'multiple selves' that cope with the complexity of modern life by compartmentalizing it into a series of multiple 'selves'. Writing in 1999, they observed that: 'In the post-World War II era . . . we had to endure . . . nearly 16 years of romantic emptiness in the persons of Richard Nixon and Ronald Reagan. Now we have the multiple Bill Clinton' (p. 29). They ask the question of whether it is necessary for therapists to go along with the 'way of being' represented by managed care, or whether it is possible to resist it.

- Caring and 'people' professions, such as nursing, medicine, teaching and social work, which had previously performed a quasi-counselling role, were financially and managerially squeezed during the 1970s and 1980s. Members of these professions no longer have time to listen to their clients. Many of them have sought training as counsellors, and have created specialist counselling roles within their organizations, as a way of preserving the quality of contact with clients.
- There is an entrepreneurial spirit in many counsellors, who will actively sell their services to new groups of consumers. For example, any personnel director of a large company will have a filing cabinet full of brochures from counsellors and counselling agencies eager to provide employee counselling services.
- Counselling regularly receives publicity in the media, most of which is positive.
- We still live in a fragmented and alienated society, in which there are many people who lack emotional and social support systems. For example, in any major city there may be large groups of refugees. Increasing numbers of people live alone.

There are, therefore, a multiplicity of factors that would appear to be associated with the expansion of counselling. What seems clear is that counselling has grown in response to social demands and pressures, rather than because research or other evidence has proved that it is effective. But what does it mean that counselling can be seen to be socially constructed in this way? What is the social meaning of counselling?

The social meaning of counselling

The historical account given here is inevitably incomplete and partial. Not enough research and scholarly attention has been devoted to the task of understanding the emergence of counselling and psychotherapy in twentieth-century society. For example, much of the historical literature on the expansion of psychotherapy in the twentieth century focuses exclusively on what happened in America. There are undoubtedly different themes and factors to be discovered through studies of the history of therapy in European countries. However, from even this limited discussion of historical factors it can be seen that the form and shape of contemporary theory and practice has been strongly influenced by cultural forces (Woolfe 1983; Pilgrim 1990; Salmon 1991; Cushman 1995). In particular, it becomes evident that the key figures in the history of counselling, such as Freud or Rogers, were not inventors of new theories as much as people who were able to articulate and give words to a way of thinking or working that was beginning to crystallize in the culture around them. A historical account also brings to the surface and illuminates some of the underlying, fundamental issues that cut across all theoretical orientations and all forms of counselling practice. These basic issues concern, first, our understanding of the *social meaning* of counselling and, second, the *image of the person* being promoted by counselling theories.

It is clear from the discussion of the origins of psychiatry that, certainly in the early years, the emphasis in psychiatric care was on the control of individuals who were seen as disruptive to the smooth running of society. Although much has changed in psychiatry, even now in most places psychiatrists have the power to enforce compulsory hospitalization. At the other extreme, humanistic counsellors aim for 'self-actualization' and assume that their clients have responsibility for their own lives and actions. There is a strong tendency for counsellors and counselling organizations to place themselves explicitly at the personal freedom and liberation end of this continuum. In practice, however, there are pressures in the direction of social conformity and control in all counselling situations. Most immediate and concrete are the values and beliefs of the counsellor regarding what behaviour is or is not socially acceptable in a client. Less tangible is the influence of who is paying for the counselling, particularly in counselling settings such as colleges, business organizations or voluntary agencies, where it is not the client who pays. Finally, in extreme cases, where clients threaten to harm themselves or others, there are powerful social pressures and sanctions that urge the counsellor to take control and do something.

Some writers have regarded their approach to counselling or psychotherapy as providing a critique of existing social norms, or even as a means of bringing about social change. The radical psychoanalyst Kovel (1981), for example, has argued that classical Freudian theory represented a powerful tool for political change, and regretted the ways in which second-generation, post-Freudian theorists adapted Freudian ideas, particularly in the USA:

> what was great in Freud – his critical ability to see beneath, if not beyond, the established order – was necessarily jettisoned; while what was compatible with advanced capitalist relations – the release of a little desire, along with its technical control and perversion – was as necessarily reinforced.

The argument that the radical edge of Freudian theory has been lost is also made by Holland (1977), and the idea of counselling or therapy as a vehicle for social change has been evoked by Rogers (1978). Within contemporary practice, the alliance between therapy and social action has been made most effectively by feminist and gay counsellors, and practitioners from ethnic minority groups (see Chapter 7). However, these attempts to radicalize counselling all necessarily confront the same contradiction: that of seeking social change through a medium that individualizes and 'psychologizes' social problems (Conrad 1981).

Another critical aspect of the social nature of counselling concerns the division of power between client and counsellor. Historically, the counsellor–client relationship has modelled itself on the doctor–patient and priest–parishioner relationships. Traditionally, doctors and priests have been seen as experts and authority figures, and the people who consulted them expected to be told what to do. In the counselling world, by contrast, many practitioners would espouse the ideal of 'empowering' clients and would agree to a greater or lesser extent with the statement by Carl Rogers that 'it is the client who knows what is right'. Nevertheless, the circumstances of most counselling interviews reproduce aspects of the doctor–patient power relationship. The meeting takes place on the territory of the counsellor, who has the power to begin and end the session. The counsellor knows everything about the client; the client knows little about the counsellor. Some counsellors have been so convinced of the unhelpfulness of the counsellor–client power imbalance that they have advocated self-help counselling networks (see Chapter 17), where people take it in turns to counsel each other. It is also relevant to note here that numerically by far the greatest number of counselling contacts are made through telephone counselling agencies, in situations where the client has much more control over how much he or she is known and how long the session will last.

Many writers in recent years have drawn attention to the ways in which power can be abused in the counselling relationship: for example, through sexual exploitation of clients. One of these writers, Masson (1988, 1992), has compiled a substantial dossier of instances of abuse of clients. He argues that this kind of abuse does not merely consist of an occasional lapse in ethical standards, but is in fact an intrinsic and inevitable consequence of any therapeutic contract. Masson (1988: 296) has written that 'the profession itself is corrupt . . . The very mainspring of psychotherapy is profit from another person's suffering', and suggests that the abolition of psychotherapy is desirable. While few would agree with this position of absolute condemnation, it is nevertheless impossible to deny, in the face of the massive evidence he presents, that his arguments deserve serious consideration. The fact that so many of the examples of abuse that Masson (1988, 1992) has uncovered relate to situations of men abusing women invites comparison with the more general social phenomenon of male violence against women, expressed through physical violence, rape and pornography.

The social nature of counselling permeates the work of the counsellor in three ways. First, the act of going to see a counsellor, and the process of change arising from counselling, will always have some effect on the social world of the client. Second, the power and status of the counsellor derive from the fact that he or she occupies a socially sanctioned role of 'healer' or 'helper'. The specific healing or helping role that the counsellor adopts will depend on the cultural context. For example, therapists in hospital settings use the language of science to describe their work, while those employed in holistic or alternative health clinics use the language of growth and spirituality. Third, client and counsellor re-enact in their relationship the various modes of social interaction they use in the everyday world.

These three dimensions to the social or cultural basis of counselling interlock and interact in practice. An example of how these ideas can be brought together to construct an understanding of the way that counselling operates within a social context is provided by the 'status accreditation' model of Bergner and Staggs (1987). They suggest that therapists are viewed as members in good standing of the community. To be a therapist is to have received endorsement that one is rational, significant, honest and credible. Any attributes or characteristics that the therapist assigns to the client are therefore likely to be believed and accepted. Bergner and Staggs (1987) point out that in a positive therapeutic relationship the

> The political dimension of counselling is explored more fully in Chapter 14

therapist will behave towards the client as if he or she is someone who makes sense, who is worthy of attention, who has the power to choose and who has strengths. The attribution or assignment of these characteristics from a high status person (such as a counsellor or therapist) has the effect on clients of 'confirming them in new positions or "statuses" that carry with them expanded eligibility for full participation in society' (Bergner and Staggs 1987: 315). Frank (1974: 272) presents the same point of view in writing that 'since the therapist represents the larger society, all therapies help to combat the patient's isolation and reestablish his sense of connectedness with his group, thereby helping to restore meaningfulness to life.' From this perspective, therapy can be viewed as a social process that offers people accreditation of their status as sane, worthy members of society. The process can be seen as the opposite of the 'labelling' by which people deemed to be 'mentally ill' are stigmatized as dangerous, irrational outsiders (Scheff 1974).

Images of the person implicit in counselling approaches

At a practical level an approach to counselling such as psychoanalysis or behaviour therapy may be seen to consist merely of a set of strategies for helping. Underneath that set of practical procedures, however, each approach represents a way of seeing people, an image of what it is to be a person, a 'moral vision' (Christopher 1996). Back in the days of the asylums, lunatics were seen as being like animals: irrational, unable to communicate, out of control. Some of these meanings were still present in the Freudian image of the person, except that in psychoanalysis the animal/id was merely one, usually hidden, part of the personality. The behaviourist image of the person has often been described as 'mechanistic': clients are seen as like machines that have broken down but can be fixed. The image of the counselling client in cognitive approaches is also mechanistic, but uses the metaphor of the modern machine, the computer: the client is seen as similar to an inappropriately programmed computer, and can be sorted out if rational commands replace irrational ones. The humanistic image is more botanical. Rogers, for example, uses many metaphors relating to the growth of plants and the conditions which either facilitate or inhibit that growth.

Each of these images of self has a history. In the main, counselling has emerged from a long historical journey in the direction of self-contained *individualism* (Baumeister 1987; Logan 1987; Cushman 1990, 1995). The profoundly individualistic nature of most (if not all) counselling limits its applicability with clients who identify with collectivist cultural traditions.

The question of the kind of world that is represented by various approaches to counselling goes beyond the mere identification of the different 'root metaphors' or images of self that lie at the heart of the different theoretical systems. There is also the question of whether the counselling model reflects the reality of the world as we experience it. For example, psychoanalytic theory was the product of an acutely male-dominated society, and many women writers and practitioners have asserted that they see in it little that they can recognize as a woman's reality. Humanistic approaches represent a positive, optimistic vision of the world, which some critics would see as denying the reality of tragedy, loss and death. It could also be said that virtually all counselling theories embody a middle-class, white, Judaeo-Christian perspective on life.

The importance for counselling of the image of the person or world-view represented by a particular approach or theory lies in the realization that we do not live in a social world that is dominated by a unitary, all-encompassing set of ideas. An essential part of the process of becoming a counsellor is to choose a version of reality that makes sense, that can be lived in. But no matter which version is selected, it needs to be understood that it is only one among several possibilities. The client, for example, may view the world in a fundamentally different way, and it may be that this kind of philosophical incompatibility is crucial. Van Deurzen-Smith (1988: 1) has suggested that

> every approach to counselling is founded on a set of ideas and beliefs about life, about the world, and about people . . . Clients can only benefit from an approach in so far as they feel able to go along with its basic assumptions.

The different root metaphors, images or basic assumptions about reality that underlie different approaches to counselling can make it difficult or impossible to reconcile or combine certain approaches, as illustrated by the debate between Rogers and Skinner on the nature of choice (Kirschenbaum and Henderson 1990). Historically, the development of counselling theory can be seen as being driven at least in part by the tensions between competing ideologies or images of the person. The contrast between a biological conception of the person and a social/existential one is, for example, apparent in many theoretical debates in the field. Bakan (1966) has argued that psychological theories, and the therapies derived from them, can be separated into two groups. The first group encompasses those theories that are fundamentally concerned with the task of understanding the *mystery* of life. The second group includes theories that aim to achieve a *mastery* of life. Bakan (1966) views the 'mystery–mastery complex' as underlying many debates and issues in psychology and therapy.

Finally, there is the question of the way the image of the person is used in the therapeutic relationship, whether the image held by the counsellor is imposed on the client, as a rigid structure into which the client's life is forced, or, as Friedman (1982) would prefer, the 'revelation of the human image . . . takes place *between* the therapist and his or her client or *among* the members of a group.'

Conclusions

To understand the ways in which counselling is understood and practised requires an appreciation of the history of counselling and its role in contemporary society. Members of the public, or clients arriving for their first appointment, generally have very little idea of what to expect. Few people can tell the difference between a psychiatrist, psychologist, counsellor and psychotherapist, never mind differentiate between alternative approaches to counselling that might be on offer. But behind that lack of specific information, there resonates a set of cultural images, which may include a fear of insanity, shame at asking for help, the ritual of the confessional and the image of doctor as healer. In a multicultural society the range of images may be very wide indeed. The counsellor is also immersed in these cultural images, as well as being socialized into the language and ideology of a particular counselling approach or into the implicit norms and values of a counselling agency. To understand counselling requires moving the horizon beyond the walls of the interview room, to take in the wider social environment within which the interview room has its own special place. In the following chapters, this critical perspective is further developed through an examination of some of the most significant areas of contemporary theory and practice.

Chapter summary

- Counselling emerged in the second half of the twentieth century. To understand what counselling is, and what counsellors do, it is necessary to have an appreciation of the historical origins and development of this form of helping.

- In pre-industrial times, people with emotional problems were helped either by their priest or by other members of their community.

- In the nineteenth century, following the Industrial Revolution, and the increasing secularization of society, there emerged new institutions and professions devoted to problems of 'mental illness'.

- During the middle years of the nineteenth century, mesmerism (hypnosis) was a widely used form of psychological therapy.

- Towards the end of the nineteenth century, Freud integrated many different strands of psychological, medical and philosophical thought into the first fully developed system of psychotherapy, known as psychoanalysis.

- Psychoanalysis remained a marginal activity until it was enthusiastically espoused by many sectors of American society in the 1920s and 1930s.

- The *client-centred* theory of Carl Rogers represented a more popular, accessible approach, that did much to bring counselling to the masses.

- The rapid expansion and popularity of counselling in the USA can be attributed to high levels of social mobility and consumerism, which produced a lack of meaning, or *empty self*, that therapy helped to fill.

- Other important strands in the evolution of counselling include vocational guidance in educational settings, and the voluntary sector.

- It is important to recognize that counselling plays a role in society of promoting an image of the person as an intrinsically autonomous and separate being, and in supporting strategies for dealing with social problems at an individual level.

- Counselling is an activity that is inextricably bound up with the culture of Western industrial societies, and is therefore not necessarily relevant to the problems experienced by members of other cultural groups.

Topics for reflection and discussion

1 Select a counselling agency with which you are familiar. What do you know about the historical development of that agency? To what extent can its creation be understood in terms of the themes discussed in this chapter? What is the social role of the agency within its community?

2 Ask people you know to give you their definition of terms such as 'counsellor', 'psychotherapist', 'hypnotherapist' and 'psychiatrist'. Invite them to tell you what they believe happens when someone consults one of these professionals. What are the origins of the images and ideas you elicit?

3 What is the relationship between religious beliefs and counselling in your own life, and in the lives of other counsellors you know or have read about?

Key terms and concepts

asylums
behaviourist perspective
capitalism
client-centred approach
culture
cure of souls
empty self
hypnosis
image of the person
individualism
industrialization
mesmerism

moral treatment
moral vision
postmodernism
psychiatry
psychoanalysis
secularization
self-improvement
social meaning
trade in lunacy
workhouse system
world-view

Suggestions for further reading

The book that brings together many of the themes of this chapter in a compelling and authoritative manner is Phillip Cushman's (1995) *Constructing the Self, Constructing America: A Cultural History of Psychotherapy*. This is possibly the only book currently available that offers an overview of the historical development of therapy. It is largely American-oriented, and has little to say about Europe, or indeed about counselling. But it is a rattling good read. Thought-provoking and horizon-widening.

There are a number of useful collections of historical and autobiographical chapters written by therapists (see, for example, Dryden and Spurling 1989; Dryden 1996; Goldfried 2001) which are worth reading. The biography of Carl Rogers by Kirschenbaum (1979) gives a very full account of a key period in the emergence of the counselling profession.

3 Counselling theories: diversity and convergence

Introduction

During the twentieth century, the development of counselling and psychotherapy came to be organized around a number of distinct theoretical models or 'approaches'. Historically, the most important of these approaches or 'schools' of therapy have been psychodynamic, cognitive–behavioural and humanistic. However, these are merely the most popular of a wide range of theoretical orientations presently in use. The current situation in counselling and psychotherapy is one of great theoretical diversity and creativity. Just as quickly as new theories are spawned, new attempts are enjoined to unify, combine or integrate them. The proliferation of theories and approaches is often confusing for people learning about counselling, whether clients or students. The aim of this chapter is to make sense of theoretical diversity, and the role of theory in counselling. The topic is tackled by first establishing just what is meant by 'theory', then looking at the *uses* of theorizing in counselling (Why do we need theory? How is theory used in practice?). The discussion moves on to consider the factors that have contributed to the apparent diversity among counselling theories, and then shifts to an analysis of the underlying similarities between all counselling approaches.

This chapter builds on the ideas presented in Chapters 1 and 2, in arguing that it is important to understand theories within their social context. Chapters 4 to 11, which follow, review the most widely used theories and approaches within contemporary counselling, ranging from the beginnings of psychotherapy in the work of Sigmund Freud, to the most recent developments in narrative therapy and philosophical counselling. These chapters on different approaches can be read as free-standing descriptions of distinctive and contrasting ways of understanding the aims and process of counselling. It is to be hoped, however, that the ideas introduced here will make it possible to look at these established approaches with a spirit of open inquiry and questioning. Theories of counselling and psychotherapy do not represent immutable truths, but are perhaps better regarded as providing tools for understanding. It is essential for each counsellor to develop his or her own *personal* approach, consistent with his or her own life experience, cultural values and work setting.

There are some key ideas that run through this chapter, and inform the book as a whole, in relation to the role of theory and the difference between competing 'schools' or approaches within the field of counselling and psychotherapy:

- from the point of view of the client, the experience of counselling is much the same, no matter which theoretical orientation is being used by the counsellor;
- there is little evidence that any one theory of counselling is more valid, effective or 'true' than any other;
- being able to offer a secure, confidential relationship, hopefulness and some kind of structure for exploring and resolving problems in living, and becoming more connected with other people, is more important than theory;

- it is essential for effective counselling that the practitioner has a coherent framework for understanding what he or she is trying to achieve;
- in multicultural, pluralist democratic societies, it is inevitable that competing value systems and cultural traditions will generate different ideas about human personality and the proper aims of counselling – some degree of theoretical diversity and debate is healthy and necessary;
- the current fragmentation and proliferation of counselling and psychotherapy theories is a result of (a) the current state of development of the profession, and (b) social and economic factors;
- the prevailing movement within counselling is in the direction of increased theoretical convergence and consensus.

It is essential, also, to appreciate that theories of counselling and psychotherapy reflect the ideas and concerns that are most pressing for individuals at any particular point in history. Theories of counselling and psychotherapy are continually undergoing *reconstruction* to reflect prevailing social issues and developments.

What is a theory?

The following chapters introduce and explain a number of counselling theories. To be able to arrive at an informed critical evaluation of these theories, it is important to recognize that the word 'theory' is itself a complex and disputed concept. This is not the place to attempt to develop a comprehensive account of debates around the role of theory in psychology and social science. Nevertheless, for the purposes of understanding counselling theories, it may be helpful to look briefly at three aspects of the concept of a theory. These are: a theory as a structured set of ideas; theory as a set of social practices; and the purpose of theory.

Theory as a structured set of ideas

The obvious way of looking at a 'theory' is to think about it as a set of ideas or concepts that are used to make sense of some dimension of reality: for example, Einstein's 'theory of relativity' is a set of ideas that explain the relationship between time and space. A theory is different from everyday, common-sense ideas in that it is stated formally, with clearly defined terms, has been tested or critically evaluated in some way and is consistent with other scientific ideas.

In relation to theories of counselling, it is essential to acknowledge that the set of ideas that makes up a theory is not only all of these things (useful, clearly defined, critically tested etc.), but is also *structured*. In other words, a counselling theory operates at different levels of abstraction, and the implications for a counsellor of using any particular theory depend a great deal on which level of abstraction he or she is employing.

A useful analysis of the structure of counselling theories has been carried out by the psychoanalytic writers Rapaport and Gill (1959), who argued that there are three levels to any theoretical model used in counselling and therapy. First, there are statements about *observational* data. Second, there are theoretical *propositions*, which make connections between different observations. Third, there are statements of *philosophical assumptions*, or 'metapsychology'. Rapaport and Gill (1959) looked at the theoretical structure of psychoanalysis, and came to the conclusion that statements about, for example, defence mechanisms such as projection or denial were fundamentally simple observations of behavioural events. Psychoanalytic concepts such as 'anal personality', on the other hand, went beyond mere observation, and made inferences about the connectedness of events separated by time and space. For example, the idea of anal personality implies a link between childhood events (potty training) and adult behaviour (obsessionality), and this association is inferred rather than directly observed. However, in principle, given good enough research, the truth of the inference could be tested through research. Finally, concepts such as the 'unconscious' and 'libido' referred to philosophical abstractions that could not be directly observed but were used as general explanatory ideas. In psychoanalysis, the reason why potty training can result in obsessional adult patterns of behaviour is because potty training operates to shape or fixate certain libidinal impulses, which then unconsciously determine the way that the person behaves in adult life. However, 'libido' and 'the unconscious' are not factors that can be measured or researched, but represent a level of highly abstract, philosophical theorizing about the meaning of being a person.

Rapaport and Gill's (1959) discussion of these issues has a number of implications for the application of theory in practice. The use of lower-level, observational constructs can be seen to carry relatively little in the way of theoretical 'baggage'. For example, describing a client as 'using the defence mechanism of projection' might be an effective shorthand means of giving information to a supervisor or colleagues in a case conference. However, it would be a straightforward matter to use everyday ordinary language to communicate the same information. Different counselling theories tend to include their own uniquely phrased observational labels, and counsellors often find it helpful to use these labels. In doing so, they are not necessarily using the theoretical model from which the label is taken, but may be merely borrowing a useful turn of phrase. At the same time, it is important to recognize that there may be times when using observational constructs may result in making assumptions about the client, and missing useful information. Categorizing a client's behaviour as 'resistance', for example, may prevent a counsellor from reflecting in a more open-ended way about different possible meanings of what the client might be doing, and why. The danger of using 'observational' concepts, therefore, can be that they can result in jumping to conclusions (by just 'labelling' a phenomenon) rather than thinking more deeply, or with more curiosity, about what might be happening.

Higher-level constructs and concepts, by contrast, cannot be as easily taken out of the context of the theoretical model within which they fit. A term such as 'libido' (Freudian theory) or 'self-actualization' (Rogerian theory) cannot be used without making a substantial number of philosophical assumptions about what it means to be a person. As a result, any attempt to combine 'libido' and 'self-actualization' in the same conversation, case study or research project is likely to lead to confusion. Thinking about people as basically driven by libidinous desires (Freud) or as basically driven by a drive to wholeness and fulfilment (Rogers) are very different philosophical positions.

The 'middle' level of theory, which involves theoretical propositions such as Freud's explanation of the 'anal personality', or Rogers' model of the 'core conditions' for therapeutic change, is potentially the most useful level of theory for practitioners, because it deals in supposedly tangible cause-and-effect sequences that give the counsellor a 'handle' on how to facilitate change. The difficulty here is whether the particular explanation offered by a theoretical model can be believed to be true, or be viewed as just one among many competing interpretations. For example, psychoanalysts claim that rigid patterns of potty training produce obsessional people (this is an over-simplification of the theory). However, if a link can be demonstrated between potty training and adult behaviour, this connection could be explained in many ways, such as being a result of obsessional attitudes being reinforced by obsessional parents (behavioural explanation), or by the acquisition of 'conditions of worth' around tidiness (Rogerian explanation).

It can be seen, therefore, that learning and using a theory of counselling involves different kinds of tasks and challenges. On the one hand, to become familiar with a theory it is necessary to learn how to detect or label observational phenomena such as 'defences', 'transference', 'empathy', 'irrational beliefs' and so on. On the other hand, it is also necessary to become immersed enough in the underlying 'image of the person' or philosophy of a theory to appreciate what is meant by 'the unconscious', 'self-actualization' or 'reinforcement'. Finally, there is the task of understanding how observational and philosophical concepts are brought together in the form of specific theoretical propositions. All this is made even more difficult because few theories of counselling and psychotherapy are ever formulated in a manner that allows their structure to be clearly identified. For example, writers such as Rogers or Freud conveyed their ideas through case studies, through essays on specific topics and (in Rogers' case) in research papers. The structures of therapy theories are often more clearly explained not in therapy and counselling books, but in personality textbooks such as those by Monte (1998) and Pervin and Johns (2000).

Theory as a set of social practices

There is no doubt that a theory of counselling can be written out in the form of a scientific formula, with all constructs being operationally defined, and cause-and-effect sequences clearly specified. In the 1950s, Carl Rogers, the founder of client-centred and person-centred counselling, and one of the leading figures in humanistic psychology, was invited to do just this by the American psychologist Sigmund Koch. The resulting scientific statement was published (Rogers 1957), and comprises a set of fundamental theoretical propositions. If this can be done for a humanistic theory that emphasizes the freedom of the person to make choices, it can certainly be done for other therapy theories. It is interesting, however, that few other leading counselling and psychotherapy theorists have opted to follow the example of Rogers and write up their theories in the form of testable hypotheses and propositions.

Despite the undeniable fact that theories exist as sets of ideas, there is an increasing appreciation that there is a human, or social, side to any theory, not only in psychology and social sciences, but also in the physical sciences such as physics, chemistry and biology. The social dimension of science has been highlighted in the writings of the philosopher Thomas Kuhn (1962). At the heart of his argument is the idea that theories are created and sustained by *scientific communities*, and that it is impossible fully to understand a theory without participating in the activities of that community. Kuhn noticed that, when scientists are trained, they do not just learn about ideas, but are socialized into a way of seeing the world, and a way of doing things. Learning about theory in chemistry, for example, involves doing experiments, learning how to interpret the results produced by particular equipment, knowing when results 'feel wrong' and learning about which problems or issues are understandable and solvable by the theory, and which are anomalous or viewed as irrelevant. A scientific community is organized around textbooks, journals and conferences. In other words, there is a whole *community of practice* that physically embodies and perpetuates the theory. The philosopher Polanyi (1958) introduced the term 'implicit knowledge' to refer to the kind of knowing used by people who belong in a community of scientists. Implicit or 'tacit' knowledge is picked up informally and unconsciously rather than being explicitly written down.

The social dimension is extremely important for an understanding of theories of counselling. Learning about counselling involves seeing, hearing and doing. Participating in a training course, or receiving supervision, represents the transmission of an *oral tradition* that is passed on from one practitioner to another. There are many concepts that, it can be argued, can only be understood by being experienced. For example, many psychoanalysts would say that a real understanding of the idea of 'transference' could only be obtained by undergoing personal psychoanalysis (a 'training analysis'). Many person-centred counsellors would assert that a full appreciation of the meaning of 'congruence' within person-centred theory requires participating in person-centred 'encounter' groups. There are aspects of personal presence, way of talking and way of being that can only be conveyed through actually meeting experienced practitioners or trainers. Certainly, these implicit or tacit dimensions of theory cannot be adequately communicated in a textbook (such as this one) or research report.

There are several implications of a social perspective that are significant for understanding how theory is created and used in counselling. First, the oral tradition is always broader than what is written about it. Writers such as Freud and Rogers were influential because they were able to put into words, better than anyone else at the time, the ways of understanding and working with clients that were being generated in their oral communities. But, even in their cases, there was always more that could be said. Both Freud and Rogers struggled, throughout their careers, to find the best ways to articulate in words what they *knew* at an implicit level. Some of the apparent theoretical debates and differences in counselling and psychotherapy can therefore be viewed not so much as arguments over the substance of what is happening in therapy, but as disputes around the best language to use in talking about these happenings. Another key implication is that, much of the time, it is more accurate to talk about counselling *approaches* rather than theories. The idea of an 'approach' is a reminder that there is more to a way of doing counselling than merely applying a set of ideas: an approach embraces philosophical assumptions, style, tradition and tacit knowing.

The third, and in some way most important, implication of a social perspective is to suggest that in many ways a theory is like a *language*: psychodynamic theory is the language used by one group of practitioners, cognitive–behavioural theory is a language used by another group and so on. The idea of theory as language is a fertile metaphor. It does not imply that one theory is right and another one is wrong. However, it does admit the possibility that it is easier to talk about some things in certain languages rather than others. Learning a language involves knowing about formal rules, acquiring everyday idioms and practising with other speakers. And it also introduces the issue of *translating* between different languages, in order to communicate with colleagues in other communities: to be able to translate, practitioners need to know about different theories, rather than remaining monolingual. There is also the question as to whether it might ever be possible, or desirable, to develop a common language for all therapies (a kind of counsellors' Esperanto?), as suggested by Ryle (1978, 1987). Finally, by regarding a theory as a language-system, it becomes easier to appreciate how processes of power and oppression can occur in counselling. If, for example, a theory does not contain language for talking about homosexuality in positive terms, then gay and lesbian counsellors and clients are silenced and excluded. If a theory does not include words to describe spiritual experience, then it becomes much harder to talk about that dimension of life in counselling or supervision. In fact, both homosexuality and religion/spirituality were largely suppressed in the language of mid-twentieth-century therapy, and it has been a long and hard struggle to allow these voices to be heard.

The purpose of theory: explanation or understanding?

There are differences in the way that the *purpose* or function of theory can be understood. From a traditional, scientific-technological standpoint, a good theory represents as close as we can get to nature, to objective external reality. A theory allows us to *explain* events, by specifying a single set of causal factors responsible for the event, and to *predict* (and therefore control) future events by applying this causal framework to the design of machines and technology. For instance, the design of a car engine is based on very precise predictions about that will happen when petrol is sparked in a cylinder etc. There is, however, another way of looking at theory. From this alternative perspective, a theory provides a way of interpreting events, with the aim of *understanding* them. A theoretical understanding involves a kind of sensitive appreciation of the multiple factors that could plausibly have contributed to an event. The possession of such an understanding can never give certain prediction, but can provide a capacity to anticipate what will happen in the future, at least in terms of considering possibilities. Theory-as-understanding opens out the possible *reasons* why something might have happened. Note here that the idea of a 'reason' allows for the possibility of human intentionality and purpose, while the idea of 'cause' refers to a mechanical or automatic process, with no space for human willingness or choice.

Does counselling theory provide explanation or understanding? In many cases, it would appear that counselling and psychotherapy theories would appear to claim the status of scientific explanations. Many people who support particular theories often behave as if they believe that their ideas reflect objective truths, and singular, true explanations for the problems that people have in their lives. Some theorists have sought confirmation in 'hard' scientific research in biology, genetics and neurology to back up their claims of objective, explanatory truth. One of the approaches that has been active in trying to secure objective scientific confirmation, since the days of Freud, has been psychoanalysis. Within the psychoanalytic and psychodynamic approach, an important and influential essay was published by Rycroft (1966). In this paper, Rycroft suggested that there are profound differences between theories of therapy and scientific theories in fields such as physics and chemistry. The latter can yield cause-and-effect statements that can be used to predict future events. The former are used by people largely to attribute meaning to events that have already taken place. Rycroft argued that, despite his genius, Freud was caught between two incompatible goals: that of establishing an objective psychology, and that of creating a rich and powerful interpretive framework. Rycroft concluded that, when looked at closely, none of Freud's ideas stood scrutiny in terms of scientific criteria for causal explanations, but that his ideas did provide a solid framework for understanding. Rycroft suggested that psychoanalytic theory is all about the *reasons* why people behave in the ways that they do, not about the *causes* of their behaviour. For example, Freud's classic work is called *The Interpretation of Dreams*, not the 'causes of dreams'.

Another psychoanalyst who arrived at a similar conclusion was Donald Spence (1982), who introduced the distinction between *narrative truth* and *historical truth*. Historical truth results from inquiry into past events that uncovers objective evidence of earlier events that preceded later events. Spence argued that, although they might believe that their methods revealed evidence of what had taken place in a client's childhood, psychodynamic therapists were very rarely (if ever) able to collect objective evidence. The best that could be hoped for, according to Spence, was a believable story, a 'narrative truth' that enabled the client to understand their life better by providing a plausible account of some of the possible reasons for their current difficulties.

The philosopher Richard Rorty (1979) offers another way of looking at the explanation versus understanding debate. He suggests that scientific theorists have been too much caught up in thinking about their work in terms of trying to create theories that function as 'mirrors of nature'. Rorty proposes that a more fruitful metaphor is that of the *conversation*: a theory is better viewed as an ongoing conversation, in which those involved in constructing, testing and using a theory continually discuss, debate and refine their ideas. The idea of a theory as an agreement between interested stakeholders around what 'works', in a pragmatic sense, rather than as an 'objective truth', also lies behind the writings of Fishman (1999).

The trend in recent years within the field of counselling and psychotherapy has been in the direction of regarding theories as interpretive frameworks, or 'lenses' through which people and therapy might be viewed and understood more clearly, rather than as constituting explanatory models in a traditional scientific sense. For some people, however, the drift towards an interpretive or 'constructivist' stance in relation to theory is worrying, because it raises the spectre of relativism: is everything true? Is there no objective reality at all? Some of the most important current debates within the field have focused on this dilemma (Fishman 1999; Downing 2000; Rennie 2000). However, it would be reasonable to conclude that, even if some therapists and psychologists believe that it *should* be possible to construct a scientific-explanatory theory of therapy, there seems little doubt that none of the theories presently available are able, at this point in time, to provide such a level of theoretical certainty. The theories we have, for now, are ones that generate *understanding* rather than explanation.

Why do we need theory? The uses of conceptualization in counselling practice

What do counsellors do when they make use of theory? Do we need theory? What is theory *for*? These are fundamental questions, which open up an appreciation of the relationship between theory and practice.

Something to hang on to: the need of the counsellor for structure in the face of chaos

The experience of being a counsellor is, typically, one of attempting to respond adequately and helpfully to complex and confusing sources of information. A client makes an appointment for a counselling session, apparently a wish to engage in a therapeutic process, and then sits slumped in his chair and says nothing. A highly successful professional woman enters counselling to deal with issues around work stress but soon talks about, and exhibits, the fear she feels about anything that reminds her of powerful memories of being a victim of violence. These are two examples of the sometimes dramatic contradictions that can be encountered in the counselling room. On some occasions, too, clients move beyond contradictions and beyond any attempt to maintain a coherent and consistent social self. In exploring painful experiences, control can be lost. Often, a client will report being stuck and hopeless, unable to see any way forward or to imagine any viable future. It is at these moments that a counsellor needs to draw deeply on a belief in his or her capacity to be helpful, and in the general capacity of human beings to learn and develop. But it can also be vital to be able to use a theoretical framework so as to begin to place what is happening into some kind of context. At difficult moments, theory gives a counsellor a basis for reflecting on experience, and a language for sharing that experience with others (for example, colleagues, a supervisor) and thus enlisting support and guidance.

Offering the client a way of making sense

One of the striking themes within the development of counselling in recent years has been the increasing emphasis given to didactic learning. Traditionally, counselling approaches such as psychodynamic and person-centred have largely relied on experiential learning and on insights or new understandings that are framed in the client's own language and the dialogue between counsellor and client. Recently, more and more counsellors and therapists have found that it is valuable for clients to acquire a theoretical framework within which they can make sense of their difficulties. Transactional Analysis (TA) is one example of a therapy approach that has generated a wide range of client-oriented books and pamphlets, and that encourages therapists to explain TA concepts to clients. Many cognitive–behavioural therapists operate in a similar manner, and claim that the best evidence of whether a client has gained from therapy is when they can quote the theory back to the therapist and explain how they apply it in their everyday life. Even in therapies that do not overtly encourage clients to learn the theory, there is no doubt that many clients do, on their own initiative, carry out a certain amount of background reading and study.

Establishing professional status

One of the characteristics of professions (such as law, medicine, the Church), as opposed to less formally established occupational groups, is that they can claim privileged access to a specialist body of theory and knowledge. Counsellors and psychotherapists who operate within professional networks would almost certainly be regarded as lacking in status and credibility if they lacked the 'special' knowledge and insight provided by a good theory.

The creation of knowledge communities

Theorizing is an active, subtle, personal and interpersonal process, which is embedded in social life; the written word inevitably abstracts ideas and concepts from their actual usage. A great deal of the learning that informs the work of counsellors comes from talking with colleagues, supervisors and tutors rather than reading books and journals (Morrow-Bradley and Elliott 1986). As suggested above, it is possible to view counsellors and therapists who adhere to a particular approach, such as person-centred counselling, as members of a language community. Within this language community, much of what is said and done may be written down, particularly by key figures such as Rogers, but the oral tradition from which the writing emerges always contains a richer, more comprehensive, more open-textured version of what is known and believed. Books and articles convey a version of the approach, rather than the approach in its entirety. The basis for critical debate within the profession often arises from the discrepancy between the linear, logical, systematized version of theory that appears in books, and the theory as used in practice. It is also difficult to reflect, at least in a sustained and systematic manner, without using concepts to organize one's fleeting impressions and thoughts.

The relationship between theoretical concepts and feelings is explored by Gendlin (1962). The writings of Gendlin on this topic are particularly relevant for counsellors, since so much of counselling practice is based on the counsellor's capacity to use his or her feeling or emotional sensitivity in the interests of the client. The model of experiencing devised by Gendlin (see Chapter 6) within the client-centred or person-centred approach proposes that meaning arises from the symbolization of a 'felt sense'. The 'felt sense' is a bodily, multifaceted area of feeling that the person experiences in response to events. This felt sense contains all the diverse meanings that the event might have for the person, but these meanings can only be accessed through symbolization, usually in words, but potentially also through images. When a symbol – for example, a word or phrase – captures the meaning contained within a feeling, there is a sense of fit, and then a sense of movement or change as this clarification of meaning allows other meanings to emerge. This approach to understanding experiencing has been highly influential within person-centred counselling (see Chapter 6). However, Gendlin (1966) has also pointed out that it provides a framework for validating the use of theory, through the process of 'experiential explication'. He suggests that the test of whether a concept or idea is helpful in therapy depends on whether its use brings about a shift in the felt sense of a problem. Gendlin is proposing that theories and concepts have a subjective truth value as well as an objective, scientifically verified validity. His framework also draws attention to the importance of using language in a creative and sensitive manner. The technical language of much counselling theory does not mean a great deal to clients, and it is essential for counsellors to communicate their ideas through a mutually constructed 'feeling language' (Hobson 1985) that makes sense to the client. One of the implications of Gendlin's analysis of theory-use is that it is important for concepts in counselling to be 'experience-near' rather than 'experience-far'. If a concept is too abstract, it will not function in the manner described by Gendlin, as a means of symbolizing and articulating implicit meanings, and thereby communicating to colleagues (and also clients) his or her subtly sensed understandings that are at the 'edge' of awareness.

It can be seen, therefore, that theory plays an invaluable role in enabling counsellors to communicate with each other. It is through a web of language and concepts that counsellors remain in contact with a collective community of practice. It is through belonging in such a community that the work of individual practitioners can be sustained and supported.

The diversity of theorizing in counselling

Why are there so many theories of counselling and psychotherapy? One widely publicized survey, by Karasu (1986), found more than 400 different named approaches to therapy. It is very difficult to accept that there are, in reality, so many unique ways to practise therapy. The proliferation of counselling and psychotherapy theories arises from a number of factors, which are discussed in this section.

Alternative 'images of the person'

One very fundamental source of theoretical complexity is that any psychological theory, or approach to counselling, ultimately relies on a root 'image of the person', a set of basic assumptions about the very nature of what it is to be human. Shotter (1975) has suggested that two of the dominant images of the person used in psychology have been the image of the machine ('the best way to understand people is to view them as mechanical objects') and the image of the organism ('the best way to understand people is to view them as animals, biological entities'). These two images can certainly be found running through different counselling approaches, from the mechanistic thinking of traditional behaviourism to the many references to bodily functioning in classical psychoanalysis. The ideas of existential philosophy have, more recently, introduced the image of the person not as an organism or mechanism but as a social being. The influence of Eastern philosophies has introduced the image of the person as spiritual being. It can be difficult to reconcile underlying images, and so at least some of the differences between counselling theories can be attributed to the different images of the person that underpin them. The situation is even further complicated by the fact that the same theory can encompass more than one root image. For example, psychoanalysis contains mechanistic ideas (e.g. defence mechanisms) and organismic/biological ideas (e.g. libido, oral fixation). Person-centred theory contains organismic images (e.g. the organismic valuing process, the self-actualization motive) as well as existential ones (e.g. congruence, empathy).

Any approach to therapy can be distilled into one or two core 'images'. Bioenergetics draws upon a strong image of the embodied, sexual person. Jungian and transpersonal approaches draw upon an image of the person as spiritual being. For systemic approaches, the person is primarily a social being. The medical model, used in psychiatry, views the person in terms of an 'illness' metaphor or image.

There is a danger, in relation to considering theories in terms of underlying images or metaphors, of over-simplifying complex sets of ideas. On the other hand, in each case the root image or metaphor captures an essential truth about a theoretical approach. We live in a culture that supports a rich diversity of images of the person, and as a result generates a rich diversity of therapy theories.

The personal dimension of theory

In other disciplines, theories and ideas tend to be identified in terms of conceptual labels, rather than being known through the name of their founder. Even in mainstream psychology, theoretical terms such as behaviourism or cognitive dissonance are employed, rather than the names of their founders (J. B. Watson, Leon Festinger). In counselling and psychotherapy, by contrast, there is a tradition of identifying theories very much with their founders. Terms such as Freudian, Jungian, Adlerian, Rogerian or Lacanian are commonplace. There are probably many reasons for this. However, one factor is certainly the recognition that theories of therapy typically reflect, to a greater or lesser extent, the personality and individual world-view of the founder. Huge amounts have been written, for instance, about the links between Freud's own life and circumstances, and the ideas that came together in his psychoanalytic theory. It may be that theories of therapy are necessarily so personal, that it is impossible to write and formulate them without importing one's own personal experience and biases. One of the reasons for the multiplicity of therapy theories, therefore, is that many individual therapists and counsellors find that the personal tenor of established theories does not quite chime with their own experience, with the result that they are driven to write down their own, personal 'version' of the theory. The intimate connection between theorizing in therapy and the personality of the theorist is explored in a classic book by Atwood and Stolorow (1993).

The social context of theory construction

The idea of the 'reconstruction' of therapy in response to changing social and cultural forces has already been mentioned. In Chapter 2, some of the important social factors responsible for the invention of psychotherapy in the nineteenth century were mentioned: the secularization of society, the movement away from authority-base relationships, the moves in the direction of greater individuality. All of these factors helped to determine the shape of psychoanalytic therapy. In more recent times, the increasing economic pressures facing health care systems and the political momentum of equal opportunities advocacy have required theories of therapy to accommodate new ideas around time limits and cultural identity. As the rate of social change continues to accelerate, it seems certain that theories of therapy will continue to proliferate, as theorists develop new ideas appropriate to the delivery of counselling in new situations.

The mental health industry: brand names and special ingredients

Another way of interpreting theoretical diversity in counselling is in commercial terms. It can be argued that all counsellors and therapists are essentially offering clients the same basic product. The exigencies of the market place, however, mean that there are many pressures leading in the direction of product diversification. It is obvious to anyone socialized into the ways of the market economy that in most circumstances it is not a good idea merely to make and sell 'cars' or 'washing powder'. Who would buy an unbranded car or box of detergent? Products that are on sale usually have 'brand names', which are meant to inform the customer about the quality and reliability of the commodity being sold. To stimulate customer enthusiasm and thereby encourage sales, many products also boast 'special ingredients' or 'unique selling features', which are claimed to make the product superior to its rivals.

This analogy is applicable to counselling and therapy. The evidence on the non-specific hypothesis implies that counsellors and therapists are, like car manufacturers, all engaged in selling broadly similar products. But for reasons of professional identity, intellectual coherence and external legitimacy there have emerged a number of 'brand name' therapies. The best known of these brand name therapies have been reviewed in earlier chapters. Psychodynamic, person-centred and cognitive–behavioural approaches are widely used, generally accepted and universally recognized. They are equivalent to the Mercedes, Ford and Toyota of the therapy world. Other, smaller, 'firms' have sought to establish their own brand names. Some of these brands have established themselves in a niche in the market place.

The main point of this metaphor is to suggest the influence of the market place, the 'trade in lunacy', on the evolution of counselling theory. The huge expansion in therapies was associated with the post-war expansion of modern capitalist economies. This economic growth has slowed and stopped, as the costs of health and welfare systems, struggling to meet the needs of an ageing population and an increasing demand for more costly and sophisticated treatments, have had to be kept within limits. At this time, when counselling and therapy services are under pressure to prove their cost-effectiveness, there are strong pressures in the direction of consolidating around the powerful brand names, and finding ways to combine resources through merger or integration.

It can be seen that there are many reasons for the diversity and fragmentation that exists within counselling and psychotherapy theory. It needs to be recognized that the modern industrial societies that have given birth to counselling and psychotherapy have themselves been fragmented and complex. Ideas from different political ideologies, such as capitalism, socialism, liberalism and feminism, have exerted an influence on therapy theorists, as have ideas from science and religion. It would be unrealistic, therefore, to expect therapy in a 'postmodern' world to comprise a monolithic universal theory.

The underlying unity of approaches to counselling

Alongside the multiple theories and voices that dominate the therapy scene, there are also writers and practitioners who argue that there is a fundamental unity to therapy. These individuals argue that, behind the specific ideas put forward by theorists, there lies a bedrock of common practice. The notion that therapy can be understood in terms of a core set of 'common' or 'non-specific' factors has become increasingly influential in recent years.

'Common' or 'non-specific' therapeutic factors

From the very beginnings of the emergence of counselling and psychotherapy as mainstream human service professions, there have been people who have pointed out that the similarities between approaches were much greater than the differences. For example, in 1940 the psychologist Goodwin Watson organized a symposium at which well known figures such as Saul Rosenzweig, Carl Rogers and Frederick Allen agreed that factors such as support, a good client–therapist relationship, insight and behaviour change were common features of all successful therapy (Watson 1940). An early piece of research by Fiedler (1950) found that therapists of different orientations held very similar views regarding their conception of an ideal therapeutic relationship.

Perhaps the most influential writer in this area has been Jerome Frank (1973, 1974), who argued that the effectiveness of therapy is not primarily due to the employment of the specific therapeutic strategies advocated by approaches (e.g. free association, interpretation, systematic desensitization, disowning irrational beliefs, reflection of feeling), but is attributable instead to the operation of a number of general or 'non-specific' factors. Frank (1974) identified the principal non-specific factors as being the creation of a supportive relationship, the provision of a rationale by which the client can make sense of his or her problems and the participation by both client and therapist in healing rituals. Frank (1974: 272) writes that although these factors are delivered in different ways by different counselling approaches, they all operate to 'heighten the patient's sense of mastery over the inner and outer forces assailing him by labeling them and fitting them into a conceptual scheme, as well as by supplying success experiences.'

The 'non-specific' hypothesis has stimulated extensive debate within the field (Parloff 1986; Strupp 1986; Hill 1989), since it directly challenges the beliefs of most counsellors and therapists that their own specific techniques and intervention strategies do have a positive effect on clients. Some of the research into this issue is reviewed in Chapter 18 and in the discussion of non-professional therapists in

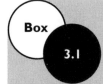

Box 3.1

'Demoralization' as a common factor in therapy

One of the great gifts of Jerome Frank has been his capacity to describe the process of therapy in ways that transcend the limits of any one single approach, yet apply to all approaches. A good example of this strategy lies in his use of the concept of *demoralization* to account for the reasons why a person might seek therapy in the first place. Frank (1974: 271) asserts that:

> the chief problem of all patients who come to psychotherapy is demoralization and . . . the effectiveness of all psychotherapeutic schools lies in their ability to restore patients' morale . . . Of course, patients seldom present themselves to therapists with the complaint that they are demoralized; rather, they seek relief for an enormous variety of symptoms and behavior disorders, and both patients and therapists see relief or modification of these as the prime goal of therapy. However, surveys of general populations, confirmed by clinical experience, indicate that only a small proportion of people with psychopathological symptoms come to therapy; apparently something else must be added that interacts with their symptoms. This state of mind, which may be termed 'demoralization', results from the persistent failure to cope with internally or externally induced stresses that the person and those close to him expect him to handle. Its characteristic features, not all of which need be present in any one person, are feelings of impotence, isolation and despair. The person's self-esteem is damaged, and he feels rejected by others because of his failure to meet their expectations . . . The most frequent symptoms of patients in psychotherapy – anxiety and depression – are direct expressions of demoralization.

The concept of demoralization, as used here by Frank, not only accounts for widely accepted ideas about therapy (e.g. anxiety and depression in clients), but also helps to explain a fact that is generally ignored by therapy theories (why relatively few people who are anxious and depressed make use of therapy). The use of 'remoralization' or 'restoration of morale' as the primary goal of therapy also brings together apparently conflicting theoretical points of view: restoring morale involves not only the recovery of self-esteem, but also developing the means to 'cope with internally or externally induced stresses that . . . those close to him expect him to handle.'

Chapter 17. One of the outcomes of this scholarly activity has been the generation of a large number of suggestions regarding a whole range of non-specific factors not mentioned by Frank (1974). The literature on non-specific or 'common' factors has been reviewed by Grencavage and Norcross (1990), who compiled a list of all the factors mentioned by at least 10 per cent of the fifty articles and books included in their review (Table 3.1). Grencavage and Norcross (1990) identified

Table 3.1 Non-specific or common factors that facilitate therapeutic change

Client characteristics

Positive expectations, hope or faith
Distressed or incongruent client
Client actively seeking help

Therapist qualities

The personal qualities of the therapist
Cultivates hope and positive expectations
Warmth and positive regard
Empathic understanding
Being a socially sanctioned healer
Non-judgemental and accepting

Change processes

Opportunity for catharsis or ventilation of emotions
Acquisition and practice of new behaviours
Provision of a rationale/model for understanding
Foster insight/awareness
Emotional and interpersonal learning
Suggestion
Success and mastery experiences
Persuasion
Placebo effects
Identification with the therapist
Behavioural self-control
Tension reduction
Desensitization
Providing information/education
Treatment methods
Use of rituals/techniques
Focus on 'inner world'
Adherence to a theory
Creating a healing setting
Interaction between two people
Communication
Explanation of client and therapist roles

Source: Grencavage and Norcross (1990).

four broad categories of non-specific factors, reflecting client characteristics, therapist qualities, change processes and treatment methods. They found that the highest levels of consensus in this review of professional opinion were concerning the therapeutic alliance (with 56 per cent of authors citing this factor), the opportunity for catharsis (38 per cent), acquisition and practising of new behaviours (32 per cent), the client having positive expectations (26 per cent), the qualities of the therapist (24 per cent) and the provision of a rationale (24 per cent).

There are three important sources of evidence that lend support to the non-specific hypothesis. The first arises from research which demonstrates that different theoretical orientations, using different specific strategies, report similar success rates (Luborsky *et al.* 1975). The second is that non-professional counsellors, who have not received enough training to be able to claim mastery of specific techniques, appear to be as effective as highly trained professional therapists (Hattie *et al.* 1984). The third piece of evidence arises from studies of the experiences of clients in counselling. When clients are asked what they find most helpful (e.g. Llewelyn and Hume 1979), they tend to rate non-specific elements more highly than specific techniques.

In the context of this chapter, the importance of the work on non-specific factors is that it points to a huge area of shared common ground between different therapies. It is a misunderstanding of the non-specific hypothesis to conclude that effective counselling consists only of these common factors. There are all sorts of complex interactions between common factors, specific techniques and theoretical models. But it makes sense to acknowledge that at the heart of any counselling relationship there are a set of generic, common processes. The diversity of theories and approaches can therefore be viewed as different versions of one common activity, rather than as fundamentally different activities.

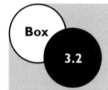

Box
3.2

Non-specific factors in action: the performance of a non-professional counsellor

In a carefully designed and controlled study, Strupp and Hadley (1979) were able to show that, under certain conditions, non-professional counsellors could be just as effective as highly trained professional therapists. The study was carried out in a university in the USA, with male clients being referred either to professional therapists or to members of academic staff with an interest in student well-being. In addition to the main report of the study published by Strupp and Hadley (1979), the research team completed intensive case study analyses in which they contrasted success and failure cases seen by the same therapist. In Strupp (1980c), an analysis is presented of the work of a non-professional counsellor who participated in the study. Dr H was a professor of statistics in his early forties. His most successful client, assessed in terms of standard outcome measures, was Sam, who was 21, mildly depressed, moderately anxious and withdrawn, and describing himself as lacking in confidence. Sam received 20 sessions of therapy, and was significantly improved at termination and follow-up.

Examination of recordings of these counselling sessions showed that Dr H adopted a robustly common-sense approach to the task. He talked a lot, took the initiative and was ready to offer advice and reassurance. For example, at the end of the first session, during which Sam had been discussing some problems with his relationship with his father, Dr H told him 'try to get along with your father over Thanksgiving weekend . . . just try . . . the world isn't lost if you don't succeed.' Although Dr H seemed quite happy to encourage Sam to talk about everyday topics such as courses, the university football team or campus politics, from time to time he would also guide him back to more conventionally therapeutic topics such as his difficulties in relating to girls or his parents, and his problems around controlling his anger. However, Sam frequently avoided talking about difficult issues, and on these occasions Dr H did not appear to possess any strategies or techniques for keeping Sam focused on therapeutic business. Dr H usually offered Sam a cup of tea. There were virtually no silences during sessions.

In many respects, therefore, Dr H did not behave in the style that might be expected from a trained counsellor. Strupp (1980c: 834) comments that, from the perspective of the research team analysing the tapes, 'many of the exchanges eventually became tedious and dreary, not unlike a conversation one might overhear in a barber-shop.' Nevertheless, Sam improved. And the benefits he gained from the therapy can be attributed to a variety of non-specific factors. Strupp (1980c: 834) sums up the case in this way:

> [Dr H] displayed a benign, accepting, and supportive fatherly attitude that extended to Sam's life, academic pursuits, and worries about the choice of a career. This was in contrast to Sam's relationship to his parents . . . A comraderie between the therapist and the patient was established, which Sam clearly enjoyed. While Dr H became Sam's ally and confidant, the therapist resisted Sam's occasional attempts to make him a partner in his cynical attitude toward the world.

Dr H's view of the case was that:

> I felt that I understood what his problems were right away and they were sufficiently minor so that they could be worked out with a little empathy and an older-brother type relationship. Mostly we just talked, and I'd encourage him to do things rather than just sit around his room. He responded fairly well to little suggestions. I think he just sort of hit a period in his life when he was lonely and just a bit depressed about breaking up with his girl . . . it was not difficult for me to put myself back at 18 or 19 and recall being in similar situations.
>
> (Strupp 1980c: 837–8)

The non-specific factors that appeared to be operating in this case were that the client was able to enter a relationship in which he was offered a high degree of respect and acceptance and was valued by a high-status member of the culture in which he lived, where the therapist acted as an effective model of how to cope with social situations, the client was allowed to tell his story and the therapist provided a framework (his own personal philosophy of life) for making sense of troubles and how to resolve them.

The movement towards theoretical integration

Historically, as a profession psychotherapy has been largely structured around distinct, separate sets of ideas or theoretical models, each backed up by its own training institute or professional association. Most counselling textbooks are organized around chapters on individual theorists, such as Freud, Rogers, Perls and Ellis, or are specifically devoted to single schools of thought. The impression given by these characteristics is that counsellors would in general be members of one or another of these sub-groups, and adhere to one specific approach. Increasingly, however, counsellors and therapists are looking beyond the confines of theoretical purity. A series of studies in the 1960s and 1970s showed that more and more practitioners were describing themselves as 'eclectic' or 'integrationist' in approach, rather than being followers of any one single model. Garfield and Kurtz (1974), for example, carried out a survey of 855 clinical psychologists in the USA, and found that 55 per cent defined themselves as eclectic, 16 per cent as psychoanalytic/psychodynamic, 10 per cent as behavioural and 7 per cent as Rogerian, humanistic and existential (the remaining 12 per cent were divided between a wide range of other orientations). Garfield and Kurtz (1977) followed up the eclectic clinical psychologists from their 1974 study and found that 49 per cent had at some time in the past adhered to a single theory and 45 per cent had always seen themselves as eclectic. Of those who had once been single approach oriented, the main shift was from psychoanalysis and Rogerian to eclecticism. Prochaska and Norcross (1983), in a survey of 410 psychotherapists in the USA, reported figures of eclectic 30 per cent, psychodynamic 18 per cent, psychoanalytic 9 per cent, cognitive 8 per cent, behavioural 6 per cent, existential 4 per cent, Gestalt 3 per cent, humanistic 4 per cent, Rogerian 2 per cent and other approaches 15 per cent. O'Sullivan and Dryden (1990) found that 32 per cent of clinical psychologists in one region in Britain designated themselves as eclectic in orientation. Hollanders and McLeod (1999) carried out a survey of over 300 counsellors and psychotherapists in Britain, drawn from a number of professional associations. Participants were allowed to describe their theoretical orientation in a way that respected the complexity of their theoretical influences. For example, when asked about the intervention techniques they used, 95 per cent showed an eclectic mix of intervention strategies. Based on their theoretical framework, 49 per cent of participants in the survey reported themselves as *explicitly* eclectic, with another 38 per cent being *implicitly* eclectic (identifying themselves with a single theoretical model but also acknowledging being influenced by other models). Only 13 per cent of the practitioners included in the Hollanders and McLeod (1999) survey could be regarded as unequivocal followers of a 'pure' approach.

The trend across all surveys of counsellors and psychotherapists has been that some form of eclecticism has emerged as the single most popular approach. One of the issues thrown up by these studies has been the sheer difficulty of finding meaningful ways of getting information about counsellors' theoretical orientations. There are so many different, often highly idiosyncratic, combinations of approaches that it is hard to design a questionnaire that will do justice to what counsellors want to say about themselves. Poznanski and McLennan (1995) have reviewed 15 different measures of counsellor orientation, and arrive at the conclusion that the only common ground is that counsellors appear to differ on where they fit on two key dimensions: analytic–experiential and objective–subjective.

The debate over the merits of integrated versus 'pure' approaches

The roots of the trend towards eclecticism and integrationism can be found in some of the earliest writings in the field. For example, as behaviourism began to be influential in the 1930s and 1940s, a number of writers, such as Dollard, Miller and Rosenzweig, were beginning to explore ways in which parallels and connections could be made between behavioural and psychoanalytic ideas and methods (see Marmor and Woods 1980). As humanistic thinking achieved prominence in the 1950s the commonalities and divergences between it and existing approaches were widely debated. It could well be argued that there is no such thing as a 'pure' theory. All theorists are influenced by what has gone before. Freudian ideas can be seen as representing a creative integration of concepts from philosophy, medicine, biology and literature. The client-centred model encompasses ideas from psychoanalysis, existential and phenomenological philosophy, and social psychology. The cognitive–behavioural approach is an example of an overt synthesis of two strands of psychological theory: behaviourism and cognitive psychology (and, more recently, constructivist philosophy).

The emergence of the idea that all therapies might largely function through the operation of common or 'non-specific' factors, discussed above, further reinforced the movement towards eclecticism and integration. The argument put forward by Frank (1973) that therapy, alongside other forms of behaviour change, achieved its effectiveness through very general processes, such as the provision of a rationale for understanding life problems, the instillation of hope and the opportunity for emotional release, made it easier to see the common ground between therapies and to begin to consider ways in which they might fit together.

Nevertheless, even though there has been an integrationist 'underground' within the field of counselling, it is probably reasonable to suggest that the dominant view until the 1960s was that different models and approaches provided perfectly viable alternative ways of working with clients, and that, on the whole, theoretical 'purity' was to be preferred. The situation today is more complex. Many practitioners, influenced not only by their own experience with clients but also by research which has shown different approaches to be equivalent in their effectiveness (Smith *et al.* 1980), have been convinced that no one model was adequate in itself. These practitioners looked beyond their initial training in a single approach and sought to acquire skills and ideas from other approaches. As a result, increasing numbers now describe themselves as eclectic in orientation. This trend is matched by the parallel development of the institutionalization of eclecticism and

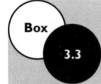

Box 3.3

Integrationism in a postmodern world

How do counsellors and psychotherapists actually use theory on a day-to-day basis? What are the strategies that are employed either to maintain a unitary theoretical stance or to integrate ideas from different theoretical models? Polkinghorne (1992) interviewed several therapists in Los Angeles, and carried out an analysis of books on therapy practice. He found that, on the whole, previous clinical experience was used as the primary source of knowledge. While theories were seen to function as useful models and metaphors that 'assist in constructing cognitive order' (p. 158), there was no sense that any theory could ever capture the complexity of human existence. These therapists were 'comfortable with the diversity of theories' (p. 158). There was feeling among several therapists that their theoretical knowledge was necessarily 'unfinished'. They might be able to anticipate how a client might respond to an intervention, but there was always the possibility that something different and unexpected might happen. They were aware that their theoretical ideas were personal constructions or 'templates', grounded in concrete instances and cases, rather than formal systems based on scientific thought and proof. The main criterion for assessing the value of a theoretical idea was pragmatic: does it work? Polkinghorne (1992) argues that these features of the way that practitioners use theory are consistent with a postmodern perspective (Kvale 1992; Lyon 1994). The belief in progress, rationality and the ultimate validity of scientific theories is seen as characteristic of modernity. Philosophical and sociological writers such as Polkinghorne have suggested that, in contrast, the currently emerging postmodern era is associated with a movement towards foundationlessness, fragmentariness, constructivism and neo-pragmatism. Polkinghorne finds all these elements in the 'psychology of practice' employed by contemporary psychotherapists. The implication here is that the movement in counselling and psychotherapy away from the modernist 'grand theories' of those such as Freud, Rogers and Berne, and towards a much more fragmented, locally or personally constructed integrationist or eclectic approach to knowledge, could be a reflection of a much broader social and cultural shift.

integrationism through the formation of the Society for the Exploration of Psychotherapy Integration (SEPI) in 1983, the inauguration in 1982 of the *International Journal of Eclectic Psychotherapy* (later renamed the *Journal of Psychotherapy Integration*), the establishment of systematic training in integrative therapy (Clarkson 1992) and the publication of a number of important books on the topic (Norcross 1986; Dryden 1992; Stricker and Gold 1993).

In opposition to this movement, a significant number of practitioners remained convinced that eclecticism or integrationism was associated with muddle and confusion, and that it was necessary to stick to one consistent approach. Voices speaking out against the integrationist trend included Eysenck (1970: 145), who vividly asserted that to follow in the direction of theoretical integration would lead us to nothing but a

> mishmash of theories, a huggermugger of procedures, a gallimaufry of therapies and a charivaria of activities having no proper rationale, and incapable of being tested or evaluated. What are needed in science and in medicine are clear-cut theories leading to specific procedures applicable to specific types of patients.

Eysenck (1970) argued that, in his view, only behaviour therapy could provide the kind of logically consistent and scientifically evaluated approach he believed was necessary. Another critic of integrationism, but this time from a psychoanalytic perspective, has been Szasz (1974: 41):

> The psychotherapist who claims to practice in a flexible manner, tailoring his therapy to the needs of his patients, does so by assuming a variety of roles. With one patient, he is a magician who hypnotizes; with another, a sympathetic friend who reassures; with a third, a physician who dispenses tranquilizers; with a fourth, a classical analyst who interprets; and so on . . . The eclectic psychotherapist is, more often than not, a role player; he wears a variety of psychotherapeutic mantles, but owns none and is usually truly comfortable in none. Instead of being skilled in a multiplicity of therapeutic techniques, he suffers from what we may consider, after Erikson, 'a diffusion of professional identity'. In sum, the therapist who tries to be all things to all people may be nothing to himself; he is not 'at one' with any particular method of psychotherapy. If he engages in intensive psychotherapy, his patient is likely to discover this.

Theoretical purists argue that there are conflicting philosophical assumptions underlying different approaches, and that any attempt to combine them is likely to lead to confusion (Eysenck) or inauthenticity (Szasz). For example, within psychoanalysis the actions of a person are regarded as ultimately determined by unconscious motives arising from repressed childhood experiences. By contrast, humanistic theories view people as capable of choice and free will. It could be argued that these are irreconcilably opposing ways of making sense of human nature, and can only breed contradiction if combined into one approach to counselling (Patterson 1989). Another type of confusion can be created by taking ideas or techniques out of context. For example, systematic desensitization is a therapeutic technique that has been developed within a behavioural perspective in which anxiety is understood in terms of a conditioned fear response to a stimulus. A humanistic counsellor who understood anxiety in terms of threat to the self-concept might invite the client to engage in a process that could superficially resemble systematic desensitization, but the meaning of the procedure would be radically different. A final source of confusion that can result from an eclectic approach reflects the difficulties involved in mastering concepts and methods from different theories. It is hard enough, according to this line of argument, to be a competent counsellor within one approach, without attempting to achieve a depth of understanding and experience in them all.

If the main objection to eclecticism is that it can result in confusion and misunderstanding, a secondary objection is that it may undermine effective training, supervision and support. If a theoretical model provides a language through which to discuss and reflect on the complex reality of work with clients, it is surely helpful to work with trainers, supervisors and colleagues who share the same language. Similarly, research or scholarship in a field of study are facilitated when everyone involved can agree on the meaning of terminology. This is a strong argument in favour of at least a strong degree of theoretical purity. The language of psychoanalysis and the psychodynamic approach, for example, is over 100 years old, and constitutes a rich and extensive literature on just about every aspect of human psychological and cultural functioning that can be imagined. Only specialists within a psychodynamic approach, it is argued, can really make effective use of these resources. Integrationist practitioners with a more superficial grasp of psychodynamic language would be much less able to find their way through this material.

The field of counselling and psychotherapy is therefore currently involved in an important debate over the relative merits of theoretical purity as against integration or eclecticism. Behind this debate is a much larger question, of whether it is even in principle possible to create a universally acceptable framework for understanding human behaviour. It would seem plausible to many people trained within Western science and philosophy that advances in human understanding arise from attempts to assess the validity of competing theories, or to refute the predictions of a dominant theory. For observers with these values and beliefs, the absence of debate over fundamental assumptions about human nature and society is associated with totalitarian and authoritarian states. From another point of view, however, the Western tendency to divide reality into competing dualisms can be seen as equally dangerous.

The issue is further complicated, however, by the fact that there are important differences between eclecticism and integrationism, and also several different types of integrationism.

Eclecticism and integrationism

An eclectic approach to counselling is one in which the counsellor chooses the best or most appropriate ideas and techniques from a range of theories or models, in order to meet the needs of the client. Integration, on the other hand, refers to a somewhat more ambitious enterprise in which the counsellor brings together elements from different theories and models into a new theory or model. To be an eclectic it is merely necessary to be able to recognize or identify what you like in the approaches on offer. To be an integrationist it is necessary not only to identify what is useful, but also to weld these pieces into a whole. Some of the differences in meaning between the two terms are presented in Table 3.2. The term 'eclectic' was more fashionable in the 1960s, but subsequently has perhaps dropped out of

Table 3.2 A comparison of the meanings of eclecticism and integrationism

Eclecticism	Integrationism
Technical	Theoretical
Divergent (focus on differences)	Convergent (interest in commonalities)
Choosing from many	Combining many
Applying what is	Creating something new
Collection	Blend
Selection	Synthesis
Applying the parts	Unifying the parts
Empirical more than theoretical	More theoretical than empirical
Sum of parts	More than sum of parts
Realistic	Idealistic

Source: Norcross and Grencavage (1989).

favour. 'Integrative' and 'integrationist' imply to many people a greater degree of intellectual rigour. However, there have recently been attempts to rehabilitate the concept of eclecticism. In practice, both concepts depend on an act of combining, and signify that the counsellor involved is not satisfied with a single-theory approach to his or her work.

Pathways to integration

So far, the general principle of combining or unifying counselling approaches has been discussed, but not the practicalities. How can different theories and techniques be combined? Within the counselling and psychotherapy literature, the urge to create a broader, more all-encompassing approach has taken a number of contrasting forms. The options for integration have been described by a number of writers. For example, Mahrer (1989) argues that there have been six distinctively different strategies for achieving integration:

1 *The development of a substantive new theory*. This strategy involves the ambitious and complex endeavour of creating a genuinely new way of looking at human beings, one that will encompass and satisfactorily replace all existing theories. This approach to integration is the equivalent of a scientific revolution, such as the replacement of Newtonian with Einsteinian ideas about time, space and gravity, and is obviously extremely difficult to achieve. However, the identification of 'transtheoretical' constructs or frameworks goes some way towards this goal.

2 *The development of one of the current theories* to the point where it would be capable of assimilating all other competing or alternative theories. This strategy is fundamentally mistaken, according to Mahrer (1989), because each of the current theories is based upon a radically different image of the person.

3 *Development of a common language*. To concentrate on the vocabularies, the sets of words, phrases and concepts used in different approaches, and work at the

development of a common language for counselling and therapy (e.g. Ryle 1978, 1987). This strategy is valuable in enabling counsellors from different orientations to communicate effectively with each other.

4 *Identify transtheoretical concepts.* To focus on areas of agreement or commonality between different approaches, in order to produce integrative concepts and techniques within specific domains or components of therapy, rather than at the level of the theory or approach as a whole. Areas of commonality that have been explored in this manner include the therapeutic alliance (Bordin 1979) and the formulation of stages of change (Prochaska and DiClemente 1982).

5 *Identify common techniques.* More extensive sharing between practitioners of specific techniques or 'operating procedures'. In this strategy, counsellors and therapists would observe each other at work (for example, on tape) and acquire new ways of working with clients, but at a practical, not theoretical, level.

6 *Concentrate on 'what works'.* Using research findings to enable practitioners to identify those intervention techniques that are most effective with specific client problems and issues. Perhaps the most fully articulated version of this strategy is contained in Beutler and Clarkin (1990). Mahrer (1989) describes this version of integration as 'diagnose-the-problem-and-prescribe-the-treatment'. Dryden (1984) has used the term 'technical eclecticism' to describe this approach.

The framework offered by Mahrer (1989) reflects the complexity of the current debate over eclecticism and integrationism. These six strategies for combining approaches can be placed on a continuum, which at one end involves close attention to concepts and theory-building, and at the other end represents a primarily atheoretical, pragmatic and empirical approach. In the middle of the continuum are counsellors and therapists who are neither solely technicians nor grand theorists, but are grappling with problems of translating one approach or theory into another. These are counsellors who are trying to learn from each other, by asking questions such as 'What does that concept mean to me?' or 'How does that way of working with a client fit into my scheme of things?'

This chapter has examined in some detail the debate over integrationism and theoretical purity, focusing on the many aspects of this complex issue. It would seem reasonable to ask, at this point, whether integrationist counsellors and therapists do anything different from practitioners who operate within a single model. The answer must be that, to a large extent, they do not do anything significantly different. They are, after all, drawing upon the same pool of therapeutic resources. There would appear to be two distinctive features of integrative work as it is currently practised. The first is a concern with client assessment, which is a central feature of technical eclecticism. The second is the use of 'transtheoretical' concepts.

The use of client assessment in integrative approaches

The basic rationale for client assessment within integrative approaches derives from the fact that the integrationist or eclectic practitioner has at his or her disposal a range of intervention tools and techniques. The form of intervention that is chosen will depend on the particular needs and personality of the client. By contrast, the single-theory practitioner, it could be suggested, can only work with each client in the same way. One of the most explicit examples of this kind of assessment can be found in multimodal therapy (Lazarus 1989a, b; Eskapa 1992). Within the multimodal approach clients are viewed as presenting problems that can be located within seven distinctive areas: behaviour, affect, sensation, imagery, cognition, interpersonal relationships, drugs/biology. Lazarus (1989a, b), the founder of the approach, uses the term 'BASIC-ID' as a mnemonic for these areas. The task of the counsellor is to identify the main focus for client work, using an assessment interview and the multimodal life history questionnaire, and then choose the relevant intervention techniques, based on research findings.

The multimodal approach is a good example of what can be called 'technical eclecticism' (Dryden 1984). In other words, it is a framework for selecting therapeutic techniques. One major advantage that this perspective on integration can claim is that it is atheoretical and thus avoids pointless debate over the compatibility (or otherwise) of theoretical constructs. A major disadvantage, on the other hand, is that, strictly speaking, it relies on the existence of sound research evidence concerning the effectiveness of particular techniques with particular categories of client. Such evidence is frequently not available, forcing the clinician to rely on his or her personal experience, which will have been at least partly shaped by theoretical assumptions and suppositions. Many other eclectic or integrationist therapists use rigorous client assessment procedures without specifically following the multimodal model (see, for example, the work of Norcross described in Dryden 1991).

The use of 'transtheoretical' concepts in integrative approaches

In practice, the main strategy for achieving integration has been to find a central theoretical concept or framework within which some or all existing approaches can be subsumed. Barkham (1992) has suggested that integrationist counsellors and therapists attempt to identify higher-order constructs that can account for change mechanisms beyond the level of any single model. The aim is to produce a cognitive 'map' that will enable the links and connections between ideas and techniques to be understood. There are several examples of approaches to counselling and therapy that employ such higher-order or transtheoretical constructs.

One example of a transtheoretical approach to integration, which is widely used within counselling, is the 'skilled helper' model constructed by Egan (1990). The key integrating concept chosen by Egan is that of problem management. Egan suggests that clients who seek assistance from counsellors and other helpers are experiencing difficulties in coping with problems in their lives, and that the primary task of the helper is to enable the person to find and act on appropriate solutions to these problems. The emphasis is therefore on a problem-solving process, which involves three stages. First, the client is helped to describe and explore the 'present scenario', the problem situation that he or she is faced with at present. The second stage is to articulate a 'preferred scenario', which includes future goals and objectives. The third stage is to develop and implement action strategies for moving from the current to the preferred scenario. Egan (1990) describes sub-stages within each stage, and identifies the client tasks and helper skills necessary to facilitate this problem-solving process.

The Egan model can usefully be viewed as a 'map' through which the usefulness of relevant elements of other approaches can be located and evaluated. For example, the concept of empathy is taken from client-centred theory and regarded as a communication skill essential to the helping process, and the idea of congruence is included under 'immediacy'. From a psychodynamic perspective, the aim of insight is included in Egan's goal of identifying and challenging 'blind spots' in the client. Many counsellors and therapists have used the Egan model as a framework through which they can employ techniques and methods from a wide range of approaches: for example, Gestalt exercises as a way of challenging blind spots or assertiveness training as a way of developing action strategies. The brief case study in Inskipp and Johns (1984) illustrates some of the ways in which various ideas can be included within the skilled helper model.

The main strengths of the skilled helper model are that it offers an intensely practical and pragmatic approach to working with people, and that it is applicable to a wide variety of situations, ranging from individual counselling to organizational consultation. As an integrationist approach, its limitation is that it is primarily based in a cognitive–behavioural perspective. Although the model clearly encompasses some elements of humanistic and person-centred thinking, through such concepts as respect, immediacy and empathy, it includes very little from the psychodynamic approaches. Key concepts from psychodynamic approaches, such as the importance of childhood object relations, the idea of defence mechanisms and unconscious processing or the notion of transference, are all absent.

Another integrative approach that employs a central unifying concept as a device for combining different approaches is the self-confirmation model developed by Andrews (1991). The core idea in this model is that the individual acts in the world to reaffirm his or her self-concept. The process of self-confirmation involves a feedback loop consisting of a number of stages. The self-concept of the person represents the way he or she perceives his or her attitudes, feeling states, ways of acting in situations and all other dimensions of 'what is me'. This sense of self generates characteristic needs and expectations. For example, a person who views herself as 'dominant' may experience a need or drive to be powerful and controlling in relationships, and will expect other people to follow her directives. Patterns of behaviour and action will ensue that are consistent with the underlying needs and expectations and even more fundamental self-concept. This behaviour is, in turn, perceived and reacted to by others, some of whom are people with whom the person is actually in relationship (e.g. friends, colleagues) but some being 'internalized others' (e.g. mental images of parents or other significant others). The person then perceives the response of these others, and not only cognitively interprets that response but also has a feeling or emotional reaction to it. These inner experiences are assimilated into the self-concept, and the process resumes.

At the heart of the self-confirmation model is that at all these stages the person acts in order to prevent outcomes that are dissonant or in conflict with his or her self-concept. Problems in living occur when the person engages in distortion at one or more of the stages in the feedback loop, in order to protect the self-concept from contradictory information from the environment. The objective of counselling or psychotherapy is, therefore, to enable the client to understand how self-confirmation operates in his or her life, and to change what is happening at those stages of the loop where the most serious distortion is occurring. The model enables an integration of a wide variety of therapeutic concepts and strategies, by providing a model that combines all of the issues (self-concept, motivation, behaviour, object relations and so forth) from all other models.

A third transtheoretical approach is cognitive-analytic therapy (CAT) (Ryle and Cowmeadow 1992; Ryle 1995; Ryle and Kerr 2002), originally developed by Ryle (1990). This model is based on some recent ideas from cognitive psychology, concerning the ways that people engage in intentional activity through sequences of mental and behavioural acts. In pursuing their life goals, people run into trouble when they encounter traps, dilemmas and snags. The psychoanalytic dimension of this model includes the Freudian idea of defence mechanisms as examples of cognitive 'editing', and takes account of the origins of traps, dilemmas and snags in early parent–child interactions. In practice, CAT is implemented through brief (16-session) therapy, which begins with an exploration of the life-history and current functioning of the client. This leads on to a reformulation of the difficulties being experienced by the client, in which the counsellor or therapist identifies targets for change.

By considering together these three integrative approaches – the Egan skilled helper model, the Andrews self-confirmation model and Ryle's CAT – some of the fundamental difficulties involved in integration can be examined. Although all three models successfully integrate previously existing sets of ideas, they all arrive at a different result regarding a suitable overarching concept or principle. In effect, Egan, Andrews and Ryle have arrived at new theories of therapy. In doing so, they have inevitably fragmented the counselling and therapy world even further. It is noticeable, for example, that little or no research has been conducted into the Egan model, even though it has been in use for some time, and there exists a wealth of research studies into cognitive–behavioural therapy, which it resembles in important respects. The other notable feature of these integrative approaches is that they bring together some ideas but clearly reject others; they are partial integrations of previous theory.

The missing dimension: counsellor development

The search for ways to combine or synthesize the massive array of ideas and techniques in counselling and therapy is probably an inevitable consequence of the explosion of writing on therapy in the past 30 years. It seems reasonable to assume that these writers have not in reality all uncovered insights that are fresh and unique. There must be a broad area of common ground between many competing approaches. However, it may be inappropriate to assume that the integrationist urge must necessarily take the form of creating new theories, such as those presented by Egan, Andrews and Ryle. A more fertile approach to understanding integrationism may be to view it as a personal process undertaken by individual counsellors and therapists.

Several writers have commented that one of the central tasks for any counsellor is to develop his or her own personal approach. Smail (1978) and Lomas (1981) have been particularly insistent that theory and techniques must be assimilated into the person of the therapist. Lomas (1981: 3) writes that the essence of counselling or therapy is 'the manifestation of creative human qualities' rather than the operation of technical procedures. In Chapter 19, the idea of the counsellor's journey is introduced as a way of understanding the development in counsellors of a professional identity. On this journey, there may be times when particular areas of theory and technique may resonate with developments in the personal life of the counsellor, and lead to the cultivation of particular knowledge and skills, or the adoption of a specific approach. The autobiographical essays included in Dryden and Spurling (1989) and Goldfried (2001) illustrate some of the ways in which professional interests interact with personal needs to create a unique professional identity.

It would appear to be necessary, therefore, to regard eclecticism and integration not as abstract theoretical exercises, but as choices intimately connected with the process of counsellor development. Significantly, the literature on therapeutic convergence is dominated by the writings of mature 'master' therapists who have had the benefit of extensive training and are able to employ a sophisticated and highly differentiated conceptual map in making sense of the similarities and differences between alternative theories and techniques. Such individuals are not in the majority in the world of counselling. Often, counsellors working in an eclectic mode may be relatively inexperienced and have limited training in the techniques they are employing. A great many counsellors have been trained within a generic skills model, of the kind described by Culley (1992). This kind of training package usually consists of a combination of ideas from person-centred and cognitive–behavioural approaches, but focused on practical skills at the expense of theoretical understanding. Although research evidence is lacking, it is not uncommon for counsellors initially trained in a generic model to choose later in their career to specialize in a pure, brand name approach, as a means of consolidating their professional identity and sense of competence.

The future of integration

It should be clear that there is no one 'eclectic' or 'integrated' approach to counselling. There is, rather, a powerful trend towards finding ways of combining the

Box
3.4

The experience of pioneering a new form of integration

One form of theoretical and practical integration that has received increasing attention in recent years has been to bring together ideas and techniques from the domain of spiritual healing alongside methods of counselling and psychotherapy (Sollod 1993). In a series of interviews and group discussions, West (1997) asked counsellors and psychotherapists who regarded themselves as both healers and therapists about their experiences of working across this boundary. Most of them talked about difficulties in labelling and describing what they did. For example, one reported that 'in terms of making my living, I find it easier to present myself as a psychotherapist.' Another informant stated that 'I don't call myself an anything.' Linked to these dilemmas in defining their professional identity were issues in finding appropriate supervision:

> I know that my normal supervision has been useless.

> Did I write this up in my case notes? Or mention it in my group servision, or to my personal supervisor. No!

> The loneliness I feel in respect of the split I have between doing counselling and psychotherapy and doing healing, most especially with my psychotherapy supervision, is very painful.

The results of this study bring into focus some of the challenges faced by counsellors seeking to pursue an integrationist path. If, as a counsellor, it is impossible to find words to describe or label the approach that is being used, it will clearly be difficult for clients to enter counselling with a fully informed appreciation of what they are committing themselves to. There are ethical issues here. Further, even if a counsellor has developed a personal understanding of how different approaches might be integrated, he or she still needs to find other people who share that understanding, to receive supervision and support and to avoid isolation.

valuable ideas and techniques developed within separate schools and approaches. At the same time, however, there are also strong forces within the counselling and psychotherapy world acting in the direction of maintaining the purity of single-approach training institutes, professional associations and publications networks. The only prediction that would appear warranted would be that this tension between integration and purity is unlikely to disappear, and that it is to be welcomed as a sign of how creative and lively this field of study is at this time.

Beyond the current debates over eclecticism and integrationism is a broader historical perspective. The intellectual history of counselling and psychotherapy is not extensive. Psychoanalysis is about 100 years old, humanistic approaches have been established for 50 years, cognitive models came on the scene less than 40 years ago. If the founders of an approach, and their first generation of students, usually fight to establish the distinctiveness and uniqueness of their creation, and subsequent generations of adherents become secure enough to feel less threatened about making links with other approaches, then we are only just entering a period when such collaborations are even possible. This trend has, of course, been complicated and slowed down by the tendency towards splitting and factionalism in the therapy world. But it may well be that we are seeing the beginnings of an emergent consensus over the aims, concepts and methods of counselling and psychotherapy. Yet true consensus is only possible when differences are acknowledged and respected. There is also a requirement, within any profession or discipline that is intellectually alive and socially responsive, for a certain degree of creative tension.

Conclusions: counselling theories – tools or truths?

It can be seen, from the ideas and debates reviewed in this chapter, that there is no simple way of understanding the role of theory in counselling. Because counselling and psychotherapy have largely developed in a professional and academic context that emphasizes the value of rigorous scientific method (which involves creating and testing theories), there has been a tendency for the leading figures in the therapy world to explain their work in scientific terms, and construct formal theories. The Western societies in which counselling evolved during the twentieth century placed great emphasis on progress and the achievement of objective truth. All of the mainstream therapy approaches that emerged in the early and mid-twentieth century were built around core ideas that their founders believed to be objectively and universally true. For Freud, the unconscious mind and the relationship between childhood events and adult neuroses were objective truths. For behaviourists such as Skinner, learning through stimulus-response reinforcement was an objective truth. For Rogers, the self-concept and the actualizing tendency were objective realities that could in principle be observed and measured. One consequence of believing in the ultimate validity of such 'truths' was the conclusion that people who did not share the chosen belief were wrong and mistaken. These others then needed to be converted to the one truth, or their heresies needed to be defended against, or, as a last resort, they could be ignored. The legacy of these attitudes has been that, to this day, the world of counselling and psychotherapy remains divided – between major schools or approaches that dispute the validity of each other's work, and then into many smaller sects.

In the most recent phase of the development of counselling, there has been a greater emphasis on the common factors and methods shared by all counselling practitioners, rather than on the differences between them. This trend reflects important movements within society as a whole, away from the belief in rationality and scientific progress that dominated the *modern* era (the nineteenth and twentieth centuries), and towards a much more sceptical stance, which characterizes *postmodern* ways of thinking. Although there are lively debates within sociology around the meaning of 'postmodernity' (for a good introduction to these debates, see Lyon 1994), there is agreement that, in a world in which ideas and information circulate at a global level, 'grand theories' such as communism and psychoanalysis, which offer a single, monolithic, authoritative version of reality, have become less convincing for many people. In place of these grand theories, there appears to be a movement towards a pragmatic knitting together of ideas that work, at a local level. The implications for counselling and psychotherapy of this cultural shift are explored by Kvale (1992) and Downing (2000).

Finally, it might be helpful to look at theory from a non-scientific domain: music. If someone is learning to play a musical instrument, and goes to classes on 'music theory', then what they acquire is a capacity to understand and follow a set of instructions for performing a musical score in the correct manner. But it is possible to be a creative and entertaining musician without knowing any music 'theory'. And being expert in music theory does not guarantee a satisfying performance – a good player needs to be able to interpret the score, appreciate the composer's intentions and the tradition he or she was composing within, make human contact with the audience and fellow players, and so on.

The following chapters present a series of alternative theoretical perspectives from which counselling and psychotherapy can be practised. In reading this theory, it is necessary, as with music, to interpret the text in the light of the composer, his or her intentions and the tradition that he or she worked within, and to remember that the theory is merely a vehicle for making contact with the audience (client) and fellow players (colleagues).

Chapter summary

- There exist a great many different theories of counselling. The aim of this chapter is to make sense of why there are so many theories, and to reflect on the role of theory in counselling.

- To some extent, different theories of counselling reflect alternative images of the person, or underlying philosophical beliefs about human nature: for example, whether people are seen as machines, or organisms, or social beings.

- A significant factor in the proliferation of theories has been the wide range of phenomena they have been attempting to explain. Typically, any one theory is better at explaining some events and processes than others.

- In practice, the use of theory by counsellors must be seen as part of a process of understanding the client, in which the counsellor draws upon his or her own feelings and personal experience as well as on ideas and concepts. Some of the theoretical ideas used by counsellors (e.g. the concept of 'defence mechanism') are designed to help them to classify and understand what is immediately happening in the counselling session. Other concepts (e.g. 'the unconscious') are more abstract, and are more likely to be used to provide a general frame-work for making sense of therapy as a whole.

- Ultimately, counsellors need theory to help them to begin to make sense of the chaos, confusion and crisis presented by some clients. Theoretical understandings allow counsellors to 'go beyond the information given' and develop a perspective from which to understand client material, the counselling process or their own reactions to the client. However, it is not helpful to regard counselling theory as similar to a scientific model that leads easily to prediction, control and explanation. Counselling theories must be integrated with the personal experience of the counsellor, and are better seen as comprising a set of heuristic tools that, when used wisely, may lead to understanding and a deepening of the therapeutic relationship.

- Another way of understanding theoretical diversity is to look at therapy as a market place. To 'sell' a counselling 'product' it is necessary to package it with a unique 'brand name' and the promise of unique 'special ingredients'.

- An important contribution to the debate on the role of theory in therapy was made by Jerome Frank, who argued that therapeutic change could be attributed to the operation of 'non-specific' or generic factors (such as the therapeutic relationship, or the opportunity to express feeling) rather than to specific therapeutic techniques.

- Although theoretical models such as psychodynamic, person-centred and cognitive–behavioural have dominated training and research, an increasing number of counsellors and psychotherapists describe themselves as integrative or eclectic in orientation, choosing to combine ideas and techniques from different approaches.

- Critics such as Szasz and Eysenck have argued that there is a danger that combining approaches can lead to confusion and superficiality.

- Eclecticism involves the counsellor selecting the best or most appropriate ideas and techniques from a range of theories or models, in order to meet the needs of the client. Integration refers to a somewhat more ambitious enterprise where the counsellor brings together elements from different theories and models into a new theory or model.

- There exist a variety of strategies for combining ideas and techniques – there is no one way to be eclectic or integrationist.

- A distinctive feature of eclectic approaches has been the systematic use of client assessment to identify which method will be most suitable for each client.

- Typically, integrationist approaches such as the Egan model or cognitive analytic therapy (CAT) rely on the use of 'transtheoretical' concepts that provide an overarching framework within which ideas and methods from other models can be placed.

- In practice, perhaps most integration takes place in the context of counsellor personal and professional development. As counsellors proceed through their careers, they find themselves drawn towards new ideas and training opportunities to keep their approach 'fresh', and end up with a synthesis of different approaches, which they blend together into their own personal style of working.

- Although it is clear that the trend toward integration will continue, the movement away from unitary or 'purist' approaches does present problems in the areas of training, supervision and research.

Topics for reflection and discussion

1 Make a list of the theoretical terms and concepts you routinely use in talking about counselling. Identify which you employ as 'observational' labels and which refer to more abstract theoretical assumptions. What does this tell you about the theoretical model(s) you use in practice?

2 What is the theoretical 'language' used in the agency in which you do you work as a counsellor (or attend as a client)? Alternatively, what is the theoretical 'language' of the training course you are, or have been, participating in? To what extent is this language coherent (i.e. are apparently contradictory ideas used alongside each other)? How are new people socialized into the language? What happens if or when someone uses a different language?

3 How important are non-specific or common factors? Do you believe that they are more influential than the actual techniques used by therapists? What are the implications of this perspective for the ways that counsellors work with clients? What are the implications for counsellor training?

4 Where do you stand on the question of eclecticism and integration? In terms of your own current counselling work, do you find it more useful to keep to one approach, or to combine different approaches? Can you envisage circumstances under which your position might change in the future?

5 John Norcross (in Dryden 1991: 13) has stated that 'a single unifying theory for all psychotherapies is neither viable nor desirable in my opinion.' Do you agree?

6 How useful do you find Frank's concept of 'demoralization' as a means of explaining why people enter therapy? Does it apply in all cases? What might be the advantages and limitations of adopting Frank's perspective?

Key terms and concepts

brand names
common factors
communities of practice
constructivism
conversation
demoralization
eclecticism
explanation
historical truth
hope
image of the person
implicit knowledge
integration
language
mental health industry

metapsychology
modernity
narrative truth
non-specific factors
oral tradition
personal approach
philosophical assumptions
postmodernity
scientific community
symbolization
theoretical orientation
theory
transtheoretical concepts
understanding

Suggested further reading

The classic book that has influenced much of the work described in this chapter is *Persuasion and Healing* by Jerome Frank (1973; new edition, Frank and Frank 1991). This book is well worth reading, and still has a great deal to say that is relevant and stimulating. Two recent books that are well informed and easy to read, and that represent the current wave of thinking about convergence between approaches to counselling are Miller *et al.* (1997) and Hubble *et al.* (1999).

The *Handbook of Psychotherapy Integration*, edited by Norcross and Goldfried (1992), remains relevant, while good sources of information on recent perspectives on integrationism are the *Journal of Psychotherapy Integration*, and the conferences sponsored by the Society for the Exploration of Psychotherapy Integration (SEPI).

One of the best ways to develop an appreciation of the issues involved in applying theoretical constructs in counselling is to look at how experienced counsellors and psychotherapists would approach the same case or client. One very interesting experiment of this type has been published by Lazarus and Messer (1988). In this paper Lazarus (an eclectic/behaviourist) and Messer (a psychoanalyst) conduct a dialogue over their perceptions of a case in which Lazarus worked with a young woman who was experiencing various relationship difficulties and exhibiting behaviour problems in the form of compulsive handwashing and a driving phobia. What is fascinating about the debate between Lazarus and Messer is the ways in which they agree over some aspects of the case, while having quite opposing views over other aspects. They suggest that in counselling situation the practitioner will encounter 'choice points' at which his or her theory will dictate different courses of action. The series of books by Moira Walker and Michael Jacobs (Jacobs 1995, 1996; Walker 1995, 1996) are structured around the presentation of detailed case material on a client, which is then separately analysed by six therapists from very different orientations. These therapists are able to communicate further questions to the client, and finally the client makes a comment on how valuable she found each report written by each of them. The particular value of this series of books lies in the very detailed and comprehensive account each of the therapists is able to give of his or her approach to the same person. Finally, Salzman and Norcross (1990) have assembled a book in which a series of case vignettes are discussed by therapists from contrasting theoretical backgrounds. All of these books and articles are reflections of an increased willingness on the part of counsellors and psychotherapists to engage in dialogues across theoretical boundaries, and to find a common language and meeting ground.

Readers interested in looking more deeply into philosophical issues associated with the use of theory in counselling will find that Downing (2000) provides a thoughtful and well informed elaboration of some of the themes touched on in the early part of this chapter.

4 Themes and issues in the psychodynamic approach to counselling

Introduction

The psychodynamic approach to counselling represents one of the major traditions within contemporary counselling and psychotherapy. Psychodynamic counselling places great emphasis on the counsellor's ability to use what happens in the immediate, unfolding relationship between client and counsellor to explore the types of feelings and relationship dilemmas that have caused difficulties for the client in his or her everyday life. The aim of psychodynamic counselling is to help clients to achieve insight and understanding around the reasons for their problems, and translate this insight into a mature capacity to cope with any future difficulties. To enable this process to take place, the counsellor needs to be able to offer the client an environment that is sufficiently secure and consistent to permit safe expression of painful or shameful fantasies and impulses.

Although psychodynamic counselling has its origins in the ideas of Sigmund Freud, current theory and practice have gone far beyond Freud's initial formulation. While Freud was convinced that repressed sexual wishes and memories lay at the root of the patient's problems, later generations of practitioners and theorists have developed a more social, relationship-oriented approach. Psychodynamic methods have been applied to understanding and treating a wide range of problems, and have been adapted to a variety of ways of working, including brief therapy, group therapy and marital/couples counselling.

The aim of this chapter is to introduce some of the main ideas and methods involved in the theory and practice of psychodynamic counselling. The chapter begins with an account of Freud's ideas. Freud remains a key point of reference for the majority of psychodynamic counsellors and psychotherapists, and later developments in psychodynamic counselling can all be viewed as an ongoing debate with Freud – sometimes disagreeing markedly with his positions, but always returning to his core ideas. Subsequent sections in the chapter review the significance of object relations and attachment theory, and other important themes in psychodynamic thinking.

The origins of psychodynamic counselling: the work of Sigmund Freud

Sigmund Freud (1856–1939) is widely regarded as being not only one of the founders of modern psychology, but also a key influence on Western society in the twentieth century. As a boy Freud had ambitions to be a famous scientist, and he originally trained in medicine, becoming in the 1880s one of the first medical researchers to investigate the properties of the newly discovered coca leaf (cocaine). However, the anti-Semitism in Austrian middle-class society at that time meant that he was unable to continue his career in the University of Vienna, and he was forced to enter private practice in the field that would now be known as psychiatry. Freud spent a year in Paris studying with the most eminent psychiatrist of the time, Charcot, who taught him the technique of hypnosis. Returning to Vienna, Freud began seeing patients who were emotionally disturbed, many of them suffering from what was known as 'hysteria'. He found that hypnosis was not particularly effective for him as a treatment technique, and gradually evolved his own method, called 'free association', which consisted of getting the patient to lie in a relaxed position (usually on a couch) and to 'say whatever comes to mind'. The stream-of-consciousness material that emerged from this procedure often included strong emotions, deeply buried memories and childhood sexual experiences, and the opportunity to share these feelings and memories appeared to be helpful for patients. One of them, Anna O., labelled this method 'the talking cure'.

Further information about the development of Freud's ideas, and the influence on his thought of his own early family life, his Jewishness, his medical training and the general cultural setting of late nineteenth-century Vienna, can be found in a number of books (e.g. Wollheim 1971; Gay 1988; Jacobs 1992).

Freud's method of treatment is called psychoanalysis. From the time his theory and method became known and used by others (starting from about 1900) his ideas have been continually modified and developed by other writers on and practitioners of psychoanalysis. As a result, there are now many counsellors and psychotherapists who would see themselves as working within the broad tradition initiated by Freud, but who would call themselves psychodynamic in orientation rather than psychoanalytic. Counsellors working in a psychodynamic way with clients all tend to make similar kinds of assumptions about the nature of the client's problems, and the manner in which these problems can best be worked on. The main distinctive features of the psychodynamic approach are:

1 An assumption that the client's difficulties have their ultimate origins in childhood experiences.
2 An assumption that the client may not be consciously aware of the true motives or impulses behind his or her actions.
3 The use in counselling and therapy of interpretation of the transference relationship.

These features will now be examined in more detail.

The childhood origins of emotional problems

Freud noted that, in the 'free association' situation, many of his patients reported remembering unpleasant or fearful sexual experiences in childhood, and, more-over, that the act of telling someone else about these experiences was thera-peutic. Freud could not believe that these childhood sexual traumas had actually happened in reality (although today we might disagree), and made sense of this phenomenon by suggesting that what had really happened had its roots in the child's own sexual needs.

It is important to be clear here about what Freud meant by 'sexual'. In his own writing, which was of course in German, he used a concept that might more accurately be translated as 'life force' or, more generally, 'emotional energy' (Bettelheim 1983). While this concept has a sexual aspect to it, it is unfortunate that its English translation focuses only on this aspect.

Freud surmised, from listening to his patients talk about their lives, that the sexual energy, or libido, of the child develops or matures through a number of distinct phases. In the first year of life, the child experiences an almost erotic pleasure from its mouth, its oral region. Babies get satisfaction from sucking, biting and swallowing. Then, between about two and four years of age, children get pleasure from defecating, from feelings in their anal region. Then, at around five to eight years of age, the child begins to have a kind of immature genital longing, which is directed at members of the opposite sex. Freud called this the phallic stage. (Freud thought that the child's sexuality became less important in older childhood, and he called this the latency stage.)

The phases of psycho-sexual development set the stage for a series of conflicts between the child and its environment, its family and, most important of all, its parents. Freud saw the parents or family as having to respond to the child's needs and impulses, and he argued that the way in which the parents responded had a powerful influence on the later personality of the child. Mainly, the parents or family could respond in a way that was too controlling or one that was not controlling enough. For example, little babies cry when they are hungry. If the mother feeds the baby immediately every time, or even feeds before the demand has been made, the baby may learn, at a deep emotional level, that it does not need to do anything to be taken care of. It may grow up believing, deep down, that there exists a perfect world and it may become a person who finds it hard to accept the inevitable frustrations of the actual world. On the other hand, if the baby has to wait too long to be fed, it may learn that the world only meets its needs if it gets angry or verbally aggressive. Somewhere in between these two extremes is what the British psychoanalyst D. W. Winnicott has called the 'good enough' mother, the mother or caretaker who responds quickly enough without being over-protective or smothering.

Freud suggests a similar type of pattern for the anal stage. If the child's potty training is too rigid and harsh, it will learn that it must never allow itself to make a mess, and may grow up finding it difficult to express emotions and with an obsessional need to keep everything in its proper place. If the potty training is too permissive, on the other hand, the child may grow up without the capacity to keep things in order.

The third developmental stage, the phallic stage, is possibly the most significant in terms of its effects on later life. Freud argues that the child at this stage begins to feel primitive genital impulses, which are directed at the most obvious target: its opposite sex parent. Thus at this stage little girls are 'in love' with their fathers and little boys with their mothers. But, Freud goes on, the child then fears the punishment or anger of the same-sex parent if this sexual longing is expressed in behaviour. The child is then forced to repress its sexual feelings, and also to defuse its rivalry with the same-sex parent by identifying more strongly with that parent. Usually, this 'family drama' would be acted out at a largely unconscious level. The effect later on, in adulthood, might be that people continue to repress or distort their sexuality, and that in their sexual relationships (e.g. marriage) they might be unconsciously seeking the opposite-sex parents they never had. The basic psychological problem here, as with the other stages, lies in the fact that the person's impulses or drives are 'driven underground', and influence the person unconsciously. Thus someone might not be consciously aware of having 'chosen' a marriage partner who symbolically represents his or her mother or father, but his or her behaviour towards the partner may follow the same pattern as the earlier parent–child relationship. An example of this might be the husband who as a child was always criticized by his mother, and who later on seems always to expect his wife to behave in the same way.

It may be apparent from the previous discussion that, although Freud in his original theory emphasized the psycho-sexual nature of childhood development, what really influences the child emotionally and psychologically as he or she grows up is the quality of the relationships he or she has with his or her parents and family. This realization has led more recent writers in the psychodynamic tradition to emphasize the psycho-social development of the child rather than the sexual and biological aspects.

One of the most important of these writers is the psychoanalyst Erik Erikson, whose book *Childhood and Society* (1950) includes a description of eight stages of psycho-social development, covering the whole lifespan. His first stage, during the first year or so of life, is equivalent to Freud's 'oral' stage. Erikson, however, suggests that the early relationship between mother and child is psychologically significant because it is in this relationship that the child either learns to trust the world (if his or her basic needs are met) or acquires a basic sense of mistrust. This sense of trust or mistrust may then form the foundation for the type of relationships the child has in later adult life.

Another writer who stresses the psycho-social events of childhood is the British psychoanalyst John Bowlby (1969, 1973, 1980, 1988). In his work, he examines the way that the experience of attachment (the existence of a close, safe, continuing relationship) and loss in childhood can shape the person's capacity for forming attachments in adult life.

Although subsequent theorists in the psychodynamic tradition have moved the emphasis away from Freud's focus on sexuality in childhood, they would still agree that the emotions and feelings that are triggered by childhood sexual experiences can have powerful effects on the child's development. However, the basic viewpoint that is shared by all psychoanalytic and psychodynamic counsellors and therapists is that to understand the personality of an adult client or patient it is necessary to understand the development of that personality through childhood, particularly with respect to how it has been shaped by its family environment.

The importance of the 'unconscious'

Freud did not merely suggest that childhood experiences influence adult personality; he suggested that the influence occurred in a particular way – through the operation of the unconscious mind. The 'unconscious', for Freud, was the part of mental life of a person that was outside direct awareness. Freud saw the human mind as divided into three regions:

- The id ('it'), a reservoir of primitive instincts and impulses that are the ultimate motives for our behaviour. Freud assumed that there were two core drives: life/love/sex/Eros and death/hate/aggression/Thanatos. The id has no time dimension, so that memories trapped there through repression can be as powerful as when the repressed event first happened. The id is governed by the 'pleasure principle', and is irrational.
- The ego ('I'), the conscious, rational part of the mind, which makes decisions and deals with external reality.
- The superego ('above I'), the 'conscience', the store-house of rules and taboos about what you should and should not do. The attitudes a person has in the superego are mainly an internalization of his or her parents' attitudes.

There are two very important implications of this theory of how the mind works. First, the id and most of the superego were seen by Freud as being largely unconscious, so that much of an individual's behaviour could be understood as being under the control of forces (e.g. repressed memories, childhood fantasies) that the person cannot consciously acknowledge. The psychodynamic counsellor or therapist, therefore, is always looking for ways of getting 'beneath the surface' of what the client or patient is saying – the assumption is that what the person initially says about himself or herself is only part of the story, and probably not the most interesting part.

Second, the ego and the other regions (the id and superego) are, potentially at any rate, almost constantly in conflict with each other. For example, the id presses for its primitive impulses to be acted upon ('I hate him so I want to hit him') but the ego will know that such behaviour would be punished by the external world, and the superego tries to make the person feel guilty because what he or she wants to do is wrong or immoral. It is, however, highly uncomfortable to live with such a degree of inner turmoil, and so Freud argued that the mind develops defence mechanisms – for example, repression, denial, reaction formation, sublimation, intellectualization and projection – to protect the ego from such pressure. So, not only is what the person consciously believes only part of the story, it is also likely to be a part that is distorted by the operation of defence mechanisms.

The therapeutic techniques used in psychoanalysis

The Freudian or psychodynamic theory described in the previous sections originally emerged out of the work of Freud and others on helping people with emotional problems. Many aspects of the theory have, therefore, been applied to the question of how to facilitate therapeutic change in clients or patients. Before we move on to look at the specific techniques used in psychoanalytic or psychodynamic therapy and counselling, however, it is essential to be clear about just what the aims of such treatment are. Freud used the phrase 'where id was, let ego be' to summarize his aims. In other words, rather than being driven by unconscious forces and impulses, people after therapy will be more rational, more

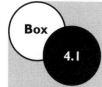

Box

4.1

The mechanisms of defence

Anne Freud, the youngest child of Sigmund Freud, trained as a psychoanalyst and went on to be one of the pioneers of child analysis. Anna Freud also made a major theoretical contribution to psychoanalysis by elaborating and refining her father's ideas about the role of *defence mechanisms*. This increasing attention to the ways in which the ego defends itself against emotionally threatening unconscious impulses and wishes represents an important step away from the original biologically oriented psychoanalystic 'drive' theory, in the direction of an 'ego' psychology that gave more emphasis to cognitive processes. The key defence mechanisms described by Anna Freud (1936/1966) in her book *The Ego and the Mechanisms of Defence* included:

- *Repression* (motivated forgetting): the instant removal from awareness of any threatening impulse, idea or memory.

- *Denial* (motivated negation): blocking of external events and information from awareness.

- *Projection* (displacement outwards): attributing to another person one's own unacceptable desires or thoughts.

- *Displacement* (redirection of impulses): channelling impulses (typically aggressive ones) on to a different target.

- *Reaction formation* (asserting the opposite): defending against unacceptable impulses by turning them into the opposite.

- *Sublimation* (finding an acceptable substitute): transforming an impulse into a more socially acceptable form of behaviour.

- *Regression* (developmental retreat): responding to internal feelings triggered by an external threat by reverting to 'child-like' behaviour from an earlier stage of development.

While it may often be straightforward to identify these kinds of patterns of behaviour in people who seek counselling (and in everyday life), it is less clear just how best a counsellor might respond to such defences. Is it best to draw the client's attention to the fact that they are using a defence mechanism? Is it more effective to attempt gently to help the person to put into words the difficult feelings that are being defended against? Is it useful to offer an interpretation of how the defensive pattern arose in the person's life, and the role it plays? Or is it better to respond in the 'here-and-now', perhaps by reflecting on how the counsellor feels when, for example, certain assumptions are projected on to him or her? From a psychodynamic perspective, there are many issues and choices involved in knowing how to use an awareness of the mechanisms of defence in the interests of the client. The writings of the British analyst David Malan (1979) provide an invaluable guide to ways of using the interpretation of defences to help clients to develop insight and, eventually, more satsifying relationships.

aware of their inner emotional life and more able to control these feelings in an appropriate manner. A key aim of psychoanalysis is, then, the achievement of insight into the true nature of one's problems (i.e. their childhood origins). But genuine insight is not merely an intellectual exercise – when the person truly understands, he or she will experience a release of the emotional tension associated with the repressed or buried memories. Freud used the term 'catharsis' to describe this emotional release.

There are a number of therapeutic techniques or strategies used in psychoanalytic or psychodynamic therapy:

Further discussion of psychodynamic ideas about the therapeutic relationship can be found on pages 298–9

1 *Systematic use of the relationship between the counsellor and client.* Psychoanalytic counsellors and therapists tend to behave towards their clients in a neutral manner. It is unusual for psychoanalytically trained counsellors to share much of their own feelings or own lives with their clients. The reason for this is that the counsellor is attempting to present himself or herself as a 'blank screen' on to which the client may project his or her fantasies or deeply held assumptions about close relationships. The therapist expects that as therapy continues over weeks or months, the feelings clients hold towards him or her will be similar to the feelings they had towards significant, authority figures in their own past. In other words, if the client behaved in a passive, dependent way with her own mother as a child, then she could reproduce this behaviour with her therapist. By being neutral and detached, the therapist ensures that the feelings the client has towards him or her are not caused by anything the therapist has done, but are a result of the client projecting an image of his or her mother, father etc. on to the therapist. This process is called transference and is a powerful tool in psychoanalytic therapy, since it allows the therapist to observe the early childhood relationships of the client as these relationships are re-enacted in the consulting room. The aim would be to help the client to become aware of these projections, first in the relationship with the therapist but then in relationships with other people, such as his or her spouse, boss, friends and so on.

2 *Identifying and analysing resistances and defences.* As the client talks about his or her problem, the therapist may notice that he or she is avoiding, distorting or defending against certain feelings or insights. Freud saw it as important to understand the source of such resistance, and would draw the patient's attention to it if it happened persistently. For example, a student seeing a counsellor for help with study problems, who then persistently blames tutors for his difficulties, is probably avoiding his own feelings of inadequacy, or dependency, by employing the defence mechanism of projection (i.e. attributing to others characteristics you cannot accept in yourself).

3 *Free association or 'saying whatever comes to mind'.* The intention is to help the person to talk about himself or herself in a fashion that is less likely to be influenced by defence mechanisms. It is as though in free association the person's 'truth' can slip out.

4 *Working on dreams and fantasies.* Freud saw the dream as 'the royal road to the unconscious', and encouraged his patients to tell him about their dreams. Again,

the purpose is to examine material that comes from a deeper, less defended, level of the individual's personality. It is assumed that events in dreams symbolically represent people, impulses or situations in the dreamer's waking life. Other products of the imagination – for example, waking dreams, fantasies and images – can be used in the same way as night dreams in analysis.

5 *Interpretation.* A psychoanalytic counsellor or therapist will use the processes described above – transference, dreams, free association etc. – to generate material for interpretation. Through interpreting the meaning of dreams, memories and transference, the therapist is attempting to help clients to understand the origins of their problems, and thereby gain more control over them and more freedom to behave differently. However, effective interpretation is a difficult skill. Some of the issues that the therapist or counsellor must bear in mind when making an interpretation are:

- Is the timing right? Is the client ready to take this idea on board?
- Is the interpretation correct? Has enough evidence been gathered?
- Can the interpretation be phrased in such a way that the client will understand it?

6 *Other miscellaneous techniques.* When working with children as clients, it is unrealistic to expect them to be able to put their inner conflicts into words. As a result, most child analysts use toys and play to allow the child to externalize his or her fears and worries. Some therapists working with adults also find it helpful to use expressive techniques, such as art, sculpture and poetry. The use of projective techniques, such as the Rorschach Inkblot Test or the Thematic Apperception Test (TAT), can also serve a similar function. Finally, some psychodynamic therapists may encourage their clients to write diaries or autobiographies as a means of exploring their past or present circumstances.

Although the number of actual psychoanalysts in Britain is small, the influence on counselling in general of psychoanalysis and the psychodynamic tradition has been immense. It is probably true to say that virtually all counsellors have been influenced at some level by psychoanalytic ideas. It should be acknowledged that the understanding of Freud in Britain and the USA is a version filtered through his translators. Bettelheim (1983) has suggested that the ideas and concepts introduced by Freud in his original writings (in German) have been made more 'clinical' and more mechanical through translation into English.

The account of Freudian theory and practice given here can provide no more than a brief introduction to this area of literature. The interested reader who would wish to explore psychoanalytic thinking in more depth is recommended to consult Freud's own work. The Introductory Lectures (Freud 1917), New Introductory Lectures (Freud 1933) and case studies of the Rat Man (Freud 1909), Schreber (Freud 1910) and Dora (Freud 1901) represent particularly accessible and illuminating examples of the power of Freudian analysis in action. The writings of Jacobs (1986, 1999) and McLaughlin (1995) offer valuable examples of the application of psychodynamic ideas in counselling settings.

The post-Freudian evolution of the psychodynamic approach

It is well documented that Freud demanded a high level of agreement with his ideas from those around him. During his lifetime, several important figures in psychoanalysis who had been his students or close colleagues were involved in disputes with Freud and subsequently left the International Association for Psycho-Analysis. The best known of these figures is Carl Jung, who was regarded as Freud's 'favourite son' within the psychoanalytic circle, and was expected in time to take over the leadership of the psychoanalytic movement. The correspondence between Freud and Jung has been collected and published, and illustrates a growing split between the two men which became irrevocable in 1912. The principal area of disagreement between Freud and Jung centred on the nature of motivation. Jung argued that human beings have a drive towards 'individuation', or the integration and fulfilment of self, as well as more biologically based drives associated with sexuality. Jung also viewed the unconscious as encompassing spiritual and transcendental areas of meaning.

Other prominent analysts who broke off from Freud included Ferenczi, Rank, Reich and Adler. Ferenczi and Rank were frustrated with the lack of interest Freud showed in the question of technique, of how to make the therapy a more effective means of helping patients. Reich left to pursue the bodily, organismic roots of defences, the ways in which the sexual and aggressive energy that is held back by repression, denial and other defences is expressed through bodily processes such as muscle tension, posture and illness. The theme that Adler developed was the significance of social factors in emotional life: for example, the drive for power and control, which is first experienced in situations of sibling rivalry.

The disagreements between Freud and his followers are misunderstood if they are regarded as mere personality clashes, examples of Freud's irrationality or attributable to cultural factors such as the Austrian Jewishness of Freud as against the Swiss Protestantism of Jung. These disagreements and splits represent fundamental theoretical issues within the psychodynamic approach, and although the personalization of the debate during the early years can obscure the differences over ideas and technique, it also helps by making the lines of the debate clear. The underlying questions being debated by Freud and his colleagues were:

- What happens in the early years of life to produce later problems?
- How do unconscious processes and mechanisms operate?
- What should the therapist do to make psychoanalytic therapy most effective for patients or clients (the question of technique)?

While Freud was alive he dominated psychoanalysis, and those who disagreed with him were forced to set up separate and independent institutes and training centres. The results of these schisms in psychoanalysis persist to this day, in the continued existence of separate Jungian, Adlerian and Reichian approaches. After the death of Freud in 1939, it became possible to re-open the debate in a more

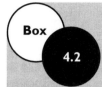

Box 4.2

The Jungian tradition in psychodynamic counselling and psychotherapy

The Jungian approach, also known as *analytic psychology*, was created by C. G. Jung (1875–1961). Jung was a Swiss psychiatrist who was one of the earliest members of the circle around Freud, the 'favourite son' who was predicted to take over from Freud as leader of the psychoanalytic movement. Jung split with Freud in 1912 through disagreement over theoretical differences. In particular, Jung diverged from the Freudian position on the predominance of sexual motives in the unconscious. Jung developed a concept of the 'collective unconscious', which he saw as structured through 'archetypes', symbolic representations of universal facets of human experience, such as the mother, the trickster, the hero. Perhaps the best known of the Jungian archetypes is the 'shadow', or animus (in women) or anima (in men), which represents those aspects of the self that are denied to conscious awareness. Another difference between Freud and Jung was highlighted in their views on development. Freudian thinking on development is restricted largely to events in childhood, particularly the oral, anal and Oedipal stages. Jung, on the other hand, saw human development as a lifelong quest for fulfilment, which he called 'individuation'. Jung also evolved a system for understanding personality differences, in which people can be categorized as 'types' made up of sensation/intuition, extraversion/introversion and thinking/feeling.

There is substantial common ground between psychodynamic approaches to counselling and the 'analytic' approach of Jung, in the shared assumptions regarding the importance of unconsious processes and the value of working with dreams and fantasy. There are, however, also significant areas of contrast, centred on the understanding of the unconscious and ideas of development and personality. Jung was also highly influenced by religious and spiritual teachings, whereas Freud was commited to a more secular, scientific approach. In recent years there has been a strong interest in Jungian approaches within the counselling and psychotherapy community. There has been a proliferation of new texts elaborating Jungian concepts and methods. The application of a Jungian perspective to gender issues has been a particularly successful area of enquiry. Although the process of Jungian analysis is lengthy, and more appropriate for the practice of psychotherapy than for counselling (at least as counselling is defined in most agencies), many counsellors have read Jung or interpreters of his work (such as Kopp 1972, 1974) and have integrated ideas such as the 'shadow' into their own way of making sense of therapy. The Jungian model of personality type has also influenced many counsellors through the use in personal development work of the Myers–Biggs Type Indicator (MBTI), a questionnaire devised to assess personality type in individuals.

The most accessible of Jung's writings are his autobiography, *Memories, Dreams, Reflections* (Jung 1963), and *Man and His Symbols* (Jung 1964). Other valuable introductory texts are Fordham (1986), Kaufmann (1989) and Carvalho (1990).

open fashion, and to reintegrate some of the ideas of the 'heretics' into a broader-based psychodynamic approach. It would be impossible to review here all the interesting and useful elements of contemporary psychodynamic thinking about counselling and psychotherapy. However, three of the most important directions in which the approach has evolved since Freud's death have been through the development of a theoretical perspective known as the 'object relations' approach, the work of the British 'Independents' and the refinements to technique necessary to offer psychodynamic counselling and therapy on a time-limited basis.

The object relations school

The 'object relations' approach to psychoanalysis and psychodynamic counselling and psychotherapy has been highly influential. It is based on direct observation of the behaviour of babies and infants, and in its application involves a relationship-oriented approach to therapy (Gomez 1996).

The origins of object relations theory in child observation

The originator of the object relations movement within the psychodynamic approach is usually accepted to be Melanie Klein. Born in Austria, Klein trained with a student of Freud, Sandor Ferenczi, in Hungary, and eventually moved to Britain in 1926, becoming an influential member of the British Psycho-Analytical Society. The work of Klein was distinctive in that she carried out psychoanalysis with children, and placed emphasis on the relationship between mother and child in the very first months of life, whereas Freud was mainly concerned with the dynamics of Oedipal conflicts, which occurred much later in childhood. For Klein, the quality of relationship that the child experienced with human 'objects' (such as the mother) in the first year set a pattern of relating that persisted through adult life. The original writings of Klein are difficult, but H. Segal (1964), J. Segal (1985, 1992) and Sayers (1991) present accessible accounts of her life and work.

Before Klein, very few psychoanalysts had worked directly with children. Using drawings, toys, dolls and other play materials, Klein found that she was able to explore the inner world of the child, and discovered that the conflicts and anxieties felt by children largely arose not from their sexual impulses, as Freud had assumed, but from their relationships with adults. The relationship with the mother, in particular, was a centrally important factor. A young child, in fact, cannot survive without a caretaker, usually a mother. Another child psychoanalyst working within this tradition, D. W. Winnicott (1964), wrote that 'there is no such thing as a baby', pointing out that 'a baby cannot exist alone, but is essentially part of a relationship'.

From the point of view of the baby, according to Klein, the mother in the first months is represented by the 'part-object' of the breast, and is experienced as either a 'good object' or a 'bad object'. She is 'good' when the needs of the baby are being met through feeding. She is 'bad' when these needs are not being met. The baby responds to the bad object with feelings of destructive rage. The first few months are described by Klein as a 'paranoid-schizoid' period, when the baby feels very little security in the world and is recovering from the trauma of birth. Over time, however, the baby begins to be able to perceive the mother as a more realistic whole object rather than as the part-object of the breast, and to understand that good and bad can coexist in the same person. The early phase of splitting of experience into 'good' and 'bad' begins to be resolved.

The next phase of development, according to Klein, is characterized by a 'depressive' reaction, a deep sense of disappointment and anger that a loved person can be bad as well as good. In the earlier phase, the baby was able to maintain the fantasy of the 'good mother' as existing separate from the 'bad'. Now he or she must accept that the bad and the good go together. There is a primitive sense of loss and separation now that the possibility of complete fusion with the 'good' mother has been left behind. There may be a sense of guilt that it was the child himself or herself who was actually responsible for the end of the earlier, simpler, phase of the relationship with the mother.

It is essential to recognize that the infant is not consciously aware of these processes as they happen. The awareness of the child is seen as dream-like and fragmented rather than logical and connected. Indeed, it is hard for adults to imagine what the inner life of a child might be like. In her effort to reconstruct this inner life, Klein portrays a world dominated by strong impulses and emotions in response to the actions of external 'objects'. The assumption is that the emotional inner world of the adult is built upon the foundations of experience of these earliest months and years.

One of the key characteristics of this inner world, according to the object relations perspective (and other theories of child development, such as that of Piaget), is the inability of the child to differentiate between what is self and what is the rest of the world. In the beginning, the child is egocentric in the sense that it believes it has power over everything that happens in its world; for example, that food arrives because I cry, it is morning because I wake up, or Grandad died because I didn't take care of him. It is this 'self-centredness', which may become expressed in grandiose or narcissistic patterns of relating to others, that forms the underlying cause of many of the problems that the person may encounter in adult life.

The application of an object relations perspective in therapy

It should be apparent, from the discussion of Klein's ideas presented here, that her work represents a subtle but highly significant shift in psychoanalytic thinking. Rather than focusing their attention primarily on the operation of biological/ libidinal impulses, Klein and her colleagues were beginning to take seriously the quality of the *relationships* between the client/patient and others:

within object relations theory, the mind and the psychic structures that comprise it are thought to evolve out of human interactions rather than out of biologically derived tensions. Instead of being motivated by tension reduction, human beings are motivated by the need to establish and maintain relationships. It is the need for human contact, in other words, that constitutes the primary motive within an object relations perspective.

(Cashdan 1988: 18)

Object relations theorists adopted the term 'object' in acknowledgement of the fact that the person's emotionally significant relationships could be with an actual person, with an internalized image or memory of a person with *parts* of a person or with a physical object:

an approximate synonym for 'Object Relations' is 'Personal Relationships'. The reason why the latter, more readily understandable phrase is not used is because psychodynamic theory also attaches significance to the *object* of a person's feelings or desires, which may be non-human (as Winnicott used the term 'transitional object') or part of a person (the breast, for example, in the earliest mother–baby relationship). Apart from relationships to whole persons, the psychodynamic therapist and counsellor is therefore concerned to understand the relationships the client has to her or his internal objects (. . . internalised aspects of the personality . . .); to what are known as 'part-objects' (parts of the body, as well as persons who are perceived only partially, and not as a whole); and to non-human objects (such as a child's security blanket as in some sense 're-presenting' the nurturing, but temporarily absent, parent).

(Jacobs 1999: 9)

The use of the term 'object' also implies that the client may be relating to another person not in a 'real' or 'authentic' way, but in a way that is selective or objectifying.

One of the most fundamental of the dysfunctional patterns by which people relate to 'objects' is *splitting*. The idea of splitting refers to a way of defending against difficult feelings and impulses that can be traced back to the very first months of life. Klein, it will be recalled, understood that babies could only differentiate between the wholly 'good' and wholly 'bad' part-object of the breast. This object was experienced by the baby as one associated with pleasurable and blissful feelings while feeding, or with feelings of rage when it was absent or taken away. Correspondingly, the psychological and emotional world of the baby at this very early stage consisted only of things that were good or bad; there were no shades of feelings in between. The fundamental insecurity and terror evoked by the feelings of 'bad' led Klein to characterize this as a 'paranoid-schizoid' position.

As the child grows and develops, it becomes able to perceive that good and bad can go together, and therefore it can begin to distinguish different degrees of goodness and badness. When this development does not proceed in a satisfactory manner, or when some external threat re-evokes the insecurity of these early months, the person may either grow up with a tendency to experience the world as 'split' between objects which are all good or all bad, or use this defence in particular situations.

It is not difficult to think of examples of splitting in everyday life, as well as in the counselling room. Within the social and political arena, many people see only good in one political party, soccer team, religion or nationality, and attribute everything bad to the other. Within relationships and family life, people have friends and enemies, parents have favourite and disowned children, and the children may have perfect mothers and wicked fathers. Within an individual personality, sexuality may be bad and intellect good, or drinking reprehensible and abstinence wonderful.

For the psychodynamic counsellor, the client who exhibits splitting is defending against feelings of love and hate for the same object. For example, a woman who idealizes her counsellor and complains repeatedly in counselling of the misdeeds and insensitivity of her husband may have underlying strong feelings of longing for closeness in the marriage and rage at the way he abuses her, or an underlying need to be taken care of by him coupled with anger at his absences at work. As with the other defences described earlier in the chapter, the task of the counsellor is first of all to help the client to be aware of the way she is avoiding her true feelings through this manoeuvre, then gently to encourage exploration and understanding of the emotions and impulses that are so hard to accept. From a psychodynamic perspective, the reason why the person needs to use the defence is that some aspects of the current situation are similar to painful childhood situations, and are bringing to the surface long buried memories of early events. Although the client may be a socially and professionally successful and respons-ible adult, the inner emotional turmoil she brings to counselling is the part of her that is still a child, and only has available to it infantile ways of coping, such as splitting. So, in the case of the woman who idealizes her counsellor and scorns her husband, it may eventually emerge that, perhaps, the grandfather who was sup-posed to look after her when mum was out actually abused her sexually, and she could only deal with this by constructing a 'good' grandad object and a 'bad' one.

The defence mechanism of splitting is similar to the classic Freudian ideas of defence, such as repression, denial and reaction formation, in that these are all processes that occur within the individual psyche or personality. The Kleinian notion of projective identification, however, represents an important departure, in that it describes a process of emotional defence that is interpersonal rather than purely intrapersonal. Being able to apply the idea of projective identification is therefore a uniquely valuable strategy for psychodynamic counsellors who view client problems as rooted in relationships.

The concept of 'projection' has already been introduced as a process whereby the person defends against threatening and unacceptable feelings and impulses by acting as though these feelings and impulses only existed in other people, not in the person himself or herself. For example, a man who accuses his work colleagues of always disagreeing with his very reasonable proposals may be projecting on to them his own buried hostility and competitiveness. The counsellor who persists in assuming that a depressed client really needs to make more friends and join some clubs may be projecting her own fear of her personal inner emptiness.

Projective identification occurs when the person to whom the feelings and impulses are being projected is manipulated into believing that he or she actually has these feelings and impulses. For instance, the man who accuses his colleagues may unconsciously set up circumstances where they have little choice but to argue with him: for example, by not explaining his ideas with enough clarity. And the counsellor may easily persuade the depressed client that she herself does want to make friends.

From an object relations perspective, the dynamics of projective identification have their origins in very early experience, in the time when the child was unable to tell the difference between self and external objects. In projective identification, this blurring of the self–other boundary is accompanied by a need to control the other, which comes from the early state of childhood grandiose omnipotence.

Cashdan (1988) has identified four major patterns of projective identification, arising from underlying issues of dependency, power, sexuality and ingratiation. He describes projective identification as a process that occurs in the context of a relationship. In the case of dependency, the person will actively seek assistance from other people who are around, by using phrases such as 'What do you think?' or 'I can't seem to manage this on my own.' The person is presenting a relationship stance of helplessness. Usually, however, these requests for help are not based on a real inability to solve problems or cope, but are motivated by what Cashdan (1988) calls a 'projective fantasy', a sense of self-in-relationship originating in disturbed object relations in early childhood. The dependent person might have a projective fantasy which could be summarized as a fundamental belief that 'I can't survive'. The great reservoir of unresolved childhood need or anger contained within this fantasy is what gives urgency and force to what may otherwise appear to be reasonable requests for assistance. The recipient of the request is therefore under pressure, and may be induced into taking care of the person. Similar processes take place with other unconscious needs. In any patterns of projective identification, the outcome is to re-create in an adult relationship the type of object relations that prevailed in childhood. The dependent person, for instance, may possibly have had a mother who needed to look after him or her all the time.

The idea of projective identification provides psychodynamic counsellors with a useful conceptual tool for disentangling the complex web of feelings and fantasies that exist in troubled relationships. The unconscious intention behind projective identification is to induce or entice the other to behave towards the self as if the self was in reality a dependent, powerful, sexual or helpful person. This interpersonal strategy enables the person to deny that the dependency, for example, is a fantasy which conceals behind it a multiplicity of feelings, such as resentment, longing or despair. There may be times when the projection is acceptable to the person on the receiving end, perhaps because it feeds his or her fantasy of being powerful or caring. But there will be times when the recipient becomes aware

Box

4.3

The goal of therapy, from an object relations perspective

The Scottish psychoanalyst Ronald Fairbairn (1889–1964) was one of the leading figures in the development of an object relations approach within psychoanalysis. Fairbairn was particularly interested in the difficulties that many of his patients had in making 'real' contact either with him or with anyone else in their lives. He came to describe the inner worlds of such patients as 'closed systems'. Towards the end of his career, he characterized the aim of psychoanalysis in the following terms: 'the aim of psychoanalytic treatment is to effect breaches of the closed system which constitutes the patient's inner world, and thus to make this world accessible to the influence of outer reality' (Fairbairn 1958: 380).

Fairbairn pointed out that the idea of 'transference' implied a process taking place within a closed system. If a person was able to make genuine contact with another, then he or she would treat that other person as a unique individual, and no transference would occur. However, for a person trapped inside a 'closed' psychological world, contact with another person can only be made by acting as though that person was treated as an 'internal object' (i.e. an internalized representation of a pattern of childhood experience). Fairbairn (1958) believed that his view held important implications for the practice of therapy:

> The implication of these considerations is that the interpretation of transference phenomena in the setting of the analytic situation is not in itself enough to promote a satisfactory change in the patient. For such a change to accrue, it is necessary for the patient's relationship with the analyst to undergo a process of development in which a relationship based on transference becomes replaced by a realistic relationship between two persons in the outer world. Such a process of development represents the disruption of the closed system within which the patient's symptoms have developed and are maintained, and which compromises his relationships with external objects. It also represents the establishment of an open system in which the distortions of inner reality can be corrected by outer reality and true relationships with external objects can occur.
>
> (p. 381)

> . . . psycho-analytical treatment resolves itself into a struggle on the part of the patient to press-gang his relationship with the analyst into the closed system of the inner world through the agency of transference, and a determination on the part of the analyst to effect a breach in this closed system.
>
> (p. 385)

These passages from Fairbairn capture the enormity of the shift in psychoanalytic practice represented by the object relations approach. The significance of this shift can too easily be lost in the abstract language used by the majority of psychodynamic/psychoanalytic theorists. It is clear that what Fairbairn is referring to is an *active* therapist, who is seeking to move beyond transference and use a 'realistic relationship' to 'breach' the closed system of the client's inner world.

that there is something not quite right, and resists the projection. Or there may be times when the projector himself or herself becomes painfully aware of what is happening. Finally, there will be occasions in counselling when projective identification is applied to the counsellor, who will be pressured to treat the client in line with fantasy expectations. These times provide rich material for the counsellor to work with.

The British Independents: the importance of counter-transference

The psychodynamic approach to counselling in the post-Freudian era has been marked by the emergence of a range of different writers who have developed the theory in different directions. One of the significant groupings of psychodynamic therapists has been the British 'Independent' group. The origins of the Independents can be traced back to the beginnings of psychoanalysis in Britain. The British Psycho-Analytical Society was formed in 1919, under the leadership of Ernest Jones. In 1926, Melanie Klein, who had been trained in Berlin, moved to London and became a member of the British Society. From the beginning Klein was critical of conventional psychoanalysis. She pioneered child analysis, insisted on the primary importance of destructive urges and the death instinct, and paid more attention to early development than to Oedipal issues. The contrast between the views of Klein and her followers, and those of more orthodox Freudians, came to a climax with the emigration of Freud and his daughter Anna Freud, along with several other analysts from Vienna, to London in 1938. Anna Freud represented the mainstream of Freudian theory, and in the years immediately following the death of Freud in 1939, the relationship between her group and the Kleinians became tense. In the 1940s there were a series of what came to be known as 'controversial discussions' in the Society. The drama of this period in psychoanalysis is well captured by Rayner (1990: 18–19):

> by 1941 the atmosphere in scientific meetings was becoming electric . . . It is puzzling that there should be such passion on matters of theory in the midst of a world war. The situation was that London was being bombed nearly every night, and many did not know whether they would survive, let alone what would happen to analysis – to which they had given their lives. They felt they were the protectors of precious ideas which were threatened not only by bombs but from within their colleagues and themselves. Also, it was hardly possible to go on practising analysis, which is vital to keep coherent analytic ideas alive. Ideological venom and character assassination were released under these circumstances. Where many people found a new communality under the threats of war, the opposite happened to psychoanalysts in London.

In what can be seen as a reflection of the British capacity for compromise, the Society decided by 1946 to divide, for purposes of training, into three loose groups: the Kleinians, the Anna Freud group and the 'middle' group, who later became known as the Independents. The rule was introduced that analysts in training must be exposed to the ideas and methods of more than one group. This principle has resulted in a tradition of openness to new ideas within the British psychodynamic community. The influence of the 'independent mind' in psycho-analysis has been documented by Kohon (1986) and Rayner (1990).

Although the Independents have inevitably generated new ideas across the whole span of psychodynamic theory (Rayner 1990), the group is particularly known for its reappraisal of the concept of counter-transference. It is not without significance that a group of therapists who had gone through the kind of personal and professional trauma described by Rayner (1990) should become particularly sensitive to the role of the personality and self of the therapist in the therapeutic relationship. The contribution of the Independents has been to draw attention to the value of the feelings of the counsellor in the relationship with the client. Previously, counter-transference had been regarded with some suspicion by ana-lysts, as evidence of neurotic conflicts in the analyst. Heimann (1950) argued, by contrast, that counter-transference was 'one of the most important tools' in analysis. Her position was that 'the analyst's unconscious understands that of the patient. This rapport on a deep level comes to the surface in the form of feelings which the analyst notes in response to [the] patient.'

Another member of the Independent group, Symington (1983), suggested that 'at one level the analyst and patient together make a single system'. Both analyst and patient can become locked into shared illusions or fantasies, which Symington (1983) argues can only be dissolved through an 'act of freedom' by the analyst. In other words, the analyst needs to achieve insight into the part he or she is play-ing in maintaining the system. The approach to counter-transference initiated by the independents involved a warmer, more personal contact between client and therapist (Casement 1985, 1990), and anticipated many of the developments associated with time-limited psychodynamic counselling. However, there still exist many debates over the nature of counter-transference and how it can be used in counselling and psychotherapy (see Box 4.4).

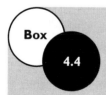

Box

4.4

What are the sources of therapists' counter-transference feelings?

In the early years of psychoanalysis, the analyst or therapist was generally regarded as a neutral, *blank screen* upon which the patient projected his or her fantasies based on unresolved emotional conflicts from the past (the 'transference neurosis'). In the recent writings on psychoanalytic and psychodynamic counselling and psychotherapy, however, it has become widely accepted that the emotional response of the therapist to the client, the 'counter-transference', is an essential source of data about what is happening in the therapy. But where does counter-transference come from? Holmqvist and Armelius (1996) suggest that within the psychoanalytic literature there are three competing perspectives on counter-transference. First, there is the classical Freudian view of counter-transference, which is that it derives from the personality of the therapist, in particular from unresolved conflicts that the therapist has not analysed and understood, which therefore interfere with the therapeutic process. This is the view that counter-transference is a distortion in the blank screen. The second perspective is to explain counter-transference as the response of the therapist to the patient's characteristic ways of relating to other people. The feelings that the therapist experiences in relation to the client or patient are, from this perspective, invaluable clues to the client's relationship style or inner life. Third, some contemporary psychodynamic writers have argued that counter-transference is a *shared* interpersonal reality that client and therapist create between them.

Some research by Holmqvist and Armelius (1996) and Holmqvist (2001) throws new light on this debate. They used a checklist of feeling words to assess the emotional reactions of therapists to their patients. The therapists were employed in treatment units for severely disturbed people, and each patient in the unit was seen by several therapists in the team. The checklist asked therapists to think about a specific client and then to choose from a list of adjectives to indicate their response to the trigger question 'when I talk with (this client), I feel . . .' Data were gathered on several occasions for each group of therapists and patients. The hypothesis was that if these therapist emotional reactions were dominated by patient transference projections (Perspective 2), then different therapists would rate each individual patient in the same way (i.e. the ratings would be dominated by a fixed way in which the patient reacted with everyone). If, on the other hand, the emotional response of a therapist to a patient was dominated by therapist personal style or unresolved conflicts (Perspective 1), then individual therapists would rate each of their patients in the same way. Finally, if counter-transference was indeed a uniquely new emotional reality with each patient (Perspective 3), then there would be what are known as statistical 'interaction effects' in the pattern of ratings. Analysis of the data showed some support for all three perspectives. In other words, there was evidence that the way that a therapist felt about a specific patient would be influenced by the patient, by the therapist and by a combination of the two. However, the single most important factor determining the therapist's emotional response was the personal style of the therapist (Perspective 1). Holmqvist (2001: 115) has concluded from his research that 'the therapist's reactions [belong] primarily to his or her own emotional universe.' This research suggests that it is a mistake to over-simplify the notion of counter-transference (evidence for all three sources of counter-transference was found) but that the therapist's 'habitual feeling style' lies at the heart of the way he or she responds emotionally to clients.

The American post-Freudian tradition: ego psychology and self-theory

The development in Britain, by Klein, Fairbairn and others, of an object relations approach that emphasized the importance of the client's relationships, rather than his or her libido-based drives, was matched in the USA by the writings of Margaret Mahler, Heinz Kohut and their colleagues, who were beginning to take a similar line.

The model of child development provided by Klein can usefully be supplemented by that offered by Margaret Mahler (1968; Mahler *et al.* 1975), whose approach is generally described as 'ego psychology'. Mahler views the child in the first year of life as being autistic, without any sense of the existence of other people. Between two and four months is the 'symbiotic' stage, in which there is the beginning of recognition of the mother as an object. Then, from about four months through to three years of age, the infant undergoes a gradual process of separation from the mother, slowly building up a sense of self independent from the self of the mother. At the beginning of this process the infant will experiment with crawling away from the mother then returning to her. Towards the end of the period, particularly with the development of language, the child will have a name and a set of things that are 'mine'.

By observing both 'normal' and disturbed children, Klein, Mahler and other post-Freudian practitioners have been able to piece together an understanding of the emotional life of the child that is, they would assert, more accurate than that reconstructed by Freud through interpretation of the free associations of adult patients in therapy. However, like Freud they regard the troubles of adult life as being derived ultimately from disturbances in the developmental process in childhood. Winnicott used the phrase 'good enough' to describe the type of parenting that would enable children to develop effectively. Unfortunately, many people are subjected to childhood experiences that are far from 'good enough', and result in a variety of different patterns of pathology.

It can be seen here that the theoretical framework being developed by Mahler and her colleagues includes a strong emphasis on the idea of 'self', a concept which was not extensively used by Freud. Where Freud, influenced by his medical and scientific training, saw personality as ultimately determined by the biologically driven stages of psycho-sexual development and biologically based motives, theorists such as Klein and Mahler came to view people as fundamentally social beings.

Another important strand of recent psychoanalytic thinking is represented by the work of Kohut (1971, 1977) and Kernberg (1976, 1984), whose ideas are referred to as 'self' theory. Kohut (1971) and Kernberg (1975) initiated a re-evaluation of the problem of narcissism within psychoanalysis. The concept of narcissism was originally introduced by Freud, who drew upon the Greek legend of Narcissus, a youth who fell in love with his own reflection. Freud viewed over-absorption in self as a difficult condition to treat through psychoanalysis, since it was almost impossible for the analyst to break through the narcissism to reach the underlying conflicts. Kohut (1971) argued that the narcissistic person is fundamentally unable to differentiate between self and other. Rather than being able to act towards others as separate entities, in narcissism other people are experienced as 'self-objects', as little more than extensions of the self. Other people only exist to aggrandize and glorify the self. For Kohut, the solution to this lay in the transference relationship between client and therapist. If the therapist refrained from directly confronting the falseness and grandiosity of the client, but instead empathized with and accepted the client's experience of things, a situation would be created that paralleled the conditions of early childhood.

Kohut (1971) argued that, just as the real mother is never perfect, and can only hope to be 'good enough', the therapist can never achieve complete empathy and acceptance. The client therefore experiences, at moments of failure of empathy, a sense of 'optimal frustration'. It is this combination of frustration in a context of high acceptance and warmth that gradually enables the client to appreciate the separation of self and other. Although the model proposed by Kohut (1971, 1977) has much more to say on the matter than is possible here, it should be apparent that his approach has made a significant contribution to the understanding and treatment of this disorder.

Another important area of advance has been in work with 'borderline' clients. This label is used to refer to people who exhibit extreme difficulties in forming relationships, have been profoundly emotionally damaged by childhood experiences and express high levels of both dependency and rage in the relationship with the therapist. One of the meanings of 'borderline' in this context refers to the idea of 'borderline schizophrenic'. Traditionally, people with this kind of depth and array of problems have not been considered as viable candidates for psychodynamic therapy, and have generally been offered long-term 'supportive' therapy rather than anything more ambitious. The work of Kernberg (1975, 1984) and others from an object relations/self perspective has attributed the problems of borderline clients to arrested development in early childhood. These people are understood to be emotionally very young, dealing with the world as if they were in the paranoid-schizoid stage described by Klein, where experience is savagely split between 'good' and 'bad'. The task of the therapist is to enable the client to regress back to the episodes in childhood that presented blocks to progress and maturity, and to discover new ways of overcoming them. This type of therapy can be seen almost as providing a second chance for development with a special kind of parenting, with the therapeutic relationship acting as a substitute for the nuclear family.

Therapy with borderline clients is often conducted over several years, with the client receiving multiple sessions each week. The intensity and challenge of this kind of therapeutic work, and the generally moderate success rates associated with it, mean that practitioners are often cautious about taking on borderline clients, or limit the number of such clients in their case load at any one time (Aronson 1989).

The European tradition

It is important to recognize that there exists an important European tradition in psychoanalytic psychotherapy. For example, psychodynamic and psychoanalytic approaches to therapy dominate therapy provision in Gemany, Sweden and France, and are represented in all other European countries. The tradition of psychodynamic therapy that has developed in Germany and Sweden has reflected the influence of British and American writers discussed earlier in this chapter. However, Germany is unusual in the respect to which its psychological therapy service has developed psychodynamic therapy for patients with psychosomatic disorders. The majority of these patients are treated on an inpatient basis – Germany is unique in having more than 8,000 short-term inpatient psychotherapy beds (Kachele *et al.* 1999). The generosity of the German health care system is also reflected in the number of sessions of publicly funded psychodynamic therapy that are available to patients: 'analytic psychotherapy should as a rule achieve a satisfactory result in 160 sessions, and special cases, up to 240 sessions. Further extension to 300 sessions is possible under exceptional circumstances, but must be supported by detailed arguments' (Kachele *et al.* 1999: 336). German and Swedish researchers have been responsible for a substantial number of studies of psychoanalytic therapy. One of the most important recent research studies into the effectiveness of psychoanalysis and psychoanalytic psychotherapy has been carried out in Stockholm (see Box 4.5).

The development of psychoanalysis in France has, however, followed a different pathway. The French analyst Jacques Lacan (1901–81) drew heavily on concepts from philosophy and linguistics, as well as advocating a return to what he perceived to be some of the basic ideas of Freud. Lacan (1977, 1979) placed a great deal of emphasis on the concept of *desire*, and the categorization of consciousness into three modes of apprehending the world: the *imaginary*, the *symbolic* and the *real*. For Lacan the task of therapy was to use language (the symbolic) to bridge the gap between two fundamentally non-linguistic realms: the imaginary and the real. Lacan also advocated innovations in technique, such as the use of short sessions. A key theme in Lacanian theory is the limits of an understanding that is based solely on language, and much of his work explores the limitations of language. An accessible example of the application of a Lacanian framework can be found in Shipton (1999).

Attachment theory

The ideas of the British psychoanalyst John Bowlby (1969, 1973, 1980, 1988) have become increasingly influential within psychodynamic counselling and psychotherapy in recent years. Although trained as an analyst, Bowlby was also an active researcher. The main focus of his work was around the process of *attachment* in human relations. In his research and writing, Bowlby argued that human beings, like other animals, have a basic need to form attachments with others throughout life, and will not function well unless such attachments are available. The capacity for attachment is, according to Bowlby, innate, but is shaped by early experience with significant others. For example, if the child's mother is absent, or does not form a secure and reliable bond, then the child will grow up with a lack

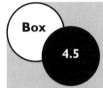

Box 4.5

Are psychoanalysis and psychodynamic therapy effective? The Stockholm study

There have been many research studies into the effectiveness of various types of psychodynamic counselling and psychotherapy. Reviews of this research can be found in Henry *et al.* (1994) and Roth and Fonagy (1996). However, the majority of these studies reflect situations where the therapy that is provided has been set up by a research team in a clinic, and delivered and monitored under tightly defined conditions. It can be argued that such 'controlled' studies may not fully represent what happens in everyday practice. The *Stockholm Outcome of Psychoanalysis and Psychotherapy Project* (STOPPP) is a research study that was set up to evaluate the effectiveness of psychoanalysis and psychodynamic psychotherapy as it is delivered in ordinary conditions (Sandell *et al.* 2000). There is a strong tradition of psychodynamic therapy in Sweden, and the health authorities subsidize long-term therapy delivered by private-practice therapists. The STOPPP study was designed to track the progress of *all* clients receiving either classical psychoanalysis or psychodynamically oriented psychotherapy within Stockholm County over a period of several years. Information on clients, at the waiting list stage and then during and after treatment, was collected through questionnaires that measured psychiatric symptoms, quality of social relationships/adjustment, optimism/morale and various demographic factors. Some clients participated in in-depth open-ended interviews following completion of therapy. Data on absence from work and health care utilization were collected from health service records. All therapists completed questionnaires on their training, attitude and approach to therapy, and use of personal therapy and supervision. The report by Sandell *et al.* (2000) draws on information collected over an eight-year period from 554 clients at the waiting list stage, 408 people who had completed therapy (331 in psychodynamic psychotherapy, 74 in psychoanalysis) and 209 therapists. All the clients in the study received long-term therapy. The psychoanalysis clients received, on average, 3.5 sessions each week over 54 months, while the psychodynamic therapy clients received an average of 1.5 sessions per week over 46 months. In general, clients were people with fairly severe problems, with many having made previous use of inpatient, drug treatment and other types of psychological therapy. The clients in analysis and those in therapy reported equal levels of symptoms at the waiting list stage, but those who had chosen to enter analysis were slightly older and better educated, and more likely to be male, than those who had opted for psychotherapy.

How effective was the therapy received by these clients? The STOPPP project team collected a great deal of data, which can be analysed in many different ways. However, the main findings reported by Sandell *et al.* (2000) were that major positive gains were found in levels of symptoms, and morale, for both groups of clients. The extent of benefit was equivalent to that found in other studies of the effectiveness of therapy: at the beginning of therapy all clients showed high levels of symptoms, while at the final follow-up period the majority were within the range of symptoms/

problems exhibited by the 'normal', non-clinical population. Improvement in social functioning was less dramatic, with only moderate benefits found in quality of social relationship/adjustment and general health. The clients who had received psychoanalysis did better than those who had been in psychodynamic therapy, particularly at follow-up. Both groups had improved significantly by the end of treatment, but the clients who had received psychoanalysis continued to improve several months after treatment had concluded. At follow-up interviews, psychoanalysis clients were much less likely than psychotherapy clients to be interested in seeking further therapy.

The research team also looked at the factors associated with good outcomes, in terms of the characteristics of therapists who had worked with high-gain clients, and those who had moderate or low-gain cases. Better results were associated with analysts and therapists who were older and more experienced, and were female. Poorer results were associated with analysts and therapists who had undergone *more* personal therapy and supervision – the researchers speculated that some of these practitioners were people who understood that they were not operating effectively, and were seeking ways of compensating for their limitations. For psychoanalysts, the personal style and attitudes of the analysts did not appear to make a difference to outcome – it appeared as though the 'discipline' and structure of the analytic session were more important than the personal qualities of the analyst. However, for psychotherapists, style and attitude had a major influence on outcome. Psychodynamic therapists who were more kindly, supportive, involved and self-disclosing, and who emphasized coping strategies (i.e. were more like humanistic and cognitive–behavioural therapists in style and attitude), were more effective than those who displayed the more classically psychoanalytic value of neutrality. In other words, the more *eclectic* the psychotherapists (but not the analysts) were, the better they did. Sandell *et al.* (2000: 940) suggested that: 'We are led to the conclusion that there is a negative transfer of the psychoanalytic stance into psychotherapeutic practice, and that this negative transfer *may be* especially pronounced when the psychoanalytic stance is not backed up by psychoanalytic training.'

The Stockholm study therefore raises important questions about the relationship between psychoanalysis and psychodynamic therapy, and points towards significant differences in the processes involved in each of these approaches. The implication from this study is that a 'pure' psychoanalytic approach can be very effective with clients who have chosen to engage in it on a four-sessions-per-week basis, but that the majority of clients, who opt for once-per-week therapy, appear to need a more 'sociable' and supportive stance on the part of their therapists. It would also seem that therapists who behave in an 'over-analytic' manner in once-per-week therapy are significantly less effective than those who deliver a form of psychodynamic therapy that combines psychoanalytic ideas with a relationship style and practice that is also informed by other therapeutic approaches.

of trust and a general inability to form stable, close relationships. If, on the other hand, the mother or other family members have provided the child with what Bowlby calls a 'secure base' in childhood, then later close relationships will be possible.

Similarly, according to Bowlby, early experiences of loss can set an emotional pattern that persists into adulthood. Bowlby and Robertson (Bowlby *et al.* 1952) observed that children separated from their parents – for example, through hospitalization – initially respond through protest and anger, then with depression and sadness, and finally by behaving apparently normally. This normality, however, masks a reserve and unwillingness to share affection with new people. If the parents return, there will be reactions of rejection and avoidance before they are accepted again. For the young child, who is unable to understand at a cognitive level what is happening, this kind of experience of loss may instil a fear of abandonment that makes him or her either cling on to relationships in later life or even avoid any relationship that might end in loss or abandonment. For the older child, the way he or she is helped (or not) to deal with feelings of grief and loss will likewise set up patterns that will persist. For example, when parents divorce it is quite common for a child to end up believing that he or she caused the split and subsequent loss, and that consequently he or she is a 'bad' person who would have a destructive impact on any relationship. Such a person might then find it hard to commit to relationships later in their life.

Bowlby (1973) suggested that the person develops an 'internal working model' to describe his or her internal representation of the social world, his or her main attachment figures within that world, himself or herself and the links between these elements. It can be seen that the idea of the 'internal working model' is similar to the notion of internalized 'object relations' used by Klein and Fairbairn and other 'object relations' theorists. There were, however, three important differences in emphasis between Bowlby and the object relations theorists. First, he argued that a biologically based mechanism of attachment had a central part to play in the inner life of the person. Second, he always maintained that attachments were the result of actual behaviour by another person (i.e. not solely internal). Third, Bowlby strongly believed that evidence from scientific research was just as important as insight derived from clinical practice.

Inspired by Bowlby, researchers in different parts of the world have sought to develop deeper understandings of the way that attachment operates, and how this idea can be applied in therapy. The most important lines of research are associated with the work of Mary Ainsworth, Mary Main and Peter Fonagy.

With the aim of looking more closely at attachment behaviour in young children, Mary Ainsworth carried out a series of studies using the 'strange situation' procedure (Ainsworth *et al.* 1978; Bretherton and Waters 1985). The 'strange situation' is a laboratory laid out like a playroom, where infants can be systematically observed from behind a mirror while the mother twice leaves, and then returns. The behaviour of infants in this situation has been shown to be similar to their behaviour in real-life (home) situations when they are left alone. Infant responses can be categorized into four types:

- *Secure*. The child shows signs of missing the parent, then seeks contact when she returns and settles back into playing normally.
- *Insecure–avoidant*. The infant shows few signs of missing the parent, and avoids her upon reunion.
- *Insecure–ambivalent*. The child is highly distressed and angry when the parent leaves, and cannot be settled when she returns.
- *Insecure–disoriented*. The child shows a range of stereotyped and frozen patterns of behaviour.

Ainsworth found that the behaviour of infants in the strange situation experiment could be explained by the behaviour of their mothers. For example, 'secure' children had mothers who were sensitive to their emotional signals, while 'insecure' children had mothers who could be observed to be insensitive, rejecting or unpredictable.

While Ainsworth's research provided a convincing picture of the powerful nature of attachment patterns in early childhood, it is not possible to observe adult patterns in such a clear-cut manner in a laboratory experiment. Mary Main therefore developed the *Adult Attachment Interview* (*AAI*) as a means of assessing patterns of attachment later in life (Main 1991; Hesse 1999). The AAI consists of a 15-item clinical interview, which will normally take around two hours to complete. The questions asked in the interview (see Table 4.1) are intended to

Table 4.1 Questions asked in the Adult Attachment Interview

 1 Who was in your immediate family? Where did you live?
 2 Describe your relationship with your parents, starting as far back as you can remember.
 3 Can you give me five adjectives or phrases to describe your relationship with your mother and father during childhood?
 4 What memories and experiences led you to choose these adjectives?
 5 To which parent did you feel closer, and why?
 6 What you were upset as a child, what did you do, and what would happen?
 7 Could you describe your first separation from your parents?
 8 Did you ever feel rejected as a child? What did you do?
 9 Were your parents ever threatening toward you?
10 How do you think your early experiences may have affected your adult personality?
11 Why do you think your parents behaved as they did in your childhood?
12 Who were the other adults who were close to you in your childhood?
13 Did you experience the loss of a parent, or other close loved one as a parent, or in adulthood?
14 Were there many changes in your relationships with your parents between childhood and adulthood?
15 What is your relationship with your parents like for you currently?

Note: This is an abbreviated list of questions. The actual AAI is based on an extensive protocol, with follow-up questions.
Source: Hesse (1999).

'surprise the unconscious'. In other words, the person will find himself or herself saying things, or contradicting themselves, in ways that are beyond their conscious control. For participants, the interview is similar to a therapy session, in that they are invited to talk openly, and at length, about childhood experiences and memories that may be quite painful. Analysis of the interview depends less on the content of what the person says, but is largely derived from the style or manner in which the person tells the story of their early life.

Coding of the AAI yields four types of attachment pattern that are broadly similar to the categories used in the 'strange situation' test:

- *Secure/autonomous*. The person's story is coherent, consistent and objective. He or she is able to collaborate with the interviewer.
- *Dismissing*. The story is not coherent. The person tends to be dismissive of attachment-related experiences and relationships. Tendency to describe parents as 'normal' or ideal.
- *Preoccupied*. The story is incoherent, and the speaker may appear angry, passive or fearful, and preoccupied with past relationships. Sentences often long, vague and confusing.
- *Unresolved disorganized*. Similar to dismissive or preoccupied, but may include long silences or overtly erroneous statements (for example, talking as though someone who died is still alive).

A large amount of research has been carried out using the AAI, and has found strong correlations between the attachment styles of parents and their children, and differences in the process of counselling with people exhibiting different attachment styles (Hesse 1999).

From the point of view of counselling and psychotherpy, one of the most significant aspects of research using the AAI was the discovery by Mary Main that people who had experienced secure attachments, and who functioned well in their lives, were able to talk about their past in a coherent and collaborative way. Main suggested that 'securely attached' people are able to do this because they are able to engage in 'metacognitive monitoring': they are able to 'step back' from the situation and reflect on what they are saying. It is as though the person is able to look objectively at their own thought processes. This is only possible, according to Main and other AAI researchers, because the person has been able to develop a single, coherent 'internal working model', rather than multiple models:

> Multiple models of attachment are formed when the acknowledgement of disturbing feelings or memories threatens the self or current relationships; distortion and incoherence are the cognitive and linguistic manifestations of multiple contradictory models . . . coherence is also a critical element in the intergenerational transmission of attachment: the mother who is able to openly acknowledge, access and evaluate her own attachment experiences will be able to respond to her child's attachment needs in a sensitive and nurturing way.
>
> (Slade 1999: 580)

The contribution of Peter Fonagy and his colleagues has been to elaborate the implications of Main's notion of metacognitive monitoring for the practice of counselling and psychotherapy. Fonagy (1999) argues that is the capacity to learn how to *reflect* on experience that lies at the heart of effective therapy. The development within therapy of what Fonagy calls the 'reflexive function', the ability to think about and talk about painful past events, helps the person to protect himself or herself against the raw emotional impact of these events, without having to use defenses such as denial or repression.

Bowlby's ideas on attachment have not resulted in the creation of a specific 'attachment therapy'. The impact of attachment theory on psychodynamic counselling and psychotherapy has taken a number of forms. A knowledge of attachment theory helps practitioners to become more aware of the possible origins of patterns of relationships described by their clients, and assists them to their way of being with clients (i.e. their own characteristic attachment styles, which may be differentially triggered by different clients). A series of research studies (Kivlighan *et al.* 1998; Tyrrell *et al.* 1999; Eames and Roth 2000; Kilmann *et al.* 1999; Rubino *et al.* 2000) have provided convincing evidence for the role of both client and therapist attachment style in shaping the process of therapy. Research has also established the biological mechanisms responsible for patterns of attachment behaviour (Cassidy and Shaver 1999), which has enhanced the scientific plausibility of psychoanalytically oriented theories of therapy. Most important of all, perhaps, attachment theory and AAI research enable counsellors to become more sensitive to the ways in which their clients tell their story – it opens up links between the style of telling the story and broader patterns of relating with others. Particularly useful accounts of how attachment theory can be applied in therapy practice can be found in the writings of the British therapist Jeremy Holmes (2000, 2001).

Other psychodynamically oriented approaches to narrative are examined on pages 227–30

Psychodynamic counselling within a time-limited framework

In the early years of psychoanalysis, it was not assumed by Freud or his colleagues that patients need necessarily be in treatment for long periods of time. For example, Freud is reported to have carried out in 1908 successful therapy of a sexual problem in the composer Gustav Mahler in the course of four sessions (Jones 1955). However, as psychoanalysts became more aware of the problem of resistance in patients, and more convinced of the intractable nature of the emotional problems they brought to therapy, they began to take for granted the idea that psychoanalysis in most cases would be a lengthy business, with patients attending therapy several times a week, perhaps for years.

Among the first psychoanalysts, however, there were some critics of this trend, who argued for a more active role for the therapist, and definite time limits for the length of therapy. The two most prominent advocates of this view were Sandor Ferenczi and Otto Rank. There was strong opposition to their ideas from Freud and the inner circle of analysts, and eventually both men were forced to leave. Within psychoanalytic circles, the ideas of Ferenczi appear to have been neglected for many years, but have recently received an increasing amount of attention from counsellors and psychotherapists interested in developing a more collaborative, active approach to working with clients (see Box 4.6).

A further important event in the progress of the debate about psychoanalytic technique came with the publication in 1946 of a book by Alexander and French, which advocated that psychoanalysts take a flexible approach to treatment. Over a period of seven years at the Chicago Institute for Psychoanalysis, they had experimented with a range of variations of standard psychoanalytic technique: for example, trying out different numbers of sessions each week, the use of the couch or chair and the degree of attention paid to the transference relationship. The Alexander and French book was highly influential and, in the spirit of openness to new ideas that followed the death of Freud in 1939, it stimulated many other analysts to tackle the issues of technique involved in offering psychodynamic therapy or counselling on a time-limited basis. The main figures in the subsequent development of what is often known as 'brief therapy' are Mann (1973), Malan (1976, 1979), Sifneos (1979) and Davanloo (1980).

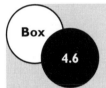

Box 4.6

The rehabilitation of Sandor Ferenczi

Sandor Ferenczi (1873–1933) was born in Hungary, the eighth of 12 children. He trained in medicine, worked in Budapest, specializing in neurological problems, and developed an early interest in hypnosis. Ferenczi met Freud in 1908, when Freud had already published some of his greatest works. Ferenczi came to be described as the 'most loved' of Freud's inner circle. He was analysed by Freud himself, and frequently accompanied the Freud family on vacation. He was a close companion to Freud on the famous visit to the USA in 1909, and was part of the 'secret committee' (Freud, Ernest Jones, Ferenczi, Karl Abraham, Otto Rank, Max Eitington and Hans Sachs) who met regularly together in Vienna, and shared special rings that Freud had made for them. Ferenczi and Otto Rank published a book in 1923, *The Development of Psychoanalysis*, which fore-shadowed ideas that were only to come to fruition many years later: brief therapy, the active involvement of the therapist, flexibility in the use of technique and increased equality in the doctor–patient relationship. Ferenczi did not enjoy good health, and died in 1933. Towards the end of his life, his relationship with Freud became strained. Following his death much of his work remained unpublished, or not translated into English, for many years. His ideas were quickly marginalized within the psychoanalytic movement, and only began to receive wider attention in the 1980s with the publication in English of some of his key writings (Ferenczi 1980a, b), his clinical diaries and his correspondence with Freud, all these followed by influential studies of his approach in Aron and Harris (1993) and Rachman (1997). But why did Ferenczi, once such a central figure in the psychoanalytic movement, suffer 'death by silence'? And why have his ideas become so popular among contemporary psychoanalysts and psychotherapists?

In the 1930s those critical of Ferenczi, primarily Ernest Jones (the biographer and Freud and a key figure in the dissemination of psychoanalytic ideas in Britain and America) portrayed him as dangerous, and someone who was possibly even mentally ill. In his analysis with Freud, Ferenczi vacillated over whether he should marry his mistress (Gizella Palos) or her daughter (Elma). The key events, as summarized by Gabbard (1996: 1122–4) were:

Ferenczi had previously analyzed Gizella, a married woman, with whom he had had an affair. Ferenczi fell in love with Elma in the course of analyzing her, and finally persuaded Freud to take over the case . . . What ensued was a rather remarkable series of boundary violations. Freud made regular reports to Ferenczi regarding the content of the psychoanalytic treatment of Elma and specifically kept Ferenczi informed of whether or not Elma continued to love him. Ultimately, Ferenczi tool Elma back into analysis, but she married an American suitor while Ferenczi himself married Gizella in 1919 . . . Despite this messy situation, Freud subsequently took Ferenczi into analysis . . . the analytic relationship occurred in parallel with other relationships, including mentor–student, close friends, and travelling companions. Moreover, Freud apparently wished that Ferenczi would ultimately marry his daughter.

Gabbard (1996: 1115) observed that 'Freud and his disciples indulged in a good deal of trial and error as they evolved psychoanalytic technique.' Ferenczi was the member of the original psychoanalytic 'inner circle' who experimented most widely in relation to psychoanalytic technique, including the development of what he called 'mutual analysis'. It is therefore perhaps not surprising that, in a period in the 1930s where psychoanalysis was striving to become 'respectable', and was faced by the growth of fascist sentiment in the general public, there was a tacit agreement to 'forget' Ferenczi when he died.

However, in among the behaviour that would now be regarded as professionally unethical, Ferenczi was responsible for some remarkable contributions to psychoanalysis. He unequivocally asserted his belief (in defiance of Freud) that many patients had indeed been sexually abused in childhood, and wrote sensitively about the 'confusion of tongues' that is associated with such a patient's attempts to talk to their therapist about such memories. He argued that analysis should pay attention to the current realities of the person's life, as well as their early years, and that it could be useful for the analyst to make suggestions for action that the client could take to resolve current difficulties. He engaged in dialogue with his patients, and wrote about the importance of the analyst being willing to learn from the patient and develop a 'real' relationship. The fascination that Ferenczi holds for many contemporary psychotherapists is that what he wrote anticipated what was later to become the increasing convergence between psychoanalysis and other forms of 'talking' therapy, particularly the humanistic therapies. And he wrote in a very human, direct style, with a great deal of humility, as someone who was the first to make these discoveries and who found himself, almost by accident, in the territory of a new type of therapy.

It is essential to recognize that the emergence of brief psychodynamic therapy and counselling arose as much from the pressures of social need and client demand as from the deliberations of therapists themselves. In the 1940s in the USA, for example, counsellors and psychotherapists were being expected to help large numbers of members of the armed forces returning from war with emotional problems. In the 1960s there was substantial political pressure in the USA to move mental health facilities into the community, and to make them more readily available for large numbers of clients. Even clients seeing therapists in private practice did not want 'interminable' therapy. For example, Garfield (1986), in a review of studies of the length of treatment in a variety of therapy settings, found that the largest group of clients were those who came for five or six sessions, with the majority seeing their counsellor or therapist on fewer than 20 occasions. These factors led counsellors and therapists from all orientations to examine closely the problem of time-limited interventions, and the literature on brief psychodynamic work is paralleled by writings on brief cognitive, client-centred and other modes of work.

Writers on brief psychodynamic therapy have different ideas about what they mean by 'brief', which can refer to anything between three and 40 sessions. Most are agreed that brief treatment is that involving fewer than 25 sessions. More fundamental, however, is the idea that the number of sessions is rationed, and that a contract is made at the start of counselling that there will only be a certain number of sessions. Although there are many styles of brief psychodynamic work that have been evolved by teams of therapists in different clinics (see Gustafson (1986) for a review of some of the main currents of thought within this movement), there is general agreement that brief work is focused on three discrete stages: beginning, the active phase and termination (Rosen 1987). If the time to be spent with a client is limited, then the maximum use must be made of each and every client–counsellor interaction. The beginning phase is therefore a site for a variety of different kinds of counsellor activity, encompassing assessment, preparing the client, establishing a therapeutic alliance, starting therapeutic work and finding out about the life history and background of the client. The first meeting with the client, and indeed the first words uttered by the client, can be of great significance. This point is well made by Alexander and French (1946: 109):

> The analyst during this period may be compared to a traveller standing on top of a hill overlooking the country through which he is about to journey. At this time it may be possible for him to see his whole anticipated journey in perspective. When once he has descended into the valley, this perspective must be retained in the memory or it is gone. From this time on, he will be able to examine small parts of this landscape in much greater detail than was possible when he was viewing them from a distance, but the broad relations will no longer be so clear.

It is generally assumed that time-limited counselling is appropriate only for particular kinds of clients. For example, clients who are psychotic or 'borderline'

Client assessment
is also discussed
on pages 329–33

are usually seen as unlikely to benefit from time-limited work (although some practitioners, such as Budman and Gurman (1988), would dispute this, and would view all clients as potentially appropriate for time-limited interventions). In brief counselling or therapy it is therefore necessary to carry out an assessment interview. The objectives of the assessment session might cover exploration of such issues as:

- the attitude of the client towards a time-limited treatment contract;
- motivation for change and 'psychological-mindedness';
- the existence of a previous capacity to sustain close relationships;
- the ability to relate with the therapist during the assessment interview;
- the existence of a clearly identifiable, discrete problem to work on in therapy.

Positive indications in all, or most, of these areas are taken to suggest a good prognosis for brief work. Techniques for increasing the effectiveness of the assessment interview include asking the client to complete a life history questionnaire before the interview, recording the interview on video and discussing the assessment with colleagues, and engaging in 'trial therapy' during the interview. The last refers to the practice of the interviewer offering some limited interpretation of the material offered by the client during the interview (Malan 1976), or devoting a segment of the assessment time to a very short therapy session (Gustafson 1986).

It is of course important that care is taken with clients who are assessed as unsuitable for brief work, and that alternative referrals and forms of treatment are available. Special training is usually considered necessary for those carrying out assessment interviews. The beginning stage of brief work also encompasses negotiation with the client over the aims and duration of the counselling or therapy contract, and preparation of the client for what is to follow by explaining to the client the nature of his or her therapeutic responsibilities and tasks.

One of the principal tasks of the brief therapist is to find a focus for the overall therapy, and for each particular session. The therapist is active in seeking out a focus for the work, and in this respect differs from the traditional psychoanalyst, who would wait for themes to emerge through free association. In finding a focus, the counsellor brings to the session some assumptions about the type of material with which he or she is seeking to work. These assumptions are derived from psychoanalytic and object relations theory, and guide the counsellor in the choice of which threads of the client's story to follow up. For example, Budman and Gurman (1988) describe an 'IDE' formula which they use in deciding on a focus for a session. They view people as inevitably grappling with developmental (D) issues arising from their stage of psycho-social development, involved in interpersonal (I) issues arising from relationships and faced with existential (E) issues such as aloneness, choice and awareness of death. Gustafson (1986) emphasizes the central importance of finding a focus when he writes that 'I will not go a step until I have the "loose end" of the patient's preoccupation for today's meeting.'

It is often valuable, in finding the focus for client work, to consider the question 'Why now?' In brief psychodynamic work it is assumed that the problem the client brings to therapy is triggered off by something currently happening in his or her life. The client is seen as a person who is having difficulties coping with a specific situation, rather than as a fundamentally 'sick' individual. The question 'Why now?' helps to begin the process of exploring the roots of the troublesome feelings that are evoked by current life events. Sometimes the precipitating event can be something that happened many years ago, which is being remembered and relived because of an anniversary of some kind. For example, a woman who requested counselling because of a general lack of satisfaction with her relationship with her husband reported that what seemed to be happening now somehow seemed to be associated with her daughter, who was 16 and starting to go out to parties and have boyfriends. The client found herself remembering that, when she had been 16, she had become pregnant and quickly found herself with all the responsibilities of a wife and mother. Her daughter was now at that same stage in life, and bringing home to the client her buried feelings about the stage of development in her life she had missed out on. This case illustrates how the question 'Why now?' can open up developmental issues.

Another set of central issues that are often the focus for brief work arise from experiences of loss. The case just mentioned in fact included a component of grieving for the loss of youth and adolescence. The events that stimulate people to seek counselling help encompass many different types of loss. The death of someone in the family, being made redundant, leaving home or the surgical removal of a body part are all powerful loss experiences. Usually, loss themes in counselling encompass both interpersonal and existential dimensions. Most experiences of loss involve some kind of change in relationships as well as change in the way the person experiences self. The experience of loss particularly challenges the illusion of self as invulnerable and immortal (Yalom 1980). The other existential facet of loss is that it can throw the person into a state of questioning the meaningfulness of what has happened: 'nothing makes sense any more'. Finally, current experiences of loss will reawaken dormant feelings about earlier losses, and may thereby trigger off strong feelings related to early childhood events.

The aims of the counsellor or therapist working with loss from within a brief psychodynamic approach will include uncovering and working through. The uncovering part of the counselling will involve the client exploring and expressing feelings, and generally opening up this whole area of inner experience for exploration. Techniques for assisting uncovering may include retelling the story of the loss, perhaps using photographs or visits to evoke memories and feelings. The working through phase involves becoming aware of the implications of what the loss event has meant, and how the person has coped with it personally and interpersonally. In the latter phase, the counsellor may give the client information about the 'normal' course of reactions to loss.

It can be seen that, although the active phase of brief psychodynamic therapy involves the use of interpretation of current feelings in terms of past events, it also includes encouragement from the therapist or counsellor to express feelings in the here-and-now setting of the counselling room. The aim is to allow the client to undergo what Alexander and French (1946) called a 'corrective emotional experience'. They saw one of the principal aims of therapy as being 'to reexpose the patient, under more favorable circumstances, to emotional situations which he/she could not handle in the past' (Alexander and French 1946: 66). So, for example, a client who had always been afraid to express his anger at the loss of his job, in case his wife could not handle it, can allow this feeling to be shown in the presence of the counsellor, and then, it is hoped, become more able to have this type of emotional experience with his wife or other people outside the counselling room. Part of the active stance of the brief therapist is therefore to assist the communication of feelings that are 'under the surface' by using questions such as 'What do you feel right now?' and 'How do you feel inside?' (Davanloo 1980).

In any kind of time-limited counselling, the existence of a definite date after which therapy will no longer be available raises a whole range of potential issues for clients. The ending of counselling may awaken feelings associated with other kinds of endings, and lead the client to act out in the relationship with the counsellor the ways he or she has defended against previous feelings of loss. The end of counselling may similarly have a resonance for the client of the separation/individuation stage of development (Mahler 1968), the stage of leaving the protective shell of the parental relationship and becoming a more autonomous individual. There may also be a sense of ambivalence about the end of a counselling relationship, with feelings of satisfaction at what has been achieved and frustration at what there still is to learn. The fact of a time limit may bring into focus the client's habitual ways of living in time: for example, by existing only in a future-orientation (in this case, being obsessed with how much time there is left) and being unwilling to be in the present or with the past. The intention of the brief therapist is to exploit the time-limited format by predicting that some of these issues will emerge for the client, and actively challenging the client to confront and learn from them when they do.

The ending of a counselling relationship can also raise issues for the counsellor, such as feelings of loss, grandiosity at how important the therapy has been for the client or self-doubt over how little use the therapy has been. Dealing with termination is therefore a topic that receives much attention in the counsellor's work with his or her supervisor.

It should already be clear that the role of the counsellor in brief psychodynamic work is subtly different from that in traditional psychoanalysis. In the latter, the therapist takes a passive role, acting as a 'blank screen' on to which may be projected the transference reactions of the client. In brief work, by contrast, the therapist is active and purposeful, engaging the client in a therapeutic alliance in which they can work together. The use that is made of the transference relationship is therefore of necessity quite different.

In long-term analysis, the therapist encourages the development of a strong transference reaction, sometimes called a 'transference neurosis', in order to allow evidence of childhood relationship patterns to emerge. In brief work, strategies are used to avoid such deep levels of transference: for example, by identifying and interpreting transferences as soon as they arise, even in the very first session, and by reducing client dependency by explaining what is happening and maintaining a clear focus for the work. In brief therapy, the here-and-now feeling response of the client towards the therapist or counsellor, the transference, is used instead as the basis for making links between present behaviour with the therapist and past behaviour with parents (Malan 1976).

Some useful principles for the interpretation of transference behaviour have been established by Malan (1979) and Davanloo (1980). The triangle of insight (Davanloo 1980) refers to the links between the behaviour of the client with the therapist (T), with other current relationship figures (C) and with past figures such as parents (P). Clients can be helped to achieve insight by becoming aware of important T–C–P links in their lives. For example, a woman who treats her counsellor with great deference, depending on him to solve her problems, may make the connection that her mother was someone who had a strong need to take care of her. The next step might be to unravel the ways in which she is deferential and dependent with her husband and work colleagues. The triangle of insight would allow this client to understand where her behaviour pattern came from, how it operates (through careful, detailed exploration of how she is in relationship to her counsellor) and what effects the pattern has in her current life.

It can be seen here that the basic techniques of psychoanalysis – transference, resistance and interpretation – are used in brief psychodynamic work, but with important modifications. Just as in any kind of psychoanalytic work, the effectiveness of these techniques will depend on the skill of the therapist.

The conversational model

Another significant development within psychodynamic counselling in recent years has been the evolution of a *conversational* model. This approach was originally developed in Britain by Bob Hobson and Russell Meares (Hobson 1985), and has become increasingly influential. There are three key features of the conversational model, which, taken together, distinguish it from other psychodynamic approaches. First, it is based on contemporary ideas about the meaning and role of language that are quite different from the assumptions and concepts of mainstream psychodynamic theory. Second, it is intended to be applied within a limited number of sessions. Third, the effectiveness of the model is supported by the results of research. While other psychodynamic models can claim achievements in one or perhaps two of these domains, the conversational model is the only current psychodynamic approach to have been simultaneously innovative in the areas of theory, service delivery and research. In addition, there has been research into how best to train people in this approach (Goldberg *et al.* 1984; Maguire *et al.* 1984).

The main text for the conversational model is *Forms of Feeling: The Heart of Psychotherapy* by Hobson (1985). This is an unusual and creative book, in which

Hobson draws on lengthy case descriptions and makes frequent use of literary sources. It is clear from the way the book is written that Hobson is presenting the approach not as an abstract theoretical or intellectual system, but as a set of principles that can help to focus the task of constructing what he terms the 'special friendship' that is therapy. It is also appears as though Hobson is unwilling to present the theory as a fixed and definitive set of ideas. Tentativeness and uncertainty are highly valued. Knowledge and understanding are to be achieved through dialogue rather than by authoritative assertion.

At the core of the conversational model is the idea that people need to be able to talk about their feelings. The troubles that people bring to therapy stem from an inability to engage in dialogue with others around their feelings. The dialogue or conversation is crucial to well-being because it is through conversation that a person can act on feelings (language is a form of action; words 'do things'), and because the dialogue with another person dissolves the loneliness that is associated with holding feelings to oneself: for example, grieving in isolation. A primary task of the counsellor or psychotherapist is to develop a mutual 'feeling language' through which client and therapist can conduct a conversation about how the client feels. The counsellor does this by paying attention to the actual or implicit feeling words and metaphors employed by the client. The counsellor also uses 'I' statements as a way of communicating the presence of another person, and therefore extending an invitation to dialogue. Here, the counsellor eschews neutrality and 'owns' what he or she says to the client, and through this way of talking hopes to act as a model for the client, thereby encouraging the client to 'own' their feelings too. The counsellor suggests tentative hypotheses that suggest possible links between the feelings of the client and the events or relationships in his or her life. All of this is built around the idea of the mutual conversation. The client has a 'problem' because in that area of their life they are unable to engage in a mutual conversation with anyone. Therapy offers the chance to open up such a mutual conversation, with the possibility that it might extend after therapy into other relationships.

Hobson, Meares and many of their colleagues involved in the development of the conversational model had a background in psychoanalytic and Jungian psychotherapy, and versions of many key psychodynamic and psychoanalytic concepts can be found in the model. However, these concepts are restated and reworked to fit with the more interpersonally and linguistically oriented assumptions underlying the conversational approach. For example, the Freudian notion of defence appears as 'avoidance'; transference becomes 'direct enactment'; insight becomes 'personal problem-solving'; an interpretation is a 'hypothesis'. Although the concept of counter-transference does not appear in the index of the Hobson (1985) book, the whole of the conversational approach relies on the counsellor's awareness of his or her input to the relationship. Meares and Hobson (1977) have also discussed negative aspects of counter-transference in terms of their concept of the 'persecutory therapist' (see Chapter 15). The goals of therapy in the conversational approach are defined as:

to facilitate growth by removing obstructions . . . the reduction of fear associated with separation, loss and abandonment . . . an aspiration toward an ideal state of aloneness-togetherness . . . an increase of individual awareness with 'inner' conversations between 'I' and many 'selves' in a society of 'myself' . . . the discovery of a 'true voice of feeling'.

(Hobson 1985: 196)

Quite apart from the established psychodynamic concepts of separation and loss, also apparent here are traces of the influence of humanistic theory ('growth', 'awareness'), existentialism ('aloneness-togetherness') and personal construct theory: for example, Mair's (1989) notion of a 'community of selves'.

An example of how the conversational model works in practice is given in Box 4.7. This case vignette is taken from a study of the effectiveness of the conversational model with hospital patients suffering from chronic irritable bowel syndrome (IBS). Chronic IBS is a debilitating condition that is believed to have a strong psychosomatic component, but that has proved in previous studies to have been fairly intractable to counselling or psychotherapy. Guthrie, however, found that a limited number of sessions of conversational model therapy could significantly help these patients. The other main studies of the conversational model have been carried out in the context of the Sheffield Psychotherapy Project,

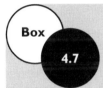

Box

4.7

'I can't keep it in . . . my guts are churning': psychodynamic conversations about bowel problems

Irritable bowel syndrome (IBS) is a condition that consists of abdominal pain and distension, and altered bowel habits, in the absence of any identifiable underlying organic cause. Many of those suffering from IBS respond well to medical treatment, but about 15 per cent are not helped by drugs or dietary regimes. It seems likely that the problems of many of these 'refractory' IBS patients are psychosomatic in nature, and that counselling may be of value to them. Guthrie (1991) carried out a study of of the effectiveness of Hobson's (1985) conversational model of therapy with 102 hospital outpatients diagnosed as cases of refractory IBS. Half of the patients received therapy, which comprised one long (3–4-hour) initial session, followed by six sessions of 45 minutes spread over the following 12 weeks. The other half were allocated to a control group, and met with the therapist on five occasions over the same period of time to discuss their symptoms, but without receiving actual therapy. The results of the study demonstrated the effectiveness of conversational model psychodynamic counselling with this group of people. The account of one case described by Guthrie (1991) offers a good illustration of the way that the conversational model operates in practice.

Bob was 49, and had suffered from abdominal pain and loose motions for several years. He had been unable to work for the previous three years. Bob was an only child, brought up by a 'strict and unaffectionate' mother; his father had left home when he was six. He saw himself as a 'loner', and he was far from convinced that counselling could help him. He spoke for a long time in the first session about his symptoms:

My guts are always churning.

I can't work, I always have to keep rushing to the loo.

It's awful, everything just explodes away from me.

I just have to go, it's awful, I'm frightened to go out.

The counsellor did little more than feed back his words:

Can't keep things in.

When things come out . . . no control.

Frightened . . . no control . . . awful . . . just have to go.

Guthrie (1991: 178) comments that:

gradually Bob came to realise that, although I was using virtually the same words that he was using to describe bowel symptoms, I was actually talking about feelings. After he had made this connection, he began to talk more freely about himself. He described in some depth how humiliated he felt by his first wife, who had particularly belittled his sexual performance, and how dominated he had felt by his mother. After a long pause I tentatively enquired whether he was worried that I would humiliate him in some way. At this point he suddenly got up and rushed out of the room saying he had to go to the toilet.

When he returned to the counselling room, Bob acknowledged that he had been feeling frightened of the counsellor, and then 'smiled with relief'. Over the following sessions, he became more able to see his bowel symptoms as a metaphor for how he felt inside. As a result of making this connection, he began to talk to his wife about his fear, and his symptoms improved. Soon, he was able to return to work, even though his symptoms had not completely disappeared.

The case of Bob captures the way that the conversational approach works. The counsellor engages in a conversation around whatever is most meaningful for the client, in this instance bowel symptoms. The counsellor and client develop a mutual feeling language, and through being able to use this language the client is enabled to stop avoiding what is difficult or painful in his or her life. The counsellor is tentative, yet direct and personal.

a large-scale comparison of the efficacy of time-limited psychodynamic–interpersonal (i.e. conversational) and cognitive–behavioural therapies for people who were depressed. Because of factors associated with the politics of psychotherapy research, in these studies the conversational model was given the more generic title of 'psychodynamic–interpersonal'. The results of this research programme strongly confirmed the effectiveness of conversational therapy for this group of clients (Shapiro *et al.* 1994).

The conversational model is an approach to counselling and psychotherapy that is likely to grow in importance over the next few years. Its use of philosophical, literary and constructivist concepts has revitalized psychodynamic theory and practice, and it is attractive to many counsellors eager to espouse a broadly integrative approach that draws on the humanistic/existential as well as psychodynamic traditions (Mackay *et al.* 2001). Recent developments in theory, research, practice and training in relation to the conversational model are reviewed in Barkham *et al.* (1998), and include the application of this approach in work in cases of deliberate self-harm (Guthrie *et al.* 2001) and with people with longstanding mental health difficulties (Guthrie *et al.* 1998, 1999; Davenport *et al.* 2000).

An appraisal of the psychodynamic approach to counselling

Psychodynamic group therapy is described on pages 445–6

Psychoanalysis has provided a set of concepts and methods that have found application in a wide variety of contexts. Psychodynamic ideas have proved invaluable not only in individual therapy and counselling, but also in groupwork, couples counselling and the analysis of organizations. The ideas of Freud have been robust and resilient enough to withstand critique and reformulation from a number of sources. Psychodynamic perspectives have made a significant contribution to research into the process of counselling and therapy. Throughout this book there are many examples of the ways psychodynamic ideas have been used in different contexts and settings. All counsellors and therapists, even those who espouse different theoretical models, have been influenced by psychodynamic thinking and have had to make up their minds whether to accept or reject the Freudian image of the person.

There are clearly innumerable similarities and differences between psychodynamic and other approaches. The most essential difference, however, lies in the density of psychodynamic theory, particularly in the area of the understanding of development in childhood. Cognitive–behavioural theory is largely silent on child development, and the person-centred approach, in its use of the concept of 'conditions of worth', is little more than silent. Psychodynamic counsellors, by contrast, have at their disposal a highly sophisticated conceptual net.

In practice, psychodynamic counselling involves a form of therapeutic helping that draws on the theories of psychoanalysis, as a means of deepening and enriching the relationship between counsellor and client, rather than being dominated by these theories. The use of these ideas can be summarized in terms of a set of key principles:

1 People have troubled relationships because they are repeating a destructive relationship pattern from the past. When a person meets someone new, there is a tendency to treat that person not as an individual, but as if they represented someone from the person's past (transference). People in authority (counsellors, nurses, teachers) often find that their clients project or transfer on to them their images of their father, mother, uncle etc.

2 The person may seek to control or hide difficult or unacceptable internal desires, memories and feelings by defending against them. 'Defence mechanisms', such as transference, projection, denial, repression, sublimation, splitting and projective identification, are used to divert attention from threatening 'internal' material.

3 It is important for helpers to be aware of their feelings, fantasies and impulses in relation to the person they are helping. This inner response (counter-transference) is evidence of (a) the kind of feelings that the person typically evokes in others, and/or (b) the kind of emotional world in which the person lives their life. In either case, 'counter-transference' feelings are valuable sources of evidence concerning the inner life, and relationship patterns, of a person seeking help.

4 The person's problems can often be understood as representing unresolved developmental tasks (for example, separating from the mother/parents). Freud proposed a series of biologically focused stages of development: oral, anal, Oedipal. Erikson suggested more socially oriented stages: trust, autonomy, initiative, industry, identity, intimacy, generativity, integrity. However, the underlying theory is the same: if a person has an unsatisfactory experience at one stage, they will continue to try to deal with this developmental issue for the rest of their lives (or until they gain some insight into it).

5 People have a need for secure, consistent emotional attachments. If a person's attachments are disrupted in early life (parental absence, illness etc.) they may grow up being insecure about forming attachments, and exhibit a pattern of difficulty in committing to relationships, ambivalence within a relationship, difficulty in parenting consistently etc.

These principles provide a powerful set of strategies for helping people first to understand and then to change conflictual and self-defeating ways of relating to others.

Chapter summary

- The psychodynamic approach to counselling is ultimately derived from the psychoanalytic theory of Sigmund Freud. It is essential both to recognize the value of Freud's ideas and to acknowledge the extent to which his theories are a product of a particular culture and historical time and place.

• The key assumptions made by Freud were that (a) emotional problems have their origins in childhood experiences, (b) people are usually not conscious of the true nature of these experiences and (c) unconscious material emerges indirectly in counselling through the transference reaction to the counsellor and in dreams and fantasy.

• The role of the counsellor is to interpret unconscious mental content to enable the client to achieve insight.

• Many of Freud's closest colleagues, such as Jung and Adler, disputed important aspects of his theory, such as his emphasis on the sexual nature of unconscious memories.

• In the 1940s and 1950s, the *object relations* school of psychoanalysis, inspired by Klein, Mahler and others, evolved a psychodynamic approach that paid more attention to the relationships between the client and significant others (objects) in his or her life. This approach remains highly influential.

• A group of British psychoanalysts, including Heimann and Casement, contributed new understandings of the role of the counsellor or psychotherapist, through their writings on the value of working actively with the counsellor's counter-transference reaction to the client.

• An important recent trend in psychodynamic counselling has been the development of time-limited methods, involving much more active participation by the counsellor and a focus on key themes such as attachment and loss.

• The *conversational model* of psychodynamic counselling, created by Hobson, Meares and their colleagues in Britain and Australia, represents a research-based, integrative approach that draws upon many different elements in the psychoanalytic tradition.

• The psychodynamic approach to counselling is a broad perspective that includes many different schools of thought. It is one of the leading perspectives in counselling and psychotherapy, has been applied successfully to many different client groups and is backed up by a rich literature and well established methods of training.

Topics for reflection and discussion

1 Coltart (1986: 187) has written of 'the need to develop the ability to tolerate not knowing, the capacity to sit it out with a patient, often for long periods, without any real precision as to where we are, relying on our regular tools and our faith in the process, to carry us through the obfuscating darkness of resistance, complex defences, and the sheer unconsciousness of the unconscious.' Discuss this statement in the light of the themes introduced in this chapter.

2 To what extent does time-limited counselling dilute the distinctive aims and meaning of psychodynamic work?

3 What are the main similarities and differences between psychodynamic counselling and the other approaches introduced in the following chapters?

4 Strupp (1972: 276) has suggested that the psychodynamic counsellor or psychotherapist 'uses the vantage point of the parental position as a power base from which to effect changes in the patient's interpersonal strategies in accordance with the principle that *in the final analysis the patient changes out of love for the therapist.*' Do you agree?

5 Think about your relationship with someone you have found difficult to deal with at an interpersonal level. Make some brief notes about what happened, and what was difficult about your contact with this person. Analyse what you have written about this relationship in psychodynamic terms. What could have been the psychodynamic processes occurring in the patient, and in you, that made this relationship problematic? In what ways might the psychodynamic perspective on what happened help you in dealing with a similar situation in the future?

Key terms and concepts

anal stage	defence mechanisms
attachment	dream analysis
borderline personality disorder	ego
brief therapy	free association
British Independents	hysteria
catharsis	id
conversational model	IDE formula
corrective emotional experience	individuation
counter-transference	interpretation

libido	psycho-sexual development
loss	psycho-social development
narcissistic character disorder	resistance
object relations approach	self-theory
oral stage	splitting
phallic stage	superego
projective fantasy	T–C–P links
projective identification	transference
projective techniques	

Suggested further reading

Anyone who is seriously interested in making sense of what psychodynamic counselling is really about needs to read some of Freud's original writings, rather than rely on second-hand textbook accounts. Freud was a wonderfully vivid and persuasive writer, who inexorably draws the reader into his search for psycho-analytic truth. A good place to start might be the *Five Lectures on Psycho-analysis* (Freud, 1910/1963), first delivered at Clark University in Massachussetts in 1909. Here, Freud was trying to explain his ideas to an enthusiastic, but also sceptical, audience of American psychologists and psychiatrists. Beyond the *Five Lectures*, it is worth looking at one of the classic case studies – Dora, the Rat Man, the Wolf Man, Schreber – all of which are included in the widely available *Standard Edition of Freud's Works*.

The literature on psychodynamic counselling is so wide and varied that it is not easy to recommend specific books without generating an endless list. Jacobs (1999) provides an excellent, easy-to-read introduction to this approach, and McLoughlin (1995) explores specific psychodynamic issues in a highly accessible style. The recent movement in psychoanalysis and psychodynamic therapy in the direction of a more 'relational' approach is discussed well by Kahn (1997) and Mitchell (1986). The journals *Psychodynamic Counselling* (now renamed *Psychodynamic Practice*) and *British Journal of Psychotherapy* contain stimulating combinations of clinical material, theoretical papers and research articles that reflect the broad scope of psychodynamic work. Books that perhaps communicate the spirit of contemporary psychodynamic thought are *On Learning from the Patient* by Patrick Casement (1985), *Mothering Psychoanalysis* by Janet Sayers (1991) and *Cultivating Intuition* by Peter Lomas (1994).

There are many voices critical of the psychoanalytic and psychodynamic traditions. Among the most useful books in this category are *Demystifying Therapy* by Ernesto Spinelli (1994), *Final Analysis: The Making and Unmaking of a Psychoanalyst* by Jeffrey Masson (1991) and *The Drama of Being a Child* by Alice Miller (1987).

5 From behaviourism to constructivism: the cognitive–behavioural approach to counselling

Introduction

The *cognitive–behavioural* tradition represents an important approach to counselling, with its own distinctive methods and concepts. This approach has evolved out of behavioural psychology and has three key features: a problem-solving, change-focused approach to working with clients; a respect for scientific values; and close attention to the cognitive processes through which people monitor and control their behaviour. In recent years, many counsellors and psychotherapists trained in cognitive–behavioural methods have become interested in a *constructivist* perspective. Constructivism gives particular attention to the language that people use to create the reality in which they live, and constructivist therapists seek to help clients to become more aware of that language, and change it. Nevertheless, in practice constructivist therapy retains the cognitive–behavioural emphasis on practical problem-solving, even if this interest is more likely to be framed in terms of generating *solutions* rather than dissecting problems. This chapter begins by reviewing the roots of these approaches in academic behavioural and cognitive psychology.

The origins of the cognitive–behavioural approach

To understand the nature of cognitive–behavioural counselling, it is necessary to examine its historical emergence from within the discipline of academic psychology. The cognitive–behavioural approach represents the most overtly 'scientific' of all the major therapy orientations. The behavioural dimension of the cognitive–behavioural approach has its origins in behavioural psychology, which is widely seen as having been created by J. B. Watson, particularly through the publication in 1919 of *Psychology from the Standpoint of a Behaviorist*.

Watson was a psychology professor at the University of Chicago at a time when psychology as an academic discipline was in its infancy. It had only been in 1879 that Wilhelm Wundt, at the University of Leipzig, had first established psychology as a field of study separate from philosophy and physiology. The method of research into psychological topics, such as memory, learning, problem-solving and perception, that Wundt and others such as Titchener had used was the technique known as 'introspection', which involved research subjects reporting on their own internal thought processes as they engaged in remembering, learning or any other psychological activity. This technique tended to yield contradictory data, since different subjects in different laboratories reported quite dissimilar internal events when carrying out the same mental tasks. The weakness of introspection as a scientific method, argued Watson, was that it was not open to objective scrutiny. Only the actual subject could 'see' what was happening, and this would inevitably result in bias and subjective distortion. Watson made the case that, if psychology was to become a truly scientific discipline, it would need to concern itself only with observable events and phenomena. He suggested that psychology should define itself as the scientific study of actual, overt behaviour rather than invisible thoughts and images, because these behaviours could be controlled and measured in laboratory settings.

Watson's 'behavioural' manifesto convinced many of his colleagues, particularly in the USA, and for the next 30 years mainstream academic psychology was dominated by the ideas of the behavioural school. The main task that behaviourists like Guthrie, Spence and Skinner set themselves was to discover the 'laws of learning'. They took the position that all the habits and beliefs which people exhibit must be learned, and so the most important task for psychology is to find out how people learn. Moreover, they suggested that the basic principles of learning, or acquisition of new behaviour, would be the same in any organism. Since there were clearly many ethical and practical advantages in carrying out laboratory research on animals rather than human beings, the behaviourists set about an ambitious programme of research into learning in animal subjects, mainly rats and pigeons.

All this may seem strange from a contemporary perspective. The assumption that the psychology of people can be explained through studies of the behaviour of animals is one that few people would now see as sensible. In fact there have been many attempts to make sense of the behaviourist era in psychology. Many writers have suggested that these psychologists were merely following a model of science, known as 'logical positivism', which was dominant in academic circles at that time. Other observers have suggested that behavioural psychology became popular in the USA because it was consistent with the growth of the advertising industry, with its need for techniques for controlling and manipulating the behaviour of consumers. It is perhaps significant that J. B. Watson himself left academic life to become an advertising executive.

In his analysis of the social origins of behaviourism, Bakan (1976) points out that many of the behaviourists, like Skinner, had grown up around animals and machines, and were therefore inevitably attracted by the idea of carrying out laboratory experiments on small animals. There were also powerful pressures in academic life to pursue 'pure' science (Bakan 1976), and the experimental approach adopted by the behaviourists enabled them to conform to this academic norm. Another factor in the development of behaviourism was the parallel growth at this time in the influence of psychoanalysis, which was viewed by behavioural psychologists as dangerously unscientific and quite misguided. To some extent the threat of becoming like psychoanalysis served to keep the attention of behaviourists firmly on the objective and observable rather than subjective and unconscious aspects of human experience.

Although the behaviourist movement, in the form in which it existed in the 1930s and 1940s, may appear to many people involved in counselling and psychotherapy to represent an impoverished and inadequate vision or image of the human person, it is essential to acknowledge the immense influence it had over psychologists in the USA. Anyone from this era who entered counselling or psychotherapy with a psychology background (for example, Carl Rogers) brought at least some residue of behavioural thinking and behaviourist attitudes. Within behaviourism itself, however, there came to be a recognition that a stimulus-response model was insufficient even to account for the behaviour of laboratory animals. Tolman (1948), in a series of experiments, had demonstrated that rats who had originally learned to swim through a flooded laboratory maze could later find their way through it successfully on foot. He pointed out that the behaviour they had acquired in the first part of the experiment – a series of swimming movements – was in fact irrelevant to the second task of running round the maze. What they must have learned, he argued, was a 'mental map' of the maze. In this manner, the study of inner mental events, or cognitions, was introduced to the subject matter of behavioural psychology. The new interest in cognition within behaviourism was matched by the work in Switzerland of Piaget, who initiated the study of the development of thinking in children, and at Cambridge by Bartlett, who examined the ways in which people 'reconstruct' the events they recall from long-term memory. These pioneering studies in the 1930s, by Tolman, Bartlett, Piaget and a few others, eventually resulted in what has been labelled the 'cognitive revolution' in psychology. By the 1970s, academic psychologists as a whole had in effect reversed the tide of behaviourism, and were no longer locked into a stimulus-response analysis of all human action. The preoccupation of the introspectionists with inner, cognitive events had returned to dominate psychology once more, but allied now to more sophisticated research methods than naive introspection.

The application of behavioural ideas in clinical practice

Throughout their history, behavioural psychologists looked for ways to apply their ideas to the explanation of psychological and emotional problems. Probably the first theorist to look at emotional problems from a behavioural perspective was Pavlov, a Russian physiologist and psychologist working at the end of the nineteenth century, who noted that when he set his experimental dogs a perceptual discrimination task that was too difficult (for example, they would be rewarded with food for responding to a circle, but not when the stimulus was an ellipse) the animals would become distressed, squeal and 'break down'. Later, Liddell, carrying out conditioning experiments at Cornell University, coined the phrase 'experimental neurosis' – a pattern of behaviour characterized by swings from somnolence and passivity to hyperactivity – to describe the behaviour of his experimental animals exposed to monotonous environments. Watson himself carried out the well known 'Little Albert' experiment, where a conditioned fear of animals was induced in a young boy by frightening him with a loud noise at the moment he had been given a furry animal to hold. Masserman, in a series of studies with cats, found that 'neurotic' behaviour could be brought about by creating an approach-avoidance conflict in the animal: for example, by setting up a situation where the animal had been rewarded (given food) and punished (given an electric shock) at the same area in the laboratory.

Skinner (1953) found that when animals were rewarded or reinforced at random, with there being no link between their actual behaviour and its outcome in terms of food, they began to acquire 'ritualistic' or obsessional behaviour.

More recently, Seligman (1975) has conducted studies of the phenomenon of 'learned helplessness'. In Seligman's studies, animals restrained in cages and unable to escape or in any other way control the situation are given electric shocks. After a time, even when they are shocked in a situation where they are able to escape, they sit there and accept it. They have learned to behave in a helpless or depressed manner. Seligman views this work as giving some clues to the origins of depression. Further documentation of the origins of behaviour therapy in experimental studies can be found in Kazdin (1978).

To behaviourists, these studies provided convincing evidence that psychological and psychiatric problems could be explained, and ultimately treated, using behavioural principles. However, the strong identification of the behavioural school with the values of 'pure' science meant that they restricted themselves largely to laboratory studies. It was not until the years immediately after the Second World War, when there was a general expansion of psychiatric services in the USA, that the first attempts were made to turn behaviourism into a form of therapy. The earliest applications of behavioural ideas in therapy drew explicitly upon Skinner's operant conditioning model of learning, which found practical expression in the behaviour modification programmes of Ayllon and Azrin (1968), and on Pavlov's classical conditioning model, which provided the rationale for the systematic desensitization technique devised by Wolpe.

Behavioural methods in counselling

Behaviour modification is an approach that takes as its starting point the Skinnerian notion that in any situation, or in response to any stimulus, the person has available a repertoire of possible responses, and emits the behaviour that is reinforced or rewarded. This principle is known as operant conditioning. For example, on being asked a question by someone, there are many possible ways of responding. The person can answer the question, he or she can ignore the question, he or she can run away. Skinner (1953) argued that the response which is emitted is the one which has been most frequently reinforced in the past. So, in this case, most people will answer a question, because in the past this behaviour has resulted in reinforcements such as attention or praise from the questioner, or material rewards. If, on the other hand, the person has been brought up in a family in which answering questions leads to physical abuse and running away leads to safety, his or her behaviour will reflect this previous reinforcement history. He or she will run off. Applied to individuals with behavioural problems, these ideas suggest that it is helpful to reward or reinforce desired or appropriate behaviour, and ignore inappropriate behaviour. If a behaviour or response is not rewarded it will, according to Skinner, undergo a process of extinction, and fade out of the repertoire.

Ayllon and Azrin (1965, 1968) applied these principles in psychiatric hospital wards, with severely disturbed patients, using a technique known as 'token economy'. With these patients specific target behaviours, such as using cutlery to eat a meal or talking to another person, were systematically rewarded by the ward staff, usually by giving them tokens that could be exchanged for rewards such as cigarettes or visits, or sometimes by directly rewarding them at the time with chocolate, cigarettes or praise. At the beginning of the programme, in line with Skinner's research on reinforcement schedules, the patient would be rewarded for very simple behaviour, and the reward would be available for every performance of the target behaviour. As the programme progressed, the patient would only be rewarded for longer, more complex sequences of behaviour, and would be rewarded on a more intermittent basis. Eventually, the aim would be to maintain the desired behaviour through normal social reinforcement.

The effectiveness of behaviour modification and token economy programmes is highly dependent on the existence of a controlled social environment, in which the behaviour of the learner can be consistently reinforced in the intended direction. As a result, most behaviour modification has been carried out within 'total institutions', such as psychiatric and mental handicap hospitals, prisons and secure units. The technique can also be applied, however, in more ordinary situations, like schools and families, if key participants such as teachers and parents are taught how to apply the technique. It is essential, however, that whoever is supplying the behaviour modification is skilled and motivated so that the client is not exposed to contradictory reinforcement schedules. Furthermore, because behaviour modification relies on the fact that the person supplying the reinforcement has real power to give or withhold commodities that are highly valued by the client, there is the possibility of corruption and abuse. It is not unusual for people with only limited training in behavioural principles to assume that punishment is a necessary component of a behaviour modification regime. Skinner, by contrast, was explicit in stating that punishment would only temporarily suppress undesirable behaviour, and that in the long term behaviour change relies on the acquisition of new behaviour, which goes hand-in-hand with the extinction of the old, inappropriate behaviour.

Another way in which behaviour modification can be abusive in practice is by too much emphasis on the technique known as 'time out'. In residential settings, problematic behaviour patterns, such as aggressive and violent behaviour, can be interrupted by placing the person in a room to 'cool off'. The intention is that their violence is not rewarded by attention from staff or other residents, but that resumption of rationality is rewarded by the person being allowed out of the room. In principle this can be a valuable intervention strategy, which can help some people to change behaviour that can lead them into severe trouble. The danger is that staff may use time out in a punitive manner, keeping a resident quiet to discharge their own anger at him or her. This technique may result in an abuse of the rights and civil liberties of the client.

Behaviour modification does not sit easily within a counselling relationship, which is normally a collaborative, one-to-one relationship in which the client can talk about his or her problems. Nevertheless, the principles of behaviour modification can be adapted for use in counselling settings, by explaining behavioural ideas to the client and working with him to apply these ideas to bring about change in his own life. This approach is often described as 'behavioural

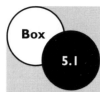

Behaviour modification in a case of bulimia

Binge eating followed by self-induced vomiting is characteristic of the condition labelled as *bulimia nervosa*. This pattern of behaviour lends itself to behavioural intervention, since the behaviours in question are overt and take place over a relatively extended period of time on a regular, predictable basis. There are thus multiple opportunities to disrupt the sequence of behaviour and introduce new responses and reinforcers. In addition, clients suffering from this condition are often desperate to change, and are therefore highly motivated to comply with a behavioural regime. In a case study reported by Viens and Hranchuk (1992), a 35-year-old woman with longstanding difficulties in eating was offered behavioural treatment. She had previously undergone surgery for weight reduction, and now was compulsively bingeing and vomiting her food. She had lost any capacity to control her eating behaviour, which was negatively reinforced by the effect that it kept her overall body weight at a personally accept-able level. However, disapproval of her eating by significant others in her life had resulted in an increasing problem of social isolation.

The initial phase of the treatment involved rigorous self-monitoring of her eating behaviour for a period of three weeks. She wrote down what she ate, how many mouthfuls she took each meal and how many times she vomited her food during and after each meal. On the basis of this information, a behavioural regime was set up, which included:

* at mealtimes, eating two spoonfuls, then resting for 30 seconds while practising a relaxation exercise, then another two spoonfuls;
* weighing herself daily in the morning, entering the weight data on a graph and reporting the results to her therapist once each week;
* continued self-monitoring of what was eaten, mouthfuls and vomiting episodes;
* engaging in some kind of physical activity every day, and reporting her progress to the therapist at their weekly meeting;
* her boyfriend was briefed on the rationale for the therapy.

This client's vomiting reduced markedly within six weeks, and remained low over the six-month period of treatment. These gains had been maintained at a one-year follow-up interview. Viens and Hranchuk (1992) suggest that this case demonstrates that behavioural change in an eating disorder can be achieved in the absence of any cognitive intervention. Moreover, there was only a minimal therapist involvement, mainly comprising being available on a weekly schedule to reinforce the client's gains and progress. They ascribe the effectiveness of the behavioural intervention not only to the fact that the client's actual eating behaviour was modified, but to the fact that this set of changes led to secondary reinforcement of the new eating pattern as she became more willing to socialize, and as people she met commented favourably on her weight loss.

self-control', and involves functional analysis of patterns of behaviour, with the aim not so much of 'knowing thyself' as of 'knowing thy controlling variables' (Thoresen and Mahoney 1974). The assumption behind this way of working is that, following Skinner, any behaviour exhibited by a person has been elicited by a stimulus, and is reinforced by its consequences. The client can then be encouraged to implement suitable change at any, or all, of the steps in a sequence of behaviour.

A simple example of what is known as functional analysis (Cullen 1988) of problem behaviour might involve a client who wishes to stop smoking. A behaviourally oriented counsellor would begin by carrying out a detailed assessment of where and when the person smokes (the stimulus), what he does when he smokes (the behaviour) and the rewards or pleasures he experiences from smoking (the consequences). This assessment will typically identify much detailed information about the complex pattern of behaviours that constitutes 'smoking' for the client, including, for example, the fact that he always has lunch with a group of heavy smokers, that he offers round his cigarettes and that smoking helps him to feel relaxed. This client might work with the counsellor to intervene in this pattern of smoking behaviour by choosing to sit with other, non-smoking colleagues after lunch, never carrying more than two cigarettes so he cannot offer them to others and carrying out an 'experiment' where he smokes one cigarette after the other in a small room with other members of a smoking cessation clinic, until he reaches a point of being physically sick, thus learning to associate smoking with a new consequence: sickness rather than relaxation.

The other technique that represented the beginning of a behavioural approach to counselling and therapy was the systematic desensitization method pioneered by Wolpe. This approach relies on Pavlov's classical conditioning model of learning. Pavlov had demonstrated, in a series of experiments with dogs, that the behaviour of an animal or organism includes many reflex responses. These are unlearned, automatic reactions to particular situations or stimuli (which he called 'unconditioned stimuli'). In his own research he looked at the salivation response. Dogs will automatically salivate when presented with food. Pavlov discovered, however, that if some other stimulus is also presented at the same time as the 'unconditioned' stimulus, the new stimulus comes to act as a 'signal' for the original stimulus, and may eventually evoke the same reflex response even when the original, unconditioned stimulus is not present. So Pavlov rang a bell just as food was brought in to his dogs, and after a time they would salivate to the sound of the bell even when there was no food around. Furthermore, they would begin to salivate to the sound of other bells (generalization) and would gradually lessen their salivation if they heard the bell on a number of occasions in the absence of any association with food.

Wolpe saw a parallel between classical conditioning and the acquisition of anxiety or fear responses in human beings. For a vivid example, imagine a person who has been in a car crash. Like one of Pavlov's dogs, the crash victim can only passively respond to a situation. Similarly, he experiences an automatic reflex response to the stimulus or situation, in this case a reflex response of fear. Finally, the fear response may generalize to other stimuli associated with the crash: for instance, travelling in a car or even going out of doors. The crash victim who has become anxious or phobic about travelling, therefore, can be understood as suffering from a conditioned emotional response. The solution is, again following Pavlov, to re-expose the person to the 'conditioned' stimuli in the absence of the original fear-inducing elements. This is achieved through a process of systematic desensitization. First of all, the client learns how to relax. The counsellor either carries out relaxation exercises during counselling sessions, or gives the client relaxation instructions and tapes to practise at home. Once the client has mastered relaxation, the client and counsellor work together to identify a hierarchy of fear-eliciting stimuli or situations, ranging from highly fearful (for example, going for a trip in a car past the accident spot) to minimally fearful (for example, looking at pictures of a car in a magazine). Beginning with the least fear-inducing, the client is exposed to each stimulus in turn, all the while practising his relaxation skills. This procedure may take some time, and in many cases the counsellor will accompany the client into and through fear-inducing situations, such as taking a car journey together. By the end of the procedure, the relaxation response rather than the fear response should be elicited by all the stimuli included in the hierarchy.

Although systematic desensitization takes its rationale from classical conditioning, most behavioural theorists would argue that a full account of the development of maladaptive fears and phobias requires the use of ideas from operant, or Skinnerian, as well as classical conditioning. They would point out that, while the initial conditioned fear response may have been originally acquired through classical conditioning, in many cases it would have been extinguished in the natural course of events as the client allowed himself to re-experience cars, travel and the outside world. What may happen is that the person actively avoids these situations, because they bring about feelings of anxiety. As a result, the person is being reinforced for avoidance behaviour – he is rewarded or reinforced by feeling more relaxed in the home rather than outside, or walking rather than going in a car. This 'two-factor' model of neurosis views the anxiety of the client as a conditioned emotional response that acts as an avoidance drive. Through systematic desensitization, the counsellor can help the client to overcome his avoidance.

The techniques of behavioural self-control and systematic desensitization are explicitly derived from the behavioural 'laws of learning' of operant and classical conditioning. However, in a process that reflected the general movement within psychology towards a more cognitivist approach, critics such as Breger and McGaugh (1965) and Locke (1971) began to question whether the therapeutic processes involved in these techniques could actually be fully understood using behaviourist ideas. In the words of Locke (1971), the issue was: 'Is behaviour therapy "behaviouristic"?' Behavioural therapists and counsellors typically asked their clients to report on and monitor their inner emotional experiences, encouraged self-assertion and self-understanding, and aimed to help them to develop new

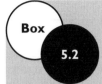

Box 5.2

Combining behavioural and cognitive techniques in a case of competitive sport performance anxiety

Houghton (1991) has published a case report on his work with an elite athlete suffering from performance-related anxiety. The athlete was a male archer who had represented his country at Olympic and World Championship competitions. On several occasions, when left needing a high scoring final arrow to complete a competition successfully, he 'froze' on the signal to shoot, waited too long, went through his routine up to five times without shooting and then hurriedly released three arrows in quick succession. He reported feeling 'anxious and negative' when needing a 'gold' (10 points) on his final arrow, and always said to himself 'Why couldn't it be a 9 instead of 10?' This athlete received 12 sessions of counselling from a sport psychologist, using a combination of behavioural and cognitive techniques. First, his behaviour during competitions was carefully observed. Following an analysis of this baseline information, he was introduced to the method of progressive relaxation, and was taught a technique of visualization that involved cognitive rehearsal of a successful performance. Finally, he was encouraged to make positive self-statements. These techniques were practised during training and at competition. Finally, he made an audio tape recording of his elation following a successful shot, and played it back daily. Following this cognitive–behavioural intervention, his scores during competition increased significantly, even in important events being televised by the BBC. As well as demonstrating the way in which behavioural and cognitive techniques can be used together, this case illustrates the preference of therapists using this approach for trying to find objective measures of change in key target behaviours. This archer was not asked whether he felt better about himself as a result of the treatment: the proof of effectiveness lay in his actual performance.

plans or strategies for dealing with life. These activities encompass a wide variety of cognitive processes, including imagery, decision-making, remembering and problem-solving. The thrust of this critique is that behavioural approaches may have generated many useful techniques, but these techniques draw heavily upon the capacity of clients to make sense of things, to process information cognitively, and that a more cognitive theory is needed in order to understand what is going on. There arose an increasing acceptance among behaviourally oriented counsellors and therapists of the need for an explicit cognitive dimension to their work. The social learning theory approach of Bandura (1971, 1977) made an important contribution to these developments. This interest in cognitive aspects of therapy coincided with the emergence of the cognitive therapies, such as rational emotive therapy (RET) (Ellis 1962) and Beck's (1976) cognitive therapy.

The cognitive strand

The development of the 'cognitive' strand of cognitive–behavioural counselling is well described in Ellis (1989). One of the earliest attempts to work in a cognitive mode with clients took place, Ellis (1989) points out, within the field of sex therapy. The pioneers of sex therapy found that, of necessity, they needed to give their clients information about sexuality and the varieties of sexual behaviour. In other words, they needed to challenge the inappropriate fantasies and beliefs that their clients held about sex. The aim of helping clients to change the way they think about things remained the central focus of all cognitive approaches.

Both Ellis, the founder of rational emotive therapy, and Beck, the founder of cognitive therapy, began their therapeutic careers as psychoanalysts. Both became dissatisfied with psychoanalytic methods, and found themselves becoming more aware of the importance of the ways in which their clients thought about themselves. The story of his conversion to a cognitive therapeutic perspective is recounted by Beck (1976) in his book *Cognitive Therapy and the Emotional Disorders*. He notes that he had 'been practising psychoanalysis and psychoanalytic psychotherapy for many years before I was struck by the fact that a patient's cognitions had an enormous impact on his feelings and behavior' (p. 29). He reports on a patient who had been engaging in free association, and had become angry, openly criticizing Beck. When asked what he was feeling, the patient replied that he felt very guilty. Beck accepted this statement, on the grounds that, within psychoanalytic theory, anger causes guilt. But then the patient went on to explain that while he had been expressing his criticism of Beck, he had 'also had continual thoughts of a self-critical nature', which included statements such as 'I'm wrong to criticize him . . . I'm bad . . . He won't like me . . . I have no excuse for being so mean' (pp. 30–1). Beck concluded that 'the patient felt guilty because he had been criticizing himself for his expressions of anger to me' (p. 31).

Beck (1976) described these self-critical cognitions as 'automatic thoughts', and began to see them as one of the keys to successful therapy. The emotional and behavioural difficulties that people experience in their lives are not caused directly by events but by the way they interpret and make sense of these events. When clients can be helped to pay attention to the 'internal dialogue', the stream of automatic thoughts that accompany and guide their actions, they can make choices about the appropriateness of these self-statements, and if necessary introduce new thoughts and ideas, which lead to a happier or more satisfied life. Although Beck had been a psychoanalyst, he found that his growing interest in cognition was leading him away from psychoanalysis and in the direction of behaviour therapy. He cites some of the commonalities between cognitive and behavioural approaches: both employ a structured, problem-solving or symptom reduction approach, with a highly active therapist style, and both stress the 'here-and-now' rather than making 'speculative reconstructions of the patient's childhood relationships and early family relationships' (Beck 1976: 321).

Albert Ellis had, a decade earlier, followed much the same path. Also trained in psychoanalysis, he evolved a much more active therapeutic style characterized by high levels of challenge and confrontation designed to enable the client to examine his or her 'irrational beliefs'. Ellis argued that emotional problems are caused by 'crooked thinking' arising from viewing life in terms of 'shoulds' and 'musts'. When a person experiences a relationship, for example, in an absolutistic, exaggerated manner, he or she may be acting upon an internalized, irrational belief, such as 'I must have love or approval from all the significant people in my life.' For Ellis, this is an irrational belief because it is exaggerated and overstated. A rational belief system might include statements such as 'I enjoy being loved by others' or 'I feel most secure when the majority of the people in my life care about me.' The irrational belief leads to 'catastrophizing', and feelings of anxiety or depression, if anything goes even slightly wrong in a relationship. The more rational belief statements allow the person to cope with relationship difficulties in a more constructive and balanced fashion.

Following the lead provided by Ellis (1962) and Beck (1976; Beck *et al.* 1979; Beck and Weishaar 1989), many other clinicians and writers within the cognitive–behavioural tradition have contributed to the further elaboration and construction of this approach to counselling. The cognitive–behavioural approach is historically the most recent of the major therapy orientations, and is perhaps in its most creative phase, with new ideas and techniques being added to it every year (Dryden and Golden 1986; Dryden and Trower 1988; Dobson 1988; Freeman *et al.* 1989). In this brief review of the most important developments within the cognitive behavioural domain it will be necessary to divide the field into three main areas of work: cognitive processes, maladaptive beliefs and strategies for cognitive intervention.

Cognitive processes

In directing her attention to cognitive aspects of the client's way of dealing with problems in living, the cognitive–behavioural counsellor recognizes that there are two distinct types of cognitive phenomenon that are of interest. First, people differ in the way in which they process information about the world. Second, people differ in the beliefs they hold about the world, in their cognitive content. Cognitive–behavioural counsellors have devised intervention strategies for addressing issues in both of these domains.

The best known model of cognitive processing used by cognitive–behavioural counsellors is that of Beck (1976), which is known as the cognitive distortion model. In this framework, it is assumed that the experience of threat results in a loss of ability to process information effectively:

Individuals experience psychological distress when they perceive a situation as threatening to their vital interests. At such times, there is a functional impairment in normal cognitive processing. Perceptions and interpretations of events become highly selective, egocentric and rigid. The person has a decreased ability to 'turn off' distorted thinking, to concentrate, recall or reason. Corrective functions, which allow reality testing and refinements of global conceptualisations, are weakened.

(Beck and Weishaar 1989)

Beck (1976) has identified a number of different kinds of cognitive distortion that can be addressed in the counselling situation. These include over-generalization, which involves drawing general or all-encompassing conclusions from very limited evidence. For example, if a person fails her driving test at the first attempt she may over-generalize by concluding that it is not worth bothering to take it again because it is obvious that she will never pass. Another example of cognitive distortion is dichotomous thinking, which refers to the tendency to see situations in terms of polar opposites. A common example of dichotomous thinking is to see oneself as 'the best' at some activity, and then to feel a complete failure if presented with any evidence of less than total competence. Another example is to see other people as either completely good or completely bad. A third type of cognitive distortion is personalization, which occurs when a person has a tendency to imagine that events are always attributable to his actions (usually to his shortcomings), even when no logical connection need be made. For example, in couple relationships it is not unusual to find that one of the partners believes that the mood of the other partner is always caused by his or her conduct, despite ample proof that, for instance, the irritation of the partner is caused by work pressures or other such external sources.

These cognitive distortions are similar in practice to the 'absolutistic' and 'catastrophizing' thinking described by Ellis (1962). The ideas behind these cognitive–behavioural concepts are familiar ones within the broader field of cognitive psychology. For example, it has been demonstrated in many studies of problem-solving that people frequently make a 'rush to judgement', or over-generalize on the basis of too little evidence, or stick rigidly to one interpretation of the facts to the point of avoiding or denying contradictory evidence. The concept of 'personalization' is similar to the Piagetian notion of egocentricity, which refers to the tendency of children younger than about four years old to see everything that happens only from their own perspective – they are unable to 'decentre' or see things from the point of view of another person. It is to some degree reassuring that the phenomena observed by cognitive–behavioural therapists in clinical settings should also have been observed by psychological researchers in other settings. On the other hand, these researchers, particularly in the studies of problem-solving, were studying ordinary adult people who were not under emotional threat or suffering from psychological problems. If cognitive distortions are part and parcel of the way that people cope in everyday life, it is difficult to make a case that they should necessarily be regarded as factors that cause emotional problems, and therefore as elements to be eliminated from the cognitive repertoire of the client.

The cognitive distortion model of cognitive processing is similar in many respects to the Freudian idea of 'primary process' thinking. Freud regarded human beings as capable of engaging in rational, logical thought ('secondary process' thinking), but also as highly prone to reverting to the developmentally less mature 'primary process' thinking, in which thought is dominated by emotional needs. The crucial difference between the primary process and cognitive distortion models is that in the former emotion controls thought, whereas in the latter thought controls emotion.

Another important dimension of cognitive distortion lies in the area of *memory*. Williams (1996) has carried out research which shows that people who are anxious, or who have undergone difficult life experiences, often find it difficult to remember painful events in detail. Their memories are over-generalized, so they recall that 'something happened', but they are unable to fill in the detail. Williams (1996) argues that this kind of memory distortion is due to the linkage between recalled events and negative emotions. Since it may often be necessary in cognitive–behavioural counselling to construct detailed micro-analyses of specific events, counsellors need to be aware of the difficulties that clients can have with this type of recall task.

The other main approach to understanding cognitive process within cognitive–behavioural counselling and therapy is concerned with the operation of meta-cognition. This refers to the ability of people to reflect on their own cognitive processes, to be aware of how they are going about thinking about something, or trying to solve a problem. A simple example to illustrate metacognition is to reflect on your experience of completing a jigsaw puzzle. You will find that you do not just 'do' a jigsaw in an automatic fashion (unless it is a very simple one) but that you will be aware of a set of strategies from which you can choose as needed, such as 'finding the corners', 'finding the edges' or 'collecting the sky'. An awareness of, and ability to communicate, metacognitive strategies is very important in teaching children how to do a jigsaw, rather than just doing it for them. Metacognition is a topic widely researched within developmental psychology in recent years.

Although the name of Meichenbaum (1977, 1985, 1986) is most closely associated with the issue of metacognition in counselling and therapy, the principle of metacognitive processing is in fact central to the work of Ellis, Beck and other cognitive–behavioural practitioners. For example, Ellis (1962) has devised an A–B–C theory of personality functioning. In this case, A refers to the activating event, which may be some action or attitude of an individual, or an actual physical event. C is the emotional or behavioural consequence of the event, the feelings or conduct of the person experiencing the event. However, for Ellis A does not cause C. Between A and C comes B, the person's beliefs about the event. Ellis contends that events are always mediated by beliefs, and that the emotional consequences of events are determined by the belief about the event rather than the event itself. For example, one person may lose her job and, believing that this event is 'an opportunity to do something else', feel happy. Another person may lose her job and, believing that 'this is the end of my usefulness as a person', feel deeply depressed.

The significance of the A–B–C formula in relation to metacognition is that the RET counsellor will teach the client how to use it as a way of monitoring cognitive reactions to events. The client is then able to engage in metacognitive processing of his or her thoughts in reaction to any event, and is, ideally, more able to make choices about how he or she intends to think about that event.

Cognitive content

Cognitive–behavioural counsellors and therapists have been active in cataloguing a wide variety of cognitive contents, referred to by different writers as irrational beliefs (Ellis 1962), dysfunctional or automatic thoughts (Beck 1976), self-talk or internal dialogue (Meichenbaum 1986) or 'hot cognitions' (Zajonc 1980). One of the central aims of much cognitive–behavioural work is to replace beliefs that contribute to self-defeating behaviour with beliefs that are associated with self-acceptance and constructive problem-solving. The following set of 'irrational beliefs', as identified by Ellis, provides the counsellor with a starting point for exploring the cognitive content of the client.

I *must* do well at all times.

I am a bad or worthless person when I act in a weak or stupid manner. I *must* be approved or accepted by people I find important.

I am a *bad, unlovable* person if I get rejected.

People *must* treat me fairly and give me what I need.

People who act immorally are undeserving, rotten people. People *must* live up to my expectations or it is terrible.

My life *must* have few major hassles or troubles. I *can't stand* really bad things or difficult people. It is awful or horrible when important things don't turn out the way I want them to.

I *can't* stand it when life is really unfair.

I *need* to be loved by someone who matters to me a lot.

I *need* immediate gratification and always feel awful when I don't get it.

The belief statements used in RET reflect the operation of a number of distorted cognitive processes. For example, over-generalization is present if the client believes he or she *needs* to be loved *at all times*. Cognitive therapists would dispute the rationality of this statement, inviting the client perhaps to reframe it as 'I enjoy the feeling of being loved and accepted by another person, and if this is not available to me I can sometimes feel unhappy.' Other cognitive distortions, such as dichotomous thinking ('if people don't love me they must hate me'), arbitrary inference ('I failed that exam today so I must be totally stupid'), personalization ('the gas man was late because they all hate me at that office') are also evident in irrational beliefs.

Within RET approaches to working with cognitions, the counsellor is looking out for examples of deeply held general statements that sum up the assumptions the client holds about the world. Another approach, used by Meichenbaum (1985, 1986) and other cognitive–behavioural counsellors, is to uncover the statements that accompany actual behaviour. For example, a client who has problems dealing with job interviews may be carrying on an 'internal dialogue' during the interview, which might include messages such as 'I will fail', 'Here we go again, its just like the last time' or 'I know that was the wrong thing to say'. These beliefs or self-statements are very likely to undermine the performance of the interview candidate, by initiating and reinforcing feelings of anxiety, and by devoting attention to internal states rather than listening to the questions being asked by the interviewer.

One of the difficulties in this area of cognitive–behavioural counselling lies in gaining access to the beliefs or self-statements of the client. Some of the main techniques used in the assessment of cognitions (Hollon and Kendall 1981; Kendall and Hollon 1981) are:

- unobtrusive tape-recording of spontaneous speech;
- recording speech following specific instructions (e.g. 'imagine you are taking an exam');
- 'thinking out loud' when doing a task;
- questionnaires (e.g. assertiveness self-statements test);
- thought listing;
- dysfunctional thoughts record (worksheet on which client records details of the activating event, belief and behavioural consequences).

It is important to be aware of the fact that the process of eliciting beliefs may in itself have an impact. For example, there is evidence that depressed people report more negative thoughts if asked to report on what they were thinking in the past, but will produce more positive cognitions if reporting what they are thinking in the here-and-now (Hollon and Kendall 1981). Verbal communication would also appear to be more productive than writing thoughts down (Blackwell *et al.* 1985).

The principal strategy for facilitating change in beliefs, once they have been brought out into the open, is to encourage the client to experiment with alternative beliefs or self-statements in particular situations, to discover for himself or herself the effects of acting according to a different set of guiding assumptions. This strategy demonstrates the behavioural as well as cognitive nature of cognitive–behavioural counselling. The client is not merely engaged in 'thought exercises', but is given opportunities to learn about the behavioural consequences of the cognitions, and to extend the available repertoire of behaviours in problem situations.

It is apparent that maladaptive cognitive processes and maladaptive cognitive contents are linked. It may be useful to see both as aspects of the operation of an overall cognitive structure (Meichenbaum 1986), schema or model of the world. The task of the cognitive–behavioural counsellor can be viewed as assisting the client to act as a scientist in discovering the validity of this personal map or model, and in making choices about which elements to keep and which to change.

The techniques and methods of cognitive–behavioural counselling

Unlike the psychodynamic and person-centred approaches to counselling, which place a great deal of emphasis on exploration and understanding, the cognitive–behavioural approach is less concerned with insight and more oriented towards client action to produce change. Although different practitioners may have different styles, the tendency in cognitive–behavioural work is to operate within a structured stage-by-stage programme (Kuehnel and Liberman 1986; Freeman and Simon 1989). Such a programme might encompass:

1 Establishing rapport and creating a working alliance between counsellor and client. Explaining the rationale for treatment.
2 Assessing the problem. Identifying and quantifying the frequency, intensity and appropriateness of problem behaviours and cognitions.
3 Setting goals or targets for change. These should be selected by the client, and be clear, specific and attainable.
4 Application of cognitive and behavioural techniques.
5 Monitoring progress, using ongoing assessment of target behaviours.
6 Termination and planned follow-up to reinforce generalization of gains.

Persons (1993) argues that in cognitive–behavioural work it is helpful to integrate all this information into an overall case formulation or conceptualization. This is a kind of mini-theory of the individual client and his or her problems. Persons (1993) suggests that it is only when the counsellor has fully conceptualized the case that potential obstacles to treatment become apparent, and can be overcome.

The cognitive–behavioural counsellor will usually employ a range of intervention techniques to achieve the behavioural objectives agreed with the client (Haaga and Davison 1986; Meichenbaum 1986). Techniques that are frequently used include:

1 Challenging irrational beliefs.
2 Reframing the issues; for example, perceiving internal emotional states as excitement rather than fear.
3 Rehearsing the use of different self-statements in role plays with the counsellor.
4 Experimenting with the use of different self-statements in real situations.

5 Scaling feelings; for example, placing present feelings of anxiety or panic on a scale of 0–100.

6 Thought stopping. Rather than allowing anxious or obsessional thoughts to 'take over', the client learns to do something to interrupt them, such as snapping a rubber band on his or her wrist.

7 Systematic desensitization. The replacement of anxiety or fear responses by a learned relaxation response. The counsellor takes the client through a graded hierarchy of fear-eliciting situations.

8 Assertiveness or social skills training.

9 Homework assignments. Practising new behaviours and cognitive strategies between therapy sessions.

10 *In vivo* exposure. Being accompanied by the counsellor into highly fearful situations; for example, visiting shops with an agoraphobic client. The role of the counsellor is to encourage the client to use cognitive–behavioural techniques to cope with the situation.

Further examples of cognitive–behavioural methods can be found in Kanfer and Goldstein (1986), Kuehnel and Liberman (1986) and Freeman *et al.* (1989).

Another set of ideas and techniques that have come to be widely used by cognitive–behavioural counsellors is associated with the concept of *relapse prevention*. Marlatt and Gordon (1985) observed that while many clients who are helped, through therapy, to change their behaviour may initially make good progress, they may at some point encounter some kind of crisis, which triggers a resumption of the original problem behaviour. This pattern is particularly common in clients with addictions to food, alcohol, drugs or smoking, but can be found in any behaviour-change scenario. Marlatt and Gordon (1985) concluded that it is necessary in cognitive–behavioural work to prepare for this eventuality, and to provide the client with skills and strategies for dealing with relapse events. The standard approaches to relapse prevention involve the application of cognitive–behavioural techniques. For example, the 'awful catastrophe' of 'relapse' can be redefined as a 'lapse'. The client can learn to identify the situations that are likely to evoke a lapse, and acquire social skills in order to deal with them. Marlatt and Gordon (1985) characterize three types of experience as being associated with high rates of relapse: 'downers' (feeling depressed), 'rows' (interpersonal conflict) and 'joining the club' (pressure from others to resume drinking, smoking etc.). Clients may be given written instructions on what action to take if there is a threat of a lapse, or a phone number to call. Wanigaratne *et al.* (1990) describe many other ways in which the relapse prevention concept can be applied in counselling.

These examples of techniques and strategies illustrate the fundamental importance of scientific methods in cognitive–behavioural counselling. There is a strong emphasis on measurement, assessment and experimentation. This philosophy has been called the 'scientist-practitioner' model (Barlow *et al.* 1984), because it stresses that therapists should also be scientists and integrate the ideas of science into their practice. At the time this perspective on counselling and therapy was also known as the 'Boulder model', since it emerged from a conference held at Boulder,

Box 5.3

Overcoming fear of flying: what helps?

Cognitive–behavioural methods are well suited to helping people who are experiencing overwhelming fears in specific areas of their life. Fear of flying is a good example of the type of problem that can often be addressed effectively from a cognitive–behavioural approach. But when a client receives a cognitive–behavioural intervention to combat fear of flying, what is it that helps? Does change occur because irrational beliefs about air travel have been altered? How important is the fact that the client has acquired a new repertoire of behaviours: for example, relaxation skills? And how significant is the relationship with the cognitive–behavioural counsellor? Do people get better because they trust the counsellor, or want to please him or her? Borrill and Foreman (1996) explored these issues in a series of interviews with clients who had successfully completed a cognitive–behavioural fear of flying programme. The programme comprised an initial session where the origins of the fear for the individual client were explored, and they were taught about the nature of anxiety. The second session was an accompanied return flight from the UK to Europe, on a normal scheduled service. When asked about their experience of therapy, these clients had a lot to say about the process of mastering their fear and panic. They reported that therapy had helped them to be able to understand their emotional arousal, and to apply a cognitive–behavioural model of anxiety in a way that made a real difference to how they felt. They became able cognitively to relabel difficult emotions. Fear and anxiety now became discomfort or excitement, or both. They became able to think rationally about their experience of flying. Actually facing up to fear, by undertaking a flight, was also a valuable source of confidence. For example, one client recalled that:

> then she [the psychologist] said 'I want you to walk the length of the plane'. Normally I've got superglue on the bottom of my shoes. I went up there and I was so proud that I had done it.
>
> (Borrill and Foreman 1996: 69)

These experiences are consistent with cognitive–behavioural theory. Coping skills, cognitive reframing and self-efficacy are central features of the cognitive–behavioural model. What was more surprising, from a strict cognitive–behavioural perspective, was the degree to which these clients reported that their relationship with the therapist had been crucial to the success of their therapy. The therapist was perceived as trustworthy, open and warm, and also *informal*. A client stated that:

> she comes over as being very casual and relaxed and enjoying it all immensely . . . it was all terribly laid back. It's just that she doesn't give the impression that there is anything to worry about.
>
> (Borrill and Foreman 1996: 65)

The therapist legitimized their fear, she accepted that they were terrified, in contrast to friends or family members who had dismissed their feelings. However, what seemed crucial was the sense that clients had of the therapist as being in control. This enabled them to feel confidence in her, and thus to feel confidence in themselves. As one client put it:

> what got me through it is this thing of someone having trust in you – her saying 'of course you can do it'. It's like *borrowing someone's belief in you to actually believe in yourself.*
>
> (Borrill and Foreman 1996: 66)

The authors of this study conclude that a strong therapeutic relationship was a necessary component of this treatment, but that this relationship operated in a somewhat paradoxical way: 'empowerment comes from being prepared to relinquish power and control, to trust the psychologist and follow her instructions' (p. 66).

Colorado, in 1949 to decide the future shape of training in clinical psychology in the USA.

An appraisal of the cognitive–behavioural approach to counselling

Cognitive–behavioural concepts and methods have made an enormous contribution to the field of counselling. Evidence of the energy and creativity of researchers and practitioners in this area can be gained by inspection of the ever-increasing literature on the topic. Kuehlwein (1993), Rosen (1993), Mahoney (1995a) and Salkovskis (1996) have reviewed recent developments in this field. Cognitive–behavioural approaches appeal to many counsellors and clients because they are straightforward and practical, and emphasize action. The wide array of techniques provide counsellors with a sense of competence and potency. The effectiveness of cognitive–behavioural therapy for a wide range of conditions is amply confirmed in the research literature.

There are, however, two significant theoretical areas in which the cognitive–behavioural approach is particularly open to criticism. The first of these concerns the notion of the therapeutic relationship. Cognitive–behavioural therapists take very seriously the necessity of establishing a good working alliance with the client (Burns and Auerbach 1996). This relationship is often characterized as educational rather than medical: teacher–student as opposed to doctor–patient. Unfortunately, this practical awareness of the relationship factor is not extended to the realms of theory and training. For example, there is no cognitive–behavioural concept equivalent to 'counter-transference' in psychodynamic theory or 'congruence' in person-centred theory. Nor is there, usually, any requirement for cognitive–behavioural counsellors to undergo personal therapy as part of their training, with the aim of facilitating the development of appropriate self-awareness in the counselling relationship. The absence of a real appreciation of the impact of the self or person of the counsellor is all the more regrettable when it is realized that the approach gives counsellors permission to challenge and confront clients. At these moments, can the cognitive–behavioural counsellor be sure of for whose benefit the challenge or confrontation is being made? From a psychodynamic perspective, for example, the achievement of a rational, equal relationship between counsellor and client would be seen as the end-point of very successful work, rather than as something that could be readily set up before the real work begins. Many clients come to counselling because of relationship difficulties, and these difficulties can often be acted out in the counselling room itself.

A second issue that presents theoretical dilemmas for cognitive–behavioural counsellors concerns the way cognition is understood and conceptualized. A basic tenet of the approach is that change in thinking can result in change in behaviour and feelings. The research evidence to support this position is, however, not without problems. For example, in a study of cognitive processes in people who were depressed, Alloy and Abramson (1982) found that these individuals exhibited thinking which was pessimistic and negative, but which was in fact less distorted than the cognitive processing of 'normal' people. They argued that depressed people see the world accurately, while non-depressed people view things through 'rose-tinted lenses'. In their experiment, depressed people remembered both good and bad information about self, while non-depressed people remembered only the positive information. In another study, Lewinsohn *et al.* (1981) followed up a group of people over a one-year period. Some of these people developed symptoms of depression during that time, but there was no correlation between irrational beliefs and cognitive processes measured at the beginning and the subsequent development of depression. Lewinsohn *et al.* (1981) interpreted these findings to mean that distorted cognitions were not a cause of depression, as Beck *et al.* (1979) would assume, but were by-products of it. Beidel and Turner (1986) draw the conclusion from these studies that cognitive processes are secondary to behavioural processes in the development of emotional problems, and that the 'cognitivist' revolution is misguided. This point of view is supported by Cullen (1991) and by Wolpe (1978: 444), who has reasserted the radical behaviourist, determinist position in stating that 'our thinking is behaviour and is as unfree as any other behaviour . . . all learning takes place automatically . . . we always do what we must do.' Beidel and Turner (1986) also suggest that the cognitive strand of cognitive–behavioural counselling and therapy could be strengthened by paying more attention to new developments in cognitive psychology.

Both the issue of the nature of the counsellor–client relationship in cognitive–behavioural therapy and the question of the validity of the theoretical assumptions employed in the approach can be understood as deriving from the same ultimate source. Compared to most other mainstream approaches to counselling and therapy, the cognitive–behavioural orientation is more of a technology than a framework for understanding life. Recurring themes in cognitive–behavioural writings are management, control and monitoring. It is a highly effective way of 'fixing' people quickly, of helping individuals to get on with their lives.

The constructivist revolution

Having become established as the form of psychological therapy most favoured by health care providers in the USA and in many European countries, it is perhaps surprising that the cognitive–behavioural approach should then be shaken to its roots by a theoretical revolution. Over the past decade or more, key figures in the cognitive–behavioural tradition, such as Michael Mahoney and Donald Meichenbaum, have taken to calling themselves *constructivist* therapists. What does this mean?

Constructivism can perhaps be characterized as resting on three basic assumptions. First, the person is regarded as an active knower, as purposefully engaged in making sense of his or her world. Second, language functions as the primary means through which the person constructs an understanding of the world. Constructivist therapists are therefore particularly interested in linguistic products such as stories and metaphors, which are seen as ways of structuring experience. Third, there is a developmental dimension to the person's capacity to construct their world. These three core assumptions mark a significant contrast between the older cognitive and cognitive–behavioural therapies and the newer constructivist alternative, although it can be seen that there is also a great deal of common ground. Constructivism would appear to be a direction in which cognitive–behavioural counselling is heading, rather than a fundamentally different approach. Some of the main points of contrast between cognitive and constructivist theories of therapy are depicted in Table 5.1.

The main historical precursor of constructivist therapy has been the *personal construct psychology* originally devised by Kelly (1955) and later developed by Bannister, Fransella, Mair and their colleagues, largely in Britain (Bannister and Fransella 1985). This theory proposes that people make sense of, or 'construe', the world through systems of personal constructs. A typical example of a personal construct might be 'friendly–unfriendly'. Such a construct enables the person to differentiate between people who are perceived as 'friendly' and those who are 'unfriendly'. This construct will function to channel the person's behaviour; he or she will behave differently towards someone construed as 'friendly', in comparison to how they might act towards someone who is 'unfriendly'. A construct is embedded within a system. In some circumstances, the 'friendly–unfriendly' construct would be subsumed under a core construct such as 'reliable–unreliable'. Each construct also has its own range of convenience. For instance, 'friendly–unfriendly' can be used to construe people, but not (presumably) food. Kelly and

Table 5.1 Comparison between cognitive and constructivist approaches to counselling

Feature	Traditional cognitive therapies	Constructivist therapies
Target of intervention and assessment	Isolated automatic thoughts or irrational beliefs	Construct systems, personal narratives
Temporal focus	Present	Present, but more developmental emphasis
Goal of treatment	Corrective: eliminate dysfunction	Creative; facilitate development
Style of therapy	Highly directive and psycho-educational	Less structured and more exploratory
Therapist role	Persuasive, analytical, technically instructive	Reflective, intensely personal
Interpretation of emotions	Negative emotion results from distorted thinking; represents problem to be controlled	Negative emotion as informative signal of challenge to existing constructions; to be respected
Understanding of client 'resistance'	Lack of motivation, viewed as dysfunctional	Attempt to protect core ordering processes

Source: Neimeyer (1993, 1995b).

his colleagues invented a technique known as the repertory grid to assess the unique structure and content of the construct systems of individuals, and also devised a number of methods for applying personal construct principles in therapeutic practice. The best known of the techniques is *fixed role* therapy. Clients are asked to describe themselves as they are, and then to create an alternative role description based on a different set of constructs. They are then encouraged to act out this role for set periods of time. A more detailed account of personal construct therapy can be found in Fransella and Dalton (1996).

One of the unusual aspects of personal construct psychology was that Kelly published his ideas as a formal theory, with postulates and corollaries. The most important of these statements was Kelly's *fundamental postulate*:

a person's processes are psychologically channelized by the way in which he anticipates events.

Later writers and theorists have gradually moved away from Kelly's formal system, while remaining true to the spirit of his approach. Constructivist counselling and therapy can be seen in this light, as true to the spirit of Kelly but including many new ideas and insights that did not appear in his original theory.

At this point in time, constructivism is still evolving, and it is not possible to specify a set of core procedures or techniques that all constructivist counsellors and psychotherapists would use. In this respect it is quite different from the cognitive–behavioural approach, which possesses a toolkit of familiar techniques with known effectiveness. Constructivist therapy is principle-driven rather than technique-driven. Constructivism also appears to be a currently fashionable label,

Box

5.4

The use of metaphor in constructivist therapy

The behavioural and cognitive traditions in counselling and psychotherapy have been shaped by the behaviourist need to deal with tangible, preferably observable, behaviours and irrational thoughts. Counsellors operating from a constructivist perspective are more interested in *meaning*, and in the ways that people create or find meaning in their lives. When a client in counselling talks about events that were traumatic and emotionally painful, it will usually be very difficult for him or her to find the words to capture just how they felt, or what happened. To convey to their counsellor or therapist some sense of the meaning of the event, the client will often use *metaphors*. Unable to articulate what happened directly, a metaphor at least makes it possible to say what the event was *like*. Attention to metaphor is an important theme in constructivist therapy. In his guide to therapy with people suffering from post-traumatic stress disorder (PTSD), Meichenbaum (1994: 112–14) places great emphasis on sensitivity to the role of metaphor. He gives long lists of metaphors employed by PTSD clients: 'I am a time bomb, ready to explode. I walk a thin red line. Over the edge. Enclosed in a steel ball. A spectator to life. Hole in my life. My life is in a holding pattern. Prisoner of the past and occasionally on parole. Vacuum in my history.' Meichenbaum (1994) also provides a list of healing metaphors that clients and therapists have used in their attempts to overcome PTSD. Among the therapist metaphors are:

> Someone who has experienced a traumatic event [is] like someone who *emigrates* to a new land and must build a new life within a new culture from the one left behind.

> When a flood occurs, the water does not continue forever. There is a rush, but it is temporary and eventually the storm stops, the land dries up, and everything begins to return to normal. Emotions can be viewed in the same way.

> Just as you can't force a physical wound to heal quickly, you can't force a psychological wound to heal either.

Other examples of the intentional use of metaphor in constructivist therapy can be found in Scott and Stradling (1992) and Goncalves (1993).

with many groups of therapists from diverse backgrounds competing over its ownership. This can make it hard to know just what the term constructivism means. It is as though anything and everything that might happen in the therapy room is, or could be, constructivist therapy. Finally, there is not only a tension between constructivist therapy and what Mahoney (1995b) has termed the older 'rationalist' cognitive therapies, there is also an area of significant contrast between the construct*ivist* approach being described here and the social construct*ionist*

Other constructivist theories are introduced on pages 230–4

approach outlined in Chapter 9. Social constructionism is less individualist than constructivism, giving more attention to the culture, history and social systems within which the person exists. On the other hand, rationalist cognitive therapy as represented by Beck and Ellis is *more* individualized and psychologized than constructivism, in that it concentrates largely on internal cognitive processes rather than on the interpersonal use of language. Constructivism is located between these two poles, pulled in both directions. Is this an uncomfortable place to be? Is it a source of creative tension?

Solution-focused therapy

In recent years, *solution-focused therapy* has become possibly the most influential of the various emergent constructivist approaches to counselling and psychotherapy. The range and scope of the approach is well illustrated in *The Handbook of Solution-focused Therapy* (Miller *et al.* 1996), and in a series of papers edited by Hoyt (1994). An excellent overview of solution-focused therapy can be found in O'Connell (1998).

Solution-focused brief therapy is mainly associated with the work of Steve de Shazer (1985, 1988, 1991, 1994) at the Brief Family Therapy Centre in Milwaukee, and a group of colleagues and collaborators, including Insoo Kim Berg (Miller and Berg 1995; Berg and Kelly 2000), Yvonne Dolan (1991) and Bill O'Hanlan (O'Hanlan and Weiner-Davis 1989; Rowan and O'Hanlan 1999). de Shazer has a background in social work and music, and in his training as a psychotherapist was strongly influenced by the theory and research carried out by the Mental Research Institute (MRI) in Palo Alto, California. The Palo Alto group were the first, during the 1950s, to study interaction patterns in families, and their approach borrowed heavily from anthropological and sociological ideas as opposed to a psychiatric perspective. de Shazer acquired from his exposure to the ideas of the Palo Alto group a number of core therapeutic principles found in systemic family therapy: a belief that intervention can be brief and 'strategic'; appreciation of the use of questioning to invite clients to consider alternative courses of action; and the use of an 'observing team', which advises the therapist during 'time out' interludes (see Chapter 7). Like many other family therapists (including members of the Palo Alto group), de Shazer became fascinated by the unique approach to therapy developed by Milton H. Erickson (see Box 5.5). The case studies published by Erickson convinced de Shazer that it was possible to work strategically and briefly with individual clients, not just with families, and that for each client there could exist a unique 'solution' to their own unique difficulties. Over the course of a number of years, de Shazer came to develop his own coherent approach, which emphasized the role of language in constructing personal reality. In working out the implications of placing language ('words', 'talk') at the heart of therapy, de Shazer made use of the ideas of philosophers such as Wittgenstein and Lyotard, and the French psychoanalytic thinker Jacques Lacan. The essence

Box 5.5

The enigma of Milton Erickson

Milton H. Erickson MD (1902–80) was an intriguing figure who played a significant role in the history of psychotherapy. Erickson worked for most of his career in Phoenix, Arizona, seeing patients in the living room of his three-bedroom home. He made major contributions to the field of medical hypnosis in his early career, and in the 1950s wrote the *Encyclopaedia Brittanica* entry on hynosis. Erickson was considered by those who knew him to be a heroic and magical individual. He overcame polio twice in youth, and developed an approach to therapy that 'cured' clients in ways that were almost impossible to understand, let alone replicate. Although he was originally best known for his use of hypnosis, it became clear to Erickson, and to those who studied with him, that the effectiveness of his approach to therapy did not rely on the use of suggestions made to patients while in trance states, but to his sensitive and creative use of language, metaphor and stories, his capacity to observe the fine detail of the client's behaviour and his ability to form a collaborative relationship with his clients.

Erickson's methods were popularized by the family therapist Jay Haley (1973), and have influenced many constructivist therapists (Hoyt 1994), as well as the solution-focused approach of Steve de Shazer. Further examples of Erickson's unique style of therapy can be found in Haley (1973), Rossi (1980), Rosen (1982) and Lankton and Lankton (1986).

of de Shazer's approach to therapy concentrates on the idea that 'problem talk' perpetuates the 'problem', maintains the centrality of the problem in the life and relationships of the person and distracts attention from any 'solutions' or 'exceptions' to the problem that the person might generate. The task of the therapist, therefore, is to invite the client to engage in 'solution' talk, while respectfully accepting (but not encouraging) the client's wish to talk about their distress and hopelessness, or the general awfulness of their problem. From de Shazer's point of view, therefore, solution-focused sessions are best thought of as conversations involving language games that are focused on three interrelated activities: namely, producing exceptions to the problem, imagining and describing new lives for clients and 'confirming' that change is occurring in their lives.

The solution-focused approach to therapy is built up from a range of strategies designed to enable the client to articulate and act on the widest possible range of solutions to their problems. These strategies include the following.

Focusing on change. The idea that change is happening all the time is an important concept in solution-focused therapy. Solution-focused therapists assume therefore that change is not only possible but inevitable. In practice this means that therapists will usually ask new clients about changes in relation to their presenting concerns prior to their first session – often referred to as 'pre-session change'. During therapy the therapist will usually begin each session by asking the client about changes since the last session: for example, 'What's better even in small ways since last time?' If the client describes any changes, even apparently minor ones, then the therapist will use a range of follow-up questions to amplify the change and resourcefulness of the client: for instance, 'How did you do that?'; 'How did you know that was the right thing to do/best way to handle the situation?' Should the client not be able to identify any change, the therapist might use 'coping questions' to invite the client to talk about how they are managing to survive or cope despite the problem.

Problem-free talk. At the beginning of a session, a counsellor might engage the client in talk about everyday activities, as a means of gaining some appreciation of the client's competencies and positive qualities.

Exception finding. Fundamental to the solution-focused approach is a belief that no matter how severe or all-pervasive a person's problem may appear there will be times when it does not occur, is less debilitating or intrusive in their lives. Such instances again point to clients' strengths and self-healing abilities, which when harnessed allow clients to construct their own unique solutions to their difficulties and concerns. Practitioners will therefore deliberately seek out exceptions by asking clients questions like: 'When was the last time you felt happy/relaxed/loved/confident etc. etc.?' 'What have you found that helps, even a little?' Exception finding questions help to deconstruct the client's view of the problem and at the same time to highlight and build on the client's success in redefining themselves and their lives.

Use of pithy slogans. There are a number of short, memorable statements that help to communicate to clients (and trainee therapists) the basic principles of a solution-focused approach. Typical solution-focused messages include: 'If it isn't broken, don't fix it', 'If it's not working stop doing it', 'If it's working, keep doing it', 'Therapy need not take a long time', 'Small changes can lead to bigger changes'.

The 'miracle question'. Typically, in a first session, a solution-focused counsellor will ask the client to imagine a future in which their problem has been resolved: 'Imagine when you go to sleep one night a miracle happens and the problems we've been talking about disappear. As you were asleep, you did not know that a miracle had happened. When you woke up, what would be the first signs for you that a miracle had happened?' (de Shazer 1988). This catalytic question allows the person to consider the problem as a whole, to step into a future that does not include the problem and to explore, with the therapist, how they would know that the problem had gone, how other people would know and how such changes had been brought about. The image of a 'miracle' is also a potent cultural metaphor that helps the client to remember what they learned from this discussion that follows the asking of the question.

Scaling. Scaling questions are designed to facilitate discussion about and measure change, and are used to consider a multitude of issues in client's lives. For instance, to assess a client's readiness or motivation to change, their coping abilities, self-esteem, progress in therapy and so on. Typically, the client is asked to rate their problem (e.g. depression) on a 0–10 scale, where 0 is as bad as it can be ('rock bottom') and 10 is ideal. Once the client places themselves at a point on the scale (a 2, for example), the therapist will first of all enquire about what has helped to get them to a 2 or what the client is doing to prevent themselves from slipping back to 'rock bottom'. Subsequently the therapist will work with the client to negotiate further small goals by inviting them to consider what will be different when they are at 3 on the scale and so on in subsequent sessions until the client reaches a point where they are ready to end therapy.

Homework tasks – exploring resources. Towards the end of each session, the therapist will either leave the room to consult with co-workers who have been observing the session, or (if working alone) take a few minutes to reflect in silence. In the final segment of the session, the therapist restates his or her admiration for positive achievements that the client has made, and then prescribes a task to be carried out before the next session. The homework task is designed to enable the person to remain focused on solutions. An example of a homework task that might be used following the first session of therapy is: 'Until the next time we meet, I'd like you just to observe what things are happening in your life/family/work that you'd like to see continue, then come back and tell me about it.'

These are some of the many ways in which a solution-focused therapist will structure the therapeutic conversation to allow the client to identify and apply their own personal strengths and competencies. Some of key points of contrast between a problem-focused and a solution-focused approach to therapy are highlighted in Table 5.2.

It is important to appreciate the wider issues associated with the solution-focused approach. Solution-focused therapy exists as a distinct approach to therapy, which is practised by Steven de Shazer, Insoo Kim Berg and many other practitioners they have trained. However, the solution-focused approach also has a wider significance, in representing a radical perspective in relation to a number of

Table 5.2 Comparison between a problem-focused and a solution-focused approach to counselling

Problem-focused	*Solution-focused*
How can I help you?	How will you know when therapy has been helpful?
Could you tell me about the problem?	What would you like to change?
Is the problem a symptom of something deeper?	Have we clarified the central issue on which you want to concentrate?
Can you tell me more about the problem?	Can we discover exceptions to the problem?
How are we to understand the problem in the light of the past?	What will the future look like without the problem?
How many sessions will be needed?	Have we achieved enough to end?

Source: O'Connell (1998: 21).

the key issues that have dominated debates within counselling and psychotherapy during the past 50 years. The historical account of the development of therapy offered in Chapter 2 described the emergence of psychoanalysis, the earliest form of psychotherapy, from a medical-psychiatric context that emphasized the necessity of diagnosing and assessing the patient's problem as the first step in effective treatment. In psychoanalysis, much of the effectiveness of therapy is attributed to the achievement of suitable levels of insight and understanding of the origins of the presenting problem: for example, its roots in childhood experience. The next generation of therapies that emerged in the mid-twentieth century – humanistic and cognitive–behavioural – retained an interest in understanding the roots of the person's problem, but, compared to psychoanalysis, paid much more attention to what the person might be seeking to be able to do in the future. Both self-actualization and behaviour change are 'future-oriented' constructs. Solution-focused therapy represents a radical further movement in this direction. In solution-focused therapy, the 'problem' is not particularly interesting. What is important is to focus on the solutions and strengths that the person already possesses, or is able to devise, in relation to living the kind of life they want to live.

Why is this a radical shift? Surely, it could be argued, even 'problem-focused' or 'assessment-oriented' therapies such as psychoanalysis use the process of analysing and understanding a problem as a means of arriving at the best solution to that problem? Even if the work of therapy concentrates largely on unravelling the connections between past experience and present troubles, in gaining insight the patient or client is effectively creating a space within which new options or solutions can be adopted. de Shazer does not share this view. For de Shazer, the concept of 'problem', as employed in counselling and psychotherapy theory, implies a notion of the person as structured in terms of a set of internal mechanisms (mind, unconscious, self, schemas) that have 'gone wrong' and need to be fixed. de Shazer, and other solution-focused therapists, *do not view people in these terms*. For them, the person exists within the way they talk, within the stories that they tell to themselves and other people. From this perspective, any attempt to explore and understand the 'problem' is merely encouraging 'problem talk', the maintenance of relationships characterized by a story-line of the 'I have a problem' type, and the suppression of stories that offer an account of the person as resourceful, capable, in control and so on. In addition, one of the by-products of an extended exploration of a 'problem' with a therapist is that the person begins to apply the language of psychology and psychotherapy not only as a means of accounting for this specific problem, but as a way of talking about other aspects of their life: the person becomes socialized into a 'problem-sensitive' way of talking about himself or herself. Moreover, de Shazer would reject any assumption that there is a necessary cause and effect relationship between studying a problem and arriving at its solution: a solution is a kind of unpredictable 'creative leap'. This way of looking at therapy seriously challenges any notion of the 'scientific' knowability of what happens in therapy. If clients get 'better' by following their own, idiosyncratic solutions, then what role is left for scientific models of dysfunction and change?

What de Shazer is doing can be seen as a rigorous attempt to conduct therapy from a postmodern standpoint. The idea that there exist internal psychological structures that determine behaviour is an essentially 'modern' way of making sense of the world. A postmodern sensitivity argues that these theories/structures are no more than another kind of story. They are stories that are associated with the power that professions and institutions have to define individuals as 'cases', as exhibiting 'deficits' (Gergen 1990). Like other postmodern writers, de Shazer adopts a role of challenging and questioning established ideas, with the aim of opening up possibilities for individuals to create their own personal or 'local' truths, rather than become assimilated into any theoretical framework that claims universal truth.

In contrast to the mainstream approaches to counselling (psychodynamic, cognitive–behavioural and person-centred), solution-focused therapy has never generated a formal theory, and has not cultivated a base within the university/research system. Although some research has been carried out into the effectiveness of solution-focused therapy (Gingerich and Eisengart 2000), there have been no large-scale studies of research programmes into this approach. As a result, although this research is generally supportive of the effectiveness of solution-focused therapy, it has received little attention within the psychotherapy research community. The published literature on solution-focused therapy mainly comprises fragments of philosophical analysis, rather than any attempt to assemble a definitive theoretical model or 'manual', supplemented by numerous case examples (which rely almost entirely on session transcripts) and dialogues between practitioners (see Hoyt 1994, 1996a).

It is important to acknowledge the difference between solution-focused therapy, which de Shazer describes as a *brief* therapy, and the imposition of limits on the number of sessions available to clients, associated with many workplace counselling schemes, managed care services in North America and counselling in primary care in the UK. The intention of solution-focused therapy is to respect the personal resourcefulness of the client by asking them whether they have achieved what they need, or inviting them to say what would need to happen for them to know they were ready to finish therapy. A solution-focused therapist would argue that it is a mark of their profound belief in the resourcefulness of people that they can accept that one session of therapy may be sufficient. However, they acknowledge that, for some people, *many* sessions may be required: it is up to the person. In this sense, solution-focused therapy is not time-*limited*, even though it is usually *brief*.

Perhaps because of the radical, 'outsider' status of solution-focused therapy, there is sometimes a sense that writers and practitioners operating within this approach are unwilling to accept the common ground between what they do and the practices of therapists from competing traditions, or to deviate from the cardinal 'rules' of solution-focused therapy, such as asking the 'miracle question' in the first session. Nylund and Corsiglia (1994) make the point that solution-focused therapy work can risk becoming solution-*forced* rather than solution-*focused*, and suggest that some clients may find its relentless future-oriented optimism persecutory and unhelpful. Bill O'Hanlan, one of the pioneers within this approach, now describes his method as *possibility* therapy (Hoyt 1996b), and argues that it is necessary to integrate Rogerian qualities of empathy and affirmation in order to offer a more caring relationship to clients.

It is difficult to predict the long-term impact of solution-focused therapy on the field of counselling and psychotherapy as a whole. Probably thousands of counsellors and psychotherapists in Europe and North America have attended workshops on solution-focused therapy, and have read de Shazer's books. It is impossible to know how many of these practitioners have attended workshops because they are curious about what may seem an odd or – in their eyes – mistaken way to conduct therapy. There are many others who would be drawn to specific techniques, such as the miracle question or scaling, that they might apply within a cognitive–behavioural, humanistic or integrative approach. It remains to be seen whether the contribution of de Shazer and his colleagues lies in the construction of a radically constructivist, postmodern approach to therapy, or whether their legacy is more properly understood in more modest (but nevertheless valuable) terms, as comprising the invention of a number of techniques for inviting clients to imagine desirable future scenarios.

Conclusions

The cognitive–behavioural tradition represents an enormous resource for counsellors. The practical and pragmatic nature of this approach means that there exists a wealth of therapeutic techniques and strategies that can be applied to different clients and their problems. The creativity of the cognitive–behavioural tradition can be seen in its recent embrace of constructivist and solution-focused thinking, and in the willingness on the part of many writers and therapists from this perspective to dialogue with others in a search for integration. An important theme in all the therapy models discussed in this chapter, from behaviour modification to solution-focused therapy, is the consistent focus on the strengths of the client, and his or her capacity to change, rather than on lengthy exploration of 'problems'. These therapies are in the vanguard of a newly emerging emphasis on *positive psychology* (Seligman and Csikszentmihalyi 2000). The cognitive–behavioural approach has always had a healthy respect for the value of research as a means of improving practice, and this has enabled practitioners to be critical and questioning in a constructive way, and to learn quickly from the discoveries of their colleagues. From a psychodynamic or humanistic point of view, the main weakness of cognitive–behavioural and constructivist approaches can be seen as their lack of interest in the dynamics and quality of the relationship between counsellor and client. Although in practice many cognitive–behavioural counsellors are well aware of the role of the relationship, and can be highly effective in establishing an egalitarian working alliance with the client, concepts such as transference, empathy and congruence have no place within cognitive–

behavioural theory. The image of the person implicit in the cognitive–behavioural tradition is of someone who is managing a life, who has a set of instrumental goals or targets that he or she seeks to achieve. While constructivist thinking has broadened out this image considerably, to include an awareness of life as involving a search for meaning, the underlying sense of cognitive–behavioural counselling is that it is intended to help individuals to manage, to cope, to get by in a difficult world.

Chapter summary

- Cognitive–behavioural counselling is an approach that has grown out of developments in behavioural and cognitive psychology.

- In recent years, many cognitive–behavioural counsellors and psychotherapists have begun to describe their approach as *constructivist*, to reflect the way that people actively create or construct their reality.

- The behavioural origins of the approach emphasize processes of learning through operant and classical conditioning, direct observation of behaviour and a scientific attitude to monitoring behavioural change.

- These behavioural principles are applied in counselling through techniques such as systematic desensitization and behavioural self-control.

- In the 1960s Beck and Ellis were influential in introducing a cognitive dimension to this approach, through attention to dysfunctional thought processes and irrational beliefs.

- Cognitive–behavioural counsellors advocate a purposeful, structured approach, drawing on a wide range of specific techniques such as homework assignments, relaxation exercises, self-monitoring and relapse prevention.

- The new constructivist model of counselling draws on the ideas of Kelly's personal construct theory, but goes beyond Kelly in its use of metaphor, language and narrative to explore the person's meaning-system.

- Solution-focused therapy represents a radical constructivist approach which concentrates on encouraging 'solution talk' in clients.

- Cognitive–behavioural, constructivist and solution-focused approaches to counselling are widely used in a variety of settings, and are supported by substantial research evidence.

Topics for reflection and discussion

1 Does it make sense to understand cognition as a type of behaviour? What are the implications for counselling practice of taking this idea seriously?

2 Ellis (1973: 56) has suggested that 'there are virtually no legitimate reasons for people to make themselves terribly upset, hysterical or emotionally disturbed, no matter what kind of psychological or verbal stimuli are impinging on them.' Do you agree? What is the 'image of the person' implicit in this statement? What might be the implications for the therapeutic relationship when a counsellor believes that there is 'no legitimate reason' for a client to be upset?

3 What are the advantages and disadvantages of the explicitly scientific emphasis of the cognitive–behavioural approach?

4 To what extent does constructivism represent a radically new departure from the basic concepts of behavioural and cognitive–behavioural therapies?

5 In so far as they all aim to produce behaviour change, rather than insight, do you believe that a *solution-focused* approach is fundamentally different from cognitive behavioural and constructivist models of therapy?

Key terms and concepts

A–B–C theory
automatic thoughts
behaviour
behavioural self-control
classical conditioning
cognitive content
cognitive distortion model
cognitive processes
cognitive revolution
cognitive therapy
conditioning
constructivist perspective
experimental neurosis
fixed role therapy
functional analysis
introspection
irrational beliefs
laws of learning

learned helplessness
logical positivism
maladaptive beliefs
memory
metacognition
operant conditioning
overgeneralization
personal construct psychology
rational emotive therapy
reinforcement
relapse prevention
schema
scientist-practitioner
self-statements
solutions
stimulus-response
strategies for cognitive intervention
systematic desensitization

Suggested further reading

One of the most consistently interesting and thought-provoking writers in the cognitive–behavioural tradition is Donald Meichenbaum. His book on post-traumatic stress disorder (Meichenbaum 1994) is an excellent illustration of the application of cognitive–behavioural and constructivist ideas and methods to a difficult clinical problem.

Recent developments in cognitive–behavioural counselling are explored in Dobson and Craig (1996) and Scott *et al.* (1995). It can be hard to keep up with the ever-expanding field of constructivist counselling and psychotherapy, but Mahoney (1995a, b), Hoyt (1994, 1996a) and Sexton and Griffin (1997) provide a good selection of the work of key theorists.

6 Theory and practice of the person-centred approach

Introduction

The brief account in Chapter 2 of the social and cultural background that shaped the work of Carl Rogers gives some indication of the extent to which his approach to counselling was rooted in the values of American society. The approach associated with Rogers, called at various times 'non-directive', 'client-centred', 'person-centred' or 'Rogerian', has not only been one of the most widely used orientations to counselling and therapy over the past 50 years, but has also supplied ideas and methods which have been integrated into other approaches (Thorne 1992). The emergence of client-centred therapy in the 1950s was part of a movement in American psychology to create an alternative to the two theories which at that time dominated the field: psychoanalysis and behaviourism. This movement became known as the 'third force' (in contrast to the other main forces represented by the ideas of Freud and Skinner), and as 'humanistic' psychology. Apart from Rogers, the central figures in early humanistic psychology included Abraham Maslow, Charlotte Buhler and Sydney Jourard. These writers shared a vision of a psychology that would have a place for the human capacity for creativity, growth and choice, and were influenced by the European tradition of existential and phenomenological philosophy. The image of the person in humanistic psychology is of a self striving to find meaning and fulfilment in the world.

Humanistic psychology has always consisted of a broad set of theories and models connected by shared values and philosophical assumptions, rather than constituting a single, coherent, theoretical formulation (Rice and Greenberg 1992; Cain 2002; McLeod 2002a). Within counselling and psychotherapy, the most widely used humanistic approaches are person-centred and Gestalt, although psychosynthesis, transactional analysis and other models also contain strong humanistic elements. The common ingredient in all humanistic approaches is an emphasis on experiential processes. Rather than focusing on the origins of client problems in childhood events (psychodynamic) or the achievement of new patterns of behaviour in the future (behavioural), humanistic therapies concentrate on the 'here-and-now' experiencing of the client. It can be a source of confusion that the label 'experiential' has been used as a general term to describe all such approaches, but has also been employed as a label for one particular approach (Gendlin 1973; Watson *et al.* 1998b).

Following a period in which the humanistic tradition appeared to be waning as a source of influence and inspiration in counselling and psychotherapy, there are signs of a revival in this approach. The edited collections by Greenberg *et al.* (1998a) and Cain and Seeman (2002) bring together an impressive body of research into person-centred, experiential and humanistic therapies. The *Handbook of Humanistic Psychology*, edited by Schneider *et al.* (2001), provides a valuable overview of the many different strands of contemporary humanistic theory and practice.

The evolution of the person-centred approach

The birth of the person-centred approach is usually attributed to a talk given by Rogers in 1940 on 'new concepts in psychotherapy' to an audience at the University of Minnesota (Barrett-Lennard 1979). In this talk, which was subsequently published as a chapter in *Counseling and Psychotherapy* (Rogers 1942), it was suggested that the therapist could be of most help to clients by allowing them to find their own solutions to their problems. The emphasis on the client as expert and the counsellor as source of reflection and encouragement was captured in the designation of the approach as 'non-directive' counselling. In the research carried out at that time by Rogers and his students at the University of Ohio, the aim was to study the effect on the client of 'directive' and 'non-directive' behaviour on the part of the counsellor. These studies were the first pieces of psychotherapy research to involve the use of direct recording and transcription of actual therapy sessions.

In 1945 Rogers was invited to join the University of Chicago, as Professor of Psychology and Head of the Counseling Center. At this time, the ending of the war and the return from the front line of large numbers of armed services personnel, many of them traumatized by their experiences, meant that there was a demand for an accessible, practical means of helping these people to cope with the transition back to civilian life. At that time, the dominant form of psychotherapy in the USA was psychoanalysis, which would have been too expensive to provide for large numbers of soldiers, even if there had been enough trained analysts to make it possible. Behavioural approaches had not yet emerged. The 'non-directive' approach of Rogers represented an ideal solution, and a whole new generation of American counsellors was trained at Chicago, or by colleagues of Rogers at other colleges. It was in this way that the Rogerian approach became quickly established as the main non-medical form of counselling in the USA. Rogers was also successful in attracting substantial funding to enable a continuing programme of research.

These developments were associated with a significant evolution in the nature of the approach itself. The notion of 'non-directiveness' had from the beginning implied a contradiction. How could any person in a close relationship fail to influence the other, at least slightly, in one direction or another? Studies by Truax (1966) and others suggested that supposedly non-directive counsellors in fact subtly reinforced certain statements made by clients, and did not offer their interest, encouragement or approval when other types of statement were made. There were, therefore, substantial problems inherent in the concept of non-directiveness. At the same time, the focus of research in this approach was moving away from a concern with the behaviour of the counsellor, to a deeper consideration of the process that occurred in the client, particularly in relation to changes in the self-concept of the client. This change of emphasis was marked by a renaming of the approach as 'client-centred'. The key publications from this period are *Client-centered Therapy* by Rogers (1951) and the Rogers and Dymond (1954) collection of research papers.

The third phase in the development of client-centred counselling came during the latter years at Chicago (1954–7), and can be seen as representing an attempt to consolidate the theory by integrating the earlier ideas about the contribution of the counsellor with the later thinking about the process in the client, to arrive at a model of the therapeutic relationship. Rogers' 1957 paper on the 'necessary and sufficient' conditions of empathy, congruence and acceptance, later to become known as the 'core conditions' model, was an important landmark in this phase, as was his formulation of a 'process conception' of therapy. The book that remains the single most widely read of all of Rogers' writings, *On Becoming a Person* (Rogers 1961), is a compilation of talks and papers produced during this phase.

In 1957 Rogers and several colleagues from Chicago were given an opportunity to conduct a major research study based at the University of Wisconsin, investigating the process and outcome of client-centred therapy with hospitalized schizophrenic patients. One of the primary aims of the study was to test the validity of the 'core conditions' and 'process' models. This project triggered a crisis in the formerly close-knit team around Rogers (see Kirschenbaum (1979) for a lively account of this episode). Barrett-Lennard (1979: 187), in his review of the historical development of the person-centred approach, notes that 'the research team suffered internal vicissitudes'. The results of the study showed that the client-centred approach was not particularly effective with this type of client. There were also tensions between some of the principal members of the research group, and, although the project itself came to an end in 1963, the final report on the research was not published until 1967 (Rogers *et al.* 1967).

Several significant contributions emerged from the schizophrenia study. New instruments for assessing concepts such as empathy, congruence, acceptance (Barrett-Lennard 1962; Truax and Carkhuff 1967) and depth of experiencing (Klein *et al.* 1986) were developed. Gendlin began to construct a model of the process of experiencing that was to have a lasting impact. The opportunity to work with highly disturbed clients, and the difficulties in forming therapeutic relationships with these clients, led many of the team to re-examine their own practice, and in particular to arrive at an enhanced appreciation of the role of congruence in the therapy process. Client-centred therapists such as Shlien discovered that the largely empathic, reflective mode of operating, which had been effective with anxious college students and other clients at Chicago, was not effective with clients locked into their own private worlds. To make contact with these clients, the counsellor had to be willing to take risks in being open, honest and self-disclosing. The increase in emphasis given to congruence was also stimulated by the phase of the project where the eight therapists involved made transcripts of sessions available to other leading practitioners, and engaged in a dialogue. In the section of the Rogers *et al.* (1967) report that gives an account of this dialogue, it can be seen that these outside commentators were often highly critical of the passive, 'wooden' style of some of the client-centred team. The fruits of these more experiential sources of learning from the schizophrenia study are included in Rogers and Stevens (1968).

The Wisconsin project has more recently been criticized by Masson (1988), who argues that the acceptance and genuineness of the client-centred therapists could never hope to overcome the appalling institutionalization and oppression suffered by these patients:

> [The] patients lived in a state of oppression. In spite of his reputation for empathy and kindness, Carl Rogers could not perceive this. How could he have come to terms so easily with the coercion and violence that dominated their everyday existence? Nothing [written by Rogers] indicates any genuinely human response to the suffering he encountered in this large state hospital.
>
> (Masson 1988: 245)

In defence, it can be pointed out that Rogers *et al.* (1967) discuss in great detail the issues arising from working in a 'total institution', and were clearly attempting to deal with the problem that Masson (1988) describes. Rogers *et al.* (1967: 93) commented that

> one of the unspoken themes of the research, largely evident through omission, is that it was quite unnecessary to develop different research procedures or different theories because of the fact that our clients were schizophrenic. We found them far more similar to, than different from, other clients with whom we have worked.

This passage would indicate that at least one of the elements in the power imbalance, the existence of labelling and rejection, was not an important factor. The end of the Wisconsin experiment also marked the end of what Barrett-Lennard (1979) has called the 'school' era in client-centred therapy. Up to this point, there had always been a definable nucleus of people around Rogers, and an institutional base, which could be identified as a discrete, coherent school of thought. After the Wisconsin years, the client-centred approach fragmented, as the people who had been involved with Rogers moved to different locations, and pursued their own ideas largely in isolation from each other.

Rogers himself went to California, initially to the Western Behavioral Sciences Institute, and then, in 1968, to the Center for Studies of the Person at LaJolla. He became active in encounter groups, organizational change and community-building and, towards the end of his life, in working for political change in East–West relations and in South Africa (Rogers 1978, 1980). He did not engage in any further developments of any significance regarding his approach to one-to-one therapy. The extension of client-centred ideas to encompass groups, organizations and society in general meant that it was no longer appropriate to view the approach as being about clients as such, and the term 'person-centred' came increasingly into currency as a way of describing an approach to working with larger groups as well as with individual clients (Mearns and Thorne 1988).

Of the other central figures at that time, Gendlin and Shlien went back to Chicago, the former to continue exploring the implications of his experiential approach, the latter to carry out research in the effectiveness of time-limited client-centred therapy. Barrett-Lennard eventually returned to Australia, and remained active in theory and research. Truax and Carkhuff were key figures in creating new approaches for training people in the use of counselling skills. In Toronto, Rice was the leader of a group that explored the relationship between client-centred ideas and the information-processing model of cognitive psychology. Various individuals, such as Gendlin, Gordon, Goodman and Carkhuff, were instrumental in setting up programmes with the aim of enabling ordinary, non-professional people to use counselling skills to help others (see Larson 1984).

The post-Wisconsin developments in client-centred theory and practice are summarized by Lietaer (1990), who notes that while there have been many useful new directions, the approach as a whole has lacked coherence and direction in the absence of the powerful, authoritative voice provided by Rogers. So, although the periodic reviews of client-centred and person-centred theory, research and

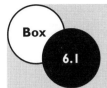

Box 6.1

Gestalt therapy: an alternative humanistic approach

Gestalt therapy represents an alternative humanistic approach to counselling. The differences and similarities between person-centred counselling and Gestalt therapy are reflected in the lives of their leading theorists: Carl Rogers and Fritz Perls. As described in this chapter, Rogers was essentially the product of a conventional, small-town America upbringing who worked for most of his life within social services and educational organizations. By contrast, Fritz Perls (1893–1970) was born in a Berlin Jewish ghetto. His father, a wine salesman, became financially successful, and Friz Perls enjoyed a middle-class upbringing. Although he was actively involved in theatre, he entered medical school. He was drafted into the German army in the First World War, and spent nine months in the trenches as a medical orderly, narrowly escaping death. He qualified as an MD in 1920, and became part of the Bauhaus group of dissident artists and intellectuals. After entering psychoanalysis in 1926, with Karen Horney, he decided to become an analyst. Fritz Perls made his living as an analyst between 1929 and 1950, first in Germany, then in South Africa (where he emigrated in 1936 as a result of the rise of fascism in Germany) and finally in New York. His mother and sister died in concentration camps. Throughout his life, he openly experimented with different types of sexual experience, and was associated in the USA with 'counter-culture' figures such as Paul Goodman, and with radical theatre groups.

The approach to therapy that was developed by Fritz and Laura Perls, Paul Goodman and Ralph Hefferline was similar to Rogers' client-centred therapy in that both rejected psychoanalytic ideas, and embraced humanistic values represented by existentialism and the celebration of individual freedom, creativity and expression of feeling. However, while Rogers has been described as a 'quiet revolutionary', the early Gestalt therapists were much more radical in their approach. Perls and his colleagues imported ideas from drama that involved the client physically *enacting* the emotional issues they presented. Another key theme in the approach was its emphasis on *conflict* between parts of the self, mirroring the personal and social conflict experienced by Perls throughout his life.

A distinctive feature of this orientation to counselling is that it draws heavily on the 'Gestalt' school of psychology, which was an influential force in the field of the psychology of perception and cognition in the period 1930–50 (Kohler 1929; Koffka 1935). Gestalt is a German word that means 'pattern', and the key idea in this psychological model is the capacity of people to experience the world in terms of wholes, or overall patterns, and, more specifically, to have a tendency to complete unfinished patterns. The actual Gestalt psychologists were primarily interested in studying human perception and thought, and were responsible for familiar ideas, such as 'mental set' (viewing later phenomena as if they were similar to the first configuration the viewer had originally encountered) and the 'Zeigarnik effect' (having a better recollection of tasks that had not been completed than of tasks that had been fully finished). Fritz Perls saw the relevance of these ideas for psychotherapy, in terms of the 'wholeness' of the person, and Gestalt therapy was established with the publication of *Ego, Hunger and Aggression* (Perls 1947) and *Gestalt Therapy* (Perls *et al.* 1951). The later writings of Perls (1969, 1973) mainly articulated the approach through examples of his work with clients, rather than through a formal theoretical presentation, although Perls also demonstrated his work extensively in training workshops. An essential feature of Gestalt therapy as practised by Fritz Perls was an extreme hostility to over-intellectualization, or what he called 'bullshit'. His approach, therefore, focused rigorously on the here-and-now experiencing or awareness of the client, with the aim of removing the blocks to authentic contact with the environment caused by old patterns ('unfinished business').

The emphasis on working with immediate experience, combined with Fritz Perls's rejection of theorizing, has meant that Gestalt therapy is often considered as a source of practical techniques for exploring current awareness, and enabling clients to express buried feelings, rather than as a distinctive theoretical model. There is some validity to this view, since Gestalt has been responsible for a wide range of techniques and exercises, such as two-chair work, first-person language and ways of working with art materials, dreams and guided fantasies. Nevertheless, this approach includes a theoretical framework that contains many important ideas.

The writings of Fritz Perls do not present a particularly balanced view of the Gestalt approach. He has been described as a 'brilliant, dramatic, controversial and charismatic teacher' (Parlett and Page 1990) who modelled a style of working with clients that was significantly more confrontational and anti-intellectual than that adopted by subsequent Gestalt practitioners (see Shepard 1975; Masson 1992). More recently, Gestalt practice has moved in the direction of work based on the relationship between client and therapist, and the development of awareness and understanding of contact disruptions within this relationship, and uses dramatic enactments rather less often than previously. Contemporary Gestalt practitioners tend to describe themselves as employing a *dialogical* or interpersonal approach (Wheeler 1991; Hycner and Jacobs 1995; Yontef 1995, 1998).

It can be seen, therefore, that many of the same humanistic themes are present in person-centred and Gestalt therapy: the importance of process, a belief in authenticity and self-fulfilment, a rejection of labelling or interpreting the client's experience, emphasis on self-acceptance and an assumption of the validity of organismic 'gut' feelings. There are two important differences between these approaches. First, Gestalt therapists believe that it is helpful to invite the client to 'experiment' with different forms of behaving and awareness; person-centred counsellors view such interventions as an unwarranted 'directiveness' that shifts therapy away from the frame of reference and 'track' of the client. Second, Gestalt practice focuses on 'splits' or polarities in the self; person-centred theory (until recently) has largely regarded the self as a unitary structure. An excellent discussion of the points of convergence between person-centred/client-centred and Gestalt approaches can be found in Watson *et al.* (1998b).

practice compiled by Hart and Tomlinson (1970), Wexler and Rice (1974), Levant and Shlien (1984) and Lietaer *et al.* (1990) contain much useful material, there is also a sense of a gradual drifting apart and splitting, and consequent reduction in impact. The client-centred or person-centred approach has been becoming less influential in the USA, partly because its central ideas have been assimilated into other approaches, although it remains a major independent force in Britain, Belgium, Germany and Holland (Lietaer 1990).

The evolution of the person-centred approach over a 50-year period illustrates many important social and cultural factors. Client-centred therapy was created from a synthesis of European 'insight' therapy and American values (Sollod 1978). The emphasis in the model on self-acceptance and its theoretical simplicity made it wholly appropriate as a therapy for soldiers returning from war, and allowed it to gain a peak of influence at that time. In the post-war years in the USA, the increasing competitiveness of the 'mental health industry' resulted in the gradual erosion of this influence, as other therapies that could claim specific techniques, special ingredients and rapid cures became available. Moreover, the insistence of insurance companies in the USA that clients receive a diagnosis before payments for therapy could be authorized went against the grain of the client-centred approach. Finally, the failure to maintain a solid institutional base, either in the academic world or in an independent professional association, contributed further to its decline. In other countries, and, for example, in Europe, counsellors and therapists working in state-funded educational establishments and in voluntary agencies were largely protected from these pressures, enabling the person-centred approach to thrive. In these other countries there have also been Rogerian institutes and training courses.

The image of the person in person-centred theory

The main concern of Rogers and other person-centred theorists was to develop an approach that was effective, rather than to engage in speculation on theoretical matters. Compared to the massive edifice of psychodynamic theory, the conceptual apparatus of the person-centred approach is an insubstantial scaffolding. It is important to recognize that this apparent absence of theoretical content necessarily accompanies any attempt to pursue a phenomenological approach to knowledge. Phenomenology is a method of philosophical inquiry evolved by Husserl, and widely employed in existential philosophy, which takes the view that valid knowledge and understanding can be gained by exploring and describing the way things are experienced by people. The aim of phenomenology is to depict the nature and quality of personal experience. Phenomenology has been applied to many areas of study other than therapy: for example, the experience of the social world. The technique of phenomenology involves 'bracketing off' the assumptions one holds about the phenomenon being investigated, and striving to describe it in as comprehensive and sensitive a manner as possible. The act of 'bracketing off' or 'suspending' assumptions implies that the phenomenological researcher (or therapist) does not impose his or her theoretical assumptions on experience. As a result, theory in phenomenological approaches to counselling, such as the person-centred approach, acts more as a general pointer towards potentially significant areas of experience, rather than making any assumptions about the actual content of that experience.

The person, in the person-centred approach, is viewed as acting to fulfil two primary needs. The first is the need for self-actualization. The second is the need to be loved and valued by others. Both these needs are, following Maslow, seen as being independent of biological survival needs. However, the person is very much seen as an embodied being, through the concept of 'organismic valuing'.

The idea of the 'self-concept' has a central place in person-centred theory. The self-concept of the person is understood as those attributes or areas of experiencing about which the person can say 'I am . . .' So, for example, a client in counselling may define himself or herself in terms such as 'I am strong, I can be angry, I sometimes feel vulnerable.' For this person, strength, anger and vulnerability are parts of a self-concept, and when he or she feels vulnerable, or angry, there will usually be a congruence between feelings and resulting words and actions. But if this person does not define himself or herself as 'nurturing', and is in a situation where a feeling of care or nurturance is evoked, he or she will not be able to put that inner sense or feeling accurately into words, and will express the feeling or impulse in a distorted or inappropriate way. Someone who is not supposed to be nurturing may, for instance, become very busy 'doing things' for someone who needs no more than companionship, comforting or a human touch. Where there is a disjunction between feelings and the capacity for accurate awareness and symbolization of these feelings, a state of incongruence is said to exist. Incongruence is the very broad term used to describe the whole range of problems that clients bring to counselling.

Why does incongruence happen? Rogers argued that, in childhood, there is a strong need to be loved or valued, particularly by parents and significant others. However, the love or approval that parents offer can be conditional or unconditional. In areas of unconditional approval, the child is free to express his or her potential and accept inner feelings. Where the love or acceptance is conditional on behaving only in a certain way, and is withdrawn when other behaviour or tendencies are exhibited, the child learns to define himself or herself in accordance with parental values. Rogers used the phrase 'conditions of worth' to describe the way in which the self-concept of the child is shaped by parental influence. In the example above, the person would have been praised or accepted for being 'useful', but rejected or scorned for being 'affectionate' or 'soft'. Incongruence, therefore, results from gaps and distortions in the self-concept caused by exposure to conditions of worth.

Another idea that is linked to the understanding of how the self-concept operates is the notion of 'locus of evaluation'. Rogers observed that, in the process of making judgements or evaluations about issues, people could be guided by externally defined sets of beliefs and attitudes, or could make use of their own internal feelings on the matter, their 'organismic valuing process'. An over-reliance on external evaluations is equivalent to continued exposure to conditions of worth, and person-centred counselling encourages people to accept and act on their own personal, internal evaluations. Rogers had a positive and optimistic view of humanity, and believed that an authentic, self-aware person would make decisions based on an internal locus of evaluation that would be valid not only for himself or herself, but for others too. Although it is perhaps not explicitly articulated in his writings, his underlying assumption was that each person carried a universal morality, and would have a bodily sense of what was right or wrong in any situation.

It is perhaps worth noting that the simple phrase 'conditions of worth' encompasses the entirety of the person-centred model of child development. The person-centred counsellor does not possess a model of developmental stages into which to fit the experience of the client. The simple idea of conditions of worth merely points the counsellor in the direction of anticipating that some unresolved childhood process may be around for the client. The task is not to go looking for these childhood episodes, but to allow the client to pursue an understanding of them if he or she chooses to do so. Also of interest is the fact that childhood experiences are seen as leaving an enduring influence in the form of internalized values and self-concepts. This is clearly different from the psychodynamic idea that people grow up with internalized images of the actual people who were formative in childhood, usually the mother and father (see Chapter 4).

The person-centred theory of the self-concept suggests that the person possesses not only a concept or definition of self 'as I am now', but also a sense of self 'as I would ideally like to be'. The 'ideal self' represents another aspect of the consistent theme in Rogers' work concerning the human capacity to strive for fulfilment and greater integration. One of the aims of person-centred therapy is to enable the person to move in the direction of his or her self-defined ideals.

One of the distinctive features of the person-centred image of the person is its attempt to describe the 'fully functioning' person. The idea of the 'actualized' or fully functioning individual represents an important strand in the attempt by humanistic psychologists to construct an alternative to psychoanalysis. Freud, reflecting his background in medicine and psychiatry, created a theory that was oriented towards understanding and explaining pathology or 'illness'. Rogers, Maslow and the 'third force' regarded creativity, joyfulness and spirituality as intrinsic human qualities, and sought to include these characteristics within the ambit of their theorizing. The main features of the fully functioning person were described by Rogers (1963: 22) in the following terms:

> he is able to experience all of his feelings, and is afraid of none of his feelings. He is his own sifter of evidence, but is open to evidence from all sources; he is completely engaged in the process of being and becoming himself, and thus discovers that he is soundly and realistically social; he lives completely in this moment, but learns that this is the soundest living for all time. He is a fully functioning organism, and because of the awareness of himself which flows freely in and through his experiences, he is a fully functioning person.

The person envisioned here is someone who is congruent, and is able to accept and use feelings to guide action. The person is also autonomous rather than dependent on others: 'the values of being and becoming himself'.

One of the difficulties involved in grasping the person-centred image of the person is that textbook versions of what is meant are inevitably incomplete. This is an area of counselling theory where the gap between the lived, oral tradition and the written account is particularly apparent (see Chapter 3). For Rogers, the actualizing tendency or formative tendency is central, the person is always in process, always becoming, ever-changing. The task for psychological theory was not to explain change, but to understand what was happening to arrest change and development. The idea of 'becoming a person' captures this notion. From a person-centred perspective, any conceptualization of the person that portrays a static, fixed entity is inadequate. The aim is always to construct a process conceptualization. In this respect, it could well be argued that some of the earlier elements in the theory, such as the idea of the self-concept, place too much emphasis on static structures. It would be more consistent to talk about a 'self-process'. The image of the fully functioning person can similarly give an impression that this is an enduring structure that can be permanently attained, rather than part of a process that can include phases of incongruence and despair. The process orientation of the model is also expressed through the absence of any ideas about personality traits or types, and the strong opposition in person-centred practitioners to any attempts to label or diagnose clients.

The significance of the image of the person employed by this approach is underlined by the fact that this orientation attaches relatively little importance to the technical expertise of the counsellor, and concentrates primarily on the attitude or philosophy of the counsellor and the quality of the therapeutic relationship (Combs 1989).

The therapeutic relationship

At its heart, person-centred counselling is a relationship therapy. People with emotional 'problems in living' have been involved in relationships in which their experiencing was denied, defined or discounted by others. What is healing is to be in a relationship in which the self is fully accepted and valued. The characteristics of a relationship that would have this effect were summarized by Rogers (1957: 95) in his formulation of the 'necessary and sufficient conditions of therapeutic personality change'. For constructive personality change to occur, it is necessary that these conditions exist and continue over a period of time:

1 Two persons are in psychological contact.
2 The first, whom we shall term the client, is in a state of incongruence, being vulnerable and anxious.

3 The second person, whom we shall term the therapist, is congruent or integrated in the relationship.
4 The therapist experiences unconditional positive regard for the client.
5 The therapist experiences an empathic understanding of the client's internal frame of reference, and endeavours to communicate this to the client.
6 The communication to the client of the therapist's empathic understanding and unconditional positive regard is to a minimal extent achieved.

The nature of the person-centred therapeutic relationship is also explained on pages 300–1

No other conditions are necessary. If these six conditions exist, and continue over a period of time, this is sufficient. The process of constructive personality change will follow.

This formulation of the therapeutic relationship has subsequently become known as the 'core conditions' model. It specifies the characteristics of an interpersonal environment that will facilitate actualization and growth.

The three ingredients of the therapeutic relationship that have tended to receive most attention in person-centred training and research are the counsellor qualities of acceptance, empathy and genuineness. In the list above the term 'unconditional positive regard' is used, rather than the everyday idea of 'acceptance'.

The core conditions model represented an attempt by Rogers to capture the essence of his approach to clients. It also represented a bold challenge to other therapists and schools of thought, in claiming that these conditions were not just important or useful, but sufficient in themselves. The view that no other therapeutic ingredients were necessary invited a head-on confrontation with psychoanalysts, for example, who would regard interpretation as necessary, or

Box 6.2

Pre-therapy: a person-centred method of making contact with individuals who find relationships difficult

The theory of 'necessary and sufficient conditions' proposed by Rogers (1957) has generally been interpreted as highlighting the importance of empathy, congruence and unconditional positive regard as basic ingredients of a productive therapeutic relationship. Less attention has been given to the opening statement in Rogers' model: 'two persons are in psychological contact'. In a great many counselling situations, it may be reasonable to take for granted the existence of a sufficient degree of basic psychological connectedness. No matter how anxious or depressed a person is, usually he or she will retain some capacity to take account of the psychological reality represented by whoever else is in their immediate proximity, whether this be a counsellor or someone else. However, there are some people for whom basic contact with another human being is hugely problematic. These may be people who have been damaged by life experiences, who are profoundly anxious, institutionalized or sedated, or who suffer from cognitive impairment. Persons regarded as schizophrenic or learning disabled may fall into this category. Few attempts have been made to provide counselling to clients from these groups. Within the person-centred approach, the pioneering work carried out at the University of Wisconsin by Rogers and his colleagues into the process of counselling with hospitalised schizophrenic patients (Rogers *et al.* 1967) has been continued in the form of the approach to pre-therapy developed by Prouty (1976, 1990; Prouty and Kubiak 1988). Rogers (1968a: 188) wrote that the Wisconsin project taught him that 'schizophrenic individuals tend to fend off relationships either by an almost complete silence . . . or by a flood of overtalk which is equally effective in preventing a real encounter.' Prouty has designed ways of counteracting that degree of 'fending-off' by reflecting back to the client, in very simple ways, the counsellor's awareness of the client's external world, self and feelings, and communication with others. The aim is to restore the client's capacity to be in psychological contact, and as a result to enable them to enter conventional therapy. Two examples from van Werde (1994: 123–4) illustrate how this technique functions in practice:

Christiane walks into the nurses' office, stands still, and stares straight ahead. She is obviously in a kind of closed, locked-up position, but nevertheless she has come to the office or to the nurses. Instead of immediately telling her to go back to her room or pedagogically instructing her first to knock at the door and then come in, one of the nurses empathically reflects what is happening: 'You are standing in the office. You look in the direction of the window. You are staring.' These reflections seem to enable Christiane to contact her feelings and free herself from whatever had been on her mind in a way that she could not master. She now says: 'I am afraid that my mother is going to die!' Then she turns herself around and walks toward the living room. The semi-psychotic mood is processed and she is once again in control of herself.

[At] the twice-weekly patient-staff meeting . . . approximately twenty people are sitting in a large circle. Suddenly a patient, Thierry, comes in with a Bible in his hand, walks straight up to me, shows me a page and says 'I can make the words change'. I make eye contact, also point at the Bible and reflect 'I can make the words change. Thierry, we are sitting in a circle. You're standing up next to me and are showing me the Bible'. Reflecting all this enables Thierry to realise that he is doing something odd, given the context of the situation, and he is able to anchor himself back into the shared reality by taking a chair and sitting quietly at the edge of the circle.

Although pre-therapy has been used mainly in work with severely damaged individuals, it is equally applicable during moments when more fully functioning individuals withdraw from relationship. Pre-therapy draws on core person-centred principles of respect, acceptance, willingness to enter the frame of reference of the other and belief in a process of actualization.

behaviourists, who would see techniques for inducing behaviour change as central. The model stimulated a substantial amount of research, which has broadly supported the position taken by Rogers (Patterson 1984). However, many contemporary counsellors and therapists would regard the 'core conditions' as components of what has become known as the 'therapeutic alliance' (Bordin 1979) between counsellor and client.

In the person-centred approach there is considerable debate over the accuracy and comprehensiveness of the necessary and sufficient conditions model. For example, Rogers (1961: Chapter 3) himself described a much longer list of characteristics of a helping relationship:

- Can I be in some way which will be perceived by the other person as trustworthy, as dependable or consistent in some deep sense?
- Can I be expressive enough as a person that what I am will be communicated unambiguously?
- Can I let myself experience positive attitudes towards this other person – attitudes of warmth, caring, liking, interest, respect?
- Can I be strong enough as a person to be separate from the other?
- Am I secure enough within myself to permit his or her separateness?
- Can I let myself enter fully into the world of his or her feelings and personal meanings and see these as he or she does?
- Can I accept each facet of this other person when he or she presents it to me?
- Can I act with sufficient sensitivity in the relationship that my behaviour will not be perceived as a threat?
- Can I free the other from the threat of external evaluation?
- Can I meet this other individual as a person who is in the process of becoming, or will I be bound by his past and by my past?

This list includes the qualities of empathy, congruence and acceptance, but also mentions other important helper characteristics, such as consistency, boundary awareness, interpersonal sensitivity and present-centredness. Later, Rogers was also to suggest that therapist 'presence' was an essential factor (Rogers 1980). Thorne (1991) has argued that 'tenderness' should be considered a core condition. These modifications of the model may be seen as attempts to articulate more clearly what is meant, or to find fresh ways of articulating the notion of a uniquely 'personal' relationship (van Balen 1990), but do not change the basic framework, which has remained the cornerstone of person-centred practice (Mearns and Thorne 1988).

Empathy

The importance attributed to empathic responding has been one of the distinguishing features of the person-centred approach to counselling. It is considered that, for the client, the experience of being 'heard' or understood leads to a

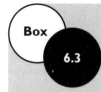

Box

6.3

How did Carl Rogers do therapy?

One of the significant contributions made by Carl Rogers and his colleagues was to initiate the practice of taping counselling sessions, so that they could later be used for purposes of research and teaching. An important by-product of this policy is that there exist several tapes of Carl Rogers doing therapy. These tapes are an invaluable archive, which has been widely used by scholars and researchers interested in the nature of person-centred counselling and psychotherapy. Farber *et al.* (1996) have compiled a book in which ten of Rogers' cases are presented, alongside commentary from both person-centred practitioners and representatives of other schools of therapy. Two of the editors of the book, Brink and Farber (1996), offer an analysis of the different kinds of responses that Rogers made to the clients in these cases. These are as follows.

Providing orientation. Rogers tended to start sessions by giving himself and the client an opportunity to orient themselves to the task. For example, Rogers started one counselling session by saying, 'Now, if you can get your chair settled . . . I need to take a minute or two to kind of get with myself somehow, okay? . . . Then let's just be quiet for a minute or two. [Pause] Do you feel ready?'

Affirming attention. Rogers frequently let his client know that he was present and listening, by leaning towards the client, saying 'm-hm, m-hm' or nodding affirmatively.

Checking understanding. Often Rogers would check whether he had correctly understood the meaning of what the client was saying.

Restating. Sometimes Rogers' words seemed directly to mirror what the client had said. On other occasions, a restatement would take the form of a short statement that clarified the core of what the client was expressing, as in the example below.

Client: And I allow myself to, and I don't regret caring, and I don't regret loving or whatever, but you know, like, I'm like a kid, you know, I'm a kid in a way, I like to be loved too, some reciprocity. And I'm going to start, I think, expecting that, you know, without being cold or anything like that. But I have to, you know, start getting something back in return.

Carl Rogers: You want love to be mutual.

Client: For sure, for sure.

There would be times when Rogers would phrase a restatement in the first person, as if speaking as the client.

Acknowledging clients' unstated feelings. This response involved making reference to feelings that were expressed in either non-verbal behaviour or voice quality, but were not explicitly verbalized by the client.

Providing reassurance. In the widely known Gloria case, there are several moments of reassurance. For example:

Gloria: I don't get that as often as I like . . . I like that whole feeling, that's real precious to me.

Carl Rogers: I suspect none of us get it as often as we'd like.

There were times, too, when Rogers would convey reassurance by touching a client, or responding to a request to hold the client's hand.

Interpreting. On rare occasions Rogers made interpretations, defined as venturing beyond the information being immediately offered by the client.

Confronting. Sometimes Rogers would confront clients who appeared to be avoiding a difficult or painful issue.

Direct questioning. An example of this response was made to a client who had mentioned feeling different. Rogers invited further exploration of the topic by asking her: 'and what are some of those differences?'

Turning pleas for help back to the client. When a client asked for guidance or answers, Rogers would often turn the request back to the person. For example:

Gloria: I really know you can't answer for me – but I want you to guide me or show me where to start or so it won't look so hopeless . . .

Carl Rogers: I might ask, what is it you wish I could say to you?

Maintaining and breaking silences. In some sessions Rogers could be seen to allow silences to continue (in one instance for as long as 17 minutes!). On other occasions he appeared to be willing to interrupt a silence.

Self-disclosing. For example, with one client Rogers stated: 'I don't know whether this will help or not, but I would just like to say that – I think I can understand pretty well – what it's like to feel that you're just no damned good to anyone, because there was a time when – I felt that way about myself. And I know it can be really tough.'

Accepting correction. When a client indicated that one of Rogers' responses was not accurate, he would accept the correction, try again to get it right and then move on.

Brink and Farber (1996) do not claim that this list of responses represents an exhaustive or comprehensive analysis of all of the therapeutic strategies or techniques used by Rogers. They do suggest, however, that the list illustrates some of the different forms through which the facilitative conditions of empathy, congruence and acceptance can be expressed within a relationship. They also observe that Rogers behaved differently with different clients. He was able to adapt his style to the needs and communication styles of specific clients. Finally, it is clear that the Brink and Farber taxonomy includes responses that are not strictly consistent with person-centred therapy, notably reassurance and interpretation. The lesson here is that perhaps it is more important to be human than it is to adhere rigorously to the dictates of a theoretical model.

greater capacity to explore and accept previously denied aspects of self. However, there were a number of difficulties apparent in the conception of empathy contained within the 'core conditions' model. When researchers attempted to measure the levels of empathic responding exhibited by counsellors, they found that ratings carried out from different points of view produced different patterns of results. A specific counsellor statement to a client would be rated differently by the client, the counsellor and an external observer (Kurtz and Grummon 1972). It was difficult to get raters to differentiate accurately between empathy, congruence and acceptance: these three qualities all appeared to be of a piece in the eyes of research assistants rating therapy tapes. Finally, there were philosophical difficulties arising from alternative intepretations of the concept. Rogers characterized empathy as a 'state of being'. Truax and Carkhuff defined empathy as a communication skill, which could be modelled and learned in a structured training programme.

Many of these issues associated with the concept of empathy are addressed in the 'empathy cycle' model proposed by Barrett-Lennard (1981):

Step 1: *Empathic set by counsellor.* Client is actively expressing some aspect of his or her experiencing. Counsellor is actively attending and receptive.

Step 2: *Empathic resonation.* The counsellor resonates to the directly or indirectly expressed aspects of the client's experiencing.

Step 3: *Expressed empathy.* The counsellor expresses or communicates his or her felt awareness of the client's experiencing.

Step 4: *Received empathy.* The client is attending to the counsellor sufficiently to form a sense or perception of the counsellor's immediate personal understanding.

Step 5: *The empathy cycle continues.* The client then continues or resumes self expression in a way that provides feedback to the counsellor concerning the accuracy of the empathic response and the quality of the therapeutic relationship.

In this model, empathy is viewed as a process that involves intentional, purposeful activity on the part of the counsellor. It can be seen that the perceptions of different observers reflect their tendency to be aware of what is happening at particular steps in the process rather than others. The counsellor will consider himself or herself to be in good empathic contact with the client if he or she is 'set' and 'resonating' in response to what the client has expressed (steps 1 and 2). An external observer will be most aware of the actual behaviour of the counsellor (expressed empathy – step 3). The client, on the other hand, will be most influenced by the experience of 'received' empathy (step 4). The Barrett-Lennard (1981) model also makes sense of the definition of empathy as communication skill or way of being. In so far as the counsellor needs to be able to receive and resonate to the expressed feelings of the client, empathy is like a state of being. But in so far as this understanding must be offered back to the client, it is also a communication skill.

The empathy cycle raises the question of the interconnectedness of the core conditions. The Barrett-Lennard model describes a process that includes non-judgemental openness to and acceptance of whatever the client has to offer. It also describes a process in the counsellor of being congruently aware of his or her inner feelings, and using these in the counselling relationship. In the flow of the work with the client the effective person-centred counsellor is not making use of separate skills, but is instead offering the client a wholly personal involvement in the relationship between them. There is a sense of mutuality, or an 'I–thou' relationship described by Buber (van Balen 1990). Bozarth (1984) has written that, at these points in counselling, an empathic response to a client may bear little resemblance to the wooden 'reflection of meaning' statements much favoured in the early years of client-centred therapy. For Bozarth (1984), the ideal is to respond empathically in a manner that is 'idiosyncratic' and spontaneous.

Another important development in relation to empathy has been to examine the impact of an accurate, well timed and sensitive empathic reponse. Barrett-Lennard (1993: 6) observes that:

> the experience of being literally heard and understood deeply, in some personally vital sphere, has its own kind of impact – whether of relief, of something at last making sense, a feeling or inner connection or somehow being less alone, or of some other easing or enhancing quality.

Vanaerschot (1990, 1993) has examined the therapeutic 'micro-processes' released by effective empathic responses. These include: feeling valued and accepted; feeling confirmed in one's own identity as an autonomous, valuable person; learning to accept feelings; reduction in alienation ('I am not abnormal, different and strange'); learning to trust and get in touch with one's own experiencing; cognitive restructuring of chaotic experiencing; and facilitating recall and organization of information.

Finally, there has been some intriguing research into the way that the counsellor or psychotherapist formulates an empathic communication. Bohart *et al.* (1993) carried out a study that suggests that it can be helpful to employ empathic reflections that are future-oriented in meaning, that link current concerns with future directions and intentions.

These recent contributions to the person-centred theory of empathy have moved the emphasis away from a definition of empathy as a trainable skill, and back towards a wider meaning of empathy, understood as a component of an authentic committment to be engaged in the world of the other. This notion implies more of a unity of the 'core conditions', and is to some extent a return to the very earliest formulation of the principles of client-centred therapy. Before Rogers and his colleagues began to use terms like empathy, congruence and unconditional regard, they described the approach as an attitude or philosophy of 'deep respect for the significance and worth of each person' (Rogers 1951: 21).

Congruence and presence

In practice, possibly the single most distinctive aspect of the person-centred approach to counselling lies in the emphasis that is placed on congruence. The influence of Rogers' ideas has meant that versions of such classic person-centred notions of empathy, self, therapeutic relationship and experiencing have entered the vocabularies of other approaches. However, no other approach gives as much importance to the realness, authenticity and willingness to be known of the counsellor as do person-centred therapy and other contemporary humanistic therapies. In the early years of client-centred therapy, Rogers and his colleagues based their way of doing counselling on principles of non-directiveness, respect for the internal frame of reference and locus of evaluation of the client, and acceptance of self. It was largely as a result of the Wisconsin project, during which Rogers, Shlien, Gendlin and their colleagues struggled to find ways of communicating with deeply withdrawn schizophrenic inpatients, that it became apparent that the therapist's contribution to the process, his or her ability to use self in the service of the relationship, was crucial to the success of therapy (see Gendlin 1967). Perhaps because of his own training and professional socialization, the concept of congruence only really entered Rogers' language in the late 1950s, and tended, at least initially, to be explained in a somewhat technical manner (Rogers 1961). Lietaer (1993, 2001) gives an excellent account of the evolution of the concept of congruence in Rogers' writings.

Congruence was believed by Rogers (1961: 61) to occur when:

> the feelings the therapist is experiencing are available to him, to his aware-ness, and he is able to live these feelings, be them, and to communicate them if appropriate. No one fully achieves this condition, yet the more the therapist is able to listen acceptantly to what is going on within himself, and the more he is able to be the complexity of his feelings, without fear, the higher the degree of his congruence.

Mearns and Thorne (1988: 75) defined congruence as 'the state of being of the counsellor when her outward responses to the client consistently match the inner feelings and sensations which she has in relation to the client.' Gendlin (1967: 120–1) describes congruence as a process that requires a deliberate act of attention on the part of the counsellor:

> At every moment there occur a great many feelings and events in the therapist. Most of these concern the client and the present moment. The therapist need not wait passively till the client expresses something intimate or therapeutic-ally relevant. Instead, he can draw upon his own momentary experiencing and find there an ever present reservoir from which he can draw, and with which he can initiate, deepen and carry on therapeutic interaction even with an unmotivated, silent or externalised person . . . to respond truly from within me I must, of course, pay some attention to what is going on within me . . . I

require a few steps of self-attention, a few moments in which I attend to what I feel.

The research carried out by Barrett-Lennard (1986) led to an appreciation of the counsellor's *willingness to be known* as an important element of congruence. All of these writers emphasize, in their different ways, the idea that congruence is not a skill to be deployed ('I used a lot of congruence in that session . . .') but is something that is much more central to the therapeutic endeavour – a basic value or attitude, or a 'way of being'. The various strands of thinking around the concept of congruence, within the person-centred approach, are represented in Wyatt (2001).

Why is congruence therapeutic? In what ways is it helpful for clients to work with a counsellor who is congruent, genuine and willing to be known? Counsellor congruence can have a number of valuable effects on therapy:

- it helps to develop trust in the relationship;
- if the counsellor expresses and accepts his or her own feelings of vulnerability and uncertainty, then it becomes easier for the client to accept their own;
- it models one of the intended outcomes of therapy (straightforward, honest relating to others);
- if cues from speech, tone and gesture are unified or consistent, then communication is clearer and more understandable;
- the counsellor is able to draw upon unsaid or 'subvocal' (Gendlin 1967) elements in the relationship;
- it can facilitate the positive flow of energy in the relationship.

By contrast, if a counsellor is consistently incongruent, the client is likely to become confused, and lack confidence in the counselling relationship as a safe place within which he or she might explore painful or shameful experiences. On the whole, clients seek counselling because the other people in their life have responded to their 'problems in living' in a silencing, judgemental manner. An important factor in the possibility of counselling making a difference is the client's belief that their counsellor is really listening, and really accepts them as a person, and that there is no hidden condemnation waiting to be unleashed. If a counsellor appears to be open and genuine, but then tenses up or seems preoccupied whenever the counsellor touches on a sensitive subject, without offering any explanation, then the chances are that the client will learn that this subject is 'out of bounds' for the counsellor, and not to be broached.

In recent years, there has been an increasing recognition within the person-centred approach (and within other humanistic therapies – see Box 6.4) that the concept of congruence offers an over-individualized means of understanding what is a key dimension of their practice. Essentially, Rogers' idea of congruence was grounded in the extent to which inner experiences (feelings, emotions, impulses and images) were either available to the person's awareness (i.e. not suppressed or repressed) or could be expressed verbally. Useful though this formulation has

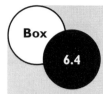

Box 6.4

The concept of presence in humanistic therapy

The quality of presence has become a central theme in the literature on humanistic therapy. For example, Kirk Schneider (1998: 111), an existential psychotherapist, has argued that:

> Presence is the *sina qua non* of experiential liberation. It is the beginning and the 'end' of the approach, and it is implicated in every one of its aspects . . . Presence is palpable. It is a potent sign that one is 'here' for the other . . . Being with another, 'clearing a space' for another, and fully permitting another to be with and clear a space for him or herself are all earmarks of presence . . . Another way to define presence is by its absence. When a therapist is distracted, when she or he is 'occupied' by matters other than the person sitting before her/him, there is a distinct weakening of the relational field. From the standpoint of the client, the field feels porous, uninviting, precarious, cold, and remote. However, when a therapist is fully present, the relational field alters radically. Suddenly, there is life in the setting. The therapist acquires a vibrant, embracing quality. The therapeutic field becomes a sanctuary . . . and the client has a sense of being met, held, heard and seen.

It is this ability to 'be' there with another person that many humanistic therapists would acknowledge as the essential quality of any good therapist.

been, many therapists believe that it does not take sufficient account of the interpersonal, relational quality of what can take place during significant moments in therapy. Towards the end of his career, Rogers (1980: 129) himself opened up the possibility of a more holistic understanding of congruence when he wrote that:

> when I am at my best, as a group facilitator or as a therapist, I discover another characteristic. I find that when I am closest to my inner, intuitive self, when I am somehow in touch with the unknown in me, when perhaps I am in a slightly altered state of consciousness, then whatever I do seems to be full of healing. Then, simply my *presence* is releasing and helpful to the other. (Italics added)

Mearns (1994, 1996) has elaborated this sense of being 'at my best' in terms of the presence of the counsellor. Mearns (1996: 307) quotes from reports written by clients:

it felt as though she was right inside me – feeling me in the same moment that I was feeling myself.

the space she created for me was huge. It made me realise how little space I usually felt in other relationships.

Mearns (1996: 309) observes that this degree of presence is risky for counsellors: 'it is one thing to have my surface relational competencies judged, but can I risk my congruent self being judged?' He compares the congruent person-centred counsellor to a 'method' actor who projects or immerses himself or herself fully in their role. In research into client and counsellor experiences during moments of congruence and incongruence, Grafanaki and McLeod (1999, 2002) were able to identify times when both participants were engaged in a process of mutual flow, and fully present to each other.

Greenberg and Geller (2001) interviewed therapists (from a range of theoretical orientations) about their experience of presence, and found that presence was typically described as comprising a series of stages. First, these therapists were consciously committed to the practice of presence in their everyday lives and relationships. Second, within a counselling session the therapist allows herself to 'respond to whatever presents itself in the moment' (p. 144). Third, the therapist then allows herself to meet, and remain engaged with, the client.

The central emphasis placed on congruence and presence by person-centred practitioners is reflected in the types of training and supervision that have evolved within this approach. For example, person-centred training typically involves substantial periods working within large groups. The large experiential group offers an environment in which most people find it difficult to be congruent, present and empathic, and in which there are plentiful opportunities for other group members to identify and feed back their perceptions of incongruent and avoidance patterns of behaviour that they witness in each other. The emphasis on congruence and presence also underscores the basic assumption of person-centred counselling, that it is within moments of authentic encounter between client and therapist that the most meaningful and significant learning takes place.

The therapeutic process

From a person-centred perspective, the process of therapeutic change in the client is described in terms of a process of greater openness to experience. Rogers (1951) characterized the direction of therapeutic growth as including increasing awareness of denied experience, movement from perceiving the world in generalizations to being able to see things in a more differentiated manner and greater reliance on personal experience as a source of values and standards. Eventually, these developments lead to changes in behaviour, but the 'reorganization of the self' (Rogers 1951) is seen as a necessary precursor to any new behaviour.

Rogers (1961) conceptualized the process of counselling as a series of stages, and his model formed the basis for subsequent work by Gendlin (1974) and Klein *et al.* (1986) and the concept of 'depth of experiencing'. In successful counselling the client will become able to process information about self and experiencing at greater levels of depth and intensity. The seven stages of increasing client involvement in his or her inner world (Rogers 1961; Klein *et al.* 1986) are summarized as follows:

1 Communication is about external events. Feelings and personal meanings are not 'owned'. Close relationships are construed as dangerous. Rigidity in thinking. Impersonal, detached. Does not use first-person pronouns.
2 Expression begins to flow more freely in respect of non-self topics. Feelings may be described but not owned. Intellectualization. Describes behaviour rather than inner feelings. May show more interest and participation in therapy.
3 Describes personal reactions to external events. Limited amount of self-description. Communication about past feelings. Beginning to recognize contradictions in experience.
4 Descriptions of feelings and personal experiences. Beginning to experience current feelings, but fear and distrust of this when it happens. The 'inner life' is presented and listed or described, but not purposefully explored.
5 Present feelings are expressed. Increasing ownership of feelings. More exactness in the differentiation of feelings and meanings. Intentional exploration of problems in a personal way, based in processing of feelings rather than reasoning.
6 Sense of an 'inner referent', or flow of feeling that has a life of its own. 'Physiological loosening', such as moistness in the eyes, tears, sighs or muscular relaxation, accompanies the open expression of feelings. Speaks in present tense or offers vivid representation of past.
7 A series of felt senses connecting the different aspects of an issue. Basic trust in own inner processes. Feelings experienced with immediacy and richness of detail. Speaks fluently in present tense.

Research using this seven-stage model has shown that clients who begin therapy at level 1 are less likely to be able to benefit from the process. Mearns and Thorne (1988) have commented on the importance of the 'readiness' of the client to embark on this type of self-exploration. Rogers (1961) also comments that the changes associated with stage 6 appear to be irreversible, so the client may be able to move into stage 7 without the help of the counsellor.

The process in the client is facilitated by the empathy, congruence and acceptance of the counsellor. For example, sensitive empathic listening on the part of the counsellor enables him or her to reflect back to the client personal feelings and meanings implicit in stage 1 statements. The acceptance and genuineness of the counsellor encourages the growth of trust in the client, and increased risk-taking regarding the expression of thoughts and feelings that would previously have been censored or suppressed. Then, as this more frightening material is exposed, the fact that the counsellor is able to accept emotions that had been long buried and denied helps the client to accept them in turn. The willingness of the counsellor to accept the existence of contradictions in the way the client experiences the world gives the client permission to accept himself or herself as both hostile and warm, or needy and powerful, and thus to move towards a more differentiated, more complex sense of self.

This process is also influenced by the growing capacity of the client to operate from a sense of their own value as a person, to employ an internal locus of evaluation. Mearns (1994) has argued that at the beginning of therapy it is likely that a client will interact with others from a perpective of an external locus of evaluation. He or she will be looking for guidance and advice from others: they know best. At this stage, the counsellor needs to be rigorous in following the client, maintaining a disciplined empathic and accepting focus on the client's frame of reference. Later, however, when the client becomes stronger in his or her locus of evaluation, becomes more internal and integrated with self, it is possible for the counsellor to be more congruent, to take risks in using his or her own experience in the counselling room. Thus it can be seen that the 'core conditions' are not static, but are expressed in response to who the client is, and their stage of the process of change.

Experiential focusing

An important framework that is widely employed in the person-centred approach as a means of understanding process is Gendlin's model of experiential focusing, which represents perhaps the single most influential development in person-centred theory and practice in the post-Wisconsin era (Lietaer 1990). The technique of focusing and the underlying theory of experiencing are supported by thorough philosophical analysis (Gendlin 1962, 1984a) and considerable psychological research (Gendlin 1969, 1984c).

The focusing process is built on an assumption that the fundamental meanings that events and relationships have for people are contained in the 'felt sense' experienced by the person. The felt sense is an internal, physical sense of the situation. In this inner sense the person knows there is more to the situation than he or she is currently able to say. According to Gendlin (1962), this 'inner referent' or felt sense holds a highly differentiated set of implicit meanings. For these meanings to be made explicit, the person must express the felt sense in a symbol, such as a word, phrase, statement, image or even bodily movement. The act of symbolizing an area of meaning in the felt sense allows other areas to come to attention. Accurate symbolization therefore brings about a 'shift' in the inner felt sense of a situation or problem.

Gendlin takes the view that the experiential process described here is at the heart of not only person-centred counselling but all other therapies too. He regards the therapeutic movement or shifts brought about by interpretation, behavioural methods, Gestalt interventions and so on to be reducible to episodes of effective experiential focusing. This experiential process is also a common feature of everyday life. The problems that bring people to counselling are caused by an interruption of the process, an unwillingness or inability of the person to achieve a complete and accurate picture of the felt sense of the problem. The basic tasks of the counsellor are therefore to help the client to stay with the inner referent rather than avoiding it, and to facilitate the generation of accurate symbols to allow expression of implicit meanings.

The process of 'focusing on a problem' can be broken into a number of stages or steps:

1 Clearing a space. Taking an inventory of what is going on inside the body.
2 Locating the inner felt sense of the problem. Letting the felt sense come. Allowing the body to 'talk back'.
3 Finding a 'handle' (word or image) that matches the felt sense.
4 Resonating handle and felt sense. Checking symbol against feeling. Asking 'does this really fit?'
5 A felt shift in the problem, experiencing either a subtle movement or 'flood of physical relief'.
6 Receiving or accepting what has emerged.
7 Stop, or go through process again.

These steps can occur, or be helped to occur, in the dialogue or interaction between counsellor or client, or the counsellor can intentionally instruct and guide the client through the process. Leijssen (1993, 1998) has provided some very clear accounts of how she integrates the use of experiential focusing into a conventional person-centered counselling session with a client (see Box 6.5). The technique has been taught to clients and used in peer self-help groups. Cornell (1993) reviews the issues involved in teaching focusing. Guidelines on how to learn practical skills in experiential focusing can be found in Gendlin (1981, 1996).

The process-experiential model of therapy

Another important development within the broad person-centred or humanistic tradition has been the process-experiential approach to counselling and psychotherapy created by Greenberg *et al.* (1993). The process-experiential approach is an integration of ideas and techniques from person-centred and Gestalt therapies, and contemporary cognitive psychology. One of the distinctive features of the approach is its emphasis on significant events within counselling sessions. Whereas Rogers' conditions of empathy, congruence and acceptance refer to interpersonal processes, or a relationship environment, that exists throughout the therapy, Greenberg and his colleagues have suggested that it can be useful to give particular attention to creating highly meaningful moments of change. A central

Box

6.5

Using experiential focusing in a counselling session: two examples

Sonia, in her twenty-fourth session of therapy, felt tense, even though it was the first day of her holidays. At the start of the session, she described herself as 'having an awful lot of things to do'. The therapist understood this statement as indicating, in terms of focusing theory, that Sonia was 'too close' to her problems to be able usefully to explore her 'felt sense' of any one of them. The therapist then initiated a simple strategy for 'clearing a space' within which Sonia could gain a clearer sense of what were the main issues for her. The therapist suggested:

> You have a notepad . . . each problem that makes you tense will receive a name, which you will write down on a sheet of notepaper, and next, you will assign the sheet – and thus the problem – a place in this room here, at a comfortable distance from yourself.

Sonia wrote and placed notes referring to each of her concerns – the carpenter coming to do some work, the heating system needing fixed, washing curtains, making an appointment with her dentist, talking to her cleaning lady . . . her loneliness, facing up to her father. In this way, the client was enabled to step back from what had seemed an overwhelming inner pressure, and to clear an emotional space in which she could discover that the underlying issue that was making her tense at the beginning of her holiday was that she no longer had an excuse to avoid visiting her father. She was then ready to look more closely at this specific issue.

Oskar was a client who tended to talk about past events in a highly rational way. He was consistently 'too far' from his feelings to be able to focus effectively on any specific issue in his life. In one session, he told a long story about how he 'thinks' he 'should' feel angry with someone he knows. The next few minutes in the session proceeded in the following manner.

Therapist: You think you should feel furious, but you don't feel any contact with it . . . Now, could you set aside for a moment everything you thought and we will start with your body and see what comes from there . . . Take your time to close your eyes and take a few deep breaths . . . [*The therapist invites the client to fully feel his body, from the feet up, asking 'what are you aware of in that part of the body?'*] . . . Just notice what you experience . . . What strikes you when you have covered the whole body?

Client: That feeling in the pit of my stomach . . . that tension there . . . that is the most powerful.

Therapist: There you experience something powerful . . . Why don't you remain there and look what else will come out of it . . .

Client: It wants to jump out of it, as a devil out of a box . . .

Therapist: Something wants to jump out . . . [*silence*].

Client: Hate . . . but that would be very unusual for me.
Therapist: You hesitate to use the word 'hate', but that is what jumps out at you?
Client: It gives me power!
Therapist: You notice that your hate is accompanied by a feeling of power.
Client: I always withdraw from my friend because he has hurt me so often [tells therapist about an incident in which he felt deeply humiliated].
Therapist: You don't want this to happen again . . . Something in you wants to keep facing him with power?
Client: Yes. That feels good . . . that is it . . . [sighs, sits more relaxed; silence]. This was the last time that I'll give him so much power over me . . . I see him tomorrow, and will make it very clear that I won't let myself be pushed aside any more . . . [client sits up straight and considers further what he wants to tell his friend].

These examples are taken from Leijssen (1998), who provides a detailed discussion of the experiential processes that are involved in each case. It is worth noting that, although the therapist in these cases is clearly following a focusing approach, she is also drawing upon a wide range of skills and competencies that can be found in other therapeutic approaches: for example, the use of empathic reflection, metaphor and symbol, ritual and externalization. The difference lies in the fact that, here, the therapist is employing all of these skills with reference to the bodily felt sense of the client (and presumably her own felt sense in relationship with the client). The aim of experiential focusing can be seen to be that of exploring and unfolding the implicit meanings that are held in bodily feeling.

assumption in process-experiential counselling is that the problems people have are based in an inability to engage in effective emotional processing. Emotions provide vital information about relationships, and are guides to action. When a person fails to express or communicate emotion, his or her capacity to interact with others is impaired. The goal of therapy is therefore to facilitate emotional processing, to enable the person to integrate how they feel into how they experience things. Greenberg *et al.* (1993) suggest that, as a client talks about his or her problems, he or she will communicate clues or 'markers' to the therapist concerning blocked or distorted emotions. The task of the therapist is to listen out for these markers and initiate an appropriate sequence of emotional processing.

An example of this kind of approach can be found in Rice's (1974, 1984) model of stages in the resolution of 'problematic incidents'. These are incidents in the client's life when he or she felt as though his or her reaction to what happened was puzzling or inappropriate. Rice (1984) has found that effective counselling in these situations tends to follow four discrete stages. First, the client sets the scene for exploration, by labelling an incident as problematic, confirming what it was that made the reaction to the incident unacceptable and then reconstructing the scene in general terms. The second stage involves the client and counsellor working on two parallel tasks. One task is to tease out different facets of the feelings experienced during the incident; the other is to search for the aspects of the event that held the most intense meaning or significance. This second stage is centred on the task of discovering the meanings of the event for the client. In the third phase, the client begins to attempt to understand the implications for his or her 'self-schema' or self-concept of what has merged earlier. The final phase involves the exploration of possible new options. Rice (1984: 201) describes this whole process as being one of 'evocative unfolding', in which 'the cognitive-affective reprocessing of a single troubling episode can lead into a widening series of self-discoveries.'

Greenberg *et al.* (1993) have conducted a substantial amount of research into emotional processing tasks in counselling and psychotherapy and have, to date, compiled protocols to guide therapists in working effectively with six types of emotional processing event:

1 Systematic evocative unfolding at a marker of a problematic reaction point.
2 Experiential focusing for an unclear felt sense.
3 Two-chair dialogue at a self-evaluative split.
4 Two-chair enactment for self-interruptive split.
5 Empty-chair work to resolve emotional 'unfinished business'.
6 Empathic affirmation at a marker of intense vulnerability.

There is evidence of the effectiveness of process-experiential therapy in marital therapy (Greenberg and Johnson 1988) and with people who are depressed (Elliott *et al.* 1990; Greenberg *et al.* 1990), and research is currently being conducted into the impact of this approach in people suffering from post-traumatic stress disorder.

The process-experiential approach is a variant of person-centred counselling that builds on the principles described by Rogers (1961) and by Mearns and Thorne (1988) but that also makes use of the practice, employed in Gestalt therapy and psychodrama, of creating highly emotionally charged moments of change. There is no doubt that process-experiential therapy is in tune with the spirit of the times. It is highly specified and trainable. It is research based. It can be readily adapted for use with clients selected according to diagnostic categories such as depression or PTSD. It is applicable within a limited number of sessions. It extends the repertoire of the counsellor, adds to the number of different ways the counsellor has of being emotionally responsive to the client. Yet, at the same time, at the heart of the Rogerian approach there has always been a profound respect for the capacity of the person to change at their own pace. There is a basic assumption about how vital it is to support the agency of the client (Rennie 1998), rather than the counsellor becoming the agent who does things to the client. Whether the methods of process-experiential therapy will turn out to threaten this key feature of the person-centred approach remains to be seen.

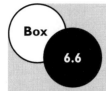

Box

6.6

Dialogue between parts of the self: an emerging theme in person-centred counselling

The idea that there exist different 'parts' of the self, representing separate aspects of the experience or identity of a person, has been central to the practice of a number of different approaches to therapy, ranging from object relations theory to transactional analysis and Gestalt therapy. However, Carl Rogers tended to describe the self as, essentially, a unitary structure that may shift in the direction of growth, fulfilment and self-actualization, but is not characterized by internal conflict. Mearns and Thorne (2000) have revisited this aspect of person-centred theory, and have argued that there has always been an implicit 'self-split' in the way that person-centred practitioners and theorists view the self. The split is between the 'growthful' part of the self and the 'not-for-growth' part. Mearns and Thorne use the term 'configurations' to describe these parts, to emphasize the individual, active and changing nature of the person's process in relation to these elements of the self. They draw out some of the implications of this new perspective for the practice of person-centred counselling, particularly in relation to the necessity for the counsellor to accept and empathize with each 'configuration', rather than favouring the vulnerable 'growing' parts of the self. From this standpoint, it is the living *dialogue* between parts of the self that constitutes growth.

An appraisal of the person-centred approach

The early phase of the development of the person-centred approach, the 'school' years (Barrett-Lennard 1979), represents a unique achievement in the history of counselling and psychotherapy. Between 1940 and 1963, Rogers and others evolved a consistent, coherent body of theory and practice that was informed and shaped by ongoing research. Despite the later fragmentation of the approach, it remains a powerful strand of thought in the contemporary counselling world. However, recent developments resulted in the appearance of some fundamental tensions between alternative conceptualizations of the legacy of Rogers.

One of these issues concerns the identity of the person-centred approach as a distinctive mode of counselling. Many counsellors and therapists regard themselves as 'client-centred' or 'person-centred' because their intention is to focus on the experience or needs of the client, rather than to impose their own definitions or structures, and because they find the ideas encompassed in the 'core conditions' model a useful framework for understanding the nature of the therapeutic alliance. However, these values are often combined with a view that, while the core conditions might be necessary, they are in themselves insufficient to bring about change (Bohart 1990; Tausch 1990). These counsellors use the core conditions as a basis for the employment of therapeutic techniques derived from other approaches. For example, Boy and Pine (1982) describe two phases of counselling. In the first phase, the counsellor employs reflective listening, genuineness and acceptance to form a good working relationship with a client. Then, in the second phase, 'the counselor adopts any pattern of responses that serve to meet the unique needs of the individual client . . . [drawing upon] the attitudes, techniques and approaches inherent in, and available from, all other existing theories of counseling' (Boy and Pine 1982: 18–19).

This approach is characteristic of that of many counsellors who use the person-centred perspective as a basis for integration (see Chapter 3). The end product is a way of working that is *a* person-centred approach rather than *the* person-centred approach. There is support for this kind of endeavour in Rogers' writings. He suggested in relation to the core conditions that empathy, congruence and unconditional positive regard could be communicated to the client in many different ways, for example through psychoanalytic interpretation (Rogers 1957). On the other hand, there is the danger that counsellors working in this fashion may merely use person-centred ideas as a gloss beneath which they are operating in a quite different fashion. For example, a rigorous interpretation of person-centred principles involves a reliance on the actualizing tendency of the client, and continual use of self in the relationship. These are characteristics that can easily become lost when ideas from other approaches are introduced.

Another central issue arising in contemporary person-centred practice concerns the role of skill and technique. Truax and Carkhuff, and others, developed structured programmes for training people in the use of empathy, acceptance and other person-centred qualities. These programmes (reviewed in Chapter 20) engage in a reduction of the person-centred approach to a set of behavioural skills. From a different direction, Gendlin and his colleagues have developed training in 'focusing' as a means of enabling people to make use of the experiential processes found in person-centred (and other) forms of therapy. These skills programmes are thoroughly consistent with the egalitarian philosophy of the person-centred approach, in that they serve to demystify the role of therapist and allow many more people to participate in and benefit from counselling. The concept of empowerment is central to these programmes: giving people the power to change their own lives.

On the other hand, the theoretical framework of the person-centred approach places great emphasis on the quality of the relationship between counsellor and client: for example, in terms of a gradual growth in trust and safety. It also states that this mode of working relies on the presence of a set of attitudes and beliefs in the counsellor, and an ability to convey these qualities in terms of a powerful, authentic presence. Clearly, brief skills training and self-help programmes can do little to address relationship and attitude issues in any serious or systematic manner. There are times when this split between technique and underlying philosophy produces uncomfortable results: for example, when managers are taught empathic listening skills in the context of organization-centred or profit-centred rather than *person*-centred relationships with employees.

A debate has emerged in person-centred counselling over the role of spiritual or transcendent dimensions of experience. Although Rogers himself had originally intended to join the ministry, for most of his career his psychological theorizing was conducted within a strictly secular humanistic framework. It was only towards the end of his life that Rogers (1980) wrote of his experience of 'transcendent unity' and 'inner spirit'. These ideas have been both welcomed (Thorne 1992) and criticized (van Belle 1990; Mearns 1996) within the person-centred movement.

In 1968, Carl Rogers was asked to speak at a symposium entitled 'USA 2000', sponsored by the Esalen Institute, the spiritual home of the humanistic psychology movement. He chose to talk about his vision of the kinds of directions in which he thought relationships between people were moving in the modern world, and about the ways in which therapy and groups could contribute to this process. His paper expresses very clearly his fundamental assumptions about the nature and role of person-centred counselling and therapy. Rogers (1968a: 266) states that 'the greatest problem which man faces in the years to come . . . is the question of how much change the human being can accept, absorb and assimilate, and the rate at which he can take it.' In this statement can be seen the central problematic for Rogers: coming to terms with change in the modern world. Rogers himself was a person who lived through huge social change, in his own life and in the world around him. His own life transitions included leaving a small rural town to go to college in New York, moving from the world of clinical practice to that of academic teaching and research, and then finally leaving that to enter a new world in California. His approach to counselling proved itself most effective with clients undergoing life transitions, such as the transition to adulthood marked by entry to university and the transition from soldier back to civilian status. The theory and method of the person-centred approach have been finely tuned to the needs of people in a changing world. Internal, personal values are to be preferred in the absence of secure external structures of meaning. Relationships must be flexible, whether in therapy or elsewhere:

> I believe there will be possibilities for the rapid development of closeness between and among persons, a closeness which is not artificial, but is real and deep, and which will be well suited to our increasing mobility of living. Temporary relationships will be able to achieve the richness and meaning which heretofore have been associated only with lifelong attachments.
>
> (Rogers 1968a: 268)

This statement sums up the immense appeal that the writing of Rogers have had to people in a world where so many factors operate to deny the possibility of lifelong attachments. The promise of rich, meaningful temporary relationships fulfils a deep longing in many people who find themselves isolated by the collapse of their familiar social ecology.

At the same time, the person-centred approach can be set alongside other counselling approaches that have resonance with other dimensions of social life. The psychodynamic and object relations approaches, for example, present an image of a person invaded by other objects and troubled not by 'conditions of worth' but by internalized representations of sometimes abusive parents. The cognitive–behavioural approach yields a portrait of a person struggling to 'manage' his or her life and be a successful, rational problem-solver. These themes can also be pursued through a person-centred perspective but are less immediately salient.

Chapter summary

- Client-centred (later known as person-centred) counselling was a key element in the 'third force' humanistic psychology movement in the 1950s and 1960s.

- The development of Carl Rogers' theory of counselling drew upon the work of colleagues such as Shlien, Raskin, Barrett-Lennard and Gendlin, and involved a creative fusion of theory, research and practice.

- Person-centred counselling is informed by phenomenological thinking and emphasises the self-concept of the person and the capacity for growth and fulfilment.

- Therapeutic change depends on the existence of a therapeutic relationship characterized by sufficient levels of acceptance, congruence and empathy (the 'core conditions').

- Barrett-Lennard has proposed a cyclical model which clarifies understanding of the key person-centred construct of empathy.

- The therapeutic process in person-centred counselling proceeds through a series of stages of deepening experiential awareness and acceptance of self.

- The method of experiential focusing developed by Gendlin can be a valuable means of facilitating this process.

- The process-experiential model of Greenberg, Rice and Elliott represents an integration of person-centred and Gestalt therapy that is becoming increasingly influential.

- Although in many ways the ideas of Rogers have permeated all of therapeutic practice, there remains a distinctive group of person-centred counsellors who are committed to developing this model further.

Topics for reflection and discussion

1 How valid do you find the 'necessary and sufficient conditions' model? Are there other 'conditions' you would want to add to Rogers' list?

2 What are the strengths and weaknesses of the person-centred approach, in comparison with the psychodynamic and cognitive–behavioural approaches described in previous chapters?

3 Kahn (1997: 38) has written that: 'Rogers spent forty years developing his view of therapy. And perhaps it would not be far off the mark to view his whole forty years' work as an attempt to shape an answer to a single question: What should a therapist do to convey to a client that at last he or she is *loved?*' In your view, how valid is Kahn's assertion?

4 To what extent can process-experiential therapy be seen as merely an extension of Rogers' ideas? Are there ways in which the process-experiential model might be in conflict with basic person-centred ideas and assumptions?

Key terms and concepts

acceptance
agency
core conditions model
depth of experiencing
emotional processing
empathy
empathy cycle model
experiential approach
experiential focusing
felt sense
fully functioning
humanistic psychology
incongruence

locus of evaluation
micro-processes
mutuality
person-centred approach
phenomenology
process model
process-experiential approach
relationship
self-actualization
self-concept
significant events
third force

Suggested further reading

There is no substitute for reading the work of important original thinkers in the field of counselling. In this field, Carl Rogers has been a dominant figure, and his 1942 book *Counseling and Psychotherapy* remains fresh and relevant. Kirschenbaum and Henderson (1990) have brought together a collection of Rogers' work from all phases of his career.

The contemporary texts that best represent current person-centred theory and practice are Mearns and Thorne (1998) and Mearns (1994). Thorne's (1992) book on Rogers supplies a useful overview of the approach, as well as discussing the various criticisms of person-centred counselling that have been made.

A book that is a pleasure to read and conveys the spirit of the person-centred approach is *Dibs*, by Virginia Axline (1971). This is an account of a version of client-centred play therapy carried out by Axline with a young boy, Dibs. More than any other piece of writing, *Dibs* communicates the deep respect for the person, and the capacity of the person to grow, that is so central to effective person-centred work.

The collections edited by Cain and Seeman (2002) and Schneider *et al.* (2001) venture beyond the person-centred approach, to encompass the many strands of contemporary humanistic therapy. Each provides a rich resource, and evidence that the 'third force' remains a potent presence.

7 Working with systems

Introduction

Most counselling has evolved as a response to individual suffering and individual needs. As discussed in Chapter 2, a historical analysis of Western societies suggests that there has been a trend during the 'modern' era, particularly during the highly industrialized, urbanized society of the twentieth and twenty-first centuries, to move in the direction of individualizing problems that had previously been dealt with at a community level. At the same time, however, the experience of living in the modern world is that of struggling to exist within large and complex social systems. So, at the same time that counselling and psychotherapy have been developing methods of working with individuals, a whole other branch of the social and physical sciences has been occupied with the problem of finding ways to understand the principles by which systems operate, and the types of intervention that can bring about change at a systemic level. The growth of a systemic perspective can be seen in a number of different fields, from the study of organizations through to research into the properties of living, ecological systems. In the field of counselling and psychotherapy, the systemic approach is mainly associated with the family therapy. The basic assumption underpinning all versions of family therapy is that the distress or maladjusted behaviour of individual family members is best understood as a manifestation of something going wrong at a systemic level: for example, through ineffective communication between family members or some distortion of the structure of the family group.

It is difficult to integrate traditional family therapy into 'mainstream' models of counselling for a number of reasons, some philosophical, some practical. The emphasis of family therapists on the structural and systemic aspects of family life, on what goes on *between* people rather that what takes place *inside* them, does not sit easily with counsellors trained to work with self, feelings and individual responsibility. From the point of view of many counsellors, too, family therapists appeared to adopt strange and alien ways of relating to their clients, often seeming to eschew the possibility of relationship. Finally, the application of classical family therapy makes a range of demands that most counsellors could not countenace: attendance by all members of the family, intervention delivered by a team of therapists, therapy rooms equipped with one-way mirrors, telephones and video. In recent years, however, there has been a gradual rapprochement between family therapy (or at least some branches of it) and the more individual-oriented therapies, and there has been an increasing acknowledgement on the part of many counsellors that it is essential to include in their work an awareness of systemic influences on the lives of their clients. The aim of this chapter is to review some of these developments. The chapter begins with a brief account of some key ideas used in understanding human systems, before moving on to examine the legacy of family therapy, the issues involved in working systemically with couples and organizations, and then, finally, the nature of a systemic approach to generic counselling practice.

Understanding human systems

The analysis of systems of one kind or another has generated a vast literature. However, it seems clear that much systemic thinking originates from the ideas of Ludwig von Bertalanffy, the founder of cybernetics, Norbert Weiner, an information theorist, and Gregory Bateson, a philosopher and anthropologist. As Guttman (1981: 41) puts it:

> general systems theory had its origins in the thinking of mathematicians, physicist, and engineers in the late 1940s and early 1950s, when technological developments made it possible to conceive of and build mechanical models approximating certain properties of the human barin. At that time, it was re-cognised that many different phenomena (both biological and non-biological) share the attributes of a system – that is, a unified whole that consists of inter-related parts, such that the whole can be identified from the sum of its parts and any change in one part affects the rest of the system. General systems theory concerns itself with elucidating the functional and structural rules that can be considered valid for describing all systems, whatever their composition.

The key ideas here are that a system comprises a whole made up of interrelated parts, and that, crucially, change in any one part affects the rest of the system. These processes can be seen to operate in social, biological and mechanical systems. For example, a motor car is a whole system made up of many sub-systems (the brakes, gear box, engine etc.). If even a minor change happens in one sub-system, such as the tyres being under-inflated, there will be consequences in other areas – in this instance higher strain on the engine leading eventually to breakdown. To take another example, a family can be viewed as a system containing, perhaps, a mother, father and two children. Each of them plays certain roles and fulfils specific tasks within the system. If, however, the mother becomes seriously ill and is not able to continue to discharge the same roles and tasks, then these functions will be redistributed among other members of the family, changing the balance of relationships.

There is another property of systems that is closely linked to the part–whole idea. Functioning systems tend to be homeostatic in the way that they operate. In other words, once a system is established, is 'up and running', it will tend to keep functioning in the same way unless some external event interferes: systems reach a 'stable state', where their parts are in balance. The most common example of homeostasis is the operation of a domestic central heating system. The room thermostat is set at a certain temperature. If the temperature rises above that level, the boiler and radiators will be turned off; if the temperature falls below, the boiler and radiators are switched on. The result is that the room, or house, is maintained at a steady temperature. This process can be understood as one in which feedback information is used to regulate the system (in the case of domestic central heating, the thermostat provides feedback to the boiler). Homeostasis and feedback also occur in human systems. To return to the example of the family in which the mother becomes seriously ill, there are likely to be strong forces within the family acting to prevent change in the system. For instance, the mother may not be physically able to wash and iron clothes but may have a belief that this is what a 'real mother' must do. Her children and spouse may share this belief. The sight of the father incompetently ironing the clothes can serve as feedback that triggers off a renewed effort on her part to be a 'real mother', but then her attempt to iron may make her more ill.

Another important idea found in general systems theory is the notion that all systems are based on a set of rules. In the example just given, the hypothetical family being described possessed powerful, unwritten rules about gender and parental roles and identities. These rules may function well for the family when it is in a state of equilibrium, but at times of change it may be necessary to revise the rules, to allow the system to achieve a new level of functioning. With this family, it would seem clear that unless they can shift their notion of 'mother', there will be a fundamental breakdown in the system brought about by the hospitalization of the mother.

A final key concept in systemic approaches relates to the notion of the life-cycle of a system. To return to the example of the motor car, a vehicle such as this comes supplied with a detailed set of rules concerning when certain parts should be inspected, adjusted or replaced. Similarly, a human system such as a family tracks its way through a predictable set of transitions: leaving home, marriage, entering the world of work, the birth of a child, the death of a parent, retirement, the death of a spouse and so on. The issue here is that while some changes to the family system (e.g. illness, unemployment, disaster) are unpredictable, there are many other potential disruptions to the system that are normative and wholly predictable. This realization brings with it important ways of understanding what is happening in a system, by looking at how it reacts to life-cycle transitions and what it has 'learned' from previous events of this sort.

It is necessary to be clear at this point that the systemic ideas presented here represent a simplified version of what is a complex body of theory. Readers interested in learning more about this perspective are recommended to consult Carter and McGoldrick (1989) and Dallos and Draper (2000) Nevertheless, it is hoped that these core systemic principles are sufficient to map out the basic outline of a powerful and distinctive style of counselling and psychotherapy. It should be clear that a systemically oriented counsellor is not primarily interested in the intrapsychic inner life of his or her client. Instead, they choose to focus on the system within which the person lives, and how this system works. Essentially, if a person reports a 'problem', it is redefined by a systemic therapist as a failure of the system to adapt to change. The goal of the systemic therapist, therefore, is to facilitate change at a systemic level: for example, by rewriting implicit rules, shifting the balance between different parts of the system or improving the effectiveness of how communication/feedback is transmitted.

The analysis and treatment of family systems

The systemic ideas described above have been applied in therapy in a variety of different ways by different groups of family therapists. It is generally agreed that there are three main schools of classical family therapy. First, there is structural family therapy, created by Salvador Minuchin (1974) and his colleagues in Philadelphia. The key concepts employed within this model to understand the structure and patterning of interaction in a family are sub-systems, boundaries, hierarchies and alliances. Second, the strategic approach to family therapy grew out of pioneering research carried out by Gegory Bateson, John Weakland, Don Jackson and Jay Haley at the Mental Research Institute at Palo Alto, California, in the 1950s. Haley later became the central figure in this approach, and introduced some of the ideas of the hypnotherapist Milton Erickson. The distinctive features of this model are the use of techniques such as paradoxical injunction, reframing and the prescription of tasks, to bring about change in symptoms. The third main grouping is known as the Milan group, featuring Palazzoli *et al.* (1978). The special contribution of this group has been to emphasize some of the philosophical aspects of family life, such as the collective construction of a family reality through shared beliefs, myths and assumptions. The Milan-systemic school makes particular use of the idea of circularity, which refers to an assumption of reciprocal causality: everything causes and is caused by everything else. All parts of the family system are reciprocally connected, and the therapy team will attempt to open up this aspect of family life through circular questions. For example, rather than ask a family member what he feels about something that has happened in the family, the therapist could ask how he feels about what his brother thinks about it, thus both introducing an awareness of the links between people and raising the possibility of generating multiple descriptions (double descriptions) of the same event. Other techniques introduced by the Milan school have been positive connotation (giving a positive meaning to all behaviour: for instance, 'how brave you were to withdraw from that situation to preserve your commitment to the family's core values . . .') and the use of therapeutic ritual. Jones (1993) offers an accessible account of the Milan-systemic approach. The similarities and differences between these models can be examined in more detail in Guttman (1981) and Hayes (1991). It should be noted, too, that there exist several well established non-systemic approaches to working with families, such as psychodynamic and behavioural.

It is probably fair to say that in recent years the divisions between these major schools of family therapy have gradually dissolved, as increasing numbers of therapists have integrated different approaches within their own practice, and as new hybrid forms of systems-oriented therapy have emerged, such as the narrative therapy of White and Epston (1990) (see Chapter 9) or the solution-focused model developed by de Shazer (1985). Further, without wishing to deny the important ideological differences between these approaches, it is possible to see significant points of convergence in the way that they have been put into action. Omer (1994) has argued that the differences between family therapy practitioners are more matters of style than of subtance. The common ground of contemporary family therapy can be taken to include:

- Active participation of all or most family members, to allow patterns of interaction to be observed and change to be shared.
- Interventions aimed at properties of the system rather than at aspects of the experiences of individuals. Techniques such as family sculpting (Satir 1972; Duhl *et al.* 1973; Papp 1976) or genograms (McGoldrick and Gerson 1985, 1989) allow the therapist to work with the family system as a whole.
- The therapist adopting a detached, neutral stance, to avoid being 'sucked in' to the system or seduced into forming an alliance with particular family members or sub-groups.
- Therapists working as team, with some workers in the room with the family and others acting as observers, to reinforce neutrality and the 'systems' orientation, and to enable the detection of subtle interaction patterns occuring in the complex dynamic of a family's way of being together.
- Use of a limited number of high-impact sessions, rather than an extended number of 'gentler' or more supportive sessions.

Another area of common ground between the competing traditions of family therapy is that many of them began as ways of attempting to carry out therapy with schizophrenic patients and their families. It is generally accepted that counselling and psychotherapy on a one-to-one basis with people diagnosed or labelled as schizophrenic is very difficult and has limited success. Basically, the behaviour

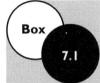

Box

7.1

Using a genogram to explore family patterns across generations

For a counsellor working with a person in the context of their family system, it can be difficult to capture and makes sense of the complexity of the relationships between family members, particularly across generations. A technique that is widely used in family and couples counselling to depict intergenerational patterns of relationships is the genogram. This is similar to a family tree or family history. Usually, the information is gathered by the counsellor and the chart is co-constructed by counsellor and family members, although it is possible to give clients instructions on how to complete a self-administered genogram. There exist a set of conventional symbols that are employed in genograms: for example, a man is represented by a square and a woman by a circle. A close relationship is designated by a double line between the individuals, and a conflictual relationship by a jagged line. Details of these symbols can be found in McGoldrick and Gerson (1985, 1989) and Papadopoulos et al. (1997). A genogram is used to map how a problem may have evolved over time, or be linked to family dynamics. The genogram can also help in highlighting events that have been significant for the family. A genogram is not only a method for gathering information, but also an intervention in itself, because participating in the construction of a genogram may well enable family members to achieve greater understanding of the role they play in the family, and the roles played by other family members.

In their account of the use of genograms in family work, McGoldrick and Gerson (1985, 1989) give many fascinating examples of analyses of the family structures of famous people. One of the most interesting of the cases they have examined is that of the family of Sigmund Freud. The genogram presented in Figure 7.1 (McGoldrick and Gerson 1989: 172) gives a sketch of the Freud family in 1859, when Sigmund Freud was three years old. Jacob and Amalia are Sigmund's parents; Schlomo, who died in 1856, is his paternal grandfather; Anna is his younger sister; John is a cousin with whom he had a close relationship.

In this genogram there are many signs of a family system under a great deal of stress. First, the family has experienced a series of losses. The grandfather, Amalia's brother Julius and the baby Julius died within the space of two years. Jacob's sons from his first marriage, Emanuel and Philip, emigrate to England. Sigmund thus loses his closest playmate, John. Moreover, the family move house twice, in 1859 and 1860, because of financial problems. Second, the Freud family constituted a mix or 'blend' of two family systems. Jacob had been married before, and had two adult

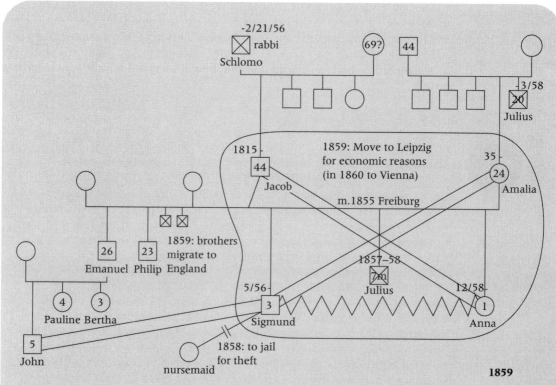

Figure 7.1 A genogram analysis of Freud's family
Source: McGoldrick and Gerson (1989).

sons, one of whom was older than his new wife. The age difference between Jacob and Amalia is further underlined by the fact that Jacob is the same age as Amalia's father. The role of Sigmund as 'special', a family myth that was to have a profound effect on his life, can perhaps be explained by imagining that he was in some sense a replacement for Schlomo, the rabbi leader of the family, who died shortly after he was born. Finally, the family contained at least one secret at this point. Jacob's second wife Rebecca, whom he married in 1852, was apparently never mentioned.

This genogram makes it possible to see some of the family factors that made Freud the person he was. It is hardly surprising that he spent his professional life attempting to make sense of the earliest experiences in his patients' lives. Nor is it surprising that he evolved a psychological theory that portrayed women in a subservient role in relation to men.

The standard introduction to the use of genograms is McGoldrick and Gerson (1985). Papadopoulos *et al.* (1997) and Stanion *et al.* (1997) provide valuable reviews of recent developments in the use of this technique, with a particular emphasis on its application in health settings.

and thought patterns of people who can be classified in this way make it hard to establish an effective therapeutic alliance. In addition, the experience of working with persons whose experience of the world is fragmented and highly fearful places a huge pressure on an individual therapist. To enter into such a world, to be empathic over an extended period time, brings the counsellor or psychotherapist into close contact with feelings of terror, engulfment and overwhelming threat. It is hardly surprising, then, that the most effective types of therapeutic intervention for people assigned the label of 'schizophrenic' have been family therapy and therapeutic communities. But the cost, at least in family therapy, has been the development of a style of doing therapy that has, to a large extent, functioned to insulate the therapist from direct person-to-person contact. This aspect of family therapy practice has changed substantially in recent years, under the influence of writers such as Bott (1994) and Reimers and Treacher (1994), who have argued for a more 'person-centred' stance.

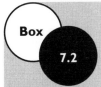

Box

7.2

What does it feel like to be in a family? Sculpting the experience of family life

A very direct way in which family members can convey their experience of being in a family is to construct a family sculpture. This is an exercise through which one family member arranges the other people in the family to represent the way that he or she sees the family. The position of the people in the family, their facial expressions and posture, closeness or distance and direction of gaze all convey the 'sculptor's' sense of what the family is like from their perspective. Sometimes, the therapist might ask the person to resculpt the family in terms of how they would ideally like it to function or how they imagined it might be in the future, or might invite other family members to create alternative sculpts. Onnis et al. (1994) give an example of the use of sculpting with a family that had been referred because Gianni, aged ten, suffered from severe chronic asthma, which had shown little improvement in response to standard medical procedures and had been diagnosed as 'untreatable'. The family comprised Gianni, his mother and father and a seven-year-old younger sister, Sabrina. Asked to sculpt his family 'as it was presently', Gianni placed an empty chair between his parents, and situated his sister in front of his mother, looking at her. He placed himself in front of the other members of the family, facing the empty chair. After completing the sculpture, he quickly ran to sit down in the empty chair between his parents. Gianni was then asked to represent the family as he thought it would be in ten years. He placed his sister at a distance, facing away from them. He said that she was facing 'towards a friend'. He then placed himself in front of his parents, with himself as the apex of a triangle, at the centre of their attention. He announced that 'they are looking at me'. The therapist asked Gianni where he was looking, and he replied 'I'm looking at the mirror' (the one-way mirror on the wall in the therapy room). His parents interjected that they did not have a mirror like that at home, and Gianni turned to his parents and said 'I'm looking at them. They're looking at me, and I am looking at them, like three pillars!' He then began to cough as he was about to have an asthma attack.

These sculptures were interpreted by the family therapy team as expressing, first of all, Gianni's feeling that there was 'a distance between Mom and Dad', and that he had to capture his father's attention and check that he stayed in position. Gianni saw his role in relation to his parents as 'neither of the two will leave if I am between them'. The therapy team understood the second sculpt as representing Gianni's fear of change. Here, Gianni reinforces his earlier message by depicting his family as a kind of immobile eternal triangle, as if he was saying:

> I can't leave my parents alone. Sabrina can perhaps look outside, have her own life, but I must stay here. I would like to see myself, reflect on myself (the desire to look into the mirror), but I cannot. If we are no longer three pillars, everything will collapse.
>
> (Onnis et al. 1994: 347)

Based on these messages, the therapy team offered the family a reframing of their situation that suggested some possibilities for positive change. This reframing statement is typical of the kind of intervention made by many family therapists:

> the sculptures you made have proven very useful to us to better understand what is happening in your family. We were particularly impressed by how Gianni sees himself in the future. Sabrina can have a friend and begin to go her own way. But Gianni cannot! Gianni must stay near his parents to sustain the family. 'We are three pillars', he said. We now understand how great an effort Gianni is making, how heavy the burden he is bearing is, an escessive burden for a child, a burden which can suffocate him, cut off his air, take his breath away. But there is one thing which remains obscure to us: why does Gianni think that his parents, alone, cannot carry this burden or organise themselves to sustain it. We believe that there is another possibility: that his parents succeed in reassuring Gianni, proving to him that they are capable of this. Perhaps then Gianni will find it easier to breathe, to begin to look at himself and find his own way.
>
> (Onnis et al. 1994: 347)

Central to this formulation is positive connotation of the symptom. The asthmatic attacks are characterized not as a problem, but as a positive sacrifice that Gianni is making in order to preserve the family unit. In this case, the family was well able to develop the alternative strategy (the parents taking up the burden) implied in the reframing statement, and soon Gianni's asthmatic crises reduced considerably.

The concept of the person's social 'niche'

The *ecological* approach to therapy, pioneered in Switzerland by Jurg Willi and his colleagues (Willi 1999; Willi *et al.* 2000) represents an important integration of psychodynamic and systemic ideas. The key idea in this approach is that the individual shapes his or her environment into a personal *niche* which allows them to meet their emotional and interpersonal needs. However, a niche which may have been highly functional at an early stage in a person's life (for example, as a young adult) may become dysfunctional as the individual develops as a person and acquires different motives or needs. Willi *et al.* (2000) present a case of a 29-year-old man who experienced frightening panic attacks, even when asleep. In his childhood and adolescence, the client had been exposed to insecurity in his relationships with his mother and father. As a result, on entering adult life he developed a niche for himself as an 'independent adventurer', through work as a sailor or odd-job man who had numerous affairs. He was generally admired by his friends in this role, and the niche he had created for himself allowed him to avoid the possibility of hurt through becoming attached to another person. In therapy, he became aware that his panic attacks had started when he had entered a relationship with a new girlfriend, who was very devoted and affectionate towards him. He had moved in with her. Most of his friends by this time had 'settled down' and started families, and they expected him to do likewise. Over the course of therapy, he came to understand that his old niche was no longer fully appropriate for him – he wished to sustain a more settled relationship. At the same time, his persistent need for independence made living with his girlfriend intolerable. He was able to develop a new niche, which encompassed some of the features of his 'early adult' way of life, but which also enabled him to continue his relationship with his girlfriend on a more distanced basis.

The ecological framework devised by Willi (1999) is firmly based in the idea that a person exists within a social system, and that constructive change involves taking into account what is happening in the system as a whole. However, it is a model that goes beyond family systems, and allows the therapist to help the client to look at other social systems within which a client lives his or her life – housing, work, leisure, physical environment etc. It is also an approach that places emphasis on the ability of the individual to create (and re-create) his or her niche.

The counsellor as consultant: working with organizational systems

So far, this chapter has discussed the issues involved for counsellors working with family systems. There are, however, other social systems in which counsellors may find themselves engaged. Many counsellors work within large organizations, and can come to see that the problems being reported by individual clients are a reflection of a dysfunctional or destructive organizational system. Some examples of this kind of work are:

- A stress counsellor employed by a large manufacturing company writes in her annual report to management that a high proportion of her clients seem to have difficulties associated with the operation of the shift system. The senior management team invite the counsellor to join a company-wide working party looking at shiftwork policy.
- A banking services group has contracted with an independent counselling provider to supply critical incident debriefing for staff subjected to armed raids. The personnel department of the bank wishes to know whether the counselling provider is giving value for money, and whether some of the members of the bank's own occupational health department might be able to do a better job.
- A social services agency in a highly multicultural city has completed a survey, which has shown high levels of day-to-day racial harrassment in some sectors of the organization. However, very few cases are being officially reported. They want to know whether counselling might help victims of harrassment to pursue complaints.
- A student counselling unit in a university discovers that a high proportion of its clients are students in one particular department. This is a department with high academic standards, and a culture of valuing research higher than teaching and pastoral support of students. One of the counsellors meets with staff from the department. They acknowledge the problem, and ask the counselling unit to advise on how to improve the situation.

The common theme running through these examples is that they all demand that the counsellor moves beyond thinking in terms of individual, personal problems and difficulties, and begins to look at issues from a systemic perspective. Just as in work with families, it is necessary to understand that organizations function as homeostatic systems, with boundaries between different parts, feedback loops, rules and myths, and a normative life-cycle. Chapter 16 is concerned with the specific organizational dynamics of counselling agencies, but many of the themes and issues touched on there can equally well be applied to other types of organizational setting.

Counselling has been becoming more established as a profession, and counsellors have started to play a more active part in facilitating organizational change. However, at the moment there is very little written about the role of counsellor as consultant. There is also an absence of appropriate training and supervision opportunities in this field. There does, of course, exist a substantial literature and professional infrastructure around management consulting and organizational behaviour that counsellors can access. Gerstein and Sturmer (1993) provide a useful outline of the opportunities and challenges facing counsellors in this line of work.

Box 7.3

Healing through ritual

One of the key features of families and other social systems is the use of ritual to mark the transition from one social role or status to another, to symbolize the bonds between group members and to express the relationship between individuals and a higher power. The family life-cycle is marked by a series of rituals – marriages, Christmas or Thanksgiving celebrations, funerals. In a modern, largely secular world, many traditional rituals have lost their meaning, or may be inappropriate in situations where families comprise people from different religious or ethnic backgrounds. Some psychologists have suggested that it is important for people to be able to invent their own rituals (Imber-Black and Roberts 1992). Family therapists have become interested in the ways that ritual occasions, such as mealtimes, exemplify the values and relationship patterns of a family, and have also developed ways of employing ritual to facilitate change in families.

Imber-Black and Roberts (1992) describe the case of Brian, 19, who went to live with his older brother when his mother died. This was a difficult time for Brian, who told his brother and sister-in-law that 'I feel I don't have a security blanket.' After reflecting on this statement, the older brother and his wife got together with other surviving members of the extended family to create a patchwork quilt for Brian, using pieces of his mother's nurse uniform, his father's marine shirt and other fabric that carried meaning for Brian. They presented the quilt to Brian on the occasion of his grandmother's eightieth birthday. It symbolized for Brian, and the family as a whole, that his brother and sister-in-law were able to give Brian the nurturing and 'security blanket' that he needed. This family ritual gave members of the family a structure through which to channel their concern for Brian, it brought them all together in a collective expression of grief and hope and, finally, it made use of a tangible physical object, a quilt, that could function as a symbol and reminder of what they had done and felt. Other physical symbols used in family rituals can include candles, places where objects or messages are buried or boxes that contain worries or joys.

Imber-Black and Roberts (1992) and Wyrostok (1995) are good sources for further reading about ways in which ritual has been employed by different therapists.

Conclusions: themes and issues in the application of systemic ideas in counselling

An appreciation of systemic concepts is invaluable for counsellors operating in any sphere. Any individual client is inevitably embedded within a social system. Usually this system is a family unit, but on some occasions it may be a work group, friendship network or hospital ward. The capacity of an individual client to make changes in his or her life will depend on the permeability of the system, on how much the pattern of relationships across that set of people can shift or even on whether the system will allow the client to leave it. All good counsellors have an intuitive sense of these issues, whether they have studied them theoretically or not.

However, at another level systemic ideas introduce a radically different way of making sense of the goals and processes of counselling. The theoretical models that have been discussed so far – psychodynamic, cognitive–behavioural and person-centred – all place the counsellor in a direct personal relationship with the client. Systemic counselling demands a realignnment of counsellor and client. There is still the necessity to form an alliance with the individual, but it is also necessary to see the individual as part of a bigger whole, and for the counsellor to relate to that system as a whole and to work with the client's relationship with it. The image of the person here is radically different from the one that underpins mainstream psychodynamic, cognitive–behavioural and person-centred counselling. These established approaches conceive of the person as a bounded, autonomous entity, essentially separate from the rest of the social world. Systemic counselling sees the person as fundamentally a relational being, as an entity that can only exist as part of a family, group or community. The theoretical approaches that are introduced in the following chapters – feminist, narrative and multicultural – have each in their own way taken up the challenge of a systemic, relational philsophy, and have applied it with differing emphases, but with the same implicit understanding that, in the end, individualism is not an adequate basis for living the good life.

Chapter summary

- Most mainstream approaches to counselling work with problems at the level of the individual person; an alternative approach is to view the person as part of a dysfunctional social or family system.

- General systems theory provides a set of concepts that can be applied to understanding patterns of relationship between people.

- These ideas have been used in therapy through the structural family therapy model of Minuchin, the strategic approach associated with Bateson and Haley and the Milan-systemic school of Palazzoli, Cecchin, Boscolo and Prata.

- Currently, many counsellors using a systemic approach draw upon elements of all of these models, using techniques such as genograms, ritual and family or group sculpting.

- The idea of the person's social 'niche' has emerged as a valuable means of applying a systems perspective in individual counselling.

- Counsellors operating from a systemic perspective have also been able to apply their skills to problems within organizations and institutions.

- Despite the power of systemic approaches, the task of adopting a relational, system-focused method remains a significant challenge for counsellors trained in traditional one-to-one insight-oriented models.

Topics for reflection and discussion

1 Take a group in which you belong. This may be a work or friendship group, or a group on a college course. Analyse the dynamics of that group in terms of some of the systemic concepts described in this chapter. What have you learned from this analysis? What does it add to your understanding of your friends or colleagues, in comparison with thinking about these people in terms of their separate individual lives and personalities? What have you learned about yourself from this exercise?

2 What might be some of the ethical issues that could be raised when working with a family or other system? How might confidentiality and informed consent operate within a system? Is the ethical principle of respect for autonomy still relevant?

3 Reflect on the implications for the counsellor–client relationship of adopting a systemic perspective. For example, from a person-centred perspective a good relationship would be characterized by high levels of congruence, empathy and acceptance. Are these concepts applicable in systemic work? How useful are psychoanalytic ideas of transference and counter-tranference?

4 Are there particular counselling issues that might be more suited to a systemic approach, and other issues that might be better dealt with at an individual level?

5 What is your own personal 'niche'? How have you negotiated change in your niche, as your needs and desires have changed at different points in your development?

Key terms and concepts

circular questioning	Milan group
equilibrium	positive connotation
family therapy	ritual
feedback	rules
genograms	sculpting
homeostasis	strategic approach
life-cycle of a system	structural family therapy

Suggested further reading

Many counsellors have found their way into a systemic perspective by reading *Families and How to Survive Them*, by John Cleese (the well known comic actor) and Robin Skynner (the family therapist).

A well established textbook that contains a wealth of relevant material on systemic approaches to counselling and psychotherapy is *The Changing Family Life Cycle* by Carter and McGoldrick (1989). The Reimers and Treacher (1995) book on user-friendly family therapy is an interesting account of their efforts to escape from the ideological rigidity that can sometimes be associated with work with families. A chapter by Hoffman (1992) captures the same spirit of 'person-centredness' that is increasingly adopted by some systemic therapists.

Both of the main research and professional journals in this field, *Family Process* and the *Journal of Family Therapy*, consistently publish papers that are stimulating and readable.

8 Feminist approaches: the radicalization of counselling

Introduction

It could well be argued that feminist perspectives have represented the most significant area of advance in counselling theory and practice over the past 20 years. The role of gender in counselling and psychotherapy has been the source of a great deal of important new theory and research. This work has explored three main areas of interest: the development of a feminist approach to counselling and psychotherapy; the impact on process and outcome of the gender match (or mismatch) of counsellor and client; and the creation of counselling models appropriate to specific areas of women's experience. The aim of this chapter is to provide an introduction to feminist counselling. First, the origins of this counselling orientation in feminist philosophy are described. This is followed by an account of how these ideas have been used to critique existing mainstream approaches to therapy.

This critique sets the scene for a discussion of the nature of feminist counselling, and a review of the implications of this approach for theory, practice and research.

Feminism as philosophy and social action

The basic assumption of feminism is that, in the great majority of cultures, women are systematically oppressed and exploited. Howell (1981) describes this state of affairs as 'the cultural devaluation of women'; other people would label it as 'sexism'. Feminists have approached the problem of sexism from several directions. The ways in which a male-dominated social order is created and maintained have been subjected to critical analysis. A language for describing and understanding the experience of women has been created. Finally, new forms of social action and social institutions have been invented with the aim of empowering women.

However, within the broad social and political approaches of feminism there exist a number of discrete strands of thought. Enns (1992) has divided the 'complex, overlapping and fluid' perspectives that operate within feminism into four main feminist traditions: liberal, cultural, radical and socialist (see Table 8.1). *Liberal* feminism can be regarded as the 'mainstream' feminist tradition, and has its roots in the struggle of the Suffragettes to gain equal rights and access. *Cultural* feminism, by contrast, has placed greater emphasis on recognizing and celebrating the distinctive experience of being a woman and promoting the 'feminization' of society through legitimating the importance of life-affirming values such as cooperation, harmony, acceptance of intuition and altruism. *Radical* feminism centres on a systematic challenge to the structures and beliefs associated with male power or patriarchy, and the division of social life into separate male and female domains. Finally, *socialist* feminism is derived from a core belief that, although oppression may be influenced by gender, it is determined at a more fundamental level by social class and race. For socialist feminists, the fulfilment of human potential will only be possible when issues of control over production and capital, and the class system, have been adequately addressed. These groupings within the feminist movement have evolved different goals, methods and solutions, and have tended to apply themselves to different sets of problems.

It is essential to acknowledge that feminism is a complex and evolving system of thought and social action. Nevertheless, it is possible to identify a set of core beliefs concerning self and society that would receive broad support from the majority of feminist-oriented counsellors. In this vein, Llewelyn and Osborne (1983) have argued that feminist therapy is built on four basic assumptions about the social experience of women:

1 Women are consistently in a position of deference to men. For example, women tend to have less power or status in work situations. J. B. Miller (1987) has observed that women who seek to be powerful rather than passive are viewed as selfish, destructive and unfeminine.

Table 8.1 The four main feminist traditions

Difference	Liberal feminism	Cultural feminism	Radical feminism	Socialist feminism
Cause of sexism and oppression	Socialization and gender conditioning, irrational prejudice	Devaluation of feminine qualities, overvaluation of masculine values and patriarchy	Male domination, patriarchy, men's control over women's bodies	Multiple oppressions based on gender, class, race distinctions; male domination embedded in economic institutions
Goal	Individual freedom, dignity, autonomy, self-fulfilment and equality	Revaluation of women's strengths, infusion of society with values based on cooperation	Transformed gender relationships, women's culture, sexual and procreative self-determination	Transformed social and gender relationships and institutions
Solutions	Reform, equal opportunity, legislation of rights education, rational argument	Women's discovery of internal truths, identification and relationships with other women, 'feminization' of culture	Formation of autonomous women's communities; separatism; celebration of women's achievements, culture and spirituality	Restructuring of education, work, parenting, economic structures and sexuality (reproductive freedom) in order to eliminate male domination and other oppressions
Key issues	Educational reform, affirmative action, reproductive rights	Non-violence, pacifism, ethics based on relationship values	Violence against women through birth technology, rape, battering, war, sterilization, intimate relationships and pornography	Race/class/gender interactions, feminization of poverty, comparable worth issues, maternity/paternity leave
Methods	Legislation of equal rights under the law, legislation that breaks up power structures, creation of gender-neutral policies	Protective legislation for women (e.g. maternity leave), organized peace efforts, cooperation with other women	Collective action, anti-violence organization, expression of anger through writing and creative expression, activism centred outside of traditional political structures	Collective action; elimination of public–private distinctions (e.g. wages for housework); redistribution of resources, so adequate schools, work and childcare are available to all

Source: Enns (1992).

2 Women are expected to be aware of the feelings of others, and to supply emotional nurturing to others, especially men.

3 Women are expected to be 'connected' to men, so that the achievement of autonomy is difficult.

4 The issue of sexuality is enormously problematic for women. This factor arises from a social context in which images of idealized women's bodies are used to sell commodities, assertive female sexuality is threatening to many men and sexual violence against women is widespread.

It is possible to see that these statements map out a distinctive agenda for feminist counselling. None of the topics highlighted by Llewelyn and Osborne is given any significant emphasis in theories of counselling such as psychodynamic, person-centred or cognitive–behavioural. The agenda of a feminist-inspired counselling brings into the counselling arena an awareness of social and economic realities, the meaning of the body and the centrality of power in relationships that is quite unique within the counselling and psychotherapy world. The first task of those women committed to putting this agenda into action was to clear themselves a space, to show how and why the ways of doing therapy that prevailed in the 1960s and 1970s were just not good enough.

The feminist critique of psychotherapy theory and practice

> To women, for whom the events in therapy resemble the events in the kitchen, overobjectification of human suffering can make identification with the field impossible. We see in many theories posturing that seems at best absurd, and at worst collusive and oppressive.
>
> (Wooley 1994: 324)

Virtually all of the key historical figures in counselling and psychotherapy have been men, and they have written, whether consciously or not, from a male perspective. There have been extensive efforts by women writers and practitioners to envision theories and approaches in counselling and psychotherapy that are more consistent with the experiences and needs of women. Many of these efforts were inspired by the consolidation of feminism in the 1960s as a central force for social change. The work of feminist authors such as Simone de Beauvoir, Germaine Greer, Kate Millett and others encouraged female psychologists and therapists to look again at established ideas in these disciplines. It would be mistaken to assume, however, that women had no voice at all in counselling and psychotherapy before that time. Within the psychoanalytic movement, Melanie Klein and Karen Horney had played a crucial role in emphasizing the part of the mother in child development. Other women therapists, such as Laura Perls, Zerka Moreno and Virginia Axline, had been important contributors to the founding of Gestalt

Box
8.1

The fate of one of the earliest women psychotherapists

In 1904 Sabina Spielrein, a 19-year-old young Russian woman from a rich Jewish family, was brought from her home in Rostov-on-Don to become a patient at one of the foremost psychiatric centres in Europe, the Burgholzi Clinic in Zurich. The physician in charge of her case was Carl Jung; she became the first person to be analysed by him. Her treatment went well, and in 1905 she enrolled as a medical student at the University of Zurich. In this role she was assigned as an assistant to Jung, to help him with his word association experiments. She became his friend, while continuing in therapy, and by 1908 probably also his lover. In February 1909 Jung's wife wrote to Spielrein's mother about the affair, which Jung then attempted to bring to an end. In 1911 Spielrein completed her studies, and moved to Vienna to work with Freud, becoming only the second female member of the Vienna Psychoanalytic Society. It appeared that Freud used material gleaned from his analysis of Spielrein's unconscious fantasies to gain evidence with which to attack Jung. Spielrein then married, and in 1916 quit psychoanalysis in order to do something 'useful' – working in a surgical clinic. She returned to psychoanalytic practice after the Great War, specializing in child analysis and at one time collaborating with the Swiss developmental psychologist Jean Piaget. She returned to Russia, to Moscow, in 1923. In 1941, in her home town of Rostov-on-Don, she was taken, along with her two daughters and the rest of the city's Jewish community, to the synagogue and shot by the Nazis.

This account of Sabina Spielrein's life is derived from a book by Kerr (1994), who argues that Spielrein played a crucial role in the early years of the psychoanalytic movement, in attempting to integrate the Freudian notion of repressed sexuality with the emerging Jungian idea of a collective unconscious. Kerr suggests that the key Jungian concept of anima is attributable to the discussions and correspondence between Jung and Spielrein. Yet, until Kerr's book, Spielrein's contribution comprised little more than a footnote in the history of psychoanalysis. And even in this book, her story is used mainly as a device through which to re-examine the famous rivalry between Freud and Jung.

therapy, psychodrama and client-centred therapy respectively, but had received much less attention than the men alongside whom they had worked.

The field of mental health affords multiple examples of the oppression and exploitation of women. There is ample evidence of experimentation on and sexual abuse of women clients and patients (Masson 1984; Showalter 1985). Studies of perceptions of mental health in women have shown that mental health workers view women in general as more neurotic and less well adjusted than men (Broverman *et al.* 1970). The psychiatric and mental health professions, which provide the intellectual and institutional context for counselling and psychotherapy, can be seen to be no less sexist than any other sector of society. It is therefore necessary to recognize that the occurence of patriarchal and sexist attitudes and practices in counselling and psychotherapy are not merely attributable to the mistaken ideas of individual theorists such as Freud, but have been part of the taken-for-granted background to most mental health care.

The evolution of feminist counselling and psychotherapy has involved a powerful re-examination of theoretical assumptions, particularly those of psychoanalysis, from a feminist point of view. Two of the fundamental ideas in psychoanalysis have received special attention: the concept of penis envy, and the formulation of childhood sexuality. The notion of penis envy was used by Freud to explain the development of femininity in girls. Freud supposed that when a little girl first saw a penis, she would be 'overcome by envy' (Freud 1905/1977). As a result of this sense of inferiority, the girl would recognize that:

> this is a point on which she cannot compete with boys, and that it would be therefore best for her to give up the idea of doing so. Thus the little girl's recognition of the anatomical distinction between the sexes forces her away from masculinity and masculine masturbation on to new lines which lead to the development of femininity.
>
> (Freud 1924/1977: 340)

These 'new lines' included a motivation to look attractive to compensate for the missing penis, and a tendency to a less mature type of moral sensitivity due to the absence of castration anxiety, which Freud saw as such an important element in male moral development.

From a contemporary perspective the penis envy hypothesis seems incredible, ludicrous and objectionable. However, such was the domination of Freud that this doctrine remained in force within the psychoanalytic movement for many years after his death (Howell 1981). It was only in the writings of Mitchell (1974) that a thorough critique of this aspect of Freudian theory was carried out.

It is possible to regard the penis envy hypothesis as an example of a lack of understanding of women in Freudian theory, an ill-conceived idea that can be reviewed and corrected without threat to the theory as a whole. The other main feminist objection to psychoanalysis is, however, much more fundamental. In the early years of psychoanalysis, Freud had worked with a number of women patients who had reported memories of distressing sexual experiences that had taken place in their childhood. Freud was uncertain how to interpret these memories, but in the end came to the conclusion that the childhood events that these women were reporting could not have taken place. It has been claimed, by Masson (1984) and others, that Freud, in the end, could not believe that middle-class, socially respectable men could engage in this kind of behaviour. Freud therefore interpreted these reports as 'screen memories', or fantasies constructed to conceal the true nature of what had taken place, which was the acting out by the child of her own sexual motives. From a modern perspective, when so much more is known about the prevalence of child sexual abuse and the barriers of secrecy, collusion and adult disbelief that confront child victims, the classical Freudian approach to this issue can be seen to be deeply mistaken. Masson (1984), one of the leading critics of this aspect of Freudian theory, was driven to label this set of ideas an 'assault on truth'. Like so many aspects of Freud's work, the truth about what actually happened in Freud's work with these patients is open to alternative interpretations, and in fact was presented in different ways by Freud on different occasions (Esterson 1998). Nevertheless, the consequences of the position that Freud took (interpreting 'scenes of seduction' described by patients as fantasies) were to be far-reaching in terms of systematic professional denial of the reality of victims of abuse.

Through time, many women therapists came to agree with Taylor (1991: 96) that 'a careful reading of Freud's writings reveals that he thoroughly rejected women as full human beings.'

At a theoretical level, the feminist re-examination of psychoanalysis carried out by Mitchell (1974) and Eichenbaum and Orbach (1982) has been followed by a steady stream of publications devoted to integrating feminist principles with psychotherapeutic (usually psychodynamic) practice. These theoretical studies have involved carrying out a systematic critique of male-dominated approaches. The feminist critique of conventional sex therapy has drawn attention to the 'phallocentric' assumptions made by most sex therapists (Stock 1988; Tiefer 1988). Waterhouse (1993) provides a carefully argued feminist critique of the application of the person-centred approach with victims of sexual violence, pointing out that the Rogerian emphasis on personal responsibility, the authentic expression of feelings and empathy pays insufficient attention to the social and political reality of women's lives, and specifically to the effects of inequalities in power. Klein (1976) has argued that the methods used for evaluating the effectiveness do not adequately reflect feminist values and women's experience.

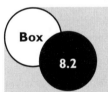

Box 8.2

Are relationships perceived as dangerous or as safe?

In a piece of research carried out at Harvard University in 1979, Pollak and Gilligan used the Thematic Apperception Test (TAT) to explore the way that men and women make sense of situations in their lives. In the TAT, participants are asked to write imaginative stories in response to a series of picture stimuli. The assumption is that the writer will spontaneously 'project' into his or her stories aspects of their attitudes and motivation of which they are not consciously aware. In this study, the stories written by a large number of male and female students were analysed in terms of gender differences in their perceptions of which situations they found particularly dangerous or threatening. Threat or dangerousness was defined in terms of the story involving a violent reaction to a situation. One of the pictures depicted a scene in which a man and a woman were sitting next to each other on a bench. In front of them was a river, with a low bridge to the side and university buildings in the background. Another picture presented an image of two women dressed in white laboratory coats, with one of them watching the other handling some test tubes. Overall, the men wrote twice as many violent stories as did the women. However, the majority of the male violence stories were in response to pictures that showed a scene depicting an intimate relationship, such as the sitting-on-the-bench scene. By contrast, the majority of the female violence stories were in response to work achievement scenes (for example, the women-in-the-laboratory picture). A typical male 'intimacy is dangerous' story was:

> Jake saw his life pass before his eyes. He could feel the cold penetrating ever deeper into his body. How long had it been since he had fallen through the ice – thirty seconds, a minute? It wouldn't take long for him to succumb to the chilling grip of the mid-February Charles River. What a fool he had been to accept the challenge of his roommate Sam to cross the frozen river! He knew all along that Sam hated him. Hated him for being rich and especially hated him for being engaged to Mary, Sam's childhood sweetheart. But Jake never realized until now that Mary also hated him and really loved Sam. Yet there they were, the two of them, calmly sitting on a bench in the river bend, watching Jake drown. They'd probably soon be married, and they'd probably finance it with the life insurance policy on Jake, for which Mary was the beneficiary.

A typical female 'achievement is dangerous' story was:

> Another boring day at the lab and that meant bitchy Miss Hegstead always breathing down the students' backs. Miss Hegstead had been at Needham Country High School for 40 years and every chemistry class is the same. She always goes over to Jane and comments to the other students that Jane is always doing the experiment right and Jane is the only student who works hard etc. Little does Miss Hegstead know that Jane is making some powerful arsenic to put in her afternoon coffee.

The messages implicit in these stories were that men construed danger as arising from connection and affiliation, while women saw danger in the isolation that results from competitive achievement. A third picture used in the study was particularly evocative in these respects. This picture showed a man and a woman in a trapeze act. The man was hanging upside down by his knees, grasping the woman's wrists. This picture, the only one to depict actual physical contact, was the one that elicited the highest perceptions of threat in the stories written by male research participants. Finally, most of the trapeze stories written by women mentioned a net, even though no net existed in the picture itself. Hardly any of the men imagined there to be a net. Pollak and Gilligan (1982: 166) conclude their report with the observation that: 'women weave nets of care to sustain connection in order to prevent violence and hurt.'

These are some of the ways in which feminist writers have contributed to a comprehensive critique of the dominant, male-oriented models of counselling. From and alongside this critique there has emerged an alternative body of feminist theory and practice.

Theory and practice of feminist counselling

Integrationist approaches

The construction of a feminist model of counselling and psychotherapy has not been an easy matter. It is probably reasonable to suppose that the majority of counsellors who have been influenced by feminist ideas actually work in counselling agencies where they are not able to deliver 'pure' feminist therapy. These counsellors can perhaps do little more than work in feminist mode with those clients with whom it is applicable. This tendency is reflected in the contemporary literature on feminist counselling and psychotherapy, much of which is avowedly eclectic or integrative in nature, drawing on a variety of ideas and techniques already employed in the field. This version of feminist counselling is advocated in widely read texts such as those of Chaplin (1988) and Worell and Remer (1992). For example, Worell and Remer encourage their readers to evolve their own 'feminist-compatible' model, by examining the theory they presently employ in terms of the kinds of feminist principles and ideas discussed in earlier sections of this chapter. In effect, this approach constitutes a kind of feminist-informed integrationism, with all the strengths and weaknesses associated with integrationist and eclectic approaches in general (see Chapter 3).

Integrative feminist approaches have been successful in identifying the distinctive goals and characteristics of feminist practice. For example, many feminist practitioners would agree with the following guidelines (Worell 1981; Worell and Remer 1992), which suggest that a feminist approach should include:

- An egalitarian relationship with shared responsibility between counsellor and client. For example, being cautious about the imposition of interpretations on the client's experience.
- Using a consciousness-raising approach. For example, differentiating between personal problems and political or social issues.
- Helping women to explore and express their personal power.
- Helping women to identify their internalized sex-role messages and beliefs, replace sex-role stereotyped beliefs with more self-enhancing self-talk and develop a full range of behaviours that are freely chosen and not dictated by sex-role stereotypes.
- Enabling women to understand that individual women's experiences are common to all women.
- Helping women to get in touch with unexpressed anger.

- Assisting women to define themselves apart from their role relationships to men, home and children.
- Encouraging women to nurture themselves as well as others.
- Promoting skills development in areas such as assertiveness and employment.

Similar principles have been identified by Israeli and Santor (2000) in their analysis of 'effective components' of feminist therapy.

The Stone Center model of feminist counselling

Worrel and Remer (1992) present an integrationist approach to constructing a feminist therapy. The other route towards a feminist model of counselling and psychotherapy has been to attempt to create a free-standing set of ideas and methods that is internally consistent and can be not only disseminated through training but also the focus of research. The group that has been most successful in achieving this goal is the Stone Center team, based at Wellesley College, in Cambridge, Massachussetts, and drawing on the work of key figures such as Miller (1976), Chodorow (1978) and Gilligan (1982).

The theoretical framework developed by Miller and her colleagues has sought to make sense of the psychological dimensions of the social inequality and powerlessness experienced by women through the use of a core concept of 'relatedness' or 'self-in-relation' (Miller 1976). In her study of gender differences in moral reasoning, for example, Gilligan (1982) found that, in general, men make moral judgements based on criteria of fairness and rights, while women assess moral dilemmas according to a sense of responsibility in relationships. The male way of looking at things, in Gilligan's (1982) words, 'protects separateness', and the female way 'sustains connections'. Gilligan goes on from this finding to suggest that men and women use different styles of constructing social reality: men fear intimacy, women fear isolation.

Miller (1976), Kaplan (1987) and other members of the Stone Center group have explored the implications of this 'relational' perspective for understanding patterns of development in childhood. They conclude that there is a basic difference between social development in boys and girls. For a girl, the relationship with the primary caretaker, the mother, is one of mutuality. Both are the same sex, both are engaged in, or preparing to be engaged in (Chodorow 1978), the tasks of mothering and nurturing. For boys the situation is one of achieving development and maturity only through increasing separation and autonomy from the mother. Men, as a result, are socialized into a separate, isolated way of being, and in counselling need help to understand and maintain relationships. Women, by contrast, spend their formative years in a world of relationships and connectedness, and in counselling seek help to achieve autonomy and also, crucially, to secure affirmation for their relatedness. The approach to therapy that has emerged from this perspective on human development has been summarized by Jordan *et al.* (1991) and Jordan (2000) in terms of a set of core ideas:

- people grow through and towards relationships throughout the lifespan;
- movement towards mutuality rather than movement towards separation characterizes mature functioning;
- relational differentiation and elaboration characterize growth;
- mutual empathy and mutual empowerment are at the core of growth-fostering relationships;
- in growth-fostering relationships, all people contribute and grow or benefit; development is not a one-way street;
- therapy relationships are characterized by a special kind of mutuality;
- mutual empathy is the vehicle for change in therapy;
- real engagement and therapeutic authenticity are necessary for the development of mutual empathy.

This emphasis on the relational nature of women's development leads also to a re-examination of some elements in the counselling process: empathy, mutuality, dependency, caring.

Jordan (1991) points out that male-dominated therapy theory has tended to emphasize the goal of developing 'ego strength', defined in terms of strong boundaries between self and other. By contrast, the feminist notion of the relational self implies much more of a sense of interconnectedness between persons. This connection is maintained through a capacity to respond empathically to the other, and the concept of empathy is therefore a central element of the Stone Center approach. However, a distinctive aspect of the use of empathy within this approach to therapy is that is takes into account the empathic sensitivity of the client as well as that of the counsellor. In the classical Rogerian 'core conditions' model (Chapter 6), empathy is regarded as a counsellor-supplied condition that can facilitate understanding and self-acceptance on the part of the client. In the Stone Center theory, empathy is viewed as a fundamental characteristic of women's ways of knowing and relating. As a result, the client's empathic engagement with others, including with the counsellor, is one of the key areas for exploration in this type of counselling (Jordan 1997b).

Women are often socialized into taking care of others, and participate in relationships where they give empathy but find it difficult to receive it back. The experience of mutuality is therefore one of the areas that a feminist model of counselling seeks to examine. As Jordan (1991: 96) puts it: 'in intersubjective mutuality . . . we not only find the opportunity of extending our understanding of the other, we also enhance awareness of ourselves.' One of the key goals of counselling is to enable the client to become more able to participate in relationships marked by high levels of mutuality. Mutuality is also expressed in the counselling relationship itself, with feminist counsellors being willing to be 'real', self-disclosing and actively helpful in the counselling room (Jordan 2000: 1015). That mutuality, based on the counsellor's willingness to let the client see how she is affected by what the client is going through, helps clients to 'develop a realistic awareness of the impact of their actions and words on other people and on relationships.'

The theme of connectedness in the Stone Center approach is also applied through a reappraisal of the concept of dependency. In the counselling and psychotherapy literature as a whole, this quality is generally considered to reflect an inability on the part of the person to take adequate control of their own life. Many men find dependency threatening to their self-esteem (Stiver 1991). From a feminist perspective, however, dependency is a basic aspect of everyday experience. The fact that it is pathologized by mental health professionals can be seen as another example of the dominance of patriarchal attitudes. In an effort to highlight the life-enhancing and constructive aspects of dependency, Stiver (1991b: 160) defines it as 'a process of counting on other people to provide help in coping physically and emotionally with the experiences and tasks encountered in the world when one has not sufficient skill, confidence, energy and/or time.' She adds that the experience of self can be 'enhanced and empowered through the very process of counting on others for help'. 'Healthy' dependency can be regarded as providing opportunities for growth and development.

Stiver (1991a) draws out some of the implications for counselling practice of the Stone Center use of empathy, mutuality and healthy dependency in her discussion of the concept of care. For her, traditional psychodynamic approaches to counselling and psychotherapy have been based on a principle of establishing relational distance between counsellor and client, in order to promote objectivity. Stiver argues that this is essentially a masculine model, which does not work well for women (or for some men), and proposes that counsellors should be willing to demonstrate that they care about their clients, that they express 'an emotional investment in the other person's well-being' (p. 265).

This is a necessarily oversimplified account of a complex and powerful theoretical model. Nevertheless, it can be seen that it points the way towards a distinctive approach to feminist counselling. The Stone Center group has placed a psychodynamic theory of development alongside a person-centred understanding of the therapeutic relationship, but has reinterpreted both sets of ideas from a feminist perspective that looks at therapy as part of a social world characterized by male domination. The notion of the relational, connected self serves as a way of effectively bridging these theoretical domains. The Stone Center model has also been used to construct an analysis of the ways that women masking their power and anger (Miller 1991a, b), and to develop a model of women's depression (Stiver and Miller 1997). Another important theme running through the work of this group has been an appreciation of women's problems in the world of work, in environments where mutual, empathic, caring relationships are difficult to sustain. Recent writings have focused on the application of the model to ethnic minority and lesbian women (Jordan 1997a). Finally, it is important to note that, even though the Stone Center model derives from the collaboration of a specific group of counsellors and psychotherapists, it nevertheless reflects many of the ideas and themes apparent in the writings of other feminist therapists: for example, the work of Taylor (1990, 1991, 1995, 1996) and the psychodynamic feminist approach represented by Lawrence and Maguire (1997).

Box 8.3

Mutuality in feminist counselling

After I had pursued a fleeting and fragile alliance with a fearful young female client, she revealed to me that she was not comfortable trusting me because she knew little about me and asked why she should have to reveal herself if I was not willing to do the same. I asked her what she would like to know that she did not know. She did not have an answer at that moment but said she would think about it.

One of the client's abiding concerns was her fear of the death of one or both of her parents. This fear, together with other stressors, resulted in a chronic, cyclical pattern of depressed mood. Three weeks after the aforementioned incident, my client asked me if I had ever lost a parent. I examined my immediate impulse, which was to inquire about why the client needed to know this. After a moment of deliberation, I decided to answer rather than inquire about her need to know. I already knew her meaning. She wanted to hear that someone who had survived this kind of loss could not only survive, but thrive. I gave her my reply, 'Yes, I have lost both of them.'

Tears appeared in my client's eyes, and she replied, 'That must feel very lonely to you sometimes.' Tearfully also, I replied, 'Yes. However, I learned to grieve, to move on and to bring other important people into my life.' We had a moment in which my client's isolation with her issues of loss was shattered and in which she felt the power and validation of her ability to empathize with me. I then added, 'And I believe that you also will learn to do that when the time comes.' Our focus then returned to my client and her fears. However, since that moment we had an alliance that permitted us to progress faster in a few weeks than we had in the previous several months.

I chose that intervention deliberately, based on therapeutic intent rather than personal need. I allowed my client to see my experience, which in turn gave her permission to reveal her own . . . In addition to allowing the client the opportunity to experience mutuality, the discrete use of counselor self-disclosure seems to promote the goal of feminist therapy that client and therapist remain as equal as possible on the power dimension.

Source: Nelson (1996: 343).

Radical feminist therapy

While being explicitly relational in emphasis, the Stone Center approach concentrates mainly on the psychological processes surrounding relationships with immediate significant others, such as parents, siblings, partners and work colleagues. It is a model that shares the psychodynamic preoccupation with the relationship between mother and child, even if it then extracts a quite different understanding of the dynamics of that relationship. Miller, Jordan and Stiver start with intimacy, and then work out towards society. Radical feminist therapy, by contrast, is primarily interested in the social and material circumstances in which women live. It starts with the social, and works back from that to arrive at an appreciation of possibilities for intimate relationships.

Perhaps the clearest account of radical feminist therapy can be found in the writing of Burstow (1992). When Burstow reviews the experience of women in contemporary society, the major theme that emerges for her is violence. The fundamental assumptions around which her approach to counselling and therapy is based are:

1 Women are violently reduced to bodies that are for-men, and those bodies are then further violated.
2 Violence is absolutely integral to our experience as women.
3 Extreme violence is the context in which other violence occurs and gives meaning to the other forms, with which it inevitably interacts.
4 All women are subject to extreme violence at some time or live with the threat of extreme violence (Burstow 1992: xv).

Childhood sexual abuse, rape and physical abuse are obvious examples of violence against women. Psychiatric treatment is a less obvious example. Depression, cutting, dissociation/splitting and problems with eating can be regarded as forms of women's responses to violence.

Radical feminist therapy understands the socialization of women as a process that is shaped by the domination of women by men, the power of men over women and the sexualization of women. A woman's experience of her body, as a sexualized object, is therefore a central topic for exploration in therapy. MacKinnon (1982: 16–17) explains the radical feminist view:

the female gender stereotype is . . . in fact, sexual. Vulnerability means the appearance/reality of easy sexual access; passivity means disabled resistance, enforced by trained physical weakness; softness means pregnability by something hard. Incompetence seeks help as vulnerability seeks shelter, inviting the embrace that becomes the invasion . . . Socially, femaleness means femininity, which means attractiveness, which means sexual availability on male terms. Gender socialization is the process through which women internalize themselves as sexual beings, as beings that exist for men . . . Women who resist or fail, including those who never did fit – for example, Black and lower-class women who cannot survive if they are soft and weak and incompetent, assertively self-respecting women, women with ambitions of male dimensions – are considered less female, lesser women.

The argument here is that the image of women as sexual objects, as 'beings that exist for men', is at the heart of women's gender roles, even though it may be overlaid by liberal rhetoric.

The application of these ideas in radical feminist practice is illustrated by the kinds of questions that Burstow (1992: 44–5) suggests a feminist counsellor or therapist should ask herself on first meeting a new client. For example, Burstow would observe whether the woman looked exhausted or frightened, wore make-up, high heels and tight clothing, or was extremely thin. These questions yield information about how oppressed the client might be. For example, a woman who wore lipstick, mascara, high heels and tight clothes could be considered to be overtly 'sexualized'. The aim of radical feminist therapy is to help the client to identify the ways in which she is oppressed, and to be empowered to bring about change. Often, the kinds of change processes that the client will be encouraged to pursue may well involve different forms of community action, and generally becoming more 'woman-identified'.

Radical feminist therapy also necessarily involves questioning the role of mainstream therapies in supporting oppressive attitudes. This is expressed particularly forcefully by McLellan (1999: 336):

> The institution of psychotherapy needs practitioners who have the courage to be fiercely independent of mainstream society, rather than its servants. Positioning ourselves apart from mainstream attitudes and culture allows us to analyse the socio-political dynamics of individual personal distress in a more objective way . . . and recognise the role of mystification and oppression . . . when honesty and the pursuit of justice are central to a therapist's work, emotional and psychological health is made possible.

A key concept here is the idea of *mystification*: the ideas and beliefs that are promoted by those in power are assimilated by those without power, in ways that lead them to deny the truth of their situation.

Therapist as outlaw: the need for a feminist ethics

The practice of feminist counselling or psychotherapy involves the practitioner in acting not only from a therapeutic standpoint, but also espousing a set of values and a political agenda. Even in an approach such as that developed by the Stone Center, which would appear to be based more in cultural feminism than in the more activist radical or socialist versions of feminism (Enns 1992), there are clear values and political elements. This tendency has led most feminist counsellors to be highly aware of the ethical dilemmas arising from their work. These dilemmas derive from a number of sources:

- Critics of feminism may accuse feminist practitioners of misusing the therapeutic relationship to promote feminist ideology or recruit members for feminist organizations.
- The political dimension of feminism makes women aware of power inequalities in general, but specifically the power difference inherent in any client–counsellor relationship.

- Feminist counsellors and psychotherapists and their clients may be drawn from relatively small communities of like-minded women, leading to greater possibilities for potentially destructive dual relationships.
- Women's moral decision-making makes use of intuition and feeling as well as logical analysis, and takes account of how moral actions have an impact on relationships. As a result, there are times when ethical codes and guidelines formulated from a male perspective may not be wholly appropriate to feminist practice.
- There can be occasions when the emphasis in feminist counselling theory on mutuality and the existence of a genuine, transparent relationship between counsellor and client may contribute to a lack of clarity in therapeutic boundaries.

These factors map out a significant area of difference between feminist practice and mainstream thinking, and have stimulated considerable debate within the feminist therapy literature.

It is important to note here that feminist counselling and psychotherapy has largely evolved in isolation from mainstream organizational and institutional settings. For many feminists, the office blocks of professional power and authority represent patriarchal structures to be subverted and opposed. As Wooley (1994: 320–1) has written, the experience of being a feminist practitioner can be similar to that of professional 'outlaw':

> many of our most fundamental values and sensibilities are at variance with the way things are 'supposed' to be . . . most female therapists have an assortment of fears related to the way they have quietly, often secretly, diverged from the dictates of their training and the official version of psychotherapy.

Taylor (1995: 109) perhaps expressed the same feelings when she wrote that 'I reached the point in my work as a psychotherapist where I could no longer stand apart from my women clients and play dumb.' It is this unwillingness to be detached, to 'stand apart', that lies at the heart of the feminist ethical dilemma.

Feminist counsellors and psychotherapists have addressed these ethical issues in two ways. First, a great deal of feminist counselling takes place in the context of 'collective' feminist organizations, such as women's therapy centres or rape crisis centres. Typically, members of these organizations are well aware of moral and ethical dilemmas associated with feminist practice, and set up effective mechanisms for reviewing the operation of their agency in the light of such issues. Second, there have been some attempts to create a feminist ethical code. The following sections are part of the ethical guidelines used by the Feminist Therapy Institute in Denver, Colorado (Rave and Larsen 1995: 40–1):

- A feminist therapist increases her accessibility to and for a wide range of clients . . . through flexible delivery of services. Where appropriate, the feminist therapist assists clients in accessing other services.
- A feminist therapist discloses information to the client which facilitates the therapeutic process. The therapist is responsible for using self-disclosure with purpose and discretion in the interests of the client.

- A feminist therapist is actively involved in her community. As a result, she is expecially sensitive about confidentiality. Recognizing that her clients' concerns and general well-being are primary, she self-monitors both public and private statements and comments.
- A feminist therapist actively questions other therapeutic practices in her community that appear abusive to clients or therapists, and when possible, intervenes.
- A feminist therapist seeks multiple avenues for impacting change, including public education and advocacy within professional organizations, lobbying for legislative actions and other appropriate activities.

These guidelines offer a useful supplement to the ethical codes published by established professional associations (see Chapter 15). The latter tend to focus mainly on the ethical implications of direct work with clients, and the impact of this work on immediate family members and significant others. The feminist code, by contrast, stresses the importance for counsellors of keeping in mind their broader social responsibilities and roles.

Conclusions: issues in feminist counselling

Feminist counselling is a relatively recent addition to the range of therapy models on offer. The progress of feminist counselling and psychotherapy over the past decade has been impressive, given the fact that it represents a radical perspective that is not likely to find any special favour in male-dominated universities, training institutes or funding agencies. There has been an explosion of new ideas and methods, books, a specialized journal (*Women and Therapy*) and applications of feminist approaches to different client groups. And, of course, many counsellors who have been influenced by these ideas and principles would not necessarily explicitly label themselves as feminist in theoretical orientation. Feminist practitioners have been in the vanguard of the movement to make counselling more socially aware and user-friendly. Feminist theory has provided a philosophical, historical and social dimension that has enabled feminist counselling to move beyond a purely psychological, individualized view of the person. At the same time, there appears to have been little or no research into feminist counselling and psychotherapy, at least in the sense of traditional outcome research. Partly this may be due to the influence of feminist critiques of mainstream 'positivist' research designs. It is certainly also due to difficulties in getting funding for such studies. But the absence of research evidence may, in the longer term, have the effect of excluding feminist therapy from settings, such as health agencies, that increasingly will only support 'evidence-based' approaches.

This chapter began by reviewing the debates within feminism, between the liberal, cultural, radical and socialist philosophical/political stances. There are other debates, too, over the relevance of Western feminisms for women from other cultures, and the significance of age and disability from a feminist perspective. There are some lesbian writers, such as Kitzinger and Perkins (1993), who argue powerfully that any form of therapy is a distraction from political and community action. But these debates are signs of the vigour of the feminist tradition.

Chapter summary

- Feminist approaches to counselling have become increasingly influential and important in recent years; feminist counselling represents an attempt to integrate political and social issues into counselling in a meaningful way.

- It is difficult to define feminist counselling because it is difficult to define feminism itself. Four major feminist traditions can be identified: liberal, cultural, radical and socialist.

- Much of the early writing of feminist-inspired theorists involved constructing a critique of male-dominated traditional psychological and psychotherapeutic theories.

- A number of distinctive approaches to contemporary feminist counselling can be identified.

- The integrative approach draws upon a wide variety of counselling techniques, but selects methods and techniques according to feminist principles.

- The Stone Center model is basically psychodynamic in orientation, but gives much more emphasis to concepts of mutuality, care and empathy.

- Radical feminist practice focuses mainly on overcoming social oppression, in particular violence against women.

- The philosophical and political stance associated with feminism has resulted in the development of a feminist ethics.

- There is a high degree of debate around feminist counselling. For example, some radical lesbian feminist writers argue that the existence of counselling and psychotherapy diverts attention away from collective political action. Others would argue that much feminist counselling reflects the experience of white middle-class women, and does not represent the reality of black women.

- While many women counsellors would claim to be influenced by feminist ideas, there is a lack of training courses or other support systems for followers of this approach.

Topics for reflection and discussion

1 Where do you place yourself in relation to the four main feminist traditions (liberal, cultural, radical and socialist)? What are the implications of this for your practice as a counsellor?

2 To what extent is feminist counselling only appropriate or helpful for women who already hold feminist beliefs? Does feminist counselling necessarily imply conversion to a feminist way of thinking?

3 In what ways can male counsellors be influenced by feminist approaches? Does it make sense for a man to call himself a feminist counsellor?

4 From a standpoint in feminist values, how would you set about assessing the effectiveness of feminist counselling? How might your research differ from that carried out (mainly by men) into other approaches to counselling and psychotherapy?

5 Some feminist therapists, such as Burstow (this chapter) or Holland (Chapter 14), have been very critical of the way in which psychiatry has oppressed women through such interventions as drug treatment, hospitalization and ECT. Should feminist counsellors reject any involvement with psychiatry? What ways might there be of developing a constructive relationship with the psychiatric profession?

6 Do any aspects of feminist ethical guidelines deserve to be transferred into the ethical codes for counselling in general?

7 The concept of the body is central in much feminist theory. For example, women's bodies are sexual objects, or may be the site for eating problems or self-mutilation. What might be the implications for counselling practice of this focus on the body?

8 Discuss Brown's (1990: 3) statement that: 'feminist therapy and feminist therapy theory have been developed by and with white women. Currently, feminist therapy theory is neither diverse nor complex in the reality it reflects. It has been deficient from the start in its inclusiveness of the lives and realities of women of color, poor or working-class women, non-North American women, women over sixty-five, or women with disabilities . . . It seems as if the lives of [these] women . . . have been too alien to comprehend, and too far from sight to be included in the theories of feminist therapists.'

Key terms and concepts

care

consciousness-raising

cultural feminism

dependency

egalitarian relationship

gender

liberal feminism

mutuality

oppression

radical feminism

relatedness

relational perspective

sexism

sexualization

socialist feminism

Stone Center

violence

Suggested further reading

A classic text, which in many ways opened up the field of women and counselling, is *Women and Mental Health,* edited by Howell and Bayes (1981). The two
books from the Stone Center collective, *Women's Growth in Connection* (Jordan *et al.*
1991) and *Women's Growth in Diversity* (Jordan 1997), present a persuasive and
coherent model of feminist practice that has been applied to a range of different
presenting problems and client groups. Jordan (2000) provides an accessible brief
introduction to this approach.

The books by Burstow (1991) and Kitzinger and Perkins (1993) describe a form
of feminist practice (or anti-practice) that is more overtly political, but that draws
upon important feminist traditions.

The journal *Women and Therapy* is also well worth reading for its coverage of
feminist research and scholarship.

9 Narrative approaches to counselling: working with stories

Introduction

One of the themes that run through this book is the relationship between counselling and science. In Chapter 2, there was some discussion of the ways in which counselling merged as a largely secular scientifically based replacement for the religious practice of 'cure of souls'. In earlier chapters on different theories and models of counselling, it was clear that some approaches, primarily the cognitive–behavioural, placed great emphasis on being able to demonstrate the scientific validity of their ideas and methods. The approach to counselling introduced in the present chapter has a somewhat different stance in relation to scientific ways of thinking. The psychologist Jerome Bruner (1990) has argued that there exist two quite different ways of knowing the world. There is what he calls *paradigmatic* knowing, which involves creating abstract models of reality. Then there is *narrative* knowing, which is based on a process of making sense of the world by telling stories. Bruner suggests that in everyday life we are surrounded by stories. We tell ourselves and each other stories all of the time. We structure, store and communicate our experiences through stories. We live in a culture that is saturated with stories – myths, novels, TV soaps, office gossip, family histories and so on. Yet, Bruner points out, on the whole social science and psychology have until recently paid very little attention to stories. Social scientists and psychologists have been intent on constructing paradigmatic, scientific models of the world. The stories told by research subjects in psychological experiments, informants in sociological surveys or clients in counselling and psychotherapy sessions have been listened to [perhaps], but have then been converted into abstract categories, concepts or variables. The actual story has been largely ignored. For Bruner, true knowledge of the world requires an interplay between both ways of knowing, between scientific abstractions and everyday stories. He suggests we should take stories more seriously.

The writings of Bruner and other key figures in what has become known as the 'narrative turn' in psychology (Sarbin 1986; Howard 1991) have stimulated an explosion of interest in narrative, which has found expression within the counselling and psychotherapy field in the form of an emerging narrative approach (McLeod 1996, 1997). The aim of this chapter is to introduce some of the key ideas and methods that have been employed within this rapidly developing approach.

Competing ways of understanding narrative

Narrative has become an enormously popular topic. There is a vast literature on narrative, written by anthropologists, sociologists, historians and scholars in linguistics, cultural studies and literary criticism, as well as by psychologists and therapists. Partly this reflects the ubiquity of narratives: stories are everywhere. But partly, too, it reflects an important aspect of what has become known as the postmodern era in which we live. The industrialized, scientific, mass society that most of us live in is dominated by the values of modernity: belief in progress, rationality, science. Many people have argued that we are moving into a postmodern era (Lyon 1994), in which the old certainties have been shattered, where it is hard to believe any more in 'grand theories' or systems of thought, such as Marxism, science or psychoanalysis. What are left to us in this postmodern world, some have said, are the stories we tell each other. We get by on local truths or local knowledges rather than espousing all-encompassing ideologies. We live in a multicultural world, which encourages an appreciation of the diversity of narratives that exist within a global community. Multiculturalism also lends an awareness that 'grand narratives' have always served to silence the voices of those in the minority, those who do not fit.

These are some of the reasons why the literature on narrative is large and complex, and potentially confusing. For instance, it is possible to find several different definitions of 'narrative' and 'story'. For the purpose of this chapter, a story is taken to be an account of a past event that is structured with a beginning, middle and end, and communicates information about a sequence of intended actions undertaken by a person or group. A story is therefore different from a mere chronicle of events. A well constructed story has some degree of dramatic quality, and conveys suspense and feeling and something about the personality of both the teller of the story and the characters within it. A story will also usually have some evaluative element. There is often a 'moral' to a story. A story is told to 'make a point'. A narrative, by contrast, is a more inclusive term that is used to describe a general process of creating an account of what has happened. A narrative may include several discrete stories, but may also include commentaries on these stories, linking passages and explanations. The whole of what a client says in a counselling session can therefore be seen as his or her 'narrative', which may be built around the telling of three or four discrete 'stories' over the course of the hour.

The concept of narrative has been used in quite different ways by representatives of competing theoretical approaches to counselling and psychotherapy. There have been three quite distinct lines of development in relation to the evolution of a 'narrative-informed' or 'narrative-oriented' model of therapy. The three theoretical orientations that have been most involved in this area are the psychodynamic, constructivist and social constructionist approaches (McLeod 1997). Most of the remainder of this chapter concentrates on the contribution of a social constructionist approach to narrative therapy, because that is the approach that has most fully exploited narrative ideas. However, before we move on to a fuller exploration of that set of ideas, it is necessary to review briefly the way that psychodynamic and cognitive/constructivist counselors and therapists have looked at story and narrative.

Psychodynamic approaches to narrative

Psychoanalytic and psychodynamic therapists and counsellors have shown a lot of interest in narrative, and have looked at this phenomenon in two main ways. First, the stories told by clients or patients have been seen as conveying information about the person's habitual ways of relating to others. Second, the role of the therapist has been viewed as that of helping the client to arrive at an alternative, and more satisfactory, way of telling their life story.

The first of these topics, the value of the client's story as a source of information about recurring patterns of conflict within their relationships, has been explored by Strupp and Binder (1984) and by Luborsky and Crits-Christoph (1990). Although Strupp and Luborsky have taken broadly similar approaches to this issue, the work of Luborsky's research group, based at the University of Pennsylvania, is better known and more extensive. The key source for these studies is Luborsky and Crits-Christoph (1990), although Luborsky *et al.* (1992, 1994) have compiled excellent short reviews of their research programme and its clinical implications.

The Luborsky group has observed that although clients in therapy tell stories about their relationships with many different people (for instance, their spouse/partner, family members, friends, the therapist), it is nevertheless possible to detect consistent themes and conflicts running through all, or most, of the stories produced by an individual. Luborsky labels this the core conflictual relationship theme (CCRT). Moreover, Luborsky suggests that these stories are structured in a particular way, around three structural elements. The story expresses the wish of the person in relation to others, the response of the other and finally the response of self. This model allows the meaning of what might be a convoluted and complex story told by a client to be summarized in a relatively simple form. An example of a CCRT analysis of a client's story is given in Box 9.1. In general, the most frequently reported client wishes are 'to be close and accepted', 'to be loved and understood' and 'to assert self and be independent'. The most common responses from others are 'rejecting and opposing' and 'controlling', and the most frequent responses of self are 'disappointed and depressed', 'unreceptive' and 'helpless' (Luborsky *et al.* 1994). In their research studies, Luborsky and his colleagues have found that clients tell an average of four stories in each session, usually about events that have taken place in the last two weeks, and that around

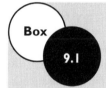

Box 9.1

Analysing a core conflictual relationship theme: the case of Miss Smithfield

To illustrate the application of the CCRT method, Luborsky *et al.* (1994) have published their analysis of the relationship themes expressed in a pre-therapy interview by a young woman, Miss Smithfield. Some examples of the stories told by this client are given below.

Story 1

> I met him at the end of my [university] programme, and I was staying, I stayed longer than the programme, but I met him at the end of my programme in Jakarta, and everything just clicked, perfectly. Both of us politically had the same mind set, emotionally had very similar mind sets, and culturally we just fascinated each other because of the diifferences . . . so we spent the rest of our time together . . . we married, and I returned to this country [the USA] not too long afterwards. The plan was that he was going to finish writing his thesis . . . come to this country till I graduated, and then we would both have gone back over . . . but he disappeared six months after I came back . . . actually I don't know exactly what has happened to him . . . Nobody knows what has happened . . . I don't know . . . I think its better for my own sanity that I don't.

I decided from after about a year from the time he disappeared that it was, I needed to get on with my own life and live it as best I could.

Story 2

I've been raped a total of five times. Four times in the past few years though. They're all knowledge rapes. People that I thought I knew, in one sense or another, and that's really put a damper on my trust . . . one of the rapes . . . happened in Indonesia. It was with a man that I had once been seeing before I met my husband, and I'd broken up with him . . . but he was still willing to help me out when I got sick, so I went down to Bandung to heal myself, and I was very weak at the time, and he expected because he was caring for me he would have sexual rights as well, and I could not fight him physically because I was very weak . . . he forced me into this position . . . he had been with another woman who had VD . . . and he knowably gave it to me because he was mad at me for breaking off with him . . .

Story 3

I was the 'school scapegoat' and was avoided and picked on . . . my parents are both highly intelligent individuals . . . they're good people, and now I'm beginning to have a better relationship with them . . . there's less pressure, there's less pressure now . . . they never really had any specific goals, but they wanted me to make it . . . I mean they did push me in my music because I was a talented oboe player for quite a while . . . they helped and supported me . . . but at times they forced me to practise an hour and a half per day or whatever to keep me going . . . I wanted to go out and play and run around in the woods with my friends and what friends I did have at that point.

On the basis of these stories, and several other stories told by this client in a lengthy and detailed interview, Luborsky et al. (1994: 178) arrived at a CCRT formulation:

I wish to resist domination and not to be forced to submit or to be over-powered. But the other person dominates, takes control and overpowers me. Then I feel dominated, submissive, helpless and victimized.

They suggest that underlying this relationship pattern there may have been a less conscious desire to submit to another, to be controlled. Such a wish can be seen to have its origins in early childhood experience: for example, in issues around separation from the mother. The analysis of Miss Smithfield's narrative shows how the CCRT approach strips the narrative from its context, and rigorously focuses in on core themes associated with emotionally very basic early object relationships. It is also worth noting that the CCRT method tends to highlight conflictual aspects of the person's story, in contrast to the approach taken by White and Epston (1990) of focusing on what the story conveys about the positive, life-enhancing capabilities of the person.

80 per cent of the responses from others and of self are clearly negative, but become more positive as therapy progresses.

The research carried out by Luborsky and his collaborators has established the importance of the CCRT as a unit for analysing therapy process. However, their model also has many implications for practice. Luborsky's main aim has been to provide therapists with a straighforward and easy-to-use method of both making interpretations and analysing transference. It has been shown (Luborsky and Crits-Christoph 1990) that interpretations accurately based on CCRT elements are highly effective in promoting insight, although overall the accuracy of therapist interpretations assessed by this technique tends to be low, and the relationship with the therapist (the transference) tends to correspond to the CCRT pattern found in stories about other people. The CCRT model therefore serves as a highly practical method for improving the effectiveness of psychodynamic counselling, by acting as a conceptual tool that counsellors and psychotherapists can use to enhance the accuracy of their interpretations.

Several other psychoanalytic theorists have made important contributions to an understanding of the role of narrative in therapy. Spence (1982) has argued for a distinction betwen narrative truth and historical truth. Whereas Freud and other early psychoanalytic therapists believed that free association and dream analysis were unearthing evidence about early childhood conflicts that actually occurred, Spence points out that it is seldom possible to verify in an objective sense whether or not these childhood events took place. He suggests that what therapists do is to help the client to arrive at a narrative truth, a story that makes sense and has sufficient correspondence with the historical data that are available. Another significant psychoanalytic writer on narrative has been Schafer (1992), who regards the interpretations made by the therapist over a period of time as comprising a 're-telling' of the client's story in the form of a psychoanalytic narrative. Eventually, the client comes to see his or her life in psychoanalytic terms. In similar fashion, Schafer would argue, a client of person-centred counselling would develop a Rogerian narrative account of their life, and a cognitive–behavioural client would acquire a cognitive–behavioural story. Finally, McAdams (1985, 1993) has explored the underlying or unconscious narrative structures, such as myths, that people use to give shape to their life as a whole.

The psychoanalytic or psychodynamic tradition has generated a wealth of powerful and applicable ideas about the role of narrative in therapy. However, for psychodynamic writers and practitioners an interest in narrative is only an adjunct to the real business of identifying unconscious material, interpreting the transference and so on. Luborsky, Schafer and others have aimed not to create a narrative therapy, but to practise psychodynamic therapy in a narrative-informed fashion.

Cognitive/constructivist approaches to narrative

The constructivist approach to counselling, introduced in Chapter 5, has been associated with many significant advances in the use of narrative in counselling and psychotherapy. The basic goal of constructivist therapy is to work with the ways that the person constructs meaning in their life. These meanings are understood as comprising cognitive schemas, and the stories that the person tells reflect the underlying structure of the cognitive schemas through which reality is interpreted. Following the roots of constructivism in the cognitive–behavioural tradition, there is a strong tendency in this approach to work very actively with the story, and to adopt techniques for bringing about change within a limited period of time. Two aspects of constructivist narrative counselling are of particular importance: identifying conflicting stories, and the use of metaphor.

The work of Russell has been influential in drawing attention to the role of cognitive conflict in therapeutic change (Russell and van den Boek 1992; Russell *et al.* 1993). Russell suggests that, in the course of therapy, a client will almost certainly tell different types of story about the same situation or relationship. For example, a client may usually refer to his inability to cope with stress at work, but may occasionally let slip some stories of how he has managed to deal with his work demands without becoming stressed. Russell suggests that at this point the client can be seen to have activated two quite different schemas relating to the same set of events. And, just as Piaget and other developmental psychologists have shown that cognitive development in childhood is triggered by the requirement to integrate competing schemas, the client may arrive at a higher level of understanding as a result of reflecting (with the help of the therapist) on the difference between these two stories. To return to the example of the stressed worker, this client may become able to construct a 'higher-order' story, which encompasses both the 'stressed at work' and 'not stressed at work stories'. A story along the lines of 'when I make sure I ask for the support and help I need, I can avoid becoming too stressed' would subsume both the previous stories, and also serve as a guide for coping better in future. Behind this new story is a new underlying schema that might feature a definition of self as worthy of support from others, in contrast to the previous underlying self-schema that centred on a sense of self as undeserving.

Another version of this theory is the solution-focused therapy of de Shazer (1985). In this approach, little attention is paid to the contrast between alternative narrative accounts of the same events. Instead, the client is invited to talk exclusively about solution stories, or positive outcome stories, and to use these stories to learn more about how they can achieve their goals in life. In some respects the solution-focused approach can appear to operate as a kind of version of behaviourism in which the client is reinforced for 'positive' behaviour, and 'negative' behaviour is ignored and therefore is extinguished. Certainly, little time is spent examining any conflicts between problem-saturated stories and solution stories. However, in the end the effect on the client is probably the same as envisaged by Russell. The energetic and unremitting pursuit by the therapist of solutions has the effect of producing a kind of cognitive crisis in the client, a realization that their problem story or stories are no longer tenable. In the aftermath of this crisis, the client is eager to find another story to tell.

The use of metaphor in constructivist counselling has already been discussed in Chapter 5. The constructivist model of narrative change proposed by Goncalves

(1995: 158) defines its goal as empowering the client to use narrative techniques to 'develop a continuous sense of actorship and authorship in his/her life'. What is particularly striking about Goncalves's work is his continuing effort to introduce incongruity and conflict into the client's way of construing the world. Over and over again, the client is invited to retell the story of key events in different ways: objectively, subjectively, metaphorically. The Goncalves (1995) model of constructivist narrative therapy takes the client through a five-stage programme:

Phase 1: *Recalling narratives.* Identification of memories of important life events, using guided imagery exercises to facilitate recall. Homework assignment involving writing key stories from each year of life. Review of collected life stories to select a 'prototype' narrative.

Phase 2: *Objectifying narratives.* Retelling important narratives in ways that 'bring the reader into the text': for example, through giving greater attention to sensory cues – visual, auditory, olfactory, gustatory, tactile. Collecting documents and artefacts (e.g. photographs, music, letters) that will further 'objectify' the story by defining its external referents.

Phase 3: *Subjectifying narratives.* The aim of this stage is to increase the client's awareness of his or her inner experience of the narrative. Exercises are used in which the therapist triggers recall of a significant story and then asks the client to focus on the inner experience of the event through instructions such as 'Allow yourself to be aware only of what you are experiencing now.'

Phase 4: *Metaphorizing narratives.* The client is trained in methods of generating metaphoric associations to stories, and then the origins of these images in his or her life are explored.

Phase 5: *Projecting narratives.* The client is given practice in constructing alternative metaphors, drawn from literature and art. These new root metaphors are implemented within sessions and then in everyday life.

An example of this approach in action is given in Box 9.2.

Box

9.2

Constructing a new life-metaphor

The process of constructivist narrative therapy is described in a case published by Goncalves (1993). The client, Fernando, was a 23-year-old single university student. Although he had initially wanted to study astronomy, he had not been accepted on to the course, so was now following a computer science programme. He had failed courses in his first year of university studies, was feeling depressed and worthless, and had started to doubt his ability. Although he had been successful in gaining a job as a substitute teacher in a school, he was unable to enjoy this role. He was the oldest of five children. He described his mother as accepting and his father as cold and distant, always involved in his work. Both his mother and father had high expectations that Fernando would be successful in his studies. He felt that 'I am already 23 and absolutely unable to make any sense out of my life.'

In the early phase of therapy, Fernando was encouraged to reflect on his recollection of the most significant narratives from any period of his life. He came up with one story that seemed particularly important to him:

> In my first day at college there was a particular incident that has marked me definitely. The door of the classroom was open, and the professor was walking restlessly and silently for 10 minutes from one side to another. Everybody was wondering what was going to happen. Suddenly, the professor closed the door and began to query the students one by one about why they had chosen computer science as a major and what was their GPA [grade point average], commenting simultaneously that if they didn't have this major as their first choice or had a low GPA they should quit right away.
>
> (Goncalves 1993: 144)

It is not hard to imagine some of the reasons why this story might have great resonance for Fernando, given his life experiences.

The next phases of therapy involved Fernando in re-experiencing the event behind this story in as much detail as possible. For example, at the moment in the story when the professor approached him to ask about his GPA grades he retold the story in these words: 'as I see the professor coming to me, I am feeling high tension in my back . . . scared and panicked . . . everybody is going to see me freezing . . . I must be an absolute piece of shit' (Goncalves 1993: 151).

Following this, the client was given some training in thinking metaphorically, and invited to generate metaphors associated with his story. The metaphor he eventually arrived at was 'a creeping, avoiding actor'. He commented that this was not only an 'ideal title' for the story of the professor, but represented 'the story of my life . . . my script'.

The final stage of therapy was to develop alternative metaphors and then to apply these new images in everyday life. Fernando initially took some time to free himself of the 'creeping, avoiding actor' life-metaphor, and experimented with various new self-images. Eventually, these experiments crystallized around a new core metaphor. Goncalves (1993: 158) describes this stage of the therapy:

> when the time came for the construction of an alternative metaphor of his prototype narrative, he came up with an interesting structural metaphor – private investigator. In fact, his hypersensitivity to social cues had allowed him to construct good observing and decentring skills. Sherlock Holmes was indeed one of his favourite characters in his past reading.

Fernando and his therapist spent the remaining time in therapy applying this new sense of self to a variety of life situations.

The work of Goncalves (1993, 1994, 1995) is representative of other constructivist approaches to working with narrative and metaphor. The therapist or counsellor takes an active role in suggesting exercises and encouraging consideration of new, alternative storylines and images. The client is guided in the direction of getting in touch with the direct experiential referents of the story. The aim is to experience the emotions and physical sensations that are associated with a story, since there are more possibilities for change generated by specific, detailed narratives than by vague and general accounts of events. The focus is on a change process occurring at the individual level. The goal is to facilitate change in how the person makes sense of the world, how they think, perceive and feel.

Social constructionist narrative therapy

Social constructionism is a philosophical position that regards personal experience and meaning as being not created merely by the individual (the constructivist position) but something embedded in a culture and shaped by that culture. People are social beings. Personal identity is a product of the history of the culture, the position of the person in society and the linguistic resources available to the individual. Social constructionism is mainly associated with the writings of Gergen (1985, 1994), although in fact it is more accurately understood as a broad movement within philosophy, humanities and the social sciences. From a social constructionist perspective, narrative represents an essential bridge between individual experience and the cultural system. We are born into a world of stories. A culture is structured around myths, legends, family tales and other stories that have existed since long before we are born, and will continue long after we die. We construct a personal identity by aligning ourselves with some of these stories, by 'dwelling within' them.

Applied to therapy, social constructionism does not look for answers in terms of change in internal psychological processes. Indeed, the whole notion that an inner psychological reality exists is questionable from a social constructionist stance. The idea of a 'true, core self' is not a fixed truth, but is part of a romantic narrative that people in Western societies tell themselves about what it means to be a person (Gergen 1991). Instead, social constructionist therapists look at what is happening within a culture or community, and the relationship between a troubled person (or client) and that community.

The main inspiration for social constructionist narrative counselling or therapy has come from the work of Michael White and David Epston. Perhaps because they live in Australia (White) and New Zealand (Epston), these therapists have been able to evolve an approach which is radically different from mainstream therapies. Although their initial training and background was in family therapy, their ideas can be and have been used in work with individuals, couples and groups. Following the publication of their main book, *Narrative Means to Therapeutic Ends*, in 1990, their approach has been extended to new audiences by books from Parry and Doan (1994) and Monk *et al.* (1996).

The key ideas that underpin social constructionist narrative therapy can be summarized as:

- people live their lives within the dominant narratives or knowledges of their culture and family;
- sometimes, there can be a significant mismatch between the dominant narrative and the actual life experience of the person, or the dominant narrative can construct a life that is impoverished or subjugated;
- one of the main taks of a therapist is to help the client to externalize the problem, to see it as a story that exists outside of them;
- the therapist also works at deconstructing the dominant narrative, reducing its hold over the person;
- another therapist task involves helping the client to identify unique outcomes or 'sparkling moments' – times when they have escaped from the clutches of the dominant narrative;
- the therapist adopts a not-knowing stance in relation to the client; the client is the expert on his or her story and how to change it (Anderson and Goolishian 1992; Hoffman 1992); at the completion of therapy the client is invited back as a 'consultant', to share their knowledge for the benefit of future clients;
- a central aim of therapy is to assist the person to re-author their story and to perform this new story within their community;
- another aim of therapy is to help the person to complete important life transitions;
- although much of the therapy is based on conversation and dialogue, written or literary communications such as letters and certificates are used because they give the client a permanent and 'authoritative' version of the new story;
- where possible, cultural resources, such as support groups or family networks, are enlisted to help a person to consolidate and live a re-authored story, and to provide supportive audiences.

Many of these features can be observed in the case of Rose (Box 9.3) (Epston *et al.* 1992). Here it can be seen that this kind of narrative therapy tends to be of fairly short duration, with high levels of therapist activity. The therapist is clearly warm and affirming, adopting a style of relating to the client that is reminiscent of Carl Rogers in the degree of hope that is transmitted, and in the implicit belief in the client's capacity to grow and change in positive ways.

Externalizing the problem

One of the distinctive features of narrative therapy is the procedure that White and Epston (1990) refer to as externalizing the problem. They argue that many clients enter counselling with a sense that the problem is a part of them, it is inherent in who they are as a person. When this happens, people can all too readily arrive at a 'totalising' position where their whole sense of self, and the

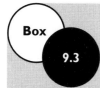

Box

9.3

Re-authoring therapy: Rose's story

An example of how the originally systemic, family-oriented approach of White and Epston can be applied in individual counselling is provided by the case of Rose (Epston *et al.* 1992). Rose had lost her job as a receptionist/video-camera operator at an advertising agency, because she would 'crack up' and burst into tears if interrupted while completing a work task. When she met David Epston, she told him that 'I don't have a base inside myself'. He replied, 'there must be a story behind this. Do you feel like telling me about it?' She then talked about the physical abuse she had received from her father, a well respected parish minister. Following this first session, Epston sent her a lengthy letter, which began:

Dear Rose,

It was a very pleasing experience to meet up with you and hear some of your story, a story of both protest and survival against what you understood to be an attempt to destroy your life. And you furthered that protest yesterday by coming and telling me that story. I would imagine that you had not been able to tell anyone for fear of being disbelieved. I feel privileged that you shared it with me and hope that sharing it relieved you of some of its weight. I can see how such a history could have left you the legacy you described – a sense of not seeming 'to have a base'.

(Epston *et al.* 1992: 103)

The rest of the letter retold the story that Rose had recounted during the counselling session, but retelling it as a story of courage, survival, and hope. The letter ended with:

I look forward to meeting you again to assist you to write a new history of events in your life, a new history that could predict a very different kind of future than your old history.

Yours sincerely,
David.

The next counselling session was one month later. During the interval, Rose had applied for and secured a job as a chef (her preferred occupation), and had been so successful in this role that the restaurant owner had left her in charge while he took his holidays. She had renewed her relationship with her mother, and had met with each of her siblings to talk through the message of the letter with them. She felt her life was 'on the right track'. After this second meeting, Epston sent another letter, which opened:

Dear Rose,

Reading the letter, which provided you with a different story, seems to have led to 'a sense of relief . . . it was normal I had problems . . . it wasn't my fault . . . I had previously felt weak and vulnerable . . . and that I should have got it all together by now.' Instead, you began to appreciate more fully that 'I felt I had made a start . . . I was definitely on the right track.' And I suspect now that you are realizing that you have been on the 'right track' for some time now; if not, as you put it, you would have become 'disillusioned . . . and ended my life'. Well, there is a lot of life in you, and it is there for all to see!

(p. 105)

There was one other counselling session, and then six months later Rose was invited to join her therapist as a 'consultant to others' so that 'the knowledges that have been resurrected and/or generated in therapy can be documented' (p. 106). During this consultation meeting, Rose gave her explanation of how she had been helped:

Having the story [the first letter] gave me a point of reference to look back at, to read it through, to think about it and form my own opinions from what we had discussed and draw my own conclusions. I remember getting the letter from the letter box, making myself nice cup of tea, sitting down and reading it. I had feelings of 'Yes . . . that's it . . . that's the whole story!' Thinking about it, re-reading it . . . and feeling a lot better about myself . . . Without it, I think I'd still be confused.

(p. 107)

way they talk about themselves, is self-blaming and 'problem-saturated'. The process of externalizing the problem involves separating oneself and one's relationships from the problem, and frees up the person to take a lighter approach to what had previously been defined as a 'deadly serious' issue.

More than this, from a narrative point of view the 'problem' is understood as arising from the 'dominant narrative' that has shaped the client's life and relationships. It is as though the dominant narrative or story is being told or enacted through the life of the client, leaving no space for alternative narratives. Externalizing the problem opens up a space for telling new types of story about the problem, for re-authoring. But how is this achieved?

The first step in externalizing is naming the problem. Ideally, the problem should be defined or phrased in language used by the client. It is normally helpful to make the problem term as specific as possible, and to use humour or imagery. So, for example, with a client who begins therapy referring to a problem as 'panic attacks' or 'depression', it may be useful to agree on a more colloquial problem label, such as 'scary stories' or 'the influence of unreachable standards of perfectionism'. Terms such as 'anxiety', 'panic attacks' or 'depression' may be elements of the dominant discourse of mental health that might have oppressed the client, so even a shift of label away from diagnostic terminology in the direction of everyday language may have the effect of beginning a process of re-authoring. The next step is to explore such issues as: how does the problem stay strong; and how does the problem influence your life? White and Epston (1990) refer to this phase as relative influence questioning. The purpose of these questions is to map out the influence of the problem, and in doing so increasingly to draw a distinction between the person and the problem story. While this is happening, the therapist is alert for the appearance of unique outcome stories, which are stories of times when the problem did not dominate the person, or was not strong. These new or 'sparkling moment' stories form the basis for re-authoring. The task of the narrative therapist is to enable the client to elaborate on these unique outcomes and find audiences for them.

In some of the writing of White and Epston (1990) there appears to be a tendency to represent externalizing as a matter of asking the client a lot of questions. This seems to be a legacy of the family therapy origins of their approach, and there does not seem to be any reason why externalizing should not take place equally well through conversation and dialogue, or through the use of ritual, artistic creations, poetry and music. Parry and Doan (1994) offer some useful examples of the flexible application of externalizing principles in therapy. Box 9.4 gives a summary of the Case of Sneaky Poo. Many famous therapists are associated with celebrated cases: for example, Freud with the Dora case, Rogers with the Gloria film. Sneaky Poo is the classic White and Epston case, and it provides a wonderful example of externalizing at its best.

Enlisting community resources and audiences

It cannot be emphasized enough that social constructionist narrative counselling or therapy is not primarily an individual-centred approach, but is a way of working in the space between the person and the community, drawing on each as necessary. Epston and White (1992) describe therapy as a *rite de passage*, through which the person negotiates passage from one status to another. In a *rite de passage*, the person first undergoes a separation stage, when they become detached from their previous niche or social role. They then enter a liminal stage, a time of exploration and confusion, and then finally proceed to reincorporation, when they re-enter society in a new role. The case of Rose (Box 9.3) illustrates this process well. At the start of therapy Rose was performing an almost child-like, dependent role in society, while at the end she had adopted a quite different, highly adult managerial role as head chef in a restaurant.

Sometimes considerable effort needs to be invested in supporting the continued existence of appropriate and life-enhancing audiences in situations where the client's problem story is enmeshed in all-pervasive cultural narratives. A good example of this kind of situation is work with women experiencing difficulties in

Box 9.4

The Sneaky Poo story

Nick was six years old, and had a long history of encopresis. Hardly a day would go by without a serious incident of soiling: the 'full works' in his underwear. Nick had befriended the 'poo'. He smeared it on walls and hid it behind cupboards. His parents, Sue and Ron, were miserable, embarrassed, despairing. They went for therapy to Michael White's clinic. Through a series of 'relative influence' questions, he discovered that the poo was:

- making a mess of Nick's life by isolating him from other children;
- forcing Sue to question her ability to be a good parent;
- profoundly embarrassing Ron and as a result making him isolate himself by avoiding visiting friends and family;
- affecting all the relationships in the family.

However, in response to further series of questions that mapped the influence of what they came to call 'Sneaky Poo' on the family, they found that:

- there were some occasions when Nick did not allow Sneaky Poo to 'outsmart' him;
- there were also times when Sue and Ron did not allow Sneaky Poo to defeat them.

White built on these 'unique outcomes' by inquiring just how the individual family members managed to be so effective against the problem. Did their success give them any ideas about 'further steps they might take to reclaim their lives from the problem'? All three of them could think of ways forward. Nick said he was 'ready to stop Sneaky Poo from outsmarting him so much'. At their next session, two weeks later, much had changed. In that time, Nick had only had one very minor accident. He had 'taught Sneaky Poo a lesson'. Sue and Ron had started to shift from their states of stress, isolation and embarassment. On the third meeting, three weeks later and at a six-month follow-up everything continued to go well. White encouraged them to reflect on what their success against Sneaky Poo said about their qualities as people, and the strength of their relationships.

Source: White and Epston (1990: 43–8).

controlling their eating. The dominant cultural and family narratives around food, women's bodies and dieting are so powerful (a major international industry) that it can be very difficult for women to find a space to develop unique outcome stories. Epston *et al.* (1995) describe the foundation of the Anti-Anorexic/Bulimic League, which has been conceived not as a support group but as an 'underground resistance movement' or 'community of counter-practice', set up to promote anti-anorexic/bulimic knowledges. Epston *et al.* (1995: 82) give an account of a ritual designed to celebrate the person's liberation from anorexia/bulimia. The new member of the League is presented with:

> The Anti-Anorexic/Bulimic League T-shirt. The recipient is asked to remember all those women executed by anorexia, all those languishing in the private 'concentration camps' throughout the Western world, and is requested to walk forward into her own 'freedom' and if it suits her, to speak out against anorexia/bulimia and all those beliefs and social practices that support it. The mood is lightened when the League's logo is revealed to them on the front of the T-shirt: A circle inside of which is the word DIET with a slash bisecting the 'T'.

The point here is that resistance to the anorexia/bulimia narrative requires joint action, sharing knowledge and resources, and that individuals stand little chance against the huge oppressive power of anorexia/bulimia.

One of the consequences of the collectivist focus of social constructionist therapy has been a questioning of the value of traditional one-to-one therapy as an effective site for constructing new stories. There are many pressures on the therapist in individual counselling and therapy to resort to an expert role, and subtly (or not so subtly) to impose his or her dominant mental health narrative on the patient or client. Gergen and Kaye (1992) and Gergen (1996) have questioned whether the privileged position of the therapist that is intrinsic to traditional modes of therapy is, in the long run, consistent with a social constructionist perspective.

Conclusions

There has been a tremendous excitement and energy surrounding the evolution of the new narrative therapies. For many therapists and clients it has been a liberating experience to be given permission to tell stories. There is a great richness and wisdom in the everyday stories that people tell. However, there has also been a certain amount of confusion and rivalry in the narrative camp: right now narrative is a hot brand name. Up to now, virtually anyone who claimed to be doing narrative counselling or psychotherapy would almost certainly have received previous training in another approach. Training in narrative methods has not been available. This situation raises a number of questions about the future of narrative therapy. Has the success of narative therapy been due to the fact that narrative therapists already possess a basis of skills and theory derived from other models, such as family therapy, psychoanalysis or cognitive therapy? Can training in a purely narrative model be sufficient? Will the formalization and subsequent institutionalization of narrative therapy stifle its creative edge?

Chapter summary

- Recent developments in psychology and social science have drawn attention to the significance of storytelling and narrative as a primary means of making sense of social experience, and communicating with others.

- Within the psychodynamic approach to counselling, stories have been seen as evidence of underlying, unconscious 'relationship themes'.

- Some psychoanalytic theorists have suggested that one of the purposes of therapy is to enable the client to retell their life story in a more satisfactory and coherent manner: for example, within a psychodynamic narrative framework.

- Cognitive–behavioural and constructivist counsellors have become increasingly interested in stories as reflections of cognitive schemas or structures.

- Constructivist counsellors use metaphor as a means of helping the client to create new, 'solution' stories in place of his or her previous 'problem-saturated' stories.

- The most comprehensive approach to narrative counselling has been developed from a social constructionist perspective, influenced by the work of Kenneth Gergen.

- Michael White and David Epston use a constructionist approach that encourages clients first to externalize their story, then to deconstruct it and finally to 're-author' a new story.

- Important and innovative facets of narrative constructionist counselling include the use of community resources and audiences, and the creation of written stories through letters and certificates.

- Narrative approaches to counselling have gained in popularity over the past decade, and many counsellors are beginning to employ narrative techniques in their work.

Topics for reflection and discussion

1 Reflect on the stories that you tell about yourself: for example, in your conversations with friends or work colleagues. How might these stories be analysed from a CCRT perspective? What is the balance between problem-focused stories and solution stories?

2 What are your favourite fictional stories (novels, fairy stories, plays etc.)? Why do these stories appeal to you? Are there ways that these stories capture aspects of your own experience of life, or sense of self?

3 What could be some of the limitations of narrative therapy?

4 Psychoanalytic therapists have criticized the White and Epston approach because it appears to ignore the importance of transference. Do you agree?

Key terms and concepts

core conflictual relationship theme (CCRT)
deconstruction
dominant narrative
externalizing the problem
historical truth
metaphor
narrative knowing
narrative truth

not-knowing stance
paradigmatic knowing
re-authoring
rite de passage
social constructionism
solution-focused therapy
unique outcomes

Suggested further reading

The classic text in this area of counselling is *Narrative Means to Therapeutic Ends* by White and Epston (1990), which is essential reading for anyone interested in understanding more about the 'narrative turn' in therapy. The other key book is *Retelling a Life* by Roy Schafer (1992). Although Schafer is a psychoanalyst, his ideas about narrative go far beyond the constraints of the psychoanalytic tradition. McLeod (1997) offers a general overview of recent developments in the theory and practice of narrative therapy, with particular emphasis on social constructionist approaches. A special issue of the *European Journal of Psychotherapy Counselling and Health* on 'Narrative therapies in Europe' provides a collection of papers representing a range of narrative-informed approaches (McLeod 2000). The book by M. Payne (1999) is an interesting example of an integration of person-centred and narrative approaches.

There are a number of short papers that can be warmly recommended as examples of aspects of narrative therapy in action. Edelson (1993), Penn and Frankfurt (1994), Wigrem (1994) and Omer (1997) give a sense of what narrative therapists and counsellors actually do.

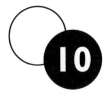

10 Multiculturalism as an approach to counselling

Introduction

One of the defining characteristics of what might be called the 'postmodern' world is the salience of cultural difference. In earlier times, it was much more possible to live as a member of a relatively isolated and self-contained social class or group, and remain relatively unaware of, and be unaffected by, the existence of different forms of life. In recent years, all this has changed. Increasingly, members of so-called 'ethnic minority' groups have become unwilling to be treated as a marginalized, disadvantaged and politically disenfranchised segment of the labour force, and have claimed their voice and their power within society. At the same time, the process of globalization, including the spread of global communications media such as satellite television and the growth of international air travel, have resulted in a huge increase in accessibility of information about other cultures. The images and sounds of other cultures are available in ways that they never have been before. It is impossible to deny that we live in a multicultural world.

Counselling has responded to the trend towards multiculturalism in two ways. The original, foundational approaches to counselling – for example, the psychodynamic, person-centred and cognitive–behavioural models – were clearly 'monocultural' in nature. They were designed and applied in the context of Western (mainly American) industrial society, and had little to say about culture or cultural difference. In the 1960s and 1970s, the counselling and psychotherapy community attempted to react to the political, legislative and personal pressures arising from the equal opportunities movement and debates over racism and equality by developing strategies for building a greater awareness of cultural issues into counselling training and practice. This phase, which generated a substantial literature on 'cross-cultural', 'transcultural' and 'intercultural' approaches to counselling and psychotherapy, represented an attempt to assimilate a cultural dimension into mainstream practice. Useful though these efforts have been in legitimating the experiences and needs of 'minority' clients and counsellors, it can be argued that they do not go far enough. A second response to the issues raised by an awareness of cultural difference has been, therefore, to strive to construct an approach to counselling that places the concept of 'culture' at the centre of its 'image of the person', rather than leaving it to be 'tacked on' as an after-thought. This new, *multicultural* approach (Pedersen 1991) starts from the position that membership of a culture (or cultures) is one of the main influences on the development of personal identity, and that the emotional or behavioural problems that a person might bring to counselling are a reflection of how relationships, morality and a sense of the 'good life' are understood and defined in the culture(s) in which a person lives his or her life. Pedersen (1991) has argued that multiculturalism should be regarded as a *fourth force* in counselling, complementing behaviourism, psychoanalysis and humanistic psychology. The aim of this chapter is to offer an overview of the theory and practice of this important, emergent approach to counselling.

What do we mean by 'culture'?

It is important to avoid any temptation to over-simplify the concept of culture. At one level, culture can be understood simply as 'the way of life of a group of people'. In any attempt to understand 'culture', it is necessary to make use of the contribution made by the social science discipline that has specialized in the task of describing and making sense of different cultures: social anthropology. The tradition in social anthropological research has always been to take the view that it is only possible to do justice to the complexity of a culture by living within it for a considerable period of time, and carrying out a systematic and rigorous set of observations into the way that the members of that culture construct the world that they know through processes such as kinship networks, ritual, mythology and language. In the words of Clifford Geertz, possibly the most influential anthropologist of recent years, culture can be understood as a:

> historically transmitted pattern of meaning embodied in symbols, a system of inherited conceptions expressed in symbolic form by means of which [people] communicate, perpetuate, and develop their knowledge about and attitudes toward life.
>
> (Geertz 1973: 89)

Geertz and other anthropologists would argue that making sense of the culture or way of life of a group of people can only be achieved by trying to understand what lies beneath the surface, the web of meaning and 'inherited conceptions' that are symbolized and expressed in outward behaviour. This external behaviour can be literally anything, from work patterns to the design of Coke bottles to the performance of religious ritual. Everything that members of a culture do represents some aspect of what life means to them. And this meaning has historical roots, it has evolved and been shaped over many years. The image that Geertz (1973) uses to capture all this is that of culture as 'thick'; an appreciation of a culture requires the construction of a 'thick description'.

This idea that the culture within which a person exists is complex and, by implication, difficult to understand has important implications for counsellors. An anthropologist would spend months or years working towards an adequate appreciation of what things mean to a person from another culture. A counsellor attempts to achieve the same goal in a much shorter period of time. Moreover, a counsellor will seldom have an opportunity to observe his or her client interacting within their own cultural milieu; counselling takes place in the world of the counsellor. For these reasons, it is necessary for counsellors to be cautious, and modest, about the extent to which they can ever hope fully to enter the cultural reality inhabited by the client.

The basis for multicultural counselling is therefore *not* exhaustive training in the culture and norms of different groups of people; this is not realistic. Instead, multicultural counsellors should be able to apply a schematic model of the ways in which the personal and relational world of the client, and the client's assumptions about helping or 'cure', can be culturally constructed. The core of multicultural counselling is a sensitivity to the possible ways in which different cultures function and interact, allied to a genuine *curiosity* (Falicov 1995) about the cultural experience of other people.

Although the lived experience of being a member of a culture is 'seamless' and unified, it is nevertheless useful for purposes of clarity to make a distinction between the underlying philosophical or cognitive dimensions of a culture and the expression of these beliefs in patterns of social behaviour. Some of the most important features of cultural identity in the area of underlying beliefs and assumptions are:

- how reality is understood, e.g. dualistic or holistic;
- concept of self (autonomous, bounded, referential versus social, distributed, indexical);
- sense of morality (e.g. choice versus fate, values);
- concept of time (linearity, segmented, future-oriented, respect for elders);
- sense of land, environment, place.

Salient aspects of externally observable dimensions of interpersonal and social life include:

- non-verbal behaviour, eye contact, distance, gesture, touch;
- use of language (e.g. reflexive and analytic versus descriptive; linearity of storytelling);
- kinship and relationship patterns (what is the most important relationship?);
- gender relationships;
- expression of emotion;
- role of healer and theory of healing.

For the multicultural counsellor, these features represent a kind of mental 'checklist' through which the world of the client can be explored, and an appropriate and helpful mutual client–counsellor world can be constructed.

Underlying cultural aspects

The concept of reality

At the most basic level of understanding and comprehension, people in different cultures possess different ideas about the fundamental nature of reality. In Western cultures, people generally hold a *dualistic* view of reality, dividing up the world into two types of entity: mind and body. The mind is 'disembodied', and consists of ideas, concepts and thought. The physical world, on the other hand, is tangible, observable and extended in space. Many writers have argued that it is this mind–body split, originally formulated by the French philosopher Descartes in the sixteenth century, that has made possible the growth of science and the resulting highly technological way of life of people in Western industrial societies. It is also a philosophical position that limits the role of religious and spiritual experience and belief, since it assigns the study of the physical world to science, and therefore places it outside of the realm of the 'sacred'. In terms of social relationships, dualism has had the impact of increasing the division between self and object, or self and other. The 'self' becomes identified with 'mind', and set against and apart from the external world, whether this be the world of things or of other people.

People who belong in many other cultures do not have a dualist conception of the nature of reality, but instead experience the world as a wholeness, as a unity. The philosophical systems associated with Buddhism, Hinduism and other world religions all adopt this position, in which the physical, the mental and the spiritual are understood as aspects or facets of a single unified reality, rather than as separate domains of being.

It might appear as though discussions of the nature of reality are esoteric and obscure, and relate only to the interests of those few people who engage in philosophical discourse and debate. Far from it. The person's understanding of reality cuts through everything that happens in counselling. For example, a dualistic Western culture has generated many terms and concepts that refer solely to mentalistic phenomena: depression, anxiety, guilt. These terms do not exist in cultures where there is a more wholistic view of things. In these cultures, the person's response to a difficult life situation will be expressed in terms that are primarily physical. An Asian person experiencing loss, for instance, might go to a doctor and complain about physical aches and pains. A European undergoing the same life event might present himself or herself as depressed. The core elements of counselling, the words that the person uses to describe their 'troubles', reflect the underlying, implicit, philosophical viewpoint of the culture to which the person belongs. Not only that, but the concept of healing espoused in a culture depends on whether it is dualist or holist. In Western dualist cultures, it makes sense merely to talk about problems, to engage in a 'mental cure'. In cultures built around a unity of mind, body and spirit, healing practices will engage the person at all these levels, possibly encompassing activities such as meditation, exercise and diet. The Hindu discipline of yoga is an example of a method of healing, learning and enlightenment that operates in this kind of holistic manner.

The sense of self

The sense of what it means to be a person varies across cultures. As indicated in Chapter 2, counselling and psychotherapy have primarily developed within cultures that espouse an understanding of the person as being an autonomous, separate individual, with strong boundaries and an 'inner', private region of experience. Landrine (1992) has described this definition of self as *referential*. The self is an inner 'thing' or area of experience: 'the separated, encapsulated self of Western culture . . . is presumed to be the originator, creator and controller of behavior' (p. 402). Landrine contrasts this notion with the *indexical* experience of self found in non-Western or 'sociocentric' cultures:

'the self' in these cultures is not an entity existing independently from the relationships and contexts in which it is interpreted . . . the self is created and re-created in interactions and contexts, and exists only in and through these.

(Landrine 1992: 406)

Sampson (1988) is among many theorists who have commented on the difference between the *individualist* concept of self that predominate in Western societies, and the *collectivist* approach that is part of traditional cultures and ways of life. The person in a collectivist community is likely to regard himself or herself as a member of a family, clan or other social group, and to make decisions in the light of the needs, values and priorities of this social network. Concepts such as self-actualization or authenticity (being true to one's individual self) do not make a lot of sense in the context of a collectivist culture. Conversely, notions of honour, duty and virtue can seem archaic within modern individualist cultures. Individualist cultures emphasize the experience of guilt, referring to an inner experience of self-criticism and self-blame. People in collectivist cultures are more likely to talk about shame, referring to situations where they have been found wanting in the eyes of a powerful other person. It can be very difficult for people from extreme individualist or collectivist cultures to understand each other (Pedersen 1994). In practice, however, most cultures, and most individuals, comprise a mix of individualist and collectivist tendencies, so that, for example, a counsellor brought up in a highly individualist environment should be able to draw on some personal experiences of collective action when working with a client from a more collectivist background. Nevertheless, the tension between an individual self with 'depth' and a relational self that is 'extended' presents a real challenge for counsellors and psychotherapists. For reasons of training, selection and personal preference, most therapists have a strong sense of the power and sanctity of the 'individual' and seek to initiate change at an individual level.

The construction of morality

Making moral choices, deciding between right and wrong, is central to life. However, the moral landscape is constructed quite differently in different cultures. The key characteristics of modern, Western morality are a belief in individual choice and responsibility, and a willingness to be guided by abstract moral principles such as 'fairness' or 'honesty'. By contrast, in traditional cultures moral issues are much more likely to be decided through consideration of the operation of *fate* (e.g. the Hindu notion of *karma*), and moral teachings or principles are embedded in stories rather than articulated through abstract concepts. The choice–fate distinction is crucial in many counselling situations. One of the goals of person-centred and other approaches to counselling is to help the person to discover or develop their 'internal locus of evaluation', their capacity to make moral choices on the basis of an individual set of values. It is not hard to make a connection between this definition of moral choice and the image of the present-day individual as consumer depicted by Cushman (1990, 1995) (see Chapter 2). Most

Box 10.1

Moroccan sense of self: the function of the *nisba*

Morocco, Middle Eastern and . . . extrovert, fluid, activist, masculine, informal to a fault, a Wild West sort of place without the barrooms and the cattle drives, is another kettle of selves altogether. My work there, which began in the mid-sixties, has been centered around a moderately large town or small city in the foothills of the Middle Atlas, about twenty miles south of Fez. It's an old place, probably founded in the tenth century, conceivably even earlier. It has the walls, the gates, the narrow minarets rising to prayer-call platforms of a classic Muslim town, and, from a distance anyway, it is a rather pretty place, an irregular oval of blinding white set in the deep-sea-green of an olive grove oasis, the mountains, bronze and stony here, slanting up immediately behind it. Close up, it is less prepossessing, though more exciting: a labyrinth of passages and alleyways, three quarters of them blind, pressed in by wall-like buildings and curbside shops and filled with a simply astounding variety of very emphatic human beings. Arabs, Berbers and Jews; tailors, herdsmen and soldiers; people out of offices, people out of markets, people out of tribes; rich, superrich, poor, superpoor; locals, immigrants, mimic Frenchmen, unbending medievalists, and somewhere, according to the official government census for 1960, an unemployed Jewish airline pilot – the town houses one of the finest collections of rugged individuals I, at least, have ever come up against. Next to Sefrou (the name of the place), Manhattan seems almost monotonous.

(Geertz 1983: 64–5)

This vivid description portrays a traditional society, one where the sense of self possessed by people might be expected to be more collectivist than individualist. Yet Geertz argues that the Moroccan sense of self is *both* individual *and* collective. When naming a person, Arabic language allows the use of a device known as the *nisba*. This involves transforming a noun into a relational adjective. For example, someone from Sefrou would be known as *Sefroui* (native son of Sefrou). Within the city itself, the person would use a *nisba* that located him or her within a particular group, for example *harari* (silk merchant). Geertz reports that he had never known a case where a person was known, or known about, but his or her *nisba* was not. He suggests that this cultural system functions to create 'contextualized persons': people 'do not float as bounded psychic entities, detached from their backgrounds and singularly named . . . their identity is an attribute that they borrow from their setting' (p. 67). Geertz's study of the Sefroui illustrates how complex and subtle the differences between Western and non-Western notions of self can be. For a Sefroui, a high degree of rugged, flamboyant individuality is made possible by the fact that one can act in virtually any way one wishes, '*without any risk of losing one's sense of who one is*' (p. 68, italics added).

counsellors would seek to challenge a client who continues to attribute his or her actions to fate, and denies any personal responsibility. Most traditional healers would, conversely, regard a person who insisted that his or her problems were due to individual choices as stubbornly self-centred and unwilling to admit the extent to which ancestors or spirit presences were determining his or her life.

Another dimension of cultural contrast can be found in the area of *moral values*. Individualist cultures tend to promote values such as achievement, autonomy, independence and rationality. Collectivist cultures place more importance on sociability, sacrifice and conformity.

The concept of time

It has been one of the great contributions of existential philosophers to review the significance for individuals and cultures of the way that *time* is experienced. From the perspective of physics, time can be treated as a linear constant, segmentable into units such as seconds, minutes and hours. From the perspective of persons and social groups, time is one of the elements through which a way of being and relating is constructed. One of the defining characteristics of modern industrial societies is the extent to which they are *future-oriented*. The past is forgotten, destroyed, built over. Oral history, the story of what a family or community achieved in the past, survives only to the most minimal degree. The past is redefined, packaged and sold as 'heritage'. Traditional, collectivist societies, by contrast, are predominantly *past-oriented*. There is a strong continuity in the oral history that is available to members of traditional cultures. It is normal to imagine that ancestors are in some sense present and can communicate with the living. In modern cultures, the notion of *progress* is given a great deal of value. The practices, lifestyle and possessions of previous generations are considered 'old-fashioned' and 'dated'. In traditional cultures, 'progress' and development can often be perceived as threatening. The forms of communication and storage of information, and types of work tasks, in different cultural settings also have an impact on the experience of time. In pre-literate cultures it makes sense to assume that everyday life was lived largely in the moment, focused on tasks that required attention in the here-and-now. In modern technological societies there is a spectrum of activities, including reading and watching television, that unavoidably shift the consciousness of the person to 'there-and-then'. There is some irony in the attempts of humanistic psychologists and therapists, in the mid-twentieth century, to create methods of enabling people to rediscover the *present*.

The influence of modern attitudes to time lies at the very heart of therapy. Implicit, and often explicit, in the practice of much psychodynamic and humanistic counselling and psychotherapy is an invitation to the client to confront and reject the authority of his or her parents, who are regarded as responsible for the inculcation of repressive and life-restricting injunctions and patterns of behaviour. This way of seeing relationships between parents and children is consistent with the pervasive ageism of contemporary society and with the need for an advanced capitalist economy to encourage citizens to consume new and different products and adopt new work patterns and roles. It does not sit easily, however, with the past-centred reverence for parents and ancestors widespread in non-Western cultures. The construction of time in different cultural settings can have very practical consequences. In cultures where linear, segmented, clock-defined time is dominant, it makes sense for counselling clients to be given hour-long appointments at the same time each week. In some other cultures these arrangements just do not make sense, and clients would expect to be able to drop in to see a counsellor when it feels right to them, rather than when the clock or calendar dictates they should.

The significance of place

The final dimension of culture to be discussed here concerns the relationship between cultures and the physical environment, the land. It is clear that the bond between person and place has been largely severed in modern urban societies. Social and geographical mobility is commonplace. People move around in response to educational and work opportunities. Transport and relocation are relatively easy. As a result, there are few people who live as adults in the same neighbourhood or community in which they grew up, and even fewer who live in the neighborhoods or communities where their parents or grandparents grew up. In modern cultures there is an appreciation of place, but often this is detached and takes the form of tourism. All this means that it can be enormously difficult for counsellors and therapists socialized into the ways of modernity to understand the meaning of place for people from different cultural backgrounds. Some of the most compelling evidence for this come from studies of native American communities. For example, Lassiter (1987) reports on the widespread psychological damage caused to Navajo peoples by forced relocation resulting from the sale of their ancestral lands to mining companies.

Research into native American and other traditional cultures has established that place and land can have a powerful emotional and social significance for people. These aspects of human experience are, however, largely ignored by Western psychology and approaches to counselling and psychotherapy. It does not need much reflection to confirm that place is often extremely important for members of modern industrial–urban societies. People invest a great deal of energy in their homes and gardens, and in their relationship with the countryside.

Externally observable cultural aspects

Turning now to more immediately observable and overt aspects of culture, it is clear that many of the underlying philosophical dimensions of different cultural 'world views' are expressed and visible in the ways that people behave. One of the observable aspects of cultural difference that has received substantial attention has been *non-verbal behaviour*. Cultures can be differentiated in terms of the way that people employ non-verbal cues such as touch, eye contact, gesture and proximity. Often, the difficulties of communication that can exist between members of separate cultural groups can be understood through an appreciation of non-verbal factors. For example, direct eye contact is considered in Western cultures as a sign of honesty and openness, but in many other cultures would be perceived as rude or intrusive. Similarly, each culture employs complex unwritten rules about who can be touched, and in what circumstances.

Important cultural differences can also be observed in patterns of *verbal behaviour*. Bernstein (1972), examining linguistic differences between working-class and middle-class subcultures in English society, found that, when asked to tell a story based on a series of pictures, middle-class people tended to use what he called an 'elaborated code', in which they explained the assumptions behind their understanding of the situation. Working-class participants in his study, by contrast, seemed to use a 'restricted code', in which they took for granted that the listener would 'know what they meant'. Landrine (1992) has suggested that people from 'referential self' cultures talk about themselves in abstract terms, as an object with attributes (e.g. 'I am female, a mother, middle-aged, tall, a librarian), whereas those immersed in 'indexical self' social life find it very difficult to do this. When asked to talk about themselves they are much more likely to recount stories of specific concrete instances and episodes that express these qualities in dramatic form. People from different cultures have quite distinct modes of story-telling. Western individuals tend to tell well ordered, logical, linear stories. People from more orally based traditional cultural groups tend to tell stories that are circular and never seem to get to the 'point'. These are just some of the many linguistic aspects of cultural difference. The key point here is that the way that a person talks, the way that he or she uses language, conveys a great deal about his or her cultural and personal identity.

A feature of social life to which anthropologists have given a great deal of attention is *kinship patterns*. There are a series of issues around this topic that are fundamental to the construction of identity in members of a culture: What is the size and composition of the family group? How are marriages arranged? Who looks after children? How is property passed on from one generation to another? From the point of view of a counsellor, the answers a person gives to these questions help to generate a picture of the kind of relational world in which he or she expects to live, or which is regarded as normal. A powerful way of illustrating differences in kinship ties is to ask: what is your most important relationship? In Western cultures the answer will often be that the most important relationship is with the spouse or life partner. In other parts of the world, the closest relationship is between parent and child.

Very much linked in with kinship patterns is the issue of *gender relationships*. The influence of gender on personal identity is immense, and some feminist theorists (see Chapter 8) would even argue that gender is more central than culture to understanding the way that a person thinks, feels and acts. Nevertheless, it is also clear that gender identity and gender roles are constructed differently in different cultures. Included within the cultural definition of gender is the extent to which a culture represses, tolerates or celebrates homosexuality.

The *expression of emotion* is a facet of enculturation that is central to counselling. Different cultures have varying understandings of which emotions are 'acceptable' and are allowed expression in public. One way that the 'emotional rules' of a culture can be observed is through the range of words that a person has available to describe emotions and feelings. It is clear, from research carried out by anthropologists and cross-cultural psychologists, that emotion or feeling words or facial expressions in one culture do not map easily on to the language of another culture. For example, in the Shona (Zimbabwe) language the term *kufungisisa* (roughly translated as 'thinking too much') is widely used to account for psychological problems, but has no direct equivalent in English. Farooq *et al.* (1995), and many other researchers, have found that people from Asian cultures tend to express depression and anxiety through bodily complaints and ailments rather than in psychological terms. Marcelino (1990) suggests that an appreciation of emotion words in communities in the Philippines is only possible if Filipino concepts of relationships are understood first. These examples represent one of the key challenges for multicultural counselling. Counselling is based on purposeful, problem-solving conversation and communication around the meanings, goals, relationships and emotions that are troubling a person. Cultural difference strikes at the heart of this endeavour. To what extent can anyone know how someone from another language community *really* feels?

The final observable manifestation of cultural difference to be discussed is the area of attitudes and practices around healing. Every culture has its own understanding of well-being, illness and cure. The *theory of healing* espoused by members of a culture can be based on scientific knowledge, as in Western industrial societies, or can be grounded in supernatural beliefs. In many cultures, traditional/spiritual and modern/scientific approaches to healing may exist side by side. For example, in Malaysia, an Asian country with an economy and educational system modelled on Western ideas, a recent survey found that over half of patients attributed their illness to supernatural agents, witchcraft and possession, and were just as likely to use the services of a traditional healer (*bomoh*) as a Western-trained physician. In his review of different varieties of psychotherapy and counselling practised in different cultures, Prince (1980) found a range of methods that extended far beyond the domain of conventional counselling, including meditation, village meetings, shamanic ecstacy and social isolation. It is futile to expect that Western approaches to counselling and psychotherapy will be seen as relevant or acceptable to people who have been brought up to view any of these kinds of ritual as the way to deal with depression, anxiety or interpersonal conflict.

The value for counsellors of possessing a model of cultural identity arises from the fact that it is impossible for a counsellor to know about all cultures. What is more useful is to know the right questions to ask. It can be dangerous to imagine that it is even possible to build up a comprehensive knowledge base about a cultural group – for instance, through attending a module or workshop on a training course – because within that cultural group there will certainly be a myriad of varying strands of cultural experience. Probably the best that can be achieved by training workshops or book chapters on the counselling needs and issues of particular groups (see, for example, the relevant sections of Ponterotto *et al.* 1995; Pedersen *et al.* 1996) is to *sensitize* the counsellor to the structures, language and traditions of that group. When working with a client from another cultural background, information on relevant cultural experiences can be gleaned from the client, from reading, from other members of that culture or from living in that culture.

The cultural identity checklist presented above gives one way of making sense of the influence of various cultural factors in the life of an individual counselling client. Falicov (1995) offers an alternative way of structuring such a cultural map, focusing on family structure and life-cycle, the living environment (ecological context) of the client and the person's experience of migration and acculturation. Hofstede (1980) has produced a way of categorizing cultures that some counsellors have found helpful (for instance, Draguns 1996; Lago and Thompson 1996). The Hofstede model describes four main dimensions of cultural difference between cultures: power distance, uncertainty avoidance, individualism–collectivism and masculinity–femininity. *Power distance* refers to the extent to which inequalities in power exist within a culture. Western industrial societies are (relatively) democratic, with power and authority being available, in principle, to all citizens. Many traditional cultures, and contemporary authoritarian regimes, are structured around major inequalities in power and privilege. *Uncertainty avoidance* distinguishes between cultures where 'each day is taken as it comes' and cultures with absolute rules and values. *Individualism–collectivism* captures the difference between cultures in which people exist as discrete, autonomous individuals, and those where there is a strong allegiance to family, clan or nation. Finally, *masculinity–femininity* reflects differences not only in the domination of conventional sex roles, but in the extent to which values of achievement and money (masculine) or quality of life and interdependence (feminine) are predominant.

There is no 'right' or 'wrong' way to understand culture, and the best that any of these guidelines or frameworks can achieve is to offer a means for beginning to make some sense of the enormous complexity of cultural identity. Effective multicultural counselling involves not only being able to 'see' people in cultural terms, but also having a capacity to apply this understanding to the task of helping people with their problems.

Multicultural counselling in practice

So far, we have mainly considered the question of how to make sense of culture, and how to develop an appreciation of how the way that a person experiences the world is built up through a multiplicity of cultural influences. We now turn to a discussion of how a multicultural approach can be applied in practice. What are the counselling techniques and strategies that are distinctive to this approach?

Some of the skills associated with multicultural counselling involve concrete, practical issues. For example, d'Ardenne and Mahtani (1989) discuss the need to review with clients the implications of using appropriate names and forms of address, deciding on whether to use an interpreter, and negotiating differences in non-verbal communication and time boundaries. Behind these tangible issues lie less concrete factors associated with the general therapeutic strategy or 'mind-set' adopted by the counsellor.

Ramirez (1991) argues that the common theme running through all cross-cultural counselling is the challenge of living in a multicultural society. He proposes that a central aim in working with clients from all ethnic groups should be the development of 'cultural flexibility'. Ramirez (1991) points out that even members of a dominant, majority culture report the experience of 'feeling different', of a sense of mismatch between who we are and what other people expect from us. The approach taken by Ramirez (1991) involves the counsellor matching the cultural and cognitive style of the client in initial meetings, then moving on to encourage experimentation with different forms of cultural behaviour. This approach obviously requires a high degree of self-awareness and cultural flexibility on the part of the therapist.

Another important strategy in multicultural counselling is to focus on the links between personal problems and political/social realities. The person receiving counselling is not perceived purely in psychological terms, but is understood as being an active member of a culture. The feelings, experiences and identity of the client are viewed as shaped by the cultural milieu. For example, Holland (1990: 262) makes a distinction between loss and expropriation:

> In my work . . . we return over and over again to the same history of being separated from mothers, rejoining mothers that they did not know, leaving grandmothers they loved, finding themselves in a totally different relationship, being sexually abused, being put into care, and so on: all the kinds of circumstances with which clinicians working in this field are familiar. That is loss, but expropriation is what imperialism and neo-colonialism does – it steals one's history; it steals all kinds of things from black people, from people who don't belong to a white supremacist race.

Holland is here writing about her work with working-class black women in Britain. But the experience of having things stolen by powerful others is a common theme in the lives of those who are gay, lesbian, religiously different, unemployed or sexually abused. Loss can be addressed and healed through therapy, but expropriation can only be remedied through social action. The theme of empowerment, within an individual life, through self-help groups or by political involvement, is therefore a distinctive and essential ingredient of multicultural counselling.

Dyche and Zayas (1995) argue that in practice it is impossible for counsellors to enter the first session with comprehensive detailed knowledge of the cultural background of their client. They suggest, moreover, that any attempt to compile such knowledge runs the danger of arriving at an over-theoretical, intellectualized understanding of the culture of a client, and may risk 'seeing clients as their culture, not as themselves' (p. 389). Dyche and Zayas argue that it is more helpful to adopt an attitude of cultural naivete and respectful curiosity, with the goal of working collaboratively with each client to create an understanding of what their cultural background means to them as an individual. Ridley and Lingle (1996) refer to a similar stance towards the client, but discuss it in terms of *cultural empathy*. David and Erickson (1990) argue that this quality of curiosity about, or empathy towards, the cultural world of others must be built upon a similar attitude towards one's own culture.

The work of Dyche and Zayas (1995), Holland (1990), Martinez (1991) and Ridley and Dingle (1996) demonstrates the point that the practice of multicultural counselling is largely driven by a set of principles or beliefs, rather than being based in a set of discrete skills or techniques. Multicultural counsellors may use different forms of delivery, such as individual, couple, family or group counselling, or may employ specific interventions such as relaxation training, dream analysis or empathic reflection. In each instance, the counsellor must take into consideration the cultural appropriateness of what is being offered. Multicultural counselling does not fit easily into any of the mainstream counselling approaches, such as psychodynamic, person-centred, cognitive–behavioural or systemic. There are some multicultural counsellors who operate from within each of these approaches; there are others who draw on each of them as necessary. Multicultural counselling is an *integrative* approach that uses a culture-based theory of personal identity as a basis for selecting counselling ideas and techniques.

One specific behaviour or skill that can be observed in effective multicultural counsellors can be described as *willingness to talk about cultural issues*. Thompson and Jenal (1994) carried out a study of the impact on the counselling process of counsellor 'race-avoidant' interventions. In other words, when working with clients who raised concerns about race and culture, these counsellors responded in ways that addressed only those aspects of the client's issue that could relate to anyone, irrespective of race, rather than acknowledging the actual racial content of what was being said. Thompson and Jenal found that this kind of 'race-neutralizing' response had the effect of disrupting or constricting the client's flow, and led either to signs of exasperation or to the client conceding or deferring to the counsellor's definition of the situation by dropping any mention of racial issues. This was a small-scale study, which needs to be repeated with other groups and clients and counsellors, and in relation to a wider range of cultural issues. Nevertheless, the findings of the study seem intuitively accurate: if the counsellor is unwilling or unable to give voice to cultural issues, then the client is silenced. Moodley (1998) uses the phrase 'frank talking' to describe the openness that is necessary in this kind of work.

Another distinctive area of competence for multicultural counsellors lies in being able to draw on therapeutic techniques and ideas from other cultures, in the service of client needs. The vignette presented in Box 10.2 gives a good example of this kind of process operating in the context of a specific case. The work of Walter (1996), in the field of bereavement counselling, provides a more

Counselling in the Chinese temple

In Taiwan, people in crisis may choose to visit the temple to seek advice through *chou-chien* (fortune-telling through the drawing of bamboo sticks). The *chien* client makes an offering to the temple god, tells the god about his or her problems, then picks up and shakes a bamboo vase containing a set of *chien* sticks. One of the sticks becomes dislodged, and is selected. The client then throws a kind of die to determine whether he or she has drawn the correct *chien*. Once sure that they have chosen the right stick, they take it over to a desk in the temple and ask for the *chien* paper corresponding to a number inscribed on the stick. On the paper there is a classical short Chinese poem describing a historical event. Often the person consults an interpreter – usually an older man – whose role is to explain the meaning of the poem in a way that he feels is helpful to the supplicant.

A young man asked whether it was 'blessed' for him to change his job. The interpreter read to him the *chien* poem on the paper he had drawn and then asked several questions before he made any interpretation, including how long he had been on the present job, why he was thinking of changing his job and whether he had any opportunities for a new job. The young man replied that he had been in his present job for only a month or so, having just graduated from school. He did not like the job because of its long hours and low pay. He had made no plans for a new job and had no idea how to go about it. Upon hearing this, the interpreter said that it was not 'blessed' for the young man to change his job at that time, that young people should make more effort than demands, and that if he worked hard and long enough he would eventually be paid more.

This account is taken from Hsu (1976: 211–12), who observes that *chien* fulfils a number of important therapeutic functions: giving hope, eliminating anxiety, strengthening self-esteem and the reinforcement of adaptive social behaviour. Hsu suggests that *chien* counselling is particularly appropriate in the Chinese cultural milieu, in which deference to authority is highly valued, and in which it is considered rude to express emotion in a direct fashion.

general example of multicultural awareness funtioning at a theoretical level. Walter (1996) notes that most Western models of grief propose that it is necessary for the bereaved person to work through their feelings of loss in order to arrive at a position where they are able to make new attachments. Within bereavement counselling, this process is facilitated by speaking to a stranger, the bereavement counsellor. Walter (1996) learned that in Shona culture, there is a tradition of keeping the spirit of the deceased person alive by continuing to acknowledge him or her as a continuing member of the family or community. This goal was achieved by a process of talking about the deceased person. People who knew the deceased spoke at length to each other about their memories of that person. At a time of

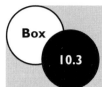

Box 10.3

The concept of *subjective culture*

Membership of a culture involves being socialized into a complex set of 'unwritten rules' about how people can be expected to think, feel and act in different situations. At one level these rules can be analysed in terms of abstract concepts: self, values and so on. However, at another level there is a lived reality, a 'structure of feeling' that differs across cultures. Standing on a street corner in Paris just *feels* different from standing on a street corner in Moscow. George and Vasso Vassiliou are psycho-therapists who have worked in the USA as well as in their native Greece, and have become very aware of what they call 'subjective culture'. They argue that even though a therapist may be well able to speak the same language as his or her clients, it is much harder for someone who does not share the same subjective culture to appreciate the *meaning* or *implications* of the words used by a client. They give an example of an experienced and expert American psychodrama trainer who conducted a workshop in Athens:

> she proposed that someone should protray 'a forty-five-year-old, elegantly dressed woman, twice divorced and ready to marry again for a third time, who brings for consultation her twenty-five-year-old, obese, unkempt, and obviously dis-turbed daughter.' When no one from the audience volunteered to portray this mother, the psychodramatist thought they were simply shying away from the task.
>
> Finally, one of the participants explained that they simply could not portray this role because they had never known such a Greek mother. 'This is unheard of,' he concluded, and, in order to convince the puzzled visitor, he proposed to play the part of the woman's brother, a Greek core-culture fifty-year-old-man, and demonstrate to her what would happen in the hypothetical case that such a mother did exist, provided that the psychodramatist was willing to play her role. The visitor, still unsuspecting, accepted. In about ten minutes she was forced to 'cut' the role-playing, pale and overwhelmed by the savage confrontation that had ensued. A merciless brother shouted that he had not come to kill 'such a creature' for dishonouring her family with her loose morals, as he said, 'because that should have been done a long time ago,' but to tell her to keep her hands off her daughter, this 'hapless, innocent victim of hers.' The psychodramatist, obviously exasperated, turned to the group, consisting mostly of girls. 'How do you stand them,' she said, 'are brothers in Greece like this?' The quite spontane-ous answer from the audience was, 'Oh, yes, to sisters like you.'
>
> (Vassiliou and Vassiliou 1973: 48)

his own personal bereavement, Walter (1996) tried out this approach, and found that it was helpful and satisfying both for him and for the other bereaved people around him. In his writing, he proposes some ways in which this Shona tradition can be integrated into Western counselling practice. Lee (2002) explores similar issues in his discussion of the integration of indigenous and Western therapies in his work with Singapore Chinese.

To summarize, it can be seen that multicultural counselling can take many forms. In responding to the needs and experiences of people from different cultural backgrounds, a multicultural counsellor must be creative and adaptive. Nevertheless, it is possible to suggest a set of guidelines for multicultural counselling practice, derived from the writings of Johnson and Nadirshaw (1993) and Pedersen (1994):

- There is no single concept of 'normal' that applies across all persons, situations and cultures. Mainstream concepts of mental health and illness must be expanded to incorporate religious and spiritual elements. It is important to take a flexible and respectful approach to other therapeutic values, beliefs and traditions: we must each of us assume that our own view is to some extent culturally biased.
- Individualism is not the only way to view human behaviour and must be supplemented by collectivism in some situations. Dependency is not a bad characteristic in all cultures.
- It is essential to acknowledge the reality of racism and discrimination in the lives of clients, and in the therapy process. Power imbalances between therapist and client may reflect the imbalance of power between the cultural communities to which they belong.
- Language use is important – abstract 'middle-class' psychotherapeutic discourse may not be understood by people coming from other cultures. Linear thinking/ storytelling is not universal.
- It is important to take account of the structures within the client's community that serve to strengthen and support the client: natural support sytems are important to the individual. For some clients, traditional healing methods may be more effective than Western forms of counselling.
- It is necessary to take history into account when making sense of current experience. The way that someone feels is not only a response to what is happening now, but may be in part a response to loss or trauma that occured in earlier generations.
- Be willing to talk about cultural and racial issues and differences in the counselling room.
- Check it out with the client – be open to learning from the client.

Cultural awareness training for counsellors

A great deal of effort has been expended within the multicultural counselling movement on the question of finding ways to facilitate the development of

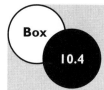

Box 10.4

A culturally sensitive approach to counselling in a case of traumatic bereavement

In the winter of 1984, about 12,000 *Falashas* (Jews of Ethiopia) were driven out of their villages in northern Ethiopia by a combination of hunger, fear of war and a desire to emigrate to Israel. On their long march through the desert and in refugee camps about 3,000 died. Eventually, the Israeli government managed to airlift the survivors to safety, but only after enormous trauma and disruption to family groups.

Some two years later, M, a 31-year-old Ethiopian woman, married with four children, and who spoke only Amharic, was referred to a psychiatric unit in Jerusalem. Although it was difficult to obtain adequate translation facilities, it emerged that she had wandered for many weeks in the desert, during which time her baby had died. She continued to carry the dead body for several days, until she arrived in Israel, when the strong-smelling corpse was taken from her and buried. For the previous two years she had been repeatedly hospitalized following 'asthmatic attacks'. Now she was agitated, fearful and depressed, and complained of 'having a snake in her leg'. She was diagnosed as suffering from an acute psychotic episode. The staff in the psychiatric unit were able to find an anthropologist familiar with M's culture and language, and it emerged that she experienced herself as 'impure' because she had never been able to undergo the purification ritual required by her religious sect for all those who have come into contact with a human corpse. Her mother-in-law had not allowed her to talk about her feelings surrounding her bereavement: 'snake in the leg' turned out to be a Falasha idiom for referring to disagreement with a mother-in-law. M received counselling that encouraged her to talk about the death of her baby, and a purification ritual was arranged. At 30-month follow-up, she was doing well and had a new baby, although admitting to still mourning her dead child.

The case of M, and the issues it raises, are described more fully in Schreiber (1995). It is case that demonstrates the strengths of a multicultural approach. Although the person in need presented with physical, somatic symptoms that could in principle be treated by medication and conventional Western psychiatry, the therapists involved in the case took the trouble to explore the *meaning* of these symptoms, and then to construct a form of help that brought together indigenous and psychotherapeutic interventions in a way that was appropriate for this individual person.

appropriate cultural awareness, knowledge and skills. Initially, much of this work concentrated solely on issues of racism, but more recent training programmes have examined a broader multicultural agenda (Rooney *et al.* 1998).

Racism is part of the value system and fabric of contemporary society, and represents a factor of enormous significance for counselling (Thompson and Neville

1999). Counselling remains a predominantly 'white' occupation, with relatively few black counsellors or black clients. It is essential for counsellors to be aware of their own stereotypes, attitudes and feelings in relation to people from other ethnic groups. Given the racist and nationalist nature of Western industrial society, it is likely that these attitudes will contain at least some elements of rejection.

The client, too, may have difficulties in accepting and trusting the counsellor. As d'Ardenne and Mehtani (1989: 78) write:

> clients who have had a lifetime of cultural and racial prejudice will bring the scars of these experiences to the [therapeutic] relationship. For the most part, counsellors are from the majority culture, and will be identified with white racist society. Thus, counsellors are seen by their clients as both part of the problem and part of the solution.

This ambivalence towards the counsellor may well be exhibited in resistance, or transference reactions.

Many training courses and workshops have been devised to enable counsellors to become more aware of their own prejudices and better informed on the needs of 'minority' clients. The case for systematic racism awareness training for counsellors is made by Lago and Thompson (1989), who also point out that such courses can be painful for participants, perhaps resulting in conflict with colleagues or family members and re-examination of core beliefs and assumptions. Tuckwell (2001) has described the underlying dynamic of cross-cultural therapy and training as involving a willingness to confront a pervasive 'threat of the other' that exists in such situations.

It is important to acknowledge that although it is essential to combat racism and prejudice, there are many aspects of cultural difference that are not necessarily bound up with the brutal rejection characteristic of racist attitudes. LaFramboise and Foster (1992) describe four models for providing training that explores a more general cultural awareness curriculum. The first is the 'separate course' model, where trainees take one specific module or workshop in cross-cultural issues. The second is the 'area of concentration' model, where trainees undertake a placement working with a particular ethnic minority group. The third is the 'interdisciplinary' model, in which trainees go outside the course and take a module or workshop run by an external college department or agency. Finally, there is the 'integration' model, which describes a situation where cross-cultural awareness is addressed in all parts of the course rather than being categorized as an option, or as outside the core curriculum. LaFramboise and Foster (1992) observe that, while integration represents an ideal, resource constraints and lack of suitably trained staff mean that the other models are more widely employed.

Harway (1979) and Frazier and Cohen (1992), writing from a feminist perspective, have suggested a set of revisions to existing counsellor training courses to make them more responsive to the counselling needs of women. Their model is just as appropriate as a way of promoting awareness of the needs of other 'minority' or disadvantaged client groups. They propose that training courses should:

- employ a significant proportion of 'minority' staff;
- enrol a significant proportion of 'minority' students;
- provide courses and placement experiences of the type outlined by LaFramboise and Foster (1992);
- encourage research on topics relevant to counselling with disadvantaged groups;
- provide library resources in these areas;
- require experiential sessions for both staff and students to facilitate examination of attitudes and stereotypes;
- encourage staff to use culturally aware language and teaching materials.

It is difficult to assess the effectiveness of cultural awareness training programmes. Few courses have been run, and there is an absence of research evidence regarding their impact on counselling practice. However, in one study, Wade and Bernstein (1991) provided brief (four-hour) training in cultural awareness to four women counsellors, two of whom were black and two white. Another four women counsellors, who did not receive the training, acted as a comparison group. The effectiveness of these counsellors was assessed by evaluating their work with 80 black women clients, who had presented at a counselling agency with personal and vocational problems. Results showed large differences in favour of the culturally trained counsellors, who were seen by clients as significantly more expert, attractive, trustworthy, empathic and accepting. The clients of the culturally aware counsellors reported themselves as being more satisfied with the counselling they had received, and were less likely to drop out of counselling prematurely. For this group of black women clients, the impact of training was more significant than the effect of racial similarity; the black counsellors who had received the training had higher success rates than those who had not. The Wade and Bernstein (1991) study illustrates that even very limited cultural awareness training can have measurable effects on counselling competence. Other studies are needed to assess the generalizability of this finding to other training packages and client groups.

Any form of multicultural training raises the question of how it is possible to know whether the training has been effective, whether the trainee actually has the relevant skills and competencies. Assessment of the effectiveness of multicultural competence has been greatly facilitated by the publication by Sue *et al.* (1992) of a statement of multicultural counselling competencies and standards that has become widely accepted in the field, and has led to the production of a number of standardized questionnaire and rating scale measures of multicultural awareness, beliefs and skills (see Pope-Davis and Dings 1995). In addition, Coleman (1996) has proposed portfolio assessment as a sensitive and flexible method of appraising such skills and qualities.

Adapting existing services and agencies to meet the needs of client groups from different cultures

Counsellor awareness training is of fundamental importance, given that ethnocentric counsellor attitudes are sure to impede the formation of a good working relationship with clients from other cultures or social groups. There are, however, limits to what can be achieved through this strategy. No counsellor can acquire an adequate working knowledge of the social worlds of all the clients he or she might encounter. In any case, many clients prefer to have a counsellor who is similar to them in sexual orientation, social class or gender, or they may not believe that they will find in an agency someone who will understand their background or language. In response to these considerations, some counsellors have followed the strategy of aiming for organizational as well as individual change. To meet the needs of disadvantaged clients, they have attempted to adapt the structure and operation of their agencies.

Rogler *et al.* (1987) and Gutierrez (1992) describe a range of organizational strategies that have been adopted by counselling and therapy agencies to meet the needs of ethnic minority clients, and that are also applicable in other situations. One approach they describe focuses on the question of access. There can be many factors (financial, geographical, attitudinal) that prevent people from seeking help. Agencies can overcome these barriers by publicizing their services differently, employing outreach workers, hiring bilingual or bicultural staff, opening offices at more accessible sites and providing crèche facilities. A second level of organizational adaptation involves tailoring the counselling to the target client group. Services are modified to reflect the issues and problems experienced by a particular set of clients. One way of doing this is to offer courses or groups that are open to these people only: for example, a bereavement group for older women, an assertiveness class for carers or a counselling programme for women with drink problems. Rogler *et al.* (1987) describe the invention of *cuento*, or folklore therapy, as a therapeutic intervention specifically designed to be of relevance to a disadvantaged group, in this case disturbed Hispanic children. This approach is based on cognitive–behavioural ideas about modelling appropriate behaviour, but the modelling is carried out through the telling of Puerto Rican folktales, followed up by discussion and role play.

A further stage in the adaptation of a counselling agency to the needs of minority clients occurs when the actual structure, philosophy or aims of the organization are changed in reaction to the inclusion within it of more and more members of formerly excluded groups. When this happens, initiatives of the type described above can no longer be marginal to the functioning of the organizations, but come to be seen as core activities. Gutierrez (1992: 330) suggests that without this kind of organizational development, 'efforts toward change can be mostly symbolic and marginal'.

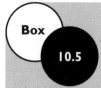

Box

10.5

How relevant are Western ideas about counselling to people living in Islamic societies?

In many predominantly Islamic societies, such as Saudi Arabia, Kuwait, Qatar and Malaysia, counselling has become an accepted component of health and social services provision (Al-Issa 2000a). In these countries, exposure to Western ideas through trade, education, travel and the global media has resulted in the adoption of ideas about counselling and psychotherapy taken from European and North American sources. Nevertheless, some leading Islamic psychologists have argued that it is essential to acknowledge the necessity to adapt therapeutic approaches to the needs and world-view of people who follow traditional Islamic teachings. Al-Issa (2000b) points out that there exists a rich history of Islamic psychiatry and psychotherapy, which pre-dates Western psychiatry, and which in general is more accepting of abnormal behaviour than its Western equivalent. As a result, counselling clients who have an Islamic cultural identity will bring into counselling distinct images and expectations regarding the role of the healer, and process of help. Al-Abdul-Jabbar and Al-Issa (2000) also suggest that 'insight-oriented' approaches to therapy, and therapy that involves questioning parental values and behaviour, may be hard to accept for many Islamic clients brought up in a strongly patriarchal culture. They offer a case history of Nawal, a 28-year-old married woman who complained of being constantly anxious and losing control of her emotions. In therapy, Nawal disclosed that she had entered into an affair with another man, and was feeling guilty about this situation. The therapist used mainly open-ended questions to help the client to explore and reflect on her feelings and choices in this situation. However, her symptoms deteriorated the longer therapy continued. Al-Abdul-Jabbar and Al-Issa (2000: 280–1) reported that:

> At this stage, the therapist decided to use direct guidance to solve address her pressing problem. The therapist now considered the problem as an approach-avoidance conflict: she had to choose between keeping her despised husband or her lover. Although she was left to make the final choice, the therapist as a patriarch (i.e., representing the father) suggested the alternative that is compat-ible with societal demands (i.e., staying with her husband). The patient decided with the help of the therapist that having a stable and good social front with her husband was more valuable to her than pursuing her sensual needs. This deci-sion was followed by a gradual disappearance of her symptoms.

Al-Abdul-Jabbar and Al-Issa (2000) propose that non-Islamic counsellors working with Islamic clients need to be aware of the importance of religious and collective values for these clients. They emphasize that the role of the counsellor must involve a willingness to be assertive, direct and advisory: 'the learning experience during therapy is "teacher-based" rather than "student-based"' (p. 283). The counsellor should also be able to express his or her own emotions, and to console the client.

Finally, the counsellor should remember that the client is seeking to find solutions that strengthen their interdependence with other family members, rather than promoting independence and self-actualization:

> The emphasis is not on the client's individuality or personal beliefs, but on the extent to which they conform to accepted norms ... there is no expectation that the client's behaviour must be consistent with their own personal beliefs. They are expected to express the common beliefs and behave in a socially acceptable fashion ... The outcome of treatment is often assessed by the ability of the clients to carry out their social roles and meet their social obligations. The emotional states of the client are given less attention by the family than daily functioning.
>
> (p. 283)

The values expressed in this statement present a significant challenge for any of the mainstream Western therapies – psychodynamic, humanistic, cognitive–behavioural. In using ideas and methods derived from mainstream Western therapies, if what an Islamic counsellor was seeking to do was basically to attempt to deflect the clients away from their personal beliefs and emotions, and move in the direction of fulfilling their social obligations (as in the case of Nawal), their practice would appear to be quite different from anything that a Western counsellor might intend. Yet, at the same time, surely there are parallels between the principles of Islamic therapy described by Al-Abdul-Jabbar and Al-Issa (2000) and the theme of 'connectedness' highlighted by feminist therapists such as Jean Baker Miller and Judith Jordan (see Chapter 8). And the definition of counselling as an activity which gives the client an opportunity to 'explore, discover and clarify ways of living more satisfyingly and resourcefully' (see Chapter 1) would apply well enough to an Islamic as a Western approach. The literature on Islamic therapy reviewed in Al-Issa (2000a) is perhaps best seen not as an instance of the straightforward application of Western ideas in a different cultural context, but as an instance of active appropriation by Islamic individuals and groups of an approach to helping that they have assimilated into their way of life, and have made their own.

Creating new specialist agencies

Within the world of counselling and therapy, existing agencies have generally had great difficulty in responding to the demands of minority clients. The direction that many socially aware counsellors have taken has been to set up specialist agencies that appeal to specific disadvantaged groups. There is a wide array of agencies that have grown up to provide counselling to women, people from different ethnic and religious communities, gay and lesbian people and so on.

These services are based on the recognition that many people will choose to see a counsellor who is similar to them. One of the difficulties these agencies face is that, usually, they are small and suffer recurring funding crises. They may also find it difficult to afford training and supervision. Nevertheless, there is plentiful evidence that people who identify strongly with a particular set of cultural experiences often do choose to consult counsellors and psychotherapists who share these experiences. On these grounds it can be argued that it is vitally important to maintain a diversity of counselling provision, and to find ways of encouraging the development of effective specialist agencies.

Promoting research into multicultural counselling

Racial and ethnic minority research is significantly under-represented in the professional literature (Ponterotto 1988). There is some evidence from research studies to suggest that black clients seeking help from 'majority culture' agencies will drop out of treatment more quickly than white clients (Sattler 1977; Abramowitz and Murray 1983). There is also evidence that in these situations black clients receive more severe diagnostic labels and are more likely than white clients to be offered drug treatment rather than therapy, or to be referred to a non-professional counsellor rather than a professional (Atkinson 1985). Research studies have also shown that clients tend to prefer counsellors from the same ethnic group (Harrison 1975). In one study, Sue *et al.* (1991) checked the client files of 600,000 users of therapy services from the Los Angeles County Department of Mental Health between 1973 and 1988. Ethnic match between client and therapist was strongly associated with length of stay in treatment (i.e. fewer early drop-outs). For those clients whose primary language was not English, ethnic match was also associated with better therapy outcomes.

Other studies of multicultural processes and methods have been described earlier in this chapter (for example, Wade and Bernstein 1991; Thompson and Jenal 1994). Atkinson and Lowe (1995) and Sue and Sundberg (1996) offer valuable reviews of other studies. However, it is clear that most of these studies refer to clients and counsellors in North American settings. In a field in which the research base as a whole is sparse, there is a significant absence of European studies.

Conclusions

In recent years there has developed an increasing awareness in counselling of the importance of cultural differences between counsellors and clients. The work in this area has been variously described as concerned with 'cross-cultural' (Pedersen 1985), 'intercultural' (Kareem and Littlewood 1992) or 'transcultural' (d'Ardenne and Mahtani 1989) counselling, or focused on 'cultural difference' (Sue 1981) or 'ethnic minorities' (Ramirez 1991). Each of these labels has its own unique meaning, but all these approaches are essentially exploring the same set of issues regarding the impact of cultural identity on the counselling process. In this chapter, the term 'multicultural' has been intentionally used to imply a broader perspective, which takes as its starting point the assumption that an appreciation of cultural identity and difference is at the heart of all counselling practice. Although multicultural counselling is a new, emergent approach, it has already generated a number of major textbooks (Ponterotto *et al.* 1995; Lago and Thompson 1996; Pedersen *et al.* 1996) and a thriving literature.

Each cultural group contains its own approach to understanding and supporting people with emotional and psychological problems. Counsellors can draw upon these resources, such as traditional healers, religious groups and social networks, when working with clients (d'Ardenne and Mahtani 1989; Lee and Armstrong 1996). The possibility of integrating indigenous and Western counselling approaches, to create a model of help that is tailored to meet the needs of a specific client group, offers great promise as a means of extending and renewing the practice and profession of counselling.

Multicultural counselling has received relatively little attention in the research literature. In addition, many counselling agencies and individual counsellors in private practice have so many clients applying from their majority cultural group that there is little incentive for them to develop expertise in multicultural work. The multicultural nature of contemporary society, and the existence of large groups of dispossessed exiles and refugees experiencing profound hopelessness and loss, make this an increasingly important area for future investment in theory, research and practice.

Chapter summary

- Social and political change, the expansion of global communication networks and the existence of ethnic minority critiques of mainstream approaches to counselling have all set the scene for the development of multiculturalism as a distinctive counselling orientation.

- The concept of *culture* is complex and multidimensional, encompassing the concepts of reality, morality, self and time held by a group of people, as well as patterns of behaviour and relationship.

- It is important for counsellors to be able to apply a framework for understanding culture (including their own cultural identity); it is not realistic to expect a counsellor to possess detailed knowledge of a range of cultures.

- In practice, multicultural counselling is sensitive to the links between personal problems and social context; effective counsellors are those who demonstrate cultural empathy, are willing to talk about cultural issues and can work alongside traditional belief systems and healing methods.

- Multicultural counselling is an integrative approach that draws upon ideas and techniques from existing theories of counselling, and builds them into a culture-informed and culture-sensitive model of practice.

- One way in which multicultural counselling has been promoted is through the provision of training experiences for counsellors. Typically, these programmes include an examination of racism as a key factor in cross-cultural communication.

- Another important strategy for promoting multiculturalism in counselling has been the movement to address issues of ethnic representation on the staff of counselling agencies, and where necessary to set up counselling agencies run by and for members of specific cultural groups.

- The emergence of multicultural counselling represents a significant example of how counselling ideas and methods have adapted to social conditions and demands. However, there is a long way to go before the counselling profession as a whole fully recognizes the necessity of awareness of cultural factors in therapy. Research is important for identifying the role that culture can play in relation to counselling processes and outcomes.

Topics for reflection and discussion

1 It can be argued that mainstream approaches to counselling (psychodynamic, person-centred, cognitive–behavioural) are so intrinsically bound up with Western assumptions about human nature that they are just not relevant to people from traditional, non-Western cultures. Do you agree?

2 How would you describe your own cultural identity? How does your cultural identity influence your approach to counselling? For example, does it lead you to prefer to employ some ideas and techniques rather than others? Does it lead you to be more comfortable, or effective, with some clients than with others?

3 Is Pedersen correct in suggesting that multiculturalism should be regarded as a 'fourth force'?

4 Reflect on the way that counselling agencies operate in your town or city. If appropriate, collect any leaflets that they use to advertise their services. How sensitive to multicultural issues are these agencies? What effect might their attitude to multiculturalism have on the clients who use their service, and on the way they are perceived in the community?

5 Is racism the real issue? Is there a danger that the term 'multicultural' might distract attention from the experiences of violence, oppression and expropriation that are caused by the ideology of racism?

Key terms and concepts

collectivist self
cultural empathy
cultural flexibility
culture
dualism
expression of emotion
fourth force
gender relationships
indexical self
individualist self

kinship patterns
moral values
multicultural approach
multiculturalism
non-verbal behaviour
racism
referential self
theory of healing
verbal behaviour

Suggested further reading

There are two major edited collections that provide an invaluable resource for anyone interested in extending their knowledge of multicultural counselling: Pedersen *et al.* (1996) and Ponterotto *et al.* (1995). Both of these books tend to reflect the North American experience of multicultural issues in counselling, which will be ideal for some readers but perhaps slightly off-focus for others. The chapter by Allen Ivey in Ponterotto *et al.* (1995) presents an empowerment model that captures much of the spirit and unique potential of the multicultural movement in counselling. Alternative overviews of counselling and culture, written from a European perspective, can be found in Lago and Thompson (1996), and in the collection of papers edited by Palmer (2002). An excellent summary of types of therapy in different cultures, and how they might be combined, can be found in Tseng (1999).

Several writers in the feminist tradition have made useful contributions to the literature on multicultural counselling. The chapters in Jordan (1997a) are particularly recommended.

The book by Ridley (1995), *Overcoming Unintentional Racism in Counseling and Therapy: A Practitioner's Guide to Intentional Intervention*, offers a very effective synthesis of theory and practical application. Ridley stays close to the reality of what happens in the counselling room, and supplies a wealth of vivid and relevant case examples. In many ways this is an excellent book on how to be a good counsellor. A powerful paper written in the same spirit is Moodley (1998).

Philosophical counselling

Introduction: the relevance of philosophy for counselling and psychotherapy

One of the most significant developments in counselling within the past decade has been the emergence of a growing interest among counsellors and psychotherapists in the relevance of philosophical insights and ideas. In the past, counselling and psychotherapy, along with most branches of psychology, social science and medicine, maintained a kind of arm's-length relationship with philosophy. Although the writings of philosophers might be useful for the purpose of clarifying ethical dilemmas, or to add a gloss of intellectual sophistication to theory, for the vast majority of therapists the domain of the philosophical held little practical relevance when it came to actual work with clients. This position has started to change in recent years. An increasing number of counsellors are realizing that the personal issues and dilemmas that their clients present in the therapy room can in fact be addressed using philosophical ideas and methods. A new approach – philosophical counselling – has become established, with its own textbooks, journals, training programmes and professional associations.

Why has this happened? Why has philosophy suddenly become a useful resource for counsellors? Probably the strongest explanation for the growth of philosophical counselling can be found in the recognition that, in previous eras, philosophy was indeed applied to everyday problems, and was widely used as a form of 'therapy'. According to this line of argument, it was really only in the nineteenth and twentieth centuries that philosophy became highly technical and 'academic', and out of reach of the majority of people. In Ancient Greece, by contrast, philosophers were actively used by members of their communities to help to sort out difficult life issues and conflicts. Eastern philosophical traditions – for example, Zen Buddhism and the study of the Vedas – still remain rooted to local communities and the concerns of ordinary people. The growth of philosophical counselling can therefore be understood as a revival of ancient values and practices, fuelled by the enthusiasm of philosophers eager to demonstrate the practical utility of their skills.

An alternative explanation for the interest in philosophy among counsellors and psychotherapists can be found within recent developments in the therapy world itself. As evidenced by the earlier chapters of this book, there are now many competing psychological models of therapy. Can all these theories be valid? How are we to make sense of the similarities and differences between theories? Answering questions such as these requires access to a meta-perspective, from which psychological ideas can in turn be analysed and understood. Philosophy provides such a meta-perspective. It seems almost inevitable, then, that as theoretical diversity and integrationism have gained in force, so too has the impetus to cultivate a philosophically informed debate about the nature of therapy. Postmodern ideas, which are discussed in a later section of this chapter, have been at the forefront of the drive to construct this kind of meta-perspective.

A third factor that has influenced the philosophical counselling movement has been the continued popularity of existential approaches to counselling and psychotherapy. Existential therapy has never found its way into the list of mainstream 'brand name' therapies, such as psychodynamic and cognitive–behavioural. The number of specialist practitioners trained in existential therapy remains small. Nevertheless, the writings of existential therapists such as Rollo May, R. D. Laing, Irvin Yalom, Emmy van Deurzen and Ernesto Spinelli have had an impact far beyond the community of existential therapists and scholars. There is something in the work of these writers that seems to capture, for many counsellors, a crucial aspect of the essence of what happens in good therapy. So, even though most existential therapists may wish to distance themselves from what has become known as philosophical counselling (which they regard as too eclectic), their work has had the effect of enabling many counsellors to appreciate the value of a philosophically informed approach to therapy.

The aim of this chapter is to introduce some of the main themes within philosophical counselling, and to suggest ways in which these ideas may be useful even to practitioners who do not wish to adopt an explicitly philosophical approach. The chapter also illustrates some of the ways in which philosophical counselling represents a genuine challenge to established approaches to counselling and psychotherapy.

The range and scope of philosophical analysis

The immense scope and range of philosophical writing can make it hard for counsellors to make meaningful use of philosophy as a resource. It is important to recognize that professional philosophers undergo many years of scholarly training in order to achieve a mastery of their discipline, and even then will tend to specialize in a particular area. Some counsellors and psychotherapists, of course, have studied philosophy before entering therapy training, and will have a solid basis from which to use philosophical insights in therapy. For those counsellors who do not possess such a background, it may be helpful to offer a brief outline of the range and scope of the philosophical literature, at least in so far as it has been explored in relation to counselling and psychotherapy. It is possible to identify four main groups of philosophers whose work has proved to be of value to therapists.

Classical Greek philosophy. The thought of Greek philosophers such as Aristotle, Socrates and Plato can be considered as the intellectual bedrock of Western civilization. Philosophy was used and respected in Greek civic life, and the issues and debates that concerned classical philosophers, and the methods they used to examine these issues, remain relevant today.

Enlightenment philosophers. Around the seventeenth and eighteenth centuries, Europe was in the process of moving from a traditional social system based on religion, feudalism and an agricultural economy, to an era of modernity characterized by cities, literacy, democracy and scientific values. The key figures here are Descartes, Locke, Hume and Kant. The central concern of these philosophers was exploring how it is possible to achieve knowledge, and behave morally, in a world that is no longer dominated by religious certainties and traditional prejudices.

Critics of modernity. In the twentieth century, the place of scientific rationality became so firmly established that some philosophers were drawn in the direction of analysing the limitations and contradictions of modern ways of life and thought. Wittgenstein, who argued that human realities are constructed through our 'form of life', and Heidegger, who sought to uncover the meaning of the dimensions of being and existence that lay behind everyday activities, have probably been the main influences on this branch of contemporary philosophy. Among the many other important writers who have questioned the assumptions of modernity are Taylor, MacIntyre, Macmurray and Rorty. A very significant sub-group within this movement has been the existentialists – such as Sartre and Merleau-Ponty – who were influenced by the nineteenth-century pioneer of existentialism, Kierkegaard. Another important sub-group has been made up of postmodern thinkers such as Derrida, Foucault and Lyotard.

Non-Western philosophical traditions. The main non-Western philosophical tradition that has been influential within the development of Western counselling and psychotherapy is Buddhism. There have also been attempts to apply within therapy ideas from Vedantic, Sufi and other philosophical systems.

This summary cannot do justice to the rich and diverse philosophical literature that is available. A useful account of the development of philosophical ideas can be found in Solomon (1988). For counsellors, an invaluable starting point is the book by Howard (2000), which introduces the main ideas of philosophers 'from Pythagoras to Sartre', and discusses the implications of these ideas for the practice of counselling and psychotherapy.

Existential psychotherapy as a philosophical approach

The counselling orientation that most vividly illustrates the application of philosophical ideas is the existential approach, which draws upon the ideas of existential philosophers such as Heidegger, Kierkegaard, Sartre and Merleau-Ponty (see Macquarrie 1972; Moran 2000). There have been several important strands within the development of existential therapy. The first has evolved from the work of European therapists such as Boss (1957) and Binswanger (1963). This body of work influenced the work of the widely read Scottish psychiatrist and psychotherapist R. D. Laing (1960, 1961). Another significant strand consists of American therapists such as May (1950), Bugental (1976) and Yalom (1980). The work of Viktor Frankl, a European psychotherapist who lived for many years in the USA, is also a valuable resource for counsellors interested in an existential approach. Although the model of therapy developed by Frankl is described as 'logotherapy', it is in fact existentially informed. Finally, more recently the writings of Emmy van Deurzen and Ernesto Spinelli have comprised important contributions to existential psychotherapy and counselling. The Society for Existential Analysis functions as a vehicle for current developments within this approach, and operates a journal.

The aim of existential philosophy is to understand or illuminate the experience of 'being-in-the-world'. Existential thinkers use the method of phenomenological reduction to 'bracket-off' their assumptions about reality, in an attempt to arrive closer to the 'essence' or truth of that reality. The aim is to uncover the basic dimensions of meaning or 'being' that underpin everyday life, and by doing this to be better able to live an *authentic* life. The results of existential inquiry appear to suggest a number of central themes to human existence or being. First, human beings exist in time. The present moment is constituted by various horizons of meaning derived from the past. The present moment is also constituted by the various possibilities that stretch out into the future. Individual worlds are constructed with different orientations to past, present and future. The presence and acceptance of death is factor in the capacity of a person to exist fully in time; people who deny death are avoiding living fully, because they are limiting the time horizon within which they exist. A second key theme that derives from existential analysis is that to be a person is to exist in an *embodied* world. Our relationship with the world is revealed through our own body (our feelings and emotions, perception of the size or acceptability of our body, general awareness of parts of the body etc.) and the way we organize the space around us. A third major theme emerging from existential philosophy is the centrality of *anxiety*, *dread* and *care* in everyday life. For existential philosophers, anxiety is not a symptom or sign of psychiatric disorder, but instead is regarded as an inevitable consequence of caring about others, and the world in general. From this perspective, it is a lack of anxiety (revealed as a sense of inner emptiness or alienation) that would be viewed as problematic. Existential philosophy emphasizes that to be a person is to be alone and at the same time to be always in relation to other people. Understanding the quality of a person's existential contact with the *other* is therefore of great interest to existentialists: is the person capable of being both alone and in communion with others? From an existential point of view, authentic being-in-the-world requires an ability to take responsibility for one's own actions, but also a willingness to accept that one is 'thrown' into a world that is 'given'. Much of the focus of existential analysis is on the 'way of being' of a person, the qualitative texture of his or her relationship with self (*Eigenwelt*), others (*Mitwelt*) and the physical world (*Umwelt*).

The brief summary of existential ideas offered here cannot claim to do justice to the richness and complexity of this body of thought. Unlike some other philosophical approaches, which perhaps emphasize a process of logical abstraction from the everyday world, existential philosophers seek to enter into the realm of everyday experience. In principle, existential philosophy should be accessible and understandable to everyone, because it is describing and interpreting experiences (anxiety, fear of death, taking responsibility) that are familiar to us all. In practice, much of the writing of existential philosophers such as Heidegger, Sartre and Merleau-Ponty is difficult to follow, because, in trying to reach beyond the ways in which we ordinarily speak of things, they frequently find it necessary to invent new terminology. Nevertheless, the insights of existential philosophy represent an enormously fertile resource for counsellors and psychotherapists, in providing a framework for enabling clients to explore what is most important for them in their lives.

The goals of existential therapy have been described by van Deurzen-Smith (1990: 157) in the following terms:

1 To enable people to become truthful with themselves again;
2 To widen their perspective on themselves and the world around them;
3 To find clarity on how to proceed into the future whilst taking lessons from the past and creating something valuable to live for in the present.

It can be seen that this is an avowedly exploratory approach to counselling, with a strong emphasis on the development of authentic understanding and action, and the creation of meaning. One of the distinguishing features of the existential approach is its lack of concern for technique. As van Deurzen-Smith (2001: 161) observes: 'the existential approach is well known for its anti-technique orientation . . . existential therapists will not generally use specific techniques, strategies or skills, but . . . follow a . . . philosophical method of inquiry.' At the heart of this 'philosophical method' is the use of phenomenological reduction. Phenomenology is a philosophical method, initially devised by Edmund Husserl, which aims to get beyond a 'taken-for-granted' way of looking at things, and instead achieve the 'essential' truth of a situation of feeling. Spinelli (1989, 1994) has described this method as comprising three basic 'rules'

- The rule of *bracketing*, or putting aside (as best we can) our own assumptions in order to clear our perceptions and actually hear what the other person is expressing.
- The rule of *description* – it is important to *describe* what you have heard (or observed) rather than rushing in to theoretical explanation.
- The rule of *horizontalization* – the therapist seeks to apply no judgement, but to try to hear *everything* before allowing importance to be attributed to any part of the experience.

Using a phenomenological approach, the goal of the existential counsellor or therapist is to explore the meaning for the client of problematic areas of experience. In line with some of the findings of existential philosophy, this exploration of meaning may focus on the significance for the person of broad categories of experience, such as choice, identity, isolation, love, time, death and freedom. Often, such exploration will be associated with areas of crisis or paradox in the current life situation of the person. The basic assumption being offered to the client is that human beings create and construct their worlds, and are responsible for their lives.

May *et al.* (1958) remains a core seminal text in existential psychotherapy, and offers a thorough grounding in the European roots of this approach. This book is, however, a difficult read, and more accessible introductions to the principles and practice of existential counselling are to be found in Bugental (1976), Yalom (1980) and van Deurzen-Smith (1988). Yalom (1989) has also produced a collection of case studies from his own work with clients. The growth of interest within British counselling and psychotherapy in existential ideas is reflected in books by Cohn (1997), Cohn and du Plock (1995), van Deurzen-Smith (1996), Strasser and Strasser (1997), Du Plock (1997) and Spinelli (1997), and chapters by van Deurzen-Smith (1990, 1999) and Spinelli (1996). Useful introductions to the broader field of existential–phenomenological psychology, which provides an underlying framework for existential counselling, have been produced by Valle and King (1978) and Schneider and May (1995).

Although existential counselling and psychotherapy is an approach that is grounded in the philosophical traditions of phenomenology and existentialism, the majority of existential therapists would be reluctant to describe what they do as 'philosophical counselling'. There are basically two reasons for the adoption of this stance by existential therapists. First, the practice of existential therapy is informed by a highly developed theory of existential and phenomenological *psychology*, while the adherents of philosophical counselling are explicitly attempting to evolve a non-psychological mode of helping. Second, the philosophical

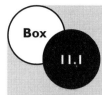

Box

11.1

Yalom's 'missing ingredients'

In the introduction to *Existential Psychotherapy*, Irvin Yalom tells the story of enrolling in a cooking class taught by an elderly Armenian woman who spoke no English. He found that, as much as he tried, he could not match the subtlety of flavouring that his teacher achieved in her dishes, and was unable to understand why. One day, he observed that, en route from the table to the oven, she 'threw in' to each dish various unnamed spices and condiments. Yalom reports that he is reminded of this experience when he thinks about the ingredients of effective therapy:

> Formal texts, journal articles and lectures portray therapy as precise and systematic, with carefully delineated stages, strategic technical interventions, the methodical development and resolution of transference, analysis of object relations, and a careful, rational program of insight-offering interpretations. Yet, I believe deeply that, when no one is looking, the therapist throws in the 'real thing'.
>
> (Yalom 1980: 6)

What is the 'real thing', the essential 'missing ingredient' in counselling? Yalom suggests that the important 'throw-ins' include compassion, caring, extending oneself and wisdom. He characterizes these ingredients as central existential categories, and goes on to argue that the most profound therapy is that which addresses one or more of the four 'ultimate concerns' in life:

* confronting the tension between the awareness of the inevitability of death, and the wish to continue to be;
* acceptance of the possibilities of freedom, including the terrifying implication that each of us is responsible for our actions;
* the ultimate experience of isolation – 'each of us enters existence alone and must depart from it alone';
* meaninglessness – what meaning can life have, if there are no pre-ordained truths?

Yalom (1980) takes the view that all effective counsellors are sensitive to these 'ultimate concerns' and ingredients, but the study of existential thought enables a counsellor or psychotherapist to place these elements 'at the centre of the therapeutic arena'.

counselling movement has drawn on a wide and eclectic range of philosophical sources, rather than being identified with any single philosophical 'school of thought'. Philosophical counselling represents the use of 'philosophizing' within the therapeutic context, rather than the application of a specific set of philosophical constructs. Existential therapy, therefore, can be seen as a therapeutic approach that, though philosophically oriented, has harnessed a particular set of philosophical ideas to a broadly exploratory, conversational approach to therapy, which is similar in many ways to contemporary psychodynamic, person-centred and constructivist models.

Philosophical counselling

The emergence over the past 30 years of philosophical counselling represents a radical break with mainstream approaches to counselling and psychotherapy. The origins of the philosophical counselling movement are generally attributed to the German philosopher Gerd Achenbach (see Jongsma 1995; Lahav 1995a), who opened the first philosophical counselling practice in Bergisch Gladbach, near Cologne, in 1981. The German Association for Philosophical Practice was formed in 1982. In 1984, a group of students at the University of Amsterdam became interested in the application of philosophy in counselling; their efforts led to the opening of the Hotel de Filosoof (The Philosopher Hotel) in Amsterdam in 1988, and the establishment of the Dutch Association for Philosophical Practice in 1989. There are now philosophical counsellors practising in most European countries, North America and Australia. The development of philosophical counselling has been supported by the publication of key texts such as Lahav and da Venza Tillmanns (1995), Schuster (1999) and Raabe (2001), as well as a number of training programmes, websites and conferences.

It would be a mistake to regard philosophical counselling, at the present time, as representing a unified and coherent approach to counselling and psychotherapy. It is a new, emergent form of therapy, and there is active debate over how it should be properly understood and practiced. Perhaps the main point of convergence within this debate is that philosophical counselling is a form of helping that requires prior training in philosophy: it is something that people who are already philosophers do, rather than being a method that can be acquired by counsellors who do not already have a thorough grounding in philosophy. It is possible to identify three main themes within the practice of philosophical therapy: the aim of world-view clarification, the use of dialogue and the teaching of philosophical skills.

The use of philosophical counselling as a means of clarifying or exploring the world-view of a person has been proposed by Lahav (1995b) as fundamental to this approach to therapy. Lahav argues that each individual has their own 'personal philosophy' or world-view, which represents the totality of their views of self and the world. These concepts may be explicitly articulated, or may be implicit in the way that the person lives their life. Lahav (1995b: 9) suggests that:

It is possible to interpret everyday problems and predicaments – such as meaning crises, feelings of boredom and emptiness, difficulties in interpersonal relationships, anxiety, etc. – as expressing problematic aspects of one's worldview: contradictions or tensions between two conceptions about how life should be lived, hidden presuppositions that have not been examined, views that fail to take into account various considerations, over-generalizations, expectations that cannot realistically be satisfied, fallacious interpretations, and so on.

Philosophers possess highly developed skills in relation to the task of analysing conceptions of the world, and are therefore well placed to assist people in a process of world-view interpretation and clarification. It is important to accept, according to Lahav, that this endeavour does not involve interpreting the *psychological* motives or mechanisms of the person, but helping the person to examine the basic assumptions or concepts around which his or her 'world' or 'reality' is constructed: 'One is likely to find among psychologists a tendency to deal with *feelings* of worthlessness instead of the *concept* of worthlessness, and with the *experience* of freedom rather than the *concept* of freedom' (Lahav 1995b: 14). It is by paying attention to the *concepts* that the person uses to make sense of his or her life that a more meaningful, coherent world-view can be constructed.

More recently, Lahav (2001) has moved beyond his original formulation of philosophical counselling as being essentially concerned with world-view interpretation. Lahav (2001) suggests that, while world-view interpretation remains fundamental to any philosophical counselling approach, it 'falls short of the much greater potential that philosophising can have in our lives' (p. 4). The 'greater potential' that can be achieved involves the *search for wisdom*, encompassing a 'journey beyond the person', and beyond the particular horizons of understanding within which he or she lives his or her everyday life. For Lahav, active engagement with philosophy can make this possible because it opens up a 'dialogue with an infinite network of ideas'.

A second core activity in philosophical counselling can be described as *entering into dialogue*. The use of dialogue as a way of exploring assumptions and opening up alternative ways of viewing the world is associated with the work of Socrates and many other philosophers down the centuries. One of the goals of dialogue is to demonstrate that there are always different ways of looking at an issue or problem. In Achenbach's (1995) words, the aim is to 'maintain philosophical skepticism concerning everything which . . . considers itself "true" and which therefore wants to abolish all further questioning', since it this attitude of scepticism that can foster a 'renewed interest' rather than stuck, passive acceptance.

A third key element in philosophical counselling involves the client learning to 'philosophize', both through the therapist acting as a model for how to question assumptions, and through reading philosophical texts selected by the counsellor. When struggling with a particular issue in their own life, a person may find that reading about how a philosopher approaches the same concept (e.g. Sartre on 'the emotions') gives them the means to generate new perspectives on their own situation.

Unlike other therapeutic approaches, which specify certain techniques and methods that should be used, practitioners of philosophical counselling have been reluctant to acknowledge that they espouse any kind of well defined 'method'. Indeed, Achenbach (1995: 68) has argued that a philosophical approach to therapy is 'beyond method':

> If there is anything that characterizes philosophy, it is that it does not accumulate insights, knowledge or stores of truths which only wait to be called up when needed . . . philosophical reflection does not produce solutions but rather questions them all.

From this perspective, anything that claimed to be 'the method' of philosophical counselling would itself be open to question. Schuster (1999: 96) describes her work as involving 'a free, spontaneous developing conversation for which no method can exist'. But what does it mean that 'no method can exist', or to claim to operate 'beyond method'? Clearly, philosophical counsellors can be seen to operate according to a set of principles, such as world-view interpretation and dialogue. But to tie these practices down to a defined method would be to deny the intrinsic open-endedness and creativity of a genuinely philosophical spirit of inquiry. The denial of 'method' may also be part of an attempt to distance philosophical counselling from psychological counselling and psychotherapy. It is perhaps significant that philosophical counsellors such as Achenbach and Schuster do not talk about 'clients' or 'patients' but instead use the term 'visitors'. A 'visitor' is someone who joins in a convivial exchange, rather than someone who buys a service or has a 'method' applied to their 'problem'. The desire to keep the options open regarding the role of the counsellor is captured well in Achenbach's image of the counsellors as pilot of a boat (see Box 11.2).

The work of Raabe (2001) represents an attempt to integrate these various ideas into a set of stages within philosophical counselling. Raabe has identified four stages within the philosophical counselling process:

1 *Free floating*. The counsellor listens, and encourages the client to talk, as a means of expressing and *discovering* the important elements of his or her world-view.
2 *Immediate problem resolution*. There is increasing dialogue between counsellor and client, in an attempt to interpret the meaning of the 'problem' presented by the client.
3 *Teaching as an intentional act*. The client is invited to read philosophical texts, and encouraged to apply critical analysis to issues that have been explored.
4 *Transcendence*. The client acquires an ability to reflect systematically on his or her beliefs and values: a philosophical stance becomes a 'way a living'.

An example of the application of Raabe's approach within a single case is provided in Box 11.3.

This brief account of some of the main ideas of philosophical counselling can supply little more than an introduction to an evolving approach, which includes within it a number of different themes and voices. Nevertheless, it seems clear that the significance of philosophical counselling for contemporary

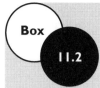

Box 11.2

Counselling 'beyond method'

Many philosophical counsellors appear to have struggled with Achenbach's insistence that this type of therapy is 'beyond method'. By way of elucidation, Raabe (2001: 57) reports on an explanation offered by Achenbach himself, when he compared being a philosophical counsellor to being the pilot of a boat:

> the philosophical counsellor is not the pilot whose job it is to take the place of the true captain of a boat long enough to steer the boat past dangers which he knows lie hidden beneath the surface of a particularly dangerous body of water. The philosophical counsellor is more a trained pilot who steps aboard a ship which has 'lost its speed or direction or both', and 'sits together' with its captain, exploring old and new maps, inspecting the compass, sextant and telescope, chatting with the captain about prevailing winds, sea currents, and the stars, over hot cups of coffee. Only later in the evening do they discuss questions such as whether he is in fact captain of this ship, and what it means to be the captain. The 'pilot' may tell the 'captain' what men in the past have said about being captain, and what those in other parts of the world have said about it. Conversation drifts from seriousness to laughter and back again until the captain once again takes up the controls of his ship, increases his speed, and goes his way 'over the unreliable sea'.

Achenbach uses this metaphor to invite reflection on the question of 'where is the method in all this?' Is the 'method' to be found in the 'intelligent talks about navigation', or in the 'view of the stars'? Or could the method be located in the 'laughter and coffee at the end'?

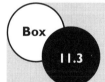

Box 11.3

Philosophical counselling in action: the case of Margot

Margot was in her late forties and worked as a health and diet advisor. She had a humanities degree, and had been in therapy before. She was an only child, who had two sons. Her main problem lay with one of her sons. She had many arguments with him, which resulted in a breakdown in their relationship that was highly distressing to her. She was also troubled by some aspects of her job. During the first two sessions, Margot told the story of her life, and described her current problems in detail. In the third session, the philosophical counsellor initiated a dialogue with Margot about the meaning of parent–child relationships, and gave her an article to read on this topic before the following session. The session included an extended discussion of the meaning of concepts such as 'love', 'responsibility' and 'karma'. The next few sessions followed a similar pattern, with exploration of the meaning of concepts relevant to Margot's idea of the 'good life' (e.g. her image of the 'perfect family') and world-view, with some discussion around how the concepts she used were associated with some of the difficulties in her life. Session 9 contained a discussion that was to be highly meaningful to Margot, concerning the question of the criteria for being a 'successful person'. She worried whether *she* was a 'successful person', and also whether her younger son would ever be successful. Her therapist's account of this conversation was:

> I wondered if simply *being*, as the Buddhists suggest, might be enough for some individuals. But Margot said he can't simply *be* when he's barely surviving in the real world. I told her that the seventeenth-century philosopher John Locke argued that so-called eccentrics are an important part of society, because they can make us wonder about those values, like success, that we often take for granted. But Margot said that a successful family is surely one in which everyone communicates with each other, whereas her sons are not friends and haven't spoken to each other for a long time, because their values are so different. Margot saw herself as being a failure for not having created a successful family. She told me about the failed 'little projects' of her younger son, and the great success of her older son. And yet she admired what her younger son was attempting to accomplish, despite his not making a lot of money at it. So we came back to the issue of how success is measured – what 'measuring stick' do we use? Is it money; is it happiness; is it living according to social norms, or what?
>
> (Raabe 2001: 241)

In the next two sessions, Margot said she wanted to continue learning about 'thinking tools', and worked with the counsellors around the principles of a 'good argument' and the 'fallacy of hasty conclusion'. She began to apply these skills to her own situation, and realized the extent to which she arrived at 'hasty conclusions' in relation to her younger son and her workplace problems. Margot appeared, as a result, to be able to resolve these difficult interpersonal issues in a manner that was satisfactory for her. The twelfth and final session was devoted to more general issues, around relativism and what Margot called 'cosmic truths', and appeared to represent a celebration and consolidation of her use of philosophical skills.

A more detailed account and interpretation of this case can be found in Raabe (2001). It seems evident that there were many aspects of what took place in this work that were very unlike the usual practices of counselling: reading philosophical texts, discussing ideas rather than feelings, learning the 'principles of a good argument'. But there is also evidence of the creation of a trusting, collaborative relationship, within which Margot was able to talk freely about what troubled her. There is also evidence that Margot achieved both understanding and self-acceptance – outcomes that are central to any form of therapy.

theory and practice is substantial. Philosophical counselling appears to be acceptable to clients, and effective, at least in terms of the evidence of its increasing popularity. But how can this be? How can an approach that does not put forward a model of 'dysfunction' or 'intervention', and that operates without any reference to psychological constructs at all, actually operate? What makes it work?

To understand how it can be that philosophical counselling can be, in principle, as effective as psychological approaches such as psychoanalysis, person-centred counselling or cognitive–behavioural therapy, it is necessary to take into account the following key issues:

1 Philosophical counselling has come into existence at a time when the majority of consumers or users already possess an understanding of what to expect from therapy, and how it operates. Clients (or visitors) therefore enter philosophical counselling with a capacity and willingness to use whatever is being offered. From this perspective, it is possible to see that some of the 'theory' that surrounds mainstream therapies operates as a means of convincing clients of the legitimacy of the particular approach, and even as a means of enabling therapists to socialize individuals into the role of client. It may be that, in the early twenty-first century, these facets of theory are not necessary.

2 Philosophical counselling may be a better way of delivering some of the experiences and activities that have been shown, through research, to be responsible for good outcomes in established therapy approaches. For example, philosophical counsellors place great emphasis on a collaborative, collegial way of working, while retaining credibility as 'experts' in relation to philosophical knowledge. The consistent use of dialogue may enable clients to 'externalize' their problem (see Chapter 9) rather than identifying the problem as intrinsic to their sense of self. Philosophers are likely to be much better trained than cognitive therapists in identifying and challenging irrational beliefs and dysfunctional (non-logical) thought processes, because all of their training has emphasized this skill. Finally, the process of exploring a client's world-view is similar to the Rogerian notion of empathic engagement. It may be, therefore, that even though it does not explicitly base itself on what can be understood as the common or essential factors responsible for therapeutic change (see Chapter 3), philosophical counselling in fact represents a highly sensitive means of making these helpful experiences available to clients.

3 Philosophical counselling may possess 'added value'. It may be that philosophical counselling encompasses at least two elements that are not found in other approaches to counselling. First, by eschewing psychological theories of dysfunction, philosophical counselling does not appear to possess any possible means of labelling a client in terms of underlying 'deficit'. Some clients may be reassured or empowered by this. Second, philosophical counsellors are in a position to introduce visitors to the immense cultural resource represented by the philosophy literature. This is a resource that could not be offered by counsellors who lack a philosophy training. There is good evidence that

'bibliotherapy' can be therapeutically useful for many clients (see Chapter 17). However, reading philosophy surely has the potential to take clients far beyond the self-help texts that are currently recommended by therapists.

It is necessary to acknowledge that philosophical counselling is a newly emerging approach, and could yet develop in a number of directions. It seems unlikely, given the diversity of philosophical thinking, that this approach to counselling will ever adopt the status of claiming to be a unitary 'theory', such as psychoanalysis. However, moves in the direction of professionalizing philosophical counselling – for example, by setting up training courses, may introduce a greater degree of conformity. At present, philosophical counsellors appear to have been at pains to keep themselves separate from psychologically based counsellors and psychotherapists. It may be in future that there is more communication and joint working across this boundary, and it will be fascinating to see what kinds of new ideas arise from such collaboration.

Postmodern therapy

On the whole, counselling and psychotherapy are practices that are embedded in what many sociologists (and philosophers) would call *modernity*. The 'modern' world that was created through and from the time of the Industrial Revolution was in many ways different from the traditional social world that had existed before. 'Modernity' was associated with the replacement of religious beliefs and values with those of science and rationality. People became fascinated by the promise of 'progress' and improvement, made possible by advances in science and technology. People became much more aware of their existence as autonomous individuals, capable of change and development, rather than as members of a family or community in which they were expected to 'know their place'. The modern world that came into full expression during the twentieth century was firmly rooted in both individualism and an assumption of the validity of scientific theories and progress.

Much of this began to change towards the end of the twentieth century. Many people began to see that globalization associated with modernity threatened many traditional values and rituals, and forms of community, that were essential to well-being. There was increasing scepticism about science and technology, which were perceived as being destructive to the planet. People appeared to find it hard to believe in anything. The sociologist Jean-François Lyotard described this state of affairs as the 'postmodern condition', characterized by an 'incredulity towards metanarratives'. An increasing circle of sociologists and philosophers, following Lyotard, also began to develop their own analyses of what appeared to them to be the gradual breakdown of modernity, as an organizing 'metanarrative' for social and cultural life, and its replacement by something else. But the 'something else', the new form of social life that was to come, was not at all easy to define or describe – it was in the process of happening. An accessible discussion of nature of postmodernity can be found in Lyon (1994).

The idea of 'postmodernity' introduces a different way of looking at persons and also at therapeutic practices. For example, it becomes hard to accept the idea that a person needs to be understood in terms of internal structures (the unconscious, the self-concept, schemas etc.). These theories become viewed as 'grand narratives' to be treated with scepticism. They are stories that are told within particular cultural enclaves, rather than constituting universal scientific 'truths'. The attention of postmodern therapists and psychologists therefore turns in the direction of an interest in how 'clients' and 'therapists' use these stories or discourses in order to construct relationships and guide action. The focus is much more on what happens *between* people, rather than on what takes place *within* them. In a postmodern, globalized, changing world, there are many differing identities on offer to a person. Indeed, the person may effectively espouse different identities at work and at home, or at different stages of their life. In therapy, this leads to a concern to explore how a person can live with such diversity: there is no assumption that there is a core, 'true' self beneath all this. Therapy becomes much to do with the ways in which the person constructs realities using language and metaphor.

Important figures in the struggle to evolve a postmodern approach to therapy have been Michael White and David Epston (1990), Steve de Shazer (1994) and Kenneth Gergen (Gergen and Kaye 1992). Other useful sources include McNamee and Gergen (1992), Polkinghorne (1992) and Sass (1992). Their effort has been strongly informed by a philosophical perspective, in developing a critique of the assumptions implicit in the ideas of 'modernist', mainstream therapies, and then finding ways of adapting the terminology of postmodern thinkers to the purpose of revisioning the aims and process of therapy.

The value of conceptual analysis for counsellors and psychotherapists

The use of *conceptual analysis* represents an intrinsic aspect of any attempt to apply a philosophical perspective. Conceptual analysis involves examining the *meaning* of an idea or concept, with the aim of moving beyond an everyday or 'taken-for-granted' understanding and arriving instead at a richer appreciation of how a word or concept is used. The assumption is that, much of the time, we do not reflect deeply on the ideas and concepts that we use, and can end up thinking and acting in contradictory and self-defeating ways because we do pay sufficient attention to the underlying or hidden meanings that are subtly conveyed when we employ certain concepts. Conceptual analysis is a particularly important tool for counsellors and psychotherapists, for two reasons. First, clients often use words and ideas that are familiar to us, but in ways that do not quite 'fit' with our own usage. It is useful, at these times, to be able to explore the many possible meanings of such concepts. Second, the professional, theoretical and research literature tends to be structured around debates that centre on differing inter-pretations of key concepts such as 'self' or 'emotion'. The complex, multicultural and 'multivoiced' nature of contemporary society means that many ideas are *contested*. To be able to participate fully in theoretical and professional conversa-tions it is not enough to know the dictionary definitions of the terms that are used: it is also necessary to be able to 'deconstruct' how these terms are deployed by different interest groups to serve different purposes.

Many examples could be given of the application of conceptual analysis within the domain of counselling and psychotherapy. For reasons of space, the discussion here focuses on two key concepts: 'self' and 'mental illness'. These are terms that are central to the practice of therapy, and each of them has been the focus of considerable critical attention.

The concept of 'self' has been much debated within social science and philo-sophy. One of the potential sources of confusion associated with this concept is whether it refers to a 'thing' or 'object' that can be known (as in the adage 'know thyself') or whether it denotes an entity with active agency ('he was self-motivated'). The social philosopher George Herbert Mead was probably the first to describe 'self' as comprising an active 'I' and passive 'me'. However, this redescrip-tion of the properties of self (into 'I' and 'me') does not really address the question of how it can be that self is both active knower and known (an object of know-ledge). One strategy for beginning to make sense of how this apparent contradic-tion might be understood is to explore where the concept came from. An analysis of the historical origins and development of a concept can often throw light on apparently puzzling aspects of its current usage. The most thorough study of the historical development of ideas of self can be found in the writings of the philo-sopher Charles Taylor (1989), who has shown that the competing notions of self that exist within modern society result from fundamental debates over morality, concerning what is involved in living a 'good life'. For example, a belief that the good life involves making one's way in society (a moral position that might be described as utilitarianism or instrumentalism) is associated with a view of self as active and purposeful (the self of behaviourism and cognitive psychology). By contrast, a belief that the good life involves being true to one's feelings and in touch with nature (a position that might be described as Romantic expressivism) is more consistent with a view of self as comprising an inner space or territory to be explored (e.g. the 'self' of psychoanalysis and humanistic psychology). For Taylor, an adequate understanding of notions of 'self' as used by contemporary counsellors and psychotherapists can only be achieved by unravelling underly-ing meanings, which comprise a kind of living 'residue' of older arguments and debates. Another approach to conceptual analysis is to consider the different meanings of related words. For example, within psychotherapy discourse, 'self' may be used interchangeably with terms such as 'person', 'ego', 'identity' or 'individual', or used in combination with other terms (for example, 'self-schema', 'self-actualization', 'self-harm', 'self-efficacy'). Unpicking the implications of such 'linked' meanings can reveal a great deal about the assumptions embodied within a concept (see Box 11.4).

Box

11.4

Conceptual analysis in action: self or ego?

Within theories of counselling and psychotherapy, there are many concepts that appear to refer to rather similar phenomena or processes. It can often be difficult to know whether these different 'labels' merely refer to different ways of describing the same thing, or whether they actually reflect quite different meanings or understandings of what is being discussed. On some occasions, too, it can almost seem as though there is an element of fashion in the use of terminology – some ideas are popular but then go out of fashion and become replaced by others. In psychoanalytic theory, the words 'ego' and 'self' are both used to refer to the core, conscious identity of the person. But are 'ego' and 'self' the same? A useful example of conceptual analysis in action is offered in a passage written by the psychoanalyst Sheldon Bach (2001):

> For those of us who were trained almost 40 years ago, hardly anybody at all had a self. To be exact, most patients had egos, which varied on a dimension from weak to strong, but hardly any of them had selves. Today, by contrast, if I can believe what my students and patients tell me, most people have selves, which vary on a dimension from true to false, but hardly any of them have egos. Are we simply witnessing a passing change in fashion, like short hemlines, tango dancing or tulipomania, or is a substantive addition being made to our knowledge and understanding of human nature? . . .
>
> Freud, who at the time was just inventing psychoanalysis and had learned to live with ambiguity, deliberately used the term *das ich* to mean both *self*, an experience-near, subjective and phenomenological construct, and *ego*, an experience-far, objective, and theoretical construct . . .
>
> The ego is a scientific fantasy of the psychoanalyst. It is a construct that integrates observations made of the subject's behavior from the viewpoint of psychic determinism, drive motivation, and conflict – that is, from the *intrapsychic* viewpoint of structural theory, isolated from the external context. It provides an impartial, objective, structurally equidistant and dispassionate view of the person as object of our scrutiny and investigation – a view, as it were, from the moon.
>
> The self, in its common usage, is an experiential construct. It integrates observations about the subject's experience from a phenomenological and subjective point of view – that is, from the viewpoint of free will rather than determinism because the person feels that his or her actions are free rather than determined – and from the viewpoints of spontaneity, activity and intentionality rather than of drive, conflict and compromise formation. The self provides a partisan, subjective, and impassioned view of the person as perceiver of his own experience. The self is one pole of an interpersonal or *interpsychic* theory, the other pole being the object.

> Both these points of view or perspectives are necessary to fully understand a human being, just as position and velocity are necessary to specify an atomic particle.
>
> (Bach 2001: 45–7)

Here, Bach clarifies the differences between these two concepts by showing how each has a different use, and how each embodies contrasting assumptions about the nature of reality (e.g. objectivity versus subjectivity). He closes his argument by suggesting that the two concepts are complementary and necessary – it is not the case that one is 'right' and the other is 'wrong'. There is no doubt that Bach's analysis does not offer any kind of closure around the meaning of 'self' as an idea used by therapists – there are other dimensions of 'self' that he does not attempt to unravel here. Nevertheless, what he has written makes a significant contribution to our understanding of these concepts because he helps us all to be more precise in how we use these terms, and the meanings and assumptions implied by each of them. His discussion is an example of how a philosophical approach that carefully considers the meanings of ideas can be helpful for counsellors and psychotherapists.

The concept of 'mental illness' represents an idea that lies at the heart of the network of assumptions which legitimate the very notion of psychological therapy. Many counsellors and psychotherapists would wish to make a sharp distinction between what they do and the practices and assumptions of medical model psychiatry. Nevertheless, whenever therapy is described as a 'treatment', or a client is considered to be suffering from a 'disorder', then the idea of mental illness is being invoked. The language of 'mental illness' permeates European and North American culture, and it is obviously important for counsellors and psychotherapists to be aware of what these ideas mean, and what they *do* at a conceptual level.

A sustained and systematic critique of the concept of 'mental illness' can be found in the writings of the psychoanalyst Thomas Szasz (1961), who argues that to describe what he calls 'problems in living' as symptoms of an 'illness' involves the use of metaphor. It is as if the person were saying: 'the pattern of behaviour and feeling that we call "depression" is *like* an illness, because it involves an incapacity to function in society, and a need for assistance from other people.' In these senses, Szasz would admit, depression is *like* a medical condition such as measles. But the analogy, or metaphor, has very strict limits. A 'problem in living' such as depression is *not* similar to an illness such as measles in many ways: it cannot be prevented by vaccination, its biological cause is not known and so on. Depression is also very *unlike* measles in that it can be helped through conversation (counselling or psychotherapy), whereas measles cannot be resolved in this manner at all. One of the central points that Szasz is making is that, although the metaphor of mental illness is superficially attractive, it actually conceals more than it reveals, and in the end leads to confusion and mystification.

However, although the idea that mental 'illness' is a metaphor is easy to grasp, and is readily understood by most people, it has remained the dominant way of talking about 'problems in living' within Western society for around 200 years. Why is this? There are no doubt many reasons that can be given. For one thing, many people would regard the attribution of 'illness' an advance on other, traditional explanations for troubled behaviour. Explanations along the lines of moral laxity (religious metaphors) or genetic weakness (eugenic metaphors) have often been associated with highly punitive approaches to those who are troubled. Moreover, there are many people who believe that mental 'illness' actually is an illness, with biological causes and treatments that will be discovered in due course. But there are perhaps additional, political reasons for the popularity of the illness metaphor. By being able to argue that 'personal troubles' are due to individual causes (like faulty mental functioning), it is possible to deflect attention from the idea that such troubles may result from social factors, such as oppression, racism or poverty. It is easier and more convenient for political elites to arrange for counselling or drug treatment to be provided to 'patients' than to ensure the rights of all citizens. By labelling someone as 'ill', it is also possible to justify the use of medical and legal restraints on his or her freedom, by arguing that the person's 'illness' means that they are no longer capable of making rational decisions, and that compulsory 'treatment' is required.

This critique of the concept of 'mental illness' illustrates some important principles of conceptual analysis. First, it is useful to consider the possibility that ideas might have originated as metaphors (figurative comparisons), which have 'reified' (become taken as 'real'). Second, it is valuable to examine the way a concept is *used* within society; what social practices does it support or legitimate? Many constituent aspects of the 'mental illness' metaphor have been studied. For example, Hallam (1994) offers a fascinating account of the ways in which the concept of 'anxiety' has been historically constructed and used within society. Stiles and Shapiro (1989) have discussed the implications, within the field of psychotherapy research, of the adoption of a medical model in the form of what they call the 'drug metaphor'. In much research, psychotherapy is studied as if it were a drug, with investigations focusing on the effect of differing 'doses' of the drug, or the inclusion of different 'ingredients'. Stiles and Shapiro (1989) argue that this way of looking at therapy results in a distorted picture, because it ignores the active involvement of the client, and the importance of the therapeutic relationship.

Conceptual analysis represents the attempt to open up the meaning of a concept by considering an idea or term from four perspectives: how its meaning has evolved over time; thinking about the concept as a metaphor; comparing its meaning to that of cognate terms; and observing how the idea is currently used within social groups. The technique of conceptual analysis is a valuable, but underutilized, tool within contemporary counselling and psychotherapy, and has a great deal to offer in relation to clarifying the underlying issues surrounding the similarities and differences between the many therapy theories that have been devised.

Conclusions

This chapter has explored some of the ways in which contemporary counselling and psychotherapy has developed a productive relationship with philosophy. There are many approaches to counselling, such as rational emotive therapy, cognitive therapy and the person-centred approach, which make use of discrete elements of philosophical thinking (for example, references to phenomenology in person-centred counselling). Existential counselling and psychotherapy represents a form of therapy that is rigorously grounded in a specific 'school' of philosophy, and involves the direct application of this set of ideas in explaining the causes of clients' problems, understanding the process of therapy and outlining the type of therapeutic method and relationship adopted by the practitioner. Although existential therapy has in practice been influenced by other, somewhat similar, 'conversational' approaches such as psychoanalysis, psychodynamic psychotherapy and the humanistic therapies, it remains firmly based in existential philosophy, and continues to draw inspiration from that body of ideas. However, existential therapy can be regarded as comprising, essentially, psychologists employing existential ideas to interpret their clients' 'symptoms'. The *philosophical counselling* movement, by contrast, involves philosophers interacting directly with clients (or, as many of them would prefer, 'visitors'). Philosophical counsellors are at pains to point out that what they do is *not* psychology or psychotherapy. Their aim is to offer visitors the opportunity to participate in philosophical discourse, characterized by dialogue, questioning assumptions and the use of philosophical texts. Up to now, no research has been carried out into the extent to which this approach actually benefits people. On the other hand, the number of practicing philosopher counsellors has increased steadily over the past 20 years, and the case studies provided by writers such as Schuster (1999) and Raabe (2001) offer plausible accounts of good outcomes. There is no reason to believe that philosophical counselling should turn out to be any less effective than any other form of therapy. From a 'common factors' perspective (see Chapter 3), a philosophical approach could well turn out to be an excellent vehicle for delivering 'non-specific' therapeutic elements such as a collaborative relationship, conveying hope and problem-solving skills.

Postmodern therapies, and the use of conceptual analysis, can be viewed as examples of the use of a philosophical perspective for *critical* purposes. It is necessary to be continually reconstructing therapy, in response to a changing society and culture. The ideas and techniques that were creative and generative for one generation all too readily become commonplace for members of the following generation. Therapy concepts, such as 'complex', 'libido' and 'empathy', become assimilated into general usage and lose much of their power to act as catalysts for therapeutic change. Methods, such as long-term therapy or the analyst sitting behind the head of the patient lying on a couch, become unappealing or unacceptable to people whose lifestyle and values are much different from those of the original founders of psychotherapy. Philosophy clearly has a major part to play in the reconstruction of therapy, by asking basic questions about what is happening, and what it means. Philosophy can be regarded, here, as a kind of cultural tool for 'fresh thinking'. For example, within the group of therapists who describe themselves as 'postmodern', the drive does not seem to be to consolidate yet another 'approach' to therapy, but to think the unthinkable: What else could therapy be? What comes after therapy? Can there be a postpsychological way of doing things?

The growing appreciation of the relevance of philosophy for counselling and psychotherapy raises some important questions for training. At the moment, philosophical themes and texts are given little or no space on training courses. There are no texts, apart from Howard (2000), that attempt to create a bridge between the world of therapy and the world of philosophy at an introductory level. The integration of philosophy, in some guise, into the therapy training syllabus remains a key task for the future.

Chapter summary

- Philosophical thought offers a rich cultural and intellectual resource which can contribute to counselling in several ways.

- Existential counselling and psychotherapy represents a well established philosophically informed approach.

- Existential therapy centres on the exploration of the client's sense of being-in-the-world.

- Philosophical counselling has developed in recent years as a form of applied philosophy.

- In practice, philosophical counsellors invite clients to examine the basic assumptions that underpin their 'world-view', and engage in dialogue about alternative ways of making sense of problems.

- In a more general sense, the methods of philosophical analysis can be used to clarify the meaning of concepts that are used in therapy, such as 'self' or 'anxiety'.

- The movement within therapy towards greater integration is likely to lead to a greater interest in philosophical ideas on the part of counsellors and psychotherapists.

Topics for reflection and discussion

1 This chapter offered a brief introduction to the conceptual analysis of two important concepts: self and mental illness. What would you add to the analyses offered here? Are there other aspects of the meanings of these concepts that you believe are important? In your own experience, how do you observe these concepts being used in everyday conversation?

2 One of the most widely read books in the field of counselling is *On Becoming a Person*, by Carl Rogers (1961). By highlighting, then reflecting on, relevant passages of this book, analyse what Rogers means by the term 'person'. Are there any apparent contradictions or tensions within his use of this term? Are there other meanings of 'person' that are excluded by Rogers? Why might this be?

3 Lahav, and other philosophical counsellors, insist that they do not deal with *psychological* processes. Do you believe that this is possible? Can people be helped to overcome their problems without considering psychological factors?

Key terms and concepts

authenticity
being-in-the-world
conceptual analysis
dialogue
Eigenwelt
existentialism
logotherapy
Mitwelt
modernity

phenomenology
philosophical analysis
philosophical counselling
postmodernism
scepticism
Umwelt
utilitarianism
world-view

Suggested further reading

Philosophy represents a vast and multifaceted area of study. Blackburn (1999) and Hospers (1997) offer accessible introductions to the methods of philosophical analysis. *The Story of Philosophy*, by Magee (1998), presents an entertaining excursion through the great philosophers, and has the advantage of being lavishly illustrated. Howard's (2000) book *Philosophy for Counselling and Psychotherapy* is the only attempt, so far, to provide an overview of philosophical ideas and their relevance for therapy practice. Howard's book is consistently interesting, and is very much written for practitioners. It is probably the single current 'must read' item in this area at the moment. The paper by Messer and Woolfolk (1998) effectively addresses the application of philosophy to a number of key issues in therapy, using a case study approach.

A somewhat more advanced discussion of philosophical issues in counselling and psychotherapy theory, practice and research can be found in *Between Conviction and Uncertainty: Philosophical Guidelines for the Practicing Psychotherapist* (Downing 2000). The collections of essays edited by Mace (1999a) and King-Spooner (1999) also include a range of stimulating and thoughtful contributions on a range of philosophical topics. Sass (1988) provides an excellent philosophical critique of humanistic psychology and therapy.

Sources of the Self: The Making of Modern Identity, by Charles Taylor, is an important book that should be read by all therapists at some point in their careers. However, it is a complex and demanding piece of writing. Somewhat briefer excursions into the same territory can be found in Baumeister (1987) and Logan (1987).

Schuster (1999) and Raabe (2001) are two recent texts that review current developments and practices in philosophical counselling. Both contain sections that are likely to be challenging for readers who lack any training in philosophy. Nevertheless, each also contains a wealth of useful ideas and insights, and both use carefully chosen case materials to illustrate the application of philosophical counselling in action. The best brief introduction to existential counselling and psychotherapy is to be found in van Deurzen (1999).

12 The counselling relationship

Introduction: the counselling relationship as a key theme in contemporary theory and practice

The actual contact between a counsellor and a person who is seeking help lies at the heart of what counselling is about. Although a counsellor may be able to use theory to make sense of the client's difficulties, and may have a range of techniques at his or her disposal for revealing and overcoming these difficulties, the fact remains that theory and technique are delivered through the presence and being of the counsellor as a person: the basic tool of counselling is the person of the counsellor. An interest in the nature of the therapeutic relationship represents a common concern of all therapy practitioners and theorists. Even if different approaches to counselling make sense of the client–therapist relationship in different ways, they all agree that effective counselling depends on how this kind of relationship operates, what happens when it goes wrong and how to fix it.

The relationship between a client and patient and their therapist is probably unique for the majority of people who enter counselling. Even in short-term counselling, the person is exposed to a situation in which another person will listen to him or her for several hours, will make every effort to see issues and dilemmas from the speaker's perspective, will treat what is said with extreme respect and confidentiality and will abstain from seeking to gratify any of their own needs during this time. There is a deep caring, and sense of being 'special', that is unusual or even absent from the experience of most people in Western industrial societies. Of course, such an experience may be hard to accept: can the counsellor really be trusted? Is he or she genuinely interested in what I am saying? How can I take so much without giving something back? The intensity with which many therapy clients experience their relationship with their therapist is captured well in a study by Lott (1999), who interviewed women around their feelings about their therapists, and by Wachholz and Stuhr (1999), who found that, 12 years after the end of therapy, clients still held vivid memories of their therapist and the qualities of their relationship with him or her (see Box 12.1).

The importance of the counsellor–client relationship has been reflected in the findings of many research studies. Research that has invited clients to describe what has been helpful or unhelpful for them in counselling has consistently found that clients identify relationship factors as being more important than the use of therapist techniques. In the eyes of the client, it is the quality of their relationship with their therapist that has made the largest contribution to the value of therapy for them. McLeod (1990) has reviewed this research literature. Another line of research has involved measuring the strength of the client–therapist relationship early in therapy, and looking at whether a strong therapeutic alliance predicts a subsequent good outcome. This research, which has been reviewed by Orlinsky et al. (1994), repeatedly demonstrates a high positive correlation between the quality of the therapeutic relationship and the amount the client gains from therapy. These research findings have been interpreted as providing support for the role of non-specific factors in therapy, which were discussed in Chapter 3: the relationship between client and therapist is a core non-specific factor existing in all forms of therapy (Hubble et al. 1999).

Why is the therapeutic relationship so important? There are several ways of making sense of what happens in the relationship between a counsellor and a client. There are some counsellors, often influenced by the cognitive–behavioural tradition, or by ideas about professional–client relationships in occupations such as medicine, teaching or social work, who regard the building of 'rapport' to be an initial step in counselling, of significance mainly as a platform from which structured therapeutic interventions can be made. In contrast, there are other

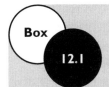

Box

12.1

The intensity of the therapeutic relationship: the client's internalization of the counsellor

Any therapy which continues for more than two or three sessions represents a situation in which an intense relationship between client and counsellor is likely to develop. The experience of being the focus of attention of another person, continuously for a whole hour at a time, and becoming more and more *known* to this person, in terms of highly personal and private information (but for the other person to remain largely unknown), is almost certain to be unique for the majority of people. For many clients, the experience is one of becoming exposed and vulnerable, of taking risks. As a client, one is highly sensitive to what the counsellor or therapist has to say. In all probability, the counsellor says little (compared to the client's output of words), so what he or she does say takes on a special significance. The client may wonder why the counsellor replies in a particular way, and what it signifies about the kind of person the counsellor might be, outside of the therapy room. And as a client, as one begins to speak of things that one may never have talked about before, things that have hitherto been held within an inner, private dialogue, the voice of the counsellor comes to be added to the voices within that inner space. Most of us can 'hear', within us, the voices of some or all of our parents, siblings, life partner and children. Being in therapy can often result in the addition of the voice of the therapist to this inner chorus.

In a qualititive study carried out by Knox *et al.* (1999), 13 people in long-term therapy were interviewed about their 'internal representation' of their therapist. These clients reported a range of different types of internal representation. Some described vivid, detailed internal 'conversations' with their therapist. For others, their inner therapist was described in more dream-like terms. The frequency of occurrence of these internal images varied a great deal, with some clients using their 'inner therapist' on a daily basis, and others only monthly. One of the main themes emerging from this study was the significant degree to which clients deliberately used such internal images to continue the therapeutic process outside of sessions. Examples of such usage included:

> One client invoked a literal and complete re-creation of the therapy setting in her mind when she felt anxious as she drove in heavy traffic. She repeated words that her therapist had told her about being a good problem solver. These words enabled her to avert a full-blown panic attack, and allowed her to do the things she wanted to do in her life . . .
>
> Another client reported envisioning her therapist extending her arms to the client, beseeching her to come for help when she considered self-mutilation.
> (Knox *et al.* 1999: 248)

On the whole, the clients interviewed in this study regarded this process of internal representation of the therapist as a beneficial aspect of therapy, although some were concerned that it might indicate an over-dependence on the therapist, or reflect the absence of other supportive individuals in their life. Few of these clients had mentioned these between-session experiences to their therapist, possibly because they believed that such occurrences were not 'normal'.

The Knox et al. (1999) study presents the internal representation of the therapist in a positive light. However, their study was carried out on a small sample of clients still in therapy, who probably volunteered to participate in the research because they were comfortable with their therapists and their progress in therapy. By contrast, Wachholz and Stuhr (1999; Stuhr and Wachholz 2001) interviewed 50 clients who had completed therapy 12 years previously, within the outpatient department of the Hamburg University Hospital. Half of these clients had received psychodynamic therapy, and half had received client-centred therapy. Some of the cases had been successful, while in other cases the therapy appeared to have only limited benefit for the client. Wachholz and Stuhr (1999) found that the internalized 'images of the therapist' that emerged in the follow-up interviews could be analysed in terms of eight 'types':

1 *Therapist as 'mature mother' object.* There was a trusting relationship, which satisfied the client's needs. Over the course of therapy, however, the client developed a more differentiated image of the therapist, as someone who had both good and bad sides. The relationship at termination was therefore both realistic and honest.
2 *Therapist as 'symbiotic mother'.* The therapist is exclusively a 'good', warm voice that is wholly attuned to the client's needs and never challenges the client's attitudes.
3 *Therapist as 'insufficient mother'.* The therapist fails to accept the client's needs to be accepted and supported: 'this permanent frustration proves intolerable for patients . . . they react by breaking off therapy, or by subsequently searching for better and more understanding mothers in countless additional therapies' (p. 334).
4 *Therapist as 'unattainable father'.* At the outset of therapy, some women clients perceive their male therapist as the partner they have always longed for: loving, understanding, accepting. As therapy progresses, these clients become increasingly disappointed and angry, and 'regard themselves as the victims of an obscure game whose rules they do not understand' (p. 334).
5 *Therapist as 'stern demanding father'.* The client's inner image is of a father whose affection and esteem she vainly struggles to win.
6 *Therapist as 'devalued object'.* The client does not feel understood or accepted at all, and is internally critical of the therapist.
7 *Therapist as 'repressed object'.* The client finds it impossible to re-create a detailed image of the therapist at all.
8 *Therapist as 'unreachable, ideal object'.* The therapist is represented as an omniscient, wise figure who stands on a pedestal and is beyond reach.

The internalized images associated with therapists who had been 'motherly' in a constructive manner (types 1 and 2) were described by clients as 'warm memories' and 'what they had been looking for'. All of the other internalized images were, to a greater or lesser extent, relatively unhelpful for clients. The research carried out by Wachholz and Stuhr (1999) conveys a sense of the complexity of the therapeutic relationship, and the degree to which the client's internalized image of the therapist is a product of the therapist's style, the client's needs and the interaction between them both. Their findings also point towards fascinating aspects of the role of gender and theoretical orientation in therapy. Both types of therapy (psychodynamic and client-centred) and all combinations of client and therapist gender were found across all the 'image types' except two: the 'stern demanding fathers' (type 5) were all male psychodynamic therapists with female clients, and all the clients who had negative father images (types 4 and 5) were female, with male therapists.

counsellors, working within the psychoanalytic tradition, who see the relationship as an arena in which the client acts out dysfunctional relationship patterns, thus enabling the therapist to observe these patterns and set about remediating them. Finally, there are counsellors operating within the humanistic tradition who regard authentic contact or encounter between persons as intrinsically healing. Some counsellors move between these types of relationship, depending on the client with whom they are working, or the stage of the work.

The aim of this chapter is to examine the different images of the therapeutic relationship that have been proposed in the counselling and psychotherapy literature, and to explore the ways in which these ideas have been applied in practice.

Images of the therapeutic relationship

It is useful to think about the different types or style of therapeutic relationship in terms of *images*, rather than as lists of attributes or theoretical models. By reflecting on images of relationship, it is possible to consider a wide array of cultural images that lie behind, or may fuse with, the approach to the counsellor–client relationship advocated by different theorists. For example, images of the counsellor or helper as confessor, priest, healer, shaman or friend are also present in contemporary theory and practice, but are generally referred to in an implicit rather than explicit fashion. The notion of 'image' also reminds us that the ideas of Freud, Rogers and others arise from their imagination. Any relationship between two people is played out at a number of levels: social, emotional, linguistic, physical etc. Theories of what goes on between counsellor/therapist and client are inevitably a partial representation of the relationship, one among many possible versions of reality. It is important to recognize that ideas such as transference and empathy are *ways of describing* some of what is happening in therapy, rather than constituting objective truths. Finally, the idea of 'image' also reminds us that the intensity and focus of an image can vary. In short-term counselling, there may not be time for an intense relationship to become established. In longer-term counselling, the relationship may become stronger and more sharply defined, but may at the same time begin to be overlaid by other images, as counsellor and client get to know each other in different ways.

The psychoanalytic concept of transference: therapist as container

The earliest attempt to make sense of what was happening in the relationship between a psychotherapist and a patient was made by Freud. When Freud and Breuer, in the 1880s, began their experiments with what they called the 'talking cure', they became aware that their patients often responded to them in terms of strong emotional reactions: admiration, erotic attraction, anger, hatred. Initially, it was hard for Freud and Breuer to make sense of why this was taking place: these emotional responses did not seem to arise from anything in the therapy itself. Eventually, they reasoned that these reactions had their origins in unresolved childhood conflicts, desires and emotional needs, which were now finding expression, many years later, in the safe environment of the therapy session. Freud (1917/1973: 494–6) eventually came to use the term *transference* to describe this phenomenon:

> a phenomenon which is intimately bound up with the nature of the illness itself . . . known by us as *transference* . . . We mean a transference of feelings on to the person of the doctor, since we do not believe that the situation in the treatment could justify such feelings. We suspect, on the contrary, that the whole readiness for these feelings is derived from elsewhere, that they were already prepared in the patient, and upon the opportunity offered by the analytic treatment, are transferred on to the person of the doctor. Transference can appear as a passionate demand for love . . . a proposal for an inseparable friendship . . . jealousy of everyone close to [the doctor] in real life . . . It is out of the question for us to yield to the patient's demands deriving from the transference . . . We overcome the transference by pointing out to the patient that his feelings do not arise from the present situation and do not apply to the person of the doctor, but that they are repeating something that happened to him earlier. In this way we oblige him to transform his repetition into a memory. By that means the transference, which, whether affectionate or hostile, seemed in every case to constitute the greatest threat to treatment, becomes its best tool, by whose help the most secret compartments of mental life can be opened.

This discovery, by Freud, of how to unlock 'the most secret compartments of mental life' became a cornerstone of psychoanalytic, and later psychodynamic, therapy. One of the core tasks of the therapist was, according to this approach, to create a relationship within which transference reactions could be powerfully and consistently exhibited by the client.

Freud and his colleagues then observed that these expressions of feeling on the part of the patient often triggered off corresponding responses within the analyst. For example, if a patient was expressing hostility towards the therapist, he or she might find himself or herself being angry in return, or seeking to defend his or her actions. If a patient commented on the attractiveness of the analyst, it would be natural to feel flattered, or to become seduced. Freud and those who worked alongside him in the early years of the development of psychoanalysis came to describe these therapist reactions as *counter-transference*. For a long time, psychoanalysts tended to view counter-transference as an unwelcome source of bias on the part of the therapist, and suggested that sufficient personal analysis would enable a therapist to be able to be free of these reactions, and achieve a state of absolute neutrality in response to the patient. Although the Hungarian analyst Sandor Ferenczi argued vigorously in the 1930s that the analyst should be willing to make active use of his or her counter-transference response to the client, it was only in the 1950s, through the work of British analysts such as Heimann and Symington (see Chapter 4), that counter-transference came to be regarded as a valuable source of therapeutic material.

The image that is used by many psychoanalytic and psychodynamic counsellors and psychotherapists to convey their sense of the type of relationship they seek to construct with clients is that of the *container*. The relationship becomes a place within which the most painful and destructive feelings of the client can be expressed and acted out, because they are held safe there. Psychodynamic counsellors also draw on the image of the *boundary*, or *frame*, to characterize the therapeutic relationship. It is only when the edges of the container are clearly defined that the client knows that they are there. If these edges are permeable or indistinct the client will be left with uncertainty about whether their desire or rage can in fact be contained and held effectively. The image of the container itself evokes and is associated with aspects of *parenting*: for example, the parent making sure that a toddler having a tantrum does not harm himself or herself, or the setting of limits for teenagers experimenting with sex or alcohol. The container image also implies that, as in parenting, one of the functions of the therapist is to *frustrate* the client/child. Within the therapeutic space, it is acceptable to express any kind of desire, but not to consummate it. It is therapeutically valuable to show anger with the therapist – for example, by being late for sessions, but if the therapist is provoked into an argument with the client ('You are wasting my time by being late every week') the client is merely repeating a destructive pattern, and has lost the opportunity to gain insight into it: the task of psychodynamic therapy is to arrive at an understanding of the meaning and origins of behaviour. The therapist therefore frustrates the unconscious desire of the client to get into a fight, and instead offers an interpretation of what has taken place between them.

The notion of the therapeutic relationship as a container or vehicle for emotional learning linked to the development of new insight into childhood patterns of relations with authority figures is described by Hans Strupp (1969: 209–10) in this passage:

Learning in psychotherapy, almost by definition, occurs within the context of a personal relationship, in the course of which the patient typically becomes dependent on the therapist as an authority, teacher and mentor . . . Learning by identification and imitation is probably the single most important aspect of the therapeutic influence . . . the patient's learning is to a large part experiential but it is also cognitive. However, cognitive learning is seen as maximally effective when the feelings have become mobilized, most notably feelings about the therapist and the therapist–patient interaction . . . I am convinced that interpretation of resistances, that is, those roadblocks which the patient erects to prevent a more open and closer relationship with the therapist, are of the greatest significance and are tremendously important in facilitating the identificatory process . . . For therapeutic learning to occur, the most important precondition is the patient's *openness* to the therapist's influence . . . in an important sense he [the patient] also complies to earn the therapist's approval which becomes an excruciatingly crucial leverage . . . [in] the agonizing process of subordinating himself to a powerful parent figure whom (following his past experiences) he never fully trusts.

Here, although Strupp acknowledges that cognitive learning is important, he also implies that the core of psychodynamic work involves a re-experiencing, in the relationship with the counsellor or psychotherapist, of the emotional responses that the person typically has in relation to significant others, such as his or her parents. The sense of the *struggle* involved in this process, a struggle that needs to be contained if it is to reach a satisfactory conclusion, is conveyed in Strupp's use of terms such as 'roadblocks', 'excruciating' and 'agonizing'.

It is probable that the image of the container is so central to the psychodynamic tradition that any practitioner working within this approach will adopt this way of seeing the therapeutic relationship to a greater or lesser extent. However, contemporary psychodynamic therapists who believe in the usefulness of counter-transference are inevitably drawn in the direction of viewing the relationship as much more of a reciprocal process, with the wishes and feelings of both participants contributing to the creating of what Gill (1994) has called a 'two-person field'. If the therapist is actively involved in sharing what he or she feels, the relationship becomes less focused on holding and containing, and more attuned to processes of mutuality and collaboration. Nevertheless, it would appear that, for therapists working in this tradition, what is created is a mutuality that emerges out of boundaried containment rather than being an open collaboration from the start.

Creating the conditions for growth: therapist as authentic presence

The emergence of humanistic psychology, and the development of the person-centred approach to counselling, have been discussed in Chapter 6. For Carl Rogers during the 1930s and 1940s as he formed the key ideas of client-centred therapy, and then those who worked alongside him at the University of Chicago in the 1950s, the image of the psychoanalytic relationship was alien to their values and cultural experience. Rogers had been brought up in a Midwest American community that emphasized individual autonomy and equality between people, and as a result he was never comfortable with what he perceived as the expert-driven nature of psychoanalysis. So, although client-centred (and then person-centred) counselling is similar to the psychodynamic approach in emphasizing the disclosure of feelings and difficult experiences in the context of a trusting relationship, it has evolved a very different image of the kind of relationship that should exist between counsellor and client.

In contemporary writing about person-centred counselling, much emphasis has been placed on what Rogers (1959) called the 'necessary and sufficient conditions' for therapeutic change, which have subsequently become known as the 'core conditions': the perception by the client of high enough levels of therapist-provided acceptance, congruence and empathy. Much effort has been devoted by person-centred theorists and researchers to the task of clarifying just what these concepts mean, and to identifying the various facets of the experience of congruence and empathy (see Chapter 6). However, it is important to recognize that the 'core conditions' model arose from an attempt by Rogers (1959), in response to an initiative headed by the psychologist Sigmund Koch, to devise a scientifically testable formulation of an approach to therapy that was already successful and widely used. For most of his career, Rogers worked within the professional environment of an academic psychological establishment that was grounded in a behavioural approach. The core conditions formula, and much of the other published work produced by Rogers and his colleagues, is expressed in a behavioural stimulus-response form of language. To understand the image of relationship that underpins this model, it is necessary to search around the edges of the literature on the client-centred/person-centred approach.

A fascinating glimpse of the root image of the person-centred relationship can be found in a section of *Client-centered Therapy* (Rogers 1951), which comprises a lengthy passage written by a junior colleague of Rogers, Oliver Bown. Here, it is suggested that 'love . . . is a basic ingredient of the therapeutic relationship' (Rogers 1951: 160). What is meant here is a non-sexual love that is reflected in a willingness to move beyond pretence and role-playing, to a relationship in which we are not threatened by the other person, and understand him or her. This involves openness on the part of the therapist to his or her own needs and feelings in the therapeutic situation. Rogers was strongly affected by the writings of the philosopher Martin Buber (see Kirschenbaum and Henderson 1990), who promoted the idea that authentic encounter depends on allowing oneself to 'meet' the other. Buber believed in the transformative power of the 'I–Thou' relationship, in which the other person is experienced without labels or conditions. An important paper by Schmid (1998) relates this dimension of person-centred thinking not only to the ideas of Buber, but also to the writings of Emmanuel Levinas and other philosophers.

The principal relationship quality suggested by these ideas is *presence*. It is through being present, in the current moment, with the client that the counsellor is able to be empathic, accepting and congruent. The commitment to be present, in the 'here-and-now', is a continual challenge to any counsellor, because it is easy to revert to evaluating the client in terms of professional and theoretical categories, to slip into thinking ahead ('What is the possible outcome?' 'Is this useful?'), or to lack the courage to respond honestly to the other. The image of the therapeutic relationship as being distinctive in its level of *authentic presence* lies at the heart of the humanistic tradition in psychology and psychotherapy. It is consistent with the existentially informed therapy of key humanistic psychologists such as Bugental (1976), the adoption of meditative spiritual practices by some humanistic practitioners (Claxton 1996) and the more recent emphasis on the importance of client agency (Bohart and Tallmann 1999; Rennie 2000b, 2001). The concept of presence also corresponds to the aim in Gestalt therapy of achieving genuine contact between person and environment.

Therapist as teacher, coach, scientist and philosopher

Within cognitive and cognitive–behavioural approaches to counselling, a good relationship between therapist and client is considered to be necessary for effective therapy to take place, but the relationship is not regarded as a central focus of the therapeutic process. Whereas psychodynamically and humanistically informed counsellors tend to see the relationship as both a here-and-now arena in which emotional issues are expressed and a source of healing, cognitive–behavioural therapists take a much more pragmatic view of what takes place between counsellor and client. The primary aim of cognitive–behavioural therapies is to help the person to change their performance in social situations in the external, 'real' world, typically through using structured exercises and interventions. Although the relationship between client and counsellor needs to be 'good enough' to enable these interventions to be applied appropriately, the focus of CBT is mainly on the interventions, rather than the relationship. Goldfried and Davison (1976: 55) put it in these terms:

> Any behavior therapist who maintains that principles of learning and social influence are all that one needs to know in order to bring about behavior change is out of contact with clinical reality. We have seen therapists capable of conceptualizing problems along behavioral lines and adept at the implementation of the various behavior therapy techniques, but they have few opportunities to demonstrate their effectiveness; they often have difficulty keeping their clients in therapy, let alone getting them to follow through on behavioral assignments.

For Goldfried and Davison (1976), the bond between therapist and client is important because it helps to keep the client in treatment long enough for the intervention to take effect.

The image that pervades much cognitive–behavioural practice is the counsellor–client relationship as similar to that of a coach or teacher and student. A coach is someone who supports a person in learning new skills, by demonstrating or modelling these skills, but also by reinforcing and celebrating achievements and successes, giving encouragement and acting as a source of motivation. A good coach also promotes positive expectations, by conveying their confidence in the capacity of the student to do well.

In addition, some cognitive–behavioural therapists, and many cognitive therapists, regard their role as being like that of a scientist or philosopher, who is trying to challenge the basic, dysfunctional beliefs and cognitive schemas held by the client. Homework assignments can be understood, within this perspective, as 'experiments' in observing the effects of new ways of behaving in social situations. Cognitive therapists, and practitioners using rational–emotive behaviour therapy (REBT) often use the image of the 'Socratic dialogue' to describe the way they work. The counsellor takes on the role of the Greek philosopher Socrates, in engaging in a process of challenging, sometimes with humour, the irrationality or arbitrariness of the beliefs or patterns of logic that the client has used to create and maintain their state of anxiety or depression.

A central theme that runs through cognitive–behavioural thinking about the nature of the therapeutic relationship is *collaboration* (Raue and Goldfried 1994; Sanders and Wills 2002). The counsellor and client work *alongside* each other to find solutions to a problem that is 'out there'. Some of the metaphors that may be used by the counsellor to explain this way of working to the client are that therapy is a 'team effort' or that 'two heads are better than one'.

Some interesting findings have emerged from research into the therapeutic relationship in cognitive–behavioural therapy (CBT). Comparative studies (for example, where CBT is compared with psychodynamic therapy) have shown that the quality of the relationship in CBT is as strong as, and sometimes significantly stronger than, the ratings derived from the more 'relationship-oriented' therapies (see Raue and Goldfried 1994). There is also consistent evidence that the quality of the relationship in CBT is associated with outcome; CBT counsellors who fail to establish collaborative relationships with their clients end up with poor results (Raue and Goldfried 1994). The research results can perhaps be understood as consistent with the idea that clients experience the type of relationship that cognitive and cognitive–behavioural counsellors offer them as being fairly comfortable, in that it resembles other types of relationship they might have come across in their lives. CBT-oriented counsellors also provide clients with a relatively high degree of structure within sessions, and focus on developing solutions to problems and symptoms, rather than exploring the inner experience of painful issues to any great extent. All these factors may suggest that the therapeutic relationship in CBT is on the whole smoother and more predictable than it may at times become in psychodynamic and person-centred therapy.

The 'not-knowing' stance: therapist as editor

Developments in narrative therapy (White and Epston 1990) have been accompanied by a distinctive and different approach to the therapeutic relationship. One of the central principles of narrative therapy is the idea that the freedom and individuality of the person has been limited as a consequence of conformity to 'dominant narratives', which define the way the person 'should' behave in various circumstances. The goal of narrative therapy is, instead, to enable the person to be 'the author of their own story'. From this perspective, any theoretical perspective (such as psychodynamic or person-centred theory) can be viewed as a dominant narrative ready to be imposed on the person. The kind of relationship that is consistent with a narrative approach is described by Anderson and Goolishian (1992). They describe the therapist as a 'participant–facilitator of the therapeutic conversation' (p. 27). At the heart of this way of being a therapist is the concept of *not-knowing*:

> the excitement for the therapist is in learning the uniqueness of each individual client's narrative truth, the coherent truths in their storied lives . . . therapists are always prejudiced by their experience, but . . . they must listen in such a way that their pre-experience does not close them to the full meaning of the client's descriptions of their experience. This can only happen if the therapist approaches each clinical experience from the position of not-knowing. To do otherwise is to search for regularities and common meaning that may validate the therapist's theory but invalidate the uniqueness of the clients' stories and thus their very identity.
>
> (Anderson and Goolishian 1992: 30)

A 'not-knowing' stance may appear to be similar in intention to the empathic phenomenological listening found in person-centred counselling or the 'free-floating attention' of the psychoanalyst. However, whereas in person-centred counselling or psychoanalysis the open listening of the therapist is used to gather material that is then understood in terms of either respective theoretical model, in narrative therapy the aim is to not arrive at a final formulation or interpretation of the 'problem', but to 'keep understanding *on the way*'. What this means is that the therapist is 'led by the expertise of the client', and is seeking to work with the client to keep the dialogue open, as a means of creating an ever-richer narrative.

The role of the therapist here is to suggest strategies that the client might use to deconstruct, reconstruct and retell his or her story. These strategies can involve questioning, using metaphor or writing. The relationship between therapist and client is akin to that between a writer and his or her editor. It is the writer who *creates* and *imagines* the story into existence; the editor helps to give it shape, and nurture it into publication.

Integrative models: the all-purpose therapist

The images of the therapeutic relationship discussed so far have derived from attempts to fashion distinctive approaches to therapy. Each approach, in its own way, has sought to maximize the difference between itself and other competing 'brands' of therapy by specifying a different quality of relationship between counsellor and client. However, there have also been theorists who have tried to bring together apparently competing ideas about the therapeutic relationship, with the aim of producing an integrative understanding of the relationship. There have been two particularly influential integrative models of the therapeutic relationship: Bordin's (1979) *working alliance* model, and the *relationship multiplicity* framework of Clarkson (1990, 1995).

Although currently regarded as providing an *integrative* framework for understanding the therapeutic relationship, the title of Bordin's (1979) paper – 'The generalizability of the psychoanalytic concept of the working alliance' – clearly indicates that the origins of his thinking lie within psychoanalysis. What Bordin was essentially able to do was to take psychoanalytic ideas about the therapeutic relationship and redescribe them in everyday language. The concept of the 'alliance' has been highly significant within psychodynamic counselling:

> The concept of the therapeutic alliance has historically played an important role in the evolution of the classic psychoanalytic tradition, insofar as it has provided a theoretical justification for greater technical flexibility . . . By highlighting the importance of the real, human aspects of the therapeutic relationship, the therapeutic alliance has provided grounds for departing from the idealized therapist stance of abstinence and neutrality.
>
> (Safran and Muran 2001: 165)

Bordin (1979) proposed that a functioning working alliance between a therapist and a client comprised three features: an agreement on *goals*; an assignment of a task or series of *tasks*; and the development of a *bond*. Bordin proposed that all forms of therapy were built around goals, tasks and bonds, even if the relative weighting of each element varied in different approaches. For example, he argued that: 'some basic level of trust surely marks all varieties of therapeutic relationships, but when attention is directed toward the more protected recesses of inner experience, deeper bonds of trust and attachment are required and developed' (p. 254).

The model outlined by Bordin has proved highly resilient in informing research and practice over a 30-year period. While it is clear that goals, tasks and bonds are quite separate features of the therapeutic enterprise, it is also certain that they interconnect in complex and reciprocal ways. For example, the degree to which a painful therapeutic task can be successfully completed may depend on the quality of the bond between therapist and client. Yet, at the same time, the successful achievement of tasks may in itself contribute to a stronger bond. In his original paper, Bordin emphasized his three key features as representing *challenges* to both counsellor and client, and he speculated that the link between the personality of the counsellor or client and their performance in therapy was mediated through the way that their personality characteristics might influence their approach to each element of the working alliance. For example, he

Box

12.2

Picturing the therapeutic relationship: how is the furniture arranged?

The philosopher and social critic Paul Goodman (1962: 157–61) has commented on the significance of the seating arrangements associated with different approaches to therapy. For example, he suggests that the room layout in classical Freudian psycho-analysis, where the patient lies on a couch with the analyst sitting in a chair at the head of the couch, out of the patient's line of sight, has the effect of 'by-passing' the actual relationship between patient and therapist:

> the patient does not see the therapist . . . any social contact with the therapist as though he were a 'person' is frowned on . . . there is thus developed the transference, infantile relationship, and treatment is largely management of this transference.

Goodman contrasts this arrangement with the situation where therapist and client sit face-to-face across a desk:

> the purpose of the seating plan is to appeal to that part of the patient's person-ality that can respond man-to-man and lay problems of the table to be discussed objectively. The table is a protective barrier, e.g., concealing the genitals.

Finally, Goodman (who worked with Fritz Perls on the early development of Gestalt therapy theory – see Perls et al. 1951) considers the seating arrangements in Gestalt therapy, where:

> the seating is freely altered as occasion arises, and any of the following may occur: the therapist might be unseen. He might have left the room. Patient and therapist might change places. There might be a group.

In this form of therapy, Goodman suggests, 'interpersonal relations with the therap-ist, or other patients, are neither encouraged nor avoided, but used as they arise; and the result hoped for is a more closely contacting social style.'

The key issue that Goodman raises concerns the extent to which the therapeutic relationship can be understood solely in terms of the verbal interactions between coun-sellor and client (i.e. through analysis of a transcript of the tape of a therapy session), or whether it is also necessary to take into account the physical environment. It is surely relevant that, compared to the time when Goodman was observing therapy (the late 1950s), the mode of contemporary practice has largely converged on a seating arrange-ment whereby the counsellor and client sit in comfortable chairs, either facing each other directly or at a slight angle. There seems little scope for physical movement in this configuration (unlike the Gestalt setting described by Goodman). Moreover, for the whole time the client is very much the object of the counsellor's gaze, and is aware of this fact. For many users of therapy, the situation might be likened to what they have seen on TV interviews or chat shows. What might these factors imply about the type of relationship that could be created between therapist and client?

observes that a humanistic therapist might be a person who was drawn towards the therapeutic task of self-disclosure. Such a therapist might be effective with clients who had similar needs, while a behaviour therapist (low self-discloser) might be more helpful for a client who did not wish to disclose feelings and personal material.

It is of interest that Bordin developed his model of the working alliance in the mid-1970s, at a time when research into Rogers's necessary and sufficient conditions' theory was at its peak. Yet, although he definitely knew of this research, he did not refer to it in his classic 1979 paper. There were perhaps two reasons for this (Horvath 2000). First, Bordin was intent on developing a framework that would transcend any specific theoretical orientation; he regarded Rogers' theory as primarily relevant to client-centred therapy. Second, he wished to emphasize that the therapeutic alliance was truly *bidirectional*, and equally influenced by both client and therapist, whereas the 'core conditions' model focuses mainly on the attitudes and qualities of the therapist alone.

Clarkson (1990, 1995) has proposed an integrative framework, which envisages five different kinds of therapeutic relationship, all potentially available to the counsellor and client. These are:

1 The working alliance.
2 The transferential/counter-transferential relationship.
3 The reparative/developmentally needed relationship.
4 The person-to-person relationship.
5 The transpersonal relationship.

Implicit in Clarkson's model is a sense that there is a developmental movement across these relationship types: an 'alliance' is viewed as a basic functional level of communication, while a 'transpersonal' relationship is characterized as a 'higher-level' type of contact. Her writing is poetic and creative, rather than research-informed, and seeks to convey the distinctive emotional environment created within each of these contrasting types of relationship. In her view, all of these relationships are possible and implicit in any therapy, and training should prepare practitioners to operate comfortably across the entire range.

The practicalities of relationship competence: how to develop an effective therapeutic alliance

Although the images of the therapeutic relationship that have been reviewed above offer a valuable range of different ways of making sense of what happens between a client and a counsellor, they tend to be fairly silent on the question of what a counsellor should actually *do* to establish a robust alliance with a client. Some of the more recent theory and research around the topic of the therapeutic relationship has focused on identifying and developing practical strategies that can be applied by counsellors to build and maintain constructive relationships with clients.

Adopting a collaborative style: being congruent and using metacommunication

A limitation of much of the writing on the person-centred concept of congruence is that it has been described almost as a mystical state or 'way of being' (see Wyatt 2001). It is helpful to realize that, on a moment-to-moment basis, congruence can be expressed in the *way the counsellor talks*. Most of the time in counselling, both counsellor and client talk in a manner that refers to the topic of the client's 'problem'. By also including talk that refers to the process and activity of talking, it becomes possible to weave in to the conversation a continual flow of statements about aspects of the relationship between counsellor and client.

This 'talking about the process of talking' has been discussed by Rennie (1998) as the skill of *metacommunication*: 'the act of communicating about communication . . . stepping outside the flow of communication to appraise it.' Examples of therapist-initiated metacommunication would be when the therapist:

- talks about his or her own plans, strategies, assumptions;
- asks the client to focus on his or her plans, strategies, assumptions;
- shares his or her assumptions about what the client thinks and intends;
- invites the client to share his or her assumptions or fantasies about what the counsellor thinks or intends;
- reviews the relationship in all these ways when stuck, or in a therapy 'crisis';
- explores the impact of the client on counsellor (the feelings, action tendencies and fantasies that are evoked by the client's behaviour);
- explores the impact of the counsellor on the client.

Each of these ways of talking opens up a layer of the 'unspoken' or implicit relationship between counsellor and client, and makes it possible for both participants in that relationship to reflect on what is happening between them, and if necessary change it. The use of metacommunication represents the application in therapy of the relationship framework developed by Laing *et al.* (1966).

On the whole, counsellors do not engage in metacommunication to any great extent within therapy – this is a neglected skill. Kiesler (1988) concluded, as a result of his research into this topic, that 'therapist interventions incorporating metacommunicative feedback have been almost universally overlooked in the individual psychotherapy literature.'

Repairing ruptures in the alliance

It is seldom that a therapist and client meet, form a good working relationship and then continue through several sessions of therapy without any challenge or disruption to the bond between them, or their agreed goals and tasks. This kind of 'ideal' relationship (in therapy as in any other area of life) is a myth. What is more usual is for the relationship, and the therapeutic work, to 'hit the buffers' now and again. Participants in counselling – both clients and counsellors – may report that they have reached an 'impasse', or that there has been a 'rupture' in the relationship. In these circumstances it is necessary for the counsellor to be able to call on strategies for 'repairing' the relationship. A significant amount of recent theory and research has begun to address the question of how best a therapist or counsellor can repair or retrieve the therapeutic relationship when it goes through a bad patch.

The work of Jeremy Safran (Safran 1993a, b; Safran and Muran 1996, 2000a, b, 2001) has been at the forefront of attempts to investigate the processes and implications of 'ruptures' in the therapeutic alliance. For Safran, the single most important strategy for the therapist in such situations is *metacommunication* – it is necessary to stand back from what is happening, name and discuss the problem, and then negotiate around it. Safran has identified a series of steps or stages that can be observed in the effective repair of a therapeutic alliance. First, the therapist needs to be sensitive to the presence of rupture in the alliance. Typically, a client will express confrontation (anger with the therapist or criticism of the progress of therapy), withdrawal (disengagement from the therapist or the therapeutic process) or a combination of these two responses. The task of the therapist at this point is to draw attention to what is happening within the here-and-now relationship, for example by asking 'What are you experiencing . . . ?' or 'I have a sense that you are withdrawing from me. Am I right?' The acknowledgement by both the therapist and the client that there is a difficulty moves the repair process on to the next stage, which involves helping the client to describe their negative feelings, or what it is they believe is blocking them or hindering progress. The therapist may need to acknowledge at this point, in an undefensive way, how he or she might be contributing to the rupture. The final stage involves encouraging the client to access their primary feelings (typically anger or sadness), and to express to the therapist their underlying needs or wishes. One of the tasks of the therapist at this stage is to affirm the importance of these needs and wishes.

Successfully resolving a rupture in a therapeutic alliance can have a number of benefits for the client. Clearly, it strengthens the relationship, and makes it possible to continue therapy in a productive direction. But it also gives the client an opportunity to learn about how to sort out relationship difficulties in general, and how to ask/demand what they need in a relationship. Finally, for people who may be more familiar with rivalrous conflict-ridden relationships, it provides a model of collaborative, give-and-take relatedness.

A case study published by Agnew *et al.* (1994) explored the process of resolving a rupture in the therapeutic alliance within a case of psychodynamic therapy. This case took place in the context of a research study in which all sessions were taped and transcribed, and both client and therapist completed questionnaires on several aspects of process and outcome. It was possible, therefore, to examine the stages of rupture resolution in great detail. In this case, the breach between client and therapist emerged towards the end of session 2, when the client angrily confronted the therapist with her uneasiness about their 'roles', specifically claiming that the therapist had adopted a role of an 'expert' and a 'superior' man. Agnew *et al.* (1994) were able to identify the following stages in the repair process:

1 *Acknowledgement.* Therapist acknowledges client's feelings.
2 *Negotiation.* Therapist and client develop a shared understanding of their roles and responsibilities.
3 *Exploration.* Client and therapist explore parallel situations outside therapy (e.g. the client's relationship with her father).
4 *Consensus and renegotiation.* Therapist and client develop a consensus over the origins of the client's dissatisfaction and renegotiate the terms of their working relationship.
5 *Enhanced exploration.* Further exploration of parallel situations outside therapy.
6 *New styles of relating.* Therapist and client discuss alternative styles of relating in these situations.

As in the Safran model, the therapist's willingness to accept responsibility for his part in the rupture (stage 2 of the Agnew model) was a crucial element in overcoming the relationship breakdown. Agnew *et al.* (1994) emphasized that, in this case, it was also important that the therapist explained to the client *why* it might be useful to explore the similarities between their current dilemma and other relationship impasses that she had experienced in her life.

The work of Safran, Agnew and others is beginning to contribute to an appreciation of the value in therapy of being able to face up to, and learn from, tensions within the client–counsellor relationship. These models reinforce the key idea that, for clients, the interpersonal arena of therapy provides unique opportunities for learning about needs and relationships in ways that can then generalize to everyday life.

The embodiment of the relationship: transition objects

The British psychoanalyst D. W. Winnicott carried out a great deal of observation of the emotional and social behaviour of young infants. He noted that, from about the age of six months, a young child may come to have a favoured possession, such as a teddy bear, blanket or bundle of wool, which appears to represent its 'emotional security'. If the object is lost or taken away, the child exhibits a grief reaction. Winnicott reasoned that the object represents the security of the mother's breast, and operates as a defence against anxiety during the period where the child is being asked to move away from its symbiotic relationship with the breast, and become a more autonomous individual. Winnicott coined the term *transition object*, in recognition of the important role of such objects at this crucial stage of transition in the child's life. Winnicott's account of the dynamics of transition objects is explained in his popular book *Playing and Reality* (Winnicott 1971).

A transition object represents a physical embodiment of a relationship. When the other person is not available, the object can remind us of his or her continuing existence and qualities. Sometimes, when a client in therapy develops a strong relationship with his or her therapist, he or she may wish to possess some object that will remind them of the therapist, and perhaps bring strength between sessions. This phenomenon is known to most experienced therapists (and clients), but has seldom been studied in a systematic manner. Arthern and Madill (1999) interviewed six experienced therapists (three Gestalt therapists and three psychodynamic therapists) about their understandings of the role of transition objects in their relationships with clients. Although not selected on the basis of having been known to use or promote transition objects, all of them could recall examples of the use of transition objects by their clients.

These therapists considered that transition objects were particularly helpful for clients who experienced separation anxiety between sessions, and who were working on painful interpersonal issues, and needed to 'internalize a sense of a nourishing relationship'. They believed that the objects served not only to remind clients of the existence of a safe, constant relationship in their life, but also provided something to 'play' with, in the sense of reflecting on the meaning of the object, and using it as a trigger for learning about personal needs and relationship patterns.

What kinds of objects were used by clients? The therapists interviewed in this study reported a wide range of objects, including greetings cards and postcards (written from therapist to client), formal letters, books and pens, through to a soft toy, a therapist's cardigan and a piece of a therapist's jewellery. Arthern and Madill (1999) compared the characteristics of objects reported by Gestalt therapists and those reported by psychodynamic clients. The psychodynamic transition objects tended to be verbal (cards, pens, messages); the Gestalt objects tended to be soft, personal or wearable. All three of the psychodynamic therapists reported feeling that they had 'broken the rules' (i.e. violated a therapeutic boundary) by allowing a client to retain an object. None of the Gestalt therapists mentioned rule violation.

It is important to note that the Arthern and Madill (1999) study refers only to instances in which therapists were aware that transition objects had been created. No doubt there are many clients who 'acquire' such objects without letting their therapist know that they are doing so.

One of the key conclusions drawn by Arthern and Madill (1999) is that transition objects can be hugely significant for clients and therapists. They suggest that these objects serve as a means of *embodying* the therapeutic relationship, and function as a practical means of supporting those clients for whom trusting relationships can be problematic.

The concept of boundary

One useful way to begin to make sense of the relationship between a therapist and client is to consider the way in which the *boundary* between the two participants is created and maintained. Although the concept of boundary was not used by any of the 'founders' of therapy (e.g. Freud, Jung, Rogers), it has become widely used in recent years as a means of describing important aspects of the therapeutic relationship. In common-sense terms, a boundary marks the limits of a territory, and the line where one territory or space ends and another one begins. In counselling and psychotherapy, the concept of 'boundary' is clearly a metaphor – there are no actual boundary posts, markers or lines laid out in a therapy room.

In a therapy situation, boundaries can be identified in reference to a range of different dimensions of the relationship. For example, boundaries can be defined around:

- Time. The beginning and end of a therapy session.
- Physical space. How close (or far apart) should the client and counsellor sit; how extensive is each participant's 'personal space'?
- Information. How much should the client know about the counsellor?
- Intimacy. How emotionally close should the counsellor and client be? Does the level of intimacy within the relationship extend to touching, or even to sexual contact?
- Social roles. How does the counsellor acknowledge the client if they meet in another setting? How should the counsellor respond to a client's request to form a relationship outside of the therapy room?

The idea of boundary also allows other significant aspects of the therapeutic relationship to be discussed. Boundaries can be rigid or permeable. Counsellors differ in the personal style, with some favouring strictly regulated boundaries, and others being more flexible. Some counsellors may 'loosen' their boundary in the later stages of therapy with a client. Many different forms of behaviour (the client being late or 'forgetting' to pay the fee; the counsellor touching the client) can be interpreted as boundary 'violations' or 'transgressions', and links can be made with other boundary issues reported by the client in his or her everyday life.

The concept of boundary has been particularly widely used within contemporary psychodynamic and psychoanalytic thinking. The psychoanalytic psychotherapist Robert Langs (1988) has been prominent in arguing for the strict imposition of clearly defined boundaries in therapy as a core principle of therapy. Langs believes that definite boundaries create a strong therapeutic frame within which the client will be safe to explore painful and threatening personal material.

Many humanistically oriented counsellors and psychotherapists have had reservations about the way in which the idea of 'boundary' is used within therapy as a justification for a distanced, detached stance in relation to the client. For example, Hermansson (1997: 135) has argued that 'the very nature of the counselling process demands a measure of boundary crossing . . . counsellor aloofness, often promoted by boundary rigidity, is in itself potentially abusive.' Jordan (2000:

1015) acknowledges that she has: 'trouble with [a] "boundary language" . . .
anchored in [a] view of separation as safety. We need to look at boundaries as
places of meeting, and we need to think of safety as residing in the development
of growth-fostering connections.' In a similar vein, Mearns and Thorne (2000: 50)
have written that:

> there are certainly psychodynamic practitioners who would have no dif-
> ficulty in defining the person-centred attitude toward boundaries and the
> therapeutic relationship to be . . . unethical . . . The willingness of person-
> centred therapists to extend sessions, increase frequency of sessions, allow
> telephone contact, engage in home visits, and respond to client requests for
> mild physical contact like a hug, are all so manifestly inappropriate within
> other theoretical models that they are automatically taken as evidence of
> therapist inadequacy, or, indeed, *over-involvement*. It is fascinating that ethical
> challenges are made on the basis of over-involvement, yet there are no
> codes which describe a pattern of systematic therapist *under-involvement*.
> It seems strange that a profession which emphasises the power of relation-
> ship should not be prepared to challenge members who offer clients such a
> degree of detachment in the face of pain that the client experiences this as
> abusive.

The emphasis in person-centred and humanistic therapy, clearly evident in these
passages, on the value of authentic contact or encounter between counsellor and
client leads to a view of a boundary not as a 'rule for remaining separate' but as
an indicator of a place where contact and 'meeting' might occur.

One of the disappointing features of much recent writing around the concept
of boundary in therapy is that it has focused to a major extent on the issue of
boundary violation, specifically on violations in relation to sexual exploitation
of clients. This form of boundary violation is highly destructive, and undoubtedly
deserves attention. However, a consequence of highlighting sexual boundary
violations has been implicitly to promote a confusion and conflation of boundary issues and ethical issues. *Some* boundary issues (such as sex with clients)
have definite ethical dimensions, but others (e.g. extending the length of a session) do not. Potentially, the metaphor of an interpersonal 'boundary' provides
practitioners with a powerful conceptual tool with which the nature of the
therapeutic relationship with a client can be examined. The construction and
maintenance of boundaries present practitioners with a series of choices that
have implications for the quality of the help that is offered to clients. There are,
no doubt, dangers in both therapeutic relationships that are insufficiently
boundaried and those that are over-boundaried. But the more interesting question is: what is the optimal set of boundaries for each specific counsellor–client
relationship? As Hartmann (1997) has shown in his research studies, individuals
have different boundary needs or boundary 'thickness' or 'thinness': the boundary setting that may be right for one client (or counsellor) may not be right for
another.

Measuring the therapeutic relationship

A great deal of research has been carried out around the topic of the therapeutic relationship. This research is of interest to counsellors for three reasons. First, it confirms the importance of the therapeutic relationship, as a factor that makes a significant contribution to the success of therapy with a client. Second, the statements used in questionnaires that have been employed to measure the therapeutic alliance and other aspects of the relationship provide a succinct summary of what the therapeutic relationship means in practice. Third, research has generated tools that can be used by counsellors to evaluate their own work.

Several questionnaires have been devised to measure dimensions of the therapeutic relationship. These questionnaires list a series of statements; the person completing the scale is required to indicate the extent to which they agree or disagree with each statement, typically using a five-point scale. Versions of most of these questionnaires have been developed for counsellors, clients and external observers (e.g. listening to a tape recording of the session) to complete. Normally, the questionnaire is completed by the counsellor or client immediately following the end of a session. The most widely used questionnaires are: the Working Alliance Inventory (WAI; Horvath and Greenberg 1986, 1994), which measures Bordin's bond, task and goal dimensions; the Barrett-Lennard Relationship Inventory (BLRI; Barrett-Lennard 1986), which assesses the Rogerian core conditions; and the Penn Helping Alliance Scales (HA; Alexander and Luborsky 1986), which evaluates the overall strength of the helping alliance between counsellor and client.

The association between client–therapist relationship and outcome has been demonstrated in a number of studies (see Horvath and Symonds 1991). In addition to documentation of the importance of the therapeutic alliance, the other striking finding to emerge from research has been that there are often low levels of agreement between the client, the counsellor and external observers on how they rate the therapeutic relationship in any individual case. It seems as though the different participants in therapy have quite different ways of interpreting the same events, or different criteria for judging these events. Another conclusion generated by research has been that there is a great deal of overlap between all of the therapeutic relationship scales, and between the sub-factors (i.e. bond, goals and tasks) within these scales. The implication here is that clients, in particular, may have a sense that their relationship is 'good', but are vague about the various dimensions that may constitute that 'goodness'. An excellent review of research into the therapeutic relationship can be found in Agnew-Davies (1999).

The process of developing a valid and reliable questionnaire is time-consuming and intricate. Essentially, the aim is to create a questionnaire with the smallest possible number of carefully worded questions. The task of the test compiler, therefore, requires checking with many people in order to arrive at a set of statements that accurately capture the meaning of the factor that is being measured

Table 12.1 Defining the therapeutic relationship: statements from research questionnaires

Working Alliance Inventory

The therapeutic bond
> I believe my counsellor is genuinely concerned for my welfare.
> *I have the feeling that if I say or do the wrong things, my counsellor will stop working with me.

Therapeutic task agreement
> I am clear on what my responsibilities are in therapy.
> *I find that what my counsellor and I are doing in therapy is unrelated to my concerns.

Therapeutic goals
> My counsellor and I are working toward mutually agreed goals.
> As a result of these sessions, I am clearer as to how I might be able to change.

Barrett-Lennard Relationship Inventory

Positive regard
> The counsellor cares for me.
> *I feel the counsellor disapproves of me.

Empathy
> The counsellor wants to understand how I see things.
> When I am hurt or upset, the counsellor can recognize my feelings exactly without becoming upset himself/herself.

Unconditionality of regard
> How much the counsellor likes or dislikes me is not altered by anything that I tell him/her about myself.
> I can (or could) be openly critical or appreciative of my counsellor without him/her really feeling any different towards me.

Congruence
> I feel that my counsellor is real and genuine with me.
> *I believe that my counsellor has feelings that he/she does not tell me about that are causing difficulty in our relationship.

Penn Helping Alliance Questionnaire

> I feel I am working together with my therapist in a joint effort.
> I believe we have similar ideas about the nature of my problems.

---

* Negatively phrased items; agreement with this statement indicates a *low* level of the factor

(or 'operationalized'). Table 12.1 gives examples of items taken from some of the more widely used relationship measures. This set of statements expresses quite clearly the main themes in the therapeutic relationship that are experienced by clients.

The role of money in the relationship

The issue of payment can have a significant impact on the relationship between a counsellor and a client. In a relationship in which a person talks about an emotional difficulty or crisis to a friend or family member, the question of payment does not arrive. The implicit assumption, when using a friend in this way, is that the relationship is reciprocal: at some point in the future the roles will be reversed. Clearly, counselling is not like this. Although the experience of being listened to, and being encouraged to explore feelings, may be very similar, in the end the counsellor is there not because of feelings of friendship or family loyalty, but because he or she is, in some way or another, being paid to be there. In some voluntary agencies and self-help groups, the counsellor and client may be regarded as having a 'gift relationship': the helper is 'giving' because he or she believes they are making a contribution to the common good. In many (but not all) countries, being a blood donor is an example of a pure form of 'gift relationship'. When such a relationship is clearly understood by both parties in these terms, monetary issues may recede into the background. But even in many self-help groups and voluntary agencies in which helpers or counsellors are freely giving their time, the client may be asked to make a 'donation' to cover the running costs of the organization. And, of course, in the majority of counselling situations the issue of payment is highly salient: the counsellor is being paid a fee or salary to listen. So, it is probably reasonable to conclude that payment is a meaningful (if hidden) dimension of most counselling relationships.

The hidden nature of the financial relationship between counsellor and client ultimately derives from the high level of secretiveness and ambivalence that exists in most modern industrialized societies in relation to the topic of money. For most people, the incomes and savings of even their closest friends and family members remain unknown. Yet, at the same time, we live in a society in which financial success is highly valued.

Within the counselling and psychotherapy literature, a number of different ideas have been proposed concerning the effect of payment and fees on the therapeutic relationship (Herron and Sitkowski 1986; Cerney 1990). First, Freud and other psychoanalysts have argued for the 'sacrificial' nature of the fee. The assumption here is that, as a means of maximizing the motivation of the patient for therapy, and signalling the importance of their commitment to therapy, a fee should be set that is the maximum affordable by the patient. This implies that sliding fees should be operated: a fee that represented a major personal commitment for one client might be insignificant for another, more affluent client. From a psychoanalytic perspective, it has also been argued that the fee is a therapeutic tool which symbolizes the strict boundaries within which therapy is conducted: no matter what happens, the fee must be paid. The existence of the fee also makes a bridge between therapy and the 'real' world, and provides motivation for completing therapy rather than becoming dependent on the therapist. From a psychodynamic perspective, therefore, the fact of a client directly paying a fee makes a positive contribution to the therapeutic process.

However, it is also possible to argue that direct payment can have a counterproductive impact on the therapeutic relationship. A client who is paying for therapy may doubt the authenticity of their counsellor's acceptance: 'he/she is only pretending to value me because they are being paid' (Wills 1982). If a counsellor's income is contingent on a client remaining in therapy, he or she might subtly find ways to prolong treatment (Kottler 1988).

Being involved in the collection of fees is a role that many therapists find troubling. Some therapists experience 'fee guilt' (Herron and Sitkowski 1986) arising from the conflict between being wanted to perceived as a 'helper' and being involved in a business that involves making a living and a profit. Counsellors and psychotherapists in private practice often report conflict around negotiating and charging fees, sending out reminders etc.

If psychoanalytic theory around the 'sacrificial' role of direct fee payment were correct, there should be evidence that therapy is more effective when fees are paid by clients, as compared to situations where there is a third-party paying (e.g. student counselling in a university, workplace counselling) or where the therapist is working for free. There is no evidence that any such a difference in effectiveness exists (Herron and Sitkowski 1986), in terms of studies that have made comparisons between fee payment and free services. Moreover, there is a huge amount of evidence that counselling and psychotherapy provided within workplace counselling schemes (McLeod 2001) or state-run health services in Britain and other European countries (which are free at the point of delivery) is just as effective as therapy that is delivered in classical private practice settings.

Does this mean that we should dismiss psychoanalytic ideas about the impact of fees on the therapeutic relationship? Not at all. The 'sacrifice' theory of payment predicted that the quality of the client's investment in the therapeutic relationship would depend on the level of fee they paid. While there may be some truth in this idea in some cases, it fails to take account of the profound meaning that therapy has for many people, in terms of creating a worthwhile life, or in some instances even as means of survival. The intrinsic meaningfulness and value of therapy is surely diminished by assuming that it can only be beneficial if it is being directly paid for. Instead, the question of money is important for the client–counsellor relationship because it represents a potentially vital area of 'things not said' (Cerney 1990). In counselling settings in which the client directly pays a fee to the counsellor, he or she may wonder 'am I worth it?', 'is my well-being or future worth it?' In settings where the counsellor's fee or salary is being paid by a third party, the client may reflect on 'does he or she really care about me, or is it just a job?', or 'if the university/hospital/company is paying his or her salary, won't they want to know about just how disturbed I am?' The counsellor, in either situation, may wonder 'am I worth what I'm being paid?' or even 'do I only tolerate this person because it's my job?' In addition, the meaning of money may be linked to the cultural or social class background of the client and counsellor. Some people are brought up in environments where self-esteem and value are bound up with 'paying your own way' or using economic power always to have 'the best'. Others have grown up in collectivist cultures in which helping others is valued in its own terms, and 'profiting' from the distress of another person would be questionable. In addition, there are wide variations around the extent to which different social groups find it acceptable to talk openly about money. Bringing underlying issues about money into the therapy conversation can therefore represent an effective method for exploring cultural identities and assumptions.

There is some evidence of gender differences in therapist attitudes and behaviour around fee payment. Lasky (1999) found that women therapists tended to charge less than male colleagues of similar levels of experience, while Parvin and Anderson (1999) reported that women therapists were more flexible in negotiating fees than their male colleagues. Lasky (1999) also found that, among the therapists she interviewed, male practitioners were able to gloss over potential internal conflicts over fees, while female practitioners tended to be 'acutely aware' of such dilemmas, and saw themselves as trapped in a three-way conflict:

(1) needing to support themselves and their families, (2) feeling torn between working additional hours to earn more money and wanting to spend the time with friends and family, and (3) focusing more on the client's financial needs than their own.

(Lasky 1999: 9)

These studies are based on small samples of therapists in the USA, and it would be interesting to learn the extent to which they generalize to other settings. Nevertheless, they illustrate the possibility that males and females approach this aspect of the therapeutic relationship in different ways.

The question of money represents a challenge to the therapeutic relationship because unspoken thoughts and feelings about money can impede full client–counsellor collaboration. For example, a workplace counselling client who assumes that their counsellor is, ultimately 'in the pocket' of management because that is who pays their wages may (consciously or unconsciously) screen out oversensitive information, and not permit the counsellor to learn about the depth of their despair or destructive behaviour. It is a particularly acute challenge for some counsellors, who experience 'fee guilt'. But it is also a difficulty for all counsellors, to the extent that the social and cultural meaning of money is an issue that has been largely neglected within therapy theory, research and training.

Implications of relationship theories for counsellor training and development

There is a substantial consensus within the counselling and psychotherapy literature that the quality of the relationship between client and counsellor is a central

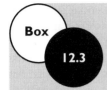

Box

12.3

Hidden dimensions of relationship: Shlien on empathy

For many counsellors, the attempt consistently to respond empathically to a client lies at the heart of the kind of relationship they seek to offer. Within the counselling and psychotherapy literature, empathy has generally been understood in terms of sensitivity to the language used by the client. Counsellor training has tended to emphasize the development of skill in responding appropriately to verbal cues. The recent writing of John Shlien (1997) opens up other dimensions of empathic relating. Shlien was a student, then colleague of Carl Rogers, who describes himself as 'privileged to be a participant observer, a sort of bystander and witness, to the development of the theory of empathy as it took place at the University of Chicago after World War II' (Shlien 1997: 67). Over a period of many years, Shlien was involved in the research on empathy and the 'core conditions' carried out by Rogers and his group. Drawing on this experience, he has arrived at the conclusion that responding fully to another person requires not merely a verbal response, but a 'whole body' reaction:

> empathy operates on such data as smell, sight, and sound: the smell of fear; the sight of tears, of blushing, and of yawning; and the sound of cadences, tones, sighs and howls. It operates at what we might think of as primitive levels, cellular, glandular, olfactory, chemical, electromagnetic, autonomic, postural, gestural, and musical-rhythmical, more than lexical.
>
> (Shlien 1997: 77)

Shlien argues that recent models of empathy have promoted the 'supremacy of brain over body', and that a proper understanding of this phenomenon will require the restoration of an appreciation of the 'whole person'. For Shlien, the experience of attunement to the kind of 'primitive' signals listed above is best described as *sympathy* rather than empathy. He suggests that sympathy involves a type of moral commitment to the other person: 'empathy alone, without sympathy, and even more, without understanding, may be harmful' (p. 67).

Shlien's ideas will be provocative and challenging for many counsellors. Even if only partially true, they carry the implication that the current ways in which counsellors and psychotherapists understand the therapeutic relationship may be inadequate, and possibly even unhelpful.

element in effective therapy, no matter what theoretical model is being applied. It is therefore essential that counsellor training takes seriously the issue of enabling trainees or students to acquire an understanding of how relationships function in general terms, and to develop an appreciation of their own style of relating. Most counselling training programmes promote student learning in these areas through a requirement to undertake personal therapy, participate in experiential groupwork and contribute to meetings of the whole course community (see Chapter 20). Mearns (1997) has argued that, in the past, counselling training courses have not done enough to facilitate trainee integration and reflection of learning across these different domains. There is also a lack of reading and training materials that focus specifically on relationship issues. Josselson (1996) is one of the few texts explicitly to place therapeutic learning within a relationship context. On the whole, writers on counsellor training have tended to frame the experiential elements of training programmes in terms of *personal* development or *self*-awareness, rather than discussing these themes from a *relational* or *self-in-relation* perspective.

Conclusions: the complexity of the therapeutic relationship

The theory and research discussed in this chapter reflects the importance of the client–counsellor relationship in all approaches to therapy. It is clear that counsellors trained in the use of different theoretical models employ quite different ways of understanding the therapeutic relationship. It also seems clear, however, that there are fundamental 'truths' about the client–counsellor relationship, relevant for all approaches to counselling, captured in the ideas of Rogers (1957) and Bordin (1979), and in Freud's concepts of transference and counter-transference. It also seems likely that some clients respond better to some types of relationship than others, depending on their own personal history and needs. The therapeutic relationship *makes a difference* in counselling – the quality of the relationship has been shown to contribute significantly to the eventual outcome of counselling, and to the ability to help distressed people to stay in counselling. It is essential, therefore, for any counsellor to be aware of where his or her strengths lie, in term of making and maintaining helpful ways of relating to clients, and also to keep striving to become more responsive to the endless variety of relationship patterns that may be presented by clients. Therapeutic relationships are complex, and operate at a number of different levels at the same time. It is difficult to 'de-centre' sufficiently from one's own viewpoint to develop an accurate understanding of how one behaves in relationships. For any counsellor, building an understanding of how he or she engages in relationship with clients is greatly facilitated by the use of opportunities, such as training groups, or supervision, which provide feedback and challenge on his or her way of being with others.

Chapter summary

- The importance of the quality of the relationship between counsellor and client is emphasized in all approaches to counselling and psychotherapy.

- There are several alternative ways of making sense of the therapeutic relationship, associated with different theoretical orientations.

- Bordin and Clarkson have formulated useful integrative models of the therapeutic relationship.

- In practice, the creation and maintenance of a strong relationship between counsellor and client can involve the use of metacommunication (reflecting on the process of the relationship), the use of strategies for resolving impasses and the embodiment of the relationship in physical objects kept by the client.

- The concept of boundary provides a valuable framework for understanding many important aspects of the therapeutic relationship.

- There are many issues raised within a relationship between a counsellor and client around the role of fees and payment.

- The importance of the relationship within counselling is reflected in the prominence given to experiential work within counselling training.

- The complexity of the therapeutic relationship means that practitioners of counselling and psychotherapy must be prepared to continue learning about their style of relating to others, throughout their working life.

Topics for reflection and discussion

1 Think about a person who has helped you to overcome or resolve an emotional issue in your life. How would you describe your relationship with this person? Think about someone you know but from whom you would be very reluctant to seek emotional support. How would you describe this relationship? How well can these personal experiences be explained in terms of the models and images of therapy relationships introduced in this chapter?

2 Research mentioned in this chapter has shown that a good relationship between therapist and client, in the early stages of counselling, is highly predictive of a good outcome at the end of therapy. Does this finding necessarily mean that the relationship is the *cause* of the eventual outcome? How else might you explain the fact that clients (and therapists) who give positive ratings of the strength of the 'therapeutic alliance' at the third or fourth session of therapy also report, several weeks later, that therapy has been successful?

3 Many counsellors and psychotherapists working in private practice operate a 'sliding fee' system, where what the client pays is adjusted according to their income and circumstances. In some situations, clients may suggest that they

pay their therapist in goods and services rather than money. For example, a client who is a farmer may be able to offer produce of a higher value than any possible cash payment that he or he she could afford. What are the potential implications for the therapeutic relationship of establishing a barter contract? What ethical issues might need to be addressed? (A useful source of further reading on this topic is Hill 1999).

4 Safran and Muran (2001: 165) have suggested that: 'strains in the therapeutic alliance tap into a fundamental dilemma of human existence – the tension between the need for agency and the need for relatedness – and the process of working through these strains can provide patients with a valuable opportunity to constructively negotiate these two needs.' How useful do you find this way of understanding relationships? Reflect on a relationship you have experienced that has been difficult. (This could be a counselling relationship, or one in another area of your life.) What was the tension within that relationship between the need for agency (being in control, following your own purposes and intentions) and the need for relatedness (being in contact) for both you and the other person? Was this tension resolved (or could it have been resolved) through a process similar to Safran's model of resolution?

Key terms and concepts

acceptance	holding relationship
authenticity	involvement
bond	not-knowing
collaboration	presence
congruence	relational depth
container	task
core conditions	therapeutic alliance
counter-transference	therapeutic relationship
empathy	transference
empowerment	transition object
goal	

Suggested further reading

The classic book on the therapeutic relationship, which is essential reading for anyone interested in counselling, is *Between Therapist and Client: The New Relationship*, by Michael Kahn (1997). Kahn captures the essence of psychodynamic and person-centred approaches to the relationship in a sensitive and highly readable manner, and demonstrates how Freudian and Rogerian ways of understanding the relationship have converged in the work of recent writers such as Merton Gill and Heinz Kohut.

Lott (1999) offers an invaluable insight into the client's perspective on the therapeutic relationship. Deborah Lott interviewed women about their feelings for their therapists, and also draws on her own experience. One of the questions raised by this book is: do men experience the therapeutic relationship with the same intensity as women?

The Space between Us: Exploring the Dimensions of Human Relationships by Ruthellen Josselson (1996) is not specifically a book about counselling and psychotherapy, but includes examples drawn from therapy, and will be of interest to both counsellors and users of counselling. Josselson suggests that many people lack a 'map' or conceptual framework for understanding relationship issues. Her book provides such a framework, based loosely on the ideas of the psychoanalytic theorist Erik Erikson but written in a way that makes sense to those who are not necessarily adherents of psychodynamic models.

Finally, an edited book by Feltham (1999) introduces notions of the therapeutic relationship applied within a wide range of therapeutic approaches. The opening chapter, by Colin Feltham himself, offers a masterful overview of the historical origins and development of the idea of the 'therapeutic relationship'. Anyone wondering why discussions of the therapy relationship can so often be complex and dense will find Feltham's chapter a useful tool for deciphering the multiple discourses that exist in this domain of knowledge.

13 The process of counselling

Introduction: defining the concept of _process_

In previous chapters, different approaches to making sense of counselling were introduced, and some of the issues involved in combining or integrating these approaches were discussed. One of the themes that emerged from this examination of competing theories and models of counselling was that, despite their undoubtedly contrasting emphases, there is in fact a fair amount of common ground. What actually happens in counselling and psychotherapy may depend less on the theoretical orientation of the specific counsellor, than on a set of more general features of the counselling situation as a particular type of helping

Table 13.1　Some process variables that have been studied in recent research

Goal consensus
Client role preparation
Client suitabilty
Personality, age, ethnic and gender match between client and therapist
Therapist willingness to talk about race and culture
Therapist skills
Extent of therapist adherence to a training manual
Focus during therapy on life problems and core personal relationships
Accuracy of transference interpretations
Frequency of transference interpretations
Client adherence to homework instructions
Therapeutic alliance
Ruptures in the therapeutic alliance
Impasse between client and therapist
Use of metaphor
Client expressiveness and open-ness
Therapist self-disclosure
Client deference to the therapist
Treatment duration
Fee structure

Main source: Orlinsky *et al.* (1994).

relationship. This sense that there may exist a common core to all forms of counselling has perhaps achieved its fullest expression in the growing research and theoretical literature on the *process* of counselling.

The concept of 'process' is defined and understood in several different ways in the literature, which can lead to confusion. Four main meanings of 'process' can be identified. First, there is a very broad sense in which any activity involving change can be described as being a 'process'. This meaning of the term merely refers to the idea that what happens in therapy is not static, and that there is some sort of sequence of events that takes place. A second meaning of 'process' has been employed mainly in the research literature, to refer to a very wide set of factors that may promote or inhibit therapeutic effects in clients. The use of the term contrasts 'process' with 'outcome': therapeutic 'processes' are the ingredients that contribute to outcomes. A list of some of the process factors investigated in recent research studies is given in Table 13.1. It can be seen that researchers have not lacked imagination in coming up with the widest possible list of what might be considered as 'process'.

A third meaning of 'process' is found mainly within humanistic perspectives on therapy. This definition characterizes process as an essential human quality of being and becoming. Rogers (1961: 27) captures this sense of process in writing that:

Life, at its best, is a flowing, changing process in which nothing is fixed. In my clients and in myself I find that when life is richest and most rewarding it is a flowing process. To experience this is both fascinating and a little frightening. I find I am at my best when I can let the flow of my experience carry me, in a direction which appears to be forward, towards goals of which I am dimly aware . . . Life is . . . always in process of becoming.

This way of understanding process, almost as a value dimension, is also expressed by contemporary narrative social constructionist therapists. For example, Anderson and Goolishian (1992: 29) describe their aim in therapy as being 'to facilitate an emerging dialogic process in which "newness" can occur'. This sense of process, as moments of flowing newness where 'nothing is fixed', represents an important way in which the concept is used by many therapists.

A fourth sense of 'process' that is sometimes used by counsellors and psychotherapists describes the way that clients in therapy attempt to comprehend or assimilate difficult experiences in their lives. This use of the term can be likened to a metaphoric analogy. The work that clients and therapists do in making meaning out of raw feelings of loss, trauma or stress can be seen as similar to the manufacturing process, in which raw materials are transformed into finished, usable products. For instance, the *emotional processing* model employed by Greenberg *et al.* (1993) involves 'doing things' to and with emotions: naming them, expressing them, reflecting on their meaning.

There would appear to be little value in attempting to nominate any one of these definitions of 'process' as more valid than the others. Not only are all of these meanings of process used by practitioners and theorists, but they all refer, in different ways, to an underlying sense that counselling is concerned with change, and that at some level this change is created by the actions and intentions of both clients and counsellors working collaboratively. Finally, implicit in these various ideas of process is the notion that to be a counsellor it is necessary not only to be able to make sense of what is happening in an abstract, conceptual manner (e.g. knowing about 'the unconscious', or 'second order change') but to have a handle on the practicalities (e.g. making an interpretation, offering an empathic response, negotiating a therapeutic contract).

It is clear that counselling process represents a huge topic. Any of the processes that have been mentioned can be explored from the point of view of the client or the therapist, or through the eyes of an external detached observer. Moreover, what takes place can occur simultaneously at different levels of awareness and visibility: there is always a hidden, covert process unfolding inside the consciousness of each participant. Elliott (1991) suggests that it can be helpful to break down the ongoing flow of the process occurring in counselling into different types of units demarcated by their time boundaries:

- The speaking turn (interaction unit), encompassing the response of one speaker surrounded by the utterances of the other speaker. This can be regarded as a *microprocess* that lasts for perhaps no more than one or two minutes.
- The episode, comprising a series of speaking turns organized around a common task or topic. This process unit is sometimes described as a therapeutic *event*, and can last for several minutes.

- The session (occasion unit).
- The treatment (relationship unit): the entire course of a treatment relationship.

Each of these units can be regarded as representing a different way of 'seeing' what takes place in counselling. Analysing microprocesses is like looking at counselling through a microscope; examining the process of a whole treatment is like constructing a map by using a telescope to view the furthest horizons.

This chapter introduces some of the theoretical and research material on counselling process that has been particularly influential in recent years. There is potentially a huge area to be covered here, and readers interested in learning more are recommended to consult Greenberg and Pinsof (1986), Hill (1991) and Orlinsky *et al.* (1994) to gain access to the research literature on this topic. The issues involved in systematically studying the counselling process, including the demanding question of how it is possible to record, measure or otherwise observe process factors without intruding unhelpfully into the actual counselling relationship, are discussed in Chapter 18.

The process of counselling: beginnings and endings

It makes most sense to begin by looking at models for understanding the process of treatment in its entirety, since other, smaller-scale processes at the session, event or microprocess level are always embedded in the wider context supplied by the process of counselling as a whole. Many writers on counselling have tended to divide up the process of treatment into three broad phases. For example, Mearns and Thorne (1988) talk about 'beginnings', 'middles' and 'ends'. Egan's (1994) 'problem management' approach is structured around three main stages: helping clients to identify and clarify problem situations; developing programmes for constructive change; and implementing goals.

The opening and concluding phases of counselling can be split into further sets of discrete component elements or tasks. For example, the beginning phase may include negotiating expectations, assessment of suitability for counselling, the formation of a therapeutic alliance, agreeing a contract, helping the client to tell their story and so on. The final phase may entail negotiating the ending, referral, dealing with issues of loss, ensuring transfer of learning into real-life situations, anticipating and preventing relapse and planning follow-up meetings. Each of these aspects of the counselling process raises key issues for theory and practice.

Negotiating expectations

The question of client *expectations* has received a considerable amount of attention in the literature. An appreciation of the social and historical origins of counselling

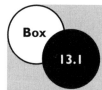

Box 13.1   Counsellors' images of the process of therapy

It is clear that there are very different ways of making sense of the process of counselling, reflected in the range of counselling theories that are currently in use. However, what kinds of images or metaphors do counsellors and therapists themselves employ when thinking about their work? Najavits (1993) carried out a survey of 29 counsellors, working in a variety of settings and using a number of different theoretical models. In this study, counsellors were provided with a list of 16 metaphors derived from a review of the literature, and were asked to use a five-point scale to endorse the metaphors they thought were most or least applicable to their work, to circle their own favourite metaphor and finally to write in any additional metaphors of their own that they used. Analysis of results identified seven clusters of metaphors, or what Najavits (1993) labelled as 'meaning systems':

- *Task-oriented, professional*: counselling process likened to teaching, acting, science, selling.
- *Primal, fantasy*: play, a spiritual quest, handling wastes.
- *Taking responsibility*: hard labour, parenting.
- *Healing arts*: art, healing.
- *Intellectual*: writing a novel, philosophical dialogue.
- *Alteration of consciousness*: meditation, intuition.
- *Travel*: voyage, exploration.

No relationship was found between the metaphors endorsed by the counsellor and their theoretical orientation, work setting or satisfaction with their job. In general, counsellors gave higher ratings to the metaphors they generated themselves, rather than the ones in the list provided by Najavits (1993). Moreover, there were extreme disagreements between those who completed the questionnaire. For example, some counsellors rated 'art', 'healing', 'science' and 'spiritual quest' as *highly* appropriate metaphors for the therapy process, whereas others rated these metaphors as being completely irrelevant. The only metaphors that were generally seen as reasonably applicable, by the majority of counsellors, were 'teaching' and 'parenting'. The diversity of opinion uncovered by these results seems to imply that counsellors tend to hold relatively idiosyncratic views about the process of therapy, with little apparent linkage between their images and the theoretical model they describe themselves as using. Of course, this study is based on a small sample of counsellors in the USA – it would be interesting to know how counsellors in other countries, or drawn from a wider variety of backgrounds, 'imagined' their work. And it would be valuable, too, to know more about the images of counselling held by clients. How many clients see their counsellor as a parent or teacher? How many experience counselling in terms of images of war?

(see Chapter 2) suggests that there exist many other culturally available forms of help – for example, spiritual and religious guidance, medical intervention and even neighbourly advice – that are much more directive and overtly authoritarian than is counselling. In addition, people from non-Western cultures may hold beliefs about self that are very difficult to incorporate within counselling models (see Chapter 10). There is, therefore, often a need on the part of the counsellors and counselling agencies to take these factors into account.

Research into expectations for counselling has shown significant differences in the extent to which people perceive different approaches as credible or preferable (Shapiro 1981; Rokke *et al.* 1990; Galassi *et al.* 1992; Pistrang and Barker 1992; Wanigaratne and Barker 1995). There is also evidence that clients who receive a form of counselling that matches their expectations are more likely to do well, particularly in time-limited counselling (Morrison and Shapiro 1987; Hardy *et al.* 1995). It also clear that people seek psychological help from a range of sources, and may enter counselling with expectations that have been shaped by a previous type of treatment. This is a major issue in cross-cultural counselling, where a client may have previously consulted an indigenous healer. Particular groups of clients can have very definite expectations about what they need. For example, Liddle (1997) found that many gay and lesbian clients put a great deal of time and effort into finding an 'affirmative' counsellor or therapist.

The realization that many potential clients may not understand the way that counselling operates has led some practitioners to develop and evaluate methods of providing appropriate pre-counselling information: for example, role induction videos or leaflets. Beutler and Clarkin (1990: 187–96) offer an excellent review of the use of these techniques.

It can be argued that the importance of pre-counselling expectations and pre-ferences is often underestimated by counsellors. The settings for counselling – the agency and the counselling room – are familiar to the counsellor. The counsellor is also thoroughly acquainted with the rule of the counselling encounter. Further-more, most clients will regard counsellors as high-status 'experts'. For all these reasons, clients are likely to be dominated by the counselling situation, and find it hard to articulate their assumptions and wishes about what should happen. Often, the mismatch between client and counsellor expectations and definitions is only brought to light when a client fails to turn up for a session. In fact, as many as one in three counselling contracts end in this manner. In some of these cases, the client may well be satisfied with what he or she received. In other cases, however, the client does not return because he or she is not getting what he or she wants.

Assessment

The beginning of counselling is also marked by a process of *assessment*. Many counsellors and counselling agencies explicitly demarcate assessment or 'recep-tion' sessions as separate from actual counselling. In some places, assessment

Table 13.2   Reasons for making a formal pre-counselling assessment

Establishing rapport
Making a clinical diagnosis
Assessing the strengths and weaknesses of the client
Giving information
Enabling the client to feel understood
Arriving at a case formulation or plan
Giving hope
Gathering information about cultural needs and expectations
Explaining the way that therapy works; obtaining informed consent
Opportunity for the client to ask questions
Giving a taste of the treatment
Motivating the client; preventing non-attendance
Arranging for any further assessments that might be necessary (e.g. medical)
Selecting clients for treatment
Selecting treatments or therapists for the client
Giving the client a basis for choice of whether to enter counselling
Making practical arrangements (time, place, access)
Providing data for research or audit

is carried out by someone other than the eventual counsellor. Assessment can serve a wide variety of purposes (see Table 13.2), including evaluating whether the person will benefit from the counselling that is available, providing sufficient information for the client to make up his or her mind and agreeing times, scheduling and costs. Some counsellors employ standardized psychological tests as part of the assessment phase (Watkins and Campbell 1990; Anastasi 1992; Whiston 2000). These tests can be utilized to evaluate a wide range of psychological variables, such as anxiety, depression, social support and interpersonal functioning. Others use open-ended questionnaires that the person completes in advance of the actual assessment interview (Aveline 1995; Mace 1995a).

The nature of assessment depends a great deal on the theoretical model being used by the counsellor or counselling agency, and a wide spectrum of assessment practices can be found (Mace 1995b; Palmer and McMahon 1997). On the whole, psychodynamic counsellors and psychotherapists consider it essential to carry out an in-depth assessment of the client's capacity to arrive at a psychodynamic formulation of the key features of the case. Hinshelwood (1991), for example, proposes that such a formulation should explore three main areas of object relations: the current life situation, object-relationships in early life and the transference relationship with the assessor. Hinshelwood also suggests that other useful information that can be collected includes the assessor's counter-transference reaction to the client and the client's ability to cope with a 'trial interpretation' of some of the material that is uncovered. Coltart (1988) regards 'psychological mindedness' as a crucial criterion for entry into long-term psychodynamic therapy.

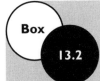

Box 13.2 Psychological mindedness: an indicator of readiness to engage in psychodynamic therapy

It is widely believed among psychoanalytic and psychodynamic therapists and coun-sellors that it is difficult, or even impossible, to work effectively with clients who lack a capacity or willingness to make sense of their actions in psychological terms. The construct of *psychological mindedness* has been used as a means of measur-ing this capacity. Appelbaum (1973: 36) has defined psychological mindedness as 'a person's ability to see relationships among thoughts, feelings and actions, with the goal of learning the meaning of . . . experiences and behavior.' McCallum and Piper (1990: 412) have defined this quality in more explicitly psychodynamic terms: 'the ability to identify dynamic (intrapsychic) components and to relate them to a person's difficulties'. When they carry out assessment or intake interviews, psychodynamic counsellors are aiming to collect evidence of the level of psychological mindedness of a client, as an indicator of readiness to engage in dynamic 'work'. A number of assessment tools have also been developed to evaluate the client's level of psy-chological mindedness (Conte and Ratto 1997). The *insight test* (Tolor and Reznikoff 1960) presents the client with a series of hypothetical situations depicting the operation of various defence mechanisms. The client then chooses between a set of four possible explanations for the situation. An example of an item from this technique is:

> A man who intensely dislikes a fellow worker goes out of his way to speak well of him.
>
> 1 The man doesn't really dislike his co-worker.
> 2 The man believes he will make a better impression on others by speaking well of him.
> 3 The man is overdoing his praise in order to cover up for his real feelings of dislike.
> 4 The man doesn't want to hurt anyone's feelings.

The situation is an example of the defence mechanism of 'reaction formation', so the third response represents the most insightful (or psychologically minded) response, while the first item represents the least insightful explanation.

McCallum and Piper (1997) have constructed a psychological mindedness assess-ment procedure that does not provide answers to the client, but instead requires them to give their own personal response. Clients are asked to watch two scenarios on video, and then asked to explain in their own words why they think the people they have observed were behaving in the way they were. McCallum and Piper (1997) then rate the person's answer in terms of nine levels of psychological mindedness. McCallum and Piper (1997) have carried out research which has shown that, in psychodynamic group therapy, clients who are more psychologically minded benefit more, and are less likely to drop out of the group prematurely.

Although psychological mindedness may be an important prerequisite for psychodynamic therapy, is it also a factor in the extent to which clients may benefit from other forms of therapy? No one really knows. Certainly, from a person-centred perspective, the client's capacity to *feel* (i.e. engage in experiential processing) might be considered to be more important than their capacity to identify defences. On the other hand, the basic ability to *reflect* on patterns of behaviour, implicit in the notion of psychological mindedness, may be a common factor in all therapies.

Behaviourally oriented counsellors, by contrast, regard assessment as necessary in order to identify realistic, achievable treatment goals (Galassi and Perot 1992). Finally, humanistic or person-centred counsellors tend to eschew formal assessment on the grounds that they do not wish to label the client or to present themselves in an 'expert' position. Some humanistically oriented counsellors may employ 'qualitative' methods of assessment, where the client will be invited to participate in learning/assessment exercises integrated into the flow of the counselling session itself. An example of this type of assessment would be the use of the Life Line as a means of eliciting the client's perceptions of significant points in his or her development, relationships with important others and values (Goldman 1992).

Halgin and Caron (1991) suggest a set of key questions that counsellors and psychotherapists should ask themselves when considering whether to accept or refer a prospective client:

- Does the person need therapy?
- Do I know the person?
- Am I competent to treat this client?
- What is my personal reaction to the client?
- Am I emotionally capable of treating the client?
- Does the client feel comfortable with me?
- Can the client afford treatment under my care?

There are times when the outcome of an assessment interview will be that the client is referred to another agency. This process can evoke powerful feelings in both clients and assessors (Wood and Wood 1990).

Cutting across these different approaches to assessment is the degree to which the counsellor will share his or her assessment with the client. Some counsellors and psychotherapists may provide the client with a written formulation (e.g. Ryle 1990), or may analyse test data together (Fischer 1978). In addition, external factors may determine the extent to which formal assessment is employed. In the

Box

13.3

The role of diagnosis in counselling and psychotherapy

Is it helpful for counsellors or psychotherapists to make a diagnosis of their clients' psychopathology? Within psychiatry and clinical psychology, it is usual to carry out a diagnostic interview at the point of assessment, and both patient statistics and research papers in these disciplines tend to be organized around diagnostic categories. There are two diagnostic systems that are currently in use. The International Classification of Diseases (ICD) diagnostic guide, published by the World Health Organization, is widely employed in Europe and many other countries. The *Diagnostic and Statistical Manual* (DSM), published by the American Psychiatric Association (APA 1994), is exclusively used in North America, and has also been adopted elsewhere. There are many similarities between the two systems. An excellent counselling-oriented account of DSM-IV (the fourth and most recent edition of the manual) can be found in Whiston (2000).

There are strong arguments for and against the use of diagnosis in counselling and psychotherapy. Those who are *against* diagnosis argue that:

- there is a danger of labelling patients;
- there is little evidence that diagnostic information is of any use in planning or choosing the right therapy for any individual client;
- diagnostic procedures introduce an expert-dominated relationship that can undermine collaborative work between client and therapist;
- defining the problem as an 'illness' may make it harder for the client to commit themselves to a therapy, which always requires active participation and taking responsibility for personal change;
- the use of diagnosis introduces a medical/biological perspective that is not consistent with the aims and processes of counselling.

The factors *in favour* of using diagnosis include:

- it enables therapists working in medical settings to communicate effectively with colleagues;
- an increasing number of treatment manuals are structured in terms of diagnostic classifications, such as depression, anxiety and borderline personality disorder;
- in some environments (e.g. managed care services in the USA), a diagnosis is a necessary precondition for being accepted for treatment;
- it helps practitioners to be clear about the limits of their competence (for example, in identifying cases where clients may require specialist referral).

The debate around the use of diagnosis is therefore multi-faceted, with strong arguments for both positions. In pragmatic terms, much counselling takes place in settings where clients attend for fewer than six sessions, and where formal diagnosis would constitute a waste of precious therapeutic time. In other settings, where counselling is delivered by volunteers or paraprofessionals, it would not be realistic to expect the counsellor to be a competent diagnostician. However, counsellors who lack information about diagnostic systems run the risk of cutting themselves off from the huge resources and accumulated knowledge of the therapies used in the medical domain.

USA, for instance, counsellors and psychotherapists are only able to claim payment from health insurance companies if they first of all diagnose their clients/ patients, and then deliver a form of treatment shown through research to be suitable for that diagnostic category.

Little evidence exists concerning the actual effects of assessment on client engagement in therapy, outcome or other variables. Frayn (1992) examined the assessments carried out on 85 people who had applied for psychoanalysis or long-term psychoanalytic psychotherapy. About one-quarter of these clients were later to drop out of therapy prematurely. Compared to the clients who had remained in therapy, those who had terminated prematurely were less motivated, possessed lower levels of psychological-mindedness and had a lower tolerance for frustration. In addition, at assessment their therapists had experienced more negative toward the clients who were later to leave early. The results of this study offer support for many of the assessment principles described earlier, including the importance of the criterion of the counsellor or therapist deciding whether he or she can accept the client sufficiently to work effectively with them.

It can be seen that there are many issues raised by the decision as to whether or not to assess, and the choice of mode of assessment. These issues are thoroughly reviewed in Mace (1995b).

Establishing a working alliance

One of the main tasks for counsellors in the initial phase of counselling, following assessment, is the establishment of a productive *working alliance* or *therapeutic alliance* with the client. The introduction of this concept is usually attributed to Bordin (1979), who suggested that there are three key aspects of the alliance that the counsellor needs to attend to in the early stages of contact with a client. First, there is agreement over the *goals* of therapy. Second, client and therapist need to reach a mutual understanding over *tasks*. What will each of the participants actually *do* during therapy, if it is to be successful? Third, there must be a good human relationship, or *bond*, between client and therapist. In Chapter 5, the origins of this model in Rogers' 'core conditions' theory was noted. There is considerable evidence that the therapeutic alliance comprises an essential element in all successful therapies (Orlinsky *et al.* 1994), even in behaviour therapy. A study by

Saltzman *et al.* (1976) found that it is necessary to consolidate the alliance by the third session – if it is not established by then it is unlikely that it ever will be.

A significant body of recent research has explored the processes associated with *ruptures* in the therapeutic alliance (Safran *et al.* 1990). In another, similar, piece of research, Hill *et al.* (1996) carried out a survey of counsellors concerning their experience of *impasse* in their work with clients. The findings of these studies are consistent with the view of Mearns (1994) that lack of therapeutic progress, or what he terms 'stuckness', is often associated with *over-* or *under-involvement* on the part of the counsellor. The issues involved in creating an effective working relationship between counsellor and client, and different perspectives on this process, are discussed in more detail in Chapter 12.

The successful negotiation of expectations, the completion of assessment and the formation of a productive working alliance lead into the main, 'working' phase of counselling. It is perhaps important to keep in mind that a significant number of clients do not turn up for their first appointment with a counsellor or psychotherapist, and there are many who only attend for one or two sessions before stopping. It seems reasonable to assume, therefore, that clients who commit themselves to more than four or five sessions are motivated to work, believe in the value of therapy as a means of helping them to overcome their problems and find their current therapist credible as a source of help. Why, under these circumstances, does therapy sometimes go wrong? Clearly, therapists can make mistakes in applying their chosen model. Research by Binder and Strupp (1997) has identified a number of common therapist sources of error. It is also useful to consider the client's view of what they have found *hindering* in therapy. In one recent study, Paulson *et al.* (2001) interviewed clients about things they believed had hindered or impeded their therapeutic progress. These clients generated a long list of hindering factors (see Table 13.3). Some of these items can be interpreted as errors in therapist technique, but others surely represented basic human weaknesses and foibles.

The existence of impasses, errors and hindrances is a reminder that, in many cases, progress in counselling does not follow a neat pathway; there can well be times when counsellor and client are forced to revisit the 'basics' of their relationship. Nevertheless, when counselling is going at least reasonably well, there will be a stage when the client and counsellor are working together to achieve productive learning, insight or behavioural change. There exist several different ways of making sense of the basic change process that occurs at this juncture. To do sufficient justice to this subject, these models of change are reviewed in a separate section below. We turn instead to the question of ending, and the processes occurring when therapy is completed.

Ending counselling

The challenge for the counsellor at the *ending* phase is to use this stage of counselling to the maximum benefit of the client. The goals of this stage include the

Table 13.3 What clients find hindering in counselling

Concerns about vulnerability

Feeling like I was going to be a guinea pig
Being concerned about confidentiality being broken
Being expected to do homework exercises outside of session
Being video-taped

Lack of commitment and motivation

Not being motivated to attend the appointments
Not starting counselling soon enough
The counsellor and I tending to become sidetracked
Doing exercises I didn't like
The counsellor asking a strange question

Uncertain expectations

Not knowing what I want from the counsellor
Not knowing what I'm supposed to get from a counsellor
Not knowing what to expect from counselling
Not knowing where I was going with counselling
Not feeling ready to open up fully
I didn't ask the proper question
Not liking where I was going in counselling
Not being 100 per cent comfortable with the notion of counselling
Expecting more specific information that I didn't get
Not knowing what I was supposed to do in counselling
Expecting the counsellor to give me answers to my questions
Sometimes wanting the counsellor to make the decision for me
Not being able to make the counsellor understand what I was feeling

Negative counsellor behaviours

Feeling that the counsellor wanted to get me out of the office as soon as possible
The counsellor having too many other things on their mind
Feeling like the counsellor didn't have the time for me
Thinking the counsellor didn't really care
The counsellor leaving with no warning
The counsellor not really listening
The counsellor using words that felt judgemental
The counsellor deciding to end counselling

Lack of connection

The counsellor was going to stop seeing me because I was going to go to sessions elsewhere at the same time
One bad counselling session disrupting sessions after that
Counselling ending before I was ready
Difficulty getting in contact with the counsellor
Not feeling connected from session to session
Not having enough in-depth discussion
Not having enough exercises in session

Barriers to feeling understood

The counsellor being paid to listen
Feeling like part of an assembly line
Being phoned by one counsellor, seen initially by another counsellor and finally assigned to somebody else
Talking to somebody who doesn't have a shared cultural experience
The counsellor not asking about the side effects of medication
The counsellor not being close to my age
My counsellor not being worldly enough
Being concerned about the counsellor's religious agenda

Structure of counselling

Not having regular sessions
An hour session is not long enough
Having long spaces between sessions
Not having enough counselling sessions
Not being able to have sessions more often when I wanted
Not being comfortable with the gender of my counsellor
Being in the room with the two-way mirror
Feeling like the counsellor was trying out a technique

Insufficient counsellor directiveness

Having more in me I wanted to say and my counsellor not asking
Not being pushed enough by my counsellor
Saying something and having the counsellor summarize it differently than I want

Table 13.3 contiuned

The counsellor not remembering details from the last session	Talking about the same thing but not moving forward with it
Asking for books and resources and not getting them	The counsellor not really doing what I expected
The counsellor trying to be my friend, but it not seeming real	My counsellor not telling me what to do
The counsellor being unaccommodating to my work hours	*Lack of responsiveness*
My counsellor not following up on suggestions made previously	The counsellor getting hung up on one pattern, and following it regardless – not tailoring counselling to my needs
The counsellor being too concerned about fees	The counsellor not being able to determine what the problem areas were
The counsellor assuming I was no longer interested in counselling	The counsellor dealing with the specific concern I came in for, but not other concerns that come up
The counsellor seeming kind of closed	The counsellor not putting very much input into the conversation
The counsellor not being very objective	
Feeling like just another statistic to the counsellor	Being over an issue and the counsellor not realizing it
The counsellor trying to tell me what to do	
My counsellor being too directive	The counsellor seeming more like a teacher
Talking for a couple of minutes and then being cut off by the counsellor	The counsellor not taking a stand on a lot of things and sitting on the fence
The counsellor just keeps pushing and pushing	

Source: Paulson *et al.* (2001).

consolidation and maintenance of what has been achieved, the generalization of learning into new situations and using the experience of loss and/or disappointment triggered by the ending as a focus for new insight into how the client has dealt with such feelings in other situations. The most fully developed strategies for working with endings are to be found in the model of *relapse prevention* that has been devised within the cognitive–behavioural tradition (see Chapter 4), and in the rigorous exploration of themes of attachment and loss associated with brief dynamic therapy (see Chapter 3). The difficult question of client readiness to end counselling is discussed by Ward (1984). Research by DeBerry and Baskin (1989) found that there were significant differences between the termination criteria used by public-sector and private-practice therapists. Therapists working in public clinics reported that the most common reasons for finishing therapy were the excessive caseload of the therapist or administrative factors. The therapists in private practice, by contrast, overwhelmingly reported that endings resulted from either the client or therapist (or both) believing that treatment goals had been achieved. It may be that the deep concerns that many counsellors and psycho-therapists express over endings are over-stated. There have been few studies of how clients feel about ending, but in one survey Fortune *et al.* (1992) found that the majority of former clients felt pride and a sense of accomplishment.

In much counselling practice, however, endings are unplanned or relatively haphazard. Sometimes the client will just cease to turn up, because they are

Box

13.4

How well do counsellors understand clients' reasons for ending?

For many counsellors and their supervisors, one way of assessing how successful therapy has been for a client is to review the reason why the decision has been made to leave counselling. Some counselling agencies keep records on clients' reasons for finishing counselling, as a means of auditing the quality of the service that is delivered. Ideally, counselling terminates when the client has sufficiently resolved his or her presenting problems, or at least has made enough progress to feel better able to cope with life.

But how aware are counsellors of the true reasons why clients may decide to finish? Research by Hunsley *et al.* (1999) suggests that, in many cases, counsellors have a somewhat skewed and over-optimistic view of the state of mind of their clients at the point of termination. The study carried out by Hunsley *et al.* (1999) was based in a therapy clinic attached to a university in Canada. Clients who used this clinic were on average in their thirties and experiencing difficulties around anxiety, depression, relationships and self-esteem, and received an average of 12 sessions of counselling, using a variety of therapeutic approaches. Reasons for termination, from the point of view of the counsellor, were identified on the basis of information held in the case files of 194 clients. Eighty-seven of these clients were interviewed by telephone and asked to describe their own perception of why they left counselling. A comparison was made between counsellors' and clients' perspectives on reasons for terminating therapy. Counsellors believed that around one-third of clients completed because they had achieved their goals, with most of the remainder stopping because of practical constraints such as moving house, lack of time and money or referral to another service. Counsellors recorded fewer than 5 per cent of cases in which clients finished because of dissatisfaction with therapy. The picture emerging from clients was quite different from the one presented by their therapists. Compared with their counsellors, a slightly higher proportion of clients (44 per cent) stated that they terminated counselling because they had achieved their goals. But a *much* higher proportion described themselves as dissatisfied. Around one in three told the interviewer that 'therapy was going nowhere', 'therapy did not fit my ideas about treatment' and they were 'not confident in my therapist's ability'. Nine per cent of these clients stated that 'therapy was making things worse'.

The findings of the Hunsley *et al.* (1999) study are consistent with results from other research into this issue. In one survey, by Dale *et al.* (1998), some clients even reported that they were afraid to leave counselling because they believed that their therapist would be angry with them if they announced that they wanted to finish. Research by Rennie (1994a, b, c) has drawn attention to the extent to which clients show deference to their counsellors, and refrain from telling them things they believe that the counsellor might not want to hear. These studies have implications for practice. As counselling comes to an end, it is important for counsellors to allow clients to be open about their disappointments, as well as to celebrate and reinforce their achievements. The possibility of being grateful to someone who has genuinely tried to help, yet being able to acknowledge openly to that person that their help has not made a difference, can be a significant learning experience in itself.

disillusioned with therapy, because they have got what they need or for practical reasons associated with housing, childcare, transport or work. Sometimes the counsellor may initiate the ending. Counsellors get other jobs, move elsewhere on training rotation, are made redundant, get pregnant, get ill, die. Each of these reasons for ending will have its own unique impact on the counselling relationship and on the client (Penn 1990).

One special type of ending is *referral* to another counsellor or agency. Referral can occur after initial assessment, or may take place after several sessions of counselling. For example, in some counselling settings, such as EAPs (see Chapter 1) clients are allowed only a limited number of sessions (sometimes no more than six), and need to be passed on to another therapist once the limit has been reached. The experience of referral is often difficult for both counsellor and client (Wood and Wood 1990).

The middle part of counselling: the process of change

Change is central to counselling, and every approach to counselling is built around a set of ideas regarding how and why change occurs, and what counsellors can do to promote change. The seven-stage model of change proposed by Rogers, Gendlin and their colleagues (Chapter 5) or the Prochaska and DiClemente stages of change model (Chapter 4) are examples of change theories identified with well-established theoretical approaches. It would be impossible to review all theories of change here. Rather, this section will attempt to provide an integrative way of understanding the change process that transcends specific theoretical approaches.

Assimilation of problematic experiences

The first model of change being considered here is the *assimilation model*, devised by Stiles and his associates (Stiles *et al.* 1990, 1992; Barkham *et al.* 1996; Honos-Webb *et al.* 1998, 1999; Stiles 1991, 2001, 2002). The basic idea behind this model is that the individual possesses a model of the world, or a set of cognitive schemas that guides that person's behaviour. New experiences need to be assimilated into that model if they are to be understood and to make sense. Experiences that do not fit into the schema or model can lead to a process of change, or accommodation, in the model itself. This theory is basically adopted from Piagetian developmental psychology, but is consistent with most models of therapy. It therefore represents a transtheoretical or integrative model.

The most interesting aspect of the assimilation model is that it specifies a series of stages, or a process, that takes place when assimilation occurs. In therapy, the most significant assimilation processes occur in relation to *problematic experiences*. The client reports an experience that is painful, or even not quite within

Table 13.4   Stages in the assimilation of a problematic experience in counselling

0   *Warded off.* Client is unaware of the problem. Affect may be minimal, reflecting successful avoidance.

1   *Unwanted thoughts.* Client prefers not to think about the experience; topics are raised by therapist or external circumstances. Affect involves strong but unfocused negative feelings; their connection with the content may be unclear.

2   *Vague awareness.* Client is aware of a problematic experience but cannot formulate the problem clearly. Affect includes acute psychological pain or panic associated with the problematic experience.

3   *Problem statement/clarification.* Content includes a clear statement of the problem – something that could be or is being worked on. Affect is negative but manageable, not panicky.

4   *Understanding/insight.* The problematic experience is formulated and understood in some way. Affect may be mixed, with some unpleasant recognitions but also some pleasant surprise of the 'aha' sort.

5   *Application/working through.* The understanding is used to work on a problem. Affective tone is positive, business-like, optimistic.

6   *Problem solution.* Client achieves a successful solution for a specific problem. Affect is positive, satisfied, proud of accomplishment.

7   *Mastery.* Client automatically generalizes solutions. Affect is positive or neutral (i.e. this is no longer something to get excited about).

Source: Barkham *et al.* 1996; Stiles *et al.* (2002).

awareness, and the task of the counsellor or therapist is to help the client to 'take it in' to their model of the world, to make it familiar, to become comfortable with an idea or feeling that initially was problematic. The assimilation process is summarized in Table 13.4. At the beginning of the process the problem is warded off, and the client does not report any strong emotion. However, as the problem begins to come into focus, through the emergence of unwanted thoughts leading to vague awareness, the client is likely to have very strong feelings. As the process continues into clarification, insight and working through, the feelings triggered off by the problem become more manageable and less intense.

The assimilation model brings together aspects of several different theoretical models. The notion that problems can be unconscious is reflected in the 'warded-off' stage. The humanistic or person-centred assumption that therapeutic change requires acceptance of feeling and working through emotion is consistent with the vague awareness stage. The importance of behavioural 'working-through' is also captured in the later stages of the model. It is important to note that not all of the problems clients work on in therapy will start at stage 0 and continue through to stage 7 in the model. A client may well enter therapy with a vague awareness of what is troubling them, or could even have arrived at a problem statement. Equally, clients may leave therapy before they have achieved mastery of the problem, either because the therapy is not long enough or because insight or even stating the problem may be sufficient for them at that point in their life. Moreover, clients may be working on two or more problematic experiences in parallel, with perhaps one of these topics as the major theme for therapy. Examples of how the assimilation model can be applied in individual cases can be found in Honos-Webb *et al.* (1998, 1999) and Stiles *et al.* (1990, 1992). The attraction of the assimilation model for practitioners is that it makes it possible to gain a sense of where the client is, in relation to an overall sense of where they might be heading. It also makes it possible to understand what has happened when a client stops talking about a particular topic: it can be because he or she has assimilated the experience, and has no further need to discuss it. The assimilation model is a useful stimulus to counsellors to reflect on their repertoire of facilitative skills. Some counsellors may be wonderful at bringing a warded-off feeling into the light of day, but may be less effective at helping the client to achieve insight. More recent developments in theory and research in relation to the assimilation model have resulted in a 'reformulation' of the model in terms of 'voices' (Honos-Webb and Stiles 1998). From this perspective, a warded-off experience can be viewed as a 'silenced' voice within the client's self. As this muted or silenced voice becomes more able to be expressed, it takes its place in the 'community of voices' that comprise the person's personal reality. An advantage of a 'voice' formulation is that it encourages the counsellor or psychotherapist to be sensitive to the actual physical characteristics and qualities of the submerged problematic experience, and thus more able to 'hear' this experience in the early stages of its emergence.

Another change model that explores similar territory is the *multiple processing* model of Bucci (1993). Wilma Bucci makes a primary distinction between the verbal and non-verbal modes of information processing. Clients in therapy may have phases where their talk is suffused by statements of feeling and emotion, imagery and communicating through facial expression, voice quality or physical gesture and movement. There are other times when they are able to talk in a rational, reflective manner, and express understanding and insight. The challenge for the counsellor or therapist is to help the client to make the journey from the first state to the second, to move from what Bucci (1995) calls *subsymbolic* processing to *symbolic* processing. The link between non-verbal and verbal information processing is achieved through *referential activity*, the use of language in such a way that abstract, symbolic concepts and gut feelings are brought together. Often, referential activity takes the form of a story. The client begins with generalized feelings, tells a story around these feelings, then reflects on the meaning of the story. Bucci is here making some very powerful suggestions about what exactly might be happening during stage 3 (problem statement/clarification) of

Box

13.5

The use of metaphor to deepen the therapeutic process

At the moment of moving another step more fully into his or her experience of a problematic issue, a client may be literally 'lost for words'. The person may just not possess a phrase or image that they have used before, that could do justice to their sense of discovering something new about self. A programme of research by Lynne Angus and Brian Rasmussen (Angus and Rennie 1988, 1989; Rasmussen and Angus 1996; Rasmussen 2000) has made a unique contribution to our understanding of some of the ways in which the use of metaphor can facilitate the therapeutic process. In their research, Angus and Rasmussen tape-recorded therapy sessions, and then invited the client and the therapist to listen to sections of the tape in which vivid metaphors were used, commenting on their experience during these events. They have found that the use of metaphor strengthens the collaborative relationship between counsellor and client, and helps them both to represent important issues in therapy. They also found that the use of metaphor can help to *deepen* the client's engagement in the process. In one case described in Rasmussen and Angus (1996: 526), a client was tearfully recalling experiences in which she had felt that her mother had behaved toward her in a dismissive fashion. The counsellor offered the following reflection:

It sounds very intense to me. The feelings in it. Like, cut right to the bone.

In the research interview conducted after the end of the therapy session, the client noted that, at this point in the session, she had been 'feeling completely lost in a sea of emotions'. When asked to comment on the counsellor's metaphor, 'cut to the bone', she stated that:

That was a good way of putting it. Very much so. It really kind of epitomizes how I am feeling right now . . . kind of the heart of the matter at that point.

This simple statement by the therapist ('cut right to the bone') was able to pull together several crucial aspects of the client's experience (the pain of what had happened, the pain being inflicted by another person, the sense that it could go no further without breaking the bone itself . . .) and thereby allow the client to develop a more coherent perspective on the issue she had been exploring.

It is of interest that this metaphor, like so many other metaphors that arise in therapy, draws on an image derived from a domain of bodily experiencing. The pervasiveness of physical, embodied metaphors was originally noted by the psychoanalyst Sharpe (1940).

the assimilation model. Like the assimilation model, Bucci's multiple code model represents an integrative theory of change:

> a common ground may be seen among cognitive-behavioural, constructivist, and experiential as well as psychodynamic treatment forms. All recognize, in different ways, the importance of experience in the nonverbal realm, the power of language in connecting to and affecting nonverbal experience, and the adaptive effects of the symbolizing process.
>
> (Bucci 1995: 119)

Change events

The models discussed in the previous section do not fit easily into the categories offered by Elliott (1991). The process of assimilation can take place over several sessions, can occur over the course of a single session or, conceivably, may even be worked through within the space of a single therapeutic 'event'. This kind of definitional problem is intrinsic to any discussion of process: it is rarely possible to be able to say with certainty when one process ends and another one begins. There is a sense in which therapeutic processes can be viewed as inseparable, overlapping, braided together. However, many counsellors and therapists find it helpful to look at process in terms of a series of significant *change events*. These events can be regarded as particularly intense, meaningful and memorable episodes within sessions. They are the moments when 'something happens'.

The most complete analysis of change events carried out so far can be found in the work of Greenberg *et al.* (1993), working within the humanistic tradition. Their ideas are reported in Chapter 6, and are based on an assumption that when a client indicates a particular type of issue (e.g. a dilemma or a tendency to be self-critical), there is a specific sequence of therapist actions or tasks that are particularly helpful and appropriate. An alternative way of comprehending helpful events has been created by Mahrer and his colleagues, who have attempted to understand the value of therapy in terms of 'good moments' (Mahrer *et al.* 1987).

Using structured exercises and interventions

As discussed in Chapter 3, both research and practical experience suggest that the most potent factors responsible for enabling therapeutic change to occur in counselling are 'non-specific': the experience of being in a supportive yet challenging relationship, the expression and exploration of feelings and emotions, the instillation of hope, the counsellor as a model of how someone might seek to engage authentically with another person. These non-specific factors are largely conveyed through generic counsellor responses such as sensitive, empathic listening, seeking clarification, encouragement, expression of caring and interpretation of meaning. However, there may be points in counselling, usually (but not always) in the middle, 'change' phase of the work, when it is helpful to use specific techniques and interventions to facilitate the development of the client. An exercise or intervention may perhaps best be viewed as providing a catalyst that allows the client to focus on and work through a specific issue. Some interventions are highly embedded in the flow of therapeutic conversation: for example, the exploration of metaphors generated spontaneously by the client (see Box 13.5). Other interventions involve stopping the flow of interaction, and concentrating on specific, structured exercises. Some of these exercises are associated with particular theoretical approaches. Examples of theory-informed exercises include the use in cognitive–behavioural therapy of the method of systematic desensitization, 'two-chair' work in Gestalt therapy and experiential focusing in person-centred counselling. Other exercises are more idiosyncratic or eclectic, and are passed on from one therapist to another informally or on training courses, or are invented by individual counsellors themselves. Examples of such exercises are the use of buttons or animal figures to represent members of a family, drawing a 'life-line', reflecting on the memories evoked by signific-ant photographs and guided fantasy. There are several books available that offer collections of widely used therapeutic exercises (e.g. Carrell 2001). In some instances, exercises may encompass homework assignments, which the client carries out between sessions. Examples of homework assignments are: keeping a diary or personal journal; spending time each day pursuing a therapeutically valuable activity such as listening to one's partner, meditating quietly or exercising; doing research on one's family history; reading a self-help book or 'inspirational' novel or watching a 'therapeutic' film.

The importance and usefulness of structured exercises vary a great deal, depending on the preferences of the particular client and counsellor involved. Some counsellors work effectively without ever using such 'props'; others find them invaluable. Some clients appreciate the structure provided by an exercise; others seem to find that it creates a distance between them and their counsellor, and prevents them from talking about what is really on their minds.

What do counsellors do? Process defined in terms of counsellor behaviour and intentions

Yet another way of looking at the process of counselling is to focus on the behaviour of the counsellor, and how this behaviour can have an effect on the client. Clearly, if is possible to identify those counsellor actions that are consist-ently associated with good outcomes, then it should be possible to train and supervise counsellors in order to maximize the frequency of occurence of these responses, and reduce the frequency of less helpful interactions. Clara Hill and her colleagues have devised widely used lists of both counsellor and client response modes (see Tables 13.5 and 13.6).

Table 13.5 Categories of therapist verbal responses

Approval. Provides emotional support, approval, reassurance or reinforcement. It may imply sympathy or tend to alleviate anxiety by minimizing the client's problems.

Information. Supplies information in the form of data, facts or resources. It may be related to the therapy process, the therapist's behaviour or therapy arrangements (time, fee, place).

Direct guidance. These are directions or advice that the therapist suggests to the client for what to do either in the session or outside the session.

Closed question. Gathers data or specific information. The client responses are limited and specific.

Open question. Probes or requests for clarification or exploration by the client.

Paraphrase. Mirrors or summarizes what the client has been communicating either verbally or non-verbally. Does not 'go beyond' what the client has said or add a new perspective or understanding to the client's statements or provide any explanation for the client's behaviour. Includes restatement of content, reflection of feelings, non-verbal referent and summary.

Interpretation. Goes beyond what the client has overtly recognized and provides reasons, alternative meanings or new frameworks for feelings, behaviours or personality. It may: establish connections between seemingly isolated statements or events; interpret defences, feelings, resistance or transference; or indicate themes, patterns or causal relationships in behaviour and personality, relating present events to past events.

Confrontation. Points out a discrepancy or contradiction but does not provide a reason for such a discrepancy. The discrepancy may be between words and behaviours, between two things a client has said or between the client's and therapist's perceptions.

Self-disclosure. Shares feelings or personal experiences.

Source: Hill (1989).

The covert dimension of process: what is going on behind the scenes

One of the most fascinating aspects of counselling process arises from the fact that both client and counsellor conceal a great deal of information from each other. Basic theoretical concepts that counsellors often use to make sense of process, ideas such as transference, counter-transference, resistance, genuineness and congruence, are grounded in the reality that, for much of the time, both participants

Table 13.6 Categories of client verbal responses

Simple response. A short, limited phrase that may indicate agreement, acknowledgement or approval of what the therapist has said, indicate disapproval or disagreement or respond briefly to a therapist's question with specific information or facts.

Request. An attempt to obtain information or advice or to place the burden of responsibility for solution of the problem on the therapist.

Description. Discusses history, events or incidents related to the problem in a storytelling or narrative style. The person seems more interested in decribing *what* has happened than in communicating affective responses, understanding or resolving the problem.

Experiencing. Affectively explores feelings, behaviours or reactions about self or problems, but does not convey an understanding of causality.

Exploration of client–therapist relationship. Indicates feelings, reactions, attitudes or behaviour related to the therapist or the therapeutic situation.

Insight. Indicates that the client understands or is able to see themes, patterns or causal relationships in his or her behaviour or personality, or in another's behaviour or personality. Often has an 'aha' quality.

Discussion of plans. Refers to action-oriented plans, decisions, future goals and possible outcomes of plans. Client displays a problem-solving attitude.

Silence. Pause of four or five seconds between therapist and client statements, or immediately after a client's simple response.

Other. Statements unrelated to the client's problem, such as small talk or comments about the weather or events.

Source: Hill (1986).

in any counselling relationship monitor what they think, select what they choose to say and attempt to control their non-verbal communication. If the aim of analysing process is to gain a fuller understanding of what is happening in a therapeutic encounter, in the interests of facilitating its effectiveness, one of the most productive strategies is to pay attention to what is *not* said. Regan and Hill (1992) carried out a number of studies in which they asked clients and counsellors at the end of each session to list 'things not said'.

In his programme of research into the client's experience of counselling, Rennie (1994a, b) found that there were many ways in which clients chose to conceal their thoughts, feelings and intentions. For example, clients might defer to the counsellor by saying nothing in a situation where they felt the counsellor had misunderstood them or asked an irrelevant question. Other clients reported to Rennie (1994b) that sometimes they overtly talked about things that were not really all that important, while covertly they might be running through another issue, or weighing up whether they felt ready to introduce into their story particular events or areas of experience that were painful or embarrassing.

The implication of these studies is to reinforce the idea that there is a lot going on 'behind the scenes' in any counselling encounter. To make sense of process, therefore, requires gaining as much access as possible to this hidden material. In training or research situations, it can be valuable to use the method of interpersonal process recall (IPR) (Kagan *et al.* 1963; Kagan 1984; Elliott 1986; Baker *et al.* 1990; Kagan and Kagan 1990), which is a systematic method for asking both participants to listen (usually separately) to the tape of a counselling session and comment on what they had been experiencing during the original interaction. If this task is carried out within 24 hours of the session, the informant is able directly to recall a lot of what went on. The longer the recall interview is delayed, the less the person will remember. In everyday ongoing counselling, ethical and practical constraints may preclude the use of IPR. In these situations the covert process of the client will only be recovered to the extent that they choose to disclose and explore it in sessions. However, it is feasible for counsellors to examine their inner experience during counselling by writing notes afterwards that focus on what they felt as well as what the client said and did, and by exploring this topic with their supervisor.

Towards a comprehensive analysis of process: bringing it all together

Many different aspects of counselling process have been discussed in this chapter. Quite possibly, the impression that has been given is that the whole topic of process is so complex and confusing that it is hardly worth serious consideration. The danger, for the counsellor, can be that of getting lost in the process, of discovering more and more layers or horizons of meaning, so that the simplest therapeutic act labours under the weight of its own significance. Nevertheless, perhaps the majority of counsellors will find that they will be required to carry out one or more 'process analyses' as part of their training. Experienced and qualified counsellors may be aware of a desire to understand more about the process of their own work with clients, perhaps in the context of supervision, or to write up for publication the process that has taken place around the use of a new technique, or in relation to working with a particularly significant or unusual client. The aim of this section is to describe some principles by which practitioners can systematically analyse the counselling process for themselves. These principles are drawn from the method of *comprehensive process analysis* (CPA), developed by Elliott (1984).

The first step in a comprehensive analysis of process is to make a taped record of a counselling session, using either audio- or video-tape. Although some counsellors are capable of making very complete and detailed process notes at the end of a session, there is no doubt that even the best notes select and 'smooth' the complex reality of what happened, and it is always better to work from a taped record whenever possible. The next stage in process analysis is usually to transcribe the tape, or key parts of the tape, to make it easier to give detailed attention to particular words, phrases and sequences, and to make notes on interesting or significant aspects of the text. The recent invention of a capacity to transfer taped material on to a personal computer, and as a result to be able to make notes that are stored and retained alongside the voice recording, may reduce the need to produce transcripts, but at the time of writing this technology is in its infancy, and it is not possible to tell whether it will in the end prove to be an effective way of conveying process information and analysis to a wider audience.

The third task in carrying out a process analysis is to scan the tape or text of the session to find a significant or interesting *event* that merits fuller interpretation and analysis. There exist a number of criteria on which events can be identified. Elliott (1984), for example, will often ask the client at the end of the session to nominate and describe the events that he or she felt were *most helpful* or *most hindering*. Mahrer *et al.* (1987) choose events considered by the therapist to represent 'good moments'. Angus and Rennie (1988, 1989), interested in the role of metaphor in therapy, directed their attention to events in which either client or counsellor employed a novel or striking metaphor. Elliott *et al.* (1990) wished to explore the meaning of insight in cognitive–behavioural and psychodynamic counselling, and so focused on insight events drawn from each of these two therapeutic modalities. These are examples from research studies. But it is striking, when reading case studies published by counsellors and therapists, or listening to counsellors present cases at supervision, that very often the discussion of a case hinges on the meaning and significance of key moments or events.

Having found an event that is, for either theoretical or practical reasons, significant or important, it is then useful to gather as much information as possible on the *covert* processes that were occurring during it, perhaps using IPR. Although in principle both client and counsellor may be invited to share their recollections of what they were thinking or feeling during the event, there are obvious ethical sensitivities involved in seeking client collaboration in this type of project. If the 'inquirer' is his or her actual counsellor there is a risk of setting up an unhelpful 'dual relationship' (see Chapter 15) in which the client is caught between the roles of research participant and recipient of therapeutic help.

Once an event has been 'filled out' with the addition of what was 'not said', it is possible to move into the analysis of its constitutive meanings and processes. This involves careful consideration of the following questions:

- What actually happened? What was the sequence of counsellor and client interactions during the event itself?
- What are the microprocesses (e.g. counsellor responses and covert reactions) that comprised the elements or 'building blocks' of the event?

- Where does the event fit in to the bigger picture represented by the session as a whole, the stage within the change process, or the therapy as a whole? In other words, what led up to the event, and what were its consequences?

Once the answers to these key process questions have been identified, it may be helpful, in bringing together the different aspects of what has been found, to draw on a pre-existing theoretical framework. In other words, it is generally useful in analysing process to make a distinction between *observation* and *interpretation*. The first step is to describe, in as much detail as possible, what happened. Although any description or observation is to some extent shaped and guided by the under-lying theoretical assumptions or conceptual language of the observer; none the less, it is still valuable to make an effort to 'bracket off' assumptions and see what is there.

In practice, there are two alternative techniques that can be helpful in organ-izing the material generated by a process analysis. The first is just to write a summary account of what happened during the event – the detailed 'story' of the event – and then in a separate section to work up the analysis and interpretation of the event. The second method is to divide the page into columns, with the transcript or descriptive account in the left-hand column and a commentary, or categorization of responses (perhaps using Hill's categories), in the right-hand column. With this method it can be helpful to number lines, so that any subse-quent analysis or interpretation can refer back to what was said at specific points in the transcript.

Examples of process analyses carried out along these lines can be found in Elliott (1983) and Elliott and Shapiro (1992). It is important to note that these published studies are rather more ambitious and time-consuming than the type of process analysis that would be feasible for a typical student or practitioner. Never-theless, the same principles can be applied in small-scale process analyses. Most people who carry out this type of process investigation report that it is enorm-ously useful to them personally, generating new insight and understanding into not only the process of counselling, but their own role in that process (Grafanaki 1996; Rennie 1996).

Conclusions: making sense of process

Counselling process is really all about the *flow* of what happens in a therapy session. Most of this flow is probably beyond any conscious control, by either party, either because it occurs so quickly or because it is so multidimensional and complex. Yet this is the environment in which a counsellor must operate. It is no good (unless you are an old-style family therapist) asking the client to wait a minute while you leave the room to consult your colleagues about what to do next or run the video-tape back to check up on what was said or done. The value of understanding process is that it can sensitize counsellors to what may be happening, it can help them to *see*. Ivey (1995) has described counselling as an *intentional* activity. All of us have probably unwittingly learned during our lives some ways of being helpful and facilitative to other people. To be a good counsellor it is necessary to be able to extend this repertoire when necessary, to be aware of when to work harder at being empathic and when to move instead into collaborative problem-solving mode. Theories and models of process, and comprehensive process analyses, are all means of slowing down and stopping the flow of process long enough to gain an appreciation of what is involved in different courses of intentional action in relation to a client.

Chapter summary

- The concept of *process* is widely used in discussions of the experience of what actually happens in counselling.

- Although there exist different meanings of process, they all refer to a sense of change, movement and activity within the counselling session.

- It is useful to break down the overall process into three broad phases: beginning, middle and end.

- Some of the key factors in the opening phase of counselling are the negotiation of expectations, assessment of the client and the formation of a therapeutic relationship.

- The key processes at the ending phase of counselling are dealing with loss, maintenance of learning and referral.

- The middle phase of counselling is the stage where most learning and change occurs.

- Two useful models of the change process are the *assimilation* model and the *multiple processing* theory.

- It can often be valuable to analyse what happens during significant helpful or hindering *events* as windows into the process of counselling.

- Some researchers have attempted to understand the process of change in counselling in terms of the set of behaviours or intentions employed by the counsellor. This approach is particularly useful in training counsellors.

- Much of the process of what happens in and between client and counsellor is covert and hidden; it can often be useful to inquire into what is *not said* in a counselling session.

- Practitioners or students/trainees interested in exploring process in the context of their own work may find that the comprehensive process analysis method provides a useful set of guidelines.

- The goal of studying and understanding process is to help counsellors to become more actively *intentional*, to be aware of what they do and to be in a position to follow the line that is most helpful for their client.

Topics for reflection and discussion

1 Looking back on your own experience as a client, or as someone being helped by another person in a less formal situation, can you identify particular *helpful* or *hindering* events? What were the main characteristics of these events that made them helpful or hindering?

2 In your view, is systematic assessment of clients necessary or useful? What might be some of the ways in which assessment might affect clients in terms of their motivation to participate in counselling?

3 Reflect on the different meanings that *ending* counselling might have for a client: for example, in a situation where there has been a preset limit of 12 sessions and the counselling has been helpful. How might the client be feeling about the ending? How might their behaviour change as the final session gets closer? How might the counsellor be acting and feeling? What might *not* be being said? How helpful would it be to bring the 'unsaid' into the conversation?

4 To what extent can the assimilation model be applied to all types of counselling? Is it a model that is most relevant to insight-oriented, exploratory approaches to counselling, such as psychodynamic and person-centred?

5 How might a client's expectations affect the way they behave in counselling? What can a counsellor do to negotiate expectations with clients?

Key terms and concepts

assessment	ends
assimilation model	expectations
beginnings	impasse
change events	interpersonal process recall
comprehensive process analysis	interpretation
emotional processing model	middles

multiple processing model
observation
preference
process
referral

relapse prevention
response modes
therapeutic alliance
working alliance

Suggested further reading

There is little to be said about the process of counselling that was not better said by Carl Rogers in the 1950s and 1960s. Most people read 'A process conception of psychotherapy' in *On Becoming a Person* (Rogers 1961). Even better is *Client-centered Therapy* (Rogers 1951).

The important topic of assessment is well covered by Mace (1995b) and Palmer and McMahon (1997). There are two research-based books that are particularly interesting and accessible. The first of these is *Therapist Techniques and Client Outcomes* by Clara Hill (1989). This book reports on analyses of the process occurring in eight cases of time-limited therapy with clients suffering from depression. Readers who might not want to work through the whole book will find that looking at one or two cases will give them plenty to think about. There is some technical information on tests completed by the clients and therapists, but there is also plenty of straightforward narrative based on interviews with both therapists and clients. Interestingly, Hill carried out this research and wrote this book because she did not believe the argument about 'non-specific' factors (see Chapter 3) and wished to prove that specific therapeutic interventions were crucial to the success of therapy. The second research book that is warmly recommended is by Toukmanian and Rennie (1992). There is much of interest in this book, but perhaps the place to start would be Rennie's own chapter looking at the hidden experience of the client, and then the chapter by Elliott and Shapiro, which presents a good example of comprehensive process analysis.

A very useful, research-informed approach to theory, practice and training in relation to counselling process can be found in two books by Clara Hill (Hill and O'Brien 1999; Hill 2001).

14 The politics of counselling: empowerment, control and difference

Introduction

The key question running through the topics covered in this chapter concerns the nature of power in the counselling relationship. Counsellors and psychotherapists are generally considered to be members of society who enjoy prestige, status and respect. Most of the time, counselling takes place within a therapeutic space defined and dominated by the counsellor: the therapist is the one who knows the 'rules of the game'. Meanwhile, clients are by definition people in need, people who are vulnerable. This vulnerability is exacerbated when the client is a member of an oppressed or 'minority' group. The counselling situation is, therefore, a situation characterized by potentially major differences in power. Yet for many practitioners and counselling agencies the goal of client empowerment lies at the heart of the counselling enterprise. How can this apparent tension be resolved? How can the power imbalance between client and counsellor be used to the advantage of the latter? What are the dynamics of power in the counselling room?

Historically, the first wave of counselling approaches – psychodynamic, person-centred and cognitive–behavioural – paid little attention to issues of power in counselling. Each of the second wave – systemic, feminist, multicultural and narrative – has promoted an appreciation of the social role of counselling. The growing literature on ethical and moral issues in counselling (Chapter 15) reflects some of the efforts being made both within counselling itself and externally through the legal system, to regulate some of the potentially oppressive aspects of counselling. The question of power in counselling, and the notion that counselling is a social and political act, can therefore be understood as highlighting issues and themes found in other chapters in this book.

This chapter first examines ideas about the nature of social power. Next, there is an exploration of the ways in which oppression and control operate in counselling, focusing particularly on the domains of social class, sexual orientation and religious orientation. The chapter concludes by reviewing some of the approaches that have been taken by counsellors and psychotherapists to combat oppression and subjugation. The overall aim of the chapter is to introduce an appreciation of the politics of counselling.

The nature of social and interpersonal power

It is no easy matter to understand the nature of interpersonal and social power. The concept of 'power' has many meanings, and is employed in different ways by different writers. Nevertheless, it is perhaps useful to focus on three basic aspects of power as a phenomenon within social life:

- power differences are universal;
- power is socially contructed;
- power is a combination of individual and structural factors.

In drawing attention to these elements of power, it is important to acknowledge the existence of an extensive social science literature on this topic. Readers interested in exploring the issue more fully could do worse than consult Dowding (1996).

The idea that power differences comprise a universal feature of human social organization is supported by research findings from many different areas. The existence of status hierarchies or a 'pecking order' in animal groups has been reported in many ethological studies. It is harder to observe hierarchical structures in human social interaction, because of its greater complexity. Nevertheless, research into the social psychology of humans also overwhelmingly supports the notion that power differentials are an unavoidable feature of human social life. However, while it might make sense to regard many of the status hierarchies observed in the animal world as determined by fairly simple genetic or biological mechanisms (e.g. size and strength), it is clear that in human groups power is socially constructed in complex ways. The power that a person is able to exert in a situation may depend on their gender, social class, ethnicity, age or role, or on combinations of these characteristics. The extent to which specific social attributes empower the individual is derived from the history of the social group concerned. For example, the oppression (disempowerment) of black people in Europe and North America can only be understood as the outcome of centuries of racism, which in turn can only be explained in terms of the religious beliefs and economic structures of Western society. Similarly, the oppression of gays, of older people or of physically disabled people are grounded in their own histories.

One implication of the social and historical construction of oppression is the realization that power differences are not merely a matter of individual attitudes, but are embedded in actual social and institutional structures and practices. Power differences are not only 'in your head', but are 'out there'. This fact has been a problem for approaches to counselling based solely in psychology. Psychological perspectives on power and oppression attempt to explain racism, sexism and ageism in terms of factors such as attitudes, perceptions and individual psychopathology. In the real lives of people who seek counselling, by contrast, the experience of racism, sexism and ageism is a tangible component of everyday life. It happens. There is a physical side to interpersonal power. Being oppressed can involve violence, fear and hunger, or the threat of these things.

The historical and social construction of power and control are the roots of authority power. A person has the power to act in a certain way because he or she possesses authority within the social system. Most interpersonal power in everyday life is of this type. Within counselling and psychotherapy, by contrast, issues of power and control have been addressed by introducing the concept of personal power. The idea of personal power is described most clearly in some of the later writings of Carl Rogers. He regarded personal power as the reverse of authority power. First, in a personal relationship such as counselling or psychotherapy, the therapist gives up influence and control based in social structure and authority: 'the politics of the client-centered approach is a conscious renunciation or avoidance by the therapist of all control over, or decision-making for, the client. It is the facilitation of self-ownership by the client . . . it is politically centered in the client' (Rogers 1977: 14). Second, personal power involves developing a particular set of values and style of relating: 'these new persons have a trust in their own experience and a profound distrust of all external authority' (p. 274). In other words, the sources of personal power come from within, rather than being drawn from external roles and statuses. Personal power depends on the capacity to be real, genuine and empathic. Rogers and many other counsellors regard themselves as 'quiet revolutionaries', and see their work as revolutionary and emancipatory. They see themselves as providing opportunities for clients to develop 'self-ownership', to make their own decision, to claim their own personal authority and voice. Ultimately, this is a form of power based in love rather than in fear.

There is no doubt a deep truth contained within the notion of personal power. However, there is also a deep contradiction. At the time that he wrote *On Personal Power*, at the age of 75, Carl Rogers was probably the most famous living psychologist in the world. During his career he had received all the honours that the American academic system could bestow. His books had sold in millions, and he was revered whenever he made a public appearance. While Rogers did, by all accounts, have a powerful personal presence and positive, facilitative impact on the lives of those who knew him, he was also a person who possessed a huge amount of authority power. The sources of this authority power were clearly identifiable in the social system. He was a leader of a major professional group. He could claim the status of a successful scientist. His reputation and prestige were promoted and marketed by the publishing industry. Yet these factors were not included in his understanding of his own powerfulness as a person. In many ways Rogers was in an ideal position from which to reflect on these matters, but he could not recognize the social bases of much of his authority and influence. The fact that it was so difficult for him to appreciate the social, as well as the individual, dynamics of interpersonal power just illustrates the scope of the problem.

The institutionalization of power and oppression in counselling

The attempt by Rogers to depict counselling (or, at least, person-centred counselling) as a subversive activity that empowers clients to take charge of their own lives presents an attractive image of a set of values to which many counsellors would aspire. It can be argued, however, that there are a number of mechanisms of social control built in to prevailing forms of counselling practice that are far from emancipatory or empowering in their effect. These mechanisms include:

• the language and concepts of counselling;
• acting as an agent of social control;
• control of space/territory/time;
• differential access to services;
• corruption of friendship.

In Chapter 15, examples are discussed of specific types of oppressive or abusive events that can occur in counselling settings, such as sexual or financial exploitation of clients, or physical violence. These kinds of occurrences can be seen as being based in the more general power dynamics being discussed here. While ethical codes and guidelines can often be effective in minimizing specific instances of mistreatment of clients, these more general issues to some extent lie beyond the remit of professional ethical codes, and are more correctly seen as intrinsic to the nature of counselling as it has developed over the past 50 years.

The language and concepts of counselling

Gergen (1990) has suggested that the way that counsellors and psychotherapists talk about their clients can be regarded as comprising a 'professionalized language of mental deficit'. He describes widely used therapeutic concepts such as 'impulsive personality', 'low self-esteem' or 'agoraphobia' as being 'invitations to infirmity', because they function in such a way that the person is identified with their 'problem'. The language of therapy, therefore, operates to:

> furnish the client a lesson in inferiority. The client is indirectly informed that he or she is ignorant, insensitive, or emotionally incapable of comprehending reality. In contrast, the therapist is positioned as the all-knowing and wise, a model to which the client might aspire. The situation is all the more lamentable owing to the fact that in occupying the superior role, the therapist fails to reveal its weaknesses. Almost nowehere are the fragile foundations of the therapist's account made known; almost nowhere do the therapist's personal doubts, foibles, and failings come to light. And the client is thus confronted with a vision of human possibility that is unattainable as the heroism of cinematic mythology . . . each form of modernist therapy carries with it an image of the 'fully functioning' or 'good' individual; like a fashion plate, this image serves as a guiding model for the therapeutic outcome.
>
> (Gergen 1990: 210)

The point being made by Gergen is that a language in which one person is characterized as a 'problem' and the other as 'problem-free' cannot help but be mirrored in the actual relationship between them. The inequality expressed in the language of counselling is carried over and acts as a 'guiding model' for the practice of counselling.

Kirkwood (1990) argues that this imbalance in power is reinforced by the use of the term client. Although he is writing about social work practice, and using the word 'need' rather than 'problem', his words capture important elements of the political and social implications of calling someone a 'client':

> identifying needs means . . . the introduction of two poles; the person with the need (to be identified and met), and the person who will identify and meet the need. The first is implicitly passive, the second active; the first known, the second a knower; the first capable, the second incapable; the first being helped, the second helping; the first receiving, the second providing

... Client is the name for this isolated human object, this recipient, this useless bag of needs ... the passive object role of the client is coming into focus ... The client is controlled by the imperial values and acts of the provider, the professional.

(Kirkwood 1990: 160–1)

For Kirkwood, to be a client is to be essentially a 'passive object', to be defined in terms of the gaze of the professional, to be not a person in the fullest sense of that word but only a 'bag of needs' or problems. Many other examples of ways in which psychological theory functions as an oppressive 'language of deficit' can be found. For example, Stock (1988) and Tiefer (1988) have argued that the language of mainstream sex therapy is fundamentally 'phallocentric', depicting men as active and women as passive. Later in this chapter, there are examples of how working-class, gay and religious persons have been described in disempowering ways in the counselling and psychotherapy literature.

The language of counselling constitutes one of the means by which the power of a high-status professional group can be employed to control those who use their services. It is important to recognize that, here, the language of counselling and psychotherapy does not refer merely to technical terms and concepts found in textbooks, and that the way that counsellors speak to their clients in everyday counselling sessions is somehow different. Several studies of psychotherapeutic discourse (for example, Davis 1986; Madill and Doherty 1994; Madill and Barkham 1997) have revealed the subtle ways in which therapeutic conversation is shaped and directed by the therapist.

The counsellor as an agent of social control

One of the ways in which counsellors can exert power over their clients is by acting as agents of social control. Ideally, in most situations counsellors strive to be as 'client-centred' as possible, regarding themselves as acting solely on behalf of their client. There are some counselling settings, however, in which the approach taken by the counsellor or the attitude of the counsellor towards the client are defined and controlled in terms of external demands. Examples of these might include:

- working with drug or alcohol users referred by the court, with the explicit aim of eliminating their addiction;
- counselling sex offenders;
- student counselling in a college where there is pressure on counsellors to maximize retention of students;
- workplace counselling in an organization where there is an expectation that those who admit to being under stress should quit.

These are all instances where a counsellor might be expected by those who pay his or her salary to influence clients in a specific direction. In these situations the pressure may be fairly overt and explicit. In other cases, however, counsellors may find themselves responding to more subtle, covert social pressures. Later in this chapter, some of the issues surrounding the provision of counselling to working-class people, gay men, lesbians and highly religious individuals are discussed. Counselling theory and counsellor training can often function according to prevailing social attitudes that are not accepting of members of these groups. When a counsellor fails to grasp the oppression that such clients have experienced, he or she is essentially functioning to reinforce social norms of rejection.

The clearest examples of counsellors operating as agents of social control can be seen in the relationship between counselling and psychiatry. Psychiatrists have the power to impose custodial, compulsory treatment on people who are assessed as being at risk to themselves or to others. From a medical perspective, such a decision can be seen as a helpful response to illness and crisis. From a sociological perspective it can be seen as a means of control. People who cause trouble are locked up, or are forced to take drugs that control their behaviour. Counsellors who refer patients to psychiatrists are agents of a system that, in extreme cases, can make use of significant state powers (laws, police) to lock people up.

It has been argued by Szasz that any involvement whatsoever by counsellors and psychotherapists in the institutions of social control (which for him would include the medical system and social services) makes meaningful therapy impossible. Szasz contends that true therapy is only possible under conditions of absolute voluntary participation by a client paying for the services of a therapist. This is an extreme position to adopt, and it does not address the issue that therapists in private practice are quite capable of imposing social norms and values on their clients (e.g. around homosexuality), even in the absence of institutional controls. It seems more helpful to acknowledge that in every counselling encounter there is some element of social control, and that it is necessary to accept that this happens, and then to find methods of ensuring that it does not have a destructive effect on the counselling process. For example, the 'user-friendly' principles devised by Reimer and Treacher (discussed later in this chapter) are one way of achieving this goal.

Control of space, territory and time

One of the most significant, but least mentioned, aspects of the politics of counselling concerns the practicalities of the typical counselling interview: where and when it happens, and how long it lasts. Counselling usually takes place on the counsellor's territory, in their office. The counsellor or a receptionist will often meet the client in a waiting area, and escort them to the counselling room. Appointments are usually made for 50-minute or one-hour sessions every two or three weeks. All of these factors are for the convenience of the counsellor or counselling agency, and are not necessarily what the user might wish, if given the choice. For example, telephone or e-mail counselling (see Chapter 17) is attractive to many people because they can contact the counsellor or counselling service at the time of their choosing, and finish the counselling session at the point where they feel they have had enough. The number of sessions that a client will receive is also often controlled by the agency. In some agencies, there can be a limit of six or eight sessions, regardless of the needs or preferences of clients. In other agencies, it is made clear to clients at the time of assessment that they will only be accepted if they make a contract for long-term therapy lasting for a year or more.

Differential access to services

Even if a counselling agency, or counsellor in private practice, is able to carry out counselling in a rigorously empowering or non-oppressive manner, their work could still be regarded as contributing to political inequality if their client group was drawn from only relatively privileged members of the community. It seems fairly clear that access to counselling services is highly correlated with various indices of social power and status. There exists only the most meagre literature, or training opportunities, in relation to counselling with people with learning disabilities or physical disabilities, older people or people labelled as severely mentally ill. Although counselling services for women (see Chapter 8), ethnic minority members (see Chapter 10), gays, lesbians and religiously committed persons (see below) have improved in recent years, it is still the case that most mainstream counselling services are staffed by white, middle-class, heterosexual, non-disabled people who attract clients with similar social characteristics. In one piece of research into access to counselling services, Crouan (1994) traced the ethnic, geographical, gender and economic circumstances of a group of 97 clients who had used a British inner-city voluntary counselling agency. She found that, despite the location of the agency near a deprived area of the city, and despite its stated mission to meet the needs of the disadvantaged, the vast majority of clients were affluent white women. In addition, black and Chinese clients who did use the agency were more likely to drop of counselling within the first few sessions.

Corruption of friendship

Research carried by Masson (1984, 1988, 1992) has uncovered a long list of examples of oppressive and abusive practice perpetrated by some of the leading members of the psychotherapy profession. Masson (1988: 24) concludes from this evidence that 'the very idea of psychotherapy is wrong', and goes on to assert that 'the structure of psychotherapy is such that no matter how kindly a person is, when that person becomes a therapist, he or she is engaged in acts that are bound to diminish the dignity, autonomy, and freedom of the person who comes for help.' Masson argues that what is wrong with therapy (and, by implication, counselling too) is that the client is offered a relationship that may appear to be a friendship, in that he or she is encouraged to share his or her closest secrets and feelings, but that is in reality a false friendship. The relationship between therapist and client, Masson points out, is a professional one, based on an inequality in power. The attempt to maintain a quasi-friendship in such conditions is, he suggests, in the end false and destructive for both therapist and client. He proposes that 'what we need are more kindly friends and fewer professionals' (Masson 1988: 30).

Unfortunately, the high profile given to Masson's writing, along with his polemical style and perhaps occasionally exaggerated claims, has meant that the simplicity of his message has become obscured (see, for example, Owen 1995). A much more straightforward account of the corruption of friendship theory of counselling and psychotherapy is offered by Kitzinger and Perkins (1993). Although they write from a lesbian perspective, and for a lesbian audience, their argument is equally relevant when applied to counselling as a whole:

> In seeking out the pseudo-frienship of a therapist, we run the risk of destroying our capacity for genuine lesbian friendships. Therapy offers us a let-out clause. With the institutionalisation of therapy, we cease to expect to have to deal with each other's distress: it is consigned to the private realm of therapy. This deprives our communities of a whole realm of experience, deprives us of the strength and ability to support each other, and deprives us of understanding the context and meaning of our distress. Therapy privatises pain and severs connections between us, replacing friendship in community with the private therapist–client relationship.
>
> (Kitzinger and Perkins 1993: 88)

From this perspective, therapy has the effect of mystifying people about the true nature of their troubles, and what needs to be done about them. Therapy individualizes, pathologizes and psychologizes what are in reality conflicts between people, and within society.

The politics of counselling have been discussed here in terms of four key factors: language, control of time and space, access and mystification. Taken together, these arguments represent a serious and profound challenge to the integrity of counselling and counsellors. An examination of theory and practice in relation to three client groups – working class, gay and lesbian, and religiously committed – suggests that concerns about inequality and discrimination in counselling are far from empty.

Counselling with economically disadvantaged people

Research in the USA, reviewed by Bromley (1983) and Garfield (1986), has found that counselling and psychotherapy services are most widely used by people in middle and upper income and social class groups, either because others do not seek therapy or because when they do seek therapy they are more likely to be refused or offered drug treatment. Lower-class clients are also more likely to drop out of counselling prematurely. Why does this happen?

From surveys carried out in both the USA and Britain, there is ample evidence that there is a strong association between social class and mental health, with people of lower social class being more likely to be hospitalized for a psychiatric problem and reporting higher levels of symptoms in community studies (Cochrane 1983). Sociologists interested in social class and mental health have proposed two alternative models for explaining these differences. The first is known as the 'social causation' hypothesis, and views the high levels of psychological disturbance in working-class people as caused by poverty, poor housing and other environmental factors. Although the social causation seems highly plausible on common-sense grounds, there is significant evidence that would appear to contradict it. Several pieces of research (for example, Goldberg and Morrison 1963) have found that although the social class distribution of psychiatric patients is weighted towards a high representation of lower-class individuals, the social class distribution of the parents of these patients resembles the class distribution in the general population. This type of result has led to the development of what is known as the 'social selection' or 'drift' hypothesis, which suggests that the high numbers of disturbed people in lower-class groups are caused by the inability of these people, because of their illness, to maintain the social class and income levels of their family of origin. In this model, the downward 'drift' is understood to be at least partly caused by genetic factors.

Substantial efforts have been expended in attempts to test these competing hypotheses but have failed to reach an unequivocal answer (see Cochrane 1983 and Lorion and Felner 1986 for reviews and further discussion). The significance of these studies for counselling is that they have a direct bearing on the aims of counselling and the attitudes of counsellors towards lower-class clients. From a social selection point of view, counselling or psychotherapy is likely to be of very limited utility for lower-class clients, because of the lack of personal resources and the history of failure experienced by the client. From a social causation perspective, by contrast, counselling may have a lot to offer in empowering clients to cope with their current situation and fulfil their potential.

The debate over social class and mental illness illustrates well the political ideologies underlying this area of research and practice. Most counsellors and psychotherapists are middle class, and have undergone several years of professional education and training. Their world-views, personal values and ways of using language are quite different from those of working-class clients. Where counselling and psychotherapy agencies use client assessment and diagnosis to screen applicants for therapy, there is evidence that working-class people are more likely to be referred elsewhere or allocated to drug treatment rather than individual therapy (Bromley 1983).

Perhaps the most obvious explanation for the different patterns of diagnosis and treatment in different social classes is the gatekeeper theory. The professional providers of counselling and psychotherapy are themselves middle class and therefore find it more congenial to work with clients or patients from similar backgrounds. Middle-class and educated clients are possibly more articulate and assertive in seeking out counselling, or may be better informed about its benefits. Finally, the costs of regular visits, which could include time off work, travel and childcare costs (even when the counselling itself might be free), to a counsellor or therapist may be beyond the means of people on low incomes.

These are all factors that prevent working-class clients from entering counselling. The attitudes and expectations of working-class clients regarding the counselling process have also received some attention. It is often said that psychoanalysis, for example, is more acceptable to highly educated intellectual and artistic clients, whereas people from lower-class or less educated groups prefer counselling that is more directive, structured and advice-giving in nature. There is, however, very little evidence to support this proposition (Bromley 1983).

Probably the most important aspect of social class in relation to counselling is that working-class clients will almost always find themselves with middle-class counsellors. As an occupational group, counsellors are almost entirely middle class. Even counsellors from families of working-class origin will usually have entered counselling through higher education or primary training in a profession such as nursing, the Church, teaching or social work. This may make it difficult for the counsellor to empathize with the needs and aspirations of the working-class client (e.g. for financial security rather than personal fulfilment).

There have been few attempts to develop a theoretical understanding of the issues involved in counselling people from lower-class groups, a situation that Pilgrim (1992) attributes to the general avoidance of political issues by counsellors and psychotherapists. However, Arsenian and Arsenian (1948) suggested that it is necessary for therapists to grasp the difference between 'tough' and 'easy' cultures. In a 'tough' social environment, people have fewer options open for satisfying their needs, those options that are available do not reliably lead to desired outcomes and the link between action and goal achievement can be difficult to identify. Living in such a culture results in feelings of frustration and low self-esteem. The lack of positive expectations for the future and belief in the efficacy of personal action resulting from socialization in a tough culture would make counselling more difficult. Meltzer (1978) has argued that social class differences in psycho-therapy are due to linguistic factors. Research carried out by Bernstein (1972) found that communication in working-class cultures took place through a 'restricted' code, which is largely limited to describing concrete, here-and-now events rather than engaging in reflexive, abstract thought. The implication for counselling of this linguistic theory is that working-class language does not lend itself to 'insight' or exploratory therapies, and that clients from this group would be better served by behaviour therapy or family therapy (Bromley 1983).

It is necessary to treat these analyses of working-class personality and commun-ication style with considerable caution. The characteristics that are interpreted as deficits of working-class culture can equally well be seen as assets. For example, middle-class people who grow up in an 'easy' culture can become narcissistic and self-absorbed. Similarly, the capacity of middle-class people to engage in abstract intellectualization, rather than describing their concrete experience, is viewed by many counsellors as a barrier to effective work. It may be more correct to regard these ideas as indicative of potential areas of mismatch between counsellors and

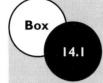

Being homeless as a counselling issue

The experience of being homeless, and its implication in relation to counselling, have been sensitively explored by Bentley (1994, 1997). In a series of interviews with homeless people in London, Bentley (1997) found a number of recurring themes. These homeless people perceived themselves as outsiders, invisible and unseen, 'a freak show on the streets'. Maintaining existence was a constant struggle. The daily threat of theft of possessions, and the difficulty of accessing food and finding a quiet safe place to sleep, were key issues. There was also a strong sense of helplessness and hopelessness. Bentley (1994) suggests that these factors make it very difficult for homeless people to commit themselves to counselling. She recounts the story of Ben, a formerly homeless man with drink and violence problems who had been resettled. His reason for accepting the offer of counselling was that 'otherwise I won't talk to anyone from one end of the week to the next'. Bentley (1994: 134) writes that:

> he continually punctuated his speech with phrases like 'I bet you're sick of me' or 'you don't have to listen to this. Do you want me to go now?' and would mask his vulnerability by cruelly mocking himself . . . On out fourth meeting he came to the session looking vibrant and alive. He announced that he'd 'given up', he'd begun drinking . . . and felt free of the pressures to master his life. He announced that I'd never have to see him again.

However, the counsellor's statement at this point that she would be willing to see him again had a deep effect on him, by letting him know that someone valued him. After a couple of weeks he resumed counselling.

Bentley (1994, 1997) suggests that effective counselling with homeless people requires either that the client has previously been found some kind of accommodation or that a 'pre-therapeutic' relationship be established first of all with a hostel or outreach worker.

clients. In this respect, it is relevant to note that, in her study *Therapy in the Ghetto*, Lener (1972) found a strong relationship between client improvement and 'democratic attitudes' in their therapists. The effective therapists in this study were those who were able to reach out across the class divide and accept their clients.

The report by Holland (1979) of a counselling centre that operated in a deprived area of London draws a number of relevant conclusions concerning the adaptation of counselling methods in such a setting. Holland noted that many clients preferred to see a counsellor once or twice, and then to return some time later for additional help, rather than entering into continuing long-term work.

Some clients would not commit themselves to a formal counselling contract, although they would talk at length to staff about themselves and their problems if given informal opportunities to do so.

The common factor in both these observations would appear to be the importance for the client of remaining in control of the counselling relationship. Working-class clients may have been on the receiving end of many welfare agencies and government departments that will have treated them as 'cases' and taken decisions on their behalf, and are as a result understandably anxious about putting themselves in the hands of professional 'helpers'.

It is evident that there does not exist a coherent body of theory and research on the psychotherapeutic issues associated with poverty, homelessness, job insecurity, powerlessness and other aspects of working-class life. Neither does there exist a comprehensive framework for practice. It would seem that counsellors and psychotherapists have tended to regard working-class people as being primarily in need of practical help, such as social work, legal advice or debt counselling. Following Maslow, therapy is for those whose needs for security and safety have already been fulfilled. It is very hard to justify this state of affairs on either moral or pragmatic grounds. The seeds of a model of class-sensitive counselling are there, in the writings of Holland (1979, 1990) and others. It is surely time for them to grow.

Power and control in counselling with lesbians, gay men and bisexual people

The social world in which counselling has developed over the past century is a world marked by a high degree of homophobia. Many industrial societies still enforce laws that restrict or criminalize homosexual behaviour, and there is widespread stigmatization of gay and lesbian relationships, despite the fact that around 10 per cent of the population is homosexual. Although gay and lesbian clients in counselling will seek help for the same wide range of general relationship, self-esteem and stress problems felt by heterosexual people, there are some distinctive issues that may be presented by clients from this group. These include dilemmas and anxieties about the process of 'coming out' and accepting a gay or lesbian identity. There may be additional problems for the heterosexual counsellor of being aware of his or her own possible homophobia, and achieving an understanding of the language and norms of gay and lesbian subcultures.

Many lesbian and gay counselling agencies have been set up to offer telephone or face-to-face counselling and self-help support networks. This trend has been motivated in part by the hostility to homosexuals shown by the mental health profession. It was only in 1974 that homosexuality ceased being classified as a psychiatric disorder by the American Psychiatric Association (Bayer 1987). The considerable opposition to this change included psychoanalysts and psychotherapists as well as 'medical model' psychiatrists. The founder of rational emotive therapy, Albert Ellis, was also in the 1950s a proponent of the view that exclusive homosexuality was a neurotic disorder that could be resolved through effective psychotherapy (Bayer 1987). Mainstream counselling research, training and practice largely ignore the existence or needs of non-heterosexual clients. For example, in a survey of articles published between 1978 and 1989 in the six most widely read and prestigious counselling psychology journals, Buhrke *et al.* (1992) found that out of a total of 6,661 articles and reports, only 43 (0.65 per cent) focused on lesbian and gay issues in any way. The majority of these articles were theoretical discussions or reviews of the literature, rather than empirical studies of counselling process or outcome. Over one-third of the articles over this 12-year period had appeared in one special issue of the *Journal of Counseling and Development* (Dworkin and Gutierrez 1989). It is clear that even research articles that are published can be written in an anti-homosexual manner. As recently as 1991, the American Psychological Association found it necessary to publish guidelines for 'avoiding heterosexist bias' in research (Herek *et al.* 1991).

Counsellors working with gay men, lesbians and bisexual people have evolved an 'affirmative' (Hall and Fradkin 1992; Davies 1996) stance towards the problems presented by their clients. A key element in the approach is to reinforce the validity and acceptability of homosexual behaviour and relationships. To accomplish this, it is often necessary to challenge the homophobic attitudes that the client has internalized through socialization. The provision of accurate information about homosexuality can often be a part of this process, as can sensitive rehearsal with the counsellor of how the client will tell others about his or her decision to come out. Many counsellors working with gay and lesbian clients adopt a developmental approach, viewing the experience of 'coming out' as a set of developmental tasks. The model of coming out constructed by Coleman (1982) has been widely utilized in counselling. Coleman (1982) postulates five developmental stages in the coming-out process: pre-coming out, coming out, exploration, first relationships and integration. Other issues that are often present in counselling gay and lesbian clients include family conflicts, sexual problems, attitudes to ageing and coping with AIDS/HIV (Harrison 1987; Coleman 1988). Recent developments in these areas are well documented by Davies and Neal (1996) and Hitchings (1997). There exists a body of literature that can enable counsellors to work creatively with homosexual clients, in contrast to the situation in the 1960s and even 1970s where most of the published theory and research functioned to pathologize members of this group.

The field of counselling and psychotherapy in relation to sexual orientation has clearly advanced substantially since the times when homosexuality was regarded as an illness to be cured. However, the existence of problems as well as progress can be seen in a series of research studies carried out by Liddle (1995, 1996, 1997). In these studies, carried out in the USA, she found that a group of counselling trainees presented with a case vignette that described the client as either heterosexual or lesbian were just as likely to give high likeability ratings to the latter (Liddle 1995). In a large-scale survey of lesbian and gay male clients of counselling and psychotherapy, she found that the majority of those who answered the questionnaire reported themselves to be generally satisfied with the therapy they had received, even when it was delivered by a heterosexual therapist (Liddle 1996), and that lesbian and gay people were likely to stay in therapy longer than a matched sample of heterosexual clients. These results suggest that the counselling profession may have overcome its earlier prejudices about homsexuality, leading to a greater trust of therapists on the part of gay and lesbian users.

Other aspects of the data collected by Liddle (1995, 1996, 1997) suggest that significant problems remain. When the sample of trainee counsellors in the Liddle (1995) study was divided into male and female sub-groups, it became apparent that the women trainees liked and admired the lesbian client more than the heterosexual client, while the result for the male trainees was the opposite: they were less likely to accept the lesbian client. In the Liddle (1996) study, even though the therapy experiences of the gay and lesbian clients was positive overall, there were still a significant minority who stated that their therapist pressurized them to renounce their homosexuality, or even terminated therapy once the client had disclosed their sexual orientation. Liddle (1997) observed that 63 per cent of gay and lesbian clients screened their therapist for gay-affirmative attitudes before committing themselves to therapy, and that the majority had a strong preference for a therapist with a similar sexual orientation.

Research conducted by Liddle (1995, 1996, 1997), Annesley and Coyle (1998) and Ryden and Loewenthal (2001) suggests that gay and lesbian consumers of therapy are aware that they need to be careful about which therapist they choose. There is still a significant amount of anti-homosexual sentiment and behaviour around among heterosexual counsellors and psychotherapists, and in counselling and psychotherapy training (Coyle *et al.* 1999). As the writings of Kitzinger and Perkins confirm, there exists a suspicion of therapy, certainly in some lesbian communities. Further, the tendency within this field to treat gay men and lesbian women as possessing parallel experiences and needs is open to question. There is still a long way to go.

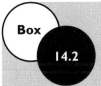

Box 14.2

Experiences of lesbians and gay men in therapy

The American Psychological Association (APA) has responded to initiatives from its membership by becoming involved in various campaigns to support the rights of gay men, bisexual men and women, and lesbians. For instance, the APA has presented legal evidence in several court cases to the effect that homosexuality is not an illness (Herek *et al.* 1991). In 1984, the APA set up a task force to investigate bias in psychotherapy with lesbians and gay men. The task force group surveyed a large number of psychologists concerning specific instances of biased and sensitive practice. Respondents in the survey were asked to describe incidents that they had experienced personally, or that had been reported to them by clients, that exemplified anti-homosexual attitudes or, alternatively, examples of informed, sensitive or gay-affirmative therapist behaviour. The survey revealed a wide variation of practitioner attitudes towards homosexuality (Garnets et al. 1991). For example, one therapist wrote that:

> I'm convinced that homosexuality is a genuine personality disorder and not merely a different way of life. Every one that I have known socially or as a client has been a complete mess psychologically. I think they are simply narcissistic personality disorders – see the description in the DSM-III – that's what they have looked and acted like – all of them.
>
> (Garnets et al. 1991: 966)

Other replies to the survey recounted stories that had been told by clients:

> A lesbian told me about her first therapist who encouraged her to date men and give up her ideas and feelings regarding women as intimate partners.

> A lesbian struggling with her sexual identity was challenged by her therapist, 'If you have a uterus, don't you think you should use it?'

> A gay male couple seeking assistance with inhibited sexual desire on the part of one partner . . . were told the problem indicated the one partner probably wasn't really gay and that the recommended intervention was to break up their relationship.
>
> (p. 967)

There were also observations of discriminatory behaviour on the part of colleagues:

> A colleague told me she 'couldn't help' expressing astonishment and disgust to a male client who 'confessed homosexuality'.

> A gay clinical psychology student was required to get aversion therapy from a professor as a condition of his remaining in the program once he was discovered.
>
> (pp. 967, 968)

While this survey also identified many examples of good practice, it is these instances of oppression and misuse of power that stick in the mind. These replies and observation come from a professional group that is highly trained and regulated. How much more bias is there in the counselling and psychotherapy profession outside of this select group?

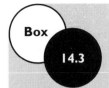

Box 14.3

The attitudes of psychoanalytic psychotherapists to working with gay and lesbian clients

A central theme that has emerged from the literature on gay and lesbian counselling is that people who are gay and lesbian who decide to enter therapy find it important to work with a therapist who will actively support and *affirm* their sexuality. A survey among British psychoanalytic psychotherapists (Bartlett *et al.* 2001; Phillips *et al.* 2001) used a combination of questionnaires and in-depth interviews to explore the attitudes of a group of experienced and highly qualified therapists to working with gay and lesbian clients. A postal questionnaire was sent to 400 randomly selected members of the British Confederation of Psychotherapists (BCP), with completed questionnaires being received from 218 (55 per cent) respondents. The questionnaire asked whether the respondent would be willing to be interviewed: 33 indicated willingness, and of this group 15 were interviewed.

The quantitative data collected in this study revealed that there were issues for many of these therapists around acceptance of gay and lesbian experience. Of the 218 therapists who completed the questionnaire, 18 declined to answer a question that invited them to describe, in their own terms, their sexual orientation. Only 30 per cent of the sample agreed that gay and lesbian clients should have a right to see a gay or lesbian psychotherapist. The open-ended comments written in response to the questionnaire, and the recordings from interviews, provided a more detailed picture of these difficulties. For example, one psychotherapist, when asked about why he chose to use the term 'homosexual' rather than 'gay', stated that:

> I've never used the word 'gay' in my life. 'Lesbian', yes, but never the word 'gay'. I've never seen the point about it, its not my business – except to be very curious about what it means to the average homosexual who changes the fact of his homosexuality to refer to it as 'gay', and I think it's part of the new sort of twist that's going on in which we are invited to consider that homosexual people behave as if they've had a choice and chosen the homosexual way of life.

When asked about the low number of gay and lesbian therapists within the training organization, this therapist replied:

> nobody sitting in the room that night at the (training organisation) was the result of a 'homosexual' love affair – each was the result of a heterosexual experience between a man and a woman, the woman becoming pregnant... in my opinion no homosexual person exists who can't be envious of such a procedure, because homosexual love doesn't produce anything creative... Homosexuality needs to be recognised as 'madness'; when it is presented as a fulfilling self choice, it is a delusion, which is about the 'impersonation' of the

ordinary heterosexual world, and of the heterosexual capacity for ordinary thinking.

(Phillips *et al.* 2001: 79)

These statements are clearly grounded in a position in which heterosexual sexuality is regarded as 'normal' and 'mature', and gay or lesbian sexuality is defined as a form of 'arrested development' and clinical entity.

Many of the therapists in the study reported that they believed that their training organization would not accept gay or lesbian people for psychotherapy training, and that gay or lesbian trainees or members of the organization kept their sexual orientation secret:

> I would have thought that as far as the training organisation is concerned, it would be a fear of exposure, and a fear of being, what's the equivalent of struck off or defrocked? There's a deep distrust about actually continuing to be respected as a colleague.

> Terror, fear. There are a lot of people, I believe, in all the trainings, that refuse gay and lesbian people.

The majority of the therapists who were interviewed said that they knew of colleagues, whom they regarded as suitable for training, who had been refused a place on the grounds of sexuality. However, some of the interviewees agreed with the policy of excluding gay men and lesbians from psychotherapy training:

> We should not play the game of this collusive idea of normalising muck and rubbish.

> It's a bit like not taking people with drugs offences into the police force.

These statements suggest a bedrock of lack of acceptance of the capacity of gay and lesbian individuals to be effective psychoanalytic psychotherapists, no matter how much they may have achieved, or how competent they might be in fields such as psychiatry, social work, clinical psychology, nursing or teaching (the typical primary professions of members of the BCP).

It is important, in a study of this kind, to be careful not to allow conclusions to be biased by the extreme views of a minority of respondents. In an attempt to offer a balanced overview of their findings, Phillips *et al.* (2001: 82–3) wrote that:

> There was some polarization of the analysts' views in that women and younger therapists were more likely to regard gay men and lesbians as valuable members of society who should have access to training as analysts and should not be 'pathologized' in psychoanalysis. However, all therapists were equivocal at some

point and were uncomfortable with the issues. The psychoanalysts interviewed found it difficult to accept gay and lesbian sexuality as one variant of the human condition. Although many of them held empathic views about gay men and lesbians and stated that they should have equal access to training as analysts, most were uncomfortable with the scenario whereby a heterosexual client may be aware that their therapist was gay. Furthermore, they were uncomfortable with the suggestion that gay people might choose a gay therapist with all that implied in terms of self-disclosure on the part of the analyst.

Phillips *et al.* (2001) further concluded that, in their opinion, 'such a wholly negative approach to gay and lesbian sexuality is unlikely to help their clients adjust positively to their life circumstances.'

What are the implications of this study for counselling? There are many openly gay and lesbian individuals who are not only participants on counselling courses, but are respected trainers on courses and senior members of the profession. The kinds of negative homophobic attitudes expressed by some of the psychoanalytic psycho-therapists in the Phillips *et al.* (2001) study would probably lead to the person being asked to leave a counselling training course. On the other hand, a similar study does not appear to have been conducted within a counselling context – perhaps similar prejudices exist in counselling, even if in a more muted form. And it is certainly true that many counsellors would regard psychoanalytic psychotherapists, such as members of the BCP, as constituting the 'elite' of the therapy profession, and would place high value on the writing, supervision and therapy offered by such colleagues.

Counselling and religious commitment

Religion may often represent a core element in the distinctive social identity of an ethnic group. Alternatively, some ethnic groups are fragmented into many competing religious sub-groups or sects, and there are world religions that unite many diverse races and ethnic groups. On the whole, counselling and counsellors have been reluctant to be explicit in addressing religious concerns. It has already been suggested in Chapter 2 that many of the values and practices of counselling have been derived from the Judaeo-Christian religious tradition. These influences have been disguised by the generally scientific, humanistic and secular framework provided by counselling theory. It would be possible to read most of the mainstream counselling and psychotherapy literature without coming across any mention of religion or spirituality. It is as though, for many therapists, the spiritual domain has been abolished. Some therapists would even go as far as to claim that clients reporting spiritual or mystical experiences were undergoing episodes of psychotic breakdown. Gradually, this anti-religious sentiment is shifting. Although surveys of religious affiliation and activity in counsellors and psychotherapists carried out in the 1960s and 1970s found lower levels of religious affiliation than in the general population (Henry *et al.* 1971; Bergin 1980), more recent surveys have found an increasing interest in and commitment to religious and spiritual values and beliefs, with counsellors and psychotherapists now demonstrating equivalent levels to the population at large (Bergin and Jensen 1990; Shafranske and Malony 1990).

Several writers and practitioners have addressed the question of how existing counselling techniques or approaches can be adapted to meet the needs of clients from particular religious groups: for example, Mormons (Koltko 1990) and Christian fundamentalists (Young 1988; Moyers 1990). These approaches have concentrated on acquiring a comprehensive understanding of the beliefs and way of life of clients from such backgrounds, to facilitate the understanding of client symptoms.

Other writers have explored the possibilities for modifying established counselling principles in work with clients with specific religious value systems and behaviours (Stern 1985). Another strategy has been to attempt to integrate ideas from both religion and counselling, with the intention of developing a new and more effective approach. One example of this type of direction is the Christian counselling movement. Johnson and Ridley (1992) have identified four sources of benefit to clients that can result from integrating Christian beliefs with counselling practice.

1 The accommodation of Christian beliefs and values within established counselling techniques and approaches. An example of this strategy can be found in a study by Propst *et al.* (1992), in which religious cognitive–behavioural therapy was offered to depressed clients, all of whom labelled themselves as actively Christian. This therapeutic intervention consisted of standard techniques derived from cognitive therapy (Beck *et al.* 1979) and RET (Ellis 1962), but with religious arguments supplied to counter irrational thoughts and religious images suggested to facilitate positive change. Clients in a comparison group received the same cognitive–behavioural treatment, but without religious imagery or rationales. Although clients in both groups reported significant benefit from the therapy, those who had received religious therapy showed slightly higher rates of improvement. One additional point of interest from the Propst *et al.* (1992) study was that even the non-religious therapists achieved good results when using a religious approach. Another example of an accommodation strategy can be found in a psychodynamic approach to pastoral counselling, in which the stories or narratives told by clients are interpreted in the light of religious stories and teachings (Foskett and Lyall 1988; Foskett and Jacobs 1989).

2 Mobilizing hope. Yalom (1980, 1986) has argued that hope can enable the client to enter and stay in counselling, and increases compliance with therapeutic interventions. Christian beliefs and practices, such as prayer, can be a powerful source of hope for the future.

3 The use of scriptural truth. Christian counsellors and clients believe that the Bible can provide guidelines for action and explanations for problems.

4 Intervention by a divine agent. Some Christian counselling approaches seek to facilitate inner healing through the acceptance of a divine agent, such as God, Jesus or the Holy Spirit.

The integration of an explicitly Christian approach to counselling can be seen to offer 'resources for mental health or well-being that are not available to the non-believer' (Jeske 1984). If the efficacy of non-religious counselling can be viewed as depending on the resources of the counsellor and client, then religious counselling introduces a third type of resource: an external, transcendent power. From a theoretical perspective, this idea is difficult to assimilate into mainstream counselling approaches. It is just not included in the 'image of the person' implicit in psychodynamic, person-centred or cognitive–behavioural theory. This discrepancy can be overcome by reinterpreting familiar counselling concepts from a Christian standpoint. For example, Malony (1983: 275) has written that 'to the degree that empathic understanding, therapeutic congruence, acceptance, permissiveness and unconditional positive regard exist in the therapeutic hour, there God is present.' It is also possible to interpret religious statements from a psychological standpoint. The 'twelve step' programme for change employed by Alcoholics Anonymous, for example, includes the suggestion that the alcoholic's behaviour is controlled by a higher power. The effects of this piece of 'cognitive reframing', according to Mack (1981), are to give the person who has difficulty controlling his or her drinking a means of 'governing the self' that is not dependent on personal will power or social sanctions.

So far this discussion has concentrated on Christian approaches to counselling. It is worth noting that there do not appear to have been any systematic published attempts to look at counselling from an Islamic, Hindu or Sikh perspective. Surprisingly, given the over-representation, compared to the general population, of practitioners from Jewish backgrounds in surveys of counsellors and therapists (Henry *et al.* 1971; Bergin and Jensen 1990; Shafranske and Malony 1990), there have been few publications on Jewish counselling. There has, however, been substantial interest in the relationship between Buddhism and Western psychotherapy and counselling (Suzuki *et al.* 1970), but this has consisted for the most part of incorporating ideas and techniques from Buddhism into therapy offered to non-Buddhist clients, rather than attempting to develop services for clients from that religious persuasion itself.

Another dimension of the relationship between religion and counselling has been the insistence of a number of practitioners and theorists that counselling itself is incomplete if it does not give serious consideration to the spiritual aspects of human existence. Bergin (1980) has made a useful distinction between spirituality and religiosity, with the former being concerned with a personal quest for transcendent meaning, while the latter refers to participation in organized religious institutions. An acknowledgement of the spiritual dimension of existence has become a highly significant theme in contemporary counselling and therapy. For example, the movement towards multiculturalism (Chapter 10) has forced many counsellors to give serious consideration to the psychological significance of the religious beliefs and practices of people from other cultures.

The past decade or so has seen something of a rapprochement between counselling and religion. However, it would be a mistake to imagine that all clients reporting religious, spiritual or mystical beliefs or experiences would be understood or well received by their counsellors. There is still a sense that these are matters that are somehow 'beyond' counselling. For instance, in the various attempts that have been made to construct a 'core battery' of tests to assess the outcomes of counselling and psychotherapy (Chapter 18), there has been an absence of any intention to include scales measuring spiritual functioning. Few counselling training courses address religious or spiritual issues. In this area, as in other areas of the application of counselling, many examples of enlightened and liberatory practice can be found, but there still remains the possibility that some religiously committed clients will have a hard time if they seek help from certain counsellors.

Other disadvantaged and marginalized groups

For reasons of space, it is not possible to offer an extended discussion of the role of counselling in relation to other oppressed and marginalized social groups. Probably the most significant among these groups are the elderly, and those with disabilities in learning or with physical disabilities. There is a growing awareness that both these groups can in fact benefit from counselling. Useful sources on counselling and older people are Knight (1986) and Hanley and Gilhooley (1986). Waitman and Conboy-Hill (1992), Segal (1996) and Reeve (2002) are excellent source of ideas about and insights into counselling and handicap. The issues in these areas are similar to those already reviewed in relation to poverty, gay and lesbian sexualities and religious commitment. First, there has been a general avoidance of the client group by counsellors and psychotherapists, and a tendency to apply labels. There then follows a slow accumulation of experience and theory in relation to counselling with members of the group, but there remains a legacy of prejudiced attitudes or negative counter-transference, and a dire need for more consciousness-raising, training and research.

Principles of anti-oppressive practice in counselling

This discussion of the experiences of people who are gay, lesbian, working class or religious demonstrates the extent to which certain groups can find themselves marginalized in relation to counselling. Counselling is based on a set of values and assumptions that reflect the world-view of its founders, almost all of whom were white, heterosexual men in secure professional-scientific jobs (Katz 1985). However, the examples discussed above also reveal the existence of a movement in the direction of beginning to recognize problems of inequality in counselling, and a willingness to do something about them. There are a number of strategies that can be adopted in the effort to achieve a form of practice that is anti-oppressive. These have included:

- developing a critique of oppressive practice;
- highlighting empowerment and emancipation as goals of counselling;
- creating a 'user-friendly' approach.

Developing a critique of mainstream, 'majority' theory and practice

Often the first steps in initiating change involve not direct action but creating a framework for understanding what is happening, and how things might be different. Counsellors and therapists committed to opening up access to counselling for members of disadvantaged groups have engaged in a number of activities designed to change the prevailing climate of opinion in their professional organizations. These activities have included publishing critical reinterpretations of theory, carrying out research into the needs and problems of the particular client group, arranging debates at conferences and in professional journals, and pressurizing committees to accept changes to discriminatory regulations and procedures. Examples of this type of enterprise can be seen in the fight to depathologize homosexuality (Bayer 1987), the publication of the classic text on cross-cultural counselling by Sue (1981) and the feminist attack on Freudian theory (Howell 1981).

This phase of change can hold dangers for those people engaged in it, who may be risking their reputations and careers by espousing unpopular causes. There is also the possibility that little may be achieved beyond recognition that there is a problem. The critique must be followed up by appropriate action if it is to have an effect on the lives of clients. However, the existence of a plausible rationale for introducing new methods and services is of inestimable value to those who are in the position of having to justify and even defend their proposals in the field.

Empowerment and emancipation as goals of counselling

The concept of empowerment plays an important part in the person-centred (Chapter 6), feminist (Chapter 8) and multicultural (Chapter 10) approaches to counselling. However, there are some counsellors and psychotherapists who have placed the goal of empowerment at the centre of their model. One of the foremost advocates of empowerment is Ivey (1995), who calls his approach *liberation psychotherapy*. Rather than the counsellor 'acting on' the client, Ivey proposes that the counsellor should work intentionally alongside the 'client colleague' to develop a mutual understanding of the social world within which they live. The aim of therapy is to help the client colleague to make sense of his or her issues in a social and historical context. A crucial stage in this process is that of naming their resistance, putting words to the experience of oppression and their ways of fighting that oppression. In practice, there are many similarities between Ivey's approach and the White and Epston (1990) narrative constructionist perspective described in Chapter 9.

Another empowerment model is the social action therapy approach developed by Holland (1990). This approach is consistent with the ideas of Ivey, but is in many ways more detailed and thought-through. One of the key aspects of this model is that it is community-based. It is not primarily a model that can be employed by individual practitioners working in isolation with individual clients, but needs to be applied in the context of a community or neighbourhood project in which several people can become involved, in different roles and at different levels and stages.

The main ideas of social action therapy are summarized in Figure 14.1. Persons who are socially oppressed are often labelled as patients, and are allocated to forms of treatment, such as behaviour therapy or psychopharmacology, that can be viewed as essentially constituting forms of social control and as 'functionalist' in character. Holland (1990) argues that it is necessary to help such a person to move to a position of accepting their own personal self, that they are indeed a worthwhile individual and that what has happened in their life has some meaning. This can be achieved by means of individual counselling or psychotherapy. Holland suggests that interpretative, psychodynamic counselling can be particularly useful at this stage, if it is regarded as being 'a tool for action, rather than an end in itself' (p. 256). However, the weakness of individual counselling is that it does not offer a good arena for exploring sociopolitical issues, so Holland includes opportunities for users to participate in groups where they can uncover their shared, collective histories and make sense of their individual experiences within a social and cultural context. This stage draws on ideas of radical humanism, encouraging the people to encounter each other and free up their energies and desires. Finally, there is a stage of radical structuralism. Holland (1990: 266) argues that making demands on social institutions and changing social and community structures is necessary 'if anything significant is to be achieved by way of change'. Members of the project act together to bring about political change and to gain access to resources that will make a difference to their lives.

There are some comments that can be made on these versions of liberatory or emancipatory counselling. Ivey (1995), Holland (1990) and other politically aware therapists such as Kirkwood (1990) have clearly been influenced by the writings of the political and educational activist Paulo Freire (1972), who constructed an approach known as conscientization. Empowerment is a theme that demands an interdisciplinary perspective. There are parallel developments within the field of community psychology (Rappaport 1987; Orford 1992; Zimmerman 1995), particularly centred on the idea of prevention; perhaps it is time for counsellors and community psychologists to engage in a dialogue. Finally, in contrast to the majority of counsellors, who perhaps might be said to espouse a limited notion of empowerment based on conventional hour-long individual sessions, those who

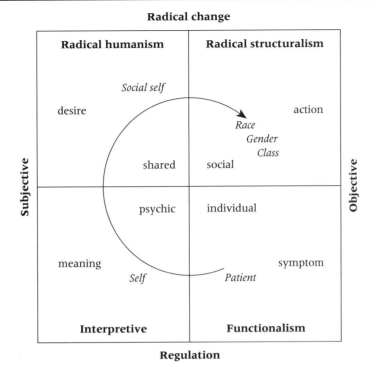

Figure 14.1 The social action model of therapy
Source: Holland (1992).

have placed empowerment higher on their agenda have found it necessary to engage in direct political action within communities.

Developing a user-friendly approach to counselling

The evidence reviewed in this chapter suggests that it is no easy matter to offer counselling in a manner that is genuinely empowering for all clients. There are many groups of people who are disadvantaged and excluded by the way that counselling is currently organized, and it is possible to make a case that even people who are not overtly oppressed by social attitudes and structures may feel intimidated by a counselling setting where the counsellor is clearly able to define the nature and limits of what will happen. The writings of Masson (1988) and other critics of counselling and psychotherapy have stimulated a search for a model of practice that reflects the values of respect and 'person-centredness' (understood in its broadest sense) espoused by the majority of counsellors. Reimers and Treacher (1995) have been at the forefront of the movement to take therapy consumers seriously. Although their own practice is based on a family therapy approach, their recommendations can be applied within any orientation to counselling. Reimers and Treacher (1995) have formulated a set of principles of good practice for any counsellor or counselling agency seeking to adopt a 'user-friendly' style of operation, encompassing the key ideas listed below. They propose that a user-friendly approach:

1 Is based on the core assumption that counsellors must accept that ethical issues are of primary, not secondary, importance in therapy. Therapy is recognized to be essentially a human encounter between participants who meet as human beings first, and therapists and users second. The crucial power difference between counsellor and user is recognized as a major source of difficulty. Failure to address this power differential opens the door to abusive practice.

2 Is based on the assumption that the building of a therapeutic alliance between user(s) and therapist(s) is usually crucial to both the success of therapy and users' reported satisfaction with therapy.

3 Recognizes that therapists generally fail to understand the stress and distress that users experience, particularly on contacting an agency for the first time.

4 Cannot treat users as though they were identical. Class, gender, sexual orientation, power, age, disability, ethnic origin, religion and socio-cultural background are some of the more obvious differences that may need to be taken into consideration if successful therapy is to be undertaken.

5 Assumes that it is integrated models of therapy that can offer users the best deal in terms of actually being offered ways of working that are likely to suit them.

6 Insists that therapists must adopt a stance of self-reflexivity. They must be willing to accept that if they themselves had difficulties they would willingly attend therapy sessions organized by therapists utilizing a model of therapy similar to their own.

7 Research needs to play a crucial role in contributing to the development of theory and practice. This is an ethical issue because therapies that fail to develop a body of research data supporting their efficacy are clearly vulnerable to criticism. Users' experiences of therapy and their satisfaction with therapy must, of necessity form a crucial part of the assessment of the value of any model of counselling or psychotherapy.

8 Stresses the crucial importance of training and professional development in influencing counsellors' attitudes. Just as therapy needs to be user-friendly, therapy training needs to be trainee-friendly.

9 Recognizes that therapy has crucial limitations in helping users. Some people need their counsellor or therapist to play a supportive role in gaining access to material resources that can be crucial to their well-being.

10 Is not simplistically user-centred. At times it is essential that the counsellor challenges users' attitudes and behaviour.

These principles represent a challenge to much contemporary practice within counselling. There are few counsellors or counselling agencies that have chosen to develop a mode of working that is fully consistent with this framework.

Conclusions

Being a client in counselling involves talking about personal concerns, areas of fear and vulnerability, secrets. This puts the counsellor in a powerful position. Many of the things that are said to a counsellor are just those thoughts and wishes that are not shared with other people in everyday life, because to do so might lead to embarrassment, shame or rejection. It is as though the person receiving counselling is opening himself or herself up to the counsellor in ways that allow the counsellor to touch him or her, emotionally and psychologically, in ways that other people have not. This process is one that gives the counsellor a large amount of power and influence over the client. What better way can there be to control someone's thoughts and beliefs than to have them share these thoughts in minute detail and allow them to be reinterpreted or reframed by someone with a strong point of view? Clients often say that they need to be able to trust their counsellor, to be confident that the counsellor will not misuse their power.

The structure of the counselling encounter reinforces the power of the counsellor. What may seem to the counsellor to be appropriate boundaries or a secure frame – time limits, an office, professional training, no contact between sessions or after counselling has ceased – also function as the components of a socially powerful role. A counsellor is someone who has been assigned the authority, within society, to deal with certain issues. After all, why does counselling exist? Why are the resources of social institutions such as colleges and the health care system invested in counselling. Partly, perhaps, to enable users of these services to flourish. But partly, also, as a means of social control.

There is always a delicate balance within counselling between the requirement that the counsellor is personally powerful, in the sense meant by Rogers (1978), and the danger of being oppressive, of putting unseen pressure on the client to conform to some set of norms and values. What is the point of going to see a counsellor unless they have the potential to have a powerful impact on your life?

Chapter summary

- Counsellors are powerful figures in the lives of their clients; many counsellors would say that they seek to empower their clients through their work together. The dynamics of power, the politics of the counselling relationship, is therefore a topic of central importance.

- Although writers such as Carl Rogers have emphasized the personal power of the counsellor, the most important source of power difference is institutional and based on authority and control.

- Counsellors control the process of what happens in counselling in a number of ways: possession of a language and labelling system; being in charge of space and time; regulating access.

- Some critics of counselling have argued that counselling supports institutional and state control of people by taking discussions of intimate and personal issues out of the family and community and opening them up to external professional governance.

- Examination of counselling theory and practice in relation to three groups (economically disadvantaged; gay, lesbian and bisexual; religiously committed) shows that members of these groups have had to struggle to have their experience and values taken seriously by the counselling profession.

- Ivey, Holland and others have developed explicit models of emancipatory, politically aware practice.

- The user-friendly approach advocated by Reimers and Treacher provides a framework for addressing issues of power and control in counselling practice.

Topics for reflection and discussion

1 Critics of counselling and psychotherapy have argued that therapy comprises an over-individualized response to personal problems and ignores the social origins and conditions which ultimately produce these problems (Smail 1991; Pilgrim 1992). Do you agree? Take any one field of counselling with which you are familiar (student, marital, workplace etc.). To what extent does the practice of counselling in that area ignore underlying social factors? Would the counselling be more effective if social factors were given more attention?

2 Discuss the strengths and weaknesses of different theoretical orientations in counselling with clients from disadvantaged or marginalized groups. Is there one theoretical perspective, or combination of perspectives, that you find most (or least) applicable in this context?

3 Think about the counselling agency where you work (or a counselling agency you have used as a client). How do you feel when you are there? Do you have a sense of being powerful and in control, or do you have a sense of being in the hands of others? What are the physical cues (e.g. notices, leaflets, layout, furniture, decoration, etc.) and behaviours that give you a feeling of being empowered, or a sense of being oppressed? Do you think a member of a different cultural group might feel differently about his agency?

4 Writing from a psychodynamic perspective, Strupp (1972: 275) suggested that: 'a fundamental problem in psychotherapy (and indeed in all human relationships) is the question of who is in control. While couching his operations in

very different terms, Freud nevertheless evolved the ingenious technique of seemingly placing the patient in control of the therapist, while in actuality creating for the latter a position of immense power. It is the judicious utilization of this power which uniquely defines the modern psychotherapist and which constitutes his expertise. The therapist's interpersonal power is deployed more or less deliberately in all forms of psychotherapy regardless of the specific techniques that may be utilized. In other words, if a symptom, belief, interpersonal strategy, or whatever is to change, a measure of external force must be applied.' Do you agree? In the end, is counselling a matter of applying 'a measure of external force' to bring about change?

Key terms and concepts

agent of social control	liberation psychotherapy
anti-oppressive practice	personal power
authority	politics
community psychology	power
conscientization	religion
corruption of friendship	social action therapy
empowerment	social causation hypothesis
gatekeeper theory	social class
gay affirmative therapy	social selection hypothesis
language	user-friendly services

Suggested further reading

The issue of power and abuse in counselling and psychotherapy was put on the agenda by Jeffrey Masson, and his book *Against Therapy: Emotional Tyranny and the Myth of Psychological Healing* (1988) remains essential reading. A thoughtful response to Masson can be found in Spinelli (1994). The *Journal of Critical Psychology, Counselling and Psychotherapy* regularly carries articles on issues of power in therapy, and seeks to promote user perspectives.

Another book that is highly recommended is *Changing Our Minds: Lesbian Feminism and Psychology* by Kitzinger and Perkins (1993). This is not a book that will only be of interest to a relatively small group of lesbian feminist readers. Kitzinger and Perkins raise fundamental issues about the relationship between therapy and community that are relevant to anyone involved in counselling at any level. In relation to counselling issues associated with gay and lesbian clients, the *Pink Therapy* series is an invaluable resource (Davies and Neal 1996, 2000; Neal and Davies 2000).

There is remarkably little writing about issues of counselling and poverty or social class. Two papers that offer stimulating reviews of issues in this area are Allen (1999) and Hannon *et al.* (2001).

Morals, values and ethics in counselling practice

Introduction

The practice of counselling includes a strong moral and ethical dimension. It is clear that one of the central characteristics of the social groups in which counselling and psychotherapy have become established is the experience of living in a world in which it is difficult to know what is the 'right' way to live. In an increasingly secular society where there may be much questioning or rejection of tradition and authority, and where different moral or religious codes coexist, individuals are required to make choices about moral issues to an extent unknown in previous generations. In Chapter 2 it was argued that much of the need for psychotherapy is due to the fact that in modern society moral controls are for the most part internalized rather than externalized. Because we do not live in communities dominated by single, comprehensive moral codes, individuals must possess within them the means of deciding what is right and wrong, and also the means of punishment – for example, feeling guilty – if they transgress these rules.

Many, perhaps even most, people who seek counselling are struggling with moral decisions. Should I finish my course or quit college? Should I stay in a marriage that is making me unhappy? Should I have this baby or arrange for an abortion? Should I come out and acknowledge that I am gay? Shall I take my own life? These, and many other counselling issues, are problematic for people because they involve very basic moral decisions about what is right and what is wrong.

One of the fundamental principles of most approaches to counselling is that the counsellor is required to adopt an accepting or non-judgemental stance or attitude in relation to the client. In general, most counsellors would agree that the aim of counselling is to help people to arrive at what is right for them, rather than attempting to impose a solution from outside. Nevertheless, at the same time counselling is a process of influence. In the end, the client who benefits from counselling will look back and see that the counselling process made a difference, and influenced the course of his or her life. The dilemma for the counsellor is to allow herself to be powerful and influential without imposing her own moral values and choices. Good counsellors, therefore, need to possess an informed awareness of the different ways in which moral and ethical issues may arise in their work.

In most societies, the principal source of moral and ethical thinking has been organized religion. Historically, there have been strong links between therapy and religion (discussed in Chapter 2). However, although Christian ideas about morality have been influential in the counselling world, it is also apparent that at least some of the people who have come into counselling from a previous religious background have done so because they have rejected elements of traditional religious thinking, or have been seeking something beyond these traditions. There has also been a steady influence on counselling and psychotherapy of non-religious moral philosophy, particularly existentialism, and of political and social movements, such as feminism. Finally, there has been a growing interest in non-Western religious thinking, particularly Buddhism.

Counsellors need to be aware of the moral dilemmas faced by their clients, and of the moral or ethical assumptions they themselves bring to their practice. However, as professionals accredited by society to deal with clients who may be vulnerable, needy and ill-informed, counsellors also have a responsibility to act towards their clients in an ethical manner. There are, therefore, two broad areas in which ethical and moral considerations are particularly relevant to counselling. The first is rooted in the actual counselling process. Clients may need help to resolve the moral issues involved in the life crises or problems that have brought them to counselling. The counsellor must also be sensitively aware of her own moral stance, and its interaction with the value system of the client. The second area is in behaving towards the client in an ethical and responsible manner.

It seems to have taken a long time for the counselling and psychotherapy professions to face up to the ethical and moral dimensions of therapeutic practice. The editor of what was probably the first comprehensive text on ethical issues in psychotherapy, Rosenbaum (1982: ix), wrote of his experience in compiling the book:

> many professionals had simply not thought about the larger issues involved in the practice of psychotherapy. This was borne out when I invited friends and colleagues who are considered major figures in the field of psychology and psychiatry to participate in my project. They reacted for the most part with anxiety and confusion. These honorable people, while aware of what they believed to be right or wrong, had great difficulty in setting this down in a form that would enable other professionals to benefit from their experiences.

The lack of attention paid to ethical issues within the profession is illustrated in the observations reported in Box 15.1 and in similar anecdotal accounts that can be found around the edges of the literature. For instance, Masson (1990: 161) quoted the famous psychoanalyst Masud Khan as saying that 'I never sleep with other analysts' patients, only my own.' Khan was living with a former patient while continuing to see her husband in analysis, and was apparently unconcerned about the ethical implications of these domestic arrangements. It was only really when the consumer movement and the women's movement gained ground in the 1980s that professional associations, in counselling and psychotherapy, as well as other fields, started to see the need to develop codes of ethical standards and procedures. The tendency for clients and patients in the USA to seek redress in the courts gave added urgency to these developments.

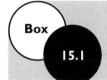

Box

15.1

Abuse in a training context

There can be situations where the potential for abuse of counselling and psychotherapy does not simply involve the mistreatment of one person by another, but takes place within a complex network of interacting social and organizational pressures and forces. McLean (1986), an anthropologist, studied training workshops run in the 1970s and 1980s in which well known family therapy experts gave 'live' therapy to an actual family in front of an audience. The advantage to the family was that it received treatment from an acknowledged expert. In addition, many therapists and trainees were able to learn at first hand how a 'master therapist' put his or her ideas into practice. Ethical problems were covered by an informed consent release signed by the family, and by the fact that proceedings were video-taped, and only presented to the audience after a two or three minute delay. McLean (1986: 180) describes events in one of these workshops, which feature two internationally renowned family systems therapists:

> During the morning of the first day, one of the therapists treated one family. In the afternoon, the second therapist treated the other family. On the second day, they exchanged families, although at points both therapists appeared together with each of the families . . . In being encouraged to participate, the families were undoubtedly informed of the rare chance they were offered to receive family therapy from two of the most recognized experts in the field. They were requested their written 'informed' consent to permit the recordings of their therapy sessions to be used in the future for professional and training purposes. They were not told, however, that for all practical purposes, their therapy sessions were being observed 'live' by several hundred people . . . [A]t breaks and at the end of each session, the therapist left the room and discussed the 'case' with the audience while the family were still in the clinic, unaware that they were currently being 'studied' by a large audience who had purchased the opportunity to observe them. This fact was almost revealed to one of the families when several persons from the audience swarmed into a rest room, discussing the morning 'case', only to discover some members of the family there. On the second day, one of the doctors, upon reviewing the situation of one family, observed the powerful position of control that the mother enjoyed in the family. He blithely declared that if the son were to be saved from becoming schizophrenic, the mother would have to 'go crazy', as would the father eventually. He then proceeded to conduct therapy with the family in a way that successfully provoked a hysterical outburst from the mother. This irate woman was understandably reacting to the demeaning manner in which she was being treated. She cried profusely, insistently demanding an explanation from the therapist for his behavior toward her. He replied smugly, '*I'm* the doctor; I don't *have* to explain myself', only intensifying her rage, as he promptly walked out with the other therapist who was present for this scene. Their exit was accompanied by support throughout the audience, as evidenced by vigorous applause.

McLean discusses the social and economic factors that have led to the treatment of a family in need as a 'commodity'. She concludes that this sort of workshop is dehumanizing for both patient and therapist. One might add that, ultimately, the audience are equally participating in a dehumanizing spectacle. Yet no one objected, no one put a stop to it. Presumably the majority of the hundreds of therapists who attended these workshops believed that what was happening was right.

Values in counselling

Ethical and moral issues in counselling are closely connected to questions of values. One of the important contributions made by the founders of humanistic psychology, such as Maslow and Rogers, has been to highlight the importance of the concept of value. A value can be defined as an enduring belief that a specific end-state or mode of conduct is preferable. Rokeach (1973) differentiates between 'instrumental' and 'terminal' values. The latter refer to desirable end-states, such as wisdom, comfort, peace or freedom. Instrumental values correspond to the means by which these goals are to be achieved: for example, through competence, honesty or ambition. Rokeach (1973) argues that most people will be in favour of a value such as 'equality', and that the best way to uncover the personal value system that guides the behaviour of an individual is to inquire about his or her value preferences. For example, one person might value equality higher than freedom, whereas another might place these two values in the other order. The study of values is, therefore, a complex matter. However, several studies have shown that the values of the counsellor influence the values held by clients. The trend shown in most studies has been for the values of the client to converge with those of the counsellor (Kelly 1989). This finding raises questions for the practice of counselling. Are counsellors imposing their values on clients? Should counselling be seen as a form of socialization into a particular set of values?

In Chapter 2, the cultural origins of counselling and psychotherapy in religious forms of helping and meaning-making were discussed. Bergin (1980) claims that the espousal by psychology of scientific beliefs and attitudes was associated with a rejection of religious values. His view is that, since many people in the general population hold strong religious views, there is a danger that therapy will be seen as irrelevant or even damaging. Bergin (1980) has carried out a systematic analysis of the differences between what he calls 'theistic' and 'clinical-humanistic' value systems (Table 15.1). The contrasts made by Bergin highlight divergences rather than acknowledging possible points of similarity and convergence, and his formulation has been criticized by Walls (1980), Ellis (1980) and Brammer *et al.* (1989). Nevertheless, his work makes it possible to see that there can be radically different views of what is 'right' or 'good'. Counsellors, trained in institutions that may embody clinical-humanistic values, may perhaps lose touch with the values of their clients. The power imbalance of the counselling situation may make it impossible for the client to assert his or her values except by deciding not to turn up. The issue of value differences is particularly relevant in multicultural counselling (Chapter 10), or when the client is gay or lesbian (Chapter 14). It is significant that many clients from these groups deliberately seek out counsellors whom they know to have a similar background and values.

In a survey carried out in the USA, Kelly (1995) found that, compared to the population as a whole, counsellors were high in the values of benevolence (concern for the welfare of others), self-direction, autonomy and self-expression, but much lower in power (defined as an aspiration towards social status and authority

Table 15.1 Comparison of religious and therapeutic value systems

Religious/theistic	Clinical-humanistic
God is supreme; humility and obedience to the will of God are virtues	Humans are supreme; autonomy and the rejection of authority are virtues
Relationship with God defines self-worth	Relationships with others define self-worth
Strict morality; universal ethics	Flexible morality; situational ethics
Service and self-sacrifice central to personal growth	Self-satisfaction central to personal growth
Forgiveness of others who cause distress completes the restoration of self	Acceptance and expression of accusatory feelings are sufficient
Meaning and purpose derived from spiritual insight	Meaning and purpose derived from reason and intellect

Source: Bergin (1980).

over others) and tradition (acceptance of and respect for customs). Almost 90 per cent of these counsellors indicated some degree of religious or spiritual orientation. Finally, there was a high degree of broadmindedness and tolerance of the beliefs and sexual choices of others, indicating that counsellors are well able to distinguish between their own value positions and those adopted by their clients. There was a high degree of consensus among the counsellors answering this questionnaire. This might indicate the existence of a distinctive 'clinical-humanistic' value profile, as proposed by Bergin (1980), or it might be the result of political correctness leading to an implied 'right' set of answers to the survey questionnaire. However, the 'clinical-humanistic' value pattern found by Kelly (1995) included a strong religious dimension, even if for many counsellors this dimension was expressed through spiritual values rather than through conventional religious observance. The finding that counsellors are not power-oriented, and question tradition, reinforces the idea introduced in Chapter 2 that counselling represents a set of moral values that are somewhat outside the mainstream of Western capitalist society, and gives credence to the notion that one of the effects of counselling and psychotherapy might be to socialize clients into this set of values.

Ethics and moral reasoning

In responding to moral and ethical questions that arise in their work, counsellors can make reference to a variety of levels of moral wisdom or knowledge. Kitchener (1984) has identified four discrete levels of moral reasoning that are drawn upon by counsellors: personal intuition; ethical guidelines established by professional organizations; ethical principles; and, finally, general theories of moral action.

Personal intuition

People generally have a sense of what feels right in any situation. This personal moral or ethical response is best understood as intuitive, since it is implicit rather than explicit, taken for granted rather than systematically formulated. Most of the time, and particularly during an actual counselling session, counsellors rely on their intuitive moral judgement of 'what feels right' rather than on any more explicit guidelines. There are, however, a number of limitations or dangers involved in relying only on this way of responding to moral choices. The first difficulty is that this kind of intuitive response is accumulated at least partially through experience, and beginning counsellors may need to have some other way of dealing with moral issues: for example, by reference to supervision or professional codes of ethics. Even for experienced counsellors, there may always be a sense in which their personal intuition is incomplete, especially in unusual or unforeseen situations. Other difficulties arise when the personal moral belief or choice of the client is outside the personal experience of the counsellor: for example, the Christian counsellor working with an Islamic client. Finally, it must be recognized that personal intuition can lead to unethical or immoral action as well as to more desirable behaviour. A counsellor in private practice, for instance, may persuade herself that a client who pays well would benefit from another ten sessions of therapy.

Despite the limitations of personal, intuitive moral reasoning, its presence is absolutely essential in counsellors. Trainers or tutors assessing candidates for counsellor training are concerned that the people they select are trustworthy, have developed a firm moral position for themselves and are capable of respecting boundaries. Counselling is an occupation in which external monitoring of ethical behaviour is extremely difficult, and therefore much depends on personal moral qualities.

Ethical guidelines developed by professional organizations

Counselling in most countries has become increasingly regulated by professional bodies. One of the functions of professional organizations such as the British Association for Counselling and Psychotherapy or the British Psychological Society is to ensure ethical standards of practice, and to achieve this objective both have produced ethical guidelines for practitioners, accompanied by procedures for dealing with complaints about unethical behaviour. In the USA, ethical guidelines have been published by the American Psychiatric Association, the American Psychological Association, the American Association for Marital and Family Therapy and the American Association for Counseling and Development. In addition, some state legislatures in the USA have constructed ethical codes, as have numerous other professional groupings and agencies. All trained and competent counsellors currently in practice should be able to indicate to their clients the specific ethical guidelines within which they are operating. The British Association for Counselling and Psychotherapy (BACP) operated, until autumn 2001, a Code of Ethics and Practice for Counsellors, which covered the nature of counselling, responsibility, competence, management of the work, confidentiality and advertising. The BACP replaced this code with an Ethical Framework for Good Practice in Counselling and Psychotherapy (2001), which places a much greater emphasis on positive virtues and values.

Although these guidelines are undoubtedly helpful in placing on record a consensus view on many of the ethical dilemmas in counselling, they are by no means unambiguous. Table 15.2 presents the key statements on confidentiality

Table 15.2 Confidentiality guidelines from three codes of ethics

British Association for Counselling (1984)

1 Counsellors treat with confidence personal information about clients, whether obtained directly or indirectly by inference. Such information includes name, address, biographical details and other descriptions of the client's life and circumstances that might result in identification of the client.
2 'Treating with confidence' means not revealing any of the information noted above to any other person or through any public medium, except to those to whom counsellors owe accountability for counselling work (in the case of those working within an agency or organizational setting) or on whom counsellors rely for support and supervision.
3 Notwithstanding the above sections, if counsellors believe that a client could cause danger to others, they will advise the client that they may break confidentiality and take appropriate action to warn individuals or the authorities.
4 Information about specific clients is only used for publication in appropriate journals or meetings with the client's permission and with anonymity preserved when the client specifies.
5 Counsellors' discussion of the clients with professional colleagues should be purposeful and not trivializing.

British Association for Counselling and Psychotherapy (2001)

1 The practice of counselling depends on gaining and honouring the trust of clients. Keeping trust requires:
   • attentiveness to the quality of listening and respect offered to clients;
   • culturally appropriate ways of communicating that are courteous and clear;
   • respect for privacy and dignity;
   • careful attention to client consent and confidentiality.
2 Situations in which clients pose a risk of causing serious harm to themselves or others are particularly challenging for the practitioner. These are situations in which the practitioner should be alert to the possibility of conflicting responsibilities between those concerning their client, other people who may be significantly affected and society generally. Resolving conflicting responsibilities may require due consideration of the context in which the service is being provided. In all cases, the aim should be to

Table 15.2   (cont'd)

ensure for the client a good quality of care that is as respectful of the client's capacity for self-determination as circumstances permit.

3 Respecting client confidentiality is a fundamental requirement for keeping trust. The professional management of confidentiality concerns the protection of personally identifiable and sensitive information from unauthorized disclosure. Disclosure may be authorized by client consent or the law. Any disclosure should be undertaken in ways that best protect the client's trust. Practitioners should be willing to be accountable to their clients and to their profession for the management of confidentiality in general and particularly for any disclosures made without their client's consent.

4 Prior consent is required from clients if they are to be observed, recorded or if their personally identifiable disclosures are to be used for training purposes.

American Association for Counseling and Development (1988)

1 Members make provisions for maintaining confidentiality in the storage and disposal of records and follow an established record retention and disposal policy. The counseling relationship and information resulting therefrom must be kept confidential, consistent with the obligations of the member as a professional person. In a group counseling situation, the counselor must set a norm of confidentiality regarding all group participants' disclosures.

2 If an individual is already in a counseling relationship with another professional person, the member does not enter into a counseling relationship without first contacting and receiving the approval of that other professional. If the member discovers that the client is in another counseling relationship after the counseling relationship begins, the member must gain the consent of the other professional or terminate the relationship, unless the client elects to terminate the other relationship.

3 When the client's condition indicates that there is clear and imminent danger to the client or others, the member must take reasonable personal action or inform responsible authorities. Consultation with other professionals must be used where possible. The assumption of responsibility for the client's behavior must be taken only after careful deliberation. The client must be involved in the resumption of responsibility as quickly as possible.

4 Records of the counseling relationship, including interview notes, test data, correspondence, tape recordings, electronic data storage, and other documents are to be considered professional information for use in counseling, and they should not be considered a part of the records of the institution or agency in which the counselor is employed unless specified by state statute or regulation. Revelation to others of counseling material must occur only upon the expressed consent of the client.

5 In view of the extensive data storage and processing capacities of the computer, the member must ensure that data maintained on a computer is: (a) limited to information that is appropriate and necessary for the services being provided; (b) destroyed after it is determined that the information is no longer of any value in providing services; and (c) restricted in terms of access to appropriate staff members involved in the provision of services by using the best computer security methods available.

6 Use of data derived from a counseling relationship for purposes of counselor training or research shall be confined to content that can be disguised to ensure the full protection of the identity of the subject client.

drawn from the BAC/BACP and AACD ethical codes. It is clear that each code highlights (and omits) different sets of issues, reflecting the fact that it is extremely difficult to formulate an ethical code that can cover *all* eventualities.

It is important to note that these ethical codes have been developed not only to protect clients against abuse or malpractice by counsellors, but also to protect the counselling profession against state interference and to reinforce its claims to control over a particular area of professional expertise. Ethics committees and codes of practice serve a useful function in demonstrating to the outside world that the counselling house is in order, that counsellors can be relied upon to give a professional service.

Ethical principles

On occasions when neither personal intuition nor ethical codes can provide a solution to a moral or ethical issue, counsellors need to make reference to more general philosophical or ethical principles. These are the ideas or more general moral injunctions that underpin and inform both personal and professional codes. Kitchener (1984) has identified five moral principles that run through most thinking about ethical issues: autonomy, non-maleficence, beneficence, justice and fidelity.

One of the fundamental moral principles in our culture is that of the *autonomy* of individuals. People are understood as having the right to freedom of action and freedom of choice, in so far as the pursuit of these freedoms does not interfere with the freedoms of others. The concept of the autonomous person is an ideal that has clearly not been achieved in many societies, in which coercion and control are routine. Nevertheless, in the societies where counselling and psychotherapy have become established, individual freedom and rights are usually enshrined in law. This concept of autonomy has been so central to counselling that many counsellors would assert that counselling cannot take place unless the client has made a free choice to participate. Another implication for counselling of the concept of autonomy lies in the notion of informed consent: that it is unethical to begin counselling, or initiate a particular counselling intervention, unless the client is aware of what is involved and has given permission to proceed.

Although it may be morally desirable to act as though clients are autonomous people capable of freedom of thought and action, there are many counselling situations in which the concept of autonomy is problematic. From a theoretical perspective, counsellors working from a psychoanalytic or radical behaviourist position would question the very possibility of individual autonomy, arguing that most of the time the behaviour of individual people is controlled by powerful external or internal forces. Counsellors influenced by feminist or family therapy perspectives would argue that in many instances autonomy may not be an ideal, and that very often clients need to move in the direction of greater relatedness or interdependence.

The freedom of choice and action of clients is also limited by a variety of practical circumstances. For example, few people would suppose that young children are capable of informed consent regarding the offer of counselling help, but it is difficult to decide at just what age a young person is able to give consent. Even with adult clients, it may be hard to explain just what is involved in counselling, which is an activity that is centred on first-hand experiential learning. Furthermore, the limits of client autonomy may be reached, at least for some counsellors, when the client becomes 'mentally ill', suicidal or a danger to others. In these situations, the counsellor may choose to make decisions on behalf of the client.

To summarize, the principle of freedom of choice and action is a theme that lies at the heart of much counselling practice. However, it is also evident that the concept of personal autonomy is not a simple one, and certainly not sufficient as a guide to action and good practice in all circumstances.

Non-maleficence refers to the instruction to all helpers or healers that they must 'above all do no harm'. Beneficence refers to the injunction to promote human welfare. Both these ideas emerge in the emphasis in codes of practice that counsellors should ensure that they are trained to an appropriate level of competence, that they must monitor and maintain their competence through supervision, consultation and training, and that they must work only within the limits of their competence.

One of the areas in which the principle of non-maleficence arises is the riskiness or harmfulness of therapeutic techniques. It would normally be considered acceptable for a client to experience deeply uncomfortable feelings of anxiety or abandonment during a counselling session, if such an episode were to lead to beneficial outcomes. But at what point does the discomfort become sufficient to make the intervention unethical? Some approaches to counselling advocate that clients be encouraged to take risks in experimenting with new forms of behaviour. The principle of autonomy might suggest that, if the client has given informed consent for the intervention to take place, then he or she has responsibility for the consequences. However, in practice it can be difficult explicitly to agree on every step in the therapy process. The counsellor or therapist may well not know about the potential riskiness of a technique, given the lack of research on many aspects of practice and the infrequency with which practitioners are influenced by research studies. Research studies also tend to focus on what works rather than on what does not work, and rarely draw attention to procedures that go badly wrong.

Moral dilemmas concerning *beneficence* are often resolved by recourse to utilitarian ideas. The philosopher John Stuart Mill defined ethical behaviour as that which brought about 'the greatest good for the greatest number'. The question of whether, for example, it was ethical to refer a highly socially anxious client to group counselling might depend on whether it could be predicted that, on balance, the benefits of this type of therapy outweighed the costs and risks. Quite apart from the uncertainty involved in ever knowing whether a therapeutic intervention will be helpful or otherwise in a particular case, the application of utilitarian ideas may conflict with the autonomous right of the client to make such decisions for himself or herself, or might lead to paternalism.

The principle of *justice* is primarily concerned with the fair distribution of resources and services, on the assumption that people are equal unless there is some acceptable rationale for treating them differently. In the field of counselling, the principle of justice has particular relevance to the question of access to services. If a counselling agency has a lengthy waiting list, is it ethical for some clients to be offered long-term counselling while others go without help? If the agency introduces a system of assessment interviews to identify the clients most in need of urgent appointments, can it be sure that its grounds for making decisions are fair rather than discriminatory? Is it just for a counselling agency to organize itself in such a way that it does not attract clients from minority or disadvantaged groups? Kitchener (1984: 50) points to the special significance of justice for counselling in writing that

> psychologists ought to have a commitment to being 'fair' that goes beyond that of the ordinary person. To the extent we agree to promote the worth and dignity of each individual, we are required to be concerned with equal treatment for all individuals.

The point here is that the conditions of trust and respect that are fundamental to the counsellor–client relationship are readily undermined by unjust behaviour.

The principle of *fidelity* relates to the existence of loyalty, reliability, dependability and action in good faith. Lying, deception and exploitation are all examples of primary breaches of fidelity. The rule of confidentiality in counselling also reflects the importance of fidelity. One aspect of counselling that is very much concerned with fidelity is the keeping of contracts. The practitioner who accepts a client for counselling is, either explicitly or implicitly, entering into a contract to stay with that client and give the case his or her best efforts. Situations in which the completion of the contract is not fulfilled, because of illness, job change or other counsellor factors, need to be dealt with sensitively to prevent breaches of fidelity.

This discussion of moral principles of autonomy, non-maleficence, beneficence, justice and fidelity has provided several illustrations of the fact that while these moral ideas are probably always relevant, they may equally well conflict with each other in any particular situation. Beauchamp and Childress (1979) have suggested that, following legal terminology, such principles should be regarded as prima facie binding. In other words, they must be abided by unless they conflict with some other principle, or there are extenuating circumstances. But when they are in conflict, or when such special circumstances do exist, what should be done?

General moral theories

Kitchener (1984) reviews some of the general theories of moral philosophy that can be called upon to resolve complex ethical dilemmas. Utilitarianism, the theoretical perspective that was mentioned in relation to beneficence, can be useful in this respect. The application of a utilitarian approach would be to consider an ethical decision in the light of the costs and benefits for each participant in the event: for example, the client, the family of the client, other people who are involved and the counsellor. Another core philosophical approach is derived from the work of Kant, who proposed that ethical decisions should be universalizable. In other words, if it is right to breach confidentiality in this case, it must be right to do so in all similar cases in the future.

A practical approach to applying Kant's principle of universality to resolving ethical issues in counselling has been put forward by Stadler (1986). She advocates that any ethical decision should be subjected to tests of 'universality', 'publicity' and 'justice'. The decision-maker should reflect on the following questions:

1 Would I recommend this course of action to anyone else in similar circumstances? Would I condone my behaviour in anyone else? (Universality)
2 Would I tell other counsellors what I intend to do? Would I be willing to have the actions and the rationale for them published on the front page of the local newspaper or reported on the evening news? (Publicity)
3 Would I treat another client in the same situation differently? If this person was a well known political leader, would I treat him or her differently? (Justice)

An alternative position developed within moral philosophy has been to argue that it is just not possible to identify any abstract moral criteria or principles on which action can be based. For example, in debates over abortion, some people support the moral priority of the rights of the unborn child, while others assert the woman's right to choose. Philosophers such as MacIntyre (1981) argue that such debates can never be resolved through recourse to abstract principles. MacIntyre (1981) suggests instead that it is more helpful always to look at moral issues in their social and historical context. Moral concepts such as 'rights' or 'autonomy' only have meaning in relation to the cultural tradition in which they operate. MacIntyre suggests that a tradition can be seen as a kind of ongoing debate or conversation within which people evolve moral positions that make sense to them at the time, only to see these positions dissolve and change as social and cultural circumstances move on. Within any cultural tradition, certain *virtues* are identified as particularly representing the values of the community. For example, in many counselling circles, authenticity is regarded as a primary virtue. In the academic community, by contrast, the key virtue is intellectual rigour or rationality.

From a 'virtues' perspective on moral decison-making, the important thing is to keep the conversation open, rather than to suppose that there can ever be an ultimately valid, fixed answer to moral questions. The implications for counselling of adopting a virtues perspective are explored in more detail by Meara *et al.* (1996). The BACP (2001: 4) Ethical Framework for Good Practice explicitly draws on a 'virtues' perspective by identifying a set of *personal qualities* that all practitioners should possess:

- Empathy: the ability to communicate understanding of another person's experience from that person's perspective.
- Sincerity: a personal commitment to consistency between what is professed and what is done.
- Integrity: personal straightforwardness, honesty and coherence.
- Resilience: the capacity to work with the client's concerns without being personally diminished.
- Respect: showing appropriate esteem to others and their understanding of themselves.
- Humility: the ability to assess accurately and acknowledge one's own strengths and weaknesses.
- Competence: the effective deployment of skills and knowledge needed to do what is required.
- Fairness: the consistent application of appropriate criteria to inform decisions and actions.
- Wisdom: possession of sound judgement that informs practice.
- Courage: the capacity to act in spite of known fears, risks and uncertainty.

The BACP Ethical Framework additionally suggests that these qualities should be 'deeply rooted in the person concerned and developed out of personal commitment rather than the requirement of a personal authority' (p. 4).

Finally, it is perhaps worth noting that the tension in the field of moral philosophy between abstract, generalized moral systems (such as utilitarianism or Kantian ethics) and the more recent tradition-based 'virtue' approach to moral inquiry is mirrored in the debate over differences between men's and women's modes of moral decision-making. Chodorow and other feminist writers have suggested that men aspire to make moral decisions on the basis of abstract principles, whereas women's moral decision-making is grounded in consideration of the impact different decisions would have on the network of relationships within which the woman lives her life (see Chapter 8). The impact of different systems of moral thinking can also be detected in debates over multiculturalism. To some extent, it can be said that Western moral and legal systems are built around utilitarian or other ideas about moral rules, understood in abstract theoretical terms, whereas most non-Western cultures approach morality from a position in which moral virtues are invested in qualities of persons. It can be seen, then, that debates over how to make sense of moral issues in fact underpin or lie behind many of the other debates and issues in counselling and psychotherapy.

Applying moral principles and ethical codes: from theory to practice

It would be reassuring to be able to take for granted that someone who is a counsellor is inevitably a person of integrity and virtue who acts in accordance

Table 15.3 Causes of malpractice costs in the USA, 1976–1986

Cause of complaint	Percentage of total insurance pay-out
Sexual contact	44.8
Treatment error	13.9
Death of patient/other	10.9
Faulty diagnosis	7.9
Loss from evaluation	3.2
Breach of confidentiality	2.8
Failure to warn or protect	2.7
Bodily injury	2.4
Dispute over fees	2.2
Assault and battery	1.8

Source: Pope (1986).

with an impeccable ethical code. This is far from being the case. There is ample evidence of ethical malpractice among counsellors and psychotherapists. Austin *et al.* (1990) report that the insurance company contracted by the American Psychological Association to provide professional cover for psychologists paid out US$17.2 million in claims in 1985. Table 15.3 indicates that over half of the cost of these claims was due to cases of unethical behaviour, such as sexual abuse of clients and breach of confidentiality, rather than technical incompetence. The statistical data collected by Austin *et al.* (1990) is brought to life in the many cases of therapist abuse of clients vividly described by Masson (1988, 1990, 1992).

The question of the ethical basis of counselling practice is not merely a topic for theoretical debate, but a matter of immediate concern for many counsellors, clients and managers of counselling agencies. The main moral issus that face counsellors in their everyday practice are reviewed in the following sections.

Whose agent is the counsellor?

One of the key ethical questions that can arise in the day-to-day practice of counselling is that of counsellor accountability. On whose behalf is the counsellor working? Is the counsellor only the agent of the client, only acting on behalf of the client? Or can there be other people who have legitimate demands on the allegiance of the counsellor? Traditionally, many counsellors have attempted to espouse a rigorous 'client-centred' ethos. Nevertheless, there are many situations where absolute client-centredness may not be morally and ethically the correct course of action. For instance, a client who is HIV positive may be engaging in unsafe sex that puts his or her partners or family at risk. A workplace counsellor being paid by a company may be under pressure to achieve a particular type of result with a client. A counsellor working with an adolescent may find the parents giving suggestions or seeking information. Agency is very often an issue in relationship or marital counselling. Some practitioners and researchers (e.g.

Hurvitz 1967) would argue that conducting therapy with one spouse is likely to lead to feelings of alienation and rejection in the other spouse, and eventually to separation and divorce. Even in work with both spouses, the interests of the children of the marriage can become a central consideration.

Conflict between fidelity to the client and other demands on the counsellor can also occur in 'third party' counselling settings, such as employee counselling or employee assistance programmes (Wise 1988). In these situations, the counsellor may be paid or employed by an organization, and may in fact be viewed by the organization as being primarily responsible to it rather than to the client (Bond 1992). There may be both overt and subtle pressures on the counsellor to disclose information about the client, or to ensure that the counselling arrives at a predetermined outcome (e.g. a troublesome employee being 'counselled' to take early retirement). Sugarman (1992) makes a number of recommendations concerning the maintenance of ethical standards in workplace counselling:

- discover the objectives the organization is attempting to fulfil by providing a counselling service;
- identify any points at which the counselling provision might benefit the organization at the expense of the individual;
- identify any points at which the organization exceeds its right to control aspects of the employee's behaviour;
- negotiate with the organization about what is to be understood by 'confidentiality', and the conditions under which it will or will not be maintained;
- discover whether the resources being allocated to counselling are sufficient to do more good than harm;
- develop a written policy statement concerning the provision of counselling within the organization.

Further discussion of the issue of accountability in workplace counselling can be found in Carroll (1996) and Shea and Bond (1997).

Another area of counselling that is associated with major dilemmas around accountability and agency is the domain of work with people who have been, or are being, sexually abused (Daniluk and Haverkamp 1993). In many countries there is a legal requirement on the counsellor to report instances of child sexual abuse to the appropriate legal authority. If a client tells the counsellor that he or she has been abused as a child, or that his or her children are being abused, the counsellor must then make a difficult decision about when and how to report this information to the authorities. Any move of this type clearly has profound implications for the relationship between client and counsellor. It also has implications for the ways that counsellors and counselling agencies carry out their work. For example, it becomes necessary to inform clients at the start of counselling that the counsellor would need to breach confidentiality in these circumstances. Levine and Doueck (1995) carried out a thorough study of the impact of 'mandated reporting' on counselling practice in the USA. Their book offers a comprehensive analysis of the issues involved in this kind of work. They found that there are

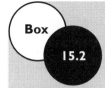

Box
15.2

The 'duty to protect and warn': ethical dilemmas arising from the Tarasoff case

In August 1969, Prosenjit Poddar was a voluntary outpatient at the university health service in Berkeley, California, receiving therapy from a psychologist, Dr Lawrence Moore. Poddar had informed his therapist of his intention to kill his girlfriend, Tatiana Tarasoff, when she returned from a trip to Brazil. In consultation with two psychiatrist colleagues, Dr Moore recommended that Poddar be committed to hospital for observation. This decision was overruled by the chief of psychiatry. Poddar moved into an apartment with Tatiana's brother, near to where she stayed with her parents. Dr Moore wrote to the chief of police asking him to confine Poddar, and verbally asked the campus security service to detain him if he was seen. They did so. Poddar assured the campus officers that he meant no harm, and they released him. Poddar subsequently murdered Tatiana Tarasoff. No warning had been given to either the victim or her family. The chief of psychiatry asked the police to return the letter written by Dr Moore and directed that the letter and case notes be destroyed. The University of California was sued by the parents of Tatiana Tarasoff, on the grounds that they should have been warned of the danger to their daughter. The defence stated that, after Poddar had been involved with the police, he had broken off all contact with the hospital, and was no longer one of their patients. A lower court rejected the case, but on appeal a higher court found for the parents.

The outcome of this case clearly carries a number of implications for counsellors and psychotherapists. Counsellors need to be willing to breach client–therapist confidentiality when the safety of others is at risk. Counsellors need to do everything possible to 'warn and protect' those in danger from their clients. Many states in the USA have enacted laws that make the failure to protect a criminal offence (Fulero 1988; Austin *et al.* 1990). Counsellors should be able to assess accurately and reliably the potential dangerousness of clients. Finally, counselling agencies must enact specific policies and procedures for dealing with such cases.

The Tarasoff case demonstrates some of the complexities of ethical decision-making in counselling, and how ethical considerations can affect the counselling process itself. The right of the client, Prosenjit Poddar, to respect for his autonomy and for the confidentiality of his disclosures to his therapist was in conflict with the fundamental duty to protect life. The information about his intention to kill his girlfriend was shared with his therapist because they had a strong therapeutic relationship, but this relationship was destroyed by the action taken in an attempt to prevent violence. The therapist himself was faced with contradictory advice and guidance from professional colleagues. The situation necessitated him liaising with the police, a course of action that he had not been trained to undertake effectively.

Many clients express anger and resentment towards others in their counselling sessions. From some theoretical perspectives, such episodes can be interpreted as 'cathartic' and beneficial. On the other hand, as the Tarasoff case and many other such cases (see Austin *et al.* 1990 for details of 17 similar cases heard in courts in the USA between 1975 and 1986) reveal, there are occasions when such client intentions are turned into action.

The Tarasoff case and the ensuing discussions over the 'duty to protect and warn' are part of a broader ethical issue relating to the problem of agency. Is the counsellor an agent only of the client, or is he or she also accountable to other people with an interest in the case?

many different strategies that counsellors adopt in an attempt to preserve the therapeutic relationship at the point of reporting, including anonymous reporting, shifting responsibility to their supervisor, child protection agency or the law and encouraging the client to self-report. Kennel and Agresti (1995) found a greater reluctance to report among female than male therapists.

Some of the most painful and difficult dilemmas over accountability arise in relation to the counsellor's 'duty to warn and protect' in cases where their client threatens violence to another person. The difficulties arising from this kind of situation are illustrated in the well known *Tarasoff* case (Box 15.2).

Issues associated with the 'duty to warn' of the counsellor are also encountered in AIDS counselling, mainly around the disclosure of HIV status to sexual partners of the client. Research by McGuire *et al.* (1995) suggests that counsellors working in this field are in fact very likely to seek to warn partners, and in some cases may even go as far as physically to detain clients who refuse to cooperate. Costa and Altekruse (1994) have compiled a valuable set of duty-to-warn guidelines for counsellors.

In most counselling theory, there is an implicit assumption that throughout the counselling process the therapist acts solely as an agent of the client. To take this view is to over-simplify the situation. An important task for the counsellor is to be aware of these other relationships and systems, and to be willing to explore, and at times defend, the appropriate boundaries. Nevertheless, there are some occasions on which the counsellor has a duty to the wider social good, and has no choice but to breach the boundary of accountability in relation to an individual client.

How far should the client be pushed or directed?
The use of persuasion, suggestion and challenge

One of the fundamental tensions in counselling and psychotherapy arises from the definition and perception of the role of the therapist. In the client-centred/person-centred and psychodynamic traditions, the position is generally taken that the role of the therapist is to be reflective and patient, and on the whole to allow the client to use the time to arrive at his or her own understandings and insights.

There is another tradition, represented by Gestalt therapy, the 'body' therapies and cognitive–behavioural approaches, which favours a much more active stance on the part of the therapist through the use of interventions that attempt to accelerate the pace of change or force breakthroughs. It is essential not to exaggerate the dichotomy between these positions: client-centred counsellors challenge clients and Gestalt therapists engage in empathic listening. However, the use of confrontative and manipulative tactics in therapy has been seen by many (Lakin 1988) as raising a number of ethical issues.

A central ethical issue here is the principle of informed consent. The ethical value of autonomy implies that clients should have a choice regarding treatment. The notion of choice rests on the idea that the person responds to information in a rational manner. The aim of confrontation techniques, by contrast, is to break through the rationalizations and intellectualized defences that the client has erected. To tell the client exactly what will happen would nullify the effectiveness of the intervention. Moreover, some techniques, such as 'paradoxical' methods, require giving the client contradictory information; for example, asking an insomniac client to check the time on an alarm clock every hour through the night.

These techniques also raise questions regarding beneficence. There is little research evidence to support the effectiveness of approaches that are highly confrontative. In fact, in their tightly controlled study of encounter groups, Lieberman *et al.* (1973) found that there were more casualties in the groups run by leaders who were high on challenge and emphasized catharsis. Lakin (1988: 13) considers that confrontation may at times be performed to meet the needs of the therapist rather than those of the client: 'active and aggressive interviewing may be based on egotistical wishes to prove one's effectiveness.'

An extreme example of a brand of highly active therapy that went beyond any acceptable limit to become overtly abusive is given by Masson (1988) in his account of the history of 'direct psychoanalysis' developed by the psychiatrist John Rosen, which included the use of physical violence, verbal assault, deception and imprisonment. Lakin (1988) describes a similar case, relating to the Centre for Feeling Therapy, where therapists again engaged in physical and verbal violence, and also encouraged extra-marital affairs among couples who were in therapy. The leading figures in both these enterprises were sued by patients, and debarred from practice. Although the levels of abuse and cruelty to clients exhibited in these cases may seem outrageous, it is important to note, as Masson (1988) and Lakin (1988) both point out, that the founders of these therapies were highly qualified and trained, had published widely and had been commended by leaders in their profession for their pioneering work.

These examples of confrontation and challenge illustrate very direct and overt attempts to control clients, to modify their beliefs and behaviour. A much more subtle form of control is implied in the issue of *false memories* of childhood sexual abuse. Most therapists are familiar with the experience of working with a client who seems suddenly to remember events from the past – for instance, memories of abuse or humiliation – that had been hidden for many years. Given that the events being recalled are in the distant past, and that quite possibly no independent or objective evidence exists concerning whether they actually happened or not, there is often an issue over whether these memories are genuine or are perhaps false and manufactured. Some people who wish to deny the prevalence of child sexual abuse in general, or are defending accusations in specific cases, have argued that some counsellors and therapists are too eager to suggest to their clients that they have been abused. These counsellors are said to be too ready to interpret feelings and images of childhood as indicators of abuse. This is not the place to review the vast literature on the veracity or otherwise of recovered memories of childhood. The interested reader is recommended to consult Enns *et al.* (1995) and Spence (1994). The point is that there are powerful moral issues here. If a therapist does plant false memories, then he or she can end up being the instigator of great harm to an individual and their family. If, on the other hand, a therapist avoids drawing conclusions about abuse, or naming the abuse, the effect on the client can be equally damaging. The connection between the use of a counselling technique and its moral consequences is very clear in this type of case. How actively should a counsellor interpret the client's experience? Should the counsellor wait until there is overwhelming evidence to support the interpretation? Under what circumstances are clinical intuition and 'hunches' allowable?

Dual relationships

Dual relationships in counselling and psychotherapy occur when the therapist is also engaged in another, significantly different, relationship with a client. Examples of dual relationships include: being a counsellor to someone who is a neighbour, friend or business partner; accepting payment from a client in the form of services (e.g. childminding); or being the landlord to a client. Pope (1991) identifies five main ways in which dual relationships conflict with effective therapy.

First, dual relationships compromise the professional nature of the relationship. Counselling depends on the creation of an environment of emotional safety created in part by the construction of reliable professional boundaries. The existence of dual relationships makes these boundaries unclear. Second, dual relationships introduce a conflict of interest. No longer is the counsellor there solely for the client. Third, the counsellor is unable to enter into a business or other non-therapy relationship on an equal footing, because of the personal material the client has disclosed and the likelihood of transference reactions, such as dependence. Finally, if it became acceptable for counsellors to engage in dual relationships after counselling had terminated, it would become possible for unscrupulous practitioners to use their professional role to set up relationships engineered to meet their needs. Research on the prevalence of dual relationships (Pope 1991; Salisbury and Kinnier 1996; Lamb and Catanzaro 1998) has shown that around one-third of therapists have at some time developed non-sexual non-therapy relationships with current or former clients. Lamb and Catanzaro (1998) found that more than half of the therapists in their survey had engaged in 'going to a client's special event' (e.g. wedding, funeral of family member, art show).

Dual relationships may be a particularly significant problem in counselling in educational settings. Bond (1992) points out that many counsellors in schools and colleges are also employed as teachers or tutors, so it is essential to be clear about the boundaries between these roles. Doyle (1997) has discussed the dual relationship dilemmas that arise when counsellors in recovery from addictions are engaged in working with clients with the same set of problems. For example, the counsellor and client may meet at a 'twelve step' meeting.

Sexual exploitation of clients

A number of surveys of psychologists and psychotherapists in the USA have discovered that sexual contact between therapists and their clients is not uncommon, despite being explicitly prohibited by all the professional associations in that country. Holroyd and Brodsky (1977), in a survey of 1,000 psychologists, found that 8.1 per cent of the male and 1.0 per cent of the female therapists had engaged in sex with clients. Some 4 per cent of their sample believed that erotic contact with clients might in some circumstances be of therapeutic benefit to the client. Pope *et al.* (1979) carried out a similar anonymous questionnaire survey of 1,000 psychotherapists, and found that 7 per cent reported having had sex with a client. Finally, Pope *et al.* (1986), in another large-scale survey of American practitioners, revealed admission of erotic contact with clients in 9.4 per cent of male and 2.5 per cent of female therapists.

The meaning of these figures is open to interpretation. The estimates made by the surveys cited must be regarded as representing a minimum estimate of the prevalence of client sexual abuse by therapists, because of the many factors that would lead respondents to conceal or under-report their involvement.

Bates and Brodsky (1989) have given a detailed account of one case of sexual exploitation of a client (see Box 15.3). This case, and other cases that have been studied in depth, support the following general conclusions regarding such events:

1 Effective therapy can include phases when the client is highly dependent on the counsellor, and open to such suggestion or manipulation.
2 Within the confidential, secretive environment of the counselling relationship it is possible for counsellors to engage in unethical behaviour with little likelihood of being found out.
3 The focus of counselling on the personality and inner life of the client may readily result in the client blaming himself or herself and his or her own inadequacies for what has happened.
4 Clients who have been sexually abused by professionals encounter great difficulty in achieving redress.

These principles make it possible to understand how sexual abuse of clients can occur, and why it is under-reported.

Box 15.3

A case of professional incest

Carolyn Bates was a client in psychotherapy who was sexually abused by her therapist over a period of months. Her story is told in a book, *Sex in the Therapy Hour*, co-written with a psychologist, Barbara Brodsky (Bates and Brodsky 1989). Their account offers a unique insight into the ways in which therapy can become transformed into a sexually abusive situation that is unethical and destructive.

Carolyn Bates was a shy, overweight teenager whose father had died after a long illness when she was 15. She 'staved off' her feelings of grief and loss by immersing herself in a church group. On leaving home to enter college, she met Steve, a Vietnam War veteran, who became her boyfriend and first sexual partner. She became dependent on him 'to ward off the feelings of depression that were nearly always encroaching upon me'. At the same time, she experienced intense guilt about engaging in pre-marital sex, in opposition to the teachings of her church. She stopped attending church. The emotional pressure built up, exacerbated by a deteriorating relationship with her mother:

> As the tenuous relationship between Steve and me progressed through the first year, my control over these newly emerging, volatile emotions began to break down. I brimmed over with disillusionment, anger, frustration, and, above all, a pervasive sense of desperation. My reactions to any hints from Steve of ending our relationship were of such inordinate proportions that, in hindsight, I know they were related to my ongoing grief over the separation by death from my father.
>
> (Bates and Brodsky 1989: 18)

After two years in this situation, with college grades dropping, Carolyn Bates entered therapy with a psychologist, Dr X, who had been recommended by one of her friends.

For the first five months of therapy, Carolyn felt a 'sense of hope and safety', and gradually opened up and explored her feelings about the death of her father and her relationship with Steve. At that point, her relationship with her therapist was close:

> I have no doubt that much of the trust and love I had for my father was directed toward Dr X, for I perceived him as having both wisdom and an unconditional concern for my well-being. I did not recognize at the time that this transference of feelings was occurring, but I did come to perceive him as a parental figure. And so I remained very dependent, working hard in therapy, in my eagerness for his acceptance and approval, believing him to be my sole source of affirmation.
>
> (Bates and Brodsky 1989: 24)

However, as time went on Dr X began to focus more and more on sexual issues during therapy sessions, encouraging Carolyn to talk about her own sexual behaviour, and explaining his own positive attitude to casual sexual intercourse. He offered an interpretation that perhaps Carolyn was repressing her sexual feelings for him. She described this later as 'the sexualization of the therapeutic relationship'. He began hugging her at the end of sessions, then kissing her goodbye. In one session he suggested that her denial of attraction to him indicated homosexuality.

During the ninth month of therapy, Dr X introduced relaxation exercises, which involved Carolyn lying down on the floor of the office. During one of these sessions he raped her. She reports 'terror', 'dissociation' and 'humiliation'. Sexual intercourse continued during eight or ten sessions over the next 12 months, always at the start of a session. During therapy, Dr X began talking more about his own problems. Eventually, some two years after entering therapy, Carolyn Bates was able to overcome her dependency and numbness and leave.

The next few months were a period of 'depression and confusion beyond hope': 'I carried with me a dark secret – I believed myself a failure in therapy . . . and blamed myself for what had occurred' (Bates and Brodsky 1989: 41). There were nightmares and suicidal thoughts. When Carolyn entered therapy with another counsellor, it became possible to confront what had happened, and to file a complaint against Dr X. Despite the fact that six other women clients of Dr X came forward to testify that they had been the victims of similar sexual exploitation, the case in the civil courts took almost five years before an out-of-court settlement was made. Court appearances involved detailed cross-examination, which was additionally humiliating and distressing. There were other painful experiences arising from appearances before the State Licensing Board, which was considering whether to revoke the professional accreditation of Dr X. The process of achieving some limited redress against this practitioner was also accompanied by media attention. At the end of it all, he reapplied for, and was granted, a licence to practise.

The damage that this type of abuse does to clients has been documented in a number of studies. For example, in her research Durre (1980: 242) observed

> many instances of suicide attempts, severe depressions (some lasting months), mental hospitalizations, shock treatment, and separations or divorces from husbands . . . Women reported being fired from or having to leave their jobs because of pressure and ineffectual working habits caused by their depression, crying spells, anger and anxiety.

One way of making sense of the prevalence of sexual acting out between clients and therapists is to regard it as an inevitable, if unfortunate, consequence of the high levels of intimacy and self-disclosure that occur in therapy. An example of this approach can be found in the work of Edelwich and Brodsky (1991), who regard sex with clients as a professional issue for which therapists should be trained to cope. They take a position of encouraging practitioners to view strong feelings for clients as normal: 'anyone who ministers to the needs of others is bound to have unsettling experiences with emotional currents that run outside the bounds of professional propriety. These crosscurrents arise from normal, universal human feelings' (Edelwich and Brodsky 1991: xiii). Difficulties arise not because counsellors have these feelings, but because they act on them inappropriately. Edelwich and Brodsky identify a number of guidelines for recognizing seductiveness in themselves and in their clients, and suggest strategies for dealing ethically with feelings of attraction:

- acknowledge your own feelings;
- separate your personal feelings from your dealings with the client;
- avoid over-identifying – the client's problems are not your own;
- don't give your problems to the client;
- talk to someone else about what is happening (e.g. colleagues or supervisor);
- set limits while giving the client a safe space for self-expression;
- don't be rejecting;
- express non-sexual caring;
- avoid giving 'double messages'.

They also point out that most sexual misconduct begins with other 'boundary violations', such as touching the client, seeing him or her socially or inappropriate counsellor self-disclosure to the client, and recommend that these apparently less significant boundaries be treated with great respect.

An alternative perspective on sexual misconduct can be developed from a Jungian–feminist standpoint. Almost all therapist–client sexual behaviour takes place between male therapists and female clients, and the professional organizations that make it difficult for women to bring perpetrators to justice are dominated by men. In his book *Sex in the Forbidden Zone*, Rutter (1989) agrees with many of the practical guidelines put forward by Edelwich and Brodsky (1991), but profoundly disagrees with their analysis of underlying causes. Rutter argues that sex between professional men (not just therapists and counsellors, but also clergy, teachers, doctors and managers) and women over whom they are in a position of power or authority results from deeply held cultural myths about what it means to be male or female. Many men, according to Rutter, suppress and deny their own emotional pain and vulnerability, but hold on to a fantasy that they can be made whole through fusion with an understanding and accepting woman. The experience of sex with a woman client is, therefore, part of an unconscious search for healing and wholeness. It is, of course only a temporary means of resolving this male dilemma, and soon the sexual intimacy will seem false and the woman will be rejected.

This interpretation of the dynamics of therapist sexual behaviour is consistent with the findings of a study carried out by Holtzman (1984), who interviewed women who had been sexually involved with their therapists. Several of these women spoke of taking care of the therapist, of being aware of gratifying his emotional needs. Searles (1975) has described this process as the client unconsciously acting as therapist to the therapist.

According to Rutter (1989), women bring to this situation a lifetime of assaults to their self-esteem, of being told they are not good enough, particularly by their fathers. The experience of being in a working relationship with a powerful man who appreciates their abilities and qualities, and seeks to help them achieve fulfilment, is, for the woman, a potentially healing encounter. The betrayal of this closeness and hope brought about by sexual exploitation is, therefore, deeply damaging. Chesler (1972) interviewed ten women who had had sexual relationships with their therapists. All were described as being insecure, with low self-regard, and all blamed themselves for what had happened. Pope and Bouhoutsos (1986) suggest that women at particularly high risk of sexual exploitation from therapists are those who have previously survived incest or sexual abuse in earlier life. This point is reinforced by Mann (1989).

Rutter (1989) is perhaps, more simply, making the point that men have a strong tendency to sexualize relationships marked by high degrees of trust and intimacy. He goes further in regarding the public silence of male colleagues in the face of sexual misconduct as evidence of the pervasiveness of the underlying myth:

> Although the majority of men holding positions of trust behave ethically in the sense that they will never have sexual contact with a woman under their care, they nevertheless hold on to the hope that one day it may actually happen . . . Men who do not engage in forbidden-zone sex participate in it vicariously through the exploits of men who do. In a tribal sense, it is as if men who violate the forbidden zone are the designated surrogates for the rest of the men in the tribe.
>
> (Rutter 1989: 62)

For Rutter, then, the existence of therapist–client sexual contact is not merely a professional issue, to be contained and addressed within the boundary of training programmes and professional associations, but something that arises from fundamental issues of gender relationships in Western culture. It is, as a result, something from which we can all learn, which casts light on all therapeutic encounters between men and women.

The issue of sexual abuse of clients has been examined at some length, to demonstrate that ethical problems in counselling are not just occasional extreme events, like the Tarasoff murder, that suddenly arise to trap the practitioner in a web of competing moral demands and practical dilemmas. Moral, ethical and value issues are there in each counselling room, in each session. Whatever the counsellor does, or does not do, is an expression of values.

Ethical issues involved in the use of touch

In her review of the views of psychoanalysts concerning the use of touch in therapy, Mintz (1969) quotes a famous analyst as asserting that 'transgressions of the rule against physical contact constitute . . . evidence of the incompetence or

Box
15.4

Impaired professional or sexual abuser?

Within the professional literature, the discussion of therapist sexual exploitation of clients has tended to focus on the development of ways of understanding and preventing this type of unethical behaviour, and on the possibility of rehabilitating those who engage in it (for example, through requiring further training or supervision). Pilgrim and Guinan (1999) have argued that the adoption of an 'impaired professional' framework detracts attention from activities that are more appropriately defined as sexual abuse. Pilgrim and Guinan (1999) examined the cases of ten British mental health professionals (nurses, psychiatrists, psychologists and hypnotherapists) who had been found guilty by their professional associations of sexual misconduct. The majority of these professionals had committed multiple abuse, were senior members of their organizations and had elected to work with vulnerable groups of patients. Pilgrim and Guinan suggest that the profile of these mental health professionals was similar to that of sex offenders, and the consequences of their actions were similar to those suffered by victims of sexual abuse. However, Pilgrim and Guinan found that the professional associations which dealt with these cases applied an 'ideology of empathic tolerance toward errant colleagues', and allowed some of them to continue practising. They point out that:

> rehabilitation of . . . paedophiles aims, at best, at their community re-integration without re-offending. It does not aim to restore or encourage their continued contact with children . . . By contrast, a rehabilitation emphasis in TSA [therapist sexual abuse] aims to restore therapists to their role and place them back once more in patient contact. The commonest scenario in this regard is the use of suspension rather than expulsion from professional bodies.
>
> (Pilgrim and Guinan 1999: 163)

For Pilgrim and Guinan, it is important to acknowledge that professional groups tend to operate a process of collective self-preservation that can result in sexually exploitative colleagues being viewed as 'patients-to-be-understood', and treated with leniency and mitigation. They question whether such an approach is publicly justifiable.

criminal ruthlessness of the analyst.' This strong rejection of the possibility of touching the client pervades the therapy literature; even therapists who *do* touch their clients find it difficult to admit to this practice (Tune 2001). The main underlying fear appears to be that touch will lead to sexual gratification on the part of the client, the therapist or both. Another ethical concern is that the client may feel violated, and accept being touched against his or her true wishes. For example, a person who has been physically or sexually abused may have a great terror of being touched, but may have little or no capacity to assert their own needs. Other people may have cultural or religious prohibitions in relation to being touched by a stranger, or by a member of the opposite sex. An additional concern, for some counsellors, arises from anxiety about being accused by clients of being over-intimate or exploitative. This can result in the adoption of a defensive policy of never offering a gesture of comfort or physical contact. There are, therefore, a number of legitimate ethical issues associated with the use of touch.

In relation to the ethics of touch in therapy, the book by Hunter and Struve (1998) affords a wise pathway through these dilemmas. Hunter and Struve (1998) base their analysis on a comprehensive discussion of the physiology and meaning of touching in human beings, and the history of touch in therapy. They make a number of recommendations, which are summarized below.

Touch is clinically appropriate when:

- the client wants to touch or be touched;
- the purpose of touch is clear;
- the touch is clearly intended for the client's benefit;
- the client understands concepts of empowerment and has demonstrated an ability to use these concepts in therapy;
- the therapist has a solid knowledge base about the clinical impact of using touch;
- the boundaries governing the use of touch are clearly understood by both client and therapist;
- enough time remains in the therapy session to process the touch interaction;
- the therapist–client relationship has developed sufficiently;
- touch can be offered to all types of clients;
- consultation/supervision is available and used;
- the therapist is comfortable with the touch.

It is clinically advisable *not* to use touch when:

- the focus of therapy involves sexual content prior to touch;
- a risk of violence exists;
- the touch occurs in secret;
- the therapist doubts the client's ability to say no;
- the therapist has been manipulated or coerced into the touch;
- the use of touch is clinically inappropriate;
- the touch is used to replace verbal therapy;
- the client does not want to touch or be touched;
- the therapist is not comfortable using touch.

These guidelines provide a useful framework for evaluating the use of touch in counselling situations. It is clear, however, that much depends on the integrity of the therapist, and on the extent to which he or she has explored the meaning of touch for them personally, and indeed has arrived at an acceptance of his or her embodiment. There can be extreme disagreements between practitioners around the use of touch, as illustrated in the case presented in Box 15.5.

Box

15.5

To touch or not to touch? The case of Mrs B

The well known British psychoanalyst Patrick Casement has written at length about one of his patients, 'Mrs B' (Casement 1982, 1985, 2000). He summarized the key features of his account of this case in the following words:

> The patient . . . had been seriously scalded when she was 11 months old. At the age of 17 months she had been operated on (under local anaesthetic) to release scar tissue from the surrounding skin. During this procedure the patient's mother was holding her hand until the mother had fainted. In re-living this experience, of being left alone with the surgeon who continued to operate on her regardless of her mother's absence, the patient asked and later demanded to hold the analyst's hand if the anxiety were to become too intolerable to bear. Without this possibility she felt she would have to terminate the analysis. In considering this demand the analyst decided that it would amount to a collusive avoidance of the central aspect of the original trauma, the absence of the mother's hand after she had fainted. The restoration of the analytic 'holding', without any physical contact, and the eventual resolution of the near-delusional transference at this time in the analysis is examined in detail. The interpretation, which eventually proved effective in restoring contact with the patient's readiness to continue with the analysis, emerged from a close following of the counter-transference responses to the patient and the projective-identificatory pressures upon the analyst during the clinical sequence described.
>
> (Casement 1982: 279)

At a moment of acute psychological pain, during the reliving of an unbearably harrowing experience from childhood, a client asks her therapist to hold her hand. What would you do? Patrick Casement decided against acceding to her request, and clearly believed that he had adopted the correct course of action.

The case of Mrs B was taken as the focus for a special issue of the journal *Psychoanalytic Inquiry*, in which ten experienced analysts were invited to comment on their reading of the case. One of these commentators, Breckenridge (2000), manages to convey, within the constraints imposed by professional discourse, her contempt for the stance taken by Casement. She comments that his celebration of a 'successful' interpretation 'is an appalling, inverted justification for his having failed her'. She concludes that:

> used within ethical, cultural, and common sense constraints, physical touch communicates with a subtlety and believability that words cannot carry. Not to touch . . . also communicates; however, the communication is, I fear, about unavailable rigidity, or even worse.
>
> (Breckenridge 2000: 10)

The case of Mrs B raises two important issues in relation to the ethics of touch in counselling and psychotherapy. First, under what circumstances can it be unethical *not* to touch a client? Under what circumstances (even if not in the case of Mrs B) might withholding touch be morally wrong? Second, where is the line to be drawn between application of therapeutic theory and technique, and adherence to the highest moral values. It would be difficult to argue that, in the case of Mrs B, Casement was *technically* in error. But, even while acting as a competent analyst, was he *morally* in error?

Strategies for maintaining ethical standards

Increasing attention has been devoted by professional organizations in recent years to the question of how to maintain and enforce ethical standards. To some extent, these efforts have been motivated, particularly in the USA but also in other countries, by the recognition that media coverage of cases of misconduct was reducing public confidence and leading government agencies to impose legal penalties, thereby reducing professional autonomy. All professional organizations require their accredited members to abide by a formal code of ethics, and all enforce procedures for disciplining members who violate these codes. Increasingly, however, aspects of the enforcement of counselling standards are being taken over by the courts. In turn, some counsellors and psychotherapists have begun to develop an area of research, called 'therapeutic jurisprudence', that focuses on the impact of the law on therapy (Wexler 1990). The relationship between the therapeutic professions and the law appears to be growing in importance (Jenkins 1997). Some counsellors, however, would argue that the intrusion of legal considerations can in some cases interfere with the creation of a productive therapeutic relationship (see Box 15.6).

Ethical codes can at best only supply broad guidelines for action. There are always 'grey areas', and situations where different ethical rules might be in conflict. It is therefore necessary for counsellors to acquire an understanding of the broader ethical, moral and value considerations that inform and underpin the statements made in formal codes. Most counselling courses give considerable attention to awareness of ethical issues, drawing on standard texts such as Corey *et al.* (1988), van Hoose and Kottler (1985) and Bond (1993). This field is also served by an increasing amount of research on ethical issues (Miller and Thelen 1987; Lakin 1988). Another development within the field has been the construction of ethical codes designed to reflect the moral concerns of practitioners working within approaches such as multicultural and feminist counselling.

One of the main techniques for addressing ethical issues in counselling practice, which has already been referred to earlier in this chapter, is the use of *informed*

Box 15.6

Should counsellors be covered by professional indemnity insurance?

One of the ways in which the relationship between counselling and the law is made tangible is through the existence of professional indemnity insurance. Many counsellors pay insurance premiums that cover them against the costs of civil action on grounds of professional malpractice. Counsellors in some countries, such as the USA, are required by their professional associations to carry such cover. In other countries, such as Britain, indemnity insurance is at present optional for counsellors. Mearns (1993) has argued strongly against the spread of indemnity insurance. He points out that insurance companies insist that the counsellor should deny liability if challenged by a client. Mearns (1993: 163) points out that 'this dishonesty is likely to alienate the client and at worst it could create mystification and the compounding of any abuse the client may have experienced.' He suggests, moreover, that the idea of indemnity insurance originates in professions such as law and medicine where it is accepted that the practitioner is an *expert* on the client's problem, whereas in counselling the practitioner takes the role of *facilitator*. Insurance may therefore threaten the nature of responsibility in the counselling relationship. While Mearns supports the value of ethical codes and procedures in counselling, he suggests that it is possible to 'go too far' in the direction of institutional regulation; indemnity cover represents that step too far.

Even in the USA, where professional insurance is mandatory, some practitioners share Mearns' misgivings. Wilbert and Fulero (1988) carried out a survey of psychologists (clinical and counselling) in the state of Ohio, inviting them to complete a questionnaire on their perceptions of malpractice litigation and how it had affected their work. Many of these therapists reported that the threat of malpractice lawsuits had encouraged them to improve certain areas of their practice: for example, by using informed consent procedures and release of information forms, keeping better records, evaluating evidence of suicidal intent and making more use of supervision. However, there were other areas in which they felt that the threat of malpractice litigation had diminished their practice. Some of them said that they excluded clients who looked as though they might sue, or that they had limited their practice to a specialized clinical domain. Around one in three agreed with the statement that 'there are many times in my practice when what I do is motivated more by the need to protect myself legally than what I feel is good practice clinically.'

consent. Effective informed consent can prevent or minimize difficulties arising over issues such as disclosure of confidential information to a third party, fees and cancellation arrangements, the risks of dual relationships and the emotional or practical demands of treatment. Full informed consent is an ideal that is difficult to achieve in reality. It is difficult for some clients to enter a counselling relationship at all, and there is a danger that some people might be deterred by receiving a mass of detailed information during or at the end of their first meeting with a counsellor. Some clients may be too upset or traumatized to assimilate informed consent information. Other clients may not understand what it means. Many counsellors and counselling agencies provide clients with a leaflet explaining the principles of their therapy, outlining practical arrangements and informing them of complaints procedures. Marzillier (1993) suggests that informed consent should be seen as a process or dialogue, extending over more than one meeting, and being reviewed at later stages in ongoing therapy. Handelsman and Galvin (1988) have proposed that therapists and therapy agencies should give clients a list of questions that they should ask their therapist, with time being set aside to discuss these questions.

Some counsellors have contributed to the development of ways of helping clients who have been the victims of malpractice. This work has been mainly concentrated on the needs of clients who have been sexually exploited by therapists, and has included advocacy services, setting up self-help groups and therapy for victims (Pope and Bouhoutsos 1986). There have been serious suggestions that the best way to prevent therapist sexual abuse of clients is for all women to be seen by women therapists (Chesler 1972). What is perhaps more realistic and achievable is to ensure that all clients are informed of their rights, and that when they attempt to complain their views will be treated with respect and acted upon quickly.

Some of the research evidence on counsellor and psychotherapist malpractice suggests that errant therapists are likely to engage in multiple acts of misconduct (Gabbard 1989). It is difficult to bring charges of professional conduct against counsellors and psychotherapists, and even harder to pursue these charges to the point at which the perpetrator is forced to quit practising. It is therefore useful for the profession to establish means of rehabilitation through which damaged and damaging counsellors can work through their problems and resume practising in a safe and facilitating manner. Strean (1993) gives some interesting case examples of his therapeutic work with therapists (male and female) who have sexually exploited their clients. This kind of intervention can also yield valuable insights into the root causes of ethical misconduct. Hetherington (2000) has argued that therapists who abuse their clients not only suffer from unresolved sexual identity issues, but also harbour 'a deep antipathy toward the practice of psychotherapy'.

For many people it is not easy to accept the idea that counsellors and psychotherapists who exploit and humiliate their clients can get away with it, or even that they might be rehabilitated. It is in the nature of counselling, particularly long-term counselling, that the practitioner will experience strong feelings towards his or her client – love, lust, anger, rage, despair. Using these feelings in the service of the client is a constant challenge for any counsellor. It is not surprising that counsellors who fail to use these feelings constructively, and instead act them out in their relationship with their clients, inspire anger and outright rejection from their colleagues.

Conclusions

The discussion in this chapter of moral, ethical and value dimensions of counselling needs to be placed in the context of all the other chapters in the book. In the early years of the counselling profession, moral and ethical issues were largely taken for granted. Now, there is a thriving literature on ethical ideas and dilemmas, but set some distance apart from the everyday routine practice of counselling. The material presented in Chapter 2, on the history of counselling, makes the point that therapy evolved to fill the vacuum left by the erosion of religion in a largely secular, scientific modern world. What is surely needed now is the reintegration of moral thinking into therapy, what MacIntyre (1981) or Meara *et al.* (1996) would call the rediscovery of the 'virtues'.

Ethical counselling is more effective counselling. For example, a study by Woods and McNamara (1980) revealed that people were likely to be more open and honest about what they said about themselves if they were convinced that the information would be heard in confidence. There are many areas of counselling practice that would repay further examination from an ethical perspective. For instance, Newnes (1995) has identified significant ethical dilemmas arising from the apparently innocuous practice of note-taking. There are important moral and ethical questions to be asked about the theories that counsellors use, the kinds of research that is carried out and the way that counsellors are trained and supervised. Morals and ethics in counselling are not just a matter of deciding whether or not it is unethical to ask a client out on a date. Most of the time, the answers to this sort of question are obvious. What is more important, and what is starting to emerge within the counselling profession, is that *all* counselling is fundamentally concerned with dialogue between competing and contrasting moral visions (Christopher 1996).

Chapter summary

- Counsellors often work with the moral dilemmas faced by their clients in their lives, and can sometimes be faced with ethical issues in relation to their own practice. A knowledge of ethical and moral decision-making is therefore essential for practitioners.

- One of the questions that has received a great deal of attention has been whether counsellors as a group espouse a distinctive set of values, and whether clients are influenced in the direction of adopting these values.

- There are four types of moral reasoning that can be used by counsellors: personal intuition; ethical guidelines established by professional organizations; ethical principles; general theories of moral action.

- It is important for counsellors to possess, and be aware of, their own sense of what is right and wrong.

- Professional associations maintain codes of ethical behaviour. However, there are occasions when these guidelines can be ambiguous, or situations may occur that are not covered by the code.

- Underpinning ethical codes are a set of core moral principles: autonomy, non-maleficence, beneficence, justice and fidelity.

- An alternative model of moral reasoning that has been proposed recently is the *virtues* approach, which emphasizes the importance of the social and cultural context of debates over moral choices and argues that abstract principles always need to be interpreted in the light of the traditions of a community.

- The application of moral codes in counselling practice has highlighted five main areas of difficulty: to whom the counsellor is accountable; the legitimacy of directiveness or active persuasion and challenge; the existence of dual roles; abuse and exploitation of clients; the issue of touch.

- There are many difficulties involved in ensuring compliance with ethical guidelines in everyday counselling practice. Counselling agencies are increasingly using informed consent pro-formas, pre-counselling leaflets and complaints procedures with clients, and are instituting ethically oriented training and supervision for counsellors.

Topics for reflection and discussion

1 Consider the statements on confidentiality extracted from the Ethics Code of the British Association for Counselling (1984), the more recent British Association for Counselling and Psychotherapy (2001) *Framework for Good Practice* and the American Association for Counseling and Development code (1988). What are the main differences between these statements? How do you make sense of the different styles and emphases of these three sets of statements? What ambiguities can you identify in these guidelines – are there any situations you can imagine where one or all of these codes would not provide you with a clear-cut recommendation for action? What suggestions do you have for improving these codes?

2 In the book *Therapists' Dilemmas*, edited by Windy Dryden (1997), a number of well known counsellors and therapists are asked to describe professional dilemmas they have experienced. The interviews with John Davis, Brian Thorne, Peter Lomas, Paul Brown, Dougal Mackay and Fay Fransella touch on a range

of ethical and value issues. Explore one or more of these interviews in the light of the ethical principles and issues discussed in this chapter.

3 What counselling situations can you imagine in which your values would be in conflict with those held by a client? What might you do in such a situation?

4 What is your reaction to the list of 'personal virtues' identified by the BACP (p. 395)? Do these qualities have meaning for you? Would you wish to add further virtues?

Key terms and concepts

autonomy	informed consent
beneficence	intuition
confidentiality	justice
dual relationships	non-maleficence
duty to warn and protect	sexual contact
ethical guidelines	therapeutic jurisprudence
ethical principles	utilitarian
false memories	values
fidelity	virtues

Suggested further reading

The most widely used texts which explore moral and ethical issues in detail are Bond (2000) and Corey, Corey and Callanan (1993). Jones *et al.* (2000) is a useful book, structured around the discussion of specific moral dilemmas by a group of experienced practitioners representing different theoretical traditions in counselling. Many of the current debates about moral philosophy and its relationship to counselling and psychotherapy can be tracked in the review paper by Meara *et al.* (1996), published in a special issue of *The Counseling Psychologist* that includes commentaries on their views from other leading writers in this area.

Part of the debate about ethics has been over whether it is appropriate for different groups of people (counsellors, clients) to adopt different ethical codes. For example, in earlier chapters of this book, there was some discussion of feminist (Chapter 8) and multicultural (Chapter 10) ethical codes. Readers may wish to follow up the sources cited there, to explore the areas of contrast between the mainstream ethical principles discussed in this chapter and the more specific codes developed elsewhere.

16 The organizational context of counselling

Introduction

The theoretical models explored in earlier chapters tend to view counselling purely as a process that takes place in the immediate encounter between helper and client. The focus of these models is on what happens in the counselling room itself. They do not consider, at least in any systematic fashion, the context in which counselling takes place. When a counsellor and client meet, it is not merely two individuals, but in fact two social worlds that engage with each other. Two sets of expectations, assumptions, values, norms, manners and ways of talking must accommodate each to the other. More than this, usually it is the client who is required to enter the social world of the counsellor, by visiting his or her consulting room or office. The physical and emotional environment in which counselling takes place forms the backdrop for the counselling process, and the quality of this environment is largely determined by organizational factors.

Counselling organizations can exert a strong influence on both their clients and their staff. The type of agency or setting, and the way it is organized and managed, may have an impact on many aspects of counselling, including the:

- number, length and frequency of sessions that are offered to clients;
- approach to counselling that is employed;
- adequacy of supervision and training provided for counsellors;
- morale and motivation of counsellors;
- sex, age and ethnicity of counsellors;
- furnishing in the interview room;
- perceptions clients have of the counsellor;
- security of confidential information;
- financial cost of counselling to client.

Types of counselling organization

Much of the counselling and psychotherapy literature, influenced by the American experience, is written as though the most common type of counselling or psychotherapy organization is the private practice, which might be characterized as the simplest or most minimal form of organization, with an absence of hierarchies, committees or other structures. In private practice the client makes contact directly with a named therapist, and personally reimburses that therapist for each session or course of sessions. Some practices consist of a number of practitioners, who may set themselves up as a partnership or a limited company. The private practice as a counselling organization most clearly exemplifies the image of the counsellor as autonomous professional. The financial structure of private practice is such that it provides a service to people who can afford it, and therefore depends on fees.

Although private practice may represent an ideal for many counsellors, in that it maximizes the freedom of the therapist, it accounts for a relatively small proportion of all counselling and therapy that is offered. Most counselling is provided through larger organizations, or 'agencies'. An important type of counselling agency has traditionally been the voluntary agency, which uses unpaid or minimally paid volunteers and which, originally at least, would have a central social mission to fulfil. One of the voluntary counselling agencies in Britain that has had a significant impact on the field is Relate (formerly the National Marriage Guidance Council), which was formed in 1947 in response to what was perceived as a crisis in married life (Tyndall 1985). Similarly, Childline was formed as a telephone counselling agency in Britain in 1986 in reponse to general concern about the rising prevalence of child sexual abuse. Relate and Childline are both large voluntary agencies, with substantial budgets and hierarchical organizational structures that encompass central management, decision-making and fund-raising functions as well as local branches. Many other voluntary counselling agencies are much smaller. For example, in many cities there are locally based gay and lesbian counselling networks, women's therapy centres, rape crisis centres and bereavement counselling agencies. Some of these smaller voluntary agencies may be run by fewer than a dozen volunteers.

The difference in size between the large national voluntary agencies and the small local ones can have implications in terms of organizational structure and functioning. For example, large organizations inevitably need to develop bureaucratic procedures, whereas smaller agencies can rely on decision-making in face-to-face meetings of everyone involved. On the other hand, the larger agencies are often better placed to afford and provide good quality selection, training and supervision. There are also common organizational issues found in all voluntary agencies, regardless of size. These include: integrating the efforts of a small group of core professional staff with those of a large workforce of volunteers; maintaining standards with minimally trained volunteers; dealing with the demands of volunteers to be able to enter paid, professional positions; raising money from clients without jeopardizing access; and expending effort and energy on collecting charitable donations from the public. These pressures and dilemmas have become more acute over the past decade, as the government has cut the resources for statutory services in fields such as social work and mental health, and has come to expect more of the burden of care to be met by the voluntary sector. Lewis *et al.* (1992) have documented the operation of these organizational processes and pressures during the evolution of Relate/Marriage Guidance.

A significant amount of counselling is also provided by people employed by statutory agencies, such as the Probation Service, social services and the National Health Service. Within this statutory sector there are many different forms of organization, ranging from the lone probation officer or social worker who sees part of his or her role as counselling, to the established psychotherapy units that have been set up by some health authorities (Aveline 1990). An area of great expansion in recent years within taxpayer-funded counselling has been the use of counsellors in general practice, working as members of primary health care teams.

There are a whole range of general organizational issues encountered by counsellors working in statutory settings. One of the very basic issues is that the ethos or philosophy of the organization may be in tension with the values of a counselling approach. For example, in some NHS settings the dominance of the medical/ biological model may make it difficult for counsellors to find acceptance for work with relationships and feelings. Or in some social services settings there may be an emphasis on mobilizing resources for the client, rather than working with the client. In some instances, the legal requirements for probation officers, social workers and nurses to act as agents of the court may make it impossible to offer clients the kind of voluntary, confidential relationship that is usually considered essential in counselling. There may also be rivalry or jealousy from colleagues in these agencies, who regard counselling as part of their role. Many of these issues arise from the challenge of inter-professional work, when counsellors need to work alongside people from other professional groups who have their own roles, norms and organizational 'territories'. Some of the problems and dilemmas that can emerge when counselling is offered within a primarily non-counselling organizational setting, such as a hospital, social services department or school, are:

- being pressured to produce results desired by the agency rather than the client;
- maintaining confidentiality boundaries;
- justifying the cost of the service;
- dealing with isolation;
- educating colleagues about the purpose and value of counselling;
- justifying the cost of supervision;
- avoiding being overwhelmed by numbers of clients, or becoming the 'conscience' of the organization;
- avoiding the threat to reputation caused by 'failure' cases;
- coping with the envy of colleagues who are not able to take an hour for each client interview;
- creating an appropriate office space and reception system.

A final type of counselling setting occurs when counselling is made available to employees of large organizations. For example, many police forces, insurance companies and other commercial and service organizations have recognized that counselling is a valuable means of taking care of their 'human resources', their employees. One of the distinctive aspects of employee counselling schemes, often known as 'employee assistance programmes' (EAPs), is that counselling is set in an organizational context that is not primarily focused on caring or helping people. The tension between the values and philosophy of the organization and those of the counsellor can be even more acute than in statutory health and social services agencies, and many of the issues highlighted in the list above may apply. Employee counselling can be provided 'in-house', by counsellors employed by the organization, or can be delivered 'out-house', through an external counselling agency under contract to the organization to supply counselling for its employees. In either case, the counselling is being paid for by the employer, rather than the client himself or herself, which can lead, for example, to client suspicion over confidentiality and pressure on the counsellor to produce results consistent with the needs of the organization rather than those of the client. Counselling in educational settings, such as schools, colleges and universities, shares many of the organizational features of employee counselling.

From this brief discussion of some of the organizational issues that can arise in different types of counselling organizations, it is evident that there are many aspects of organizational life of potential relevance to counsellors. The field of organizational studies or organizational behaviour is a well established area of research, scholarship and teaching. Further, more detailed overviews of current thinking about organizations can be found in Handy (1990), Robbins (1991), Hosking and Morley (1991) and many other texts. Some of the specific issues in organizational theory that are relevant to counselling are explored in the remainder of this chapter.

The nature of counselling organizations

One of the most valuable concepts to have emerged from the field of organizational studies has been the idea of the 'open system' (Katz and Kahn 1978). From this perspective, organizations are seen as consisting of sets of overlapping and inter-connecting parts, which combine to form an organizational system. Change in any element or part of the system will affect what happens elsewhere in the system. Furthermore, the system exists in an environment, and is open to influence from external factors. The purpose of the organizational system is to produce 'through-put': there is an input of 'raw materials', which are processed and then leave the system as 'output'. A typical counselling agency, therefore, could be viewed as a system made up of clients, counsellors, supervisors, managers and administrators, receptionists and fund-raisers. The throughput of the agency is represented by the number of clients seen, and the external environment may include funding agencies, professional bodies and members of the general public. A systems perspective is particularly useful in providing a framework for beginning to understand the ways in which other parts in the system may have an impact on the client–counsellor relationship. For example, successful publicity and outreach work may increase the number of clients applying for counselling. The long waiting lists that may then result can lead to pressure to place a limit on the number of sessions offered to clients. Some of the counsellors may find this policy unacceptable, and leave. This very brief, simplified (but not fictional) example gives a sense of how an organizational system might operate. Other examples are explored later in the chapter.

In his analysis of the organization of human services providers, Hasenfeld (1992) makes two observations that are highly relevant to counselling agencies. He suggests that an appreciation of the nature of these organizations must take into account that they are engaged in 'moral' work and in 'gendered' work. Counselling organizations ultimately exist because of an assumption that certain groups of people deserve help and resources. A person who is depressed, or who is abusing drugs, is entitled to the time of a therapist. The fact that a counselling agency has been set up to provide counselling for such clients implies a value position. Other people, however, may not share this value position, and may argue on moral grounds that these problems do not deserve a share of public resources. Counselling agencies may, as a result, need to work to establish their legitimacy in the eyes of external groups, such as funding bodies and the public at large.

Historically, the task of caring for people has been work for women. In counsel-ling and other human service organizations, women predominate in frontline service delivery roles, although men are proportionally more heavily represented in management roles. This pattern is even more apparent in voluntary counselling agencies, where male counsellors can be thin on the ground. In general, female occupations enjoy lower status and rates of pay than male occupations, and this tendency can be seen in the field of counselling. Another issue arising from the gendered nature of counselling is the influence of feminist values on counselling organizations. Taylor (1983: 445) has suggested that organizations dominated by women are more likely to espouse values such as 'egalitarianism rather than hierarchy, co-operation rather than competition, nurturance rather than rugged individualism, peace rather than conflict'. This set of values is congruent with the values of counselling as a whole, and can lead to misunderstanding, tension or difficulty when counselling agencies attempt to develop hierarchical structures, or operate in host organizations that embody different beliefs.

Another set of issues that must be faced by counselling organizations concerns the position to be taken regarding professionalism and voluntarism. There is a long and respectable tradition of counselling as voluntary work. People trained and practised as counsellors on a part-time basis because of the intrinsic satisfaction of the work, and also for the altruistic motive of giving to others who were less fortunate. There is also a tradition of counselling as a profession, carried out by paid experts. Difficulties arise in situations where these traditions confront each other: for example, in voluntary agencies where some training and supervisory staff are paid, but counsellors are not, or in agencies seeking to make the transition from voluntary to professional status.

Organizational culture

Just as different nations have different cultures, so do organizations and work groups. The experience of walking through the centre of Paris is quite distinct from the experience of walking through London. There are a different language, different rules regarding physical space and contact, driving on the other side of the road, different values and ways of feeling implied by the architecture and use of leisure and so on. These are two different cultures. The social anthropologist Clifford Geertz (1973) has suggested an essential quality of any culture: it is 'thick'. By this, Geertz means that there are always many layers and levels to a culture, and that describing or understanding it is never a simple matter. The method used by social anthropologists to study cultures, known as 'ethnography', reflects their recognition of the complexity of cultures. Ethnographic studies involve immersion in the life of a group, using participant observation and interviewing, for long periods of time.

Studies of organizational cultures have looked at such aspects as the kinds of roles and relationships that exist in the organization, the language, imagery and humour of the organization, social norms and rules, and the underlying values and philosophy that underpin behaviour and decision-making. All these factors interact with each other in complex ways, to create an organizational system. In counselling agencies, the concept of organizational culture can be employed to make sense of the tension that can often exist between bureaucracy, which is associated with formal procedures and impersonal rules, and the informality and personal relationships that can be cultivated by counsellors in supervision or being trained together. The rational decision-making inherent in bureaucracy can also be at odds with the use of feelings as a guide to action, as advocated by some approaches to counselling.

Expectations about 'what is supposed to happen here' are also communicated by the culture of an agency. Crandall and Allen (1981), for example, found in one study that different drug abuse therapy agencies embodied quite different levels of demand regarding client change. In some agencies there was a strong expectation that clients' behaviour would change in basic ways. In other agencies there were low therapeutic demands on clients. The promotion of a 'culture of excellence' will be expressed through various aspects of organizational culture, such as allocation of rewards and praise, availability of training and provision of support and resources (Hackman and Walton 1986). An example of the different kinds of expectations for counselling found in organizational units with contrasting cultures and values can be found in Box 16.1.

The culture of an organization is reflected in the use of language within the organization. People in formal, hierarchical organizations, for example, address each other by title or surname; people in informal, 'flat hierarchy' organizations are more likely to be on first name terms. There may be shared images of the agency or unit that express a sense of the organizational culture: the agency may be a 'family', a 'team', a 'sinking ship'. People are usually consciously aware of the meanings of these uses of language. Some writers on organizations have suggested, however, that a group or organizational culture operates largely at an unconscious level. These theorists have borrowed from Freud the idea that the most powerful motives in people are deeply hidden and emerge only indirectly, in patterns of behaviour and in fantasies and dreams. Members of organizations may hold powerful fantasies about other people, or groups in the organization, or their clients. According to this theory, the most fundamental elements of the culture of an organization are unconscious and are revealed only through fantasies, jokes and other non-conscious processes.

Institutional defence mechanisms

One of the most influential analyses of organizational life in terms of unconscious processes has been the study of hospital nurses carried out by Menzies (1959). The very nature of the nursing task involves nurses in intimate contact with patients, through being exposed to physical and sexual bodily functions that are usually private, and to pain, anxiety and death. Menzies argued that this kind of contact can be emotionally threatening to nurses, and as a consequence they have evolved, on a collective or group basis, organizational defence mechanisms with which to cope with their emotional reactions to the job. These collective defences include 'objectifying' the patient, denying his or her humanity (e.g. 'the appendix in bed fourteen') and projecting their vulnerabilities on to other colleagues. Menzies

Box

16.1

The effect of organizational culture on the counsellor: school counsellors in Israel

Counsellors are employed in the majority of schools in Israel, and perform a variety of tasks, including advising on pupil placement and referral, and offering consultation to teachers and parents, as well as actually counselling pupils. One of the principal challenges faced by the Israeli educational system in recent years has been that of how best to respond to the needs of thousands of immigrant children, many from the former Soviet Union. In an interview-based study with 37 secondary school counsellors, Tatar (1998) found that the kind of work done by each counsellor was largely determined by the culture and values of their school. Tatar (1998) identified four counsellor roles, associated with different school philosophies:

• *The counsellor as culturally encapsulated assimilator.* The majority of schools reflected the dominant cultural values of the Israeli authorities: immigrants should rapidly assimilate the language, traditions and behavioural norms of the country. In these schools, the counsellor related mainly to immigrant children as a group, and prioritized activities that would help these pupils to learn Hebrew.
• *The counsellor as facilitator of individual development.* In some schools, each pupil was considered as an individual. One counsellor in such a school stated that 'any immigrant pupil, and any pupil at all, is a world in himself/herself'. These counsellors did not treat immigrant children as a group, but responded to them as individuals. Counsellors spent time with staff raising their awareness of individual processes of adjustment that they might encounter in children experiencing cultural dislocation and change. These counsellors reported that their approach required a significant investment of time and dedication, and was personally exhausting.
• *The counsellor as specialist.* A few counsellors had found themselves identified as the 'expert' on all immigrant issues, and advised teachers and school principals on policies and practices relating to immigrant children. In these schools, there was a tendency towards a cultural orientation of strong categorization of immigrant children as 'different'.
• *The counsellor as cultural 'translator'.* Four school counsellors (the smallest number in any of the categories) worked in schools in which the cultural heritage of immigrants was valued, and it was accepted that the host community could learn from the new arrivals. In these schools, both the immigrant and majority culture pupils were regarded by the counsellor as her 'clients' in respect of acculturation issues. These counsellors defined their role in terms such as 'cultural translator', 'bridgemaker' or 'mediator'.

Tatar's (1998) research demonstrates the extent to which counsellors with similar backgrounds, training and experience, and appointed to similar positions within an organization, can find themselves undertaking quite different kinds of work. In each school, the role of the counsellor was shaped by the prevailing school ethos and culture, reinforced by the attitudes of the school principal. Counsellors appeared to have relatively little capacity to modify school culture: Tatar (1998: 349) commented that 'only in a few cases and circumstances were counsellors able to lead and change the organisation's goals and beliefs by themselves.'

found that more senior nurses, for example, tended to view student nurses as irresponsible and unreliable, thereby projecting their unconscious fears over their own ability to cope on to this group.

These two processes, objectifying patients and blaming colleagues rather than acknowledging personal feelings of vulnerability, are of general relevance and can be found in many counselling agencies. The fundamental value placed in counselling on acceptance, respect and empathy for clients has evolved in response to the powerful tendency for busy caring professionals to lose their sense of the client as a unique individual person rather than as a representative of a category of problem. The process of blaming colleagues can also be found in counselling agencies, particularly where there is inter-professional working.

Parallel process

The key idea in Menzies's (1959) approach is that a group of staff can collectively develop a set of defences for coping with the emotional challenge of dealing with clients. This basic idea has been expanded and specifically applied to counselling and psychotherapy agencies through the concept of 'parallel process'. Crandall and Allen (1981) suggest that there can often be significant parallels between counselling issues and organizational issues. In other words, what happens between counsellor and client is influenced by what happens between counsellor and agency, and vice versa. For example, in a marriage counselling agency that works a lot with couples, counsellors often come across the combination of one rational, unfeeling spouse with a partner who is the emotionally sensitive, feeling but illogical one. This splitting of logic and feeling can become inherent in the agency itself, perhaps through managers and administrators being perceived by counsellors as unfeeling insensitive bureaucrats, and the counsellors being perceived by administrators as disorganized and unwilling to make decisions.

The parallel process can also take place in the other direction, from agency to client. For example, in an agency with an authoritarian and directive management style, where counsellors are told what to do, counsellors may find themselves becoming more structured and directive in their work with clients. Even the choice of furniture for counselling rooms in an agency can influence the counselling process. A counselling room with floor cushions gives a different message about expressing feelings than would a room with upright tubular chairs (see Rowan 1992b).

The developmental history of the agency

Another important perspective on organizational functioning is linked to the age of the organization, and its stage of development. Chester (1985) has suggested that many counselling agencies begin existence with a strong sense of mission and commitment. The agency is set up because its founders believe passionately that there is a powerful social need for something to be done about a particular problem. Chester (1985) calls this the 'social movement' stage in the development of an agency. As time goes by, however, the original excitement and sense of mission becomes diluted by the requirement to provide a service to clients. The agency then begins to move into a professional, 'service agency' stage, where expertise and professional competence is valued over commitment and passion. The work of the agency becomes consolidated and routinized. This transition can be painful and difficult, with agencies becoming 'stalemated' (Hirschhorn 1978) as opposing groups of staff adopt positions on one side or another of a movement–professionalism split.

A version of this kind of organizational crisis can be observed when an agency is set up in the first place by a charismatic, inspirational leader. Such people are more effective in the mission stage of the life of an agency than in the later consolidation phase, and may leave once the initial task is complete. But, because their influence over other staff is so strong, their departure may threaten the very existence of the service. This pattern has been observed in therapeutic communities (Manning 1989), and has led to caution about the usefulness of founders who adopt the role of 'hero-innovator'.

Counselling has not been established long enough for agencies to develop beyond the consolidation/professionalization stage. In the domain of religious life, however, there have been religious communities and organizations that have been in existence for hundreds of years. Research into the lifespan of religious orders indicates a similar early process to that observed in counselling agencies, with high levels of mission and commitment followed by consolidation and maintenance. After this stage, though, there is a further stage of decline, in which the membership of the order diminishes, and the organization may cease to function unless a new leader emerges to inspire new directions. Fitz and Cada (1975) suggest that the life-cycle of a religious congregation follows five discrete stages: foundation, expansion, stabilization, breakdown and transition. This whole process can take centuries to complete.

Role conflict

The idea of 'role' refers to the behaviour expected from a person who holds a particular position in a social group. Role conflict occurs when other people hold contradictory expectations in relation to that person. One of the guiding principles of counselling is to avoid allowing role conflicts to occur in relation to a client. For example, it is generally considered bad practice for a counsellor or therapist to be a friend, colleague or relative of a client, since the expectations and behaviours elicited through these other relationships will get in the way of the counselling relationship. This is one reason, incidentally, for the difficulty in establishing counselling agencies in rural settings where everyone knows everyone else and the kind of anonymity required for role 'purity' can be impossible to guarantee. The avoidance of role conflict is also one of the reasons why many counsellors idealize private practice. Only in private practice can the counsellor be responsible solely to the client. A counsellor who works for an agency is responsible to the agency, and can be seen as representing the agency. The counsellor who is paid by a third party, such as the employer of the client, inevitably has a role in relation to that other person or institution as well as to the client. The issue of role conflict emerges in supervision if the supervisor is also a manager or tutor of the counsellor.

Why is role conflict considered in such a negative light by counsellors? After all, it could be argued that it could in some circumstances be a valuable learning experience for the client to work out the implications of different role expectations he or she held in relation to the counsellor. A key factor involves the capacity of the counsellor to be there solely for the client. Any role other than counsellor carries with it the danger that the counsellor is using the relationship at least partially to gratify his or her needs. Counsellors working within a psychodynamic approach place particular importance on the maintenance of strict counsellor–client boundaries, since the introduction of other types of relationship into the equation makes transference more difficult to understand. Counsellors working within a humanistic or person-centred approach can be more flexible in the roles they are willing to develop in relation to a client (see, for example, Thorne 1985, 1987).

The issue of role conflict arises frequently in counselling agencies. It is impossible to work in a counselling organization of any complexity without fulfilling a range of roles: counsellor, colleague, fundraiser, peer supervision group member, friend. Sometimes the training requirements of agencies and institutes (see Chapter 20) require counsellors to be in personal therapy with another member of the same organization. It is essential, therefore, for agencies to have some means of monitoring and dealing with these issues when they arise, usually through the employment of outside consultants. Role conflict can also raise a number of ethical issues, which are discussed in Chapter 15 under the heading of 'dual relationships'.

The role of the paraprofessional or voluntary counsellor

The use of unpaid volunteer counsellors raises a number of issues in counselling organizations. Whereas paid professional employees receive a salary to reward their efforts, and may be motivated by hopes of promotion and career development, voluntary workers seek personal satisfaction and rewards intrinsic to the job itself. The perceptions and attitudes of paid and unpaid counselling staff may therefore be quite different, leading to difficulties when they work side-by-side in the same agency. Feild and Gatewood (1976) have identified a number of problems of mutual adjustment that can occur when professional and volunteer staff work together:

1 Volunteer counsellors may be given little encouragement or opportunity for career development. They may be allocated simple tasks that do not allow them to express their skills adequately, or may not be allowed to attend courses that would allow them to develop new skills.

2 Because they are only involved for a few hours each week, volunteers or paraprofessionals may have little power or influence within the agency, and may become frustrated at their inability to influence policy and practice.

3 Professionals may fear that the introduction of volunteer workers will threaten their livelihoods.

4 Volunteers may have little previous experience of working in an organization, and may find it difficult to comply with administrative procedures and expectations.

5 When a counselling agency uses volunteers selected on the basis of their similarity to the client population (e.g. sex, age, ethnicity, specific life experience), there may be a tendency for these workers to over-identify with clients, or to experience conflict between allegiance to clients and adherence to agency policies.

Feild and Gatewood (1976) suggest that counselling agencies using volunteers can overcome many of these difficulties through appropriate supervision and training (see Box 16.2).

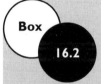

Box 16.2

How can volunteer counsellors be supported and motivated?

An important study of the factors influencing the commitment and effectiveness of volunteer alcohol counsellors has been carried out by Hunot and Rosenbach (1998), who were able to collect questionnaire data from 141 volunteer counsellors employed in 15 counselling agencies in Britain. One of the significant findings to emerge from their study was that counsellors who received both individual and group supervision felt more adequately prepared for their role, compared to counsellors who had only group supervision or only individual supervision. For these volunteers, individual supervision helped to reassure them that they were performing their counselling role adequately, while group supervision provided social support and helped them to feel part of a team. Counsellors who were supervised by agency staff were more satisfied than those who had external supervisors. It was important for these counsellors to feel that their efforts were recognized and valued by the agency. For some, an accreditation scheme operated as a tangible means of gaining recognition. The majority of counsellors in the study reported that they had not felt competent or confident about their ability during their first year working as a counsellor for the agency; it appeared to take three or four years for a sense of secure adequacy to become established. Overall, the study found that levels of commitment to remain with the agency, and job satisfaction, were strongly influenced by how proactive the agency was in providing a variety of incentives and support mechanisms.

Organizational stress and burnout

As with all organizations, working in a counselling agency can affect the health and well-being of staff. Studies of many different types of organizations have demonstrated that stress and emotional and physical ill-health can be caused by overwork, unplanned change and a poor working environment. In human service organizations, a specific type of stress has been identified, which has been labelled 'burnout' (Freudenberger 1974; Farber 1983b; Maslach and Jackson 1984). The phenomenon of burnout occurs when workers enter a human service profession (such as social work, nursing, the police or counselling) with high and unrealistic aspirations regarding the degree to which they will be able to help other people. In many instances the amount of help that can be offered, or the effectiveness of an intervention, is limited. There are also, usually, too many clients for them all to be dealt with in an ideal manner. The result is that the helper becomes caught between his or her own high standards and the impossibility of fulfilling these standards, and after a while is unable to maintain the effort and energy required in functioning at such a high level. This is the state of burnout.

Maslach and Jackson (1984) have identified three main dimensions of the burnout syndrome. People experiencing burnout report emotional exhaustion, a persistent fatigue and a state of low motivation. They also exhibit depersonalization, gradually coming to see their clients not as unique people with individual problems but as 'cases' or representatives of diagnostic categories. Finally, burnout is associated with feelings of lack of personal accomplishment, or powerlessness. Prevention of burnout has been shown, in a number of studies of different groups of human services personnel, to be correlated with the presence of support from colleagues, realistic workloads, clarity about job roles and demands, variety and creativity in the job specification and recognition and positive feedback from clients and management (Maslach and Jackson 1984).

A number of studies of burnout with counsellors and therapists have been carried out. Farber and Heifitz (1982) interviewed 60 psychotherapists about their experiences of job-related stress. The primary source of stress reported by these therapists was 'lack of therapeutic success'. Other burnout factors included overwork, work with clients raising personal issues and isolation. Most of the interviewees stated that they could only see four to six clients a day before becoming depleted, although male therapists claimed they could see greater numbers before being affected. The therapists in this study also felt they were particularly prone to burnout when under stress at home. Hellman and Morrison (1987) administered a 350-item stress questionnaire to psychologists engaged in therapy, and found that those working with more disturbed clients were likely to experience more professional doubt and personal depletion. Therapists working in institutions reported more stress from organizational factors, while those in private practice found it more stressful to deal with difficult clients. Jupp and Shaul (1991) surveyed the stress experiences of 83 college counsellors in Australia, and found that more experienced counsellors reported more burnout symptoms than their less experienced colleagues. In all of these studies, the existence of effective social support networks was associated with lower levels of stress and burnout.

Another type of occupational stress experienced by some counsellors is vicarious traumatization (Neumann and Gamble 1995; Pearlman and McIan 1995). This can happen when counsellors work with clients who are suffering from extreme trauma: for example, survivors of sexual or physical abuse, refugees who have been tortured, disaster victims or Holocaust survivors. Counsellors working in these areas can often find that they begin to experience intrusive images linked to scenes described by their clients, and other symptoms of post-traumatic stress disorder: for example, loss of trust in a safe world. This is an area in which there is a very clear link between the work counsellors are doing and the impact it has on their own personal lives. It is important for agencies offering services to these clients to be aware of the danger of vicarious traumatization, and to offer appropriate support to staff (Sexton 1999).

The potential for burnout in counselling work is considerable. Counsellors are routinely exposed to clients who are in great distress and whose problems do not readily resolve themselves in the face of therapeutic interventions. There are many references in the therapy literature to therapists who have been driven to the very depths of their personal resources through working with particular clients (e.g. Hobson 1985). The high suicide rate of psychiatrists, who are more likely to be involved with highly disturbed clients, has been noted in a number of studies (Farber 1983a). Many counselling agencies have long waiting lists and are under external pressure regarding continued funding. Feedback concerning the effectiveness of the work can sometimes be meagre.

The implementation of organizational procedures to forestall burnout is therefore of immense importance. There are a range of organizational strategies designed to prevent stress and burnout. Regular, effective supervision is essential. Opportunities for counsellor career development, through expanding interests in training, supervision, writing and research, are also helpful. Peer support, either within an agency (Scully 1983) or through training workshops and conferences, also contributes to burnout prevention. Cherniss and Krantz (1983) have argued that burnout results from the loss of commitment and moral purpose in the work. This absence of meaningfulness can be counteracted by the establishment of 'ideological communities' comprised of groups of colleagues sharing a set of beliefs and values. Boy and Pine (1980) similarly advocate the benefits of associating with committed, concerned colleagues.

It is difficult to estimate the overall prevalence of burnout in counsellors and therapists. An unknown number of trained counsellors either leave the profession or gravitate towards teaching and administration rather than frontline therapy (Warnath and Shelton 1976). Although Farber and Heifitz (1981) have argued that the majority of practitioners see therapeutic work as offering a unique opportunity for personal affirmation and fulfilment, the issue of counsellor burnout clearly requires further research attention, all the more so at a time when cut-backs in the funding of health and social service agencies have increased workloads and job insecurity.

Stability of funding

The type and quality of funding that a counselling agency receives can have a profound impact on its approach to clients. In private practice, the pressure to maintain income from client fees can lead indirectly to longer-term rather than time-limited approaches, and to an unconscious reluctance to complete the therapy of lucrative clients (Kottler 1988). The counsellor in private practice may need to develop knowledge and skills in such areas as marketing and business planning (Woody 1989). In voluntary or non-profit organizations a number of different issues may emerge.

Gronbjerg (1992) observes that most voluntary organizations rely on three sources of income: client fees; donations from individuals, trusts and companies; and contracts with government agencies. The task of maintaining stable funding is complex, with administrators or managers being required to meet the criteria and demands of three different groups. The agency may have little control over these sources of funding, and may therefore find itself periodically in crisis when a donor or government agency reduces or fails to renew its commitment to it. In addition, grants or contracts from government or local authority departments usually carry strict deadlines, formalized reporting procedures and other forms of external control. These features all result in a great deal of administrative work, and possibly the need to appoint staff who are skilled in this particular area.

In a study of six voluntary agencies in Chicago, Gronbjerg (1992) identified three contrasting strategies for dealing with funding issues. The first was to adopt a 'client-driven' approach, in which services were developed in response to client demand. This strategy was only possible for agencies whose main sources of finance were client fees and reliable private donations. The second approach was to aim for maximum flexibility and cushioning against funding jolts by continually seeking increases in grants (to counteract the possibility of cuts), finding ways of commercially marketing some services and looking for different sources of finance for the same projects. In emergencies, cash-flow problems would be dealt with by borrowing, delaying the payment of bills and delaying salary payments. The third financial strategy for voluntary agencies could be described as 'expansionist'. This approach involves engaging in political activity, attempting to establish relationships with staff in charitable trusts and forming networks and joint initiatives with other non-profit organizations. Gronbjerg (1992) suggests that although this final strategy may be effective in securing finance and resources, it does so at the risk of losing touch with client needs. On the other hand, the pure 'client-driven' approach is highly vulnerable to the vicissitudes of funding sources.

Conclusions

Theory and research in counselling have concentrated mainly on the immediate process occurring between client and counsellor. This chapter has explored some of the ways in which the 'macro' environment of the counselling agency or setting can influence the 'micro' process of the counselling interview. Many of the issues that have been discussed would be equally relevant in relation to other human service agencies, such as social services departments, hospitals, residential homes and police, fire and rescue services. However, unlike these other forms of helping, counselling claims to offer people a special kind of relationship, characterized by high levels of empathy, honesty and acceptance. The concept of 'parallel process' implies that the relationship offered to clients will reflect the relationships between people in the organization. It would seem, therefore, that counsellors have a particular responsibility for ensuring that the life of the organization models the assumptions, values and roles to which it intends that clients will aspire. Sensitivity to and awareness of organizational factors is also important because of the relatively recent expansion of counselling into many new areas of work. Many counselling agencies now in existence have only been set up very recently, and many counsellors find that they are the first people to have held their particular post. The continued health of these agencies and counsellors will depend on the establishment of appropriate organizational norms and practices.

The history of counselling includes many examples of counsellors breaking away from organizations and entering private practice. In many respects the people who become counsellors are not good followers of bureaucratic procedures. Nevertheless, the needs of socially disadvantaged groups (see Chapter 14) will never be met through private practice. If counselling is to respond to these needs, it will require further research and experimentation to find the most appropriate ways of creating organizational structures that respect the ethos of counselling but can survive in a harsh political and economic climate.

Chapter summary

- The organizational context within which counselling takes place makes a difference to the service that is offered to clients: for example, in the number of sessions they can have, the training and supervision of counsellors, even the ambience and furnishing of the counselling room.

- There are many different types of counselling agency, varying in terms of size, private practice/voluntary sector, independent or attached to a large organization such as a commercial company or university.

- A counselling organization is a social system that depends for its effectiveness on the achievement of an equilibrium both between the elements inside the system (e.g. managers, supervisors, counsellors) and between the system itself and other interacting systems (e.g. funding bodies, the local community, professional associations).

- The organizational culture of an agency is an important factor in determining the extent to which clients and counsellors have positive expectations, are able to express their feelings and feel safe.

- A useful way of making sense of organizational dynamics is through applying psychodynamic concepts such as projection, splitting, denial and parallel process. Counsellors are exposed to potentially threatening emotions and experiences, and one of the characteristics of an effective counselling organization lies in the extent to which these emotions can be dealt with openly, or are channelled into destructive forms of defensiveness.

- The developmental history of the agency can be a significant factor – some agencies become bureaucratized and lose any sense of mission and purpose.

- Other sources of difficulty in counselling agencies can be the existence of dual relationships or role conflicts, and the stress of the work.

- Many of these factors are strongly affected by stability of external funding. Counselling agencies can often be involved in a constant struggle to justify their legitimacy in the eyes of external groups.

Topics for reflection and discussion

1 Consider either the counselling setting where you currently work or another counselling setting with which you are familiar. How does the way counselling is organized limit the effectiveness of the help offered to clients? What organizational changes could be introduced to overcome these problems?

2 Is there an optimum size for a counselling agency? Discuss the advantages and disadvantages of both very large and very small agencies.

3 In what ways could the underlying theoretical orientation of a counselling organization (e.g. psychodynamic, person-centred, cognitive-behavioural, integrative/eclectic) have an effect on the way it is administered and managed? Does the theoretical orientation have an effect on the decoration of an agency, the kinds of chairs that are used and the kinds of pictures that are on the wall?

4 Reflect on the kind of humour you have observed in a counselling agency or training course in which you are involved. What kinds of jokes are shared, and in which situations? How could these jokes be interpreted in terms of the unconscious fantasies and needs of people within the organization? What do these needs and fantasies say about the *culture* of the organization?

Key terms and concepts

burnout

employee assistance programmes

funding legitimacy

open system

organizational cultures

organizational defence mechanisms

parallel process

professionalization

role conflict

service agency stage

social movement stage

vicarious traumatization

volunteers

Suggested further reading

Not enough has been written on the topic of the organization of counselling, and much of the time it is necessary to look at theory and research into other 'human service' agencies, and apply this material to counselling. A valuable source of insight is the pioneering work of Isabel Menzies Lyth, which has now been republished in two volumes, *Containing Anxiety in Institutions* (1988) and *The Dynamics of the Social* (1989). More recent papers that apply the same psychodynamically informed approach can be found in Obholzer and Roberts (1994). The other key writer on these areas is Hasenfeld (1992), who emphasizes the political and economic rather than unconscious aspects of the functioning of human service agencies.

For counsellors, many of the issues reviewed in this chapter manifest themselves as stress and hassle; the book by Dryden (1995) includes a variety of counsellor accounts of how they have suffered from, and dealt with, the stresses of the job.

There is an interesting chapter by Thomas Gordon on 'Group-centred leadership and administration' in Rogers (1951), which provides a fascinating picture of how the values of the person-centred approach can be expressed in the functioning of an organization.

Finally, a special issue of the *British Journal of Guidance and Counselling* (McLeod and Machin 1998) brings together a number of studies of how contextual and organizational factors impact on the process of counselling.

17 Alternative modes of delivery

Introduction

The somewhat clumsy phrase 'modes of delivery' refers to the differing shapes and forms that counselling can take. The chapters on core theoretical models, and the discussion of integrative approaches, are largely based on the practice of one-to-one counselling, where the counsellor and client are the only people involved. This type of counselling can be seen as representing a 'pure' form of the genre, whose principles and processes are readily identifiable and well documented. There are, however, several other formats within which counselling can occur. In this chapter some of these alternative modes of delivery are discussed, including variants of one-to-one counselling, group counselling, telephone counselling, working with couples and bibliotherapy. These approaches provide a range of fascinating challenges for counsellors primarily trained in face-to-face individual work, as well as enabling the benefits of counselling to achieve a wider impact in society.

Time-limited counselling

Normally, counselling is regarded as taking place between a trained, professional counsellor and a client over a number of meetings. The main variants on this pattern have been to limit the number of sessions and to use minimally trained volunteers rather than professional practitioners.

A considerable amount of research evidence has demonstrated that most counselling and therapy takes place within a fairly limited number of sessions, and that clients seem to benefit more from earlier than from later sessions (the literature on this topic is reviewed by Howard *et al.* 1986). These findings, as well as other theoretical and pragmatic considerations, have led to a growth in interest in developing forms of 'brief therapy', in which the client is offered a limited number of sessions. Psychodynamic brief therapy is discussed in Chapter 3, but the principle of time limits has also been applied in counselling delivered from a cognitive–behavioural or person-centred orientation (Dryden and Feltham 1992). The decision to adopt a time-limited rather than open-ended approach to working with clients has been viewed by Budman and Gurman (1988) as reflecting a shift in underlying counsellor or therapist values (see Table 17.1). Other writers who have discussed the issues involved in deciding whether to offer open-ended or time-limited counselling are Fuhriman (1992) and Tryon (1995).

Table 17.1   A comparison of the values underlying long-term and short-term counselling

The long-term therapist	*The short-term therapist*
Seeks change in basic character	Pragmatic, does not believe in concept of 'cure'
Sees preventing problems as indicative of underlying pathology	Emphasizes client's strengths and resources
Wants to be there as client makes significant change	Accepts that many changes will occur after termination of therapy, and will not be observable by therapist
Is patient and willing to wait for change	Does not accept the 'timelessness' of some approaches
Unconsciously recognizes the fiscal convenience of maintaining long-term clients	Fiscal issues often muted by the nature of the organization for which the therapist works
Views therapy as always benign and useful	Views therapy as sometimes useful and sometimes harmful
Being in therapy is the most important part of the client's life	Being in the world is more important than therapy

Source: Budman and Gurman (1988).

Recently, some researchers and practitioners have addressed the question of how few sessions are necessary to enable effective counselling to take place. The attraction of very brief counselling is that its implementation can avoid the necessity for long waiting lists. In addition, clients may also be encouraged and given hope by the assumption that they can make progress quickly. Research into very brief therapy has included examining the efficacy of a '2 + 1' model. In this approach, clients are offered two sessions one week apart, then a follow-up meeting around three months later (Barkham and Shapiro 1989, 1990a, b; Dryden and Barkham 1990). One of the aims of the study is to identify the types of client most likely to benefit from this approach. Initial results, based on counselling offered to white-collar workers referred for job-related stress and relationship difficulties, suggest that at six-month follow-up, around 60 per cent of clients exhibited significant benefits (Barkham and Shapiro 1990a).

A study of even shorter counselling by Rosenbaum (1994) focused on the effects on clients of offering single-session counselling. At the beginning of the first session, clients were told:

> We've found that a large number of our clients can benefit from a single visit here. Of course, if you need more therapy, we will provide it. But I want to let you know that I'm willing to work hard with you today to help you resolve your problem quickly, perhaps even in this single visit, as long as you are ready to work hard at that today. Would you like to do that? (p. 252)
>
> (Rosenbaum 1994: 252)

At the end of the session (which was allowed to extend to 90–120 minutes), clients were asked if they needed further sessions. Fifty-eight per cent of clients opted for the single session. When contacted at one-year follow-up, 88 per cent of these clients rated their problems as improved or much improved. Important features of the Rosenbaum (1994) approach are that it empowers clients by giving them choice in relation to the number of sessions, and that the initial introductory statement conveys positive expectations and hope, and sets the scene for an intense exploration of the client's problem.

Another variant on time-limited counselling has been to 'front-load' sessions, with perhaps three sessions in the first week, one in the second week and then a final session one month later (Zhu and Pierce 1995). The '2 + 1' model mentioned above takes this strategy. Turner *et al.* (1996) report a successful experiment, in a student counselling service, in which they retained the same number of sessions, but reduced the length of each session to 30 minutes. They found that clients seemed to gain just as much from these shorter sessions.

The practice of structuring counselling around time limits makes special demands on counsellors, and requires careful training and supervision. Counsellors and counselling agencies employing time-limited approaches also need to organize themselves to enable effective and sensitive selection of clients, and appropriate referral of clients who turn out to require longer-term work. From the wide array of theory and research into brief therapy, some central principles for time-limited counselling are clearly emerging. These include initial assessment of clients, an active approach by the counsellor, structuring the therapeutic process in terms of stages or phases, engaging the active involvement and cooperation of the client and providing the client with new perspectives and experiences (Dryden and Feltham 1992; Steenberger 1992; Elton-Wilson 1996).

Non-professional counsellors

The use of non-professional, paraprofessional or lay counsellors in one-to-one work has attracted a great deal of controversy in recent years, following the publication by Karlsruher (1974) and Durlak (1979) of reviews of studies assessing the therapeutic effectiveness of non-professional helpers. Durlak (1979), in a review of 42 studies, reported that research evidence indicated that lay or non-professional counsellors tended to be more effective than highly trained expert practitioners. This conclusion, not unexpectedly, provoked a strong reaction within the profession (Durlak 1981; Nietzel and Fisher 1981). The accumulation of further evidence has, however, supported the original position taken by Durlak (1979). In two more recent reviews of the research literature, Hattie *et al.* (1984) concluded that paraprofessionals were more effective than trained therapists, and Berman and Norton (1985), using more rigorous criteria for accepting studies as methodologically adequate, concluded that there were no overall differences in effectiveness between professional and non-professional therapists. Since the Berman and Norton (1985) review, there have been further research studies (Burlingame and Barlow 1996; Bright *et al.* 1999) and two reviews (Christensen and Jacobson 1994; Faust and Zlotnick 1995), which have essentially arrived at the same conclusion. A review by Stein and Lambert (1995) reported that training did have an effect on effectiveness, but the studies they reviewed mainly looked at the effectiveness levels of psychologists at different levels of training, rather than comparing paraprofessional and professional helpers. On the whole, therefore, the research evidence does appear to confirm that non-professional/paraprofessional counsellors are as effective as trained professional therapists in terms of the benefits that their clients gain from counselling.

Although the general trend in these studies does not confirm the prediction that most people would make, that years of professional training should lead to positive advantages, it is necessary to be cautious in interpreting the results. The studies cover a wide range of client groups, including psychiatric patients, schizophrenic people in the community, people in crisis, students with study problems and children with behavioural difficulties. The non-professional helpers have included adult volunteers, parents of children and college students. Modes of treatment have encompassed one-to-one and group counselling, behavioural methods and telephone counselling. So although the general effectiveness of non-professionals has been demonstrated, there are insufficient studies in specific areas to allow the claim that the efficacy of using volunteers for that specific client group has been established. Moreover, when the factors that are associated with effective non-professional counselling are considered, some interesting results emerge. Non-professionals who are more experienced and have received more training achieve better results (Hattie *et al.* 1984). Non-professionals did better with longer-term counselling (over 12 weeks), while professionals were comparatively more effective with short-term work (one to four weeks) (Berman and Norton 1985).

Why do non-professionals, such as volunteer counsellors, achieve such good results? The discussion of this issue has generated a number of suggestions for contributory factors:

- perceived by clients to be more genuine;
- less likely to apply professional labels to clients;
- restrict themselves to straightforward, safe interventions;
- clients will attribute success and progress to self rather than to the expertise of their therapist;
- able to refer difficult cases to professionals;
- limited case-load;
- highly motivated to help;
- may be more likely to come from similar cultural background to client;
- able to give more time to clients.

This list, derived from the writings of Durlak (1979) and Wills (1982), indicates that there are advantages in non-professional status and relative lack of experience that balance the advantages conferred by professional authority, experience and advanced training. There are also disadvantages associated with expertise, such as the danger of burnout due to overwork, and the development of professional distancing or detachment from clients. One possible explanation for the effectiveness of non-professional counsellors may be that they are selected from a pool of naturally talented, untrained listeners in the community. In a unique piece of research, Towbin (1978) placed an advertisement in the personal column of his local paper to seek out non-professional 'confidants'. The entry began, 'Do people confide in you?' Towbin interviewed 17 of those who replied. These people were self-confident and open, and had felt deeply loved as children. With regard to the relationships with those who confided in them, they saw themselves as trustworthy and able to be fully present in the situation.

Perhaps the most detailed piece of research comparing professional and non-professional counsellors is the study at Vanderbilt University carried out by Strupp and Hadley (1979). In this study, male college students seeking counselling were assessed using a standardized personality questionnaire. Those who exhibited a profile characterized by depression, isolation and social anxiety were randomly allocated either to experienced therapists or to college professors without training in counselling who were 'selected on the basis of their reputation for warmth, trustworthiness, and interest in students' (Strupp and Hadley 1979: 1126). A comparison group was formed from prospective clients who were required to wait for treatment. The effectiveness of the counselling (twice weekly, up to 25 hours) was evaluated using standard questionnaires and ratings administered at intake, termination and a one-year follow-up. In addition, sessions were either video- or audio-taped.

Both treatment groups showed more improvement than the control group, but there was no difference in outcome between those clients seen by experienced therapists and those counselled by untrained college professors. The non-professional counsellors proved to be just as helpful as their professional colleagues. However, there were marked differences in the counselling style of the two sets of helpers. The non-professionals were more likely to give advice, discuss issues other than feelings and conflicts, and run out of relevant material to explore (Gomes-Schwartz and Schwartz 1978).

In a detailed examination of counselling carried out by one of the college professors in the study, Strupp (1980c) presents a picture of a professor of statistics who was genuinely interested in his clients, offered high levels of encouragement and acceptance and communicated a sincere belief in their capacity to change for the better. With a client who was ready to try out new behaviours, he proved to be a highly effective therapist. With one of his more difficult clients, a young man who turned out to have deep-rooted difficulties arising from his relationship with his father, therapy broke down because of the counsellor's inability to understand or challenge high levels of client resistance and negative transference. The overall conclusion that can be drawn from this study is that volunteer, non-professional counsellors can achieve a great deal through 'the healing effects of a benign human relationship' (Strupp and Hadley 1979: 1135), but are less well equipped to cope with some of the dilemmas and difficulties that can occur in particular cases.

An important area requiring further research is the relationship between professional and volunteer counsellors. For example, in Strupp and Hadley's (1979) study, the college professors acting as counsellors were all carefully selected by professional therapists, and had the option of passing clients on to the university counselling service. Clearly, professionals are heavily involved in volunteer counselling schemes, through delivering training and supervision, and in taking referrals for clients whose difficulties are beyond the competence of volunteer counsellors to handle.

Unfortunately, little is known about the distinct training and supervision needs or the development of skills and awareness in volunteer counsellors. Another useful area of enquiry concerns the theoretical basis for volunteer counselling. Non-professionals with limited time to attend courses or explore the literature often lack a consistent theoretical orientation, even though they may possess good counselling skills. It is significant that theoretical models employed in training courses for volunteers, such as the Egan (1990) skilled helper model, are broadly integrative and action-oriented rather than exploratory in nature (Culley 1992).

Telephone counselling

In terms of numbers of client contacts made each year, telephone counselling agencies such as Samaritans, Childline, Nightline and Gay Switchboard do much more counselling than any other type of counselling agency. For example, Childline alone answers over 1,000 calls each day. Despite the overwhelming importance of telephone counselling as a means of meeting public needs for emotional support, there has been relatively little effort devoted to theory and research in this area. The task of supplying counselling help over a telephone raises several fundamental questions. In what ways do counselling techniques and approaches need to be modified? Do telephone counsellors have different training and support needs? How much, and in what ways, do users benefit from telephone counselling? Which problems are amenable to telephone counselling and which require ongoing face-to-face contact with a counsellor?

The circumstances of telephone counselling make it difficult to evaluate the benefits that callers may experience. In studies that have asked callers, either at the end of the conversation or at subsequent follow-up, to assess their satisfaction with the service, it has been found that consistently two-thirds or more of clients have reported high levels of satisfaction (Stein and Lambert 1984). The types of counsellor behaviour which are perceived by callers to be helpful include understanding, caring, listening, offering feedback, exhibiting a positive attitude, acceptance, keeping a focus on the problem, and giving suggestions (Slaikeu and Willis 1978; Young 1989). These counsellor behaviours are similar to effective counsellor interventions in face-to-face counselling.

There does, however, appear to be one important process dimension along which telephone counselling differs from face-to-face work. Lester (1974) has suggested that telephone counselling is a situation that increases the positive transference felt by the caller. The faceless helper is readily perceived as an 'ideal', and can be imagined to be anything or anyone the caller needs or wants. Grumet (1979) points out the elements of the telephone interview that contribute to increased intimacy: visual privacy, the speaker's lips being, in a sense, only inches from the listener's ear and a high level of control over the situation. Rosenbaum (1974) has written that 'the ringing of the phone symbolically represents the cry of the infant and there was an immediate response, namely my voice itself being equivalent to the immediate response of the mother.'

One consequence of the positive transference found in telephone counselling would appear to be to make the caller tolerant of counsellor errors. Delfin (1978) recorded the way clients responded to different types of statements made by telephone counsellors. It was found that clients appeared to react positively to counsellor responses that were viewed by trained observers as clichéd or inaccurate.

Zhu *et al.* (1996) describe a telephone counselling service set up in Calfornia to help people to quit smoking. They observed a number of advantages in operating a service of this type by telephone, rather than in more traditional one-to-one or group formats. The telephone contact allowed the counsellor to focus specifically on the needs of the individual client, something that could be difficult in many group-based smoking cessation programmes. Second, they noted, as have other counsellors, that the anonymity of the telephone enabled clients to be very honest, and therefore speeded up the counselling process. Third, they noted that the telephone format lent itself to using a standard counselling protocol, which the counsellor could add to, depending on the initial client. The existence of the protocol or manual was an effective way of ensuring counsellor competence and quality of service. Finally, they felt that the telephone allowed the counsellor to take the initiative much more:

> the telephone makes it possible to conduct proactive counseling. Once a smoker has taken the step of calling for help, all subsequent contacts can be initiated by the counselor. The fact that the counselor makes an appointment for each call and then follows through by calling at the appointed time seems to foster accountability and support. The proactive approach also reduces the attrition rate because the counselor does not share the client's possible ambivalence about following through with the sessions as planned.
>
> (Zhu *et al.* 1996: 94)

This element of proactivity is clearly a major advantage in counselling with smokers, where maintaining motivation to change is a high priority.

Most telephone counselling agencies are staffed by part-time volunteer workers who receive only very limited training and supervision, although there are increasing numbers of commercially run telephone helplines: for example, the California Smokers' Helpline described in the previous paragraph, or lines run by EAP providers. It would appear, from the research evidence already reviewed, that the personal qualities and presence of the counsellor are more important in telephone work than are technical skills. Most clients will have one contact with any individual counsellor, so some of the complexities of other forms of counselling, such as action planning, overcoming resistance to change and building a therapeutic alliance, are not present to the same extent. On the other hand, telephone counsellors need to work quickly, to be flexible and intuitive and to be able to cope with silence. Hoax calls and sex calls draw on skills that are less frequently used in face-to-face counselling. Telephone counsellors are required to enter into the personal worlds of people actually in the middle of crisis, and are thereby exposed to strong emotions. They may become remote participants in suicide. Not only are telephone counsellors involved in a potentially raw and harrowing type of work, they are also less liable to receive feedback on the results of their efforts. Indeed, they may never know whether a caller did commit suicide, or did escape from an abusive family environment. The rate of turnover and burnout in telephone counselling agencies, and the provision of adequate support and supervision, are therefore topics of some concern, which require further study and research.

From the point of view of the caller or client, telephone counselling has two major advantages over face-to-face therapy: access and control. It is easier to pick up a phone and speak directly to a counsellor than it is to make an appointment to visit a counselling agency at some time next week. Telephone counselling therefore has an important preventative function, in offering a service to people who would not submit themselves to the process of applying for other forms of help, or whose difficulties have not reached an advanced stage. Moreover, most people are ambivalent about seeking help for psychological problems. The telephone puts the client in a position of power and control, able to make contact and then terminate as he or she wishes.

Clearly, this section can offer only a brief introduction to the issues associated with telephone counselling. This is a mode of delivery that tends to be highly valued by users, who appreciate its flexibility, anonymity and accessibility. Readers interested in learning more about telephone counselling are recommended to seek out the excellent book by Rosenfield (1997).

Counselling on the Internet

The most recent mode of delivery of counselling to become established is counselling by e-mail. There are counsellors and support groups who advertise their services on the Internet, on a variety of different types of home pages, and it is possible for a client in any country to access a counsellor anywhere in the world, at any time of the day or night. Despite the amazing potential of such a service, there are a number of obvious problems, which have been reviewed by Sampson *et al.* (1997) and Robson and Robson (1998). Is it possible to establish a therapeutic relationship by e-mail? Can confidentiality be safeguarded? Can a counsellor function effectively in the absence of contextual information concerning where someone lives, how old they are etc.? How can unqualified counsellors be prevented from offering services and then exploiting clients?

Many of these difficulties appear to have been resolved by e-mail practitioners. Bloom (1998), for example, describes ways in which ethical standards can be maintained. Murphy and Mitchell (1998) report that the expression of emotion and the establishment of a therapeutic relationship can be made possible by employing a number of writing conventions: for example, regularly recording, in brackets, the emotional state of the writer. King *et al.* (1998) describe how family therapy can be facilitated by e-mail contact when there are family members living apart. Murphy and Mitchell (1998) outline some of the advantages of e-mail counselling:

- there is a permanent record of the whole of the counselling contact (this is useful for the client, and also for the counsellor and counselling supervisor);
- typing is an effective means of 'externalizing the problem' (see Chapter 9);
- the act of writing helps the person to reflect on their experience;
- power imbalances are reduced – the Internet is an intensely egalitarian medium;

- the client can express their feelings in the 'now', they can write e-mail messages when in the middle of a depression or panic attack, rather than waiting for the next counselling session to come round.

Even the briefest of explorations on the Internet will reveal a wide range of e-mail counselling services and chat rooms. The diversity and creativity of uses of the Internet for therapeutic purposes has been documented by Fink (1999).

A small number of research studies have been carried out into applications of therapy on the Internet. Lange *et al.* (2000) evaluated a structured therapeutic intervention for individuals experiencing post-traumatic stress and pathological grief, delivered through the Internet. This intervention required participants to write about traumatic or bereavement events, with limited input from their therapist in the form of feedback. The majority of clients who participated in this study reported highly significant gains at the end of therapy. Celio *et al.* (2000) compared the effectiveness of a psycho-educational programme for eating disorders, available through the Internet or through face-to-face group sessions. They found higher levels of therapeutic gain in the participants who used the Internet. Clearly, these studies need to be replicated, and research needs to be carried out on less structured forms of Internet therapy. However, the studies by Lange *et al.* (2000) and Celio *et al.* (2000) demonstrate that, in principle, Internet therapy can be just as effective as conventional face-to-face working, at least for some clients.

The technology of the Internet has only recently made e-mail counselling and Internet therapy possible. In many respects this mode of counselling appears to have as much potential as telephone counselling, or even more. It is difficult to predict just how it will evolve and develop, but it seems certain that the Internet is due to become a major resource for counsellors and psychotherapists over the next few years, as technology becomes more affordable, accessible and user-friendly.

Reading and writing as therapy

Reading and writing are important components in e-mail therapy. However, counselling based on these forms of communication have been in use for many years, as bibliotherapy and guided writing. The concept of 'bibliotherapy' refers to the therapeutic effect of reading books. In general, there are two categories of book that are used in bibliotherapy. The first category consists of explicit self-help manuals, which are designed to enable people to understand and resolve a particular area of difficulty in their lives. Self-help books will usually contain exercises and suggestions for action, and are therefore often thought of as behavioural in orientation. Other books often employed in bibliotherapy are texts, usually on a psychological topic, that essentially discuss ideas and experiences rather than being explicitly oriented towards behaviour change. These may be originally written for a professional audience, but become taken up by the general public or achieve cult status.

Examples of this second type of bibliotherapy text are *The Road Less Travelled* by Scott Peck (1978) and Alice Miller's (1987) *The Drama of Being a Child*.

The use of self-help manuals and books raises a number of theoretical issues (Craighead *et al.* 1984). Much theory and research in counselling emphasizes the importance of the therapeutic relationship, yet in bibliotherapy there is no direct relationship. Self-help manuals also assume that the same techniques will be effective for all people who experience a particular problem, rather than individualizing the intervention for separate clients. Finally, the suggestions made in self-help books must have a relatively low risk of side-effects.

Starker (1988) carried out a questionnaire survey of psychologists in the USA, asking them about their prescription of self-help books in therapy. Some 69 per cent of these therapists reported that some of their clients had been 'really helped' by such books. More than half of the practitioners at least occasionally recommended self-help books to supplement treatment. Psychodynamic therapists were less likely to use bibliotherapy than were therapists from other orientations. The most popular bibliotherapy texts were in the areas of parenting, assertiveness, personal growth, relationships, sexuality and stress.

Other studies have looked at the effectiveness of bibliotherapy. In one study, Ogles *et al.* (1991) supplied self-help books for coping with loss to 64 people who had recently experienced divorce or the break-up of a relationship. Levels of depression and psychiatric symptoms were assessed before and after reading the book. Clinically significant benefits were reported. It was also found that those readers who initially had high positive expectations that the book would help subsequently showed greater gains, which might imply that a book or self-help manual received on the recommendation of a therapist might be particularly valuable. Some projects have combined the prescription of self-help manuals with telephone counselling, either using a telephone hotline that clients can phone or calling clients at regular intervals to encourage them to use the manual (Orleans *et al.* 1991; Ossip-Klein *et al.* 1991). Although most self-help manuals are written from a cognitive–behavioural perspective, the remarkable *Barefoot Psychoanalyst* booklet (Southgate and Randall 1978) demonstrates that it is possible to employ even Kleinian and Reichian ideas in a self-help mode.

In a review of evaluative studies of self-help manuals, Craighead *et al.* (1984) came to the conclusion that, although totally self-administered manuals may be effective for some people, most clients want or need some additional personal contact with a helper. They also noted that particularly positive results had been obtained with self-help manuals for problem drinking, anxiety control, vocational guidance and study skills problems. The effectiveness of bibliotherapy in other areas, such as obesity, smoking cessation, sexual problems and assertiveness, was difficult to assess because of methodological weaknesses in the studies that had been carried out. Scogin *et al.* (1990), in a more recent review of the literature, largely confirmed these conclusions, and suggested that bibliotherapy appeared to be more effective with older, more highly educated clients.

The results of research would seem to confirm that bibliotherapy can be an effective way of facilitating insight and change in clients, particularly in combination with face-to-face counselling or telephone contact. Cohen (1994) provides some fascinating insights into the meaning of therapeutic reading for clients, and Fuhriman *et al.* (1989) have published a review of the literature on uses of bibliotherapy. Norcross *et al.* (2000) have evaluated the quality of self-help resources available in the USA, using a panel of psychologists. Finch *et al.* (2000) reported positive results following their evaluation of the delivery of self-help materials for controlling anxiety through multimedia (audio- and video-tapes).

The exploration of feelings and experiences through personal writing can also be helpful. Some therapists encourage clients to write on particular topics (e.g. Maultsby 1971; McKinney 1976). Others suggest the use of ongoing diaries or journals, perhaps using structures and techniques developed by Progoff (1975) or Rainer (1980). Lukinsky (1990) has carried out a review of different journal-writing techniques. Additional writing-based modes of counselling intervention include correspondence, poetry writing and autobiography (Greening 1977). The practice of writing letters has played a major role in narrative therapy (see Chapter 9). Lange (1994, 1996) gives some very powerful examples of the use of letter-writing in the resolution of trauma and grief. The basic effectiveness of writing as a therapeutic medium has been convincingly demonstrated in a series of studies by Pennebaker and his colleagues (Pennebaker 1993), in which people who had experienced loss or trauma were asked to do no more than write about their feelings for four or five days, for twenty minutes on each occasion. Even this minimalist intervention produced significant psychological and health benefits.

Group counselling and therapy

Group counselling and therapy represents a major area of theory, research and practice in its own right, and interested readers are recommended to learn more about the topic by consulting some of the major texts in the field (Whitaker 1985; Corey 1990; Forsyth 1990). The aim of the present discussion is to identify some of the possibilities and issues arising from this mode of delivery of counselling help, rather than attempting a comprehensive review of this area of specialization.

There are several parallel historical sources of the origins of group therapy. Early forms of groupwork were pioneered by Moreno with psychodrama, by Lewin through the invention of 'T-groups' and by Bion in his psychoanalytic groups. These various initiatives came together in the late 1940s and early 1950s to form what has become a strong tradition in the various branches of the helping professions. Group-based approaches are used in counselling, psychotherapy, social work and organizational development. The three main theoretical orientations in counselling – psychodynamic, humanistic and cognitive–behavioural – are all represented in distinctive approaches to the theory and practice of working with groups.

The first systematic psychodynamic group theory was formulated by Bion, Foulkes and Jacques, initially during the Second World War through work with psychologically disturbed and traumatized soldiers at the Northfield Hospital in

Birmingham, and later at the Tavistock Institute in London. The key idea in psychodynamic groupwork is its focus on the 'group-as-a-whole'. Bion (1961) argued that, just as individual patients in psychoanalysis exhibit defences against reality, so do groups. He coined the phrase 'basic assumptions' to describe these collective patterns of defence and avoidance in groups. At the heart of a 'basic assumption' is a shared, unconscious belief that the group is acting 'as if' some imaginary state of affairs were true. For example, a group can act 'as if' the leader was all-knowing and all-powerful (dependency), 'as if' the only option in a group was to engage in conflict with others (fight–flight), or 'as if' the main purpose of the group was the formation of two-person friendships or sexual liaisons (pairing). The role of the group leader was similar to that of the analyst in individual psychoanalyst, in saying little and thereby acting as a blank screen on to which members could project their fantasies.

The benefits to be gained from therapy in this kind of group lie in gaining personal insight from participating in a group that was learning to understand issues concerning authority, boundaries, sexuality and aggression, which emerged in the culture of the group-as-a-whole. Whitman and Stock (1958) introduced the notion of the 'group focal conflict' as a way of making sense of the link between group process and individual learning. If the group becomes emotionally engaged in, for instance, the question of whether it is acceptable for members to meet outside of sessions, this issue will resonate in each individual member of the group in so far as it resembles similar issues in their own lives. One member may bring strong feelings about betrayal, another anger about having been controlled by his parents and so on.

The process of a psychodynamic group takes time, and it may be possible to see phases or stages in the life of the group. Bennis and Shepard (1956) have constructed a model that envisages two general stages in the life of a group. The first stage is concerned with issues of control and authority, the second with issues of intimacy and interdependence. During the first stage, group members behave in the group in line with previously learned ways of coping with authority: some may be conformist, others rebellious. In the process of the group as an entity sorting out how it can reconcile these tensions, there is opportunity for individual insight and therapeutic change. The practical implications, in terms of running counselling groups, of these ideas about group dynamics are fully explored in Agazarian and Peters (1981) and Whitaker (1985), and current issues in the theory and application of this approach are discussed in Pines (1983) and Roberts and Pines (1991).

The humanistic approach to group counselling devotes particular attention to ideas of growth and encounter. The main aim of this approach is the personal development or self-actualization of group members, and traditionally there have been two contrasting methodologies employed by practitioners. Some group facilitators utilize a high degree of structure in their groups, providing the group with exercises and tasks to promote exploration and growth. This tradition has its origins in psychodrama and the T-group, or sensitivity training group, movement. The other tradition is to offer very little structure, and for the facilitator to strive to create a group environment characterized by respect, empathy and congruence. This latter tradition is associated with the work of Rogers and the person-centred approach. A central aim in much groupwork informed by humanistic thinking is the creation of a 'cultural island' where people can experiment with different behaviour, share experiences and receive feedback from others in a setting that is outside everyday life and thereby allows greater freedom.

The third of the approaches to group counselling has evolved from the cognitive–behavioural tradition, and is primarily concerned with using the group to foster behavioural change in clients. Examples of this type of groupwork are social skills groups (Trower *et al.* 1978), assertiveness training and short-term groups focused on a specific problem behaviour, such as alcohol abuse, eating or offending. Social skills training groups exhibit many of the key features of the approach. There is a didactic component, with the group leaders supplying teaching and modelling appropriate skills. Group members practise skills through exercises, simulations and role play, and will usually be given homework assignments to encourage generalization of the skill to ordinary life situations. The emphasis is on action and behaviour change rather than reflection and encounter.

These three approaches to working with groups have different aims, along a continuum with insight and personal development at one end and behaviour change at the other. The form of group that is set up will also reflect the needs of clients and the agency or organization within which it takes place. Agazarian and Peters (1981) propose a categorization of helping groups into three levels of challenge, depending on clients' needs. However, organizational factors can also have a bearing on group practice. Psychodynamic, Tavistock-oriented groups and Rogerian encounter groups, for example, will usually need to meet over many hours, to allow the dynamics of the group to develop. If the agency can only afford to allocate ten or twenty hours of staff time to running a group, then a more behaviourally oriented experience will probably be selected.

Most counsellors are initially trained to work with individual clients, and the contrast between one-to-one and group facilitation can present a significant challenge. The interactions that take place in a group are more complex than those occurring between a single client and counsellor. The group facilitator must monitor the relationships between himself or herself and the group members, but also those occurring between group members. The facilitator also needs to have a sense of what is happening to the group as a whole system. The emotional demands, or transference, that the facilitator absorbs from the group may at times be much more intense than in individual counselling. Bennis and Shepard (1956), for example, identify the 'barometric event' in the life of a group as the moment when all group members combine together to reject the authority of the leader. There are case management issues unique to groupwork: for example, designing and forming the group, selecting members, combining group and individual counselling, introducing new members once the group is under way and dealing with the process of people leaving the group (Whitaker 1985). There are distinctive ethical issues arising in groups, mainly concerning the conformity pressure that can be exerted on individuals and the difficulty of maintaining confidentiality

(Lakin 1988). Finally, it is common practice to work with a co-leader or co-facilitator when running a group, as a way of dealing with some of the complexities of the task. There is, therefore, a distinctive knowledge base and set of requirements for effective group leadership. It is unfortunate that very few formal training courses exist to prepare people to be group facilitators. Most practitioners working with groups have acquired their groupwork competence through being members of groups and acting in a co-facilitator role as an assistant or apprentice.

Groups offer a number of ways of helping clients that are not readily available in individual counselling. The group provides an arena in which the client can exhibit a much broader range of interpersonal behaviour than could ever be directly observed in a one-to-one relationship with a counsellor. In individual counselling, a client may tell a male counsellor about how he has problems in communication with women. In a group these problems can be expressed in his relationships with the women in the group. Oatley (1980, 1984) has described this process as the acting out of 'role-themes'. Group counselling, therefore, presents the counsellor with a different quality of information about the client, and different opportunities for immediacy and working with the here-and-now. In groups, moreover, there are chances for clients to help each other through clarification, challenge and support. This is useful not only in that there is more help available, but also in that the client who is able to be helpful to another will benefit in terms of enhanced self-esteem. The group setting can be viewed as akin to a drama, where the interaction between group members is a means of acting out personal and collective issues (McLeod 1984). In this drama, not all participants are on centre stage at the same time. Some will be in the role of audience, but this ability to be able to observe how other people deal with things can in itself be a powerful source of learning.

One of the most fertile lines of research into group counselling and therapy in recent years has developed out of the work of Yalom (1975) in identifying and defining the 'curative' or 'therapeutic' factors in groups. Struck by the complexity of what went on in his groups, Yalom set about reviewing the literature with the aim of bringing together ideas about the factors or processes in groups that help people. He arrived at a set of 12 factors:

- group cohesiveness;
- instillation of hope;
- universality;
- catharsis;
- altruism;
- guidance;
- self-disclosure;
- feedback;
- self-understanding;
- identification;
- family re-enactment;
- existential awareness.

The presence of these factors in a group can be assessed through questionnaire or Q-sort (a kind of structured interview) techniques devised by Yalom and others. Bloch *et al.* (1981) have developed a similar approach based on asking group members at the end of each group session to write briefly about what they found helpful. The 'curative factors' research is of particular interest to many group facilitators because it is grounded in the perceptions of clients regarding what is helpful or otherwise, and because it provides valuable pointers to how the group might be run.

While the work of Yalom (1975) and Bloch *et al.* (1981) focuses on what is helpful in groups, it is also valid to take account of group processes that may be harmful or damaging. In a large-scale, comprehensive study of 20 encounter groups run for students at Stanford University, Lieberman *et al.* (1973) found that around 10 per cent of the people who had participated in the groups could be classified at the end as 'casualties'. Being in the group had caused more harm than good to these people. This piece of evidence stimulated a lively debate in the literature, with some critics claiming that there were aspects of the Stanford study that would exaggerate the casualty estimate. Nevertheless, it is fair to say that the Lieberman *et al.* (1973) research does draw attention to some of the potentially worrying aspects of group approaches. Situations can arise in groups where individual members are put under pressure to self-disclose or take part in an exercise despite their resistance or defences against doing so. The reactions of other members of the group may be destructive rather than constructive: for example, when a group member shares his fears over 'coming out' as gay and is met by a homophobic response from others. The ensuing distress may be hidden or difficult to detect. These are some of the factors that lead group leaders to be careful about selecting people for groups, and are often keen to set up arrangements for providing support outside the group session for group members (e.g. individual counselling). There are also implications for the supervision of group facilitators themselves.

Self-help groups

A great deal of group counselling takes place in self-help groups, which consist of people with similar problems who meet together without the assistance of a professional leader. The appeal of the self-help movement can be seen to rest on two main factors. The first is that self-help groups can be created in the absence of professional resources, and can thereby transcend the budgetary limitations of health and welfare agencies. The second is that people who participate in self-help groups appreciate the experience of talking to others who 'know what it feels like' to have a drink problem, to have lost a child in a road accident or to be a carer of an infirm elderly parent.

The effectiveness of self-help groups for a variety of client groups has been well documented. In the field of alcohol dependence, there is even evidence that

Alcoholics Anonymous is on the whole more effective than individual or group counselling offered by professional experts (Emrick 1981). However, many mental health professionals remain sceptical about the value of self-help groups, and view them as opportunities for socializing rather than as arenas for serious therapeutic work (Salzer *et al.* 1999).

One of the issues that can lead to difficulties in self-help groups is the establishment of an unhelpful or inappropriate group culture. For example, the group may come to be dominated by one or two people who have covert needs not to change, and who create groups where people collude with each other to remain agoraphobic, overweight or problem drinkers. Another difficulty may be that the group does not evolve clear enough boundaries and norms, so that being in the group is experienced as risky rather than as a safe place to share feelings. Antze (1976) has suggested that the most effective self-help groups are those which develop and apply an explicit set of ground rules or an 'ideology'. Women's consciousness-raising groups, for example, can draw upon an extensive literature that details the philosophy and practice of feminist approaches to helping. Alcoholics Anonymous uses a clearly defined 'twelve-step' rulebook.

Professional counsellors may be involved in enabling self-help groups to get started, either through taking a proactive role within their organization or because people in the group seek guidance about where to meet and how to proceed. For example, student counsellors may encourage the formation of self-help groups among mature students or overseas students. Counsellors in hospitals may work with self-help groups of nursing staff suffering from work stress, or of patients with cancer. The relationship between the 'expert' and the group requires sensitive handling, with the counsellor being willing to act as external consultant rather than coming in and taking charge (Robinson 1980). The collection of papers in Powell (1994) represents an invaluable resource for readers wishing to know more about current trends and developments in the use of self-help groups.

Couples counselling

A substantial number of people seek counselling as a couple, because they recognize that their problems are rooted in their relationship rather than being attributable to individual issues. Counselling agencies specifically devoted to working with couples, or with individuals on relationship issues, have been established in many countries. Many of these agencies, like the British National Marriage Guidance Council (Relate), began life as a result of fears about the sanctity of married life, and were in their early years mainly 'marriage saving' organizations. In recent years, however, the realities of changing patterns of marriage and family life have influenced these agencies in the direction of defining their work as being more broadly based in relationship counselling in general.

The field of couples counselling is dominated by two major approaches: psychodynamic and behavioural. Useful comparisons between these styles of working with couples can be found in Paolino and McCrady (1978) and Scarf (1987). The psychodynamic approach aims to help couples gain insight into the unconscious roots of their marital choice, and into the operation of projection and denial in their current relationship. One of the fundamental assumptions of psychodynamic couples counselling is that each partner brings to the relationship a powerful set of ideas about being a spouse and being a parent, which originate in his or her family of origin. Each partner also brings to the relationship a set of interpersonal needs shaped by experience in early childhood. For example, the person whose mother died at a critical age in childhood may have a need for acceptance but a fear of allowing himself to trust. A person who was sexually abused in childhood may express needs for intimacy through sexualized relationships. The job of the counsellor is, just as in individual work, to help the couple to achieve insight into the unconscious roots of their behaviour, and to learn to give expression to feelings that had been repressed.

The psychodynamic counsellor in marital or couples work also brings to the task a set of ideas about relationships. The dynamics of the Oedipal situation, with its triangular configuration of child, same-sex parent and opposite-sex parent, can serve as a template for understanding difficulties currently experienced by the couple, such as husband, wife and wife's mother, or husband, wife and first child. Another triangular pattern in couples work is that consisting of husband, wife and the person with whom one of them is having an affair. Many counsellors find object relations theory (Chapter 4) valuable in disentangling the processes of jealousy, attachment, loss and rivalry that can occur in couples work.

The concepts of marital 'choice' and marital 'fit' help in making sense of the basis for the emotional bond between a couple. According to psychodynamic theory, a couple will choose each other because, at least partially, the unconscious needs of each will be met by the other. So, for example, a man who gets angry may find a partner who is even-tempered. However, this marital fit may become less and less comfortable as one or both of the partners develops in such a way as to claim back the unconscious territory ceded to the other. Some couples are able to renegotiate the basis of their relationship as and when such changes occur. Others are not able to do so, and after some time there is an explosion as the pressure becomes too great and the original pattern of the relationship is torn apart in a crisis of violence, splitting up or conducting an affair. It is often in such crisis that the couple will come for help.

A psychodynamic perspective brings to couples counselling a sophisticated model of personality development. Behind the conflict and dissent projected by many couples who arrive for counselling are fundamental developmental issues. A woman who married at sixteen finds herself experimenting with new partners and nightclubs when her daughter reaches the same age. A man in his midtwenties is terrified by the transition to parenthood; his wife is ready to have a child now. The Educating Rita scenario, where a woman who has missed out on her opportunity to fulfil her potential in the world of study or work, is not uncommon as a source of marital conflict.

The technique of psychodynamic couples work involves the same careful listening and exploration as in individual counselling. Some couples counsellors recommend that the counselling is provided by a pair of counsellors, a man and a woman, to facilitate different types of transference, but this is an option that is only feasible in well resourced counselling centres. On the whole, it is necessary for counsellors working in this way to be more active and interventionist than they might be with individual clients, to keep the focus of the couple on the therapeutic work rather than on acting out arguments in the counselling room. Further information about the theory and practice of psychodynamic work with couples is available in Skynner and Cleese (1983) and Clulow and Mattinson (1989).

The cognitive–behavioural approach to couples counselling is quite different. There is very little theoretical baggage, little exploration of the past and a predominant emphasis on finding pathways to changed behaviour. The central assumption in this approach is that people in an intimate relationship act as a source of positive reinforcement for each other. At the time of first meeting each other, and through courtship, there is usually a high level of positive reinforcement or reward associated with the relationship. Later on, as the couple perhaps live together, work together or bring up children, the opportunities for rewarding contact diminish and the costs of the relationship, the compromise and stress, increase. As a result, the 'reward-cost ratio' reduces, and there is a loss of satisfaction. At the same time, the couple may encounter difficulties in such areas as communication, problem-solving and sexuality.

The remedy for these problems, in a cognitive–behavioural mode, is to apply behavioural principles to initiate change, such as the use of contracts between spouses. Cognitive–behavioural methods have been particularly successful in couples work in the area of sex therapy. Other theoretical perspectives have had only a limited impact on couples work. Some couples counsellors find it valuable to think about couples in terms of family systems models. Greenberg and Johnson (1988) have developed emotionally focused couples therapy (EFT), which takes an experiential approach that is also informed by attachment theory. Johnson *et al.* (1999) provide a useful review and summary of research and practice in this approach.

One of the central issues and debates in couples counselling concerns the decision to work with partners individually, or to see them together as a couple. There are many occasions when this decision is made by the clients, when only one member of the couple is willing to see the counsellor. Even in these circumstances, however, there is an issue about how much to involve the absent partner or spouse (Bennun 1985).

This discussion of couples counselling can do no more than introduce some of the central themes running through theory and practice in this field. The reader interested in finding out more about this type of counselling is recommended to consult Dryden (1985a), Scarf (1987), Freeman (1990) and Hooper and Dryden (1991).

Conclusions

This review of alternative modes of providing counselling help for people in need indicates that there is a wide range of formats that can be used. There is scope for counsellors and counselling agencies to be creative in their use of resources. It would appear that the approaches described in this chapter have the potential to reach people who might be reluctant to seek out conventional one-to-one counselling or therapy. Each of these approaches, however, requires training and awareness based in an acknowledgement that they demand different skills and methods from counsellors. There are also underlying issues concerning the lack of theory and research into formats such as telephone and e-mail counselling and the use of reading and writing.

Chapter summary

- Previous chapters have generally assumed that counselling is carried out in a face-to-face, one-to-one format. The aim of this section of the book is to explore the contribution of other modes of delivery of counselling.

- Time limits can be used to increase the effectiveness and accessibility of counselling. Some counsellors have found that even single sessions can be helpful for some clients.

- There is substantial evidence that non-professional, volunteer counsellors can, in the appropriate circumstances, be as effective as highly trained professional therapists.

- Counselling at a distance, using the telephone or e-mail, is widely used and has the advantage of giving the client or user more control over the timing and length of the counselling session.

- Bibliotherapy (reading self-help books) and writing (for instance, keeping a journal) have been shown to be valuable adjuncts to face-to-face counselling.

- There are many problems for which group, couple or family counselling is more helpful than traditional individual work.

- Some people report that self-help groups or networks provide them with more safety and affirmation than they would receive from professional therapists, and also give them the opportunity of themselves adopting a helping role.

- It is necessary for counsellors to be aware of the range of modes of delivery that are available, and to be ready to adapt counselling service provision to meet the requirements of clients who may prefer not to meet on a regular one-to-one basis.

Topics for reflection and discussion

1 Take any one face-to-face counselling agency. How could the service offered by that agency be enhanced by introducing some of the other modes of delivery of counselling discussed in this chapter?

2 Do different modes of counselling help (e.g. groups, bibliotherapy, telephone counselling, individual face-to-face work) produce different outcomes in clients? Is the learning process for clients the same whatever type of intervention is used, or are there change elements unique to each format?

3 Discuss the extent to which alternatives to traditional individual counselling represent attempts to deal with power issues in the helper–helpee relationship. How successful are these alternative approaches in empowering clients?

4 You have been asked to run a training course intended to enable counsellors who work with individual clients in face-to-face settings to undertake telephone counselling, groupwork, or couples counselling. What would you include in the course?

5 Reflect on the experience of reading a self-help book, preferably one that you consulted some time ago. Why did you decide to use the book? Did you discuss it with anyone else, or merely work through it on your own? What impact, either in the short-term or of a more lasting nature, has the book made on you? What was it about the book that you felt was most and least helpful?

6 Do alternative modes of delivery present new ethical dilemmas? What might these be, and how could they be addressed?

7 An important theme running through the counselling litarature, and certainly something that is apparent to many experienced counsellors, is the different ways in which men and women use counselling. Are there particular modes of delivery that are likely to be more attractive or appropriate for men or for women?

8 Do you keep a diary or journal? What are the therapeutic benefits you get from it? In a group, or through discussion with other people you know, build up a picture of how journal-writing helps, and also of its limitations as a form of counselling.

Key terms and concepts

2 + 1 model	Internet
barometric event	journal writing
basic assumptions	non-professional counsellors
bibliotherapy	role-themes
brief therapy	self-help groups
couples counselling	self-help manuals
curative factors	social skills groups
e-mail therapy	telephone counselling
group counselling	time-limited counselling
group focal conflict	

Suggested further reading

This chapter deals with a diverse set of topics, and readers interested in learning more are recommended to follow up sources referenced in specific sections of the chapter. It is perhaps worth noting that at present there does not seem to be any unified model of the advantages and disadvantages of differing modes of delivery of counselling.

A book that provides valuable information, analysis and discussion of books, films and Internet resources is the Norcross *et al.* (2000): *Authoritative Guide to Self-help Resources in Mental Health*. There are also regular reviews of self-help resources in the *Counselling and Psychotherapy Journal*, published by the British Association for Counselling and Psychotherapy (BACP).

18 The role of research in counselling and therapy

Introduction

A great deal of research has been carried out into counselling and psychotherapy, particularly in the past 30 years. The existence of this body of research may seem to imply a paradox: the counselling relationship is private and confidential, while the research process involves external access to information. But it is just this hidden or secret dimension to counselling that has made research so important. Good research should, ultimately, allow the development of a better understanding of events and processes that are experienced by individual counsellors and clients, and therefore enable practitioners to learn from each other. Research can also promote a critical and questioning attitude in practitioners, and help them to improve the quality of service offered to clients. Finally, research is an international activity, and research journals are read by a world audience. Participation in such an international community of scholars helps counsellors to achieve a broader perspective on their work. The role of research in the field of counselling is complex and multifaceted.

Some of the factors that can motivate people to conduct research in this field are:

- testing the validity of theory;
- evaluating the effectiveness of different approaches or techniques;
- demonstrating to a third-party funding agency (e.g. government department, insurance company, private company) the cost-effectiveness of counselling or psychotherapy;
- enabling an individual practitioner to monitor his or her work;
- allowing individual practitioners to resolve 'burning questions';
- to get a masters degree or PhD;
- letting colleagues know about particularly interesting cases or innovations;
- establishing the academic credibility of counselling as a subject taught in universities;
- enhancing the professional status of counsellors in relation to other professional groups.

It can be seen that there are many different reasons for doing research. Some research studies are inspired by the practical concerns of practitioners. Other studies emerge from the interests of groups of people working together on a set of ideas or theory. Yet other studies are set up to meet external demands. Often, there can be more than one factor motivating a study.

Within the social sciences in general there has been considerable debate over the issue of what constitutes valid research. This debate has generated an enormous literature, which in part can be characterized as an argument between advocates of quantitative approaches and those who would favour qualitative methods of research. Quantitative research involves careful measurement of variables, with the researcher taking a detached, objective role. Qualitative research, by contrast, has as its aim the description and interpretation of what things mean to people, and to achieve this the researcher must develop a relationship with the research informants or co-participants. The differences between the quantitative and qualitative research traditions are displayed in Table 18.1. Both approaches to research have a lot to offer in the field of counselling and psychotherapy research, and they can be combined effectively (see, for example, Hill 1989; Stiles *et al.* 1990; Stiles 1991). Nevertheless, the split between qualitative and quantitative approaches has been significant for the field as a whole, and remains a source of conflict and tension (Neimeyer and Resnikoff 1982). The disciplines that have had the strongest professional and institutional influence on counselling have been psychology and psychiatry. These are both disciplines that have been associated

Table 18.1   The contrast between qualitative and quantitative approaches to research

Qualitative	Quantitative
Description and interpretation of meanings	Measurement and analysis of variables
Quality of relationship between researcher and informants important	Aims for neutral, objective relationship
Necessity for self-awareness and reflexivity in researcher	Aims for value-free researcher
Uses interviews, participant observation, diaries	Uses tests, rating scales, questionnaires
Researchers interpret data	Statistical analysis of data
Strongest in sociology, social anthropology, theology and the arts	Strongest in psychiatry and psychology
Many similar ideas to psychoanalysis and humanistic therapies	Many similar ideas to behavioural and cognitive therapies

with 'hard', quantitative research. On the other hand, the philosophy of the person and values of the qualitative research tradition are very close to those of most counselling and psychotherapy practitioners (McLeod 2001, 2002b; Frommer and Rennie 2001).

The breadth and scope of research in counselling and psychotherapy is immense. Beutler and Crago (1991), identified 41 separate research programmes in eight different countries. It would be impossible to attempt meaningful discussion of all aspects of the field in this chapter. Particular attention will therefore be given to three types of research study that have been of central importance: outcome studies, process studies and case studies. Readers interested in pursuing other aspects of research in counselling are recommended to consult Bergin and Garfield (1994), which contains an authoritative review of research findings on a wide range of topics. Reviews of current research can also be found in the *Annual Review of Psychology* (Gelso and Fassinger 1990; Goldfried *et al.* 1990). Readers interested in learning more about research design should consult Barker *et al.* (1994), McLeod (1999c, 2003) or Parry and Watts (1995), each of which examines in detail the issues involved in planning and implementing different kinds of research study. More advanced discussions of methodological issues can be found in Aveline and Shapiro (1995) and Bergin and Garfield (1994).

Outcome and evaluation research

Outcome and evaluation studies have the primary aim of finding out how much a particular counselling or therapy intervention has helped or benefited the client.

The earliest systematic research into counselling and therapy concentrated entirely on this issue. In the 1930s and 1940s, several studies were carried out into the effects of psychoanalysis. The results of these investigations suggested that, overall, around two-thirds of the psychoanalytic patients followed up improved, with one-third remaining the same or deteriorating after treatment.

These findings appeared highly encouraging for psychoanalysis and, by implication, for other forms of the 'talking cure'. However, in 1952 Eysenck published a devastating critique of this early research. Eysenck pointed out that studies of neurotic people who had not received therapy but had been followed up over a period of time also produced an improvement rate of around 60 per cent. He argued that psychoanalysis could not be considered effective if it produced the same amount of benefit as no therapy at all. Eysenck suggested that there existed a process of 'spontaneous remission', by which psychological problems gradually became less severe over time owing to non-professional sources of help in the community or because the person had learned to deal with a crisis situation that had provoked a breakdown.

The psychotherapy world reacted strongly to Eysenck's critique, but the main effect of his attack was to force researchers to design more adequate studies. In particular, it became accepted that outcome studies should include a control group of clients who do not receive treatment, so that the impact of the counselling or therapy can be compared with the levels of improvement brought about by spontaneous remission. The usual method of creating a comparison group of this kind has been to use a 'waiting list' group of clients who have applied for therapy but who are not offered their first appointment for some time, and are assessed at the beginning and end of that period to detect changes occurring in the absence of professional help.

A good example of outcome research is the Sloane *et al.* (1975) study, which compared the effectiveness of psychodynamic therapy with that of a behavioural approach. The study was carried out in a university psychiatric outpatient clinic, and applicants for therapy were screened to exclude those too disturbed to benefit or who required other forms of help. Ninety-four clients were randomly allocated to behaviour therapy, psychodynamic therapy or a waiting list group. The people on the waiting list were promised therapy in four months, and were regularly contacted by telephone. Clients paid for therapy on a sliding scale, and received an average of 14 sessions over four months. Before the beginning of therapy, each client was interviewed and administered a battery of tests. In addition, clients identified three target symptoms, and rated the current intensity of each symptom. Ratings of the level of adjustment were also made by the interviewer and a friend or relative of the client. These measures were repeated at the end of the therapy, and at one-year and two-year follow-up. Every fifth session was tape-recorded and rated on process measures of therapist qualities, such as empathy, congruence and acceptance. Speech patterns of therapists and clients were also analysed from these tapes.

The results of the Sloane *et al.* (1975) study indicated that, overall, more than 80 per cent of clients improved or recovered at the end of therapy, with these gains being maintained at follow-up. Both treatment groups improved more than the waiting list group. The quality of the therapist–client relationship was strongly associated with outcome, for both types of therapy. Behaviour therapists were rated on the whole as being more congruent, empathic and accepting than the psychodynamic therapists. There was no evidence for symptom substitution.

Many other studies have been carried out along similar lines to the Sloane *et al.* investigation, and most have arrived at similar conclusions regarding the relative effectiveness of different approaches. With the aim of determining whether the apparent equivalence of approaches was confirmed across the research literature as a whole, several literature reviews have been conducted (Luborsky *et al.* 1975). The most comprehensive and systematic of these literature reviews was the 'meta-analysis' carried out by Smith *et al.* (1980). Meta-analysis involves calculating the average amount of client change reported for each approach in each separate study, then adding up these change scores to give an overall estimate how much benefit a particular approach (such as psychoanalysis, client-centred therapy or behaviour therapy) yields over a set of studies comprising a large number of clients. In their report, Smith *et al.* (1980) conclude that they could find no consistent evidence that any one approach to counselling or therapy was any more effective than any other. Although this conclusion has been disputed by some writers (for example, Rachman and Eysenck), who continue to assert the superiority of behavioural methods over all others, there is now general agreement within counselling that different approaches are equally effective, and that counselling or therapy is significantly more beneficial than no treatment.

The story of the development of outcome research might suggest that there is little more to be learned about the effectiveness of counselling and therapy. This is far from being the case. One of the important and significant aspects of studies such as Sloane *et al.* (1975) is that they are difficult to organize and expensive to implement, and as a result have tended to be carried out in 'elite' therapy institutions, such as university psychiatry or counselling clinics. The therapists in these studies are usually experienced, highly trained and conducting therapy in accordance with 'treatment manuals' that tightly specify how they should work with their clients, as a means of monitoring their adherence to the therapeutic model being evaluated. All these factors mean that controlled studies of the *efficacy* of therapy (i.e. how well it does under ideal circumstances) can often be criticized as unrepresentative of everyday practice. There is a need, therefore, for more studies to be carried out into the effectiveness of the work done in agencies that are less well resourced and that may well serve clients who present a wider range of problems or have less counselling sophistication. Relatively few naturalistic studies of this kind have been carried out, and those that have been completed have not been able to use control groups or to follow up large numbers of clients.

Another gap in the outcome research literature arises from the lack of specificity of many studies. Paul (1967: 111) has made the point that research should be able to identify 'what treatment, by whom, is most effective for this individual with that specific problem, and under which set of circumstances.' At the present time, research evidence is not precise enough to answer these questions.

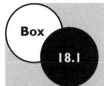

Box 18.1

The researcher's own therapeutic allegiance: a factor in outcome research

The concept of the 'experimenter effect' is familiar to anyone who has studied psychology. In a psychology experiment carried out in a laboratory, the expectations of the researcher, in relation to what he or she believes the experiment will show, can be subtly communicated to subjects, and influence their responses to stimuli or tasks (Rosnow and Rosenthal 1997). The impact of 'experimenter effects' is to skew results so that the experimenter's hypothesis will be confirmed. As a result, laboratory researchers are extremely careful to standardize what they say to subjects, how they respond to questions etc. Does the experimenter effect apply in psychotherapy outcome studies? It seems unlikely that it would, because therapy is a 'real-world' situation, and clients have strong motivation to get what they need from therapy, rather than trying to 'second guess' the expectations of the person or team running the study. The well known therapy researcher Lester Luborsky, along with a group of colleagues (Luborsky *et al.* 1999), decided to try to find out the extent to which researchers' expectations and biases might be operating in psychotherapy outcome research. They reviewed 29 studies in which the relative effectiveness of two forms of therapy was compared. They then carried out a painstaking analysis of what was known about the therapeutic allegiances of the researchers who conducted the studies. They found a significant positive relationship between allegiance and outcome. For example, in a study carried out by a psychodynamic researcher, comparing cognitive–behavioural and psychodynamic therapy, it would be virtually certain that the results would favour the psychodynamic approach. In a study carried out by a researcher positively oriented towards cognitive–behavioural, CBT would be likely to emerge as the most effective therapy. Luborsky *et al.* (1999) argue that researcher allegiances can seriously distort the findings of outcome studies, and make a number of suggestions for eliminating this possible source of bias.

The outcome and evaluation studies mentioned so far have all comprised the assessment of change in groups of clients receiving counselling or therapy from a number of practitioners. It has already been noted that these studies are complex, expensive and difficult to arrange. Several writers have advocated, by contrast, that it is desirable for individual counsellors to monitor or evaluate their own work in a systematic way. Barlow *et al.* (1984) have called for counsellors and therapists to adopt the role of 'scientist-practitioner' and to use research routinely to help them reflect on their work with clients. They point out that research instruments such as psychological tests or questionnaires may provide clinicians with invaluable information that can be used in therapy. The use of the scientist-practitioner approach normally involves gathering baseline information on the level of problem behaviour in a client, before the commencement of counselling, then continuing to monitor the level of that behaviour throughout counselling and then at follow-up. An essential element of this kind of research is clarity about the goals and objectives of treatment, which has made it more popular with the action-oriented behavioural and cognitive–behavioural approaches rather than the more insight-oriented psychodynamic and humanistic approaches.

Examples of some of the many different types of assessment tool that can be used in outcome and evaluation studies are:

- Self-monitoring of problem behaviours (e.g. eating, smoking, occurrence of paranoid or obsessional thoughts) using a notebook or diary.
- Self-ratings of moods or feelings. Examples: rating scales to assess level or intensity of tension, pain, sadness or anxiety.
- Questionnaire measures of general psychological adjustment. Examples: General Health Questionnaire (GHQ), Minnesota Multiphasic Personality Inventory (MMPI), Clinical Outcome Routine Evaluation (CORE).
- Questionnaire measures of specific variables. Examples: Beck Depression Inventory (BDI), Spielberger State-Trait Anxiety Inventory.
- Client-defined variables. Examples: Personal Questionnaire (Phillips 1986), client ratings of target symptoms (Sloane *et al.* 1975).
- Client satisfaction questionnaires (Berger 1983).
- Direct observation of the client. Examples: counting frequency of stuttering or negative self-statements during counselling session, observation of social skills performance during role play, measuring sleep duration of insomniacs.
- Post-therapy ratings of outcome from client, therapist or friends and family members of the client.

A very wide range of measures and techniques has been employed, reflecting a diversity of aims, client groups and theoretical rationales. Further information on these techniques can be found in Nelson (1981), Lambert *et al.* (1983) and Bowling (1991).

A final type of research that can be carried out in the area of evaluation concerns the assessment of quality of service provided by a counselling agency or organization. In this kind of study, many other factors are investigated in addition to the impact of counselling on individual clients. Maxwell (1984) has suggested six criteria for evaluating service provision: relevance/appropriateness, equity, accessibility, acceptability, effectiveness and efficiency. The question of acceptability introduces the perceptions and judgements of consumers of the service. The issue of efficiency brings in considerations of cost-effectiveness and cost–benefit analysis (McGrath and Lowson 1986; Mangen 1988; Tolley and Rowland 1995; Miller and Magruder 1999). For example, in the area of counselling in primary care (family medicine), studies have examined the relative costs and benefits of counselling as compared with routine GP care (Friedli *et al.* 2000). Parry (1992) has carried out a thorough review of the different methods and approaches that have been employed in service evaluation. She concludes that, in the interests of the many potential clients who might need therapeutic help but are denied it because of

Box 18.2

The CORE outcome measure – an important new evaluation tool

There are significant difficulties faced by practitioners seeking to evaluate the outcomes of their own practice. There are a large number of different questionnaires that have been used by previous researchers, and it can be hard to decide which is the most appropriate. In addition, the majority of outcome scales are copyrighted by publishing companies, with the result that they may be expensive to purchase, or access to them may be restricted to people who have completed specific training courses. As a response to these barriers to research, the Mental Health Foundation in Britain commissioned a team at the Psychological Therapies Research Centre, University of Leeds, to produce a new outcome questionnaire that embodied 'best practice' from existing scales, and could be made widely available to practitioners and researchers. The CORE (Clinical Outcomes Routine Evaluation) scale is a 34-item self-report questionnaire that measures client distress in terms of four dimensions: well-being, symptoms, functioning and risk (Mellor-Clark et al. 1999; Evans et al. 2000). It can be copied without charge, and a low-cost software package is available to facilitate data analysis. The CORE questionnaire has been widely adopted by counselling, psychotherapy and clinical psychology service providers. One of the aims of the CORE group is to collect naturalistic data on the progress of therapy with clients in a range of settings, and to build up a data set and norms that will enable 'benchmarking' of standards of effectiveness in different settings (Barkham et al. 2001; Mellor-Clark et al. 2001).

inefficient or inaccessible services, 'unmonitored practice is no longer defensible' (Parry 1992: 14).

Process research

Whereas outcome studies mainly examine the difference in the client before and after counselling, without looking at what actually happens during sessions, process studies take the opposite approach. In a process study, the researcher is attempting to identify or measure the therapeutic elements that are associated with change. Following the conclusions of reviewers such as Luborsky et al. (1975) and Smith et al. (1980) that counselling and psychotherapy is, on the whole, effective, the energies of many researchers have focused more on questions of process. Having established that therapy 'works', they are seeking to learn how it works.

Studies of process from a client-centred perspective

The client-centred approach to counselling and therapy developed by Rogers and his colleagues (Rogers 1942, 1951, 1961) has been characterized by a consistent emphasis on the process of change in clients, and the process of the client–counsellor relationship. Rogers and his colleagues at the University of Ohio (1940–5) were the first investigators to make recordings of therapy sessions, and the first to study process in a systematic way. The earliest studies within the client-centred framework explored changes in the ways that clients made references to self at different points in their therapy, and the 'directiveness' of counsellor statements, by analysing transcripts of counselling sessions (Snyder 1945; Seeman 1949). Other studies from this period focused on the experience of the client in counselling, for example through the exploration of diaries kept by clients (Lipkin 1948; Rogers 1951).

In a major piece of research carried out at the University of Chicago, Rogers and Dymond (1954) and their colleagues examined different aspects of change in clients' self-concepts during and after therapy. Self-acceptance, a key concept in Rogerian theory, was assessed using a technique known as the 'Q-sort', in which clients arrange a set of self-statements to describe 'how I see myself now' and 'how I would ideally like to be' (the difference between actual and ideal self being taken as a measure of self-acceptance). Taking a group of 29 clients, they administered the Q-sort, and a range of other tests, at a pre-therapy interview, regularly throughout therapy and at follow-up. Results showed that changes in self-perception were closely associated with good outcomes. One of the main achievements of this phase of research was to demonstrate that research could be undertaken that was phenomenological, respecting the experience of the client, yet at the same time rigorous and quantitative. For the first time, an important aspect of process, change in self-acceptance, had been measured and tracked across a course of therapy. The Rogers and Dymond (1954) report was also noteworthy in containing a systematic analysis of failure and attrition cases.

Towards the end of his stay at Chicago, Rogers integrated the fruits of research and practice in client-centred therapy and counselling into two key papers, one on the 'necessary and sufficient' relationship conditions of empathy, congruence and unconditional positive regard (Rogers 1957), the other on the process of change in therapy (Rogers 1961: Chapter 7). These papers are discussed more fully in Chapter 6. In their next major piece of research, Rogers and his collaborators set out to test these ideas in a study of client-centred therapy with hospitalized schizophrenic patients (Rogers *et al.* 1967). Rating scales were devised to measure the levels of therapists' unconditional positive regard, congruence, empathy and experiencing level observed in recordings of sessions with clients. Barrett-Lennard developed a questionnaire, the Relationship Inventory, to assess these 'core conditions' as perceived by clients, counsellors or external observers. Although the results of the schizophrenia study were ambiguous, largely due to the difficulty in achieving any degree of substantial change in disturbed clients, the Relationship Inventory and the various rating scales developed during the project have remained standard instruments in process studies (Greenberg and Pinsof 1986).

The research team around Rogers split up after he moved to California following the Wisconsin study, but the hypothesis of Rogers that the 'core conditions' of adequate levels of acceptance, empathy and congruence, once perceived by the client, represented not only necessary but also sufficient conditions for positive personality change in clients received a great deal of further study. Reviews of the work on this important theoretical claim (Patterson 1984; Watson 1984; Cramer 1992) suggest that Rogers was largely correct, even though there have been severe practical difficulties in adequately testing his model. Currently the most active research within the client-centred process model has been that concerned with 'depth of experiencing' in clients and counsellors.

The process research carried out by Rogers and his collaborators has made a significant contribution to the field, for a number of reasons. First, it demonstrated that the phenomena and processes of the counselling relationship were not something mysterious and elusive, but could appropriately and effectively be opened up for external scrutiny and research. Second, it represents what is probably still the most successful attempt in counselling and therapy to use research to test theoretical assumptions and evolve new concepts and models. Third, it supplied an example of the fruitful integration of research with practice, since all the people taking part in the research were practitioners as well as researchers. Finally, Rogers and his colleagues showed that it was possible and profitable to give the client a voice, and to explore the experience and perceptions of the client in therapy.

Studies of process from a psychodynamic perspective

Psychodynamic theory contains a wealth of ideas about the process of therapy. For example, the counselling process in psychodynamic work is likely to include instances of free association, interpretation, transference, counter-transference, analysis of dream and fantasy material, and episodes of resistance. Research that could help practitioners to understand more fully the mode of operation of these factors would be of substantial practical utility. However, research that is consistent with the basic philosophical assumptions of psychoanalysis presents a number of distinctive methodological problems. From a psychoanalytic point of view, the meaning of a client statement, or interaction between client and counsellor, can only be understood in context, and can only be interpreted by someone competent in psychodynamic methods. It is insufficient, therefore, to conduct process studies that rely on tape-recordings of segments of an interview, or to use a standardized rating scale administered by research assistants, as in other process research. Psychodynamic process studies are carried out by expert, trained practitioners, and are based on the investigation of whole cases.

One of the best examples of psychodynamic process research is to be found in the use of the core conflictual relationship theme (CCRT) method developed by Luborsky *et al.* (1986) as a technique for exploring transference. In this technique, a number of expert judges first read a transcript of an entire session. They are then asked to focus on episodes in the transcript where the client makes reference to relationships, and to arrive at a statement of three components of each episode: the wishes or intentions of the client towards the other person; the responses of the other person; and the response of the client himself or herself. Taken together, these components yield a picture of the kind of conflictual relationships, or transference patterns, experienced by the client in his or her life. The formulations of different judges are checked against each other to arrive at a consensus view.

The CCRT method has been used to investigate a number of hypotheses regarding the transference process in therapy. For example, Luborsky *et al.* (1986) compared the transference themes displayed towards other people and those expressed in relation to the therapist. Results provided strong evidence to confirm the Freudian assumption that the transference relationship with the therapist is a reflection of the way the client characteristically relates to people in everyday life. Crits-Christoph *et al.* (1988), also using the CCRT technique, showed that accuracy of interpretation, assessed by comparing CCRT formulations with therapist interpretations of relationship issues, was positively correlated with client benefit in therapy. Similar studies, in which expert readers have been employed to identify psychodynamic themes in session transcripts, have been carried out by Malan (1976), Silberschatz *et al.* (1986) and Kachele (1992).

The 'events paradigm'

Process-oriented research carried out within the client-centred perspective has become less fashionable in recent years, owing to a variety of factors that resulted in diminishing interest in the person-centred approach in the USA. Currently, researchers exploring therapy process are more likely to be working within what has become known as the 'events paradigm' (Rice and Greenberg 1984a). This approach concentrates on finding change events within therapy sessions, and identifying the therapist's or counsellor's actions or strategies that enabled these events to occur. This is quite different from the client-centred view of process, which focuses not so much on discrete events as on general conditions or the creation of a therapeutic environment.

One of the key figures in events research has been Robert Elliott, based at the University of Toledo in Ohio, who has adapted the interpersonal process recall (IPR) method (see Chapter 13) for use in research (Kagan *et al.* 1963; Kagan 1984). In this approach, a video- or audio-tape of a therapy session is played back to either the therapist or the client, with the aim of stimulating their recall of the experience of being in the session, and collecting information about their evaluation or perception of events within it. Early studies using this method looked at process elements, such as client perceptions of what is helpful and dimensions of therapist intentions (Elliott 1986). However, later research has focused on identifying and analysing actual events, with the aim of describing 'the nature and unfolding of particular types of significant change event' (Elliott 1986: 507). Another approach to studying significant events has been evolved by Mahrer *et al.* (1987). In these studies, Mahrer and his co-researchers listened to audio-tapes of therapy sessions in order to identify 'good moments' where the client showed movement, progress, process improvement or change. The distribution of these moments over the session, and the therapist's behaviour that appeared to facilitate good moments, have been explored. In yet another series of studies of events, Rice and Greenberg have looked at the tasks the therapist must carry out in order to facilitate change in different circumstances.

These studies of key events in the counselling process are all recent or still in progress, and it is too early to tell where they will lead. It is worth noting, however, that unlike the Rogerian studies, which were explicitly informed by theory, the events studies are largely non-theoretical in nature, and so far at least have been devoted to describing change events and processes rather than to developing a theoretical framework for understanding them.

The process as experienced by the client

One of the fundamental issues in research into counselling and psychotherapy concerns the question of who is observing what is happening. Rogers and Dymond (1954) pointed out that different conclusions on process and outcome could be reached depending on whether the perspective of the client, the therapist or an external observer was taken. Most research has relied on either the perspective of the therapist or that of an external observer, since to involve the client could intrude on his or her therapy, or cause distress. Most studies that have involved collecting data from clients have used standardized questionnaires or rating scales. In these studies, the experience of the client is filtered through categories and dimensions imposed by the researcher. There have been relatively few studies into the client's experience of the process of counselling as defined by the client (McLeod 1990).

Maluccio (1979) carried out intensive interviews with clients who had completed counselling. This piece of research illustrates the difficulties inherent in inviting people to talk retrospectively about the whole of their counselling experience. The informants interviewed by Maluccio produced large amounts of complex material that was difficult to interpret. Maluccio found that, on the whole, clients experienced their counselling as having passed through discrete stages. Another significant finding from this study was that clients often attributed changes in psychological and emotional well-being not to anything that was happening with their therapist, but to external events such as getting a job or moving house. This finding indicates one of the important differences between the client's and therapist's experience of counselling. The client experiences counselling as one facet of a life that may encompass many other relationships; the counsellor has no first-hand involvement with these other relationships and is limited to his or her experience of the actual sessions. The two types of experience therefore have quite different horizons.

The work of Maluccio (1979), and of other researchers such as Timms and Blampied (1985), has looked at the experience of the client over an extended time, which may span several months of counselling. Clearly, a lot can happen over the course of therapy, and this kind of research will not be able to pick up the fine-grained detail of what the client experiences on a moment-by-moment basis. In a series of studies, Rennie (1990) focused on the experiences of clients in single sessions. Rennie used a version of the Interpersonal Process Recall technique (Kagan 1984) to enable clients to relive or re-experience what they thought and felt during the session. An audio- or video-tape is made of the session, and as soon as possible after the end of the session the client reviews the tape in the presence of the researcher, stopping the tape whenever he or she remembers what was being experienced at that point. The researcher then sorts through the transcript of the inquiry interview to identify themes and categories of experience.

The client experience studies carried out by Rennie and his associates (Angus and Rennie 1988, 1989; Rennie 1990, 1992) have opened up for research an area of the counselling process that is normally inaccessible to counsellors, and have produced some striking results. One of the conclusions Rennie arrives at is that clients are responding to the counsellor on different levels. They may be telling the counsellor about some event in their life, but underneath that narrative may be considering whether or not to take the risk of talking about some previously secret piece of information. They may agree with an interpretation or intervention from the counsellor, while knowing that it is inaccurate or inappropriate.

Exploration of the world of the client, as pioneered by Maluccio (1979) and Rennie (1990), requires sensitive, ethically aware contact between researcher and client, as well as much painstaking work categorizing and interpreting themes derived from interview transcripts. The aim of this type of work is to produce 'grounded theory' (Glaser and Strauss 1967; Glaser 1978; Rennie *et al.* 1988), or generalizations and models that are demonstrably rooted in actual experience rather than imposed by the researcher. Rennie (2002) has reviewed the substantial contribution that studies of this kind have made to appreciating the extent to which the client is an active, reflexive participant in therapy.

Case studies

The final approach to research to be considered is the case study. Traditionally, case studies have been the primary vehicle for research and theory construction in psychodynamic approaches to counselling and psychotherapy. Many of the cases published by Freud, for example, have been widely debated and reinterpreted by other therapists and theorists and represent some of the basic building blocks of psychoanalytic knowledge and training. It would be unusual to find a trained and experienced psychodynamic counsellor or therapist who had not carefully read the cases of Dora (Freud 1901/1979), the Rat Man (Freud 1909/1979) or Schreber (Freud 1910/1979).

From a research point of view, however, there are many methodological issues raised by the manner in which Freud and his colleagues carried out case studies. Freud saw several patients each day, and wrote up notes of his consultations in the evening. Some of these notes were subsequently worked up as papers presented to conferences or published in books and journals. At each stage of this process of producing a case study, there was no possible check on the validity of the conclusions reached by Freud, or on any bias in his recollection or selection of evidence. Critics of Freudian theory such as Eysenck can, as a result, put forward the argument that Freud distorted the evidence to fit his theories. There is little that psychoanalysts can do to counter this charge, given the way the case studies were carried out.

The dilemma that is apparent in this debate over case studies is that, on the one hand, detailed examination of individual cases is invaluable for the development of theory and practice, but, on the other hand, finding a rigorous and unbiased way of observing and analysing individual cases is difficult. The construction of methods for systematic case study research has been a recurrent concern for researchers in the field of personality for many years (Murray 1938; DeWaele and Harré 1976; Rabin *et al.* 1981, 1990). Within the field of counselling and psychotherapy research, there have been three distinctive approaches to systematic case study investigations, reflecting the influence of behavioural, psychoanalytic and integrationist thinking.

Behavioural case studies are sometimes known as '$N = 1$' studies, and are associated with the 'scientist-practitioner' model discussed earlier in this chapter. These case studies concentrate on tracking changes in a limited number of key variables predicted to change as a result of counselling: for example, amount of time spent studying or score on a depression inventory. The principal aim of the study is to demonstrate the effectiveness of a particular type of intervention with a particular category of client, and broader process issues are not usually considered. Barlow and Hersen (1986), Barlow *et al.* (1984) and Morley (1989) provide a useful account of the procedures involved in this type of case study.

Psychoanalytic or psychodynamic systematic case study research is quite different in its aims and methods. The intention in this type of study is to replicate the capacity of the therapist or counsellor to arrive at a formulation of the unconscious dynamics of a case, but using a team of researchers to avoid the bias or distortion that could arise from relying solely on the judgement of the therapist himself or herself. Examples of this kind of study are given in the earlier section on psychodynamically oriented process research.

Case study research from a more integrationist orientation has been conducted by Hill (1989), who carried out a series of eight case studies of brief therapy with depressed women clients, with the aim of identifying the relative contribution to outcome made by non-specific factors and therapist techniques. This study is unique in the exhaustive and comprehensive information that was gathered on each case (see Table 18.2). A number of other case studies have recently been published in which cases of special interest have been selected from large-scale extensive investigations. For example, Strupp (1980a, b, c, d) presented four

Table 18.2   The intensive case study method

Pre-therapy, at termination and follow-up

Minnesota Multiphasic Personality Inventory
Hopkins Symptom Checklist (SCL-90-R)
Tennessee Self-Concept Scale
Target complaints
Hamilton Depression and Anxiety Scales
Interview

After each session researchers rated

Counsellor verbal response modes
Counsellor activity level
Client reactions during session
Client level of experiencing

Client and therapist completed

Post-session questionnaire or interview
Working Alliance Inventory
Session Evaluation Questionnaire

Client and therapist separately

Watched video of session to recall feelings and rate helpfulness of each counsellor statement

Note: Information gathered on each case by Hill (1989).

comparative pairs (one success and one failure case) of cases drawn from Strupp and Hadley (1979). A similar approach, choosing representative cases for detailed analysis, has been taken by Barkham (1989), Barkham and Shapiro (1990a) and Stiles *et al.* (1992). The distinguishing features of these integrationist case studies have been the combination of qualitative and quantitative data, the use of group comparisons as well as intensive analysis of individual cases and the adoption of a trans-theoretical perspective (see Good and Watts 1989).

Having explored some of the methods and techniques that researchers have used in studying process and outcome in counselling and psychotherapy, we can now discuss some of the underlying issues and debates in this area.

Ethical dilemmas in counselling research

The purpose of counselling is to help people, or to empower them to help themselves, and the process of counselling can often require disclosure of confidential information, experience of painful memories and emotions, and the taking of decisions that affect other people. Counsellors take great care to ensure that this sometimes risky process does not bring harm to clients. It is easy to see that research into counselling introduces additional possibilities of harm. Research may lead to information about clients being disclosed, painful feelings being restimulated or the relationship of trust with the therapist being damaged.

Most forms of counselling research contain ethical dangers. For example, in outcome studies in which there is a control group of 'waiting list' clients, the decision is taken to offer help immediately to some people, but to withhold it from others. In studies of new types of counselling intervention, clients may be exposed to therapy that is harmful. If the researcher contacts the client to request that he or she takes part in the study, the knowledge that this person is a client is transmitted beyond the counsellor or agency. If the counsellor asks the client to participate in a study, the client may be unwilling to do so but may nevertheless comply for fear of antagonizing someone upon whom he or she feels emotionally dependent. In studies where former clients are interviewed about their experience of therapy, the interview itself may awaken a need for further counselling.

For these reasons, counselling and psychotherapy research studies carried out in government agencies, such as hospitals or social services departments, or submitted for funding to charitable trusts will normally need to be assessed by ethical committees, and will need to document in detail their procedures for dealing with ethical issues. However, all research should be designed with ethical considerations in mind, and research training for counsellors and therapists should emphasize awareness of ethical factors.

The problem of reactivity

Connected with ethical issues, but also distinct from them, is the problem of reactivity in counselling research. Reactivity occurs when the research process interferes with or alters what is happening in counselling. In the study by Hill (1989), for example, clients were asked to participate in a great many activities that involved self-exploration and learning (such as watching a video of the therapy session) but were not part of the actual therapy. Hill (1989: 330) acknowledged that 'the research probably influenced the results of all eight cases . . . the [research activities] were probably therapeutic in and of themselves.' In the Sheffield Psychotherapy Research Project (Firth *et al.* 1986), which compared the effectiveness of brief 'exploratory' or 'prescriptive' therapy, all questionnaires and other data gathering were carried out by a clinic secretary or by interviewers who were independent of the therapists. However, although they knew this, many clients wrote comments on the questionnaires as though they expected their counsellors to read them. Some also admitted sabotaging the research, by completing questionnaires at random, when feeling hostile towards their counsellor.

Another dimension of reactivity is the effect of the research on the counsellor. Many counsellors can be anxious about exposing their work to colleagues, and perhaps risking criticism or censure. In many process studies, transcripts of therapy sessions may be read and rated by a number of judges. Research has shown that there can be wide differences between counsellors and therapists in their levels of effectiveness, so there is a basis in reality for these fears. In some studies, the research design requires counsellors or therapists to provide standardized treatment, and to conform to the guidelines of a treatment manual, or to offer clients a limited number of sessions. There may be times when these constraints conflict with the professional judgement of the counsellor regarding how to proceed or how many sessions the client might need.

The relevance of research for practitioners

While there may be a lot of research being carried out, the relevance or utility of that research for practitioners has been extensively questioned. In a study of psychotherapists in the USA, even though 88 per cent of a sample of 279 therapists had PhDs (which meant that they had received extensive training in research, and had carried out research), 24 per cent reported that they never read articles or books about research, and 45 per cent reported that none of the research articles they read had a significant influence on the way they worked with clients (Morrow-Bradley and Elliott 1986). It would seem highly probable that groups of practitioners in countries with less academically oriented training programmes, or therapists trained in independent institutes rather than in university departments, would report even lower levels of research utilization.

The perceived lack of relevance of much counselling and psychotherapy research has been labelled the 'researcher–practitioner gap', and has been attributed to the differing roles and professional interests and values of researchers and clinicians. Counsellors and therapists typically view research as not giving enough information about the methods of treatment used, looking at groups of clients rather than individuals and assessing differences between treatment groups on the basis of statistical rather than practical or clinical criteria for significance (Cohen *et al.* 1986; Morrow-Bradley and Elliott 1986). In addition, many practitioners may not have access to research libraries or facilities.

Behind the research–practice gap can be detected even more fundamental issues regarding the nature of knowledge about counselling. As mentioned at the beginning of this chapter, counselling and therapy research has been largely dominated by quantitative methods and assumptions borrowed from mainstream psychology and psychiatry, even though many of the ideas and assumptions of qualitative research are probably more congenial to counsellors. This situation will not be resolved until counselling achieves a more explicitly interdisciplinary approach, rather than continuing to define itself as a subdiscipline of psychology.

Box
18.3

The debate over evidence-based practice

The most significant issue to have emerged within counselling and psychotherapy research in recent years has focused on the question of which types of therapy are supported by research evidence, and which are not. Professional associations and government bodies in North America and Europe have sought to restrict therapeutic training and practice only to those approaches that are 'evidence-based' or (in North America) 'empirically validated' in terms of quantitative, 'trials'. There are several important questions linked to this debate:

- Are 'controlled', quantitative studies the best, or the only way to evaluate the effectiveness of therapy?
- How adequately do controlled trials reflect everyday therapeutic practice?
- Does the lack of positive research evidence mean that an approach to therapy is invalid, or merely that those who practice it do not have access to the resources necessary to carry out rigorous research?
- Should clients be given a choice of which kind of therapist they see, regardless of the research evidence?
- How important, in the context of this debate, is the research evidence that suggests that the quality of relationship between client and therapist is a better predictor of good outcome than is the type of therapy being offered?

In a social and political climate in which all forms of medical, nursing and social care are required to be 'evidence-based', it is surely reasonable that counselling and psychotherapy should be fully accountable. But the decisions that are taken will affect both therapists' livelihoods and clients' choices, and represent a crucial test of the trustworthiness and value of the research that has been carried out. Good sources of further reading around this critical issue are the book edited by Rowland and Goss (2000), and the special issue of *Psychotherapy Research* edited by Elliott (1998).

Another fundamental issue concerns the integration of research with theory and practice. For example, during the period spanning 1941 to *c.*1965, client-centred counselling and therapy was centred on a group of people headed by Rogers who were all active in seeing clients, teaching students, carrying out research and developing theory. The integration of these activities gave their research a high degree of coherence and impact. In more recent times, there has been a greater fragmentation of professional roles and fewer opportunities to create that kind of research environment.

The relationship between theory and research

One of the distinctive trends apparent in the counselling and psychotherapy research literature over the past 20 years has been the increased reluctance of researchers to engage with theoretical issues. In 1967 and 1968, 69 per cent of therapy research articles published in the *Journal of Consulting and Clinical Psychology* included a theoretical rationale, but this proportion had fallen to 31 per cent in 1987–8 (Omer and Dar 1992). This state of affairs can be explained in different ways. It could be that the popularity of integrationist approaches has undermined the relevance of established theoretical models in the eyes of researchers. Alternatively, it could be that the pressure of cutbacks in welfare and health funding in Europe and the USA during this period has temporarily concentrated attention on practical issues of cost-effectiveness at the expense of rather more abstract theoretical speculations.

The image of the person in therapy research

To return to some of the themes and issues introduced in Chapter 1, it can be argued that most research into counselling and therapy draws upon a medical/biological image of the person. Counselling or therapy is regarded as 'treatment' that is administered to the client, just as a drug is administered to a patient in hospital. The various dimensions of the counselling process, such as empathy or interpretation, can be seen as ingredients of the drug, and process research becomes a search for the best blend of ingredients. Howard *et al.* (1986) have written about the 'dose–effect relationship', meaning the link between the number of sessions (dose) and client improvement. Stiles and Shapiro (1989) have criticized what they call the 'abuse of the drug metaphor' in research. They argue that counselling and therapy involve active, intentional participation on the part of the client rather than passive and automatic responding to ingestion of a drug. The ingredients of therapy, such as empathic reflection, are not fixed and inert, but consist of meanings negotiated between people. These are essential aspects of therapy that do not fit a drug model. Stiles and Shapiro (1989) observe further that even if the drug metaphor is accepted, its use in therapy research is less subtle than in pharmacological research. In studies of real drugs, it is not assumed that 'more is better': some drugs are most effective in small doses, or within certain parameters. Similar effects may well apply in counselling and therapy. For example, a little self-disclosure on the part of the counsellor may be beneficial, but a lot just gets in the way.

The kinds of issues raised by Stiles and Shapiro (1989) have contributed to the need felt by many in the field of counselling and therapy research to construct research informed by alternative metaphors and images of the person.

Chapter summary

- Over the past 30 years, research has been instrumental in clarifying the main elements of the helpful counselling relationship, and in establishing counselling as a profession.

- Outcome research looks at the effectiveness of counselling. Various strategies have been developed for overcoming the ethical and practical issues involved in assessing the benefits of counselling.

- Process research focuses on the factors that contribute to good outcomes in counselling.

- Several different approaches to process research have evolved: client-centred, psychodynamic, analysis of significant change events and studies of the client's experience. These methods have led to new understandings of what happens during counselling.

- Ever since the early work of Freud, case studies have represented an important source of evidence for counsellors. Recent developments in case study methodology mean that it is possible to carry out rigorous, systematic case studies.

- The purpose of counselling is to help clients, and it is essential that research does not intrude on the counselling process in such a way that it will damage the client–counsellor relationship. Counselling researchers operate within a stringent ethical code, which emphasizes the need for informed consent from clients at all stages in a research study.

- One of the underlying problems in counselling research is *reactivity* – the extent to which the research investigation has an effect on the actual counselling. There are times when research can have the effect of increasing the effectiveness of counselling.

- Despite the increasing volume and quality of counselling research that is being produced, there is evidence that counsellors do not read research articles, and do not regard their practice as being influenced by research findings. The existence of the *research–practice gap* is a cause for concern.

- Other problematic issues in counselling research are the relative abandonment of theoretical topics by researchers and the use in research of models of the person, and research techniques, derived from psychiatry and medicine.

Topics for reflection and discussion

1 Imagine that a counselling agency (for example, a student counselling service in a college, an employee counselling unit, a Relate branch) had asked you to carry out a study of how much benefit their clients gained from counselling. What would you do? How much would it cost them? How much person time would it require? What ethical issues would need to be considered? How would these ethical issues be dealt with in the design of your study?

2 What research would you like to see carried out? List three research questions that would be of particular interest to you. Consider how you would investigate these questions from both a qualitative and a quantitative perspective.

3 How relevant is counselling research for you in your work as a counsellor, or how relevant do you think it might be in your future counselling career? In what ways do you see research positively influencing your practice, or in what ways could you see it possibly leading to confusion and poor practice?

4 Read a research article published in one of the research journals. What are the strengths and weaknesses of this particular study? Does the author arrive at conclusions that are fully justified by the evidence, or can you think of other plausible interpretations of the data that the author has not taken into account? How valuable is this piece of research in terms of informing or guiding counselling practice?

Key terms and concepts

case study
core conflictual relationship theme
cost-effectiveness
ethical issues in research
events paradigm
grounded theory
meta-analysis
N = 1 studies
outcome and evaluation studies

process studies
Q-sort
qualitative methods
quantitative methods
reactivity
research–practice gap
scientist-practitioner
spontaneous remission

Suggested further reading

The authoritative guide to all matters concerning research into counselling and psychotherapy is Bergin and Garfield (1994). This is a large and intimidating handbook. Possibly no one alive has read it cover-to-cover. However, it is a book that richly repays sampling. My own books on research (McLeod 1999c, 2001, 2003) offer expanded accounts of all of the topics introduced in this chapter. The book by Toukmanian and Rennie (1992) was recommended in Chapter 13, but is recommended again here as an accessible source of interesting examples of qualitative process research.

There are several research journals in counselling. The most consistent source of good quality research articles is the *Journal of Counseling Psychology*. The majority of the work it publishes is quantitative, but the proportion of qualitative pieces is increasing. *Counselling and Psychotherapy Research* is a journal that is seeking to create a tradition of reflexive, qualitative, practitioner-oriented research.

19 The skills and qualities of the effective counsellor

Introduction

In previous chapters, some fundamental questions were asked about the theory and practice of counselling. Ultimately, though, counselling is an activity carried out by people. Theoretical insights or research findings can only be expressed through the behaviour of counsellors. The aim of this chapter is to explore the skills and qualities associated with effective counselling.

Much attention has been given in the counselling and psychotherapy literature to the notion of counselling skills. Writers such as Ivey, Carkhuff and Egan (see Larson 1984) have attempted to identify a set of core skills that are necessary for effective counselling, and that can be acquired through systematic training. Ivey, for example, has broken down the work of the counsellor into a set of microskills (see Chapter 20). There are, however, serious limitations to the concept of skill in the context of understanding the activities of counsellors and psychotherapists. The idea of 'skill' was first developed to make sense of fairly simple, short time-scale, observable sequences of behaviour in workers performing simple manual tasks: for example, on an assembly line. The aim of an analysis of skilled performance is to break down the actions of a person into simple sequences that can be learned and mastered in isolation from each other. This approach can be seen in the Ivey model.

It can be argued that this way of looking at the task of the counsellor is inappropriate, for three reasons. The first is that many of the essential abilities of the counsellor refer to internal, unobservable processes. For example, a good counsellor is someone who is aware of how she feels in the presence of the client, or who anticipates the future consequences in the family system of an intervention that she plans to initiate with a client. Neither of these counsellor actions is easily understood in terms of observable skills. The second problem of the skills approach lies in the fact that it would appear that one of the differences between truly effective and less able counsellors is that the former are able to see their own actions, and those of the client, in the context of the total meaning of the relationship. Therefore, the 'skilfulness' of an intervention can rarely be assessed by dissecting it into smaller and smaller micro-elements. Finally, it can be argued that personal qualities, such as genuineness or presence, are at least as important as skills.

For these reasons it is desirable to find an alternative to the skills approach to understanding counsellor behaviour. A more useful concept would appear to be to adopt the much broader idea of competence, which refers to any skill or quality exhibited by a competent performer in a specific occupation. In recent years there has been an increasing amount of research interest devoted to identifying the competencies associated with success in the counselling and psychotherapy. This is an area of research that is very much in progress, and there exist competing models of counsellor competence. For example, Crouch (1992) suggests that there are four main areas of skills development: counsellor awareness, personal work, theoretical understanding and casework skills. Larson *et al.* (1992) have constructed a model that breaks down counsellor competence (which they term 'counsellor self-efficacy') into five areas: micro-skills, process, dealing with difficult client behaviours, cultural competence and awareness of values. Beutler *et al.* (1986), in a review of the literature, identified several categories of 'therapist variables' that had been studied in relation to competence: personality, emotional well-being, attitudes and values, relationship attitudes (e.g. empathy, warmth, congruence), social influence attributes (e.g. expertness, trustworthiness, attraction, credibility and persuasiveness), expectations, professional background, intervention style and mastery of technical procedures and theoretical rationale. For the purpose of this chapter, subsequent discussion is structured around consideration of a composite model consisting of seven distinct competence areas:

1 *Interpersonal skills.* Competent counsellors are able to demonstrate appropriate listening, communicating, empathy, presence, awareness of non-verbal

communication, sensitivity to voice quality, responsiveness to expressions of emotion, turn-taking, structuring time, use of language.

2 *Personal beliefs and attitudes.* Capacity to accept others, belief in the potential for change, awareness of ethical and moral choices. Sensitivity to values held by client and self.

3 *Conceptual ability.* Ability to understand and assess the client's problems, to anticipate future consequences of actions, to make sense of immediate process in terms of a wider conceptual scheme, to remember information about the client. Cognitive flexibility. Skill in problem-solving.

4 *Personal 'soundness'.* Absence of personal needs or irrational beliefs that are destructive to counselling relationships, self-confidence, capacity to tolerate strong or uncomfortable feelings in relation to clients, secure personal boundaries, ability to be a client. Absence of social prejudice, ethnocentrism and authoritarianism.

5 *Mastery of technique.* Knowledge of when and how to carry out specific interventions, ability to assess effectiveness of interventions, understanding of rationale behind techniques, possession of a sufficiently wide repertoire of Interventions.

6 *Ability to understand and work within social systems.* Including awareness of the family and work relationships of the client, the impact of the agency on the client, the capacity to use support networks and supervision. Sensitivity to the social worlds of clients who may be from a different gender, ethnic, sexual orientation or age group.

7 *Openness to learning and inquiry.* A capacity to be curious about clients' backgrounds and problems. Being open to new knowledge. Using research to inform practice.

Interpersonal skill

Being able to form a productive relationship with a client, to establish rapport or contact, is emphasized by all approaches to counselling. The original analysis of this area of competence in terms of skills led counselling trainers such as Ivey to recommend that counsellors practise listening and reflecting skills. From the broader perspective of a competency analysis, the 'therapeutic alliance' model (Bordin 1979) emphasizes three of the elements central to the formation of a good working relationship with a client: the creation of an emotional bond between client and counsellor; the achievement of agreement over the goals of counselling; and a shared understanding of the tasks to be performed to fulfil these goals.

The therapeutic alliance model provides a general framework for understanding the interpersonal competencies required in effective counselling. Other theorists have drawn attention to dimensions of interpersonal relating that contribute to the process of forming an alliance. Rogers (1957), for example, has proposed that facilitative therapeutic relationship are those in which the counsellor can provide the 'core conditions' of empathy, congruence and acceptance (see Chapter 6).

Box

19.1

Are all counsellors equally effective?

Most research into the effectiveness of counselling and psychotherapy has looked at the overall, or average, effectiveness of a group of therapists participating in a research study. Seldom do researchers publish an analysis of the differential success rates on individual therapists. Sometimes this may be because the number of clients seen by each counsellor is small, so that differences in success rates might be due to random allocation of one or two 'good' clients to one counsellor, and one or two 'difficult' clients to another. However, there are also political and even ethical barriers to research into individual success rates: who would volunteer to be a counsellor in such a study? Despite these problems, there have been a number of studies that have looked at the relative effectiveness of individual counsellors and therapists.

McLellan et al. (1988) analysed the relative effectiveness of four counsellors employed on a subtance abuse rehabilitation research project, and found marked and consistent differences in outcome. The clients of one counsellor showed significant decreases in drug use, arrest rates and unemployment. The clients seen by another counsellor, by contrast, reported higher drug use and criminality, despite the fact that their training, level of experience, supervision and client profiles were equivalent. From examining the notes and records kept by each of the counsellors in the study, McLellan et al. (1988) concluded that the more effective counsellors were those who were more highly motivated, concerned about clients and well organized, and who tended to anticipate future problems rather than merely reacting to crises.

Blatt et al. (1996) carried out a similar study, this time in the area of psychotherapy for people suffering from depression. The 28 therapists participating in this study could be placed at all points across a range of effectiveness rates. The clients seen by the most successful therapists reported clinically significant improvements; the clients seen by the least successful practitioners reported equally large levels of clinical detrioration. The more successful therapists also had a much higher percentage of clients completing therapy. The main differences between the more successful and less successful groups of therapists were that the former adopted a more psychological (rather than biological) perspective on depression, and were much better at forming a warm, empathic relationship with their clients. There was also a tendency for the more effective therapists to be female.

It needs to be kept in mind that these studies reflect the work of highly experienced, well trained and supervised counsellors and therapists participating in elite research projects. One might reasonably expect higher levels of quality control in such circumstances than would be found in normal everyday clinical practice. Presumably the variability in counsellor effectiveness is even higher in everyday practice. The results reported by McLellan et al. (1988) and Blatt et al. (1996) are not aberrant: all the published studies that have looked at individual differences in counsellor effectiveness have come up with similar results (Luborsky et al. 1997; Elkin 1999). The implication is that counsellor skills and qualities make a big difference. For a client seeking counselling, the choice of counsellor is a crucial decision.

Hobson (1985) has suggested that the bond between counsellor and client grows from the creation of a shared 'feeling language', a way of talking together that allows expression of the feelings of the client. Rice (1974) has carried out considerable research into the importance of the voice quality of the therapist or counsellor.

Relationships between people are profoundly influenced by general factors, such as social class, age, ethnicity and gender. While it is difficult to generalize about the effect on the counselling relationship of any of these variables, it does seem sensible to conclude that one of the important relationship competencies for a counsellor is that he or she should be aware of the significance of these demographic characteristics, and be able to adjust his or her style or approach accordingly.

Personal beliefs and attitudes

Since the examination by Halmos (1965) of the 'faith of the counsellors', there has been a lively interest in the idea that all effective counsellors might possess similar belief systems or ways of making sense of the world. The assumption is that counsellors are able to help people because they see the client's problems in a particular way, and that a helper who took a different perspective might hinder the growth or learning of the client.

The most coherent attempt to identify the beliefs and attitudes associated with effectiveness in counselling has been made by Combs (1986). In a series of 14 studies, using not only counsellors but also members of other human service professions such as clergy and teachers, Combs and Soper (1963) and Combs (1986) found that more effective helpers in these professions were more likely to view the world from a basically person-centred perspective.

The studies conducted by Combs (1986) have all been firmly based in a client-centred or person-centred orientation, and one of the limitations of his work has been that he restricted himself only to testing the importance of 'person-centred' attitudes. It could be that there is a wider set of beliefs that can be shown to be held by effective counsellors. But the work done by Combs (1986) is especially relevant in contributing to an understanding of the decisions by many people in professions such as nursing, social work and the ministry to change career and enter counselling: the beliefs and attitudes described by Combs may in some circumstances conflict with the practices of these other professions.

Competence in the area of personal beliefs and attitudes consists not only of having certain ways of seeing the world, but also of having accurate self-awareness regarding them. Clients may well possess quite different sets of beliefs and attitudes, and may even on occasion dispute the legitimacy of what they perceive to be the way the counsellor views things. To be able to handle these situations a counsellor needs to be able to stand back from her own philosophical position in order to let the client know she is capable of accepting his contrasting perspective. Many training courses, therefore, include work on 'values clarification', and this issue is also common in supervision.

Conceptual ability

A great deal of what happens in counselling is about understanding. Clients come to see a counsellor because they have exhausted their own capacity to make sense of what is happening, or to decide what to do about it. Many clients expect their counsellor to tell them what is happening or advise them what to do, and are disappointed when the counsellor suggests that it would be better for the client to arrive at his own understanding and decisions. Nevertheless, counsellors need to be able to work with clients in these areas of difficulty, and therefore need to be competent at thinking about what is happening.

There has been very little research on the conceptual or cognitive abilities of counsellors. In a review of the literature, Beutler *et al.* (1986) found no relationship between the academic competence of counsellors, as measured by their performance on an undergraduate degree, and their success on a training course. This is not a surprising result, since just through being graduates all of the counsellors would have demonstrated a basic intellectual competence adequate for the role of counsellor. But it does confirm the widely held view that high academic achievement does not correlate with high counselling efficacy. Whiteley *et al.* (1967) investigated differences in levels of cognitive flexibility in counsellors on a training course, and found a strong association between flexibility and overall counselling competence. Shaw and Dobson (1988) have suggested that 'clinical memory', the capacity to remember information conveyed by the client, constitutes a key cognitive competency. Although the notion of 'clinical memory' makes sense at an intuitive level, there is as yet no research that has looked at the part it plays in counselling. Martin *et al.* (1989) found that more experienced counsellors viewed clients from the basis of a more cognitively complex construct system.

In the absence of research studies into the abilities of effective counsellors, it is instructive to look at the results of studies of effective managers, a field where considerable research has been carried out. Klemp and McClelland (1986) carried out research into the competencies exhibited by effective managers in a number of different organizations, and found that a set of common, or 'generic', competencies tended to be identifiable in all successful managers. One of the main results of this study was clear evidence that more effective managers have a better capacity to conceptualize problems.

Personal 'soundness'

In contrast to the paucity of research into cognitive or conceptual competencies, there is a much more substantial research basis for any discussion of the significance of personality factors and general mental health as variables associated with counselling effectiveness. These studies have concentrated on two main issues: identifying the personality characteristics of effective therapists, and assessing the value of personal therapy for practitioners. Much of the work in this area has been carried out with the aim of giving weight to a critique of skills or technique-oriented approaches. The spirit behind these studies is captured by McConnaughy (1987: 304) in her statement that

> the actual techniques employed by the therapists are of lesser importance than the unique character and personality of the therapists themselves. Therapists select techniques and theories because of who they are as persons: the therapy strategies are manifestations of the therapist's personality. The therapist as a person is the instrument of primary influence in the therapy enterprise. A corollary of this principle is that the more a therapist accepts and values himself, or herself, the more effective he or she will be in helping clients come to know and appreciate themselves.

Numerous studies have explored the impact of the personality of the counsellor on counselling outcomes. It can be argued that the whole area of personality research is problematic, in that personality traits as measured by questionnaires tend to demonstrate low correlations with actual behaviour in all studies (see Mischel 1968 for a fuller discussion of this debate). Nevertheless, there would seem to be reliable evidence that good counsellors are people who exhibit higher levels of general emotional adjustment and a greater capacity for self-disclosure. It should be noted that personality variables that do not appear to be associated with counselling success include introversion–extraversion and dominance–submissiveness. Other studies have explored the possibility that the similarities or differences between counsellor and client personality traits might be associated with outcome. This work has been reviewed by Beutler *et al.* (1986), who found no consistent relationship between client–counsellor similarity and outcome. Many counsellor training courses advocate personal therapy for trainees as a means of ensuring personal growth in the direction of adjustment and openness. There is some evidence that personal therapy enhances the subsequent professional effectiveness of counsellors and psychotherapists by giving a reliable basis for the confident and appropriate 'use of self' (Baldwin 1987) in relationships with clients.

Personal therapy represents a unique means of learning about the therapeutic process, that it gives insight into the role of client and, finally, that it contributes to a general heightening of self-awareness in the trainee. There are, however, some fundamental difficulties that are raised by the practice of personal therapy for trainees. First, the client is required to attend, rather than depending on voluntary participation. Second, if the trainee becomes deeply caught up in therapeutic work, it may diminish her own emotional availability for her clients. Third, in some training institutes the personal therapist is a member of the training staff, and not only reports on the progress of the trainee in therapy, but, if the trainee completes the programme, will then subsequently become a colleague of the person who was a client. These practices are less prevalent now than they were in the past, but introduce unusual external pressures that may inhibit the benefits to be gained from the therapy. There are, therefore, reasons to expect personal therapy to be associated with greater counsellor competence, but also reasons to expect the reverse. Studies of personal therapy reflect this balance of views. Although, for example, Buckley *et al.* (1981) found that 90 per cent of the therapists in their sample reported that personal therapy had made a positive contribution to their personal and professional development, Norcross *et al.* (1988b) found that 21 per cent felt that, for them, personal therapy had been harmful in some way. Peebles (1980) reported that personal therapy was associated with higher levels of empathy, congruence and acceptance in therapists, while Garfield and Bergin (1971) concluded from a small-scale study that the therapists who had not received personal therapy were more effective than those who had. In an important recent study of psychoanalytic psychotherapists in Sweden, Sandell *et al.* (2000) were able to compare the personal characteristics and training, supervision and person therapy profiles of therapists who were found to be either more or less clinically effective in their work with clients. This study discovered that the *less* effective therapists reported having had *more* personal therapy than their more effective colleagues. Sandell *et al.* (2000) interpreted this result as suggesting a possibility that therapists who feel that they are not doing very well with their clients may enter person therapy as a means of enhancing their sensitivity and performance.

Surveys in the USA have suggested that around three-quarters of therapists have received at least one course of personal therapy (Norcross *et al.* 1988a). There is, therefore, a high level of professional commitment to this practice. Evidence is not available concerning the incidence of personal therapy in counsellors. With non-professional counsellors, in particular, the financial and emotional cost of personal therapy might be more difficult to justify in the light of lower caseloads and generally more limited training. None of the research evidence that is currently available addresses issues related to *how many* sessions of personal therapy should be recommended or required for either trainees or practitioners. There is also a lack of evidence concerning the consequences of *when* such therapy might take place (before, during or after training). At present, the personal therapy requirements stipulated by professional associations and licensing bodies are based on custom and practice and clinical wisdom, rather than on research evidence. Given that personal therapy is such a potentially important element of training and continuing professional development in counsellors, and also because it is so costly, the absence of research-informed policy-making is unfortunate.

Mastery of technique

There has been a substantial movement over the past few years to identify counsellor competence as primarily a matter of mastery of technique. There is some evidence that practitioners who claim to use different approaches to counselling may work with clients in an identical manner, and that there can be huge

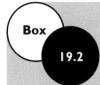

Box

19.2

How does personal therapy affect a therapist's practice?

The debate over the role of personal therapy in counselling and psychotherapy training, and the maintenance of good practice, has been hampered by the quality of the evidence that has been available. The position on personal therapy adopted by many therapists and trainers tends to be based largely on their personal experience of whether therapy has been helpful for them individually, or for colleagues they have known. This kind of 'testimonial' evidence is important, but can never be grounded in systematic analysis or sampling. The research evidence is largely derived from questionnaire surveys of therapists, which ask about their use of personal therapy and attitude to it. However, questionnaire surveys are unable to explore the *meaning* of an event or experience with any depth or complexity. In recognition of these issues, Macran et al. (1999) conducted in-depth interviews with seven experienced therapists in Britain, representing a variety of approaches (psychodynamic, person-centred, body-oriented, eclectic). Their research sought to combine the authentic testimony of participants with a process of rigorous analysis of what these informants had to say.

These interviews generated a substantial list of ways in which personal therapy had affected day-to-day practice for these therapists. Three main themes were identified in the analysis of this interview material: *orienting to the therapist (humanity, power, boundaries), orienting to the client (trust, respect, patience)* and *listening with the third ear.* The report by Macran et al. (1999) provides a detailed account of these findings, illustrated by quotes from the interviews. These therapists described many examples of the effect of personal therapy on their awareness and practice:

> I think that some therapists . . . find it very difficult to understand that somebody can exhibit severe physical pain when it might actually be about something else. Because to be absolutely honest with you, I'd never have believed it if it hadn't happened to me.

> Have a much greater trust in being able to use the transference . . . and the significance of it . . . I don't think I understood until I understood the way I transferred myself and what I experienced onto my therapist.

> The point of getting therapy yourself is to actually remind you that you are a human being and your client is a human being, and the only difference between you is the roles that you're in in this particular interaction.

> I think what a lot of my therapy has helped me to do is to just be more ordinary in some way with other people. It's like . . . I don't have to put on a face so much or a mask or a professional role, do you know what I mean? It's like I . . . can trust in me.

I think a client picks up, a client knows how far you've gone. At the unconscious level, they know if you're the kind of person who can take their rage, take their hostility, take their seductiveness . . . Unless you've been in the position of knowing about your own seductiveness, your own rage, your own hatred and whatever, it's quite difficult to sit with certain kinds of clients who will stir in you those sorts of feelings.

I've been embroiled sexually with a couple of clients. Not in the sense of actually breaking the boundaries, but it was getting rather sort of hot and steamy and uncomfortable . . . I was getting confused . . . wasn't really able to step back and see the wood for the trees . . . [Therapy] helped me be true about what was mine and what was theirs and to actually process my own feelings and my own needs on my own and not try to get my needs met in therapy.

Macran et al. (1999) suggest that therapists *translate* their experiences as clients into the 'language' of their practice. In doing this, they use observations of their personal experience (self as client) but also observations they have made of how their therapist operated. It was clear that interviewees were not merely imitating or modelling themselves on their therapists – they learned as much from negative examples as from positive ones. An important source of learning was to figure out how to avoid making the mistakes with their own clients that their therapists had made with them.

One of the intriguing aspects of this study lies in what was *not* said by these therapists. There was little sense in what was reported in the Macran et al. (1999) paper that any of these people had entered therapy in order to resolve troublesome and distressing 'problems in living'. There did not appear to be any comments around a theme of learning from personal therapy about how to resolve or live with a problem (depression, panic attacks, eating disorder, surviving abuse etc.) of the type presented by clients in everyday therapy (rather than 'personal' therapy). Macran et al. (1999) present a picture of personal therapy as a profoundly instructive and helpful learning experience, which contributes greatly to an improved awareness of the process of therapy and the role and experience of both client and therapist. But their study also implies that there is a difference between 'personal' therapy and 'everyday' therapy. The latter is typically focused more on surviving than on thriving. Of course, there are many therapists who have experienced 'everyday' therapy: for example, at a period of their life prior to deciding to train as a counsellor or psychotherapist. It would be interesting to know whether what they have learned from their therapy is similar to, or perhaps different from, the learning themes reported in Macran et al. (1999).

differences between practitioners who purport to employ the same model (see, for example, Lieberman *et al.* 1973). This kind of finding has created difficulties for researchers interested in comparing different approaches. If half the behaviourists in a study are indistinguishable from the psychoanalysts, the study can hardly constitute a comparison of behaviour therapy and psychoanalytic psychotherapy! Increasingly, therefore, researchers have constructed 'manuals' that give detailed instructions to the counsellors or psychotherapists involved in the study regarding just how to implement the particular approach being studied. The competence of the counsellor is assessed, then, in terms of how closely she is able to adhere to the manual.

Valuable though this strategy might be in some research studies, and perhaps also in some training situations, it is of limited use in assessing the competence of most counsellors, who would not claim to be even attempting to follow the dictates of any one approach. Furthermore, one of the characteristics of highly competent or gifted counsellors is that they are adept at creatively modifying techniques or exercises to meet the needs of individual clients. However, it should be noted that in studies that have used manual-instructed counsellors, poor client outcomes are correlated with persistent errors or mistakes in technique. Mastery of technique may be important, therefore, when it is absent rather than when it is present.

It might be supposed that possession of a range of techniques, or what is sometimes called an 'armoury' or 'toolkit' of techniques, would be beneficial. The founder of systematic eclecticism, Lazarus (1989a, b), would certainly recommend that competent counsellors should be familiar with a range of intervention strategies. There is very little direct research evidence on whether counsellors who employ many techniques are more effective in helping clients than are counsellors with more restricted repertoires. A series of studies by Mahrer (1989; Mahrer *et al.* 1987) would imply that a large repertoire is not necessarily desirable. Mahrer classified techniques into broad categories and used this set of categories of therapist 'operations' to analyse the behaviour of several well known 'master therapists', such as Carl Rogers and Irving Polster. He found that each of them regularly uses only a very limited range of strategies. Although further research is clearly required, the results achieved by Mahrer would seem to imply that a thorough grasp of a narrow range of techniques might be more valuable than a more superficial capacity to use a wider range. Mahrer himself would not agree with this conclusion, and sees one of the main objectives of his research programme as being to encourage counsellors and therapists to acquire a broader repertoire of operations.

Ability to understand and work within social systems

It could be argued that one of the weaknesses of most contemporary approaches to counselling is that they take an over-individualistic perspective on the counselling process. They focus on a scenario in which the client is in one chair and the counsellor sits opposite in another chair. In reality, though, there is usually an audience to this performance – encompassing, among others, the family and friends of the client, and the supervisor and colleagues of the counsellor. The counsellor and client always act within a social system, and their actions have consequences for that system. An important competence, therefore, is the capacity to be aware of the operation of social systems. In the earlier discussion of burnout it was suggested that the presence of a support system around the counsellor was a good way of avoiding burnout. In Britain, the BAC and BPS require counsellors to engage in ongoing supervision, an acknowledgement of the necessity for support.

Counsellors who work in or for organizations will be aware of the demands and pressures the organization may make upon them. These pressures, which are discussed more fully in Chapter 16, can include inducements to pass on information confided by clients, expectations to influence the behaviour of clients and restrictions on the type of work that can be done with clients. Effective counsellors in such settings need to be highly competent in dealing with the social system within which they work.

Openness to inquiry

This competence underpins all the other competence areas listed above. It is important for anyone in a counselling role to be willing to learn from his or her clients, and to be willing actively to search for knowledge and understanding in situations where the counselling process or relationship takes them beyond their existing knowledge base. Central to this competence is an ability to engage with the findings of research, and to use research evidence to inform practice.

The counsellor's journey: a developmental model of counsellor competence

The categorization and identification of the skills and qualities associated with effectiveness in counselling have largely focused on competencies exhibited by people who are already practitioners. However, the emphasis in the literature on the importance of personal factors and the value in the area of supervision of models of counsellor identity development (see Chapter 20) suggests that a developmental perspective might also be applied to the question of understanding counsellor competence. Many counsellors find meaning in the metaphor of the 'counsellor's journey' (Goldberg 1988), an image that allows them to trace the roots of their counselling role back to its earliest origins, and make sense of the different territories and obstacles encountered on the way to becoming a counsellor. The personal and professional pathways followed by counsellors are divisible into five distinct and also overlapping stages:

1 Roles, relationship patterns and emotional needs established in childhood.
2 The decision to become a counsellor.
3 The experience of training.
4 Coping with the hazards of practice.
5 Expressing creativity in the counselling role.

This model draws upon research mainly carried out on psychotherapists in the USA (Henry 1966, 1977; Burton 1970), although there is some evidence of similarities in a small-scale study of British therapists (Norcross and Guy 1989; Spurling and Dryden 1989). It is important to note that these studies were all carried out on full-time professional therapists. Research is lacking on the motivational patterns and developmental processes of non-professional or voluntary counsellors.

Studies of the childhood and family life of therapists (Henry 1966; Burton 1970; Spurling and Dryden 1989) have found a number of factors that appear to be related to later career choice. Therapists frequently come from minority groups (for example, the high proportion of Jewish therapists), have lived for some time in another country or have parents who are exiles or immigrants. As Henry (1977: 49) puts it, in childhood many therapists 'have been exposed to more than one set of cultural influences'. As children, many have experienced illness, loneliness (perhaps through being an only child or living in an isolated location) or bereavement. Conflict in family life is reported fairly often, with the therapist as child taking the role of mediator or subsitute parent. Consistent with this role, therapists often reported that they were the dominant sibling in the family.

These types of childhood experiences can be seen as creating the conditions for embarking on a career as therapist. As Brightman (1984: 295) has written, 'the role of therapist itself may constitute a reenactment of an earlier situation in which a particularly sensitive and empathic child has been pressed into the service of understanding and caring for a parent (usually depressed mother) figure.' The child in this situation grows up with a need to care for others. As the sibling most involved in the family drama, he or she is not able to escape from the responsibility to care. The experience of being a social 'outsider' introduces the additional motivation to learn about and understand relationships and interactions. As Henry (1977) noted, the motive to care on its own is more likely to lead to a career in social work, whereas therapy requires a strong interest in making sense of the inner worlds of clients. The exposure in childhood to periods of loneliness or isolation provides a capacity for exploration of inner life.

Another dimension of the childhood experience of therapists relates to what is known as the 'wounded healer' theory (Guggenbuhl-Craig 1971; Rippere and Williams 1985). This idea proposes that the power of the healer (the priest or shaman in primitive societies, the therapist in modern society) derives from his or her inner experience of pain, loss or suffering. The presence of a 'wound' in the healer gives him or her an excellent basis from which to understand and empathize with the wounds of clients. A danger is that the wound of the healer is exacerbated by the demands of those being helped, and the healer is sacrificed for their benefit. The wounded healer concept makes it possible to understand the 'search for wholeness and integration' (Spurling and Dryden 1989), which characterizes the lives of many counsellors and therapists and which makes it possible to transform the pain of negative life experiences into a resource for helping others.

The pattern of childhood experience is unique for every therapist, but if it contains some of the elements described above it can lead to a motivation to enter counselling as a career. Marston (1984) suggests that the motives for becoming a therapist can include contact, helping others, discovery, social status, power and influence, self-therapy and voyeurism. Clearly, an appropriate balance of motives is necessary. For perhaps the majority of counsellors, the pathway into the occupation unfolds over time. It is common for people to enter professions such as nursing, social work and teaching and then find themselves more and more attracted to and involved in the counselling components of their job. Undergoing personal therapy or counselling as a client can often be a catalyst for the decision to enter counselling training. The experience of meeting therapists or trainers who become influential role models can also be a factor. The decision to become a counsellor can also be facilitated by participation in introductory skills courses. It is important to acknowledge that the decision to become a counsellor is not made lightly by people. It constitutes a significant developmental stage in its own right, and many very talented counsellors do not complete this stage, and enter training, until well into their middle years.

Once the person has decided to become a counsellor, he or she enters the stage of formal training. The training process itself encompasses a developmental process (see Chapter 20) but, viewed from the perspective of the journey as a whole, the main developmental theme of training can be seen to be adequacy to the task. Through training, the counsellor needs to arrive at an answer to the question 'Am I good enough?'

To be 'good enough' to help people who are deeply damaged by life is to make a strong statement about one's own sanity, knowledge and competence. Particularly during the early phase of training, when clients may not return, or present overwhelming problems of staggering complexity and horror, all the evidence points in the direction of inadequacy rather than sufficiency. On the other hand, there is, both in the professional literature and within popular culture, 'the stereotype of the psychotherapist as all-knowing, all-loving, a fusion of the artist and scientist setting forth to battle the dark forces of the human soul' (Brightman 1984: 295). Counsellors in training may feel vulnerable and incompetent, but they know that they should aspire to the ideal of being a 'potent' role model for their clients (Egan 1986: 28).

As a means of resolving the tension between expectations of competence and inner fears of inadequacy, some therapists evolve what Brightman (1984) has called a 'grandiose professional self'. Such counsellors and therapists deal with the fears and anxieties arising from their role by identifying with the image of an all-knowing, all-powerful and all-loving therapist. The earliest observation of this phenomenon was made by Ernest Jones, the psychoanalyst who was student and biographer of Freud. Jones (1951) wrote that some analysts kept themselves aloof and mysterious, acted as if they knew everything and never admitted mistakes. He coined the term 'God complex' to describe such therapists. Marmor (1953) described this pattern as a 'feeling of superiority', and commented that it was often reinforced by the tendency of patients to idealize their analysts. Sharaf and Levinson (1964) argue that the enormous responsibility and pressure placed on new therapists result in a desperate quest for all the trappings of a professional role. An account of what it can be like to be on the receiving end of 'grandiose' therapy is given by Allen (1990), who describes her unsuccessful encounter with a therapist who was cold, sat in a chair two inches higher than her chair and in the end diagnosed her as needing hospital treatment.

The resolution of this phase of grandiosity can be facilitated by appropriate supervision and personal therapy (Brightman 1984). Often, the transition to a more realistic self-appraisal can be accompanied by depression and a sense of mourning for an idealized state that has been left behind.

The next stage, that of coping with the hazards of practice, brings with it a new set of challenges to competence. The possibility of professional burnout, brought about by high workloads and an increasing discrepancy between the capacity to help and the demands of clients, has been described in Chapter 16. Burnout, and the similar state of 'disillusionment' (Burton 1970), can be viewed as a consequence of unresolved grandiosity, of the therapist finishing training and taking on a job while still carrying a sense of omnipotence. There are other hazards of practice. Mair (1989: 281) has portrayed counselling and therapy as a trade in secrets:

> Psychotherapists occupy a remarkable position in society. We daily have access to the secrets of our clients, and therefore of the society of which they and we are part. We are secret agents, being told what others try to hide . . . We are ambiguous and liable to be suspect by many in the ordinary world.

Kovacs (1976) has similarly represented the therapist as only participating in life 'from one side', not risking genuine contact but acting as 'observer' or 'witness'. The main threat to competence during the part of the counsellor's journey that immediately follows training, or may even include the latter phase of training, is that of losing the motivation to help, as a result of burnout, detachment or alienation. Luborsky, in a study that looked at differences in effectiveness between individual counsellors, found motivation to help to be one of the central factors distinguishing effective from ineffective practitioners. McCarley (1975) and Aveline (1986) have both argued for the importance of opportunities for 'self-renewal' being made available to experienced therapists.

The final stage of the counsellor's journey is to achieve a capacity for working creatively with clients. At this stage, the counsellor is no longer merely a technician implementing a specific theoretical approach:

In the end, each therapist develops his or her own style, and the 'theoretical orientation' falls into the background. What remains salient is a unique personality combining artistry and skill. In this respect, a fine therapist closely resembles a painter, novelist or composer. As is true in all the arts and sciences, few reach the summit.

(Strupp 1978: 31)

A developmental model of counsellor competence brings into focus a number of issues. Each stage presents the counsellor with a distinctive set of challenges to competence. For the counsellor contemplating a career in counselling, important tasks include checking out the robustness of the adaptation to childhood experiences and being aware of the balance of motives. In selecting people for counsellor training courses, often the most crucial question is whether the person is ready to give help to others, or whether he or she is basically seeking therapy for himself or herself. In training, a principal challenge is to acknowledge vulnerability and accept the 'negative capability' of not knowing everything. As a qualified practitioner, competence depends on periodical renewal and rediscovery of personal meaning in the work, and on establishing sufficient support networks to avoid burning out.

As in any developmental model, the failure to resolve an issue or learning task at one stage will carry implications for the succeeding stages. So, for example, someone who has not gained insight into childhood 'wounds' will find it very difficult to arrive at a sense of being a 'good enough' counsellor. A counsellor who is struggling to meet the everyday demands of clients will lack the time and energy to move to a stage of creative self-expression through his or her work.

Chapter summary

- The role of the counsellor involves a range of tasks and competencies. The concept of *skill* captures only one component of counsellor competence.

- Counsellors need to possess good interpersonal skills in such areas as communication, listening and non-verbal behaviour.

- The capacity to accept others and believe in their capacity for change is another core area of counsellor competence.

- Research evidence suggests that effective counsellors are those who can demonstrate cognitive flexibility and an ability to conceptualize.

- Although many counsellors may have overcome loss or trauma in their own lives, it is important for counsellors to have achieved enough self-awareness and capacity to tolerate anxiety to be able to be fully present in relation to their clients.

• Counsellor competence also relies upon being able to use specific techniques in an appropriate manner.

• Competence in counselling is linked to an appreciation of the demands of working with other people, and within organizational systems.

• Rather than regarding these areas of counsellor competence as fixed and static, it is more useful to view them as part of a developmental process. It is suggested that being a counsellor is like being on a *journey*, which begins in childhood and builds on early experiences and then on training to reach a stage of professional maturity.

• A developmental model of competence reminds counsellors both of the unique strengths and weaknesses, gifts and deficits, that they bring with them into the counselling encounter, and of the fact that development is never complete.

Topics for reflection and discussion

1   To what extent, and in what ways, have your early life experiences predisposed you to have an interest in counselling? Have these childhood and adolescent events and experiences influenced your choice of theoretical orientation, or your commitment to work with particular client groups?

2   Does the metaphor of the counsellor's 'journey' apply to your life? Where are you now in terms of that journey? What might be involved in the next stage of the journey? Do any other images or metaphors capture more accurately your sense of your development as a counsellor?

3   Consider the seven areas of basic counsellor competence discussed in this chapter: interpersonal skills, personal beliefs and attitudes, conceptual ability, personal 'soundness', mastery of technique, ability to work within social systems, and openness to inquiry. Under each of these headings, list the skills or competencies that you are able to employ well, and those that are more problematic for you. You might invite someone who knows you well to comment on your self-perceptions. What are the implications of this exercise for your training needs as a counsellor?

4   Reflect on, and then discuss, the implications of Sussman's (1992: 19) statement that 'behind the wish to practice psychotherapy lies the need to cure one's inner wounds and unresolved conflicts.'

Key terms and concepts

clinical memory   personal therapy
competence   skill
counsellor identity development   therapeutic alliance
hazards of practice   values clarification
manuals   wounded healer

Suggested further reading

Readers interested in the themes explored in this chapter will find reward and pleasure in the work of Goldberg (1988) and Kottler (1988), both of whom offer a moderately heroic, yet balanced, picture of the counsellor and his or her motivation. By contrast, Sussman (1992) and Strean (1993) represent the counsellor as a demonic figure, intent on gratifying their needs at the expense of their clients. The single classic paper in this area is McConnaughy (1987).

There has not, in fact, been a great deal of research into the qualities that contribute to the making of a counsellor. Worth special mention is the study by Skovholt and Ronnestad (1992), which brings together some interesting interview material from experienced counsellors. Wosket's (1999) book on the therapeutic use of self draws on research and practice, and is likely to become a 'must read' text in this area.

Training and supervision in counselling

Introduction

The professionalization of counselling in the past two decades in Britain and Europe has seen increasing attention being devoted to the provision of training and supervision. In North America this process occurred largely during the 1950s. The requirement of professional accountability, and the existence and growing influence of professional associations, have forced colleges, agencies and training institutes to formalize arrangements for training and supervising counsellors. In Britain, for example, the first university-based counsellor training courses began operation only in 1966. In 1986 the British Association for Counselling produced its first criteria and procedures for approving counselling courses, and in 1992 the British Psychological Society published similar guidelines for courses in counselling psychology.

Despite this growth in numbers of courses, relatively little research has been carried out that would assist counselling trainers and tutors in their work. Counsellor training remains, curiously, an underdeveloped area for research and scholarship. Even the knowledge that tutors and trainers have gained through personal and professional experience is seldom written up for publication.

Historical trends in counsellor training

The history of training in psychotherapy, and psychoanalysis in particular, gives some clues to the prevalence of barriers to knowledge about what goes on in training courses. The primary training medium for psychoanalysts has been the training analysis. Trainees in psychoanalytic institutes enter analysis with a senior member of the institute. Through the period of training they may undergo training analyses with two or more analysts in this way. The training analysis was considered to be the only way in which an analyst could learn about what psychoanalysis was really like, although theoretical seminars, case discussions and child observation studies came eventually to be added to the psychoanalytic training programme in many institutes. The assessment of suitability of candidates for qualification as analysts was largely determined by the training analyst. The privacy and secretiveness of these arrangements precluded public discussion of training issues; the suitability of a candidate was assessed solely on the professional judgement, with no appeal possible. The potential oppressiveness of this kind of training has been documented by Masson (1988).

The emergence of client-centred therapy in the 1940s and 1950s brought with it a whole set of new ideas about how to train counsellors. Rogers and his colleagues brought in students to act as co-therapists in sessions with clients. Students practised counselling skills on each other. The 'T-group' or personal growth group was applied to counsellor training, with trainees participating in small experiential groups. Students watched films of sessions and analysed recordings and transcripts. This phase of development of approaches to counsellor training featured a more open and multifaceted approach to learning technique, and the introduction of other means of facilitating self-awareness (for example, encounter groups), rather than a reliance solely on personal therapy. There was also a degree of democratization in the training process, with student self-evaluations being used alongside staff appraisals.

During the 1960s and 1970s the main innovation in counsellor training consisted of the introduction of structured approaches to skills training. These approaches were used not only on counsellor training courses but also in the context of shorter skills courses designed for people in other helping or human service professions, such as teaching, nursing and management. The first of these structured approaches was the human resource development model devised by Carkhuff (1969). Other packages of a similar nature were the micro-skills model (Ivey and Galvin 1984), the skilled helper model (Egan 1984), SASHA tapes (Goodman 1984) and interpersonal process recall (Kagan *et al.* 1963). Although these models and approaches differed in certain respects, they all contained carefully structured training materials, in the form of handouts, exercises and video or film demonstrations, which would take trainees through a standard programme for learning specific counselling skills.

More recently, significant developments in counsellor training have included increased attention to the role of supervision and personal therapy in training programmes (Mearns 1997; Thorne and Dryden 1991).

Key elements in counsellor training courses

The development of different ideas and approaches to the training of counsellors and therapists has resulted in what currently appears to be a broad consensus concerning the elements that need to be included in training courses (Dryden and Thorne 1991; Dryden *et al.* 1995; Mearns 1997). Different courses may emphasize some of these activities at the expense of others, but all courses will probably include at least some input under each of the headings listed below.

Theoretical frameworks

It is widely accepted that counsellors need to be equipped with a theoretical perspective through which to understand their work with clients. The theory component of courses may include models of counselling, basic psychological theories in areas such as developmental psychology, interpersonal behaviour and group dynamics, an introduction to psychiatric terminology and some aspects of sociology relating to social class, race and gender. There is potential in counselling courses, therefore, for extensive coverage of theoretical topics, particularly when it is taken into account that specialist areas of counselling, such as marital and couples counselling or bereavement work, have their own well articulated theoretical models. The challenge of theoretical learning in counselling is further increased by the general recognition that students should not merely know about theory, but should be able to apply it in practice. The aim is to be able to use theory actively to understand clients and the reactions of the counsellor to these clients.

One of the issues that arises in this area of counsellor training is whether it is more appropriate to introduce students to one theoretical orientation in depth, or to expose them to an integration of several theoretical models (Halgin 1985; Norcross *et al.* 1986; Beutler *et al.* 1987). To some extent this issue is linked to the nature of the organization that is offering the training. Independent institutes are often created around proponents of a particular theoretical approach, so that students being trained in these institutes will inevitably be primarily taught that set of ideas. Courses operating in institutions of higher education, such as colleges and universities, are likely to be influenced by academic values concerning the necessity for critical debate between theoretical positions, and will therefore usually teach theory from an integrationist or multiple perspective stance.

Another facet of this debate addresses the question of the order in which theoretical choices should appropriately be made. Is it more helpful to organize initial counsellor training around a broad-based multiple perspective or generic perspective, and encourage counsellors to specialize in a particular approach later on in their careers when they have a solid basis for choice? Or is it more appropriate to begin training with a thorough grounding in a single coherent approach? The recent trend in Britain and other countries has been to favour intial training structured around a single core theoretical model. However, Feltham (1997) has cogently argued that this approach entails the danger of stifling dialogue, debate and creativity, by turning out counsellors who are socialized into narrow ways of understanding their clients and their role. The argument over the relative merits of training based on a core model as against training that is eclectic and integrative reflect the broader debate over integrationism discussed in Chapter 3.

Counselling skills

Training in counselling skills has been associated more with person-centred and cognitive–behavioural than with psychodynamic approaches to counselling. The concept of skill refers to a sequence of counsellor actions or behaviours carried out in response to client actions or behaviours. Implicit in the idea of skill is an assumption that it makes sense to break down the role of counsellor into discrete actions or behaviours, and this has been an assumption that is difficult to reconcile with psychoanalytic ways of thinking.

As already mentioned, a number of models of counselling skill training have been developed. Even when these models are not adopted in their entirety into training courses, the ideas and procedures contained in them are often put into service. It is therefore worthwhile to describe the main features of three of the more widely used of these approaches.

The human resource development (HRD) model (Carkhuff 1972; Cash 1984) was originally based on the Rogerian 'core conditions' of empathy, unconditional positive regard and congruence. The later evolution of the approach added 'action' skills, such as concreteness, confrontation and immediacy, to the repertoire, and placed these skills within a three-stage model of the helping process. The stages are self-exploration, understanding and action. In an HRD training programme, trainees are exposed to each of the skills in turn. A rationale is presented for the use of the skill in helping relationships, and there is a live or video demonstration of the skill in action. Trainees also take part in a small group experience designed to give them an opportunity of experiencing at first hand the impact of the core conditions.

The microcounselling or microskills training approach (Ivey and Galvin 1984) also breaks down the task of counselling into a number of discrete skills:

- attending behaviour;
- client observation skills;
- open and closed questions;
- encouraging, paraphrasing and summarizing;
- reflecting feelings and meanings;
- focusing on problems;
- influencing skills;
- confrontation;
- structuring the interview;
- integrating skills.

Trainees are given written descriptions of positive and negative examples of each skill, watch an expert demonstrating the skill on video, then engage in videotaped practice of the skills with other trainees acting as clients. Feedback is provided, and then the trainee attempts the skill once more. This sequence is repeated until the trainee reaches an appropriate level of competence in the skill. One of the primary aims of the microskills approach is to enable counsellors to function in an 'intentional' rather than 'intuitive' manner, in other words to be able to select an appropriate response from a wide repertoire rather than being restricted to only one or two modes of communication and intervention. Another area of emphasis has been the identification of skills congruent with particular cultural settings (Ivey *et al.* 1987).

Interpersonal process recall (IPR: Kagan 1984; Kagan and Kagan 1990) differs from the HRD and microskills approaches in being based on discovery learning. Trainees initially watch counsellors responding to clients using desirable skills, and briefly practise these skills in response to video-taped 'trigger' vignettes. The next phase, affect simulation, involves trainees responding to vignettes in which actors express intense and distressing emotional statements direct to camera. The final phase involves making a video-tape of a counselling session, then watching it immediately afterwards with the help of an 'inquirer' who urges the trainee to recall any thoughts, feelings or images that he or she experienced during the session. This 'stimulated recall' component is unique to IPR, and is based on an assumption that all helpers, even beginning trainees, are capable of demonstrating a wide repertoire of helpful responses but stop themselves from doing so because of anxiety or social inhibition.

It can be seen that, although there are some differences between these approaches, they nevertheless all embrace many of the same set of learning activities:

- beginning with a generic set of skills, rather than with a theoretical model;
- receiving a description of and rationale for the skill;

- observing an expert modelling the skill;
- learning to discriminate between effective and ineffective examples of the skill;
- practising the skill with a client or colleague;
- the trainee reviewing his or her performance of the skill;
- feedback from other trainees and tutor;
- desensitization of the anxiety level of the helper, particularly in relation to client expression of emotions;
- further practice of skill;
- integration of skills into the counselling role.

Research into the effectiveness of these methods in counsellor training suggests that there is good evidence to support the claims of the microskills and HRD approaches, but somewhat less evidence to confirm the value of interpersonal process recall (Baker *et al.* 1990).

Work on self

The importance of self-knowledge and self-awareness in counsellors is central to many of the mainstream theoretical approaches. Even basically skills-oriented approaches to training, such as the human resource development and interpersonal process recall models described above, place considerable emphasis on self-awareness. In psychodynamic work, for example, the counsellor must be able to differentiate between counter-transference reactions that are triggered by client transference, and those that are projections of unresolved personal conflicts. In person-centred work, the congruence of the counsellor, his or her ability to be aware of and act appropriately upon personal feelings, is considered a core condition in creating an effective therapeutic environment.

Self-awareness is also necessary in a more general sense, in enabling the counsellor to survive without burning out through the experience of holding and sharing the pain, fear and despair of clients. Most ordinary people to whom clients turn deny the depth of the emotional suffering that is presented to them, or repress their own reactions to it. Effective counsellors cannot afford these defences, but must find ways of staying with clients in their distress. Finally, it is essential for counsellors to be aware of their own motivations and pay-offs for engaging in this kind of work, in order to prevent different types of client exploitation or abuse.

The value of personal therapy is also discussed on pages 484–7

Traditionally, training courses in psychodynamic counselling, or influenced by psychodynamic approaches, have insisted that counsellors in training undergo personal therapy during the period of training. The number of sessions stipulated varies widely, from ten sessions to twice weekly over several years. The rationale for therapy is not only to promote personal development, but to give the student some experience in the role of client, and to enable first-hand observation of a therapist in action. An additional objective, in some training courses, is to enable assessment of the potential of the trainee.

The requirement for personal therapy has been criticized on several grounds. First, this arrangement does not allow the client to choose to enter therapy, which is usually considered essential for productive therapy to take place. This element of choice is particularly relevant when the trainee may have recently completed a course of therapy, before entering training, and has no wish or need to reopen personal issues. Second, if the therapy leads to the uncovering of difficult emotional material, the trainee may not be able to participate effectively in other parts of the course, such as skills training or supervised placements. Third, if the therapy does not go well – for example, if there is a mismatch between therapist and client – the trainee may feel that it is necessary to continue, at the risk of emotional damage, for the sake of completing a mandatory part of the course. Fourth, given the scarcity of counselling availability to people in real crisis, it may be difficult to justify using a significant proportion of the time of highly qualified practitioners in supplying personal therapy to trainees. Finally, the financial cost of personal therapy can place counsellor training even further out of the reach of people from socially disadvantaged groups.

None of these arguments against personal therapy is conclusive. For example, if a trainee is thrown into personal crisis as a result of personal therapy, it could be argued that it is better that it happens then rather than as a result of working with one of his or her own clients. It may be extremely valuable for someone to take time out from any kind of training course to reassess personal priorities. A strong argument for the continuation of personal therapy in training is probably that it helps to ensure the centrality of acceptance of the client role: counselling is not a set of techniques applied to others but a learning process in which counsellor as well as client participates. Another reason for including some personal therapy experience in training is that it is necessary for counsellors to know when they themselves need help, and to feel all right about seeking such help, rather than persevering with client work in an impaired state. In some respects, the completion of personal therapy can represent a professional *rite de passage* for trainee counsellors, an entry into a professional role.

Considerable research has been carried out into the impact of personal therapy on the subsequent effectiveness of counsellors and therapists (see Chapter 19). The results of this research have been inconsistent, with no clear benefit being demonstrated. It should be noted, however, that personal therapy is merely one element in a training programme, and it is difficult to identify the unique effects of this component in isolation from everything else that might be happening on a course.

Another approach to work on self that is included in many courses is experiential work in groups. These groups may be called therapy groups, T-groups or encounter groups, and may be run by external consultants or leaders, course tutors or even on a self-help or leaderless basis. The aims of such groupwork are similar to those of personal therapy, with the added dimension that the quality of relationships and support developed in the groups will benefit the learning that takes place in other areas of the course as a whole. Work in small groups can also enable counsellors to identify and clarify the values that inform their approach to clients. It is regrettable that there has been no research into the role of groupwork in counsellor training, since there are many issues and dilemmas that would repay systematic study. It would be interesting to know, for instance, whether groups that become highly supportive and cohesive contribute more to counsellor learning than do groups that are fragmented and tense. There are often also serious dilemmas presented by confidentiality boundaries in respect of the acceptability of talking in the rest of the course about topics originating in small groups.

Personal learning diaries and journals are employed in several courses to facilitate personal learning and to record the application of learning in practice (Pates and Knasel 1989). Guidelines for approaches to writing personal learning diaries can be found in Progoff (1975) and Rainer (1980). The diary or journal is particularly helpful in assisting the transfer of learning and insight beyond the course itself into the rest of the personal and professional life of the trainee. Reading and commenting on diary or journal material can, however, be a time-consuming business for trainers and tutors.

The quality and depth of personal exploration and learning on counsellor training courses can often be facilitated through the creation of suitable physical surroundings. Training groups may use residentials, which are often held in countryside settings away from the usual training premises, to construct a 'cultural island' where relationships are strengthened and new patterns of behaviour tried out. The personal meaning of counsellor training for many trainees is that it is a time of intense self-exploration and change (Battye 1991; Johns 1998), which has implications for partners, family and work roles.

The issues arising from the personal development area of counsellor training have been reviewed by Johns (1995) and Wilkins (1997), who provide more detailed explorations of the questions that have been introduced here. Research into the impact of personal development groups in training has been reviewed by Payne (1999).

Professional issues

Training courses should include careful consideration of a wide range of professional issues. Principles of ethical practice are usually given substantial attention on courses, mainly through discussion of cases. Other professional issues that are covered are: power and discrimination in counselling, particularly with respect to race, gender, disability and sexual orientation; case management and referral; boundary issues; professional accountability and insurance; interprofessional working; and the organization and administration of counselling agencies. Bond (1993) provides a thorough review of most of these areas.

Supervised practice

At some point in training students will begin work with real clients, rather than practising with course colleagues. It is generally considered essential that participants on training courses should be involved in some supervised practice, to provide them with material to use in other parts of the course, and to give them opportunities to apply skills and concepts. A broader discussion of the nature of supervision is introduced later in this chapter, but at this point it can be mentioned that the delivery of supervision to trainees can be either through regular one-to-one meetings with a supervisor or through group supervision. The quality and frequency of supervision is of vital importance to people learning to be counsellors. There are, however, aspects of training that make effective supervision difficult to achieve. The first of these arises from the anxieties and dependency that most people experience when first confronted by clients. This stage of counsellor development is more fully explored in a later section in this chapter. The second issue concerns the relationship between the supervisor and the primary trainers or tutors. It is desirable for supervisors to work with their supervisees in ways that are consistent with the aims and philosophy of a course. It is also desirable, on the other hand, for the trainee to know that he or she can be open with the supervisor, with no fear that disclosures will find their way back to those deciding who will pass or fail the course. The role of the supervisor in relation to a training course represents a challenge to achieve an appropriate balance between involvement with the course and autonomy in service of the student.

Research awareness

An exploration of the contribution of research to an understanding of the counselling process is included in many courses. This may take the form of sessions on research awareness, the ability to read research papers and draw appropriate conclusions from them, through training in research methods and ultimately to designing and implementing a piece of research. The low regard in which most practising counsellors and therapists hold the utility of research findings (reviewed in Chapter 18) would suggest that past efforts on training courses to inculcate an interest in research have not met with any great success.

Issues and dilemmas in counsellor training

Although it might be said that there exists a fair measure of agreement over the broad shape and outline of counsellor training, this apparent consensus should not conceal the fact that there is a wide range of dilemmas and issues to be resolved. In terms of issues arising from the practicalities of operating courses, the two most common dilemmas are balance and time. There are always difficult choices to be made about how much emphasis to give some course elements at the expense of others. No matter how long a course is, the time available could be filled with theory, or could be taken up wholly by experiential work. The other fundamental dilemma is related to time. The process of counsellor development takes a lot of time. People training to be counsellors need to assimilate counselling theory and skills into their own personal way of relating. It probably takes at least four years for most people to become competent as counsellors, and very few courses allow that much time. Other issues that will be addressed include selection of trainees, assessment of competence and course philosophy.

Selection of trainees

There would appear to be very little published research on the selection of applicants for training courses in counselling and psychotherapy. Many courses do little more than interview candidates and take up references. Given the poor evidence concerning the validity of selection interviewing, particularly in situations where job criteria are not clearly defined and the interview itself is not tightly structured, there can be little confidence that this approach to selection is adequate in itself. Best current practice tends to involve taking one or two days to put candidates through an 'assessment centre' procedure, similar to that used in industry, the civil service and the armed forces in the selection of senior managers (see Bray 1982), in which they are interviewed on different topics by different selectors, observed in group discussion and counselling role play situations and asked to complete tests that tap relevant aspects of personality, intelligence and counselling aptitude. This procedure gives selectors a range of indicators of counselling potential, with the expectation that such multiple sources of information (which may include peer ratings from the other candidates in the group) will prove to be more reliable and valid than 'one-shot' interviews.

The assessment of counsellor competence

The assessment of competence to practise as a counsellor generates another set of difficult issues. The approach to accreditation or licensing of counsellors as competent to practise that is currently being implemented by professional bodies places a great deal of emphasis on the completion of an acceptable training course. The methods that training courses use to assess competence therefore have important implications for the profession as a whole, and for the quality of service received by clients.

There is a wide range of sources of assessment judgements and techniques for deriving assessment information currently being used on courses. Information about the competence of a counsellor in training can be gathered from tutors or trainers, the supervisor or an external examiner or consultant. Independent panels of judges can be used to assess samples of the work handed in by the trainee, or to hold an oral assessment of case material (Stevenson and Norcross 1987). Peer and self-assessment are used on many courses. It is seldom possible to obtain ratings of trainee competence from actual clients, although often fellow students on a course will have been clients for each other, and so a form of client perspective will constitute a component of peer evaluations. All of these diverse assessment sources have a contribution to make, and all also possess limitations. For example, tutors and trainers may be excellent observers of counsellor skills, but trainees may engage in 'impression management' by presenting only their best work to these mentors. Members of the peer group are more likely than tutors to have a rounded view of the weaknesses as well as the achievements of a trainee.

There are a number of different techniques for gathering information on counselling skills and competencies. The most widely used of these techniques are:

- questionnaires and rating scales;
- video-tapes or audio-tapes of work with clients (real or role played);
- learning journals or diaries;
- examinations and tests;
- computer simulations.

Again, each of these techniques has advantages and disadvantages. The questionnaires and ratings scales that are available (e.g. Linden *et al.* 1965; Carkhuff 1969; Myrick and Kelly 1971) either have been employed mainly for research purposes or lack adequate up-to-date norms. In other words, although these questionnaires would appear to measure relevant counsellor characteristics, such as empathy, there is an absence of valid data on cut-off points, on just how high a score is 'good enough'. In addition, there are aspects of counsellor learning for which questionnaires and rating scales do not exist.

There are several problems associated with the use of tapes in counsellor assessment, including the self-consciousness of the trainee when being taped, the lack of information on internal processes and the question of whether a short tape is representative of the general approach of a counsellor. Learning journals or diaries have often been used as a way of evaluating the development of trainees and the application of learning in practice (Pates and Knasel 1989). Journals can only present the view of the student, however, and it should also be noted that some students or trainees may lack writing skills and fail to do themselves justice through this medium of communication.

Examinations and tests are used on many courses, particularly those located in academic establishments. It is clear that such techniques only assess the cognitive knowledge of students, which may or may not be associated with effectiveness with clients. Finally, computer simulations of patterns of client problems have been used to assess the skill of counsellors in clinical decision-making and case formulation (Berven and Scofield 1980; Berven 1987).

Although there is certainly a wealth of ideas about how to assess counsellor competence, the validity and reliability of most of these techniques are unknown (Scofield and Yoxheimer 1983). In a study by Chevron and Rounsaville (1983), the clinical skills of therapists were assessed through a variety of techniques. The level of agreement between the techniques was generally low, even though the raters and supervisors used in the study were highly trained and experienced.

Another key issue in the assessment of counsellor competence concerns the sensitivity of the sources and techniques that are used. Davis (1989) has argued that although counsellor errors can be judged more accurately and reliably, it is much harder to differentiate between higher levels of skill: for example, between an 'adequate' and an 'excellent' piece of counselling. Sachs (1983) has produced research results which indicate that the absence of counsellor errors is predictive of good client outcomes. It may be, therefore, that there would be advantages in restricting competency assessments merely to pass–fail distinctions.

As Purton (1991) has observed, the modes of assessment used on training courses reflect the philosophy or theoretical orientation of the course. For example, in his study he found that a person-centred course emphasized student-centred peer assessment, a psychosynthesis course emphasized the use of intuition in assessment and in a psychodynamic training course close attention was paid in assessment to unconscious personality characteristics that might impede work with clients. The culture of a training course is also significant in determining the way that assessment decisions are made. Tyler and Weaver (1981) consider that policies about access to student records, or the manner in which feedback is given to students, seriously affect the validity of the assessment information that is gathered. The openness of trainers about assessment procedures and criteria is also an important factor. Toukmanian *et al.* (1978) looked at two groups of students participating in equivalent counselling training courses. One group was provided with information about the assessment criteria being used by tutors, while the other group was given no information on this topic. The first group achieved significantly higher grades on the course.

The competency judgements arising from training courses have important implications. The successful completion of a course can often be seen by employers and clients as bestowing a licence to practise. Given the paucity of research in this area, however, it would seem appropriate to take a cautious approach to the use of assessment sources and techniques. It would seem sensible to combine as many sources and techniques as possible, to arrive at a multiperspective assessment, drawing upon a large sample of relevant behaviour. The reader interested in exploring the issues raised by counsellor assessment is recommended to consult Wheeler (1996), which offers an authoritative discussion of this topic. The important issue of assessment of multicultural competency is reviewed in Chapter 10.

Supervision

An important element in counsellor development, not only during training but also throughout the working life of the counsellor, is the use of effective and appropriate supervision. It is a requirement of most professional associations that counsellors accredited by them should receive regular supervision from a qualified person. In this context, it is necessary to emphasize that supervision has a different meaning from that in other work settings. Supervision in counselling is not primarily a management role in which the supervisee is given directions and allocated tasks, but is aimed at assisting the counsellor to work as effectively as possible with the client (Carroll 1988). The supervision role in counselling is similar to that of the tutor or consultant. Hawkins and Shohet (1989) have identified three main functions of supervision in counselling. The first is educational, with the aim of giving the counsellor a regular opportunity to receive feedback, develop new understandings and receive information. The second aspect is the supportive role of supervision, through which the counsellor can share dilemmas, be validated in his or her work performance and deal with any personal distress or counter-transference evoked by clients. Finally, there is a management dimension to supervision, in ensuring quality of work and helping the counsellor to plan work and utilize resources.

There are a number of different formats for providing supervision (Hawkins and Shohet 1989). Probably the most common arrangement is to make a contract for individual sessions over a period of time with the same person. A variant on this approach is to use separate consultants to explore specific issues: for example, going to an expert in family work to discuss a client with family problems, and using a mental health counsellor for consultation on a client who is depressed (Kaslow 1986). Another possibility is group supervision, where a small group of supervisees meet with a supervisor. The case discussion group is a type of group supervision that gives particular attention to understanding the personality or family dynamics of the client. Peer supervision groups involve a group of counsellors meeting to engage in supervision of each other, without there being a designated leader or consultant. Finally, supervision networks (Houston 1990) consist of a set of colleagues who are available for mutual or peer supervision, on either a one-to-one or a small group basis.

Each of these modes of supervision has its advantages and disadvantages. Regular individual supervision facilitates the development of a good working relationship between supervisor and supervised. On the other hand, specific consultants will have a greater depth of experience in particular areas. Group and peer group supervision enable the counsellor to learn from the cases and issues presented by colleagues. In these supervision settings, however, there may be problems in maintaining confidentiality and in dealing with the dynamics of the group. The choice of mode of supervision depends on a wide range of factors, including personal preference, cost, availability, agency policy and organization, and counselling philosophy.

The supervision process is highly dependent on the quality of information that supervisees bring to the supervision setting. Most often, the supervisee will report what he or she has been doing with clients, using notes taken after counselling sessions to augment his or her recollection. Dryden and Thorne (1991) argue that, if the focus of the supervision is to be on the skills employed by the counsellor, the supervisor needs 'actual data' from sessions. These data can be obtained from detailed process notes written immediately after a session, and video- or audio-tapes of sessions. In some situations supervisors may even be able to make live observations of the supervisee working with a client.

One of the principal dilemmas in supervision is deciding on what it would be helpful to discuss. Potentially, the supervisee might need to explore his or her understanding of the client, the feelings he or she holds in reaction to the client, the appropriateness of different interventions or techniques and many other topics. Hawkins and Shohet (1989, 2000) have constructed a model of the supervision process that usefully clarifies some of these issues. They suggest that at any time in supervision there are six levels operating:

1 *Reflection on the content of the counselling session.* The focus here is on the client, what is being said, how different parts of the life of the client fit together and what the client wants from counselling.
2 *Exploration of the techniques and strategies used by the counsellor.* This level is concerned with the therapeutic intentions of the counsellor, and the approach he or she is taking to helping the client.
3 *Exploration of the therapeutic relationship.* The aim at this level is to examine the ways in which the client and counsellor interact, and whether they have established a functioning working alliance.
4 *The feelings of the counsellor towards the client.* In this area of supervision the intention is to identify and understand the counter-transference reactions of the counsellor, or the personal issues that have been re-stimulated through contact with the client.
5 *What is happening here and now between supervisor and supervisee.* The relationship in the supervision session may exhibit similar features to the relationship between the counsellor and his or her client. Paying attention to this 'parallel process' (McNeill and Worthen 1989) can give valuable insights.
6 *The counter-transference of the supervisor.* The feelings of the supervisor in response to the supervisee may also provide a guide to some of the ways of seeing the cases that are not yet consciously articulated by supervisor or supervisee, as well as contributing to an understanding of the quality of the supervisor–supervisee relationship.

Hawkins and Shohet (1989, 2000) argue that good supervision will involve movement between all these levels. Supervisors tend to have a personal style of supervision in which they stick mainly to a particular set of levels, and the model can be used as a framework for both supervisors and supervisees to reflect on their work together and if necessary to negotiate change. The Hawkins and Shohet model has been widely used in training, but has not yet generated research.

An approach that can be used to complement the Hawkins and Shohet framework is the 'cyclical model' developed by Page and Wosket (2001). The cyclical model pays particular attention to the creation of a 'reflective space' in which the supervisee can explore dilemmas arising from his or her work, and to the crucial task of applying supervision insights in practice. Page and Wosket (2001) suggest that the work of supervision can be divided into five stages:

Stage 1: *Establishing a contract.* The counsellor and supervisor negotiate such matters as ground rules, boundaries, accountability, mutual expectations and the nature of their relationship.

Stage 2: *Agreeing a focus.* An issue is identified for exploration, and the counsellor's objectives and priorities in relation to the issue are specified.

Stage 3: *Making a space.* Entering into a process of reflection, exploration, understanding and insight around the focal issue.

Stage 4: *The 'bridge' – making the link between supervision and practice.* Consolidation, goal setting and action planning in order to decide how what is to be learned can be taken back into the counselling arena.

Stage 5: *Review and evaluation.* Supervisor and counsellor assess the usefulness of the work they have done, and enter a phase of recontracting.

Page and Wosket (2001) emphasize that this series of stages is cyclical, with each completion of the cycle leading to a strengthening of the counsellor–supervisor relationship, and concluding with the negotiation of a new contract. An appreciation of the different levels at which learning in supervision may occur, as specified by Hawkins and Shohet (1989, 2000), can inform the awareness of counsellor and supervisor at all stages of this cycle.

The Hawkins and Shohet (1989, 2000) and Page and Wosket (2001) models primarily focus on what happens within a single supervision setting. There are also processes in supervision that occur over a much longer time-span, which concern the ways in which the stage of development of the counsellor can have an impact on the counselling process. Counsellors of different degrees of experience and maturity have different supervision needs, and numerous models have been devised to portray this developmental track (see Hess 1980 or Stoltenberg and Delworth 1987 for a review of these ideas). One such model is the six-stage model of development of professional identity constructed by Friedman and Kaslow (1986). The stages, which may take several years to pass through, are described as:

1 *Excitement and anticipatory anxiety.* This phase describes the period before the counsellor has seen his or her first client. The task of the supervisor is to provide security and guidance.

2 *Dependency and identification.* The second stage commences as soon as the counsellor begins work with clients. The lack of confidence, skill and knowledge in the counsellor results in a high degree of dependency on the supervisor, who is perceived as having all the answers. The trainee counsellor at this stage will use the supervisor as a model. However, anxiety about being seen as incompetent may lead the supervisee to conceal information from the supervisor. The personality and dynamics of the client, rather than the therapeutic relationship or counter-transference, is the most common focus of supervision at this stage, reflecting the lack of confidence and awareness of the counsellor in exploring his or her own contribution to the therapeutic process.

3 *Activity and continued dependency.* This phase of development is triggered by the realization of the counsellor that he or she is actually making a difference to clients. This recognition enables the counsellor to be more active with clients, and to try out different strategies and techniques. The counsellor is beginning

to be more open to his or her own feeling response to clients, and may discuss counselling issues with colleagues and family members as a means of 'spilling affect' (Friedman and Kaslow 1986: 38). In this burst of enthusiasm for therapy, the counsellor may experiment by applying therapeutic skills and concepts to friends and family members. The primary task of the supervisor at this stage is to be able to accept the needs for dependency as well as active autonomy, and to allow the counsellor to explore different options.

4 *Exuberance and taking charge*. Friedman and Kaslow (1986: 40) write that 'the fourth phase of development is ushered in by the trainee's realization that he or she really is a therapist.' Having acquired considerable experience in working with clients, having read widely in the field and probably having embarked on personal therapy, the counsellor is actively making connections between theory and practice, and beginning to identify with one theoretical perspective rather than trying out diverse ideas and systems. In supervision, there is a willingness to explore counter-transference issues and to discuss theoretical models. The counsellor no longer needs as much support and warmth in supervision, and is ready for a higher degree of challenge. In becoming less dependent on the supervisor, the counsellor comes to view the latter more as a consultant than as a teacher.

5 *Identity and independence*. This is described as the stage of 'professional adolescence'. In beginning to envisage life without the protection and guidance of the supervisor, the counsellor becomes more willing and able to express differences of opinion. Counsellors at this stage of development are often attracted to peer supervision with others at a similar stage. The supervisee has by this time internalized a frame of reference for evaluating client work, and is in a position to accept or reject the advice or suggestions of the supervisor. The counsellor may be aware of areas in which his or her expertise exceeds that of the supervisor. It is necessary for the supervisor at this stage to remain available to the counsellor, and to accept a lack of control.

6 *Calm and collegiality*. By this stage the counsellor has acquired a firm sense of professional identity and belief in his or her competence. The counsellor is able to take a balanced view of the strengths and weaknesses of different approaches to therapy, and is able to use peers and supervisors as consultants, 'from a spirit of genuine respect among colleagues' (Friedman and Kaslow 1986: 45). At this stage counsellors begin to take an interest in taking on the supervisor role.

The process involved in the formation of a professional identity has the consequence that the focus of supervision can be qualitatively different at succeeding stages. It is helpful for both supervisors and supervisees to be aware that this kind of developmental sequence can take place, and to adjust their behaviour and expectations accordingly.

Throughout this account of the supervision process, it can be observed that the quality of the relationship between supervisor and supervisee is of paramount importance (Shohet and Wilmot 1991). Charny (1986: 20) has written that 'the greatest possibilities of growth in supervision ... [lie] in tapping candidly just what is going on in the heart, mind and body of a therapist in relation to a given case.' He adds that, for him, the most valuable question in supervision is: 'what about this case really worries me?' To undertake this kind of open exploration of self in relation to the client requires the same degree of emotional safety and the same 'core conditions' that are offered to clients. As in counselling, the freedom to choose an appropriate helper is valuable, as is the freedom to terminate. The sensitivity to relationship issues that is found in much effective supervision can also lead to the danger of straying over the boundary that separates supervision from actual therapy. The role of supervision in counsellor training and ongoing development is, therefore, closely linked to issues of how and when to structure counsellor personal therapy or work on self.

There is also an increasing appreciation that, although counselling supervision consists primarily of a secure, confidential relationship between a supervisor and an individual counsellor (or group of counsellors), the organizational context within which supervision takes place can have a profound influence on the quality and nature of what takes place. For example, a supervisor may have responsibility to report to the counselling agency management on the competence or effectiveness of the counsellor, or to ensure that the counsellor complies with agency regulations around risk assessment or the number of counselling sessions that can be offered. Further discussion of the issues associated with the interplay between supervisor, counsellor and the organization which employs (and manages) them both can be found in Hawkins and Shohet (2000) and Copeland (2000).

The requirement to engage in regular supervision has become one of the cornerstones of the commitment to the provision of quality therapy services in Britain. In other countries, supervision may be mandatory during training, with regular 'consultation' required following completion of training. Although the precise regulatory arrangements may differ in countries and within different professional groups, there can be no denying the immense commitment of time and energy that is currently devoted to supervision within the therapy professions. Recently, however, an increasing number of questions have been asked about the value of mandatory supervision. Critics have argued that supervision has the potential to be counterproductive in some circumstances (see Box 20.1).

Training and supervision in counselling: some conclusions

The development of theory and research into the practice of counselling and psychotherapy has not been matched by equivalent critical attention to the problems of training and supervision. Few studies have been carried out on the evaluation of the effects of training programmes. Major questions remain unanswered concerning methods of addressing ethical and multicultural perspectives

Box 20.1

The value of supervision: critical voices

The most widely adopted format for supervision is based on the counsellor describing his or her work with a client to an individual supervisor, or to a peer group or supervision group. It has become apparent that there are a number of potentially serious limitations inherent in this approach. Some studies have shown that supervisees are typically selective in the material they present in supervision (Ladany *et al.* 1996; Webb 2000), and may not disclose information that they feel might reflect poorly on their competence. Other research has shown that, fairly often, supervisees report that their supervision has been counterproductive (Lawton 2000; Gray *et al.* 2001), or even that they feel that they have been locked into a supervision relationship that is conflict-ridden (Nelson and Friedlander 2001) or even abusive (Kaberry 2000). In contrast, there is no research evidence to back up the claim, made by advocates of mandatory supervision, that regular supervision is associated either with improved client outcomes or with lower levels of ethical violation on the part of practitioners.

Feltham (2000) has identified the current position in counselling in Britain, in relation to supervision, as reflecting what he calls 'the dynamics of the mandatory'. He argues that:

> The logic of regular, mandatory supervision is that, along with ever-rising costs of training, personal therapy, membership fees, accreditation, registration, continuing professional development and insurance, the counselling professional closes its doors to all but the relatively affluent . . . the dynamics of the mandatory within supervision itself [also requires that] the supervisee must attend for regular supervision whether he or she usually finds this useful or not. If the supervisee does not always find it particularly useful, there is an implication that something is wrong with the supervisee, since supervision is apparently found universally and invariably helpful.
>
> (Feltham 2000: 10)

The central concern for Feltham (2000: 21) is that 'there is currently little evidence, but much emotional rhetoric, supporting the value or clarifying the purposes of supervision.' The adoption of regular supervision as a mandatory requirement for counsellors can be viewed, therefore, as pre-empting other methods of achieving a number of important goals, such as ensuring the effectiveness of therapy that is provided for clients, maximizing adherence to ethical standards and preventing counsellor burnout. There are many other ways in which these goals might be facilitated. For example, within family therapy (see Chapter 7), there is a tradition of 'reflecting teams', in which colleagues observe the work of a therapist and immediately feed back their comments to him or her (and often to the clients as well). In the early years of client-centred counselling, trainee counsellors would sit in on therapy cases of more experienced colleagues, gradually playing a more active role as an actual therapist to the client (Rogers 1951). Either of these approaches give a much more direct form of consultation than would ever be available in conventional supervision. It may be that the task of monitoring the effectiveness of therapy could be better carried out by asking clients to complete questionnaires such as the CORE outcome measure (see Chapter 18) on a regular basis. The use of information technology makes it possible for such data to be analysed and accessible to the counsellor in advance of the following session, and also for the counsellor to compare the rate of 'progress' of the client with that reported by other clients with similar presenting problems.

Among these critical voices, there is no suggestion that it is not helpful to have opportunities to reflect on work with clients in the context of a supportive relationship with an experienced colleague. The debate that has emerged over the past few years is about the formats within which such opportunities can be made available, and the wisdom of adopting a mandatory system of professional regulation built around a particular format. If a system of supervision is mandatory, there is a danger that it can degenerate into a bureaucratic ritual that evokes resistance, and that lacks sensitivity to individual needs. If, on the other hand, a system is wholly voluntary, it runs the risk of denying the all too real hazards of practice, and the grandiose fantasy of being able, on one's own, to take care of everything (Chapter 19).

in training. The implications for training of the movement towards integrationist and eclectic approaches are only beginning to be addressed. The relevance for counselling practice of research training or the adoption of a 'scientist practitioner' model has not been fully investigated. There are few courses for training trainers and supervisors. The specific training and supervision needs of non-professional or volunteer counsellors have not been assessed. There is, therefore, room for a great deal of additional theory and research in this area.

On the other hand, it is possible to assert with some confidence that the core elements of counsellor training and education are known, or are believed to be known. Competent counsellors are able to make use of accurate self-awareness, knowledge of theoretical models and a range of counselling skills.

Chapter summary

- Counselling training has become more professionalized and regulated in the post-war era. The psychoanalytic practice of structuring training largely around a period of personal analysis has been replaced by a more comprehensive approach.

- The key components of most counselling training programmes are: developing theoretical understanding; acquiring counselling skills; work on self-awareness; exploration of professional issues; supervised practice with clients; research skills and awareness of research-informed practice.

- The most controversial area of training concerns the requirement to undergo *personal therapy*. The evidence in support of this element of training is equivocal.

- The most difficult issues facing counselling trainers are those of *selecting trainees* and *assessing competence*.

- There are many different methods of assessing competence, but at present there is a lack of consensus on how to define the criteria for adequacy of performance.

- For the majority of counsellors, ongoing supervision or regular consultation with colleagues represents the main form of continuing education and training.

Topics for reflection and discussion

1 How would you organize the initial selection of people who wish to participate in counsellor training? In your view, what are the most important qualities of the person who has the potential to be an effective counsellor? How can these qualities be reliably assessed?

2 Do you agree with those who would insist on personal therapy as a requirement for all those in training as counsellors? How much personal therapy should be demanded, in your view? Should non-professional counsellors, who may be seeing only two or three clients each week, also receive personal therapy?

3 Compare the relative strengths and weaknesses of integrationist/eclectic and 'single theory' approaches to counsellor training.

4 It is generally accepted that counselling courses should contain inputs in the three areas of theory, practical skills, and work on self. In your view, what is the ideal balance between these elements?

5 How would you know whether someone is a competent counsellor?

6 Reflect on your experience as a member of an experiential group as part of a counselling course. How has this activity contributed to your learning?

Key terms and concepts

assessment centre procedure

assessment of competence

development of professional identity

human resource development

interpersonal process recall

microcounselling or microskills

personal journals

professional issues

self-awareness

supervision

theoretical orientation

training analysis

Suggested further reading

The one really powerful book in this area, a book that fundamentally changed the way that people think about supervision and training, is *Supervision in the Helping Professions*, by Hawkins and Shohet (2000). Beyond that, Dryden *et al.* (1995) bring together a good account of the current consensus concerning what should be included in counsellor training programmes, and both Mearns (1997) and Johns (1998) effectively capture the highly personal, and demanding, nature of counselling and psychotherapy training.

For those interested in what is possibly the most difficult aspect of training, the assessment of fitness to practice, Wheeler (1996) summarizes very effectively the various options that are available, and their strengths and weaknesses.

21 Beyond an introduction: continuing the conversation

Introduction

Counselling is a practice that has evolved in response to social conditions and as a result of the creativity of practitioners. Counselling can be viewed as a particular type of relationship between people, which occurs when one person has a need to tell their story or to resolve a problem in living with the help of another person who is outside their family or immediate network. All cultures have provided opportunities for this kind of relationship. In modern industrialized societies, counselling and psychotherapy have emerged as important and widely used arenas for 'therapeutic' storytelling and personal 'work'. Counselling is continually being reconstructed and reshaped to reflect the needs and circumstances of different groups of people within a society that is complex, fragmented and changing. The preceding chapters have introduced the diversity and historical development of contemporary counselling theory and practice. But what are the underlying trends and issues? Is there a coherence to counselling, despite its multiplicity of models?

This concluding chapter is structured around some key questions:

- What are the main themes that underpin debates about counselling theory and practice? What are the fundamental choices and tensions existing within the field?
- How has counselling changed over the past 50 years? What directions or trends can be seen?
- How might counselling evolve over the next 50 years? What are the potential future directions for counselling?

The metaphor of the conversation provides a number of powerful ways of understanding these issues. What goes on between counsellor and client is, at heart, a conversation. Debates between different counselling theorists can be seen as ongoing conversations about the best way to help or to make sense of the therapeutic relationship. On a longer time-scale, the images of the person implicit in counselling, and the role and positioning of counselling in society, can be seen as part of a long slow cultural conversation about what it means to be human. And, of course, the conversation never ends. There is always something new to be said. There is always scope and profit in returning to something that was said long ago: does it have a meaning that was not appreciated at the time? And, best of all, a conversation is an actual living process between people (which books can never be). So the conversation flows on, doubles back on itself, veers off at tangents. Nevertheless, there are certain central themes around which the conversation circles and to which it returns. Counselling is a conversation *about* (some of) the fundamental uncertainties of living in the modern world, of being a citizen of a capitalist industrial nation at the start of the twenty-first century. It is a conversation about deep questions for which there can be no certain answers.

Key issues in counselling theory and practice

The tension between the individual and the collective: autonomy/freedom versus relatedness/belonging

The modern world opens up staggering possibilities for individual autonomy. In traditional cultures, people depended on each other, for food, shelter and security, in very tangible and obvious ways. For the majority of people, there were very limited choices, even in relation to what they ate or where they lived. All this seems to be different in the modern world. We are individuals. We please ourselves. We have rights. We consume. As many people have observed, the growth of individualism and the growth of counselling and psychotherapy have gone hand in hand. As individual selves, we can only really deal with our anxiety, fear, depression and destiny on an individual basis, in the privacy of a confidential counselling room. Individualism is built into the fabric of society in such forms as the design of houses and cars, the organization of the tax system, the plotlines of novels, films and plays. Yet, in the end, the individualism of the modern world is false. We are all profoundly interdependent, at both personal and economic levels. Anxiety, depression and destiny are embedded in relationships with others, are understood through shared cultural conceptions, are assuaged through talking to someone who accepts and understands.

To be a person in modern society is therefore to be caught in a field of great tension, simultaneously pulled in the direction of individualism and in the direction of the communal. We live simultaneously in internal and external worlds. All aproaches to counselling, and all counsellors, have had to find their own way of addressing this question, of resolving this tension. Many approaches have attempted to deal with it by excluding or redefining the social. In person-centred theory, the social becomes a set of generalized 'conditions of worth'. In recent psychodynamic theory, the social is dealt with in terms of 'internalized objects'. By contrast, systemic and family-oriented approaches strive to exclude the individual and highlight the communal. Other approaches, such as multicultural and feminist, strive to find ways of incorporating both the social and the individual within their models of the person. What all aproaches share is the necessity of coming up with some means of talking about the tension between the individual and the collective, some way of carrying out a conversation – however stilted or partial – around this pervasive theme.

Of course, to frame this issue in terms of 'individualism' and 'community' is overly abstract. The most important relationships a person has are those of being a child and being a parent, and the most important group to which a person belongs is his or her family. In counselling, people talk about how they feel about these relationships, and try to find the best mix of giving and taking, caring and being cared for.

The nature of power and influence

What does it mean to be powerful, to be able to exert influence and control? What does it mean to be powerless, to be a victim of oppression, to be controlled by others? What is the right balance in a life between powerfulness and power-lessness, between controlling others and allowing them to control oneself, domination and submission? As human beings, we possess many powers, and are confronted by the power of others. There is an inevitability in any life to the experiencing of not only triumph and joy, but also pain and suffering. Power differences are structured around fundamental social categories, such as class, race and gender. Dilemmas and issues around the nature of power and control are intrinsic to counselling, for both counsellor and client. Does the counsellor adopt a position of expert, of client-centred equal or of 'not-knowing' witness? How much does the counsellor say in the counselling room? *What* kinds of statement does he or she make – reflection, instruction, interpretation? Is the aim of counselling self-control and self-management, or a self-fulfilment that reflects a celebration of personal power? How is the person who has been oppressed, as in childhood sexual abuse, encouraged to name their experience? Are they victims, survivors or post-traumatic stress disorder sufferers? Should this person seek to express their power through anger, or through forgiveness? These are just some of the many examples of issues of power that emerge in counselling. In reality, questions of power and powerlessness are always present in counselling: in the stories told by the client, in the counsellor–client relationship and in the relationship between both counsellor and client and the counselling organization.

Location of identity in time and history

As persons, we live in time. Our plans and aspirations stretch out into, and create, a future. The past is represented not only in our memories, our mental images and recollections, but through the meanings that external objects and places hold for us. One of the basic human dilemmas arises from the task of being able to locate oneself in time and history. There seems to be a basic human tendency or need to construct a story of one's life, with a beginning, middle and end (or possible endings). Many of the problems that people bring to counselling can be seen as distortions of the person's relationship with the time of their life: depression is a time with no hoped for future state, compulsive behaviour is warding off a feared future event, low self-esteem may entail returning again and again to a moment of failure in the past. Although different approaches to counselling must each be flexible enough to enable the client to move across past, present and future, each model has its own distinctive time slot. Humanistic approaches emphasize 'here-and-now' experiencing. Behavioural approaches are much concerned with what will happen in the future: achieving behavioural *targets*; relapse *prevention*. On the whole, most counselling models operate within the time-frame of the client's life. Some family therapy approaches stretch this personal time-frame to encompass intergenerational influences. The more culturally oriented therapies, such as feminist, multicultural and narrative counselling, operate within an extended time-frame that may include events well outside the family history of the individual client. For example, some multicultural counsellors would see relevance for some clients in studying the history of racism. In all of these approaches, counselling can be seen as a means of assisting people to construct an identity that is positioned in time and history.

The significance of bodily experience

To be a person is to be embodied, to have physical presence and sensations, to move. Living with, and within, a body presents a continual set of challenges. The person's relationship with his or her body is one of the central issues in many (perhaps all) counselling situations. The primary area in which aspects of the body dominate counselling is through the existence (or non-existence) of feeling and emotion. We feel in our bodies, and these feelings or emotions are indicators of what is most important to us. Our bodies tell us how we feel about things. And we live in a culture in which acknowledging, naming and expressing emotions is deeply problematic. Mass modern society places great value on rationality, self-control and 'cool'. For many people, the counselling room is the only place in which they have permission to allow themselves fully to feel. All approaches to counselling, in their very different ways, give emotion a high place on the thera-peutic agenda. Another crucial dimension of bodily experiencing is sexuality. The person's relationship with himself or herself as a sexual being, as someone with sexual powers and energies, can often be a core issue in counselling. Other counselling issues that centre on the body are concerns about eating, digesting, defecating, being big or small, being attractive or ugly. Finally, there are many problematic experiences that people have around health, including fertility, being ill, dealing with loss of functioning or parts of the body and the encounter with death. The common thread through all these life issues is the experience of embodiment. We are all faced with the issue of what our body means to us, and how we accept or deny different aspects of our bodily functioning. Counselling is a setting in which some of these issues can be explored and reconciled, and all counsellors and theories of counselling adopt their own particular stance in relation to the body.

The basis for knowledge, truth and moral action

How do we *know*? What counts as valid knowledge? What is the right thing to do? People act on the basis of what they believe to be true, and so the issue of what is to count as true knowledge is therefore a fundamental question with profound implications. However, knowing what is true and what is right is far from easy for members of modern technological societies. First, there are many competing sources of authoritative knowledge. In the past, most people would have accepted the teachings of their religious leader as the primary source of true knowledge. Now, of course, perhaps the majority of people would doubt the validity of religious knowledge, and would look instead to science to provide certainty and a reliable guide to action. On the other hand, scientific knowledge can be questioned in terms of the areas of human experience which it excludes. There is a reawakening in some quarters of the value of spiritual experience as a source of knowledge. Other people look to art as a source of knowledge, claiming that insight and understanding are developed through the use of creative imagination and different modes of representing reality. Finally, through all this, many people maintain a belief in the truth of their own everyday common-sense experience. Counselling reflects this multiplicity of knowledge sources, with different approaches to counselling encouraging their clients to specialize in one or another modes of knowing. For example, cognitive–behavioural therapies place great weight on objective, scientific knowing, whereas transpersonal therapies attempt to create the conditions for spiritual learning.

The five core issues that have been discussed – individualism–collectivism, power, time, embodiment and knowledge – are inevitably interlinked in practice. Experience is a unity, and these different facets or dimensions are only ways of organizing or making sense of that experience. These issues are similar to the modes of *being-in-the-world* identified by existentialist philosophers, but I have presented them in a way that highlights the importance of social context. The point is that these are perhaps some of the basic questions or dilemmas that we face as members of the society in which we live, and that counselling is one of the few arenas in which we are allowed an opportunity to reflect on how we deal with them. Counselling theories, skills and training courses provide a framework that will enable people to engage in a personal conversation about some of these issues. The issues, of course, never go away. It just seems to help to be be able to name them, to share other people's perceptions and understandings of them, to be less alone with them.

Where counselling has been: the past 50 years

No one has really written or researched the recent history of counselling to any great extent. It is difficult to make statements that characterize 'counselling' as a whole. This is a largely fragmented profession or discipline. Nevertheless, my impression is that over time there have been some significant shifts in the positions that counselling and counsellors have taken in relation to the five core issues outlined above. In terms of the question of individualism–community, there would appear to have been a steady movement in the direction of a more socially and culturally oriented approach, largely initiated by feminist and multicultural practitioners and theorists. This trend is surely also associated with the fact that counselling has grown and expanded. There are many more counsellors per head of the population, in Western industrial societies, than there were in 1950, and this has meant that counsellors have been forced to adapt their methods and ideas to accommodate many different social groups and take full account of a wider range of social and cultural identities.

The question of power and control, and how it is addressed in counselling, can be discussed on several levels. The negative, or abusive, power of the counsellor in relation to the client, as manifest in such behaviour as sexual exploitation, has been widely recognized and has led to the installation of tightly defined codes of ethics and to an increasing emphasis given to ethical issues in counsellor training. On the other hand, counsellors are probably exerting more direct control over their clients than ever before, because they are working much more often within externally defined time limits and are employing externally specified therapeutic procedures (as mediated through 'manualized' training and competency assessment). As a result, there is simply less space for the client to do whatever it is they feel they need to do in therapy. While the 1960s and 1970s saw a flowering of avowedly radical, emancipatory or liberationist therapies, such as encounter groups or the antipsychiatry of R. D. Laing, the 1990s saw a convergence of counselling and the world of business, in the form of workplace counselling and employee assistance programmes. Even in health services, a business focus has been introduced through research into the cost-effectiveness of psychological therapies. There has been an erosion of voluntarism, and the appearance in its place of a salaried profession.

It is in the actual content of counselling sessions that the issue of power has become most evident. The areas of therapeutic work that expanded most during the 1980s were therapies for survivors of sexual abuse and work with people suffering from post-traumatic stress disorder. The common theme across both of these groups of clients is the experience of powerlessness, of being controlled by an abusive other or threatening situation. It seems likely that this trend reflects two much broader social phenomena that have been dominant during the post-war era. First, the struggle to overcome sexism has meant that sexual violence against women has come into the open, has been named and discussed, with the consequence that sexual abuse of children could no longer be regarded as mere fantasy on the part of the child. Second, the enormous sensitivity to *risk* that many sociologists consider to be at the heart of late twentieth-century attitudes has contributed to a preoccupation with the psychology of trauma and danger.

In the domain of *location of identity in time and history*, there has been perhaps a slight shift in the past 50 years, again led by feminist and multicultural practitioners and theorists, in the direction of a gradual opening up of historical understandings that go beyond the individual life-course. However, most of the time most counsellors and clients probably still limit their discussion events within a one-year radius of the now.

The issue of embodiment has probably not been as fully assimilated into counselling as it might have been over the past 50 years. The majority of counsellors still operate in a relatively disembodied manner: seated, not moving very much, not touching. Outside of this mainstream armchair counselling, however, a lot has been happening. There are many therapists who use body-oriented methods such as movement, dance, massage, meditation and ritual. The therapeutic value of physical exercise is well established. But, for the most part, counselling remains centred on talking rather than doing.

The question of truth and knowledge, and the diversity of knowledge sources that exist within modern culture, has affected counselling in a number of quite different ways over the past 50 years. Some groups have attempted to make counselling as scientifically validated a procedure as they can: for example, by carrying out research into the outcomes and processes of therapy and using these results both to legitimate and to improve their approach. From another direction, there has been a rejection of scientific knowledge by counsellors who argue that science as it is practised does not produce knowledge that has an special relevance to counselling. Some counsellors have moved into the discourses of religious and spiritual experience, within traditions such as Christianity and Buddhism, to validate their work. Still others have developed versions of creative arts therapies. Counselling therefore reflects the epistemological and moral relativism that is characteristic of postmodern culture. This is a real shift since the 1950s. In the early writings of Carl Rogers, or the psychoanalysts, or the behaviourists, things seemed much simpler. One knew where one was. These earlier theories of the person told fairly straightforward, unambiguous stories about how people got problems and what could be done to help them. The prevailing mood now, by contrast, is best summed up by the *constructivist* movement. The world is what we make it. Truth is what people believe to be true.

Taking the overall picture of the historical development of counselling over the past 50 years, it is apparent that two opposing trends can be observed. On the one hand, counselling has become much more professionalized, regulated and embedded within society as a kind of service industry with links to medicine and education. It has become respectable. On the other hand, there are signs that some of the basic ideas that held counselling together and gave it some overall coherence are being increasingly questioned. The focus on the individual, the espousal of rational scientific knowledge, the creation of a site for personal reflection and problem-solving that could be separated from a world of politics and inequality, the idea that counselling involved the application of a theoretical model – all these assumptions are being challenged. There is an increasing tension between the external face of counselling – the role that it fulfils in society – and the experience of what it feels like inside that beast.

Where counselling is going: the next 50 years

I believe that it is quite likely that counselling will change significantly over the next 50 years, in response to the increasing pace of change in society. There are three scenarios that seem to me to be unlikely. First, there is the possibility that counselling might continue much as it is. I do not think that this will happen, because counselling is highly sensitive to cultural change, and in effect has been a form of caring that has moved into gaps that have appeared in pre-existing networks of social care and support. For example, bereavement and loss counselling has emerged to fill a niche caused by the increasing secularization and medicalization of death. Moreover, counselling always needs to re-create itself, as its concepts and methods become assimilated into popular culture. For example, the Jungian notion of the *complex* quickly became common usage to a point where it no longer functioned as a technical term. The concept of *empathy* is heading in the same direction. Social change seems inevitable, and as society changes it consumes psychological theories. Counsellors, psychotherapists and psychologists need to keep one step ahead of common sense. So counselling will change, one way or another.

The second possibility is that counselling may become appropriated by the state and become closely controlled and regulated in a similar manner to nursing, social work or probation. Again, this seems unlikely. Counselling as it exists today is funded from a diversity of sources – private, voluntary agency, commercial and state – and no government has the resources available to assimilate any significant portion of this activity into a statutory agency. Moreover, counselling is not important enough to be directly controlled by the state. The established human service professions, such as medicine, nursing and social work, all deal, in the end, with matters of life and death. Counselling can never plausibly make this sort of claim.

A third possibility is that counselling could become much more like a religion, and develop as a vehicle for spiritual experience and communion. To some extent this is happening, but it seems highly unlikely that such a movement could come to dominate counselling, because of the opposition on one side of existing religions, the opposition on another side of the 'scientific faction' within therapy and the opposition from a third side of the humanists. In addition, much of the funding for counselling comes through agencies that position themselves as adjuncts to health care, personnel or welfare services. To move counselling significantly in the direction of religion could endanger this source of legitimacy and economic support.

If the status quo, social work and religion are *not* likely futures for counselling, then what will happen? I anticipate that there may be five trends that could possibly exert a major influence on the shape of counselling over the next 50 years.

Increasing attention to environmentalism. If counselling acts as a reflection of what is most painful for members of a culture at a particular point in time (in Freud's era, sexuality and paternal authority; in Rogers' era, personal identity and self-acceptance; today, risk and belonging), then there is every chance that the issue that will emerge over the next decades is that of the relationship between the person and the environment. If even half of the predictions about global warming turn out to be true, the next 50 years could well be a frightening time. People will wish to change their behaviour and attitudes not in the direction of being more assertive or self-actualized, but in the direction of being more environmentally aware and responsible. Enormous feelings of loss and guilt may be evoked by the destruction of peoples, species, parts of the planet. The sense of self and embodiment that has characterized the modern person, a largely autonomous and separate self, may come to be seen as part of a pattern of life that has resulted in environmental failure. Counsellors may be called upon to work with quite different kinds of issues, in new ways.

The localization of practice. A process that has been observed by sociologists during the late twentieth and early twenty-first centuries is *globalization*. New methods of mass communication have multiplied many times over the dissemination of information across cultures and between individuals. This has brought about an increasing uniformity of cultures and economies – a McDonald's in every town or village. Globalization has also occurred within the field of counselling and psychotherapy. Indigenous methods of problem-solving and psychological healing have been replaced by Western psychiatry and psychotherapy. Training manuals and videos ensure that models of counselling are taught and delivered in the same way in every country in the world. The professionalization of counselling means that practitioners are likely to have been exposed to high status, internationally recognized approaches, rather than merely being trained to do what works and makes sense at their local level. There are signs, however, that the global apparatus of counselling is beginning to lose momentum. Fewer and fewer counsellors admit to using 'brand name' manualized approaches to therapy. More and more, practitioners describe themselves as integrationist or eclectic, willing to combine ideas and methods in ways that meet the needs of the clients they see, rather than the clients seen many years ago by the founder of a new theory. More practitioners are open to ideas drawn from older healing traditions, such as Buddhism, yoga or shamanism. There is a kind of 'reverse colonialism', where European and American counsellors seem to have become more interested in learning from other cultures. All these trends seem to point towards a growing *localization* of counselling, in which groups of practitioners work together to create services that respond to the issues faced by their actual local communities, rather than attempting to replicate models of care developed in other places for other people.

Interdisciplinarity. At a theoretical level, counselling and psychotherapy have been dominated by ideas and concepts from psychology, and have largely lived within a professional niche carved out by psychiatry and clinical psychology. It is hard to see that this state of affairs can continue. Essentially, the image of the human subject presented by psychology is too impoverished to provide counsellors with a basis for making sense of what happens in the counselling room. In that room, what client and counsellor talk about will necessarily refer to the social world within which they both live, their ideas about truth, justice and the good life, their use of language. A full enough understanding of the counselling process requires some appreciation of sociology, anthropology, philosophy, theology and the arts. Moreover, it is now clear that there are many competing psychological models: psychodynamic, humanistic, behavioural, cognitive. The differences between these models cannot be understood or resolved at a psychological level, but require the application of theories and concepts from philosophy and the social sciences in general.

The impact of technology. We live in a world characterized by high levels of technological innovation, driven largely by the research and development laboratories of international corporations seeking commercial advantage. Up to now, technology has played a relatively minor role in counselling and psychotherapy. Clients and counsellors have engaged in face-to-face contact, usually sitting in chairs in the same room. Research has mainly employed paper questionnaires filled in with a pen. The availability of Internet-mediated communications, through e-mail, chatrooms, web cameras, mobile phones, text messages etc., introduces different forms of real and virtual relationship. Different kinds of sensors can be used to measure, in real-time, aspects of a client's emotional state. Clients can respond to research questions by talking or texting; research data can be instantly available to both client and counsellor. The use of information technology widens the repertoire of ways of being in contact that are open to clients and counsellors. It may also be that communication technology changes the way that people understand themselves. For example, being in voice contact (through a mobile phone) with any friend at any moment of the day is surely very different, as a way of being a person, from working as a rural farmer in a remote, small community. The new technologies associated with assisted reproduction will almost certainly produce new identity issues. In the past, someone who had been adopted would know that he or she actually had a biological parent, an actual person who 'made' them. In the future, for some people the notion of 'biological parent' may hardly make sense. What would it be like to be like this? The implications for counselling of technological change are hard to imagine. Already, some counsellors are embracing the Internet, while others cannot accept that anything that takes place in that medium could truly be regarded as 'therapy'.

Consumer empowerment and choice. The single most important feature of the historical development of counselling has been its expansion. Compared to the 1950s, there are many more people now who have received counselling, or who know someone who has been in counselling. Many more people have studied psychology at college or university, and have acquired some appreciation of psychotherapeutic ideas. Other people may have come across counselling depicted in magazines, novels, plays and films. The result of all this is that consumers of counselling are increasingly well informed, and are increasingly able to express their preferences and wishes for specific types of help. There is even the beginning of a consumer movement, with user groups publicizing what they regard as good practice, and surveys of therapy carried out by consumers. Potential clients know what they want, and are able to find it, particularly in large metropolitan areas that are well supplied with counselling and psychotherapy services. The growth of telephone and Internet counselling opens up another avenue for consumer choice. In some areas of the USA, state funding of therapy services depends on consumer evaluations, and agencies are forced to publish reports that detail their effectiveness with different categories of clients. Given the overwhelming significance of consumption and consumer choice in all areas of modern life, it seems unlikely that counselling clients will become *less* well informed and empowered in the future. The result of this may be that the types of services that are offered become increasingly shaped by consumer preferences and choices, and that the relationship between counsellor and client may change in ways that cannot easily be anticipated.

There is only one certainty about these predictions about the future directions that counselling might take, and that is that they are wrong. No one can predict the future. But something will happen. There will certainly be some ways in which the map of counselling in 20 or 50 years is significantly different from the map that has been offered in the earlier chapters of this book. The challenge for each of us is to be willing to share our own personal visions for counselling, and by doing so to participate in a conversation that will continue to be of value to ourselves and to those who privilege us by sharing their stories of trouble.

References

Abramowitz, S. I. and Murray, J. (1983) Race effects in psychotherapy. In J. Murray and P. R. Abramson (eds) *Bias in Psychotherapy*. New York: Praeger.

Achenbach, G. B. (1995) Philosophy, philosophical practice, and psychotherapy. In R. Lahav (ed.) *Essays on Philosophical Counseling*. Lanham, MD: University Press of America.

Addis, M. E. and Krasnow, A. D. (2000) A national survey of practicing psychologists' attitudes toward psychotherapy treatment manuals. *Journal of Consulting and Clinical Psychology*, 68, 331–9.

Agazarian, Y. and Peters, R. (1981) *The Visible and Invisible Group: Two Perspectives on Group Psychotherapy and Group Process*. London: Tavistock/Routledge.

Agnew, R. M., Harper, H., Shapiro, D. A. and Barkham, M. (1994) Resolving a challenge to the therapeutic relationship: a single-case study. *British Journal of Medical Psychology*, 67, 155–70.

Agnew-Davies, R. (1999) Learning from research into the counselling relationship. In C. Feltham (ed.) *Understanding the Counselling Relationship*. London: Sage.

Ainsworth, M. D. S., Blehar, M. C., Waters, E. and Wall, S. (1978) *Patterns of Attachment: A Psychological Study of the Strange Situation*. Hillsdale, NJ: Erlbaum.

Al-Abdul-Jabbar, J. and Al-Issa, I. (eds) (2000) Psychotherapy in Islamic society. In I. Al-Issla (ed.) *Al-Junon: Mental Illness in the Islamic World*. Madison, IN: International Universities Press.

Albee, G. W. (1977) The Protestant ethic, sex and psychotherapy. *American Psychologist*, 32, 150–61.

Alexander, F. and French, T. M. (1946) *Psychoanalytic Therapy. Principles and Applications*. New York: Ronald Press.

Alexander, L. B. and Luborsky, L. (1986) The Penn Helping Alliance scales. In L. D. Greenberg and W. M. Pinsot (eds) *The Psychotherapeutic Process: A Research Handbook*. New York: Guilford Press.

Al-Issa, I. (ed.) (2000a) *Al-Junon: Mental Illness in the Islamic World*. Madison, IN: International Universities Press.

Al-Issa, I. (2000b) Mental illness in medieval Islamic society. In I. Al-Issla (ed.) *Al-Junon: Mental Illness in the Islamic World*. Madison, CN: International Universities Press.

Allen, J. (1999) Responding to unemployment and inqualities in income and health. *European Journal of Psychotherapy, Counselling and Health*, 2, 143–52.

Allen, L. (1990) A client's experience of failure. In D. Mearns and W. Dryden (eds) *Experiences of Counselling in Action*. London: Sage.

Alloy, L. B. and Abramson, L. Y. (1982) Learned helplessness, depression and the illusion of control. *Journal of Personality and Social Psychology*, 42, 1114–26.

American Association for Counseling and Development (1988) *Ethical Standards*. Alexandria, VA: AACD.

American Psychiatric Association (1994) *Diagnostic and Statistical Manual of Mental Disorders*, 4th edn. Washington, DC: American Psychiatric Association.

Anastasi, A. (1992) What counselors should know about the use and interpretation of psychological tests. *Journal of Counseling and Development*, 70, 610–15.

Anderson, H. and Goolishian, H. (1992) The client is the expert: a not-knowing approach to therapy. In S. McNamee and K. J. Gergen (eds) *Therapy as Social Construction*. London: Sage.

Anderson, W. (ed.) (1977) *Therapy and the Arts: Tools of Consciousness*. New York: Harper and Row.

Andrews, J. D. W. (1991) *The Active Self in Psychotherapy: An Integration of Therapeutic Styles*. Boston: Allyn and Bacon.

Angus, L. (1996) An intensive analysis of metaphor themes in psychotherapy. In J. S. Mio and A. Katz (eds) *Metaphor: Pragmatics and Applications*. New York: Erlbaum.

Angus, L., Levitt, H. and Hardtke, K. (1999) The Narrative Process Coding System: research applications and implications for psychotherapy practice. *Journal of Clinical Psychology*, 55, 1255–70.

Angus, L. E. and Rennie, D. L. (1988) Therapist participation in metaphor generation: collaborative and noncollaborative styles. *Psychotherapy*, 25, 552–60.

Angus, L. E. and Rennie, D. L. (1989) Envisioning the representational world: the client's experience of metaphoric expressiveness in psychotherapy. *Psychotherapy*, 26, 373–9.

Annesley, P. and Coyle, P. (1998) Dykes and psychs: lesbian women's experience of clinical psychology. *Changes*, 16, 247–58.

Ansbacher, H. L. (1990) Alfred Adler's influence on the three leading cofounders of humanistic psychology. *Journal of Humanistic Psychology*, 30(4), 45–53.

Antze, P. (1976) The role of ideologies in peer psychotherapy organisations. *Journal of Applied Behavioral Science*, 12, 323–46.

Appelbaum, A. (1973) Psychological mindedness: word, concept and essence. *International Journal of Psychoanalysis*, 54, 35–46.

Aron, L. and Harris, A. (eds) (1993) *The Legacy of Sándor Ferenczi*. Hillsdale, NJ: The Analytic Press.

Aronson, T. A. (1989) A critical review of psychotherapeutic treatments of the borderline personality: historical trends and future directions. *Journal of Nervous and Mental Disease*, 177, 511–28.

Arsenian, J. and Arsenian, J. M. (1948) Tough and easy cultures: a conceptual analysis. *Psychiatry*, 11, 377–85.

Arthern, J. and Madill, A. (1999) How do transition objects work? The therapist's view. *British Journal of Medical Psychology*, 72, 1–21.

Atkinson, D. R. (1985) Research on cross-cultural counseling and psychotherapy: a review and update of reviews. In P. Pedersen (ed.) *Handbook of Cross-cultural Counseling and Psychotherapy*. New York: Praeger.

Atkinson, D. R. and Lowe, S. M. (1995) The role of ethnicity, cultural knowledge, and conventional techniques in counseling and psychotherapy. In J. G. Ponterotto, J. M. Casas,

L. A. Suzuki and C. M. Alexander (eds) *Handbook of Multicultural Counseling*. London: Sage.

Atwood, G. and Stolorow, R. D. (1993) *Faces in a Cloud: Intersubjectivity in Personality Theory*, 2nd edn. Northvale, NJ: Jason Aronson.

Austin, K. M., Moline, M. E. and Williams, G. T. (1990) *Confronting Malpractice: Legal and Ethical Dilemmas in Psychotherapy*. London: Sage.

Aveline, M. O. (1986) Personal themes from training groups for health care professionals. *British Journal of Medical Psychology*, 59, 325–35.

Aveline, M. (1990) Developing a new NHS psychotherapy service and training scheme in the provinces. *British Journal of Psychotherapy*, 6, 312–23.

Aveline, M. O. (1995) How I assess for focal therapy. In C. Mace (ed.) *The Art and Science of Assessment in Psychotherapy*. London: Routledge.

Aveline, M. and Dryden, W. (eds) (1988) *Group Therapy in Britain*. Milton Keynes: Open University Press.

Aveline, M. and Shapiro, D. A. (eds) (1995) *Research Foundations for Psychotherapy Practice*. Chichester: Wiley.

Axline, V. (1971) *Dibs: In Search of Self*. Harmondsworth: Penguin.

Ayllon, T. and Azrin, N. H. (1965) The measurement and reinforcement of behavior of psychotics. *Journal of the Experimental Analysis of Behavior*, 8, 357–83.

Ayllon, T. and Azrin, N. H. (1968) *The Token Economy*. New York: Appleton Century Crofts.

Bach, S. (2001) Toward a theory of self. In J. C. Muran (ed.) *Self-relations in the Psychotherapy Process*. Washington, DC: American Psychological Association.

Bachelor, A. (1988) How clients perceive therapist empathy: a content analysis of 'received' empathy. *Psychotherapy*, 25, 227–40.

Badaines, A. (1988) Psychodrama. In J. Rowan and W. Dryden (eds) *Innovative Therapy in Britain*. Milton Keynes: Open University Press.

Bakan, D. (1966) *Against Method*. New York: Basic Books.

Bakan, D. (1976) Politics and American psychology. In K. Riegel (ed.) *Psychology: Theoretical–Historical Perspectives*. New York: Springer.

Baker, S. B., Daniels, T. G. and Greeley, A. T. (1990) Systematic training of graduate level counselors: narrative and meta-analytic reviews of three programmes. *Counseling Psychologist*, 18, 355–421.

Baldwin, M. (ed.) (1987) *The Use of Self in Therapy*. New York: Haworth Press.

Bandura, A. (1971) Psychotherapy based upon modeling principles. In A. E. Bergin and S. L. Garfield (eds) *Handbook of Psychotherapy and Behavior Change: An Empirical Analysis*. New York: Wiley.

Bandura, A. (1977) *Social Learning Theory*. Englewood Cliffs, NJ: Prentice Hall.

Bannister, D. and Fransella, F. (1985) *Inquiring Man*, 3rd edn. London: Routledge.

Barker, C., Pistrang, N. and Elliott, R. (1994) *Research Methods in Clinical and Counselling Psychology*. Chichester: Wiley.

Barker, P. (1992) *Basic Family Therapy*, 3rd edn. Oxford: Blackwell.

Barkham, M. (1989) Brief prescriptive therapy in two-plus-one sessions: initial cases from the clinic. *Behavioural Psychotherapy*, 17, 161–75.

Barkham, M. (1992) Research on integrative and eclectic therapy. In W. Dryden (ed.) *Integrative and Eclectic Therapy: A Handbook*. Buckingham: Open University Press.

Barkham, M., Guthrie, E., Hardy, G. E., Margison, F. R. and Shapiro, D. A. (eds) (1998) *Psychodynamic-interpersonal Therapy: Foundations of Research-based Practice*. London: Sage.

Barkham, M., Margison, F., Leach, C. *et al.* (2001) Service profiling and outcomes benchmarking using the CORE OM: toward practice based evidence in the psychological therapies. *Journal of Consulting and Clinical Psychology*, 69, 184–96.

Barkham, M. and Shapiro, D. A. (1989) Towards resolving the problem of waiting lists: psychotherapy in two-plus-one sessions. *Clinical Psychology Forum*, 23, 15–18.

Barkham, M. and Shapiro, D. A. (1990a) Brief psychotherapeutic interventions for job-related distress: a pilot study of prescriptive and exploratory therapy. *Counselling Psychology Quarterly*, 3, 133–47.

Barkham, M. and Shapiro, D. A. (1990b) Exploratory therapy in two-plus-one sessions: a research model for studying the process of change. In G. Lietaer, J. Rombauts and R. Van Balen (eds) *Client-centered and Experiential Psychotherapy in the Nineties*. Leuven: Leuven University Press.

Barkham, M., Stiles, W. B., Hardy, G. E. and Field, S. F. (1996) The assimilation model: theory, research and practical guidelines. In W. Dryden (ed.) *Research in Counselling and Psychotherapy: Practical Applications*. London: Sage.

Barlow, D. H., Hayes, S. C. and Nelson, R. O. (1984) *The Scientist Practitioner: Research and Accountability in Clinical and Educational Settings*. New York: Pergamon.

Barlow, D. H. and Hersen, M. (1986) *Single Case Experimental Designs: Strategies for Studying Behavior Change*, 2nd edn. New York: Pergamon.

Barrett-Lennard, G. T. (1962) Dimensions of therapist response as causal factors in therapeutic change. *Psychological Monographs*, 76 (whole number 562).

Barrett-Lennard, G. T. (1979) The client-centered system unfolding. In F. J. Turner (ed.) *Social Work Treatment: Interlocking Theoretical Approaches*, 2nd edn. New York: Free Press.

Barrett-Lennard, G. T. (1981) The empathy cycle – refinement of a nuclear concept. *Journal of Counseling Psychology*, 28, 91–100.

Barrett-Lennard, G. T. (1986) The Relationship Inventory now: issues and advances in theory, method and use. In L. S. Greenberg and W. M. Pinsof (eds) *The Psychotherapeutic Process: A Research Handbook*. New York: Guilford.

Barrett-Lennard, G. (1993) The phases and focus of empathy. *British Journal of Medical Psychology*, 66, 3–14.

Barrett-Lennard, G. T. (1998) *Carl Rogers' Helping System: Journey and Substance*. London: Sage.

Bartlett, A., King, M. and Phillips, P. (2001) Straight talking: an investigation of the attitudes and practice of psychoanalysts and psychotherapists in relation to gays and lesbians. *British Journal of Psychiatry*, 179, 545–9.

Bates, C. M. and Brodsky, A. M. (1989) *Sex in the Therapy Hour: A Case of Professional Incest*. London: Guilford Press.

Battye, R. (1991) On being a trainee. In W. Dryden and B. Thorne (eds) *Training and Supervision for Counselling in Action*. London: Sage.

Bauer, G. and Kobos, J. (1987) *Brief Therapy: Short-term Psychodynamic Intervention*. New York: Jason Aronson.

Baumeister, R. F. (1987) How the self became a problem: a psychological review of historical research. *Journal of Personality and Social Psychology*, 52(1), 163–76.

Bayer, R. (1987) *Homosexuality and American Psychiatry: The Politics of Diagnosis*, 2nd edn. Princeton, NJ: Princeton University Press.

Bayne, R. (1999) The counselling relationship and psychological type. In C. Feltham (ed.) *Understanding the Counselling Relationship*. London: Sage.

Beauchamp, T. L. and Childress, J. F. (1979) *Principles of Biomedical Ethics*. Oxford: Oxford University Press.

Beck, A. (1976) *Cognitive Therapy and the Emotional Disorders*. Harmondsworth: Penguin.

Beck, A. Y., Rush, A. G., Shaw, B. F. and Emery, G. (1979) *Cognitive Therapy of Depression*. New York: Guilford.

Beck, A. and Weishaar, M. (1989) Cognitive therapy. In A. Freeman, K. M. Simon, L. E. Beutler and H. Arkowitz (eds) *Comprehensive Handbook of Cognitive Therapy*. New York: Plenum Press.

Beidel, D. C. and Turner, S. M. (1986) A critique of the theoretical bases of cognitive behavioral theories and therapy. *Clinical Psychology Review*, 6, 177–97.

Bennis, W. and Shepard, H. (1956) A theory of group development. *Human Relations*, 9, 415–57.

Bennun, I. (1985) Unilateral marital therapy. In W. Dryden (ed.) *Marital Therapy in Britain, Volume 2*. London: Harper and Row.

Bentley, A. (1994) Counselling and homelessness. *Counselling*, 5(2), 132–4.

Bentley, A. (1997) The psychological effects of homelessness and their impact on the development of a counselling relationship. *Counselling Psychology Quarterly*, 10(2), 195–210.

Berg, I. K. and Kelly, S. (2000) *Building Solutions in Child Protective Services*. New York: Norton.

Berg, I. K. and Miller, S. D. (1992) *Working with the Problem Drinker: A Solution-focused Approach*. New York: Norton.

Berger, M. (1983) Toward maximising the utility of consumer satisfaction as an outcome. In M. J. Lambert, E. R. Christensen and S. S. DeJulio (eds) *The Assessment of Psychotherapy Outcome*. New York: Wiley.

Bergin, A. E. (1980) Psychotherapy and religious values. *Journal of Consulting and Clinical Psychology*, 48, 95–105.

Bergin, A. E. and Garfield, S. L. (eds) (1994) *Handbook of Psychotherapy and Behavior Change*, 4th edn. New York: Wiley.

Bergin, A. E. and Jensen, J. P. (1990) Religiosity of psychotherapists: a national survey. *Psychotherapy*, 27, 3–7.

Bergner, R. M. and Staggs, J. (1987) The positive therapeutic relationship as accreditation. *Psychotherapy*, 24, 315–20.

Berman, J. S. and Norton, N. C. (1985) Does professional training make a therapist more effective? *Psychological Bulletin*, 98, 401–7.

Berne, E. (1975) *What Do You Say After You Say Hello? The Psychology of Human Destiny*. London: Corgi.

Bernstein, B. (1972) Social class, language and socialization. In P. P. Giglioli (ed.) *Language and Social Context*. Harmondsworth: Penguin.

Berven, N. L. (1987) Improving evaluation in counselor training and credentialing through standardized simulations. In B. A. Edelstein and E. S. Berler (eds) *Evaluation and Accountability in Clinical Training*. New York: Plenum Press.

Berven, N. and Scofield, M. (1980) Evaluation of professional competence through standardised simulations: a review. *Rehabilitation Counseling Bulletin*, 179, 178–202.

Bettelheim, B. (1983) *Freud and Man's Soul*. London: Chatto and Windus.

Beutler, L. (1983) *Eclectic Psychotherapy. A Systematic Approach*. New York: Pergamon.

Beutler, L. E. and Clarkin, J. F. (1990) *Systematic Treatment Selection: Toward Targeted Therapeutic Interventions*. New York: Brunner/Mazel.

Beutler, L. E. and Crago, M. (eds) (1991) *Psychotherapy Research: An International Review of Programmatic Studies*. Washington, DC: American Psychological Association.

Beutler, L. E., Crago, M. and Arizmendi, T. G. (1986) Therapist variables in psychotherapy process and outcome. In S. L. Garfield and A. E. Bergin (eds) *Handbook of Psychotherapy and Behavior Change*, 3rd edn. New York: Wiley.

Beutler, L. E., Machado, P. P. and Neufeldt, S. A. (1994) Therapist variables. In A. Bergin and S. Garfield (eds) *Handbook of Psychotherapy and Behavior Change*. London: Wiley.

Beutler, L. E., Mahoney, M. J., Norcross, J. C. *et al.* (1987) Training integrative/eclectic psychotherapists II. *Journal of Integrative and Eclectic Psychotherapy*, 6, 296–332.

Bimrose, J. (1996) Multiculturalism. In R. Bayne, I. Horton and J. Bimrose (eds) *New Directions in Counselling*. London: Routledge.

Binder, J. L. and Strupp, H. H. (1997) 'Negative process': A recurrently discovered and underestimated facet of therapeutic process and outcome in the individual psychotherapy of adults. *Clinical Psychology: Science and Practice*, 4, 121–39.

Binswanger, L. (1963) *Being-in-the-World*. New York: Basic Books.

Bion, W. (1961) *Experiences in Groups*. London: Tavistock.

Blackburn, S. (1999) *Think*. Oxford: Oxford University Press.

Blackwell, R. T., Galassi, J. P., Galassi, M. D. and Watson, T. E. (1985) Are cognitive assessment methods equal? A comparison of think aloud and thought listing. *Cognitive Therapy and Research*, 9, 399–413.

Blatt, S. J., Sanislow, C. A., Zuroff, D. C. and Pilkonis, P. A. (1996) Characteristics of effective therapists: further analysis of data from the National Institute of Mental Health Treatment of Depression Collaborative Research Program. *Journal of Consulting and Clinical Psychology*, 64(6), 1276–84.

Bloch, S., Crouch, E. and Reibstein, J. (1981) Therapeutic factors in group psychotherapy. *Archives of General Psychiatry*, 38, 519–26.

Bloom, J. W. (1998) The ethical practice of Web counselling. *British Journal of Guidance and Counselling*, 26, 53–60.

Boadella, D. (1988) Biosynthesis. In J. Rowan and W. Dryden (eds) *Innovative Therapy in Britain*. Milton Keynes: Open University Press.

Bohart, A. C. (1990) Psychotherapy integration from a client-centered perspective. In G. Lietaer, J. Rombauts and R. Van Balen (eds) *Client-centered and Experiential Therapy in the Nineties*. Leuven: Leuven University Press.

Bohart, A. C. (2000) The client is the most important common factor: clients' self-healing capacities and psychotherapy. *Journal of Psychotherapy Integration*, 10, 127–48.

Bohart, A. C. and Greenberg, L. S. (eds) (1997) *Empathy Reconsidered: New Directions in Psychotherapy*. Washington, DC: American Psychological Association.

Bohart, A., Humphrey, A., Magallanes, M., Guxman, R., Smiljanich, K. and Aguallo, S. (1993) Emphasizing the future in empathy responses. *Journal of Humanistic Psychology*, 33, 12–29.

Bohart, A. and Tallman, K. (1996) The active client: therapy as self-help. *Journal of Humanistic Psychology*, 3, 7–30.

Bohart, A. C. and Tallman, K. (1998) The person as an active agent in experiential therapy. In L. S. Greenberg, J. C. Watson and G. Lietaer (eds) *Handbook of Experiential Psychotherapy*. New York: Guilford Press.

Bohart, A. C. and Tallman, K. (1999) *How Clients Make Therapy Work: The Process of Active Self-healing*. Washington, DC: American Psychological Association.

Bond, T. (1989) Towards defining the role of counselling skills. *Counselling*, 69 (August), 24–6.

Bond, T. (1992) Ethical issues in counselling in education. *British Journal of Guidance and Counselling*, 20, 51–63.

Bond, T. (1993) *Standards and Ethics for Counselling in Action*. London: Sage.

Boorstein, S. (ed.) (1986) *Transpersonal Psychotherapy*. Palo Alto, CA: Science and Behavior Books.

Boothe, B., von Wyl, A. and Wepfer, R. (1999) Narrative dynamics and psychodynamics. *Psychotherapy Research*, 9, 258–73.

Bordin, E. S. (1979) The generalizability of the psychoanalytic concept of working alliance. *Psychotherapy: Theory, Research and Practice*, 16, 252–60.

Borrill, J. and Foreman, E. I. (1996) Understanding cognitive change: a qualitative study of the impact of cognitive-behavioural therapy on fear of flying. *Clinical Psychology and Psychotherapy*, 3(1), 62–74.

Boss, M. (1957) *Psychoanalysis and Daseinanalysis*. New York: Basic Books.

Bott, D. (1994) A family systems framework for intervention with individuals. *Counselling Psychology Quarterly*, 7(2), 105–15.

Bourguignon, E. (1979) *Psychological Anthropology: An Introduction to Human Nature and Cultural Differences*. New York: Holt, Rinehart and Winston.

Bowlby, J. (1969) *Attachment*. London: Hogarth.

Bowlby, J. (1973) *Separation, Anxiety and Anger*. London: Hogarth.

Bowlby, J. (1980) *Loss, Sadness and Depression*. London: Hogarth.

Bowlby, J. (1988) *A Secure Base: Clinical Applications of Attachment Theory*. London: Routledge.

Bowlby, J., Robertson, J. and Rosenbluth, D. (1952) A two year old goes to hospital. *Psychoanalytic Studies of the Child*, 7, 82–94.

Bowling, A. (1991) *Measuring Health. A Review of Quality of Life Scales*. Buckingham: Open University Press.

Boy, A. V. and Pine, G. J. (1980) Avoiding counselor burnout through role renewal. *Personnel and Guidance Journal*, 59, 161–3.

Boy, A. V. and Pine, G. J. (1982) *Client-centered Counseling: A Renewal*. Boston: Allyn and Bacon.

Bozarth, J. D. (1984) Beyond reflection: emergent modes of empathy. In R. F. Levant and J. M. Shlien (eds) *Client-centered Therapy and the Person-centered Approach: New Directions in Theory, Research and Practice*. New York: Praeger.

Brammer, L., Shostrom, E. and Abrego, P. J. (1989) *Therapeutic Psychology: Fundamentals of Counseling and Psychotherapy*. Englewood Cliffs, NJ: Prentice Hall.

Braude, M. (ed.) (1987) *Women, Power and Therapy*. New York: Haworth Press.

Bray, D. W. (1982) The assessment center and the study of lives. *American Psychologist*, 37, 180–9.

Brazier, D. (1991) *A Guide to Psychodrama*. London: Association for Humanistic Psychology in Britain.

Breckenridge, K. (2000) Physical touch in psychoanalysis: a closet phenomenon? *Psychoanalytic Inquiry*, 20, 2–20.

Breger, L. and McGaugh, J. (1965) Critique and reformulation of 'learning-theory' approaches. *Psychological Bulletin*, 63, 338–58.

Bretherton, I. and Waters, E. (eds) (1985) Growing points of attachment theory and research. *Monographs of the Society for Research in Child Development*, 50(209).

Bright, J. I., Baker, K. D. and Neimeyer, R. A. (1999) Professional and paraprofessional group treatments for depression: a comparison of cognitive-behavioral and mutual support interventions. *Journal of Consulting and Clinical Psychology*, 67, 491–501.

Brightman, B. K. (1984) Narcissistic issues in the training experience of the psychotherapist. *International Journal of Psychoanalytic Psychotherapy*, 10, 293–371.

Brink, D. C. and Farber, B. A. (1996) Analysis of Carl Rogers' therapeutic interventions. In B. A. Farber, D. C. Brink and P. M. Raskin (eds) *The Psychotherapy of Carl Rogers: Cases and Commentary*. New York: Guilford Press.

British Association for Counselling (1977) *Counselling News No. 16*. Rugby: BAC.

British Association for Counselling (1984) *Code of Ethics and Practice for Counsellors.* Rugby: BAC.

British Association for Counselling (1992) *16th Annual Report 1991/92.* Rugby: BAC.

British Association for Counselling and Psychotherapy (2001) *Ethical Framework for Good Practice in Counselling and Psychotherapy.* Rugby: BACP.

Brock, G. W. and Bernard, C. P. (1992) *Procedures in Marriage and Family Therapy,* 2nd edn. Boston: Allyn and Bacon.

Brodsky, A. M. and Holroyd, J. (1975) Report on the task force on sex bias and sex-role stereotyping in psychotherapeutic practice. *American Psychologist,* 30, 1169–75.

Bromley, E. (1983) Social class issues in psychotherapy. In D. Pilgrim (ed.) *Psychology and Psychotherapy. Current Issues and Trends.* London: Routledge.

Broverman, I. K., Broverman, D., Clarkson, F. E., Rosencrantz, P. S. and Vogel, S. R. (1970) Sex-role stereotypes and clinical judgements of mental health. *Journal of Consulting and Clinical Psychology,* 34, 1–7.

Brown, L. S. (1990) The meaning of a multicultural pewrspective for theory-building in feminist therapy. *Women and Therapy,* 9, 1–21.

Brown, L. S. and Root, M. P. (eds) (1990) *Diversity and Complexity in Feminist Therapy.* New York: Harrington Park Press.

Bruner, J. (1986) *Actual Minds, Possible Worlds.* Cambridge, MA: Harvard University Press.

Bruner, J. (1990) *Acts of Meaning.* Cambridge, MA: Harvard University Press.

Bucci, W. (1993) The development of emotional meaning in free association: a multiple code theory. In A. Wilson and J. E. Gedo (eds) *Hierarchical Concepts in Psychoanalysis: Theory, Research and Clinical Practice.* New York: Guilford Press.

Bucci, W. (1995) The power of the narrative: a multiple code account. In J. W. Pennebaker (ed.) *Emotion, Disclosure and Health.* Washington, DC: American Psychological Association.

Buckley, P., Karasu, T. B. and Charles, E. (1981) Psychotherapists view their personal therapy. *Psychotherapy: Theory, Research and Practice,* 18, 299–305.

Budman, S. and Gurman, A. (1988) *Theory and Practice of Brief Psychotherapy.* London: Hutchinson.

Bugental, J. (1976) *The Search for Existential Identity.* San Francisco: Jossey-Bass.

Bugental, J. F. T. (1990) *Intimate Journeys: Stories from Life-changing Therapy.* San Francisco: Jossey-Bass.

Buhrke, R. A., Ben-Ezra, L. A., Hurley, M. E. and Ruprecht, L. J. (1992) Content analysis and methodological critique of articles concerning lesbian and gay male issues in counseling journals. *Journal of Counseling Psychology,* 39, 91–9.

Burks, H. M. and Stefflre, B. (1979) *Theories of Counseling,* 3rd edn. New York: McGraw-Hill.

Burlingame, G. M. and Barlow, S. H. (1996) Outcome and process differences between professional and nonprofessional therapists in time-limited group psychotherapy. *International Journal of Group Psychotherapy,* 46, 455–78.

Burns, D. D. and Auerbach, A. (1996) Therapeutic empathy in cognitive-behavioral therapy: does it really make a difference? In P. M. Salkovskis (ed.) *Frontiers of Cognitive Therapy.* New York: Guilford Press.

Burstow, B. (1992) *Radical Feminist Therapy: Working in the Context of Violence.* Newbury Park, CA: Sage.

Burton, A. (1970) The adoration of the patient and its disillusionment. *American Journal of Psychoanalysis,* 29, 194–204.

Cain, D. J. (2002) Defining characteristics, history and evolution of humanistic psycho-therapies. In D. J. Cain and J. Seeman (eds) *Humanistic Psychotherapies: Handbook of Research and Practice.* Washington, DC: American Psychological Association.

Cain, D. J. and Seeman, J. (eds) (2002) *Humanistic Psychotherapies: Handbook of Research and Practice*. Washington, DC: American Psychological Association.

Carkhuff, R. (1969) *Helping and Human Relations, Volume 2*. New York: Holt, Rinehart and Winston.

Carkhuff, R. (1972) *The Art of Helping*. Amherst, MA: Human Resource Development Press.

Carrell, S. E. (2001) *The Therapist's Toolbox*. Thousand Oaks, CA: Sage.

Carroll, M. (1988) Counselling supervision: the British context. *Counselling Psychology Quarterly*, 1, 387–96.

Carroll, M. (1996) *Workplace Counselling*. London: Sage.

Carroll, M. (1997) *Counselling Supervision: Theory, Skills and Practice*. London: Cassell.

Carter, B. and McGoldrick, M. (eds) (1989) *The Changing Family Life Cycle: A Framework for Family Therapy*, 2nd edn. Boston: Allyn and Bacon.

Carvalho, R. (1990) Psychodynamic therapy: the Jungian approach. In W. Dryden (ed.) *Individual Therapy: A Handbook*. Milton Keynes: Open University Press.

Casement, P. J. (1982) Some pressures on the analyst for physical contact during the reliving of an early childhood trauma. *International Review of Psycho-Analysis*, 9, 279–86.

Casement, P. (1985) *On Learning from the Patient*. London: Tavistock.

Casement, P. (1990) *Further Learning from the Patient: The Analytic Space and Process*. London: Tavistock/Routledge.

Casement, P. J. (2000) The issue of touch: a retrospective overview. *Psychoanalytic Inquiry*, 20, 160–84.

Cash, R. W. (1984) The Human Resources Development model. In D. Larson (ed.) *Teaching Psychological Skills: Models for Giving Psychology Away*. Monterey, CA: Brooks/Cole.

Cashdan, S. (1988) *Object Relations Therapy: Using the Relationship*. New York: W. W. Norton.

Cassidy, J. and Shaver, P. R. (eds) (1999) *Handbook of Attachment: Theory, Research and Clinical Applications*. New York: Guilford.

Celio, A. A., Winzelberg, A. J., Wilfley, D. E., Eppstein-Herrald, D., Springer, E. A., Dev, P. and Taylor, C. B. (2000) Reducing risk factors for eating disorders; comparison of an Internet- and a classroom-delivered psychoeducational program. *Journal of Consulting and Clinical Psychology*, 68, 650–7.

Cerney, M. S. (1990) Reduced fee or free psychotherapy: uncovering the hidden issues. *Psychotherapy Patient*, 7, 53–65.

Chaplin, J. (1988) *Feminist Counselling in Action*. London: Sage.

Charny, I. W. (1986) What do therapists worry about? A tool for experiential supervision. In F. W. Kaslow (ed.) *Supervision and Training: Models, Dilemmas and Challenges*. New York: Haworth Press.

Cherniss, C. and Krantz, D. L. (1983) The ideological community as an antidote to burnout in the human services. In B. A. Farber (ed.) *Stress and Burnout in the Human Service Professions*. New York: Pergamon.

Chesler, P. (1972) *Women and Madness*. New York: Doubleday.

Chester, R. (1985) Shaping the future: from marriage movement to service agency. *Marriage Guidance*, Autumn, 5–15.

Chevron, E. and Rounsaville, B. (1983) Evaluating the clinical skills of psychotherapists. *Archives of General Psychiatry*, 40, 1129–32.

Chodorow, N. (1978) *The Reproduction of Mothering*. Berkeley: University of California Press.

Christensen, A. and Jacobson, N. S. (1994) Who (or what) can do psychotherapy: the status and challenge of nonprofessional therapies. *Psychological Science*, 5, 8–14.

Christopher, J. C. (1996) Counseling's inescapable moral visions. *Journal of Counseling and Development*, 75, 17–25.

Clarkson, P. (1989) *Gestalt Counselling in Action*. London: Sage.

Clarkson, P. (1990) A multiplicity of psychotherapeutic relationships. *British Journal of Psychotherapy*, 7(2), 148–63.

Clarkson, P. (1991) *Transactional Analysis Psychotherapy: An Integrated Approach*. London: Tavistock/Routledge.

Clarkson, P. (1992) Systematic integrative psychotherapy training. In W. Dryden (ed.) *Integrative and Eclectic Therapy: A Handbook*. Buckingham: Open University Press.

Clarkson, P. (1995) *The Therapeutic Relationship*. London: Whurr.

Clarkson, P. and Gilbert, M. (1990) Transactional analysis. In W. Dryden (ed.) *Individual Therapy: A Handbook*. Buckingham: Open University Press.

Clarkson, P. and Gilbert, M. (1991) The training of counsellor trainers and supervisors. In W. Dryden and B. Thorne (eds) *Training and Supervision for Counselling in Action*. London: Sage.

Claxton, G. (ed.) (1996) *Beyond Therapy: The Impact of Eastern Religions on Psychological Theory and Practice*. Sturminster Newton: Prism Press.

Clulow, C. and Mattinson, J. (1989) *Marriage Inside Out. Understanding Problems of Intimacy*. Harmondsworth: Penguin.

Cochrane, R. (1983) *The Social Creation of Mental Illness*. London: Longman.

Cohen, L. H., Sargent, M. H. and Sechrest, L. B. (1986) Use of psychotherapy research by professional psychologists. *American Psychologist*, 41, 198–206.

Cohen, L. J. (1994) Phenomenology of therapeutic reading with implications for research and practice of bibliotherapy. *The Arts in Psychotherapy*, 21(1), 37–44.

Cohn, H. W. (1997) *Existential Thought and Therapeutic Practice*. London: Sage.

Cohn, H. W. and du Plock, S. (eds) (1995) *Existential Challenges to Psychotherapeutic Theory and Practice*. London: Society for Existential Analysis Press.

Coleman, E. (1982) *Developmental Stages of the Coming Out Process*. New York: Haworth.

Coleman, E. (ed.) (1988) *Psychotherapy with Homosexual Men and Women: Integrated Identity Approaches for Clinical Practice*. New York: Haworth Press.

Coleman, H. L. K. (1996) Portfolio assessment of multicultural counseling competency. *Counseling Psychologist*, 24(2), 216–29.

Collier, H. V. (1987) The differing self: women as psychotherapists. *Journal of Psychotherapy and the Family*, 3, 53–60.

Coltart, N. E. C. (1986) 'Slouching towards Bethlehem' . . . or thinking the unthinkable in psychoanalysis. In G. Kohon (ed.) *The British School of Psychoanalysis: The Independent Tradition*. London: Free Association.

Coltart, N. (1988) Diagnosis and assessment for suitability for psycho-analytical psychotherapy. *British Journal of Psychotherapy*, 4(2), 127–34.

Combs, A. W. (1986) What makes a good helper? *Person-centered Review*, 1, 51–61.

Combs, A. W. (1989) *A Theory of Therapy. Guidelines for Counseling Practice*. London: Sage.

Combs, A. W. and Soper, D. W. (1963) Perceptual organization of effective counselors. *Journal of Counseling Psychology*, 10, 222–6.

Conrad, P. (1981) On the medicalization of deviance and social control. In D. Ingleby (ed.) *Critical Psychiatry: The Politics of Mental Health*. Harmondsworth: Penguin.

Conte, H. R. and Ratto, R. (1997) Self-report measures of psychological mindedness. In M. McCallum and W. E. Piper (eds) *Psychological Mindedness: A Contemporary Understanding*. Mahwah, NJ: Lawrence Erlbaum.

Cooter, R. (1981) Phrenology and the British alienists: 1825–1845. In A. Scull (ed.) *Mad-houses, Mad-doctors and Madmen*. Pennsylvania: University of Pennsylvania Press.

Copeland, S. (2000) New challenges for supervising in organisational contexts. In B. Lawton and C. Feltham (eds) *Taking Supervision Forward: Enquiries and Trends in Counselling and Psychotherapy*. London: Sage.

Corey, G. (1990) *Theory and Practice of Group Counseling*. San Francisco: Brooks/Cole.

Corey, G., Corey, M. and Callanan, P. (1988) *Issues and Ethics in the Helping Professions*, 3rd edn. Pacific Grove, CA: Brooks/Cole.

Corey, G., Corey, M. and Callanan, P. (1993) *Issues and Ethics in the Helping Professions*, 4th edn. Pacific Grove, CA: Brooks/Cole.

Cornell, A. W. (1993) Teaching focusing with five steps and four skills. In D. Brazier (ed.) *Beyond Carl Rogers*. London: Constable.

Corsini, R. J. and Wedding, D. (eds) (1989) *Current Psychotherapies*, 4th edn. Itasca, IL: F. E. Peacock.

Costa, L. and Altekruse, M. (1994) Duty-to-warn guidelines for mental health counselors. *Journal of Counseling and Development*, 72, 346–50.

Counseling Psychologist (1994) Multicultural training. 24(2 and 3), special issues.

Counseling Psychologist (1995) Culture and counseling. 23(1), special issue.

Counseling Psychologist (1996) Multicultural challenges. 24(2), special issue.

Coyle, A., Milton, M. and Annesley, P. (1999) The silencing of gay and lesbian voices in psychotherapeutic texts and training. *Changes*, 17, 132–41.

Craighead, L. W., McNamara, K. and Horan, J. J. (1984) Perspectives on self-help and bibliography: you are what you read. In S. D. Brown and R. W. Lent (eds) *Handbook of Counseling Psychology*. New York: Wiley.

Cramer, D. (1992) *Personality and Psychotherapy: Theory, Practice and Research*. Buckingham: Open University Press.

Crandall, R. and Allen, R. (1981) The organisational context of helping relationships. In T. A. Wills (ed.) *Basic Processes in Helping Relationships*. New York: Academic Press.

Crits-Christoph, P., Cooper, A. and Luborsky, L. (1988) The accuracy of therapists' interpretations and the outcome of dynamic psychotherapy. *Journal of Consulting and Clinical Psychology*, 56, 490–5.

Crouan, M. (1994) The contribution of a research study toward improving a counselling service. *Counselling*, 5(1), 32–4.

Crouch, A. (1992) The competent counsellor. *Self and Society*, 20, 22–5.

Cullen, C. (1988) Applied behaviour analysis: contemporary and prospective agenda. In G. Davey and C. Cullen (eds) *Human Operant Conditioning and Behaviour Modification*. London: Wiley.

Cullen, C. (1991) Radical behaviourism and its influence on clinical therapies. *Behavioural Psychotherapy*, 19, 47–58.

Culley, S. (1992) Counselling skills: an integrative framework. In W. Dryden (ed.) *Integrative and Eclectic Therapy: A Handbook*. Buckingham: Open University Press.

Cushman, P. (1990) Why the self is empty: toward a historically-situated psychology. *American Psychologist*, 45, 599–611.

Cushman, P. (1992) Psychotherapy to 1992: a historically situated interpretation. In D. K. Freedheim (ed.) *History of Psychotherapy: a Century of Change*. Washington, DC: American Psychological Association.

Cushman, P. (1995) *Constructing the Self, Constructing America: A Cultural History of Psychotherapy*. Reading, MA: Addison-Wesley.

Cushman, P. and Gilford, P. (1999) From emptiness to multiplicity: the self at the year 2000. *Psychohistory Review*, 27, 15–31.

Cushman, P. and Gilford, P. (2000) Will managed care change our way of being? *American Psychologist*, 55, 985–96.

Dailey, T. (ed.) (1984) *Art as Therapy: An Introduction to the Use of Art as a Therapeutic Technique*. London: Routledge.

Dailey, T. and Case, C. (1992) *The Handbook of Art Therapy*. London: Tavistock/Routledge.

Dale, P., Allen, J. and Measor, L. (1998) Counselling adults who were abused as children: clients' perceptions of efficacy, client–counsellor communication, and dissatisfaction. *British Journal of Guidance and Counselling*, 26, 141–58.

Dallos, R. and Draper, R. (2000) *An Introduction to Family Therapy*. Buckingham: Open University Press.

Daniluk, J. C. and Haverkamp, B. E. (1993) Ethical issues in counseling adult survivors of incest. *Journal of Counseling and Development*, 72, 16–22.

d'Ardenne, P. and Mahtani, A. (1989) *Transcultural Counseling in Action*. London: Sage.

Davanloo, H. (ed.) (1980) *Short-term Psychodynamic Psychotherapy*. New York: Jason Aronson.

Davenport, S., Hobson, R. and Margison, F. (2000) Treatment development in psychodynamic-interpersonal psychotherapy (*Hobson's 'Conversational Model'*) for chronic treatment-resistant schizophrenia: two single case studies. *British Journal of Psychotherapy*, 16, 287–96.

David, A. B. and Erickson, C. A. (1990) Ethnicity and the therapist's use of self. *Family Therapy*, 17, 211–16.

Davies, D. (1996) Towards a model of gay affirmative therapy. In D. Davies and C. Neal (eds) *Pink Therapy: A Guide for Counsellors Working with Lesbian, Gay and Bisexual Clients*. Buckingham: Open University Press.

Davies, D. and Neal, C. (eds) (1996) *Pink Therapy: A Guide for Counsellors Working with Lesbian, Gay and Bisexual Clients*. Buckingham: Open University Press.

Davies, D. and Neal, C. (eds) (2000) *Therapeutic Perspectives on Working with Lesbian, Gay and Bisexual Clients*. Buckingham: Open University Press.

Davis, J. (1989) Issues in the evaluation of counsellors by supervisors. *Counselling*, 69 (August), 31–7.

Davis, K. (1986) The process of problem (re)formulation in psychotherapy, *Sociology of Illness and Health*, 8, 44–74.

DeBerry, S. and Baskin, D. (1989) Termination criteria in psychotherapy: a comparison of private and public practice. *American Journal of Psychotherapy*, 43, 43–53.

Delfin, P. E. (1978) Components of effective telephone intervention: a critical incidents analysis. *Crisis Intervention*, 9, 50–68.

de Shazer, S. (1985) *Keys to Solution in Brief Therapy*. New York: Norton.

de Shazer, S. (1988) *Clues: Investigating Solutions in Brief Therapy*. New York: Norton.

de Shazer, S. (1991) *Putting Difference to Work*. New York: Norton.

de Shazer, S. (1994) *Words Were Originally Magic*. New York: Norton.

DeWaele, J. P. and Harré, R. (1976) The personality of individuals. In R. Harre (ed.) *Personality*. Oxford: Blackwell.

Dinnage, R. (1988) *One to One: the Experience of Psychotherapy*. London: Viking.

Dobson, K. S. (ed.) (1988) *Handbook of Cognitive Behavioural Therapies*. London: Routledge.

Dobson, K. S. and Craig, K. D. (1996) *Advances in Cognitive–Behavioral Therapy*. London: Sage.

Dolan, Y. M. (1991) *Resolving Sexual Abuse: Solution Focused Therapy and Ericksonian Hypnosis for Adult Survivors*. New York: Norton.

Dowding, K. (1996) *Power*. Buckingham: Open University Press.

Downing, J. N. (2000) *Between Conviction and Uncertainty: Philosophical Guidelines for the Practicing Psychotherapist*. Albany, NY: State University of New York Press.

Doyle, K. (1997) Substance abuse counselors in recovery: implications for the ethical issue of dual relationships. *Journal of Counseling and Development*, 75, 428–32.

Draguns, J. G. (1996) Humanly universal and culturally distinctive: charting the course of cultural counseling. In P. B. Pedersen, J. G. Draguns, W. J. Lonner and J. E. Trimble (eds) *Counseling across Cultures*. London: Sage.

Dryden, W. (1984) Issues in the eclectic practice of individual therapy. In W. Dryden (ed.) *Individual Therapy in Britain*. London: Harper and Row.

Dryden, W. (ed.) (1985a) *Therapists' Dilemmas*. London: Harper and Row.

Dryden, W. (ed.) (1985b) *Marital Therapy in Britain, Volume 1. Context and Therapeutic Approaches*. London: Harper and Row.

Dryden, W. (1991) *A Dialogue with John Norcross: Toward Integration*. Buckingham: Open University Press.

Dryden, W. (ed.) (1992) *Integrative and Eclectic Therapy: A Handbook*. Buckingham: Open University Press.

Dryden, W. (ed.) (1995) *The Stresses of Counselling in Action*. London: Sage.

Dryden, W. (ed.) (1996) *Developments in Psychotherapy: Historical Perspectives*. London: Sage.

Dryden, W. (ed.) (1997) *Therapists' Dilemmas*, 2nd edn. London: Sage.

Dryden, W. and Barkham, M. (1990) The two-plus-one model: a dialogue. *Counselling Psychology Review*, 5, 5–18.

Dryden, W., Charles-Edwards, D. and Woolfe, R. (eds) (1989) *Handbook of Counselling in Britain*. London: Tavistock/Routledge.

Dryden, W. and Feltham, C. (1992) *Brief Counselling: A Practical Guide for Beginning Practitioners*. Buckingham: Open University Press.

Dryden, W. and Golden, W. L. (1986) *Cognitive–Behavioural Approaches to Psychotherapy*. Milton Keynes: Open University Press.

Dryden, W., Horton, I. and Mearns, D. (1995) *Issues in Professional Counsellor Training*. London: Cassell.

Dryden, W. and Spurling, L. (eds) (1989) *On Becoming a Psychotherapist*. London: Tavistock/Routledge.

Dryden, W. and Thorne, B. (1991) Approaches to the training of counsellors. In W. Dryden and B. Thorne (eds) *Training and Supervision for Counselling in Action*. London: Sage.

Dryden, W. and Trower, P. (eds) (1988) *Developments in Cognitive Psychotherapy*. London: Sage.

Duhl, F. J., Kantor, D. and Duhl, B. S. (1973) Learning space and action in family therapy. In D. A. Bloch (ed.) *Techniques of Family Psychotherapy: A Primer*. New York: Grune and Stratton.

Duncan, B. L. and Miller, S. D. (2000) The client's theory of change: consulting the client in the integrative process. *Journal of Psychotherapy Integration*, 10, 159–87.

Du Plock, S. (ed.) (1997) *Case Studies in Existential Psychotherapy and Counselling*. Chichester: Wiley.

Durlak, J. A. (1979) Comparative effectiveness of paraprofessional and professional helpers. *Psychological Bulletin*, 86, 80–92.

Durlak, J. A. (1981) Evaluating comparative studies of paraprofessional and professional helpers: a reply to Nietzel and Fisher. *Psychological Bulletin*, 89, 566–9.

Durre, L. (1980) Comparing romantic and therapeutic relationships. In K. S. Pope (ed.) *On Love and Losing. Psychological Perspectives on the Nature and Experience of Romantic Loss*. San Francisco: Jossey-Bass.

Dusay, J. M. and Dusay, K. M. (1989) Transactional analysis. In R. J. Corsini and D. Wedding (eds) *Current Psychotherapies*, 4th edn. Itasca, IL: F. E. Peacock.

Dworkin, S. H. and Gutierrez, F. (1989) Introduction to special issue. Counselors be aware: clients come in every size, shape, color and sexual orientation. *Journal of Counseling and Development*, 68, 6–8.

Dyche, L. and Zayas, L. H. (1995) The value of curiosity and naivete for the cross-cultural psychotherapist. *Family Process*, 34, 389–99.

Eames, V. and Roth, A. (2000) Patient attachment orientation and the early working alliance: a study of patient and therapist reports of alliance quality and ruptures. *Psychotherapy Research*, 10, 421–34.

Edelson, M. (1993) Telling and enacting stories in psychoanalysis and psychotherapy: implications for teaching psychotherapy. *Psychoanalytic Study of the Child*, 48, 293–325.

Edelwich, J. and Brodsky, A. (1991) *Sexual Dilemmas for the Helping Professional*, 2nd edn. New York: Brunner/Mazel.

Egan, G. (1984) People in systems: a comprehensive model for psychosocial education and training. In D. Larson (ed.) *Teaching Psychological Skills: Models for Giving Psychology Away*. Monterey, CA: Brooks/Cole.

Egan, G. (1986) *The Skilled Helper. A Systematic Approach to Effective Helping*, 3rd edn. Belmont, CA: Brooks/Cole.

Egan, G. (1990) *The Skilled Helper: A Systematic Approach to Effective Helping*, 4th edn. Belmont, CA: Brooks/Cole.

Egan, G. (1994) *The Skilled Helper: A Systematic Approach to Effective Helping*, 5th edn. Belmont, CA: Brooks/Cole.

Eichenbaum, L. and Orbach, S. (1982) *Outside in, Inside out. Women's Psychology: A Feminist Psychoanalytic Approach*. Harmondsworth: Penguin.

Ekstein, R. and Wallenstein, R. S. (1958) *The Teaching and Learning of Psychotherapy*. New York: International Universities Press.

Elkin, I. (1999) A major diilemma in psychotherapy outcome research: disentangling therapists from therapies. *Clinical Psychology: Science and Practice*, 6, 10–32.

Ellenberger, H. F. (1970) *The Discovery of the Unconscious: The History and Evolution of Dynamic Psychiatry*. London: Allen Lane.

Elliott, R. (1983) 'That in your hands . . .': a comprehensive process analysis of a significant event in psychotherapy. *Psychiatry*, 46, 113–29.

Elliott, R. (1984) A discovery-oriented approach to significant change events in psychotherapy: interpersonal process recall and comprehensive process analysis. In L. N. Rice and L. S. Greenberg (eds) *Patterns of Change: Intensive Analysis of Psychotherapy Process*. New York: Guilford Press.

Elliott, R. (1986) Interpersonal Process Recall (IPR) as a psychotherapy process research method. In L. S. Greenberg and W. M. Pinsof (eds) *The Psychotherapeutic Process: A Research Handbook*. New York: Guilford Press.

Elliott, R. (1991) Five dimensions of therapy process. *Psychotherapy Research*, 1, 92–103.

Elliott, R. (1998) A guide to the empirically supported treatments controversy. *Psychotherapy Research*, 8, 115–25.

Elliott, R., Clark, C., Kemeny, V., Wexler, M. M., Mack, C. and Brinkerhoff, J. (1990) The impact of experiential therapy on depression: the first ten cases. In G. Lietaer, J. Rombauts and R. Van Balen (eds) *Client-centered and Experiential Psychotherapy in the Nineties*. Leuven: University of Leuven Press.

Elliott, R., Davis, K. L. and Slatick, E. (1998) Process-experiential therapy for posttraumatic stress difficulties. In L. S. Greenberg, J. C. Watson and G. Lietaer (eds) *Handbook of Experiential Psychotherapy*. New York: Guilford Press.

Elliott, R. and Shapiro, D. A. (1992) Client and therapist as analyst of significant events. In S. G. Toukmanian and D. L. Rennie (eds) *Psychotherapy Process Research: Paradigmatic and Narrative Approaches*. London: Sage.

Ellis, A. (1962) *Reason and Emotion in Psychotherapy*. New York: Lyle Stuart.

Ellis, A. (1973) *Humanistic Psychotherapy*. New York: McGraw-Hill.

Ellis, A. (1980) Psychotherapy and atheistic values: a response to A. E. Bergin's 'Psychotherapy and religious values'. *Journal of Consulting and Clinical Psychology*, 48, 635–9.

Ellis, A. (1989) The history of cognition in psychotherapy. In A. Freeman, K. M. Simon, L. E. Beutler and H. Arkowitz (eds) *Comprehensive Handbook of Cognitive Therapy*. New York: Plenum Press.

Elton-Wilson, J. (1996) *Time-conscious Counselling and Therapy*. Chichester: Wiley.

Emrick, C. (1981) Nonprofessional peers as therapeutic agents. In M. H. Bean and N. E. Zinberg (eds) *Dynamic Approaches to the Understanding and Treatment of Alcoholism*. New York: Free Press.

Enns, C. Z. (1992) Toward integrating feminist psychotherapy and feminist philosophy. *Professional Psychology: Theory and Practice*, 23(6), 453–66.

Enns, C. Z., McNeilly, C. L., Corkery, J. M. and Gilbert, M. S. (1995) The debate about delayed memories of child sexual abuse: a feminist perspective. *The Counseling Psychologist*, 23, 181–279.

Epston, D. (1989) *Collected Papers*. Adelaide: Dulwich Centre Publications.

Epston, D., Morris, F. and Maisel, R. (1995) A narrative approach to so-called anorexia/bulimia. In K. Weingarten (ed.) *Cultural Resistance: Challenging Beliefs about Men, Women and Therapy*. New York: Haworth Press.

Epston, D. and White, M. (eds) (1992) *Experience, Contradiction, Narrative and Imagination*. Adelaide: Dulwich Centre Publications.

Epston, D. and White, M. (1995) Termination as a rite of passage: questioning strategies for a therapy of inclusion. In R. A. Neimeyer and M. J. Mahoney (eds) *Constructivism in Psychotherapy*. Washington, DC: American Psychological Association.

Epston, D., White, M. and Murray, K. (1992) A proposal for a re-authoring therapy: Rose's revisioning of her life and a commentary. In S. McNamee and K. J. Gergen (eds) *Therapy as Social Construction*. London: Sage.

Erikson, E. (1950) *Childhood and Society*. New York: W. W. Norton.

Eskapa, R. (1992) Multimodal therapy. In W. Dryden (ed.) *Integrative and Eclectic Therapy: A Handbook*. Buckingham: Open University Press.

Esterson, A. (1998) Jeffrey Masson and Freud's seduction theory: a new fable based on old myths. *History of the Human Sciences*, 11, 1–21.

Evans, C., Mellor-Clark, J. *et al.* (2000) CORE: Clinical Outcomes in Routine Evaluation. *Journal of Mental Health*, 9, 247–55.

Eysenck, H. J. (1952) The effects of psychotherapy: an evaluation. *Journal of Consulting Psychology*, 16, 319–24.

Eysenck, H. J. (1970) A mish-mash of theories. *International Journal of Psychiatry*, 9, 140–6.

Fairbairn, R. D. (1958) On the nature and aims of psycho-analytical treatment. *International Journal of Psychoanalysis*, 39, 374–85.

Falicov, C. J. (1995) Training to think culturally: a multidimensional comparative framework. *Family Process*, 34, 373–88.

Farber, B. A. (ed.) (1983a) Stress and Burnout in the Human Service Professions. New York: Pergamon.

Farber, B. A. (1983b) Dysfunctional aspects of the psychotherapeutic role. In B. A. Farber (ed.) *Stress and Burnout in the Human Service Professions*. New York: Pergamon.

Farber, B. A., Brink, D. C. and Raskin, P. M. (eds) (1996) *The Psychotherapy of Carl Rogers: Cases and Commentary*. New York: Guilford Press.

Farber, B. A. and Heifetz, L. J. (1981) The satisfactions and stresses of psychotherapeutic work: a factor analytic study. *Professional Psychology*, 12, 621–30.

Farber, B. A. and Heifetz, L. J. (1982) The process and dimensions of burnout in psycho-therapists. *Professional Psychology*, 13, 293–301.

Farooq, S., Gahir, M. S., Okyere, E., Sheikh, A. J. and Oyebode, F. (1995) Somatization: a transcultural study. *Journal of Psychosomatic Research*, 39, 883–8.

Farson, R. (1978) The technology of humanism. *Journal of Humanistic Psychology*, 18, 5–35.

Faust, D. and Zlotnick, C. (1995) Another Dodo Bird verdict? Revisiting the comparative effectiveness of professional and paraprofessional therapists. *Clinical Psychology and Psycho-therapy*, 2, 157–67.

Feild, H. S. and Gatewood, R. (1976) The paraprofessional and the organization: some problems of mutual adjustment. *Personnel and Guidance Journal*, 55, 181–5.

Feltham, C. (1995) *What Is Counselling?* London: Sage.

Feltham, C. (1997) Challenging the core theroetical model. *Counselling*, 8, 121–5.

Feltham. C. (ed.) (1998) *Witness and Vision of the Therapists*. London: Sage.

Feltham, C. (ed.) (1999) *Understanding the Counselling Relationship*. London: Sage.

Feltham, C. (2000) Counselling supervision: baselines, problems and possibilities. In B. Lawton and C. Feltham (eds) *Taking Supervision Forward: Enquiries and Trends in Counselling and Psychotherapy*. London: Sage.

Feltham, C. and Dryden, W. (1993) *Dictionary of Counselling*. London: Whurr.

Ferenczi, S. (1980a) The elasticity of psychoanalytic technique. In M. Balint (ed.) *Final Con-tributions to the Problems and Method of Psycho-analysis, Volume 3*. New York: Brunner/Mazel (original work published 1928).

Ferenczi, S. (1980b) The confusion of tongues between adults and children: The language of tenderness and passion. In M. Balint (ed.) *Final Contributions to the Problems and Method of Psycho-analysis, Volume 3*. New York: Brunner/Mazel (original work published 1938).

Fernando, S. (ed.) (1995) *Mental Health in a Multi-ethnic Society: A Multidisciplinary Handbook*. London: Routledge.

Fiedler, F. E. (1950) A comparison of psychoanalytic, nondirective and Adlerian therapeutic relationships. *Journal of Consulting Psychology*, 14, 436–45.

Finch, A. E., Lambert, M. J. and Brown, G. (2000) Attacking anxiety: a naturalistic study of a multimedia self-help program. *Journal of Clinical Psychology*, 56, 11–21.

Fine, R. (1988) *Troubled Men: The Psychology, Emotional Conflicts and Therapy of Men*. San Franciso: Jossey-Bass.

Fink, J. (1999) *How to Use Computers and Cyberspace in the Clinical Practice of Psychotherapy*. Northvale, NJ: Jason Aronson.

Firth, J., Shapiro, D. A. and Parry, G. (1986) The impact of research on the practice of psychotherapy. *British Journal of Psychotherapy*, 2, 169–79.

Firth-Cozens, J. (1992) Why me? A case study of the process of perceived occupational stress. *Human Relations*, 45, 131–43.

Fischer, C. T. (1978) Personality and assessment. In R. S. Valle and M. King (eds) *Existential–Phenomenological Alternatives for Psychology*. New York: Oxford University Press.

Fishman, D. B. (1999) *The Case for a Pragmatic Psychology*. New York: New York University Press.

Fitz, R. and Cada, L. (1975) The recovery of religious life. *Review for Religious*, 34, 690–718.

Fonagy, P. (1999) Psychoanalytic theory from the viewpoint of attachment theory and research. In J. Cassidy and P. R. Shaver (eds) *Handbook of Attachment: Theory, Research and Clinical Applications*. New York: Guilford Press.

Fordham, M. (1986) *Jungian Psychotherapy*. London: Karnac.

Forsyth, D. R. (1990) *Group Dynamics*, 2nd edn. Pacific Grove, CA: Brooks/Cole.

Fortune, A. E., Pearlingi, B. and Rochelle, C. D. (1992) Reactions to termination of indi-vidual treatment. *Social Work*, 37(2), 171–8.

Foskett, J. and Jacobs, M. (1989) Pastoral counselling. In W. Dryden, D. Charles-Edwards and R. Woolfe (eds) *Handbook of Counselling in Britain*. London: Tavistock/Routledge.

Foskett, J. and Lyall, D. (1988) *Helping the Helpers*. London: SPCK.

Foucault, M. (1967) *Madness and Civilization: A History of Insanity in the Age of Reason*. London: Tavistock.

Frank, A. W. (1998) Just listening: narrative and deep illness. *Families, Systems and Health*, 16, 197–212.

Frank, J. D. (1973) *Persuasion and Healing: A Comparative Study of Psychotherapy*. Baltimore: Johns Hopkins University Press.

Frank, J. D. (1974) Psychotherapy: the restoration of morale. *American Journal of Psychiatry*, 131, 272–4.

Fransella, F. and Dalton, P. (1996) Personal construct therapy. In W. Dryden (ed.) *Handbook of Individual Therapy*. London: Sage.

Frayn, D. H. (1992) Assessment factors associated with premature psychotherapy termination. *American Journal of Psychotherapy*, 46(2), 25–61.

Frazier, P. A. and Cohen, B. B. (1992) Research on the sexual victimization of women: implications for counselor training. *Counseling Psychologist*, 20, 141–58.

Freeman, A. and Simon, K. M. (1989) Cognitive therapy of anxiety. In A. Freeman, K. M. Simon, L. E. Beutler and H. Arkowitz (eds) *Comprehensive Handbook of Cognitive Therapy*. New York: Plenum Press.

Freeman, A., Simon, K. M., Beutler, L. E. and Arkowitz, H. (eds) (1989) *Comprehensive Handbook of Cognitive Therapy*. New York: Plenum Press.

Freeman, C. and Tyrer, P. (eds) (1989) *Research Methods in Psychiatry. A Beginner's Guide*. London: Gaskell.

Freeman, D. R. (1990) *Couples in Conflict: Inside the Consulting Room*. Buckingham: Open University Press.

Freire, P. (1972) *Pedagogy of the Oppressed*. Harmondsworth: Penguin.

Freud, A. (1936/1966) *The Ego and the Mechanisms of Defense*, rev. edn. New York: International Universities Press.

Freud, S. (1901/1979) The case of Dora. *Pelican Freud Library Volume 8: Case Histories I*. Harmondsworth: Penguin.

Freud, S. (1905/1977) Three essays on the theory of sexuality. *Pelican Freud Library Volume 7: On Sexuality*. Harmondsworth: Penguin.

Freud, S. (1909/1979) Notes upon a case of obsessional neurosis (the 'Rat Man'). *Pelican Freud Library Volume 9: Case Histories II*. Harmondsworth: Penguin.

Freud, S. (1910/1979) Psychoanalytic notes on an autobiographical account of a case of paranoia (Dementia Paranoides) (Schreber). *Pelican Freud Library Volume 9. Case Histories II*. Harmondsworth: Penguin.

Freud, S. (1917/1973) *Introductory Lecture on Psychoanalysis*. Harmondsworth: Penguin.

Freud, S. (1924/1977) The dissolution of the Oedipus complex. *Pelican Freud Library Volume 7: On Sexuality*. Harmondsworth: Penguin.

Freud, S. (1933/1973) *New Introductory Lectures on Psycho-Analysis*. Harmondsworth: Penguin.

Freudenberger, H. J. (1974) Staff burn-out. *Journal of Social Issues*, 30, 159–65.

Friedli, K., King, M. B. and Lloyd, M. (2000) The economics of employing a counsellor in general practice: analysis of data from a randomised control trial. *British Journal of General Practice*, 50, 276–83.

Friedman, D. and Kaslow, N. J. (1986) The development of professional identity in psychotherapists: six stages in the supervision process. In F. W. Kaslow (ed.) *Supervision and Training: Models, Dilemmas and Challenges*. New York: Haworth Press.

Friedman, M. (1982) Psychotherapy and the human image. In P. W. Sharkey (ed.) *Philosophy, Religion and Psychotherapy: Essays in the Philosophical Foundations of Psychotherapy*. Washington, DC: University Press of America.

Frommer, J. and Rennie, D. (eds) (2001) *Qualitative Psychotherapy Research: Methods and Methodology*. Lengerich: Pabst.

Fuhriman, A. (1992) Short-term therapy: a shift in thinking. *Counseling Psychologist*, 20, 451–4.

Fuhriman, A., Barlow, S. H. and Wanlass, J. (1989) Words, imagination, meaning: towards change. *Psychotherapy*, 26, 149–56.

Fulero, S. M. (1988) Tarasoff: 10 years later. *Professional Psychology: Research and Practice*, 19, 184–90.

Gabbard, G. (ed.) (1989) *Sexual Exploitation in Professional Relationships*. Washington, DC: American Psychiatric Press.

Gabbard, G. O. (1996) The early history of boundary violations in psychoanalysis. *Journal of the American Psychoanalytic Association*, 43, 1115–36.

Galassi, J. P., Crace, R. K., Martin, G. A., James, R. M. and Wallace, R. L. (1992) Client preferences and anticipations in career counseling: a preliminary investigation. *Journal of Counseling Psychology*, 39, 46–55.

Galassi, J. P. and Perot, A. R. (1992) What you should know about behavioral assessment. *Journal of Counseling and Development*, 70, 624–31.

Gardner, D. and Marzillier, J. (1996) Day-to-day maintenance of confidentiality: practices and beliefs of trainee and qualified clinical psychologists in the UK. *Clinical Psychology and Psychotherapy*, 3(1), 35–45.

Garfield, S. (1982) Eclecticism and integration in psychotherapy. *Behavior Therapy*, 13, 610–23.

Garfield, S. L. (1986) Research on client variables in psychotherapy. In S. L. Garfield and A. E. Bergin (eds) *Handbook of Psychotherapy and Behavior Change*, 3rd edn. London: Wiley.

Garfield, S. L. and Bergin, A. E. (1971) Personal therapy, outcome and some therapist variables. *Psychotherapy*, 8, 251–3.

Garfield, S. L. and Bergin, A. E. (eds) (1986) *Handbook of Psychotherapy and Behavior Change*, 3rd edn. New York: Wiley.

Garfield, S. and Kurtz, R. (1974) A survey of clinical psychologists: characteristics, activities and orientations. *The Clinical Psychologist*, 28, 7–10.

Garfield, S. and Kurtz, R. (1977) A study of eclectic views. *Journal of Consulting and Clinical Psychology*, 45, 78–83.

Garnets, L., Hancock, K. A., Cochran, S. D., Goodchilds, J. and Peplau, L. A. (1991) Issues in psychotherapy with lesbians and gay men. *American Psychologist*, 46(9), 964–72.

Gay, P. (1988) *Freud. A Life for Our Times*. London: Dent.

Geertz, C. (1973) *The Interpretation of Cultures*. New York: Basic Books.

Geertz, C. (1983) *Local Knowledge: Further Essays in Interpretive Anthropology*. New York: Basic Books.

Geller, S. M. (2000) Therapists' presence: the development of a model and a measure. Unpublished doctoral dissertation, York University, Toronto.

Gelso, C. J. and Carter, J. A. (1985) The relationship in counseling and psychotherapy: components, consequences and theoretical antecedents. *The Counseling Psychologist*, 13, 155–244.

Gelso, C. J. and Fassinger, R. E. (1990) Counseling psychology: theory and research on interventions. *Annual Review of Psychology*, 41, 355–86.

Gendlin, E. T. (1962) *Experiencing and the Creation of Meaning*. New York: Free Press.

Gendlin, E. T. (1964) A theory of personality change. In P. Worchel and D. Byrne (eds) *Personality Change*. New York: Wiley.

Gendlin, E. T. (1966) Experiential explication and truth. *Journal of Existentialism*, 6, 131–46.

Gendlin, E. T. (1967) Subverbal communication and therapist expressivity: trends in client-centered therapy with schizophrenics. In C. Rogers and B. Stevens (eds) *Person to Person: The Problem of Being Human*. San Francisco: Real People Press.

Gendlin, E. T. (1969) Focusing. *Psychotherapy*, 6, 4–15.

Gendlin, E. T. (1973) Experiential psychotherapy. In R. Corsini (ed.) *Current Psychotherapies*. Itasca, IL: Peacock.

Gendlin, E. T. (1974) Client-centered and experiential psychotherapy. In D. A. Wexler and L. N. Rice (eds) *Innovations in Client-centered Therapy*. New York: Wiley.

Gendlin, E. T. (1978) *Focusing*. New York: Bantam Books.

Gendlin, E. T. (1981) *Focusing*, rev. edn. New York: Bantam.

Gendlin, E. T. (1984a) The client's client: the edge of awareness. In R. F. Levant and J. M. Shlien (eds) *Client-centered Therapy and the Person-centered Approach: New Directions in Theory, Research and Practice*. New York: Praeger.

Gendlin, E. T. (1984b) The politics of giving therapy away. In D. G. Larson (ed.) *Teaching Psychological Skills: Models for Giving Psychology Away*. Monterey, CA: Brooks/Cole.

Gendlin, E. T. (1984c) Imagery, body and space in focusing. In A. A. Sheikh (ed.) *Imagination and Healing*. New York: Baywood.

Gendlin, E. T. (1990) The small steps of the therapy process: how they come and how to help them come. In G. Lietaer, J. Rombauts and R. Van Balen (eds) *Client-centered and Experiential Therapy in the Nineties*. Leuven: Leuven University Press.

Gendlin, E. T. (1996) *Focusing-oriented Psychotherapy: A Manual of the Experiential Method*. New York: Guilford Press.

Gergen, K. J. (1985) The social constructionist movement in modern psychology. *American Psychologist*, 40, 266–75.

Gergen, K. J. (1990) Therapeutic professions and the diffusion of deficit. *Journal of Mind and Behavior*, 11, 353–68.

Gergen, K. J. (1991) *The Saturated Self: Dilemmas of Identity in Modern Life*. New York: Basic.

Gergen, K. J. (1994) *Toward Transformation in Social Knowledge*, 2nd edn. London: Sage.

Gergen, K. J. (1996) Beyond life narratives in the therapeutic encounter. In J. E. Birren, G. M. Kenyon, J.-K. Ruth, J. J. F. Schroots and T. Svensson (eds) *Aging and Biography: Explorations in Adult Development*. New York: Springer.

Gergen, K. J. and Kaye, J. (1992) Beyond narrative in the construction of therapeutic meaning. In S. McNamee and K. Gergen (eds) *Therapy as Social Construction*. London: Sage.

Gerstein, L. H. and Sturmer, P. (1993) A Taoist paradigm of EAP consultation. *Journal of Counseling and Development*, 72, 178–84.

Giddens, A. (1991) *Modernity and Self-identity: Self and Society in the Late Modern Age*. Cambridge: Polity Press.

Gill, M. M. (1994) *Psychoanalysis in Transition*. Hillsdale, NJ: Analytic Press.

Gilligan, C. (1982) *In a Different Voice*. Cambridge, MA: Harvard University Press.

Gingerich, W. J. and Eisengart, S. (2000) Solution-focused brief therapy: a review of the outcome research. *Family Process*, 39, 477–98.

Glaser, B. G. (1978) *Theoretical Sensitivity: Advances in the Methodology of Grounded Theory*. Mill Valley, CA: The Sociology Press.

Glaser, B. G. and Strauss, A. (1967) *The Discovery of Grounded Theory*. Chicago: Aldine.

Glasgow, R. E. and Rosen, G. M. (1978) Behavioral bibliotherapy: a review of self-help behavior therapy manuals. *Psychological Bulletin*, 85, 1–23.

Goldberg, C. (1988) *On Being a Psychotherapist: The Journey of the Healer*. New York: Gardner Press.

Goldberg, D. P., Hobson, R. F., Maguire, G. P. *et al.* (1984) The classification and assessment of a method of psychotherapy. *British Journal of Psychiatry*, 144, 567–75.

Goldberg, D. and Huxley, P. (1992) *Common Mental Disorders: A Bio-social model*. London: Tavistock.

Goldberg, E. M. and Morrison, S. C. (1963) Schizophrenia and social class. *British Journal of Psychiatry*, 109, 785–802.

Goldfried, M. R. (1982) On the history of therapeutic integration. *Behavior Therapy*, 13, 572–93.

Goldfried, M. R. (2001) *How Therapists Change: Personal and Professional Reflections*. Washington, DC: American Psychological Association.

Goldfried, M. R. and Davison, G. C. (1976) *Clinical Behavior Therapy*. New York: Holt, Rinehart and Winston.

Goldfried, M. R., Greenberg, L. S. and Marmar, C. (1990) Individual psychotherapy: process and outcome. *Annual Review of Psychotherapy*, 41, 659–88.

Goldman, L. (1992) Qualitative assessment: an approach for counselors. *Journal of Counseling and Development*, 70, 616–21.

Gomes-Schwartz, B. and Schwartz, J. M. (1978) Psychotherapy process variables distinguishing the 'inherently helpful' person from the professional psychotherapist. *Journal of Consulting and Clinical Psychology*, 46, 196–7.

Gomez, L. (1996) *An Introduction to Object Relations*. London: Free Association Books.

Gomm, R. (1993) Issues of power in health and welfare. In J. Walmsley, J. Reynolds, P. Shakespeare and R. Woolfe (eds) *Health, Welfare and Practice: Reflecting on Roles and Relationships*. London: Sage.

Goncalves, O. F. (1993) Cognitive narrative psychotherapy: the hermeneutic construction of alternative meanings. In M. J. Mahoney (ed.) *Cognitive and Constructive Psychotherapies: Theory, Research and Practice*. New York: Springer.

Goncalves, O. F. (1994) From epistemological truth to existential meaning in cognitive narrative psychotherapy. *Journal of Constructivist Psychology*, 7, 107–18.

Goncalves, O. F. (1995) Hermeutics, constructivism and cogntive-behavioral therapies: from the object to the project. In R. A. Neimeyer and M. J. Mahoney (eds) *Constructivism in Psychotherapy*. Washington, DC: American Psychological Association.

Good, D. A. and Watts, F. N. (1989) Qualitative research. In G. Parry and F. N. Watts (eds) *Behavioural and Mental Health Research: A Handbook of Skills and Methods*. London: Lawrence Erlbaum.

Goodman, G. (1984) SASHA tapes: a new approach to enhancing human communication. In D. Larson (ed.) *Teaching Psychological Skills. Models for Giving Psychology Away*. Monterey, CA: Brooks/Cole.

Goodman, P. (1962) *Utopian Essays and Practical Proposals*. New York: Vintage Books.

Gordon-Brown, I. and Somers, B. (1988) Transpersonal psychotherapy. In J. Rowan and W. Dryden (eds) *Innovative Therapy in Britain*. Milton Keynes: Open University Press.

Grafanaki, S. (1996) How research can change the researcher: the need for sensitivity, flexibility and ethical boundaries in conducting qualitative research in counselling/ psychotherapy. *British Journal of Guidance and Counselling*, 24, 329–38.

Grafanaki, S. and McLeod, J. (1999) Narrative processes in the construction of helpful and hindering events in experiential psychotherapy. *Psychotherapy Research*, 9, 289–303.

Grafanaki, S. and McLeod, J. (2002) Experimental congruence: qualitative analysis of client and counsellor narrative accounts of significant events in time-limited person-centred therapy. *Counselling and Psychotherapy Research*, 2, 20–32.

Graham, H. (1990) *Time, Energy and the Psychology of Healing*. London: Jessica Kingsley.

Gray, L. A., Ladany, N., Walker, J. A. and Ancis, J. R. (2001) Psychotherapy trainees' experience of counterproductive events in supervision. *Journal of Counseling Psychology*, 48, 371–83.

Greenberg, G. (1994) *The Self on the Shelf: Recovery Books and the Good Life*. Albany, NY: State University of New York Press.

Greenberg, I. (ed.) (1974) *Psychodrama. Theory and Therapy*. London: Souvenir Press.

Greenberg, J. R. and Mitchell, S. A. (1983) *Object Relations in Psychoanalytic Theory*. Cambridge, MA: Harvard University Press.

Greenberg, L. S. (1984a) A task analysis of intrapersonal conflict resolution. In L. N. Rice and L. S. Greenberg (eds) *Patterns of Change: Intensive Analysis of Psychotherapy Process*. New York: Guilford Press.

Greenberg, L. S. (1984b) Task analysis: the general approach. In L. N. Rice and L. S. Greenberg (eds) *Patterns of Change: Intensive Analysis of Psychotherapy Process*. New York: Guilford Press.

Greenberg, L. S., Elliott, R. and Foerster, F. S. (1990) Experiential processes in the psycho-therapeutic treatment of depression. In C. D. McCann and N. S. Endler (eds) *Depression: New Directions in Theory, Research and Practice*. Toronto: Wall and Emerson.

Greenberg, L. S. and Geller, S. (2001) Congruence and therapeutic presence. In G. Wyatt (ed.) *Rogers' Therapeutic Conditions: Evolution, Theory and Practice. Volume 1: Congruence*. Ross-on-Wye: PCCS Books.

Greenberg, L. S. and Johnson, S. (1988) *Emotionally Focused Therapy for Couples*. New York: Guilford Press.

Greenberg, L. S. and Pinsof, W. M. (eds) (1986) *The Psychotherapeutic Process: A Research Handbook*. New York: Guilford Press.

Greenberg, L. S., Rice, L. N. and Elliott, R. (1993) *Facilitating Emotional Change: The Moment-by-moment Process*. New York: Guilford Press.

Greenberg, L. S. and van Balen, R. (1998) Theory of experience centered therapy. In L. S. Greenberg, J. C. Watson and G. Lietaer (eds) *Handbook of Experiential Psychotherapy: Foundations and Differential Treatment*. New York: Guilford Press.

Greenberg, L. S., Watson, J. C. and Lietaer, G. (eds) (1998a) *Handbook of Experiential Psycho-therapy: Foundations and Differential Treatment*. New York: Guilford Press.

Greenberg, L. S., Watson, J. C. and Goldman, R. (1998b) Process-experiential therapy of depression. In L. S. Greenberg, J. C. Watson and G. Lietaer (eds) *Handbook of Experiential Psychotherapy: Foundations and Differential Treatment*. New York: Guilford Press.

Greenberger, D. and Padesky, C. A. (1995) *Mind over Mood. Change How You Feel by Changing the Way You Think*. New York: Guilford Press.

Greening, T. C. (1977) The uses of autobiography. In W. Anderson (ed.) *Therapy and the Arts: Tools of Consciousness*. New York: Harper and Row.

Grencavage, L. M. and Norcross, J. C. (1990) Where are the commonalities among the therapeutic common factors? *Professional Psychology: Research and Practice*, 21, 372–8.

Grierson, M. (1990) A client's experience of success. In D. Mearns and W. Dryden (eds) *Experiences of Counselling in Action*. London: Sage.

Griffith, E. H., Blue, H. C. and Harris, H. W. (eds) (1995) *Racial and Ethnic Identity: Psychological Development and Creative Expression*. London: Routledge.

Gronbjerg, K. A. (1992) Nonprofit human service organizations: funding strategies and patterns of adaptation. In Y. Hasenfeld (ed.) *Human Services as Complex Organizations*. London: Sage.

Grumet, G. W. (1979) Telephone therapy: a review and case report. *American Journal of Orthopsychiatry*, 49, 574–84.

Guggenbuhl-Craig, A. (1971) *Power in the Helping Professions*. Dallas: Spring Publications.

Gustafson, J. P. (1986) *The Complex Secret of Brief Psychotherapy*. New York: W. W. Norton.

Guthrie, E. (1991) Brief psychotherapy in patients with refractory irritable bowel syndrome. *British Journal of Psychotherapy*, 8(2), 175–88.

Guthrie, E., Kapur, N. *et al.* (2001) Randomised control trial of brief psychological intervention after deliberate self poisoning. *British Medical Journal*, 323, 212–19.

Guthrie, E., Moorey, J., Barker, H., Margison, F. and McGrath, G. (1998) Brief psychodynamic–interpersonal therapy for patients with severe psychiatric illness which is unresponsive to treatment. *British Journal of Psychotherapy*, 15, 155–66.

Guthrie, E., Moorey, J., Barker, H., Margison, F. and McGrath, G. (1999) Cost-effectiveness of brief psychodynamic-interpersonal therapy in high utilizers of psychiatric services. *Archives of General Psychiatry*, 56, 519–26.

Gutierrez, L. M. (1992) Empowering ethnic minorities in the twenty-first century: the role of human service organizations. In Y. Hasenfeld (ed.) *Human Services as Complex Organizations*. London: Sage.

Guttman, H. A. (1981) Systems theory, cybernetics, and epistemology. In A. S. Gurman and D. P. Kniskern (eds) *Handbook of Family Therapy*. New York: Brunner/Mazel.

Haaga, D. A. and Davison, G. C. (1986) Cognitive change methods. In A. Kanfer and A. Goldstein (eds) *Helping People Change*, 3rd edn. New York: Pergamon.

Hackman, J. and Walton, R. (1986) Leading groups in organisations. In P. Goodman (ed.) *Designing Effective Work Groups*. San Francisco: Jossey-Bass.

Haley, J. (1973) *Uncommon Therapy: The Psychiatric Techniques of Milton H. Erickson, M.D.* New York: Norton.

Halgin, R. P. (1985) Teaching integration of psychotherapy models to beginning therapists. *Psychotherapy*, 22, 555–63.

Halgin, R. P. and Caron, M. (1991) To treat or not to treat: considerations for referring prospective clients. *Psychotherapy in Private Practice*, 8, 87–96.

Hall, A. S. and Fradkin, H. R. (1992) Affirming gay men's mental health: counseling with a new attitude. *Journal of Mental Health Counseling*, 14, 362–74.

Hallam, R. S. (1994) Some constructionist observations on 'anxiety' and its history. In T. R. Sarbin and J. I. Kitsuse (eds) *Constructing the Social*. Thousand Oaks, CA: Sage.

Halmos, P. (1965) *The Faith of the Counsellors*. London: Constable.

Handelsman, M. M. and Galvin, M. D. (1988) Facilitating informed consent for out-patient psychotherapy. *Professional Psychology: Research and Practice*, 19, 223–5.

Handy, C. (1990) *Voluntary Organisations*. Harmondsworth: Penguin.

Hanley, I. and Gilhooley, M. (eds) (1986) *Psychological Therapies for the Elderly*. London: Croom Helm.

Hannon, J. W., Ritchie, M. and Rye, D. R. (2001) Class; the missing discourse in counselling and counsellor education in the USA. *Journal of Critical Psychology, Counselling and Psychotherapy*, 1, 137–54.

Hardy, G. E., Aldridge, J., Davidson, C. *et al.* (1999) Therapist responsiveness to client attachment styles and issues observed in client-identified significant events in psychodynamic-interpersonal psychotherapy. *Psychotherapy Research*, 9, 36–53.

Hardy, G. E., Barkham, M., Shapiro, D. A. *et al.* (1995) Credibility and outcome of cognitive-behavioural and psychodynamic-interpersonal psychotherapy. *British Journal of Clinical Psychology*, 34, 555–69.

Hardy, J. (1987) *Psychology with a Soul: Psychosynthesis in Evolutionary Context.* London: Routledge and Kegan Paul.

Hardy, J. and Whitmore, D. (1988) Psychosynthesis. In J. Rowan and W. Dryden (eds) *Innovative Therapy in Britain.* Milton Keynes: Open University Press.

Hare, E. (1962) Masturbatory insanity: the history of an idea. *Journal of Mental Science*, 108, 1–25.

Harrison, D. K. (1975) Race as a counselor–client variable in counseling and psychotherapy: a review of the research. *Counseling Psychologist*, 5, 124–33.

Harrison, J. (1987) Counseling gay men. In M. Scher, M. Stevens, G. Good and G. A. Eichenfield (eds) *Handbook of Counseling and Psychotherapy with Men.* London: Sage.

Hart, J. T. and Tomlinson, T. M. (eds) (1970) *New Directions in Client-centered Therapy.* Boston: Houghton Mifflin.

Hartmann, E. (1997) The concept of boundaries in counselling and psychotherapy. *British Journal of Guidance and Counselling*, 25, 147–62.

Harway, M. (1979) Training counselors. *Counseling Psychologist*, 8, 8–10.

Hasenfeld, Y. (1992) The nature of human service organisations. In Y. Hasenfeld (ed.) *Human Services as Complex Organizations.* London: Sage.

Hattie, J. A., Sharpley, C. F. and Rogers, H. J. (1984) Comparative effectiveness of professional and paraprofessional helpers. *Psychological Bulletin*, 95, 534–41.

Hawkins, P. and Shohet, R. (1989) *Supervision in the Helping Professions. An Individual, Group and Organizational Approach.* Milton Keynes: Open University Press.

Hawkins, P. and Shohet, R. (1991) Approaches to the supervision of counsellors. In W. Dryden and B. Thorne (eds) *Training and Supervision for Counselling in Action.* London: Sage.

Hawkins, P. and Shohet, R. (2000) *Supervision in the Helping Professions*, 2nd edn. Buckingham: Open University Press.

Hayes, H. (1991) A re-introduction to family therapy: clarification of three schools. *Australia and New Zealand Journal of Family Therapy*, 12(1), 27–43.

Hays, P. A. (1996) Addressing the complexities of culture and gender in counseling. *Journal of Counseling and Development*, 74, 332–8.

Heimann, P. (1950) On countertransference. *International Journal of Psycho-Analysis*, 31, 81–4.

Hellman, I. D. and Morrison, T. L. (1987) Practice setting and type of caseload as factors in psychotherapist stress. *Psychotherapy*, 24, 427–33.

Henry, W. E. (1966) Some observations on the lives of healers. *Human Development*, 9, 47–56.

Henry, W. E. (1977) Personal and social identities of psychotherapists. In A. S. Gurman and A. M. Razin (eds) *Effective Psychotherapy: A Handbook of Research.* Oxford: Pergamon.

Henry, W. E., Sims, J. H. and Spray, S. L. (1971) *The Fifth Profession.* San Francisco: Jossey-Bass.

Henry, W. P. (1998) Science, politics, and the politics of science: the use and misuse of empirically validated treatment research. *Psychotherapy Research*, 8, 126–40.

Henry, W. P., Strupp, J. H., Schacht, T. E. and Gatson, L. (1994) Psychodynamic approaches. In A. E. Bergin and S. L. Garfield (eds) *Handbook of Psychotherapy and Behavior Change*, 4th edn. New York: Wiley.

Heppner, P. P., Kivlighan, D. M. Jr and Wampold, B. E. (1992) *Research Design in Counseling.* Belmont, CA: Wadsworth.

Heppner, P. P., Kivlighan D. M. Jr and Wampold, B. E. (1992) *Research Design in Counseling*. Pacific Grove, CA: Brooks/Cole.

Herek, G. M., Kimmel, D. C., Amaro, H. and Melton, G. B. (1991) Avoiding heterosexist bias in psychological research. *American Psychologist*, 46(9), 957–63.

Hermansson, G. (1997) Boundaries and boundary management in counselling: the never-ending story. *British Journal of Guidance and Counselling*, 25, 133–46.

Herron, W. G. and Sitkowski, S. (1986) Effect of fees on psychotherapy: what is the evidence? *Professional Psychology: Research and Practice*, 17, 347–51.

Hess, A. K. (ed.) (1980) *Psychotherapy Supervision. Theory, Research and Practice*. New York: Wiley.

Hesse, E. (1999) The Adult Attachment Interview: historical and current perspectives. In J. Cassidy and P. R. Shaver (eds) *Handbook of Attachment: Theory, Research and Clinical Applications*. New York: Guilford Press.

Hetherington, A. (2000) A psychodynamic profile of therapists who sexually exploit their clients. *British Journal of Psychotherapy*, 16, 274–86.

Hill, C. E. (1989) *Therapist Techniques and Client Outcomes: Eight Cases of Brief Psychotherapy*. London: Sage.

Hill, C. E. (1991) Almost everything you wanted to know about how to do process research on counselling and psychotherapy but didn't know who to ask. In C. E. Watkins Jr and L. J. Schneider (eds) *Research in Counselling*. New York: Lawrence Erlbaum.

Hill, C. E., Nutt-Williams, E., Heaton, K. J., Thompson, B. J. and Rhodes, R. H. (1996) Therapist retrospective recall of impasses in long-term psychotherapy: a qualitative analysis. *Journal of Counseling Psychology*, 43, 207–17.

Hill, M. (1999) Barter: ethical considerations in psychotherapy. *Women and Therapy*, 22(3), 81–92.

Hill, D. E. (ed.) (2001) *Helping Skills: The Empirical Foundation*. Washington, DC: American Psychological Association.

Hill, C. E. and O'Brien, K. M. (1999) *Helping Skills: Facilitating Exploration, Insight and Action*. Washington, DC: American Psychological Association.

Hinshelwood, R. D. (1991) Psychodynamic formulation in assessment for psychotherapy. *British Journal of Psychotherapy*, 8(2), 166–74.

Hirschhorn, L. (1978) The stalemated agency: a theoretical perspective and a practical proposal. *Administration in Social Work*, 2, 425–38.

Hitchings, P. (1997) Counselling and sexual orientation. In S. Palmer and G. McMahon (eds) *Handbook of Counselling*, 2nd edn. London: Routledge.

Hobson, R. E. (1985) *Forms of Feeling: The Heart of Psychotherapy*. London: Tavistock.

Hoffman, L. (1992) A reflexive stance for family therapy. In S. McNamee and K. J. Gergen (eds) *Therapy as Social Construction*. London: Sage.

Hofstede, G. (1980) *Culture's Consequences: International Differences in Work-related Values*. London: Sage.

Hofstede, G. (1992) *Cultures and Organizations: Software of the Mind*. London: McGraw-Hill.

Holdstock, L. (1990) Can client-centered therapy transcend its monocultual roots? In G. Lietaer, J. Rombauts and R. Van Balen (eds) *Client-centered and Experiential Therapy in the Nineties*. Leuven: Leuven University Press.

Holifield, E. B. (1983) *A History of Pastoral Care in America: From Salvation to Self-realization*. Nashville, TN: Abingdon Press.

Holland, R. (1977) *Self and Social Context*. London: Macmillan.

Holland, S. (1979) The development of an action and counselling service in a deprived urban area. In M. Meacher (ed.) *New Methods of Mental Health Care*. London: Pergamon.

Holland, S. (1990) Psychotherapy, oppression and social action: gender, race and class in black women's depression. In R. J. Perelberg and A. C. Miller (eds) *Gender and Power in Families*. London: Tavistock/Routledge.

Hollanders, H. and McLeod, J. (1999) Theoretical orientation and reported practice: a survey of eclecticism among counsellors in Britain. *British Journal of Guidance and Counselling*, 27, 405–14.

Hollon, S. D. and Kendall, P. C. (1981) *In vivo* assessment techniques for cognitive–behavioral processes. In P. C. Kendall and S. D. Hollon (eds) *Assessment Strategies for Cognitive-Behavioral Interventions*. New York: Academic Press.

Holmes, J. (1999a) Narrative, attachment and the therapeutic process. In C. Mace (ed.) *Heart and Soul: The Therapeutic Face of Philosophy*. London: Routledge.

Holmes, J. (1999b) The relationship in psychodynamic counselling. In C. Feltham (ed.) *Understanding the Counselling Relationship*. London: Sage.

Holmes, J. (2000) Attachment theory and psychoanalysis: a *rapprochement*. *British Journal of Psychotherapy*, 17, 157–72.

Holmes, J. (2001) *The Search for the Secure Base: Attachment, Psychoanalysis, and Narrative*. London: Routledge.

Holmqvist, R. (2001) Patterns of consistency and deviation in therapists' countertransference feelings. *Journal of Psychotherapy Practice and Research*, 10, 104–16.

Holmqvist, R. and Armelius, B. A. (1996) Sources of therapists' countertransference feelings. *Psychotherapy Research*, 69(1), 70–8.

Holroyd, J. C. and Brodsky, A. (1977) Psychologists' attitudes and practices regarding erotic and nonerotic physical contact with patients. *American Psychologist*, 32, 843–9.

Holtzman, B. L. (1984) Who's the therapist here? Dynamics underlying therapist-client sexual relations. *Smith College Studies in Social Work*, 54, 204–24.

Honos-Webb, L. and Stiles, W. B. (1998) Reformulation of assimilation analysis in terms of voices. *Psychotherapy*, 35, 23–33.

Honos-Webb, L., Stiles, W. B., Greenberg, L. S. and Goldman, R. (1998) Assimilation analysis of process – experiential psychotherapy: a comparison of two cases. *Psychotherapy Research*, 8, 264–86.

Honos-Webb, L., Surko, M., Stiles, W. B. and Greenberg, L. S. (1999) Assimilation of voices in psychotherapy: the case of Jan. *Journal of Counseling Psychology*, 46, 448–60.

Hooper, D. and Dryden, W. (eds) (1991) *Couple Therapy. A Handbook*. Buckingham: Open University Press.

Horvath, A. O. (2000) The therapeutic relationship: from transference to alliance. *In Session: Psychotherapy in Practice*, 56, 163–73.

Horvath, A. O. and Greenberg, L. S. (1986) The development of the Working Alliance Inventory. In L. D. Greenberg and W. M. Pinsot (eds) *The Psychotherapeutic Process: A Research Handbook*. New York: Guilford Press.

Horvath, A. O. and Greenberg, L. (eds) (1994) *The Working Alliance: Theory, Research and Practice*. New York: Wiley.

Horvath, A. and Symonds, B. D. (1991) Relation between working alliance and outcome in psychotherapy: a meta-analysis. *Journal of Counseling Psychology*, 38, 139–49.

Hosking, D. and Morley, I. (1991) *A Social Psychology of Organizing: People, Processes and Contexts*. Englewood Cliffs, NJ: Prentice Hall.

Hospers, J. (1997) *An Introduction to Philosophical Analysis*, 4th edn. London: Routledge.

Houghton, S. (1991) A multi-component intervention with an Olympic archer displaying performance related anxiety: a case study. *Behavioural Psychotherapy*, 19, 289–92.

Houston, G. (1990) *Supervision and Counselling*. London: The Rochester Foundation.

Howard, A. (2000) *Philosophy for Counselling and Psychotherapy: Pythagoras to Postmodernism*. London: Macmillan.

Howard, G. S. (1991) Culture tales: a narrative approach to thinking, cross-cultural psychology and psychotherapy. *American Psychologist*, 46, 187–97.

Howard, K. I., Kopta, S. M., Krause, M. S. and Orlinsky, D. E. (1986) The dose–effect relationship in psychotherapy. *American Psychologist*, 41, 159–64.

Howe, D. (1993) *On Being a Client: Understanding the Process of Counselling and Psychotherapy*. London: Sage.

Howell, E. (1981) Women: from Freud to the present. In E. Howell and M. Bayes (eds) *Women and Mental Health*. New York: Basic Books.

Hoyt, M. F. (ed.) (1994) *Constructive Therapies*. New York: Guilford.

Hoyt, M. F. (ed.) (1996a) *Constructive Therapies 2*. New York: Guilford.

Hoyt, M. F. (1996b) Welcome to PossibilityLand. A conversation with Bill O'Hanlan. In M. F. Hoyt (ed.) *Constructive Therapies 2*. New York: Guilford.

Hsu, J. (1976) Counseling in the Chinese temple: a psychological study of divination by *chien* drawing. In W. P. Lebra (ed.) *Culture-bound Syndromes, Ethnopsychiatry and Alternative Therapies. Volume IV of Mental Health Research in Asia and the Pacific*. Honolulu, HI: University Press of Hawaii.

Hubble, M. A., Duncan, B. C. and Miller, S. D. (eds) (1999) *The Heart and Soul of Change: What Works in Therapy*. Washington, DC: American Psychological Association.

Hunot, V. and Rosenbach, A. (1998) Factors influencing the attitudes and commitment of volunteer alcohol counsellors. *British Journal of Guidance and Counselling*, 26, 353–64.

Hunsley, J., Aubry, T. D., Verservelt, C. M and Vito, D. (1999) Comparing therapist and client perspectives on reasons for psychotherapy termination. *Psychotherapy*, 36, 380–8.

Hunter, M. and Struve, J. (1998) *The Ethical Use of Touch in Psychotherapy*. Thousand Oaks, CA: Sage.

Hurvitz, N. (1967) Marital problems following psychotherapy with one spouse. *Journal of Consulting Psychology*, 31, 38–47.

Hycner, R. (1993) *Between Person and Person: Toward a Dialogical Psychotherapy*. New York: The Gestalt Journal Press.

Hycner, R. and Jacobs, L. (1995) *The Healing Relationship in Gestalt Therapy: A Dialogical/Self Psychology Approach*. New York: The Gestalt Journal Press.

Imber-Black, E. and Roberts, J. (1992) *Rituals for Our Times: Celebrating, Healing and Changing Our Lives and Our Relationships*. New York: HarperCollins.

Inskipp, F. and Johns, H. (1984) Developmental eclecticism: Egan's skills model of helping. In W. Dryden (ed.) *Individual Therapy in Britain*. Milton Keynes: Open University Press.

Israeli, A. L. and Santor, D. A. (2000) Reviewing effective components of feminist therapy. *Counselling Psychology Quarterly*, 13, 233–47.

Ivey, A. E. (1995) Psychotherapy as liberation: toward specific skills and strategies in multicultural counseling and therapy. In J. G. Ponterotto, J. M. Casas, L. A. Suzuki and C. M. Alexander (eds) *Handbook of Multicultural Counseling*. London: Sage.

Ivey, A. E. and Galvin, M. (1984) Microcounseling: a metamodel for counseling, therapy, business and medical interviews. In D. Larson (ed.) *Teaching Psychological Skills: Models for Giving Psychology Away*. Monterey, CA: Brooks/Cole.

Ivey, A. E., Ivey, M. B. and Simek-Downing, L. (1987) *Counseling and Psychotherapy: Integrating Skills, Theory and Practice*, 2nd edn. Englewood Cliffs, NJ: Prentice Hall.

Jacobs, M. (1986) *The Presenting Past*. Milton Keynes: Open University Press.

Jacobs, M. (1992) *Sigmund Freud*. London: Sage.

Jacobs, M. (1995) *Charlie – An Unwanted Child?* Buckingham: Open University Press.

Jacobs, M. (1996) *Jitendra – Lost Connections.* Buckingham: Open University Press.

Jacobs, M. (1999) *Psychodynamic Counselling in Action,* 2nd edn. London: Sage.

James, M. and Jongeward, D. (1971) *Born to Win: Transactional Analysis with Gestalt Experiments.* Reading, MA: Addison-Wesley.

James, W. (1890) *Principles of Psychology.* New York: Holt.

Jenkins, P. (1997) *Counselling, Psychotherapy and the Law.* London: Sage.

Jennings, L. and Skovholt, T. M. (1999) The cognitive, emotional and relational characteristics of master therapists. *Journal of Counseling Psychology,* 46, 3–11.

Jeske, J. O. (1984) Varieties of approaches to psychotherapy: options for the Christian therapist. *Journal of Psychology and Theology,* 12, 260–9.

Johns, H. (1995) *Personal Development in Counselling Training.* London: Cassell.

Johns, H. (ed.) (1998) *Balancing Acts: Studies in Counselling Training.* London: Routledge.

Johnson, A. W. and Nadirshaw, Z. (1993) Good practice in transcultural counselling: an Asian perspective. *British Journal of Guidance and Counselling,* 21(1), 20–9.

Johnson, S. E., Hunsley, J., Greenberg, L. and Schindler, D. (1999) Emotionally focused couples therapy; status and challenges. *Clinical Psychology: Science and Practice,* 6, 67–79.

Johnson, W. B. and Ridley, C. R. (1992) Sources of gain in Christian counseling and psychotherapy. *Counseling Psychologist,* 20, 159–75.

Jones, C., Shillito-Clarke, C., Syme, G., Hill, D., Casemore, R. and Murdin, L. (2000) *Questions of Ethics in Cousnelling and Therapy.* Buckingham: Open University Press.

Jones, E. (1951) *Essays in Applied Psychoanalysis, Volume II.* London: Hogarth Press.

Jones, E. (1955) *Life and Work of Sigmund Freud, Volume 2.* London: Hogarth Press.

Jones, E. (1993) *Family Systems Therapy: Developments in the Milan-systemic Therapies.* Chichester: Wiley.

Jones, E., Krupnik, J. L. and Kerig, P. K. (1987) Some gender effects in a brief psychotherapy. *Psychotherapy,* 24(3), 336–52.

Jongsma, I. (1995) Philosophical counseling in Holland: history and open issues. In R. Lahav and M. da Venza Tillmanns (eds) *Essays on Philosophical Counselling.* Lanham, MD: University Press of America.

Jordan, J. V. (1991) Empathy, mutuality and therapeutic change: clinical implications of a relational model. In J. V. Jordan, A. G. Kaplan, J. B. Miller, I. P. Stiver and J. L. Surrey (eds) *Women's Growth in Connection.* New York: Guilford Press.

Jordan, J. V. (ed.) (1997a) *Women's Growth in Diversity: More Writings from the Stone Center.* New York: Guilford Press.

Jordan, J. V. (1997b) A relational perspective for understanding women's development. In J. V. Jordan (ed.) *Women's Growth in Diversity: More Writings from the Stone Center.* New York: Guilford Press.

Jordan, J. V. (2000) The role of mutual empathy in relational/cultural therapy. *Journal of Clinical Psychology,* 56, 1005–16.

Jordan, J. V., Kaplan, A. G., Miller, J. B., Stiver, I. P. and Surrey, J. L. (eds) (1991) *Women's Growth in Connection: Writings from the Stone Center.* New York: Guilford Press.

Josselson, R. (1996) *The Space Between Us: Exploring the Dimensions of Human Relationships.* Thousand Oaks, CA: Sage.

Jung, C. G. (1963) *Memories, Dreams, Reflections* (edited by A. Jaffe). New York: Pantheon Books.

Jung, C. G. (1964) *Man and His Symbols.* New York: Doubleday.

Jupp, J. J. and Shaul, V. (1991) Burn-out in student counsellors. *Counselling Psychology Quarterly,* 4, 157–67.

Kaberry, S. (2000) Abuse in supervision. In B. Lawton and C. Feltham (eds) *Taking Supervision Forward: Enquiries and Trends in Counselling and Psychotherapy*. London: Sage.

Kachele, H. (1992) Narration and observation in psychotherapy research: reporting on a 20 year long journey. *Psychotherapy Research*, 2, 1–15.

Kachele, H., Richter, R., Thoma, H. and Meyer, A.-E. (1999) Psychotherapy services in the Federal Republic of Germany. In N. E. Miller and K. M. Magruder (eds) *Cost-effectiveness of Psychotherapy: A Guide for Practitioners, Researchers and Policymakers*. New York: Oxford University Press.

Kagan, N. (1984) Interpersonal Process Recall: basic methods and recent research. In D. Larson (ed.) *Teaching Psychological Skills: Models for Giving Psychology Away*. Monterey, CA: Brooks/Cole.

Kagan, N. and Kagan, H. (1990) IPR – a validated model for the 1990s and beyond. *Counseling Psychologist*, 18, 436–40.

Kagan, N., Krathwohl, D. R. and Miller, R. (1963) Stimulated recall in therapy using videotape – a case study. *Journal of Counseling Psychology*, 10, 237–43.

Kahn, M. (1997) *Between Therapist and Client. The New Relationship*, 2nd edn. New York: W. H. Freeman.

Kahn, W. L. and Harkavy-Friedman, J. M. (1997) Change in the therapist: the role of patient-induced inspiration. *American Journal of Psychotherapy*, 51, 403–14.

Kanfer, A. and Goldstein, A. (eds) (1986) *Helping People Change*, 3rd edn. New York: Pergamon.

Kaplan, A. G. (1987) Reflections on gender and psychotherapy. In M. Braude (ed.) *Women, Power and Therapy*. New York: Haworth Press.

Kaplan, A. G. (1991) Female or male psychotherapists for women: new formulations. In J. V. Jordan, A. G. Kaplan, J. B. Miller, I. P. Stiver, and J. L. Surrey (eds) *Women's Growth in Connection: Writings from the Stone Center*. New York: Guilford Press.

Karasu, T. B. (1986) The specificity against nonspecificity dilemma: toward identifying therapeutic change agents. *American Journal of Psychiatry*, 143, 687–95.

Kareem, J. and Littlewood, R. (1992) *Intercultural Therapy*. Oxford: Blackwell.

Karlsruher, A. E. (1974) The nonprofessional as psychotherapeutic agent. *American Journal of Community Psychology*, 2, 61–77.

Kaslow, F. W. (1986) Supervision, consultation and staff training – creative teaching/learning processes in the mental health profession. In F. W. Kaslow (ed.) *Supervision and Training. Models, Dilemmas and Challenges*. New York: Haworth Press.

Katz, D. and Kahn, R. I. (1978) *The Social Psychology of Organizations*, 2nd edn. New York: Wiley.

Katz, J. (1985) The sociopolitical nature of counseling. *Counseling Psychologist*, 13, 615–24.

Kaufmann, Y. (1989) Analytical psychotherapy. In R. J. Corsini and D. Wedding (eds) *Current Psychotherapies*, 4th edn. Itasca, IL: F. E. Peacock.

Kazdin, A. E. (1978) *History of Behavior Modification: Experimental Foundations of Contemporary Research*. Baltimore: University Park Press.

Kelly, A. E. (2000) Helping construct desirable identities: a self-presentational view of psychotherapy. *Psychological Bulletin*, 126, 4754–94.

Kelly, E. W. (1995) Counselor values: a national survey. *Journal of Counseling and Development*, 73, 648–53.

Kelly, G. A. (1955) *The Psychology of Personal Constructs, Volumes 1 and 2*. New York: W. W. Norton.

Kelly, T. A. (1989) The role of values in psychotherapy: a critical review of process and outcome effects. *Clinical Psychology Review*, 10, 171–86.

Kendall, P. C. and Hollon, S. D. (1981) Assessing self-referent speech: methods in the measurement of self-statements. In P. C. Kendall and S. D. Hollon (eds) *Assessment Strategies for Cognitive–Behavioral Interventions*. New York: Academic Press.

Kennel, R. G. and Agresti, A. A. (1995) Effects of gender and age on psychologists' reporting of child sexual abuse. *Professional Psychology: Research and Practice*, 26(6), 612–15.

Kernberg, O. F. (1975) *Borderline Conditions and Pathological Narcissism*. New York: Aronson.

Kernberg, O. F. (1976) *Object Relations Theory and Clinical Psychoanalysis*. New York: Jason Aronson.

Kernberg, O. F. (1984) *Severe Personality Disorders: Psychotherapeutic Strategies*. New Haven, CT: Yale University Press.

Kerr, J. (1994) *A Most Dangerous Method: The Story of Jung, Freud, and Sabina Speilrein*. London: Sinclair-Stevenson.

Kiesler, D. (1988) *Therapeutic Metacommunication: Therapist Impact Disclosure as Feedback in Psychotherapy*. Palo Alto, CA: Consulting Psychologists Press.

Kilmann, P. R., Laughlin, J. E., Carranza, L. V., Downer, J. T., Major, S. and Parnell, M. M. (1999) Effects of an attachment-focused group preventive intervention on secure women. *Group Dynamics*, 3, 138–47.

King, S. A., Engi, S. and Pouli, S. T. (1998) Using the Internet to assist family therapy. *British Journal of Guidance and Counselling*, 26, 43–52.

King-Spooner, S. (1999) Editorial: introduction to special issue on philosophy and psychotherapy. *Changes*, 17(3), 159–60.

Kirkwood, C. (1990) *Vulgar Eloquence: From Labour to Liberation. Essays on Education, Community and Politics*. Edinburgh: Polygon.

Kirkwood, C. (2000) *The Development of Counselling in Shetland*. Stirling: COSCA.

Kirsch, I. (1978) Demonology and the rise of science: an example of the misperception of historical data. *Journal of the History of the Behavioral Sciences*, 14, 149–57.

Kirschenbaum, H. (1979) *On Becoming Carl Rogers*. New York: Dell.

Kirschenbaum, H. and Henderson, V. L. (eds) (1990) *Carl Rogers: Dialogues*. London: Constable.

Kitchener, K. S. (1984) Intuition, critical evaluation and ethical principles: the foundation for ethical decisions in counseling psychology. *Counseling Psychologist*, 12, 43–55.

Kitzinger, C. and Perkins, R. (1993) *Changing Our Minds: Lesbian Feminism and Psychology*. London: Onlywomen Press.

Kivlighan, D. M., Patton, M. J. and Foote, D. (1998) Moderating effects of client attachment on the counselor experience–working alliance relationship. *Journal of Counseling Psychology*, 45, 274–8.

Klein, J. (1987) *Our Need for Others and Its Roots in Infancy*. London: Tavistock.

Klein, M. H. (1976) Feminist concepts of therapy outcome. *Psychotherapy: Theory, Research and Practice*, 13(1), 89–95.

Klein, M. H., Mathieu-Coughlan, P. and Kiesler, D. J. (1986) The Experiencing Scales. In L. S. Greenberg and W. M. Pinsof (eds) *The Psychotherapeutic Process: A Research Handbook*. New York: Guilford Press.

Kleinman, A. (1988) *The Illness Narratives: Suffering, Healing and the Human Condition*. New York: Basic Books.

Klemp, G. and McClelland, D. (1986) What characterizes intelligent functioning among senior managers? In R. Sternberg and R. Wagner (eds) *Practical Intelligence: The Nature and Origins of Competence in the Everyday World*. Cambridge: Cambridge University Press.

Knight, B. (1986) *Psychotherapy with Older Adults*. London: Sage.

Knox, S., Goldberg, J. L., Woodhouse, S. S. and Hill, C. E. (1999) Clients' internal representations of their therapists. *Journal of Counseling Psychology*, 46, 244–56.

Koffka, K. (1935) *Principles of Gestalt Psychology*. New York: Harcourt, Brace.

Kohler, W. (1929) *Gestalt Psychology*. New York: Liveright.

Kohon, G. (ed.) (1986) *The British School of Psychoanalysis: The Independent Tradition*. London: Free Association Books.

Kohut, H. (1971) *The Analysis of the Self*. London: Hogarth.

Kohut, H. (1977) *The Restoration of the Self*. Madison, CT: International Universities Press.

Koltko, M. E. (1990) How religious beliefs affect psychotherapy: the example of Mormonism. *Psychotherapy*, 27, 132–41.

Kopp, S. (1972) *If You Meet the Buddha on the Road, Kill Him!* Palo Alto, CA: Science and Behavior Books.

Kopp, S. (1974) *The Hanged Man*. Palo Alto, CA: Science and Behavior Books.

Kottler, J. (1988) *The Imperfect Therapist*. San Francisco: Jossey-Bass.

Kovacs, A. L. (1976) The emotional hazards of teaching psychotherapy. *Psychotherapy*, 13, 321–34.

Kovel, J. (1981) The American mental health industry. In D. Ingleby (ed.) *Critical Psychiatry: The Politics of Mental Health*. Harmondsworth: Penguin.

Kuehlwein, K. T. (1993) A survey and update of cognitive therapy systems. In K. T. Kuehlwein and H. Rosen (eds) *Cognitive Therapies in Action: Evolving Innovative Practice*. San Francisco: Jossey-Bass.

Kuehnel, J. and Liberman, P. (1986) Behavior modification. In I. Kutush and A. Wolf (eds) *A Psychotherapist's Casebook*. San Francisco: Jossey-Bass.

Kuhn, T. S. (1962) *The Structure of Scientific Revolutions*. Chicago: University of Chicago Press.

Kurtz, R. and Grummon, D. (1972) Different approaches to the measurement of therapist empathy and their relationship to therapy outcomes. *Journal of Consulting and Clinical Psychology*, 39, 106–15.

Kvale, S. (ed.) (1992) *Postmodernism and Psychology*. London: Sage.

Lacan, J. (1977) *Ecrits: A Selection*. New York: W. W. Norton.

Lacan, J. (1979) *The Four Fundamental Concepts of Psycho-Analysis*. London: Penguin.

Ladany, N., Hill, C. E., Corbett, M. M. and Nutt, E. A. (1996) Nature, extent and importance of what psychotherapy trainees do not disclose to their supervisors. *Journal of Counseling Psychology*, 43, 10–24.

LaFramboise, T. D. and Foster, S. L. (1992) Cross-cultural training: scientistpractitioner model and methods. *Counseling Psychologist*, 20, 472–89.

Lago, C. and Thompson, J. (1989) Counselling and race. In W. Dryden, D. Charles Edwards and R. Woolfe (eds) *Handbook of Counselling in Britain*. London: Tavistock/Routledge.

Lago, C. and Thompson, J. (1996) *Race, Culture and Counselling*. Buckingham: Open University Press.

Lahav, R. (1995a) Introduction. In R. Lahav and M. da Venza Tillmanns (ed.) *Essays on Philosophical Counseling*. Lanham, MD: University Press of America.

Lahav, R. (1995b) A conceptual framework for philosophical counseling: worldview interpretation. In R. Lahav and M. da Venza Tillmanns (eds) *Essays on Philosophical Counselling*. Lanham, MD: University Press of America.

Lahav, R. (2001) Philosophical counselling as a quest for wisdom. *Practical Philosophy*, 4, 1–21.

Lahav, R. and da Venza Tillmanns, M. (eds) (1995) *Essays on Philosophical Counselling*. Lanham, MD: University Press of America.

Laing, R. D. (1960) *The Divided Self*. Harmondsworth: Penguin.

Laing, R. D. (1961) *Self and Others*. Harmondsworth: Penguin.

Laing, R. D., Phillipson, H. and Lee, A. R. (1966) *Interpersonal Perception – A Theory and a Method of Research*. London: Tavistock.

Lakin, M. (1988) *Ethical Issues in the Psychotherapies*. New York: Oxford University Press.

Lamb, D. H. and Catanzaro, S. J. (1998) Sexual and nonsexual boundary violations involving psychologists, clients, supervisees, and students: implications for professional practice. *Professional Psychology: Research and Practice*, 29, 498–503.

Lambert, M. J., Christensen, E. R. and DeJulio, S. S. (eds) (1983) *The Assessment of Psychotherapy Outcome*. New York: Wiley.

Landrine, H. (1992) Clinical implications of cultural differences: the referential vs the indexical self. *Clinical Psychology Review*, 12, 401–15.

Lange, A. (1994) Writing assignments in the treatment of grief and traumas from the past. In J. Zeig (ed.) *Ericksonian Methods: The Essence of the Story*. New York: Brunner/Mazel.

Lange, A. (1996) Using writing assignments with families managing legacies of extreme traumas. *Journal of Family Therapy*, 18, 375–88.

Lange, A., Schrieken, B., van de Ven, J.-P., Bredeweg, B. and Emmelkamp, P. M. G. (2000) 'Interapy': the effects of a short protocolled treatment of posttraumatic stress and pathological grief through the Internet. *Behavioural and Cognitive Psychotherapy*, 28, 175–92.

Langs, R. J. (1988) *A Primer of Psychotherapy*. New York: Gardner.

Lankton, S. and Lankton, C. (1986) *Enchantment and Intervention in Family Therapy*. New York: Brunner/Mazel.

Larson, D. (ed.) (1984) *Teaching Psychological Skills: Models for Giving Psychology Away*. Monterey, CA: Brooks/Cole.

Larson, L. M., Suzuki, L. A., Gillespie, K. N. *et al.* (1992) Development and validation of the counseling self-estimate inventory. *Journal of Counseling Psychology*, 39, 105–20.

Lasky, E. (1999) Psychotherapists' ambivalence about fees: male–female differences. *Women and Therapy*, 22(3), 5–14.

Lawrence, M. and Maguire, M. (eds) (1997) *Psychotherapy with Women: Feminist Perspectives*. London: Macmillan.

Lawton, B. (2000) 'A very exposing affair': explorations in counsellors' supervisory relationships. In B. Lawton and C. Feltham (eds) *Taking Supervision Forward: Enquiries and Trends in Counselling and Psychotherapy*. London: Sage.

Lawton, B. and Feltham, C. (eds) (2000) *Taking Supervision Forward: Enquiries and Trends in Counselling and Psychotherapy*. London: Sage.

Lazarus, A. A. (1989a) *The Practice of Multimodal Therapy*. Baltimore: Johns Hopkins University Press.

Lazarus, A. A. (1989b) Multimodal therapy. In R. J. Corsini and D. Wedding (eds) *Current Psychotherapies*, 4th edn. Itasca, IL: F. E. Peacock.

Lazarus, A. A. and Messer, S. B. (1988) Clinical choice points: behavioral versus psychoanalytic interventions. *Psychotherapy*, 25(1), 59–70.

Lee, B.-O. (2002) Chinese indigenous psychotherapies in Singapore. *Counselling and Psychotherapy Research*, 2, 2–10.

Lee, C. C. and Armstrong, K. L. (1995) Indigenous models of mental health intervention: lessons from traditional healers. In J. G. Ponterotto, J. M. Casas, L. A. Suzuki and C. M. Alexander (eds) *Handbook of Multicultural Counseling*. London: Sage.

Leijssen, M. (1993) Creating a workable distance to overwhelming images: comments on a session transcript. In D. Brazier (ed.) *Beyond Carl Rogers*. London: Constable.

Leijssen, M. (1998) Focusing microprocesses. In L. S. Greenberg, J. C. Watson and G. Lietaer (eds) *Handbook of Experiential Psychotherapy*. New York: Guilford Press.

Lener, R. (1972) *Therapy in the Ghetto*. New York: Wiley.

Lester, D. (1974) The unique qualities of telephone therapy. *Psychotherapy*, 11, 219–21.

Levant, R. F. and Shlien, J. M. (eds) (1984) *Client-centered Therapy and the Person-centered Approach: New Directions in Theory, Research and Practice*. New York: Praeger.

Levine, M. and Doueck, H. J. (1995) *The Impact of Mandated Reporting on the Therapeutic Process: Picking up the Pieces*. London: Sage.

Lewinsohn, P. M., Steinmetz, J. L., Larson, D. W. and Franklin, J. (1981) Depression related cognitions: antecedent or consequences? *Journal of Abnormal Psychology*, 90, 213–19.

Lewis, J., Clark, D. and Morgan, D. (1992) *Whom God Hath Joined Together: The Work of Marriage Guidance*. London: Routledge.

Liddle, B. J. (1995) Sexual orientation bias among advanced graduate students of counseling and counseling psychology. *Counselor Education and Supervision*, 34, 321–31.

Liddle, B. J. (1996) Therapist sexual orientation, gender, and counseling practices as they relate to ratings of helpfulness by gay and lesbian clients. *Journal of Counseling Psychology*, 43(4), 394–401.

Liddle, B. J. (1997) Gay and lesbian clients' selection of therapists and utilization of therapy. *Psychotherapy*, 34, 11–18.

Lieberman, M., Yalom, I. and Miles, M. (1973) *Encounter Groups: First Facts*. New York: Basic Books.

Lietaer, G. (1984) Unconditional positive regard: a controversial basic attitude in client-centered therapy. In R. F. Levant and J. M. Shlien (eds) *Client-centered Therapy and the Person-centered Approach: New Directions in Theory, Research and Practice*. New York: Praeger.

Lietaer, G. (1990) The client-centered approach after the Wisconsin project: a personal view on its evolution. In G. Lietaer, J. Rombauts and R. Van Balen (eds) *Client-centered and Experiential Therapy in the Nineties*. Leuven: Leuven University Press.

Lietaer, G. (1993) Authenticity, congruence and transparency. In D. Brazier (ed.) *Beyond Carl Rogers*. London: Constable.

Lietaer, G. (2001) Becoming genuine as a therapist: congruence and transparency. In G. Wyatt (ed.) *Rogers' Therapeutic Conditions: Evolution, Theory and Practice, Volume 1: Congruence*. Ross-on-Wye: PCCS Books.

Lietaer, G., Rombauts, J. and van Balen, R. (eds) (1990) *Client-centered and Experiential Therapy in the Nineties*. Leuven: Leuven University Press.

Linden, J., Stone, S. and Shertzer, B. (1965) Development and evaluation of an inventory for rating counseling. *Personnel and Guidance Journal*, 44, 267–76.

Lipkin, S. (1948) The client evaluates nondirective therapy. *Journal of Consulting Psychology*, 12, 137–46.

Littlewood, R. and Lipsedge, M. (1989) *Aliens and Alienists: Ethnic Minorities and Psychiatry*. London: Unwin Hyman.

Llewelyn, S. and Hume, W. (1979) The patient's view of therapy. *British Journal of Medical Psychology*, 52, 29–36.

Llewelyn, S. and Osborne, K. (1983) Women as clients and therapists. In D. Pilgrim (ed.) *Psychology and Psychotherapy: Current Trends and Issues*. London: Routledge.

Locke, A. (1971) Is behavior therapy 'behavioristic'? *Psychological Bulletin*, 76, 318–27.

Logan, R. D. (1987) Historical change in prevailing sense of self. In K. Yardley and T. Honess (eds) *Self and Identity: Psychosocial Perspectives*. Chichester: Wiley.

Lomas, P. (1981) *The Case for a Personal Psychotherapy*. Oxford: Oxford University Press.

Lomas, P. (1987) *The Limits of Interpretation: What's Wrong with Psychoanalysis*. Harmondsworth: Penguin.

Lomas, P. (1994) *Cultivating Intuition: An Introduction to Psychotherapy*. Harmondsworth: Penguin.

Lopez, S. R., Lopez, A. A. and Fong, K. T. (1991) Mexican Americans' initial preferences for counselors: the role of ethnic factors. *Journal of Counseling Psychology*, 38, 487–96.

Lorion, R. P. and Felner, R. D. (1986) Research on psychotherapy with the disadvantaged. In S. L. Garfield and A. E. Bergin (eds) *Handbook of Psychotherapy and Behavior Change*, 3rd edn. London: Wiley.

Lott, D. A. (1999) *In Session: The Bond between Women and Their Therapists*. New York: W. H. Freeman.

Luborsky, L., Barber, J. P. and Diguer, L. (1992) The meanings of narratives told during psychotherapy: the fruits of a new observational unit. *Psychotherapy Research*, 2, 277–90.

Luborsky, L. and Crits-Christoph, P. (eds) (1990) *Understanding Transference: The CCRT Method*. New York: Basic Books.

Luborsky, L., Crits-Christoph, P. and Mellon, J. (1986) Advent of objective measures of the transference concept. *Journal of Consulting and Clinical Psychology*, 54, 39–47.

Luborsky, L., Diguer, L., Seligman, D. A. *et al.* (1999) The researcher's own therapy allegiances: a 'wild card' in comparisons of treatment efficacy. *Clinical Psychology: Science and Practice*, 6, 95–106.

Luborsky, L., McLellan, A. T., Diguer, L., Woody, G. and Seligman, D. A. (1997) The psychotherapist matters: comparison of outcomes across twenty-two therapists and seven patient samples. *Clinical Psychology: Science and Practice*, 4, 53–65.

Luborsky, L., Popp, C., Luborsky, E. and Mark, D. (1994) The core conflictual relationship theme. *Psychotherapy Research*, 4, 172–83.

Luborsky, L., Singer, B. and Luborsky, L. (1975) Comparative studies of psychotherapies: is it true that 'everyone has one and all must have prizes'? *Archives of General Psychiatry*, 32, 995–1008.

Lueger, R. J., Saunders, S. M., Howard, K. I., Vessey, J. T. and Nunez, P. R. (1999) Entering psychotherapy: probabilities, routes and finances. In N. E. Miller and K. M. Magruder (eds) *Cost-effectiveness of Psychotherapy: A Guide for Practitioners, Researchers and Policymakers*. New York: Oxford University Press.

Lukinsky, J. (1990) Reflective withdrawal through journal writing. In J. Mezirow (ed.) *Fostering Critical Reflection in Adulthood: A Guide to Transformative and Emancipatory Learning*. San Francisco: Jossey-Bass.

Lyon, D. (1994) *Postmodernity*. Buckingham: Open University Press.

McAdams, D. P. (1985) *Power, Intimacy, and the Life Story: Personological Inquiries into Identity*. New York: Guilford Press.

McAdams, D. P. (1993) *The Stories We Live By: Personal Myths and the Making of the Self*. New York: William Murrow.

McCallum, M. and Piper, W. B. (1990) The psychological mindedness assessment procedure. *Psychological Assessment*, 2, 412–18.

McCallum, M. and Piper, W. E. (1997) The psychological mindedness assessment procedure. In M. McCallum and W. E. Piper (eds) *Psychological Mindedness: A Contemporary Understanding*. Mahwah, NJ: Lawrence Erlbaum.

McCarley, T. (1975) The psychotherapist's search for self-renewal. *American Journal of Psychiatry*, 132, 221–4.

McConnaughy, E. A. (1987) The person of the therapist in therapeutic practice. *Psychotherapy*, 24, 303–14.

Mace, C. (1995a) When are questionnaires helpful? In C. Mace (ed.) *The Art and Science of Assessment in Psychotherapy*. London: Routledge.

Mace, C. (ed.) (1995b) *The Art and Science of Assessment in Psychotherapy*. London: Routledge.

Mace, C. (ed.) (1999a) *Heart and Soul: the Therapeutic Face of Philosophy*. London: Routledge.

Mace, C. (1999b) Therapeutic questioning and Socratic dialogue. In C. Mace (ed.) *Heart and Soul: the Therapeutic Face of Philosophy*. London: Routledge.

McGoldrick, M. and Gerson, R. (1985) *Genograms in Family Assessment*. New York: Norton.

McGoldrick, M. and Gerson, R. (1989) Genograms and the family life cycle. In B. Carter and M. McGoldrick (ed.) *The Changing Family Life Cycle: A Framework for Family Therapy*, 2nd edn. Boston: Allyn and Bacon.

McGrath, G. and Lowson, K. (1986) Assessing the benefits of psychotherapy: the economic approach. *British Journal of Psychiatry*, 150, 65–71.

McGuire, J., Nieri, D., Abbott, D., Sheridan, K. and Fisher, R. (1995) Do *Tarasoff* principles apply in AIDS-related psychotherapy? Ethical decision making and the role of therapist homophobia and perceived client dangerousness. *Professional Psychology: Research and Practice*, 26(6), 608–11.

MacIntyre, A. (1981) *After Virtue: A Study in Moral Theory*. London: Duckworth.

Mack, J. (1981) Alcoholism, AA and the governance of self. In M. H. Bean and N. E. Zinberg (eds) *Dynamic Approaches to the Understanding and Treatment of Alcoholism*. New York: Free Press.

Mackay, H. C., West, W., Moorey, J., Guthrie, E. and Margison, F. (2001) Counsellors' experiences of changing their practice: learning the psychodynamic-interpersonal model of therapy. *Counselling and Psychotherapy Research*, 1, 29–40.

McKinney, F. (1976) Free writing as therapy. *Psychotherapy*, 13, 183–7.

MacKinnon, C. (1982) Feminism, Marxism, method and the state: an agenda for theory. In N. Keohane, M. Rosaldo and B. Gelpi (eds) *Feminist Theory: A Critique of Ideology*. Chicago: University of Chicago Press.

McLean, A. (1986) Family therapy workshops in the United States: potential abuses in the production of therapy in an advanced capitalist society. *Social Science and Medicine*, 23(2), 179–89.

McLellan, A. T., Woody, G. E., Luborsky, L. and Gohl, L. (1988) Is the counselor an 'active ingredient' in substance abuse rehabilitation? An examination of treatment success among four counselors. *Journal of Nervous and Mental Disease*, 176, 423–30.

McLellan, B. (1999) The prostitution of psychotherapy: a feminist critique. *British Journal of Guidance and Counselling*, 27, 325–13.

McLeod, E. (1994) *Women's Experience of Feminist Therapy and Counselling*. Buckingham: Open University Press.

McLeod, J. (1984) Group process as drama. *Small Group Behavior*, 15, 319–32.

McLeod, J. (1990) The client's experience of counselling: a review of the research literature. In D. Mearns and W. Dryden (eds) *Experiences of Counselling in Action*. London: Sage.

McLeod, J. (1996) The emerging narrative approach to counselling and psychotherapy. *British Journal of Guidance and Counselling*, 24, 173–84.

McLeod, J. (1997) *Narrative and Psychotherapy*. London: Sage.

McLeod, J. (1999a) Counselling as a social process. *Counselling*, 10, 217–26.

McLeod, J. (1999b) A narrative social constructionist approach to therapeutic empathy. *Counselling Psychology Quarterly*, 12, 377–84.

McLeod, J. (1999c) *Practitioner Research in Counselling*. London: Sage.

McLeod, J. (2000) The development of narrative-informed theory, research and practice in counselling and psychotherapy; European perspectives. *European Journal of Psychotherapy, Counselling and Health*, 3, 331–3.

McLeod, J. (2001) *Qualitative Research in Counselling and Psychotherapy*. London: Sage.

McLeod, J. (2002a) The humanistic paradigm. In R. Woolfe, W. Dryden and S. Strawbridge (eds) *Handbook of Counselling Psychology*, 2nd edn. London: Sage.

McLeod, J. (2002b) Qualitative research methods in counselling psychology. In R. Woolfe, W. Dryden and S. Strawbridge (eds) *Handbook of Counselling Psychology*, 2nd edn. London: Sage.

McLeod, J. (2003) *Doing Counselling Research*, 2nd edn. London: Sage.

McLeod, J. and Balamoutsou, S. (2000) Narrative process in the assimilation of a problematic experience: qualitative analysis of a single case. *Zeitschrift für qualitative Bildungs- Beratungs- und Sozialforschung*, 2, 283–302.

McLeod, J. and Balamoutsou, S. (2001) A method for qualitative narrative analysis of psychotherapy transcripts. In J. Frommer and D. L. Rennie (eds) *Qualitative Psychotherapy Research: Methods and Methodology*. Berlin: Pabst.

McLeod, J. and Lynch, G. (2000) 'This is our life': strong evaluation in psychotherapy narrative. *European Journal of Psychotherapy, Counselling and Health*, 3, 389–406.

McLeod, J. and Machin, L. (1998) Contexts of counselling: a neglected dimension of theory, research and practice. *British Journal of Guidance and Counselling*, 26, 325–36.

McLoughlin, B. (1995) *Developing Psychodynamic Counselling*. London: Sage.

McNamee, S. and Gergen, K. J. (ed.) (1992) *Therapy as Social Construction*. London: Sage.

McNeill, B. W. and Worthen, V. (1989) The parallel process in psychotherapy supervision. *Professional Psychology: Research and Practice*, 20, 329–33.

McNeill, J. T. (1951) *A History of the Cure of Souls*. New York: Harper and Row.

Macquarrie, J. (1972) *Existentialism*. Harmondsworth: Penguin.

Macran, S., Stiles, W. B. and Smith, J. A. (1999) How does personal therapy affect therapists' practice? *Journal of Counseling Psychology*, 46, 419–31.

Madill, A. and Barkham, M. (1997) Discourse analysis of a theme in one successful case of brief psychodynamic-interpersonal psychotherapy. *Journal of Counseling Psychology*, 44, 232–44.

Madill, A. and Doherty, K. (1994) 'So you did what you wanted then': discourse analysis, personal agency, and psychotherapy. *Journal of Community and Applied Social Psychology*, 4, 261–73.

Magee, M. (1998) *The Story of Philosophy*. London: Dorling Kindersley.

Maguire, G. P., Goldberg, D. P., Hobson, R. F. *et al.* (1984) Evaluating the teaching of a method of psychotherapy. *British Journal of Psychiatry*, 144, 575–80.

Mahler, M. S. (1968) *On Human Symbiosis and the Vicissitudes of Individuation: Infantile Psychosis*. New York: International Universities Press.

Mahler, M. S., Pine, F. and Bergman, A. (1975) *The Psychological Birth of the Human Infant*. New York: Basic Books.

Mahoney, M. J. (ed.) (1995a) *Cognitive and Constructive Psychotherapies: Theory, Research and Practice*. New York: Springer.

Mahoney, M. J. (1995b) Theoretical developments in the cognitive psychotherapies. In M. J. Mahoney (ed.) *Cognitive and Constructive Psychotherapies: Theory, Research and Practice*. New York: Springer.

Mahrer, A. (1989) *The Integration of Psychotherapies: A Guide for Practicing Therapists*. New York: Human Sciences Press.

Mahrer, A. R., Nadler, W. P., Dessaulles, A., Gervaize, P. A. and Sterner, I. (1987) Good and very good moments in psychotherapy: content, distribution and facilitation. *Psychotherapy*, 24, 7–14.

Main, M. (1991) Metacognitive knowledge, metacognitive monitoring, and singular (coherent) versus multiple (incoherent) model of attachment: findings and directions for future research. In C. M. Parkes, J. Stevenson-Hinde and P. Marris (eds) *Attachment across the Life-cycle*. London: Routledge.

Mair, M. (1989) *Between Psychology and Psychotherapy: A Poetics of Experience*. London: Routledge.

Malan, D. H. (1976) *The Frontiers of Brief Psychotherapy*. New York: Plenum.

Malan, D. H. (1979) *Individual Psychotherapy and the Science of Psychodynamics*. London: Butterworths.

Malony, H. N. (1983) God-talk in psychotherapy. In H. N. Malony (ed.) *Wholeness and Holiness*. Grand Rapids, MI: Baker.

Maluccio, A. (1979) *Learning from Clients. Interpersonal Helping as Viewed by Clients and Social Workers*. New York: The Free Press.

Mangen, S. (1988) Assessing cost-effectiveness. In F. N. Watts (ed.) *New Developments in Clinical Psychology, Volume 11*. Chichester: Wiley.

Mann, D. (1989) Incest: the father and the male therapist. *British Journal of Psychotherapy*, 6, 143–53.

Mann, J. (1973) *Time-limited Psychotherapy*. Cambridge, MA: Harvard University Press.

Manning, N. (1989) *The Therapeutic Community Movement. Charisma and Routinization*. London: Routledge.

Marcelino, E. P. (1990) Toward understanding the psychology of the Filipino. *Women and Therapy*, 9, 105–28.

Marineau, R. F. (1989) *Jacob Lery Moreno 1889–1973: Father of Psychodrama, Sociometry and Group Psychotherapy*. London: Tavistock/Routledge.

Markus, H. and Kitayama, S. (1991) Culture and the self: implications for cognition, emotion and motivation. *Psychological Review*, 98, 224–53.

Marlatt, G. A. and Gordon, J. R. (eds) (1985) *Relapse Prevention: Maintenance Strategies in the Treatment of Addictive Behaviors*. New York: Guilford Press.

Marmor, J. (1953) The feeling of superiority: an occupational hazard in the practice of psychotherapy. *American Journal of Psychiatry*, 110, 370–6.

Marmor, J. and Woods, S. M. (eds) (1980) *The Interface Between the Psychodynamic and Behavioral Therapies*. New York: Plenum.

Marsella, A., de Vos, G., Hsu, F. L. K. *et al.* (eds) (1985) *Culture and Self: Asian and Western Perspectives*. London: Tavistock.

Marston, A. R. (1984) What makes therapists run? A model for the analysis of motivational styles. *Psychotherapy*, 21, 456–9.

Martin, J., Slemon, A. G., Hiebert, B., Hallberg, E. T. and Cummings, A. L. (1989) Conceptualizations of novice and experienced counselors. *Journal of Counseling Psychology*, 36, 395–400.

Marzillier, J. (1993) Ethical issues in psychotherapy: the importance of informed consent. *Clinical Psychology Forum*, 54, 33–7.

Maslach, C. and Jackson, S. E. (1984) Burnout in organisational settings. In S. Oskamp (ed.) *Applied Social Psychology Annual 5: Applications in Organizational Settings*. London: Sage.

Masson, J. (1984) *The Assault on Truth: Freud's Suppression of the Seduction Theory*. New York: Farrar, Straus and Giroux.

Masson, J. (1988) *Against Therapy: Emotional Tyranny and the Myth of Psychological Healing*. Glasgow: Collins.

Masson, J. (1991) *Final Analysis: The Making and Unmaking of a Psychoanalyst*. London: HarperCollins.

Masson, J. (1992) The tyranny of psychotherapy. In W. Dryden and C. Feltham (eds) *Psychotherapy and Its Discontents*. Buckingham: Open University Press.

Mathieu-Coughlan, P. and Klein, M. H. (1984) Experiential psychotherapy: key events in client–therapist interaction. In L. N. Rice and L. S. Greenberg (eds) *Patterns of Change: Intensive Analysis of Psychotherapy Process*. New York: Guilford Press.

Matthews, E. (1996) *Twentieth-century French Philosophy*. Oxford: Oxford University Press.

Maultsby, M. C. (1971) Systematic written homework in psychotherapy. *Psychotherapy*, 8, 195–8.

Maxwell, R. J. (1984) Quality assessment in health. *British Medical Journal*, 288, 1470–2.

May, R. (1950) *The Meaning of Anxiety*. New York: W. W. Norton.

May, R., Angel, E. and Ellenberger, H. (1958) *Existence: A New Dimension in Psychology and Psychiatry*. New York: Basic Books.

Meadow, A. (1964) Client-centered therapy and the American ethos. *International Journal of Social Psychiatry*, 10, 246–60.

Meara, N. M., Schmidt, L. D. and Day, J. D. (1996) Principles and virtues: a foundation for ethical decisions, policy and character. *Counseling Psychologist*, 24(1), 4–77.

Meares, R. and Hobson, R. F. (1977) The persecutory therapist. *British Journal of Medical Psychology*, 50, 349–59.

Mearns, D. (1993) Against indemnity insurance. In W. Dryden (ed.) *Questions and Answers for Counselling in Action*. London: Sage.

Mearns, D. (1994) *Developing Person-centred Counselling*. London: Sage.

Mearns, D. (1996) Working at relational depth with clients in person-centred therapy. *Counselling*, 7(4), 307–11.

Mearns, D. (1997) *Person-centred Counselling Training*. London: Sage.

Mearns, D. and Thorne, B. (1988) *Person-centred Counselling in Action*. London: Sage.

Mearns, D. and Thorne, B. (1999) *Person-centred Counselling in Action*, 2nd edn. London: Sage.

Mearns, D. and Thorne, B. (2000) *Person-centred Therapy Today: New Frontiers in Theory and Practice*. London: Sage.

Meichenbaum, D. (1977) *Cognitive-Behavior Modification: An Integrative Approach*. New York: Plenum.

Meichenbaum, D. (1985) *Stress Innoculation Training*. New York: Pergamon.

Meichenbaum, D. (1986) Cognitive-behavior modification. In A. Kanfer and A. Goldstein (eds) *Helping People Change*, 3rd edn. New York: Pergamon.

Meichenbaum, D. (1994) *Treating Post-traumatic Stress Disorder. A Handbook and Practical Manual for Therapy*. Chichester: Wiley.

Mellor-Clark, J., Barkham, M., Connell, J. and Evans, C. (1999) Practice based evidence and standardized evaluation: Informing the design of the CORE system. *European Journal of Psychotherapy, Counselling and Health*, 2, 357–74.

Mellor-Clark, J., Connell, J., Barkham, M. and Cummins, P. (2001) Counselling outcomes in primary health care: a CORE system data profile. *European Journal of Psychotherapy, Counselling and Health*, 4, 65–86.

Meltzer, J. D. (1978) A semiotic approach to suitability for psychotherapy. *Psychiatry*, 41, 360–76.

Menzies, I. (1959) A case-study in the functioning of social systems as a defence against anxiety: a report on a study of the nursing service of a general hospital. *Human Relations*, 13, 95–121.

Menzies Lyth, I. (1988) *Containing Anxiety in Institutions: Selected Essays*. London: Free Association.

Menzies Lyth, I. (1989) *The Dynamics of the Social: Selected Essays*. London: Free Association.

Messer, S. B. and Woolfolk, R. L. (1998) Philosophical issues in psychotherapy. *Clinical Psychology: Science and Practice*, 5, 251–63.

Miller, A. (1987) *The Drama of Being a Child and the Search for the True Self*. London: Virago.

Miller, D. J. and Thelen, M. H. (1987) Confidentiality in psychotherapy: history, issues and research. *Psychotherapy*, 24, 704–11.

Miller, J. B. (1976) *Toward a New Psychology of Women*. Harmondsworth: Penguin.

Miller, J. B. (1987) Women and power. In M. Braude (ed.) *Women, Power and Therapy*. New York: Haworth Press.

Miller, J. B. (1991a) The construction of anger in women and men. In J. V. Jordan, A. G. Kaplan, J. B. Miller, I. P. Stiver and J. L. Surrey (eds) *Women's Growth in Connection: Writings from the Stone Center*. New York: Guilford Press.

Miller, J. B. (1991b) Women and power. In J. V. Jordan, A. G. Kaplan, J. B. Miller, I. P. Stiver and J. L. Surrey (eds) *Women's Growth in Connection: Writings from the Stone Center*. New York: Guilford Press.

Miller, N. E. and Magruder, K. M. (eds) (1999) *Cost-effectiveness of Psychotherapy: A Guide for Practitioners, Researchers and Policymakers*. New York: Oxford University Press.

Miller, S. D. and Berg, I. K. (1995) *The Miracle Method: A Radically New Approach to Problem Drinking*. New York: Norton.

Miller, S. D., Duncan, B. L. and Hubble, M. A. (1997) *Escape from Babel: Toward a Unifying Language for Psychotherapy Practice*. New York: W. W. Norton.

Miller, S. D., Hubble, M. A. and Duncan, B. L. (1996) *Handbook of Solution-focused Brief Therapy*. San Francisco: Jossey-Bass.

Milner, P. and Palmer, S. (eds) (2001) *Counselling: The BACP Counselling Reader, Vol. 2*. London: Sage.

Mintz, E. E. (1969) Touch and the psychoanalytic tradition. *Psychoanalytic Review*, 56, 365–76.

Minuchin, S. (1974) *Families and Family Therapy*. London: Tavistock.

Mischel, W. (1968) *Personality and Assessment*. New York: Wiley.

Mitchell, J. (1974) *Psychoanalysis and Feminism: A Radical Reassessment of Freudian Psychoanalysis*. London: Allen Lane.

Mitchell, S. A. (1986) *Relational Concepts in Psychoanalysis*. Cambridge, MA: Harvard University Press.

Monk, G. Winslade, J., Crocket, K. and Epston, D. (eds) (1996) *Narrative Therapies in Action: The Archeology of Hope*. San Francisco: Jossey-Bass.

Monte, C. F. (1998) *Beneath the Mask: An Introduction to Theories of Personality*. New York: Thomson.

Moodley, R. (1998) 'I say what I like': frank talk(ing) in counselling and psychotherapy. *British Journal of Guidance and Counselling*, 26, 495–508.

Moore, J. (1991) On being a supervisee. In W. Dryden and B. Thorne (eds) *Training and Supervision for Counselling in Action*. London: Sage.

Moran, D. (2000) *Introduction to Phenomenology*. London: Routledge.

Morley, S. (1989) Single case research. In G. Parry and F. N. Watts (eds) *Behavioural and Mental Health Research: A Handbook of Skills and Methods*. London: Lawrence Erlbaum.

Morrison, L. A. and Shapiro, D. A. (1987) Expectancy and outcome in prescriptive vs. exploratory psychotherapy. *British Journal of Clinical Psychology*, 26, 59–60.

Morrow-Bradley, C. and Elliott, R. (1986) Utilization of psychotherapy research by practicing psychotherapists. *American Psychologist*, 41, 188–97.

Moyers, J. C. (1990) Religious issues in the psychotherapy of former Fundamentalists. *Psychotherapy*, 27, 42–5.

Muran, J. C. (ed.) (2001) *Self-relations in the Psychotherapy Process*. Washington, DC: American Psychological Association.

Murphy, L. J. and Mitchell, D. L. (1998) When writing helps to heal: e-mail as therapy. *British Journal of Guidance and Counselling*, 26, 21–32.

Murray, H. A. (1938) *Explorations in Personality: A Clinical and Experimental Study of Fifty Men of College Age*. New York: Oxford University Press.

Myrick, R. and Kelly, F. (1971) A scale for evaluating practicum students in counseling and supervision. *Counselor Education and Supervision*, 10, 330–6.

Najavits, L. M. (1993) How do psychotherapists describe their work? A study of metaphors for the therapy process. *Psychotherapy Research*, 3, 294–9.

Neal, C. and Davies, D. (eds) (2000) *Issues in Therapy with Lesbian, Gay, Bisexual and Transgender Clients*. Buckingham: Open University Press.

Neimeyer, G. and Resnikoff, A. (1982) Qualitative strategies in counseling research. *Counseling Psychologist*, 10, 75–85.

Neimeyer, R. A. (1993) Constructivist psychotherapy. In K. T. Kuehlwein and H. Rosen (eds) *Cognitive Therapies in Action: Evolving Innovative Practice*. San Francisco: Jossey-Bass.

Neimeyer, R. A. (1995) Constructivist psychotherapies: features, foundations, and future directions. In R. A. Neimeyer and M. J. Mahoney (eds) *Constructivism in Psychotherapy*. Washington, DC: American Psychological Association.

Nelson, M. L. (1996) Separation versus connection: the gender controversy: implications for counseling women. *Journal of Counseling and Development*, 74, 339–44.

Nelson, M. L. and Friedlander, M. L. (2001) A close look at conflictual supervisory relationships: the trainee's perspective. *Journal of Counseling Psychology*, 48, 384–95.

Nelson, R. O. (1981) Realistic dependent measures for clinical use. *Journal of Consulting and Clinical Psychology*, 49, 168–82.

Nelson, S. H. and Torrey, E. F. (1973) The religious functions of psychiatry. *American Journal of Orthopsychiatry*, 43, 362–7.

Neugebauer, R. (1978) Treatment of the mentally ill in medieval and early modern England: a reappraisal. *Journal of the History of the Behavioral Sciences*, 14, 158–69.

Neugebauer, R. (1979) Early and modern theories of mental illness. *Archives of General Psychiatry*, 36, 477–83.

Neumann, D. A. and Gamble, S. J. (1995) Issues in the professional development of psychotherapists: countertransference and vicarious traumatization in the new trauma therapist. *Psychotherapy*, 32, 341–7.

Newnes, C. (1995) On note-taking. *Clinical Psychology Forum*, 53, 31–5.

Nietzel, M. T. and Fisher, S. G. (1981) Effectiveness of professional and paraprofessional helpers: a comment on Durlak. *Psychological Bulletin*, 89, 555–65.

Norcross, J. (ed.) (1986) *Handbook of Eclectic Psychotherapy*. New York: Brunner/Mazel.

Norcross, J. C. and Aranowitz, H. (1992) The evolution and current status of psychotherapy integration. In W. Dryden (ed.) *Integrative and Eclectic Therapy: A Handbook*. Buckingham: Open University Press.

Norcross, J. C. and Grencavage, L. M. (1989) Eclecticism and integration in counselling and psychotherapy: major themes and obstacles. *British Journal of Guidance and Counselling*, 17, 215–47.

Norcross, J. C. and Guy, J. D. (1989) Ten therapists: the process of becoming and being. In W. Dryden and L. Spurling (eds) *On Becoming a Psychotherapist*. London: Tavistock/Routledge.

Norcross, J. C., Beutler, L. E., Clarkin, J. F. *et al.* (1986) Training integrative/eclectic psychotherapists. *International Journal of Eclectic Psychotherapy*, 5, 71–103.

Norcross, J. C., Santrock, J. W., Campbell, L. F., Smith, T. P., Sommer, R. and Zuckerman, E. L. (2000) *Authoritative Guide to Self-help Resources in Mental Health*. New York: Guilford Press.

Norcross, J. C., Strausser, D. J. and Faltus, F. J. (1988a) The therapist's therapist. *American Journal of Psychotherapy*, 42, 53–66.

Norcross, J. C., Strausser, D. J. and Missar, C. D. (1988b) The processes and outcomes of psychotherapists' personal treatment experiences. *Psychotherapy*, 25, 36–43.

Nylund, D. and Corsiglia, V. (1994) Being solution-focused forced in brief therapy: remembering something important we already knew. *Journal of Systemic Therapies*, 13, 5–12.

Oatley, K. (1980) Theories of personal learning in groups. In P. B. Smith (ed.) *Small Groups and Personal Change*. London: Methuen.

Oatley, K. (1984) *Selves in Relation: An Introduction to Psychotherapy and Groups*. London: Methuen.

Obholzer, A. and Roberts, V. Z. (eds) (1994) *The Unconscious at Work: Individual and Organizational Stress in the Human Services*. London: Routledge.

O'Connell, B. (1998) *Solution-focused Therapy*. London: Sage.

Ogles, B. M., Lambert, M. J. and Craig, D. E. (1991) Comparison of self-help books for coping with loss: expectations and attributions. *Journal of Counseling Psychology*, 38, 387–93.

O'Hanlon, W. H. and Weiner-Davis, M. (1989) *In Search of Solutions: A New Direction in Psychotherapy*. New York: Norton.

Olfson, M. and Pincus, H. A. (1999) Outpatient psychotherapy in the United States: the national Medical Expenditure survey. In N. E. Miller and K. M. Magruder (eds) *Cost-effectiveness of Psychotherapy: A Guide for Practitioners, Researchers and Policymakers*. New York: Oxford University Press.

Omer, H. (1997) Narrative empathy. *Psychotherapy*, 25, 171–84.

Omer, H. and Dar, R. (1992) Changing trends in three decades of psychotherapy research: the flight from theory into pragmatics. *Journal of Consulting and Clinical Psychology*, 60, 88–93.

Omer, H. and London, P. (1988) Metamorphosis in psychotherapy: end of the systems era. *Psychotherapy*, 25, 171–84.

O'Neill, P. (1998) *Negotiating Consent in Psychotherapy*. New York: New York University Press.

Onnis, L., Gennaro, A. D., Cespa, G., Agostini, B., Chouhy, A., Dentale, R. C. and Quinzi, P. (1994) Sculpting present and future: a systemic intervention model applied to psychosomatic families. *Family Process*, 33, 341–55.

Orford, J. (1992) *Community Psychology: Theory and Practice*. Chichester: Wiley.

Orleans, C. T., Schoenbach, C. J., Wagner, E. H. *et al.* (1991) Self-help quitting smoking interventions: effects of self-help manuals, social support instructions and telephone counselling. *Journal of Consulting and Clinical Psychology*, 59, 439–48.

Orlinsky, D., Grawe, K. and Parks, B. K. (1994) Process and outcome in psychotherapy – noch einmal. In A. E. Bergin and S. L. Garfield (eds) *Handbook of Psychotherapy and Behavior Change*, 4th edn. Chichester: Wiley.

Osipow, S. H. and Reed, R. A. (1987) Training and evaluation in counseling psychology. In B. A. Edelstein and E. S. Berler (eds) *Evaluation and Accountability in Clinical Training*. New York: Plenum Press.

Ossip-Klein, D. J., Giovino, G. A., Megahed, N. *et al.* (1991) Effects of a smokers' hotline: results of a ten-county selfhelp trial. *Journal of Consulting and Clinical Psychology*, 59, 325–32.

O'Sullivan, K. R. and Dryden, W. (1990) A survey of clinical psychologists in the South East Thames Region: activities, role and theoretical orientation. *Clinical Psychology Forum*, 29, 21–6.

Overholster, J. (1990) Defining the boundaries of professional competence: managing subtle cases of clinical incompetence. *Professional Psychology: Research and Practice*, 21(6), 462–9.

Owen, I. R. (1995) Power, boundaries, intersubjectivity. *British Journal of Medical Psychology*, 68, 97–107.

Padesky, C. A. and Greenberger, D. (1995) *Clinician's Guide to Mind over Mood*. New York: Guilford Press.

Page, S. and Wosket, V. (2001) *Supervising the Counsellor: A Cyclical Model*, 2nd edn. Hove: Brunner-Routledge.

Palazzoli, M., Cecchin, G., Boscolo, L. and Prata, G. (1978) *Paradox and Counter Paradox*. New York: Aronson.

Palmer, S. (ed.) (2002) *Multicultural Counselling: A Reader*. London: Sage.

Palmer, S., Dainow, S. and Milner, P. (eds) (1996) *Counselling: The BAC Counselling Reader*. London: Sage.

Palmer, S. and McMahon, G. (eds) (1997) *Handbook of Counselling*, 2nd edn. London: Routledge.

Paolino, T. and McCrady, B. (eds) (1978) *Marriage and Marital Therapy: Psychoanalytic, Behavioral and Systems Theory Perspectives*. New York: Brunner/Mazel.

Papadopoulos, L., Bor, R. and Stanion, P. (1997) Genograms in counselling practice: a review (part 1). *Counselling Psychology Quarterly*, 10(1), 17–28.

Papp, P. (1976) Family choreography. In P. J. Guerin Jr (ed.) *Family Therapy: Theory and Practice*. New York: Gardner Press.

Parlett, M. and Page, F. (1990) Gestalt therapy. In W. Dryden (ed.) *Individual Therapy: A Handbook*. Buckingham: Open University Press.

Parloff, M. B. (1986) Frank's 'common elements' in psychotherapy: nonspecific factors and placebos. *American Journal of Orthopsychiatry*, 56, 521–30.

Parry, A. and Doan, R. E. (1994) *Story Re-visions: Narrative Therapy in the Post-modern World*. New York: Guilford.

Parry, G. (1992) Improving psychotherapy services: applications of research, audit and evaluation. *British Journal of Clinical Psychology*, 31, 3–19.

Parry, G. and Watts, F. N. (eds) (1989) *Behavioural and Mental Health Research: A Handbook of Skills and Methods*. London: Lawrence Erlbaum.

Parry, G. and Watts, F. N. (eds) (1995) *Behavioural and Mental Health Research: A Handbook of Skills and Methods*, 2nd edn. New York: Lawrence Erlbaum.

Parry, T. A. (1998) Reasons of the heart: the narrative construction of emotions. *Journal of Systemic Therapies*, 17, 65–79.

Parvin, R. and Anderson, G. (1999) What are we worth? Fee decisions of psychologists in private practice. *Women and Therapy*, 22(3), 15–26.

Passons, W. R. (1975) *Gestalt Approaches to Counselling*. New York: Holt, Rinehart and Winston.

Pates, A. and Knasel, E. (1989) Assessment of counselling skills development: the learning record. *British Journal of Guidance and Counselling*, 17, 121–32.

Patterson, C. H. (1984) Empathy, warmth and genuineness in psychotherapy: a review of reviews. *Psychotherapy*, 21, 431–8.

Patterson, C. H. (1989) Eclecticism in psychotherapy: is integration possible? *Psychotherapy*, 26, 157–61.

Paul, G. L. (1967) Strategy of outcome research in psychotherapy. *Journal of Consulting Psychology*, 31, 109–18.

Paulson, B., Everall, R. D. and Stuart, J. (2001) Client perceptions of hindering experiences in counselling. *Counselling and Psychotherapy Research*, 1, 53–61.

Payne, H. (1999) Personal development groups in the training of counsellors and therapists: a literature review. *European Journal of Psychotherapy, Counselling and Health*, 2, 55–68.

Payne, M. (1999) *Narrative Therapy: An Introduction for Counsellors*. London: Sage.

Peake, T. (1988) *Brief Psychotherapies: Changing Frames of Mind*. London: Sage.

Pearlman, L. A. and McIan, P. S. (1995) Vivarious traumatisation: an empirical study of the effects of trauma work on trauma therapists. *Professional Psychology: Research and Practice*, 26, 558–65.

Peck, M. S. (1978) *The Road Less Traveled: A New Psychology of Love, Traditional Values and Spiritual Growth*. New York: Simon and Schuster.

Pedersen, P. B. (ed.) (1985) *Handbook of Cross-cultural Counseling and Psychotherapy*. New York: Praeger.

Pedersen, P. B. (1991) Multiculturalism as a generic approach to counseling. *Journal of Counseling and Development*, 70, 6–12.

Pedersen, P. B. (1994) Multicultural counseling. In R. W. Brislin and T. Yoshida (eds) *Improving Intercultural Interactions: Modules for Cross-cultural Training Programs*. London: Sage.

Pedersen, P. B. (1995) Culture-centered ethical guidelines for counselors. In J. G. Ponterotto, J. M. Casas, L. A. Suzuki and C. M. Alexander (eds) *Handbook of Multicultural Counseling*. London: Sage.

Pedersen, P. B., Draguns, J. G., Lonner, W. J. and Trimble, J. E. (eds) (1996) *Counseling across Cultures*. London: Sage.

Peebles, M. J. (1980) Personal therapy and ability to display empathy, warmth and genuineness in therapy. *Psychotherapy*, 17, 252–62.

Penn, L. S. (1990) When the therapist must leave: forced termination of psychodynamic therapy. *Professional Psychology: Research and Practice*, 21, 379–84.

Penn, P. and Frankfurt, M. (1994) Creating a participant text: writing, multiple voices, narrative multiplicity. *Family Process*, 33, 217–32.

Pennebaker, J. W. (1993) Social mechanisms of constraint. In D. W. Wegner and J. W. Pennebaker (eds) *Handbook of Mental Control*. Englewood Cliffs, NJ: Prentice Hall.

Perls, F. S. (1947) *Ego, Hunger and Aggression*. London: Allen and Unwin.

Perls, F. S. (1969) *Gestalt Therapy Verbatim*. Lafayette, CA: Real People Press.

Perls, F. S. (1973) *The Gestalt Approach and Eye-witness to Therapy*. Ben Lomond, CA: Science and Behavior Books.

Perls, F. S., Hefferline, R. F. and Goodman, P. (1951) *Gestalt Therapy: Excitement and Growth in the Human Personality*. New York: Julian Press.

Persons, J. B. (1993) Case conceptualization in cognitive–behavior therapy. In K. T. Kuehlwein and H. Rosen (eds) *Cognitive Therapies in Action: Evolving Innovative Practice*. San Francisco: Jossey-Bass.

Pervin, L. and Johns, O. (2000) *Personality*, 8th edn. New York: Wiley.

Phillips, J. P. N. (1986) Shapiro Personal Questionnaire and generalized personal questionnaire techniques: a repeated measures individualised outcome measurement. In L. S. Greenberg and W. M. Pinsof (eds) *The Psychotherapeutic Process: A Research Handbook*. New York: Guilford Press.

Phillips, P., Bartlett, A. and King, M. (2001) Psychotherapists' approaches to gay and lesbian patients/clients: a qualitative study. *British Journal of Medical Psychology*, 74, 73–84.

Piercy, F. P., Sprenkle, D. H. and Wetchler, J. L. (eds) (1996) *Family Therapy Sourcebook*, 2nd edn. New York: Guilford Press.

Pilgrim, D. (1990) British psychotherapy in context. In W. Dryden (ed.) *Individual Therapy: A Handbook*. Buckingham: Open University Press.

Pilgrim, D. (1992) Psychotherapy and political evasions. In W. Dryden and C. Feltham (eds) *Psychotherapy and Its Discontents*. Buckingham: Open University Press.

Pilgrim, D. and Guinan, P. (1999) From mitigation to culpability: rethinking the evidence about therapist sexual abuse. *European Journal of Psychotherapy, Counselling and Health*, 2, 153–68.

Pines, A. (1981) Helpers' motivation and the burnout syndrome. In T. A. Wills (ed.) *Basic Processes in Helping Relationships*. New York: Academic Press.

Pines, M. (ed.) (1983) *The Evolution of Group Analysis*. London: Tavistock/Routledge.

Piper, W. E. (1988) Psychotherapy research in the 1980s: defining areas of consensus and controversy. *Hospital and Community Psychiatry*, 39, 1055–63.

Pistrang, C. and Barker, C. (1992) Clients' belief about psychological problems. *Counselling Psychology Quarterly*, 5, 325–35.

Pockock, D. (1995) Searching for a better story: harnessing modern and postmodern positions in family therapy. *Journal of Family Therapy*, 17, 149–73.

Polanyi, M. (1958) *Personal Knowledge*. London: Routledge.

Polkinghorne, D. E. (1992) Postmodern epistemology of practice. In S. Kvale (ed.) *Psychology and Postmodernism*. London: Sage.

Pollak, S. and Gilligan, C. (1982) Images of violence in Thematic Apperception Test stories. *Journal of Personality and Social Psychology*, 42(1), 159–67.

Ponterotto, J. G. (1988) Racial/ethnic minority research in the Journal of Counseling Psychology: a content analysis and methodological critique. *Journal of Counseling Psychology*, 35, 410–18.

Ponterotto, J. G., Casas, J. M., Suzuki, L. A. and Alexander, C. M. (eds) (1995) *Handbook of Multicultural Counseling*. London: Sage.

Ponterotto, J. and Pedersen, P. (1993) *Preventing Prejudice: A Guide for Counselors and Educators*. London: Sage.

Pope, K. S. (1986) New trends in malpractice cases and trends in APA's liability insurance. *Independent Practitioner*, 6, 23–6.

Pope, K. S. (1991) Dual relationships in psychotherapy. *Ethics and Behavior*, 1, 21–34.

Pope, K. S. and Bouhoutsos, J. C. (1986) *Sexual Intimacy between Therapists and Patients*. New York: Praeger.

Pope, K. S., Keith-Speigel, P. and Tabachnick, B. G. (1986) Sexual attraction to clients: the human therapist and the (sometimes) inhuman training system. *American Psychologist*, 41, 147–58.

Pope, K. S., Levenson, H. and Schover, L. R. (1979) Sexual intimacy in psychology training: results and implications of a national survey. *American Psychologist*, 34, 682–9.

Pope-Davis, D. B. and Dings, J. G. (1995) The assessment of multicultural counseling competencies. In J. G. Ponterotto, J. M. Casas, L. A. Suzuki and C. M. Alexander (eds) *Handbook of Multicultural Counseling*. London: Sage.

Porter, R. (ed.) (1985) *The Anatomy of Madness, Volumes 1 and 2*. London: Tavistock.

Powell, T. J. (ed.) (1994) *Understanding the Self-help Organization: Frameworks and Findings*. Thousand Oaks, CA: Sage.

Poznanski, J. J. and McLennan, J. (1995) Conceptualizing and measuring counselors' theoretical orientation. *Journal of Counseling Psychology*, 42, 411–22.

Prince, R. (1980) Variations in psychotherapeutic procedures. In H. C. Triandis and J. G. Draguns (eds) *Handbook of Cross-cultural Psychopathology, Volume 6*. Boston: Allyn and Bacon.

Prochaska, J. O. and DiClemente, C. C. (1982) Transtheoretical therapy: toward a more integrative model of change. *Psychotherapy*, 19, 276–88.

Prochaska, J. and Norcross, J. (1983) Contemporary psychotherapists: a national survey of characteristics, practices, orientations and attitudes. *Psychotherapy*, 20, 161–73.

Progoff, I. (1975) *At a Journal Workshop*. New York: Dialogue House.

Propst, L. R., Ostrom, R., Watkins, P., Dean, T. and Mashburn, D. (1992) Comparative efficacy of religious and nonreligious cognitive–behavioral therapy for the treatment of clinical depression in religious individuals. *Journal of Consulting and Clinical Psychology*, 60, 94–103.

Prouty, G. (1976) Pre-therapy, a method of treating pre-expressive psychotic and retarded patients. *Psychotherapy: Theory, Research and Practice*, 13, 290–4.

Prouty, G. (1990) Pre-therapy: a theoretical evolution in the person-centered/experiential psychotherapy of schizophrenia and retardation. In G. Lietaer, J. Rombauts and R. Van Balen (eds) *Client-centred and Experiential Psychotherapy in the Nineties*. Leuven: University of Leuven Press.

Prouty, G. (1998) Pre-therapy and pre-symbolic experiencing: evoluations in person-centred/experiential approaches to psychotic experience. In L. S. Greenberg, J. C. Watson and G. Lietaer (eds) *Handbook of Experiential Psychotherapy*. New York: Guilford Press.

Prouty, G. and Kubiak, H. (1988) The development of communicative contact with a catatonic schizophrenic. *Journal of Communication Therapy*, 4(1), 13–20.

Purton, C. (1991) Selection and assessment in counsellor training courses. In W. Dryden and B. Thorne (eds) *Training and Supervision for Counselling in Action*. London: Sage.

Raabe, P. B. (2001) *Philosophical Counseling: Theory and Practice*. Westport, CT: Praeger.

Rabin, A. I., Aronoff, J., Barclay, A. and Zucker, R. (eds) (1981) *Further Explorations in Personality*. New York: Wiley.

Rabin, A. I., Zucker, R. A., Emmons, R. A. and Frank, S. (eds) (1990) *Studying Persons and Lives*. New York: Springer.

Rachman, A. W. (1997) *Sandor Ferenczi: The Psychotherapist of Tenderness and Passion*. New York: Jason Aronson.

Rack, P. (1982) *Race, Culture and Mental Disorder*. London: Tavistock.

Rainer, T. (1980) *The New Diary*. London: Angus and Robertson.

Ramaswami, S. and Sheikh, A. A. (1989) Buddhist psychology: implications for healing. In A. A. Sheikh and K. S. Sheikh (eds) *Eastern and Western Approaches to Healing. Ancient Wisdom and Modern Knowledge*. New York: Wiley.

Ramirez, M. III (1991) *Psychotherapy and Counseling with Minorities: A Cognitive Approach to Individual and Cultural Differences*. Oxford: Pergamon Press.

Rapaport, D. and Gill, M. (1959) The points of view and assumptions of metapsychology. *International Journal of Psycho-Analysis*, 40, 153–62.

Rappaport, J. (1987) Terms of empowerment/exemplars of prevention: toward a theory for community psychology. *American Journal of Community Psychology*, 15, 121–48.

Rasmussen, B. (2000) Poetic truths and clinical reality: client experiences of the use of metaphor by therapists. *Smith College Studies in Social Work*, 27, 355–73.

Rasmussen, B. and Angus, L. (1996) Metaphor in psychodynamic psychotherapy with borderline and non-borderline clients: a qualitative analysis. *Psychotherapy*, 33, 521–30.

Raue, P. J. and Goldfried, M. R. (1994) The therapeutic alliance in cognitive-behavior therapy. In A. O. Horvath and L. S. Greenberg (eds) *The Working Alliance: Theory, Research and Practice*. New York: Wiley.

Rave, E. J. and Larsen, C. C. (eds) (1995) *Ethical Decision Making in Therapy: Feminist Perspectives*. New York: Guilford Press.

Rayner, E. (1990) *The Independent Mind in British Psychoanalysis*. London: Free Association Books.

Razali, S. M., Khan, U. A. and Hasanah, C. I. (1996) Belief in supernatural causes of mental illness among Malay patients: impact on treatment. *Acta Psychiatrica Scandinavica*, 94, 229–33.

Reeve, D. (2002) Oppression within the counselling room. *Counselling and Psychotherapy Research*, 2, 11–19.

Regan, A. and Hill, C. E. (1992) Investigation of what clients and counsellors do not say in brief therapy. *Journal of Counseling Psychology*, 38, 168–74.

Reimers, S. and Treacher, A. (1995) *Introducing User-friendly Family Therapy*. London: Routledge.

Rennie, D. L. (1990) Toward a representation of the client's experience of the psychotherapy hour. In G. Lietaer, J. Rombauts and R. Van Balen (eds) *Client-centered and Experiential Therapy in the Nineties*. Leuven: University of Leuven Press.

Rennie, D. L. (1992) Qualitative analysis of the client's experience of psychotherapy: the unfolding of reflexivity. In S. Toukmanian and D. Rennie (eds) *Psychotherapy Process Research*. London: Sage.

Rennie, D. L. (1994a) Clients' deference in psychotherapy. *Journal of Counseling Psychology*, 41, 427–37.

Rennie, D. L. (1994b) Storytelling in psychotherapy: the clients' subjective experience. *Psychotherapy*, 31, 234–43.

Rennie, D. L. (1996) Fifteen years of doing qualitative research on psychotherapy. *British Journal of Guidance and Counselling*, 24, 317–28.

Rennie, D. L. (1998) *Person-centred Counselling: An Experiential Approach*. London: Sage.

Rennie, D. L. (2000a) Grounded theory methodology as methodological hermeneutics: reconciling realism and relativism. *Theory and Psychology*, 10, 481–512.

Rennie, D. L. (2000b) Aspects of the client's conscious control of the psychotherapeutic process. *Journal of Psychotherapy Integration*, 10, 151–67.

Rennie, D. L. (2001) Clients as self-aware agents. *Counselling and Psychotherapy Research*, 1, 82–9.

Rennie, D. L. (2002) Experiencing psychotherapy: grounded theory studies. In D. J. Cain and J. Seeman (eds) *Humanistic Psychotherapies: Handbook of Research and Practice*. Washington, DC: American Psychological Association.

Rennie, D. L., Phillips, J. R. and Quartaro, J. K. (1988) Grounded theory: a promising approach for conceptualization in psychology? *Canadian Psychology*, 29, 139–50.

Rice, L. N. (1974) The evocative function of the therapist. In D. A. Wexler and L. N. Rice (eds) *Innovations in Client-centered Therapy*. New York: Wiley.

Rice, L. N. (1984) Client tasks in client-centered therapy. In R. F. Levant and J. M. Shlien (eds) *Client-centered Therapy and the Person-centered Approach: New Directions in Theory, Research and Practice*. New York: Praeger.

Rice, L. N. and Greenberg, L. S. (eds) (1984a) *Patterns of Change: Intensive Analysis of Psychotherapy Process*. New York: Guilford Press.

Rice, L. N. and Greenberg, L. S. (1984b) The new research paradigm. In L. N. Rice and L. S. Greenberg (eds) *Patterns of Change: Intensive Analysis of Psychotherapy Process*. New York: Guilford Press.

Rice, L. N. and Greenberg, L. S. (1992) Humanistic approaches to psychotherapy. In D. K. Freedheim (ed.) *History of Psychotherapy: A Century of Change*. Washington, DC: American Psychological Association.

Rice, L. N. and Kerr, G. P. (1986) Measures of client and therapist voice quality. In L. S. Greenberg and W. M. Pinsof (eds) *The Psychotherapeutic Process: A Research Handbook*. New York: Guilford Press.

Rice, L. N. and Saperia, E. (1984) Task analysis of the resolution of problematic reactions. In L. N. Rice and L. S. Greenberg (eds) *Patterns of Change: Intensive Analysis of Psychotherapy Process*. New York: Guilford.

Ridley, C. R. (1995) *Overcoming Unintentional Racism in Counseling and Therapy: A Practitioner's Guide to Intentional Intervention*. Thousand Oaks, CA: Sage.

Ridley, C. R. and Lingle, D. W. (1996) Cultural empathy in multicultural counseling: a multidimensional process model. In P. B. Pedersen, J. G. Draguns, W. J. Lonner and J. E. Trimble (eds) *Counseling across Cultures*. London: Sage.

Riesman, D., Glazer, N. and Denny, R. (1950) *The Lonely Crowd*. New Haven, CT: Yale University Press.

Rippere, V. and Williams, R. (eds) (1985) *Wounded Healers: Mental Health Workers' Experiences of Depression*. New York: Wiley.

Roazen, P. (1971) *Freud and His Followers*. New York: Alfred A. Knopf.

Robbins, A. (1988) *Between Therapists: The Processing of Transference/Countertransference Material*. New York: Human Sciences Press.

Robbins, S. P. (1991) *Organizational Behavior*, 3rd edn. Englewood Cliffs, NJ: Prentice Hall.

Roberts, J. and Pines, M. (eds) (1991) *The Practice of Group Analysis*. London: Tavistock/ Routledge.

Robinson, D. (1980) Self-help health groups. In P. B. Smith (ed.) *Small Groups and Personal Change*. London: Methuen.

Robson, D. and Robson, M. (1998) Intimacy and computer communication. *British Journal of Guidance and Counselling*, 26, 33–42.

Rogers, C. R. (1942) *Counseling and Psychotherapy*. Boston: Houghton Mifflin.

Rogers, C. R. (1951) *Client-centered Therapy*. Boston: Houghton Mifflin.

Rogers, C. R. (1957) The necessary and sufficient conditions of therapeutic personality change. *Journal of Consulting Psychology*, 21, 95–103.

Rogers, C. R. (1959) A theory of therapy, personality, and interpersonal relationships, as developed in the client-centered framework. In S. Koch (ed.) *Psychology: A Study of a Science. Volume 3. Formulations of the Person and the Social Context*. New York: McGraw-Hill.

Rogers, C. R. (1961) *On Becoming a Person*. Boston: Houghton Mifflin.

Rogers, C. R. (1963) The concept of the fully functioning person. *Psychotherapy: Theory, Research and Practice*, 1, 17–26.

Rogers, C. R. (1968a) Interpersonal relationships: USA 2000. *Journal of Applied Behavioral Science*, 4, 265–80.

Rogers, C. R. (1968b) Some learnings from a study of psychotherapy with schizophrenics. In C. R. Rogers and B. Stevens (eds) *Person to Person: The Problem of Being Human*. Lafayette, CA: Real People Press.

Rogers, C. R. (1975) Empathic: an unappreciated way of being. *Counseling Psychologist*, 5, 2–10.

Rogers, C. R. (1978) *Carl Rogers on Personal Power: Inner Strength and its Revolutionary Impact*. London: Constable.

Rogers, C. R. (1980) *A Way of Being*. Boston: Houghton Mifflin.

Rogers, C. R. and Dymond, R. F. (eds) (1954) *Psychotherapy and Personality Change*. Chicago: University of Chicago Press.

Rogers, C. R., Gendlin, E. T., Kiesler, D. J. and Truax, C. B. (eds) (1967) *The Therapeutic Relationship and its Impact: A Study of Psychotherapy with Schizophrenics*. Madison: University of Wisconsin Press.

Rogers, C. R. and Stevens, B. (eds) (1968) *Person to Person: The Problem of Being Human*. Lafayette, CA: Real People Press.

Rogler, L. H., Malgady, R. G., Costantino, G. and Blumenthal, R. (1987) What do culturally sensitive mental health services mean? The case of Hispanics. *American Psychologist*, 42, 565–70.

Rokeach, M. (1973) *The Nature of Human Values*. New York: The Free Press.

Rokke, P. D., Carter, A. S., Rehm, L. P. and Veltum, L. G. (1990) Comparative credibility of current treatments for depression. *Psychotherapy*, 27, 235–42.

Rooney, S. C., Flores, L. Y. and Mercier, C. A. (1998) Making multicutural eduction effective for everyone. *Counseling Psychologist*, 26, 22–32.

Rorty, R. (1979) *Philosophy and the Mirror of Nature*. Princeton, NJ: Princeton University Press.

Rosen, G. M. (1987) Self-help treatment books and the commercialization of psychotherapy. *American Psychologist*, 42, 46–51.

Rosen, H. (1993) Developing themes in the filed of cognitive therapy. In K. T. Kuehlwein and H. Rosen (eds) *Cognitive Therapies in Action: Evolving Innovative Practice*. San Francisco: Jossey-Bass.

Rosen, S. (ed.) (1982) *My Voice Will Go with You: The Teaching Tales of Milton H. Erickson*. New York: W. W. Norton.

Rosenbaum, M. (1974) Continuation of psychotherapy by 'long distance' telephone. *International Journal of Psychoanalytic Psychotherapy*, 3, 483–95.

Rosenbaum, M. (ed.) (1982) *Ethics and Values in Psychotherapy: A Guidebook*. New York: Free Press.

Rosenbaum, R. (1994) Single-session therapies: intrinsic integration. *Journal of Psychotherapy Integration*, 4, 229–52.

Rosenfield, M. (1997) *Counselling by Telephone*. London: Sage.

Rosewater, L. B. and Walker, L. E. A. (eds) (1985) *Handbook of Feminist Therapy: Women's Issues in Psychotherapy*. New York: Springer.

Rosnow, R. L. and Rosenthal, R. (1997) *People Studying People: Artifacts and Ethics in Behavioral Research*. New York: W. H. Freeman.

Rossi, E. L. (ed.) (1980) *The Collected Papers of Milton H. Erickson on Hypnosis. Volume 1: The Nature of Hypnosis and Suggestion*. New York: Irvington.

Roth, A. and Fonagy, P. (1996) *What Works for Whom? A Critical Review of Psychotherapy Research*. New York: Guilford Press.

Rothman, D. (1971) *The Discovery of the Asylum: Social Order and Disorder in the New Republic*. Boston: Little Brown.

Rowan, J. (1992a) *The Transpersonal: Psychotherapy and Counselling*. London: Routledge.

Rowan, J. (1992b) *Breakthroughs and Integration in Psychotherapy*. London: Whurr.

Rowan, J. and Dryden, W. (eds) (1988) *Innovative Therapy in Britain*. Milton Keynes: Open University Press.

Rowan, T. and O'Hanlon, B. (1999) *Solution-oriented Therapy for Chronic and Severe Mental Illness*. New York: John Wiley and Sons.

Rowland, N. and Goss, S. (eds) (2000) *Evidence-based Counselling and Psychological Therapies: Research and Applications*. London: Routledge.

Rubino, G., Barker, C., Roth, T. and Fearon, P. (2000) Therapist empathy and depth of interpretation in response to potential alliance ruptures: the role of patient and therapist attachment styles. *Psychotherapy Research*, 10, 408–20.

Russell, J. (1993) *Out of Bounds: Sexual Exploitation in Counselling and Therapy*. London: Sage.

Russell, J. (1996) Feminism and counselling. In R. Bayne, I. Horton and J. Bimrose (eds) *New Directions in Counselling*. London: Routledge.

Russell, R. L. (ed.) (1994) *Reassessing Psychotherapy Research*. New York: Guilford Press.

Russell, R. L. and van den Broek, P. (1992) Changing narrative schemas in psychotherapy. *Psychotherapy*, 29, 344–54.

Russell, R. L., van den Broek, P., Adams, S., Rosenberger, K. and Essig, T. (1993) Analyzing narratives in psychotherapy: a formal framework and empirical analyses. *Journal of Narrative and Life History*, 3(4), 337–60.

Rutter, P. (1989) *Sex in the Forbidden Zone*. London: Mandala.

Rycroft, C. (1966) Causes and meaning. In C. Rycroft (ed.) *Psychoanalysis Observed*. London: Constable.

Rycroft, C. (1985) *Psychoanalysis and Beyond*. London: Chatto and Windus.

Ryden, J. and Loewenthal, D. (2001) Psychotherapy for lesbians: the influence of therapist sexuality. *Counselling and Psychotherapy Research*, 1, 42–52.

Ryle, A. (1978) A common language for the psychotherapies? *British Journal of Psychiatry*, 132, 585–94.

Ryle, A. (1987) Cognitive psychology as a common language for psychotherapy. *Journal of Integrative and Eclectic Psychotherapy*, 6, 191–212.

Ryle, A. (1990) *Cognitive-Analytic Therapy: Active Participation in Change. A New Integration in Brief Psychotherapy*. Chichester: Wiley.

Ryle, A. (ed.) (1995) *Cognitive Analytic Therapy: Developments in Theory and Practice*. Chichester: Wiley.

Ryle, A. and Cowmeadow, P. (1992) Cognitive-analytic therapy (CAT). In W. Dryden (ed.) *Integrative and Eclectic Therapy: A Handbook*. Buckingham: Open University Press.

Ryle, A. and Kerr, I. B. (2002) *Introducing Cognitive Analytic Therapy: Principles and Practice*. Chichester: Wiley.

Sachs, J. (1983) Negative factors in brief psychotherapy: an empirical assessment. *Journal of Consulting and Clinical Psychology*, 51, 557–64.

Safran, J. D. (1993a) The therapeutic alliance rupture as a transtheoretical phenomenon: definitional and conceptual issues. *Journal of Psychotherapy Integration*, 3, 33–49.

Safran, J. D. (1993b) Breaches in the therapeutic alliance: an arena for negotiating authentic relatedness. *Psychotherapy*, 30, 11–24.

Safran, J. D., Crocker, P., McMain, S. and Murray, P. (1990) therapeutic alliance rupture as a therapy event for empirical investigation. *Psychotherapy*, 27, 154–65.

Safran, J. D. and Muran, J. C. (1996) The resolution of ruptures in the therapeutic alliance. *Journal of Consulting and Clinical Psychology*, 64, 447–58.

Safran, J. D. and Muran, J. C. (2000a) *Negotiating the Therapeutic Alliance: A Relational Treatment Guide*. New York: Guilford Press.

Safran, J. D. and Muran, J. C. (2000b) Resolving therapeutic alliance ruptures: diversity and integration. *In Session: Psychotherapy in Practice*, 56, 233–43.

Safran, J. D. and Muran, J. C. (2001) The therapeutic relationship as a process of intersubjective negotiation. In J. C. Muran (ed.) *Self-relations in the Psychotherapy Process*. Washington, DC: American Psychological Association.

Salisbury, W. A. and Kinnier, R. T. (1996) Postermination friendship between counselors and clients. *Journal of Counseling and Development*, 74, 495–500.

Salkovskis, P. M. (ed.) (1996) *Frontiers of Cognitive Therapy*. New York: Guilford Press.

Salmon, P. (1991) Psychotherapy and the wider world. *The Psychologist*, 2, 50–1.

Saltzman, C., Luetgert, M. J., Roth, C. H., Creaser, J. and Howard, L. (1976) Formation of a therapeutic relationship: experiences during the initial phase of psychotherapy as predictors of treatment duration and outcome. *Journal of Consulting and Clinical Psychology*, 44, 546–55.

Saltzman, N. and Norcross, J. C. (eds) (1990) *Therapy Wars: Contention and Convergence in Differing Clinical Approaches*. San Franciso: Jossey-Bass.

Salzer, M. S., Rappaport, J. and Segre, L. (1999) Professional appraisal of self-help groups. *American Journal of Orthopsychiatry*, 69, 536–40.

Sampson, E. E. (1988) The debate on individualism: indigenous psychologies of the individual and their role in personal and social functioning. *American Psychologist*, 43, 15–22.

Sampson, H. and Weiss, J. (1986) Testing hypotheses: the approach of the Mount Zion Psychotherapy Research Group. In L. S. Greenberg and W. M. Pinsof (eds) *The Psychotherapeutic Process: A Research Handbook*. New York: Guilford Press.

Sampson, J. P. Jr, Kolodinsky, R. W. and Greeno, B. P. (1997) Counseling on the information highway: future possibilites and potential problems. *Journal of Counseling and Development*, 74, 203–12.

Sandell, R., Blomberg, J., Lazar, A. *et al.* (2000) Varieties of long-term outcome among patients in psychoanalysis and long-term psychotherapy. A review of findings of the Stockholm Outcome of Psychoanalysis and Psychotherapy Project (STOPPP). *International Journal of Psychoanalysis*, 81, 921–42.

Sanders, D. and Wills, F. (1999) The relationship in cognitive therapy. In C. Feltham (ed.) *Understanding the Counselling Relationship*. London: Sage.

Sanders, D. and Wills, F. (2002) *Counselling for Anxiety Problems*. London: Sage.

Sarbin, T. R. (1986) The narrative as a root metaphor for psychology. In T. R. Sarbin (ed.) *Narrative Psychology: The Storied Nature of Human Conduct*. New York: Praeger.

Sass, L. A. (1988) Humanism, hermeneutics, and the concept of the human subject. In S. B. Messer, L. A. Sass and R. L. Woolfolk (eds) *Hermeneutics and Psychological Theory: Interpretive Perspectives on Personality, Psychotherapy and Psychopathology*. New Brunswick, NJ: Rutgers University Press.

Sass, L. A. (1992) The epic of disbelief: the postmodern turn in contemporary psychoanalysis. In S. Kvale (ed.) *Psychology and Postmodernism*. London: Sage.

Satir, V. (1972) *Peoplemaking*. Palo Alto, CA: Science and Behavior Books.

Sattler, J. M. (1977) The effects of therapist–client racial similarity. In A. S. Gurman and A. M. Razin (eds) *Effective Psychotherapy: A Review of Research*. New York: Pergamon.

Sayers, J. (1991) *Mothering Psychoanalysis: Helene Deutsch, Karen Horney, Anna Freud and Melanie Klein*. Harmondsworth: Penguin.

Scarf, M. (1987) *Intimate Partners*. New York: Century.

Schafer, R. (1992) *Retelling a Life*. New York: Basic Books.

Scheff, T. (1974) The labeling theory of mental illness. *American Sociological Review*, 39, 444–52.

Scher, M., Stevens, M., Good, G. and Eichenfield, G. A. (eds) (1987) *Handbook of Counseling and Psychotherapy with Men*. New York: Sage.

Schiff, J. L., Schiff, A. W. *et al.* (1975) *Cathexis Reader: Transactional Analysis Treatment of Psychosis*. New York: Harper.

Schmid, P. F. (1998) On becoming a *person*-centred approach: a person-centred understanding of the person. In B. Thorne and E. Lambers (eds) *Person-centred Therapy: A European Perspective*. London: Sage.

Schneider, K. J. (1998) Existential processes. In L. S. Greenberg, J. C. Watson and G. Lietaer (eds) *Handbook of Experiential Psychotherapy*. New York: Guilford Press.

Schneider, K. J., Bugental, J. F. T. and Pierson, J. F. (eds) (2001) *The Handbook of Humanistic Psychology: Leading Edges in Theory, Research and Practice*. Thousand Oaks, CA: Sage.

Schneider, K. J. and May, R. (1995) *The Psychology of Existence: An Integrative, Clinical Perspective*. New York: McGraw-Hill.

Schreiber, S. (1995) Migration, traumatic bereavement and transcultural aspects of psychological healing: loss and grief of a refugee woman from Begamer County in Ethiopia. *British Journal of Medical Psychology*, 68, 135–42.

Schuster, S. C. (1999) *Philosophy Practice: An Alternative to Counseling and Psychotherapy*. Westport, CT: Praeger.

Scofield, M. and Yoxheimer, L. (1983) Psychometric issues in the assessment of clinical competencies. *Journal of Counseling Psychology*, 30, 413–20.

Scogin, F., Bynum, J., Stephens, G. and Calhoon, S. (1990) Efficacy of self-administered treatment programmes: meta-analytic review. *Professional Psychology: Research and Practice*, 21, 42–7.

Scott, M. J. (1997) Post-traumatic stress disorder: a cognitive-contextual approach. *Counselling Psychology Quarterly*, 10(2), 125–37.

Scott, M. J. and Stradling, S. G. (1992) *Counselling for Post-traumatic Stress Disorder*. London: Sage.

Scott, M. J., Stradling, S. G. and Dryden, W. (1995) *Developing Cognitive–Behavioural Counselling*. London: Sage.

Scull, A. (1975) From madness to mental illness: medical men as moral entrepreneurs. *European Journal of Sociology*, 16, 218–61.

Scull, A. (1979) *Museums of Madness: The Social Organization of Insanity in Nineteenth Century England*. London: Allen Lane.

Scull, A. (1981a) Moral treatment reconsidered: some sociological comments on an episode in the history of British psychiatry. In A. Scull (ed.) *Mad-houses, Mad-doctors and Madmen*. Philadelphia: University of Pennsylvania Press.

Scull, A. (ed.) (1981b) *Mad-houses, Mad-doctors and Madmen*. Philadelphia: University of Pennsylvania Press.

Scull, A. (1989) *Social Order/Disorder: Anglo-American Psychiatry in Historical Perspective*. London: Routledge.

Scully, R. (1983) The work-settings support group: a means of preventing burnout. In B. A. Farber (ed.) *Stress and Burnout in the Human Service Professions*. New York: Pergamon.

Searles, H. (1975) The patient as therapist to his analyst. In R. C. Givaccini (ed.) *Tactics and Techniques in Psychoanalytic Treatment, Volume II*. New York: Jason Aronson.

Seeman, J. (1949) A study of the process of nondirective therapy. *Journal of Consulting Psychology*, 13, 157–68.

Segal, H. (1964) *Introduction to the Work of Melanie Klein*. London: Hogarth.

Segal, J. (1985) *Phantasy in Everyday Life: A Psychoanalytical Approach to Understanding Ourselves*. Harmondsworth: Penguin.

Segal, J. (1992) *Melanie Klein*. London: Sage.

Segal, J. (1996) Whose disability? Countertransference in work with people with disabilities. *Psychodynamic Counselling*, 2(2), 152–66.

Seligman, M. E. P. (1975) *Helplessness*. San Francisco: Freeman.

Seligman, M. E. P. and Csikszentmihalyi, M. (2000) Positive psychology – an introduction. *American Psychologist*, 55, 5–14.

Sexton, L. (1999) Vicarious traumatisation of counsellors and effects on their workplaces. *British Journal of Guidance and Counselling*, 27, 393–404.

Sexton, T. L. and Griffin, B. L. (eds) (1997) *Constructivist Thinking in Counseling Practice, Research and Training*. New York: Teachers College Press.

Shafranske, E. P. and Malony, H. N. (1990) Clinical psychologists' religious and spiritual orientations and their practice of psychotherapy. *Psychotherapy*, 27, 72–9.

Shapiro, D. A. (1981) Comparative credibility of treatment rationales: three tests of expectancy theory. *British Journal of Clinical Psychology*, 28, 111–22.

Shapiro, D. A., Barkham, M., Rees, A. *et al.* (1994) Effects of treatment duration and severity of depression on the effectiveness of cognitive-behavioral and psychodynamic-interpersonal psychotherapy. *Journal of Consulting and Clinical Psychology*, 62, 522–34.

Sharaf, M. R. and Levinson, D. J. (1964) The quest for omnipotence in professional training. *Psychiatry*, 27, 135–49.

Sharpe, E. F. (1940) Psycho-physical problems revealed in language: an examination of metaphor. *International Journal of Psycho-Analysis*, 21, 21–43.

Shaw, B. and Dobson, K. (1988) Competency judgements in the training and evaluation of psychotherapists. *Journal of Consulting and Clinical Psychology*, 56, 666–72.

Shea, C. and Bond, T. (1997) Ethical issues for counselling in organizations. In M. Carroll and M. Walton (eds) *Handbook of Counselling in Organizations*. London: Sage.

Sheikh, A. A. and Sheikh, K. S. (eds) (1989) *Eastern and Western Approaches to Healing: Ancient Wisdom and Modern Knowledge*. New York: Wiley.

Shepard, M. (1975) *Fritz*. New York: Bantam Books.

Shipton, G. (1999) Self-reflection and the mirror. In C. Mace (ed.) *Heart and Soul: The Therapeutic Face of Philosophy*. London: Routledge.

Shlien, J. (1997) Empathy in psychotherapy. A vital mechanism? Yes. Therapist's conceit? All too often. By itself enough? No. In A. C. Bohart and L. S. Greenberg (eds) *Empathy Reconsidered: New Directions in Psychotherapy*. Washington, DC: American Psychological Association.

Shohet, R. and Wilmot, J. (1991) The key issue in the supervision of counsellors: the supervisory relationship. In W. Dryden and B. Thorne (eds) *Training and Supervision for Counselling in Action*. London: Sage.

Shotter, J. (1975) *Images of Man in Psychological Research*. London: Methuen.

Showalter, E. (1985) *The Female Malady: Women, Madness and English Culture, 1830–1980*. New York: Pantheon Books.

Shweder, R. and LeVine, R. (eds) (1984) *Culture Theory: Essays on Mind, Self and Emotion*. Cambridge: Cambridge University Press.

Sifneos, P. E. (1979) *Short-term Dynamic Psychotherapy*. New York: Plenum.

Silberschatz, G., Fretter, P. B. and Curtis, J. T. (1986) How do interpretations influence the process of psychotherapy? *Journal of Consulting and Clinical Psychology*, 54, 646–52.

Skinner, B. F. (1953) *Science and Human Behavior*. New York: Macmillan.

Skovholt, T. M. and Ronnestad, M. H. (1992) *The Evolving Professional Self: Stages and Themes in Therapist and Counselor Development*. New York: Wiley.

Skynner, R. and Cleese, J. (1983) *Families and How to Survive Them*. London: Methuen.

Slade, A. (1999) Attachment theory and research: implications for the theory and practice of individual psychotherapy with adults. In J. Cassidy and P. R. Shaver (eds) *Handbook of Attachment: Theory, Research and Clinical Applications*. New York: Guilford Press.

Slaikeu, K. A. and Willis, M. A. (1978) Caller feedback on counselor performance in telephone crisis intervention: a follow-up study. *Crisis Intervention*, 9, 42–9.

Sloane, R. B., Staples, F. R., Cristol, A. H., Yorkson, N. J. and Whipple, K. (1975) *Psychotherapy versus Behavior Therapy*. Cambridge, MA: Harvard University Press.

Smail, D. (1978) *Psychotherapy: A Personal Approach*. London: Dent.

Smail, D. (1984) *Illusion and Reality: The Meaning of Anxiety*. London: Dent.

Smail, D. (1991) Towards a radical environmentalist psychology of help. *The Psychologist*, 2, 61–5.

Smith, M., Glass, G. and Miller, T. (1980) *The Benefits of Psychotherapy*. Baltimore: Johns Hopkins University Press.

Snyder, W. U. (1945) An investigation of the nature of non-directive psycho-therapy. *Journal of Genetic Psychology*, 13, 193–223.

Sollod, R. N. (1978) Carl Rogers and the origins of client-centered therapy. *Professional Psychology*, 9, 93–104.

Sollod, R. N. (1982) Non-scientific sources of psychotherapeutic approaches. In P. W. Sharkey (ed.) *Philosophy, Religion and Psychotherapy: Essays in the Philosophical Foundations of Psychotherapy*. Washington, DC: University Press of America.

Sollod, R. N. (1993) Integrating spiritual healing approaches and techniques into psycho-therapy. In G. Stricker and J. R. Gold (eds) *Comprehensive Handbook of Psychotherapy Integration*. New York: Plenum.

Solomon, R. C. (1988) *Continental Philosophy since 1750: The Rise and Fall of the Self*. Oxford: Oxford University Press.

Southgate, J. and Randall, R. (1978) *The Barefoot Psychoanalyst: An Illustrated Manual of Self-help Therapy*. London: Association of Karen Horney Psychoanalytic Counsellors.

Southwell, C. (1988) The Gerda Boyson method: biodynamic therapy. In J. Rowan and W. Dryden (eds) *Innovative Therapy in Britain*. Milton Keynes: Open University Press.

Spanos, I. (1978) Witchcraft in histories of psychiatry: a critical analysis and alternative conceptualisation. *Psychological Bulletin*, 85, 417–39.

Speedy, J. (2000) The 'storied' helper: narrative ideas and practices in counselling and psychotherapy. *European Journal of Psychotherapy, Counselling and Health*, 3, 361–74.

Spence, D. P. (1982) *Narrative Truth and Historical Truth: Meaning and Interpretation in Psycho-analysis*. New York: Norton.

Spence, D. P. (1994) Narrative truth and putative child abuse. *International Journal of Clinical and Experimental Hypnosis*, 42, 289–303.

Spinelli, E. (1989) *The Interpreted World: An Introduction to Phenomenological Psychology*. London: Sage.

Spinelli, E. (1994) *Demystifying Therapy*. London: Constable.

Spinelli, E. (1996) The existential-phenomenological paradigm. In R. Woolfe and W. Dryden (eds) *Handbook of Counselling Psychology*. London: Sage.

Spinelli, E. (1997) *Tales of Unknowing: Therapeutic Encounters from an Existential Perspective*. London: Duckworth.

Spurling, L. and Dryden, W. (1989) The self and the therapeutic domain. In W. Dryden and L. Spurling (eds) *On Becoming a Psychotherapist*. London: Tavistock/Routledge.

Stadler, H. A. (1986) Making hard choices: clarifying controversial ethical issues. *Counseling and Human Development*, 19, 1–10.

Stanion, P., Papadopoulos, L. and Bor, R. (1997) Genograms in counselling practice: constructing a genogram (part 2). *Counselling Psychology Quarterly*, 10(2), 139–48.

Starker, S. (1988) Do-it-yourself therapy: the prescription of self-help books by psycholo-gists. *Psychotherapy*, 25, 142–6.

Steenberger, B. N. (1992) Toward science–practice integration in brief counseling and therapy. *Counseling Psychologist*, 20, 403–50.

Stein, D. M. and Lambert, M. J. (1984) Telephone counseling and crisis intervention: a review. *American Journal of Community Psychology*, 12, 101–26.

Stein, D. M. and Lambert, M. J. (1995) Graduate training in psychotherapy: are therapy outcomes enhanced? *Journal of Consulting and Clinical Psychology*, 63, 182–96.

Steiner, C. (1970) *Games Alcoholics Play*. New York: Grove Press.

Steiner, C. (1971) *Scripts People Live*. New York: Grove Press.

Stern, E. M. (ed.) (1985) *Psychotherapy and the Religiously Committed Patient*. New York: Haworth.

Stevenson, J. F. and Norcross, J. C. (1987) Current status of training evaluation in clinical psychology. In B. A. Edelstein and E. S. Berler (eds) *Evaluation and Accountability in Clinical Training*. New York: Plenum Press.

Stiles, W. B. (1991) Longtitudinal study of assimilation in exploratory psychotherapy. *Psychotherapy*, 28, 195–206.

Stiles, W. B. (2001) Assimilation of problematic experiences. *Psychotherapy: Theory, Research, Practice and Training*, 38, 462–5.

Stiles, W. B. (2002) Assimilation of problematic experiences. In J. C. Norcross (ed.) *Psychotherapy Relationships that Work*. New York: Oxford University Press.

Stiles, W. B., Elliott, R., Llewelyn, S. P. *et al.* (1990) Assimilation of problematic experiences in psychotherapy. *Psychotherapy*, 27, 411–20.

Stiles, W. B., Meshot, C. M., Anderson, T. M. and Sloan, W. W. (1992) Assimilation of problematic experiences: the case of JohnJones. *Psychotherapy Research*, 2, 81–101.

Stiles, W. B. and Shapiro, D. A. (1989) Abuse of the drug metaphor in psychotherapy process-outcome research. *Clinical Psychology Review*, 9, 521–43.

Stiver, I. P. (1991a) The meaning of care: reframing treatment models. In J. V. Jordan, A. G. Kaplan, J. B. Miller, I. P. Stiver and J. L. Surrey (eds) *Women's Growth in Connection: Writings from the Stone Center*. New York: Guilford Press.

Stiver, I. P. (1991b) The meanings of 'dependency' in female–male relationships. In J. V. Jordan, A. G. Kaplan, J. B. Miller, I. P. Stiver and J. L. Surrey (eds) *Women's Growth in Connection: Writings from the Stone Center*. New York: Guilford Press.

Stiver, I. P. and Miller, J. B. (1997) From depression to sadness in women's psychotherapy. In J. V. Jordan (ed.) *Women's Growth in Diversity: More Writings from the Stone Center*. New York: Guilford Press.

Stock, W. (1988) Propping up the phallocracy: a feminist critique of sex therapy and research. In E. Cole and E. D. Rothblum (eds) *Women and Sex Therapy: Closing the Circle of Sexual Knowledge*. New York: Harrington Park Press.

Stoltenberg, C. D. and Delworth, U. (1987) *Supervising Counselors and Therapists*. San Francisco: Jossey-Bass.

Strasser, F. and Strasser, A. (1997) *Time Limited Existential Therapy: the Wheel of Existence*. Chichester: Wiley.

Strean, H. S. (1993) *Therapists Who Have Sex with Their Patients: Treatment and Recovery*. New York: Brunner and Mazel.

Street, E. and Dryden, W. (eds) (1988) *Family Therapy in Britain*. Milton Keynes: Open University Press.

Stricker, G. and Gold, J. R. (eds) (1993) *Comprehensive Handbook of Psychotherapy Integration*. New York: Plenum.

Strupp, H. H. (1969) Toward a specification of teaching and learning in psychotherapy. *Archives of General Psychiatry*, 21, 203–12.

Strupp, H. H. (1972) On the technology of psychotherapy. *Archives of General Psychiatry*, 26, 270–8.

Strupp, H. H. (1978) The therapist's theoretical orientation: an overrated variable. *Psychotherapy*, 15, 314–17.

Strupp, H. H. (1980a) Success and failure in time-limited psychotherapy. A systematic comparison of two cases: comparison 1. *Archives of General Psychiatry*, 37, 595–603.

Strupp, H. H. (1980b) Success and failure in time-limited psychotherapy. A systematic comparison of two cases: comparison 2. *Archives of General Psychiatry*, 37, 708–16.

Strupp, H. H. (1980c) Success and failure in time-limited therapy: with special reference to the performance of the lay counselor. *Archives of General Psychiatry*, 37, 831–41.

Strupp, H. H. (1980d) Success and failure in time-limited psychotherapy. Further evidence: comparison 4. *Archives of General Psychiatry*, 37, 947–54.

Strupp, H. H. (1986) The nonspecific hypothesis of therapeutic effectiveness: a current assessment. *American Journal of Orthopsychiatry*, 56, 513–20.

Strupp, H. H. and Binder, J. L. (1984) *Psychotherapy in a New Key: A Guide to Time-limited Dynamic Psychotherapy*. New York: Basic Books.

Strupp, H. H. and Hadley, S. W. (1979) Specific vs nonspecific factors in psychotherapy: a controlled study of outcome. *Archives of General Psychiatry*, 36, 1125–36.

Stuhr, U. and Wachholz, S. (2001) In search for a psychoanalytic research strategy: the concept of ideal types. In J. Frommer and D. Rennie (eds) *Qualitative Psychotherapy Research: Methods and Methodology*. Lengerich: Pabst.

Sue, D. W. (1981) *Counseling the Culturally Different: Theory and Practice*. London: Wiley.

Sue, D. W., Aredondo, P. and McDavis, R. J. (1992) Multicultural counseling competencies and standards: a call to the profession. *Journal of Counseling and Development*, 70, 477–86.

Sue, D. W. and Sue, D. (1990) *Counseling the Culturally Different*, 2nd edn. Chichester: Wiley.

Sue, D. and Sundberg, N. D. (1996) Research and research hypotheses about effectiveness in intercultural counseling. In P. B. Pedersen, J. G. Draguns, W. J. Lonner and J. E. Trimble (eds) *Counseling across Cultures*. London: Sage.

Sue, S., Fujino, D. C., Hu, L., Takenchi, D. T. and Zane, N. W. (1991) Community mental health services for ethnic minority groups: a test of the cultural responsiveness hypothesis. *Journal of Consulting and Clinical Psychology*, 59, 533–40.

Sue, S. and Zane, N. (1987) The role of culture and cultural techniques in psychotherapy: a critique and reformulation. *American Psychologist*, 42, 37–45.

Sugarman, L. (1992) Ethical issues in counselling at work. *British Journal of Guidance and Counselling*, 20, 64–74.

Sussman, M. (1992) *A Curious Calling: Unconscious Motivation for Practicing Psychotherapy*. New York: Jason Aronson.

Sutich, A. J. (1986) Transpersonal psychotherapy: history and definition. In S. Boorstein (ed.) *Transpersonal Psychotherapy*. Palo Alto, CA: Science and Behavior Books.

Suzuki, D. T., Fromm, E. and de Martino, R. (eds) (1970) *Zen Buddhism and Psychoanalysis*. New York: Harper and Row.

Symington, N. (1983) The analyst's act of freedom as an agent of therapeutic change. *International Review of Psycho-Analysis*, 10, 83–91.

Szasz, T. S. (1961) *The Myth of Mental Illness*. New York: Hoeber-Harper.

Szasz, T. S. (1971) *The Manufacture of Madness: A Comparative Study of the Inquisition and the Mental Health Movement*. London: Routledge and Kegan Paul.

Szasz, T. S. (1974) *The Ethics of Psycho-Analysis: The Theory and Method of Autonomous Psychotherapy*. London: Routledge and Kegan Paul.

Szasz, T. S. (1978) *The Myth of Psychotherapy*. Oxford: Oxford University Press.

Tang, T. Z. and DeRubeis, R. J. (1999) Sudden gains and critical sessions in cognitive–behavioural therapy for depression. *Journal of Consulting and Clinical Psychology*, 67, 894–904.

Tatar, M. (1998) Counselling immigrants: school contexts and emerging strategies. *British Journal of Guidance and Counselling*, 26, 337–52.

Tausch, R. (1990) The supplementation of client-centered communication therapy with other valid therapeutic methods: a client-centered necessity. In G. Lietaer, J. Rombauts and R. van Balen (eds) *Client-centered and Experiential Therapy in the Nineties*. Leuven: Leuven University Press.

Taylor, C. (1989) *Sources of the Self: The Making of Modern Identity*. Cambridge: Cambridge University Press.

Taylor, M. (1990) Fantasy or reality? The problem with psychoanalytic interpretation in psychotherapy with women. In E. Burman (ed.) *Feminists on Psychological Practice*. London: Sage.

Taylor, M. (1991) How psychoanalytic thinking lost its way in the hands of men: the case for feminist psychotherapy. *British Journal of Guidance and Counselling*, 19, 93–103.

Taylor, M. (1995) Feminist psychotherapy. In M. Walker (ed.) *Peta: A Feminist's Problems with Men*. Buckingham: Open University Press.

Taylor, M. (1996) The feminist paradigm. In R. Woolfe and W. Dryden (eds) *Handbook of Counselling Psychology*. London: Sage.

Taylor, V. (1983) The future of feminism in the 1980s: a social movement analysis. In L. Richardson and V. Taylor (eds) *Feminist Frontiers: Rethinking Sex, Gender and Society*. Reading, MA: Addison-Wesley.

Thomas, M. (1999) Seventeen syllables for the self. In C. Mace (ed.) *Heart and Soul: The Therapeutic Face of Philosophy*. London: Routledge.

Thompson, C. E. and Jenal, S. T. (1994) Interracial and intraracial quasi-counseling interactions: when counselors avoid discussing race. *Journal of Counseling Psychology*, 41(4), 484–91.

Thompson, C. E. and Neville, H. A. (1999) Racism, mental health, and mental health practice. *Counselling Psychologist*, 27, 155–223.

Thoresen, C. and Mahoney, M. (1974) *Behavioral Self-control*. New York: Holt, Rinehart and Winston.

Thorne, B. (1985) Interview with Brian Thorne. In W. Dryden (ed.) *Therapists' Dilemmas*. London: Harper and Row.

Thorne, B. (1987) Beyond the core conditions. In W. Dryden (ed.) *Key Cases in Psychotherapy*. London: Croom Helm.

Thorne, B. (1991) *Person-centred Counselling: Therapeutic and Spiritual Dimensions*. London: Whurr.

Thorne, B. (1992) *Carl Rogers*. London: Sage.

Thorne, B. and Dryden, W. (1991) Key issues in the training of counsellors. In W. Dryden and B. Thorne (eds) *Training and Supervision for Counselling in Action*. London: Sage.

Thorne, B. and Dryden, W. (eds) (1993) *Counselling: Interdisciplinary Perspectives*. Buckingham: Open University Press.

Tiefer, L. (1988) A feminist critique of the sexual dysfunction nomenclature. In E. Cole and E. D. Rothblum (eds) *Women and Sex Therapy: Closing the Circle of Sexual Knowledge*. New York: Harrington Park Press.

Timms, N. and Blampied, A. (1985) *Intervention in Marriage: The Experience of Counsellors and Their Clients*. Sheffield: University of Sheffield Joint Unit for Social Services Research.

Tolley, K. and Rowland, N. (1995) *Evaluating the Cost-effectiveness of Counselling in Health Care*. London: Routledge.

Tolman, E. C. (1948) Cognitive maps in rats and men. *Psychological Review*, 55, 189–208.

Tolor, A. and Reznikoff, M. (1960) A new approach to insight: a primary report. *Journal of Nervous and Mental Disease*, 130, 286–96.

Toukmanian, S., Capelle, R. and Rennie, D. (1978) Counsellor trainee awareness of evaluative criteria: a neglected variable. *Canadian Counselor*, 12, 177–83.

Toukmanian, S. and Rennie, D. (eds) (1992) *Psychotherapy Process Research: Paradigmatic and Narrative Approaches*. London: Sage.

Towbin, A. P. (1978) The confiding relationship: a new paradigm. *Psychotherapy*, 15, 333–43.

Trower, P., Bryant, M. and Argyle, M. (1978) *Social Skills and Mental Health*. London: Tavistock.

Truax, C. B. (1966) Reinforcement and nonreinforcement in Rogerian psychotherapy. *Journal of Abnormal Psychology*, 71, 1–9.

Truax, C. B. and Carkhuff, R. R. (1967) *Toward Effective Counseling and Psychotherapy*. Chicago: Aldine.

Tryon, G. S. (1995) Issues to consider when instituting time limitations on individual counseling services. *Professional Psychology: Research and Practice*, 26, 620–3.

Tseng, W.-S. (1999) Culture and psychotherapy: review and practical guidelines. *Transcultural Psychiatry*, 36, 131–79.

Tuckwell, G. (2001) 'The threat of the Other': using mixed quantitative and qualitative methods to elucidate racial and cultural dynamics in the counselling process. *Counselling and Psychotherapy Research*, 1, 154–62.

Tudor, K. (1998) Value for money? Issues of fees in counselling and psychotherapy. *British Journal of Guidance and Counselling*, 26, 477–94.

Tune, D. (2001) Is touch a valid therapeutic intervention? Early returns from a qualitative study of therapists' views. *Counselling and Psychotherapy Research*, 1, 167–71.

Turner, P. R., Valtierra, M., Talken, T. R., Miller, V. I. and DeAnda, J. R. (1996) Effect of session length on treatment outcome for college students in brief therapy. *Journal of Counseling Psychology*, 43, 228–32.

Tyler, J. and Weaver, S. (1981) Evaluating the clinical supervisee: a survey of practice in graduate training programmes. *Professional Psychology*, 12, 434–7.

Tyndall, N. (1985) The work and impact of the National Marriage Guidance Council. In W. Dryden (ed.) *Marital Therapy in Britain, Volume 1*. London: Harper and Row.

Tyrrell, C. L., Dozier, M., Teague, G. B. and Fallot, R. D. (1999) Effective treatment relationshops for persons with serious psychiatric disorders: the importance of attachment states of mind. *Journal of Consulting and Clinical Psychology*, 67, 725–33.

Ussher, J. and Nicolson, P. (1992) *Gender Issues in Clinical Psychology*. London: Routledge.

Valle, R. S. and King, M. (eds) (1978) *Existential-phenomenological Alternatives for Psychology*. New York: Oxford University Press.

Vanaerschot, G. (1990) The process of empathy: holding and letting go. In G. Lietaer, J. Rombauts and R. van Balen (eds) *Client-centred and Experiential Psychotherapy in the Nineties*. Leuven: University of Leuven Press.

Vanaerschot, G. (1993) Empathy as releasing several micro-processes in the client. In D. Brazier (ed.) *Beyond Carl Rogers*. London: Constable.

van Balen, R. (1990) The therapeutic relationship according to Carl Rogers: only a climate? a dialogue? or both? In G. Lietaer, J. Rombauts and R. van Balen (eds) *Client-centered and Experiential Therapy in the Nineties*. Leuven: Leuven University Press.

van Belle, H. A. (1990) Rogers' later move toward mysticism: implications for client-centered therapy. In G. Lietaer, J. Rombauts and R. van Balen (eds) *Client-centered and Experiential Therapy in the Nineties*. Leuven: Leuven University Press.

van de Riet, V., Korb, M. P. and Gorrell, J. J. (1980) *Gestalt Therapy: An Introduction*. New York: Pergamon.

van der Veer, G. (1992) *Counseling and Therapy with Refugees*. New York: Wiley.

van Deurzen, E. (1999) Existentialism and existential psychotherapy. In C. Mace (ed.) *Heart and Soul: The Therapeutic Face of Philosophy*. London: Routledge.

van Deurzen-Smith, E. (1988) *Existential Counselling in Practice*. London: Sage.

van Deurzen-Smith, E. (1990) Existential therapy. In W. Dryden (ed.) *Individual Therapy: A Handbook*. Buckingham: Open University Press.

van Deurzen-Smith E. (1996) *Everyday Mysteries: Existential Dimensions of Psychotherapy*. London: Routledge.

van Deurzen-Smith, E. (1999) Existentialism and existential psychotherapy. In C. Mace (ed.) *Heart and Soul: The Therapeutic Face of Philosophy*. London: Routledge.

van Deurzen-Smith, E. (2001) *Existential Counselling and Psychotherapy in Practice*, 2nd edn. London: Sage.

van Hoose, W. H. and Kottler, J. A. (1985) *Ethical and Legal Issues in Counseling and Psychotherapy*, 2nd edn. San Francisco: Jossey-Bass.

van Werde, D. (1994) An introduction to client-centred pre-therapy. In D. Mearns (ed.) *Developing Person-centred counselling*. London: Sage.

Vassiliou, G. and Vassiliou, V. G. (1973) Subjective culture and psychotherapy. *American Journal of Psychotherapy*, 27, 42–51.

Viens, M. J. and Hranchuk, K. (1992) The treatment of bulimia nervose following surgery using a stimulus control procedure: a case study. *Journal of Behaviour Therapy and Experimental Psychiatry*, 23, 313–17.

von Wyl, A. (2000) What anorexic and bulimic patients have to tell: the analysis of patterns of unconscious conflict expressed in stories about everyday events. *European Journal of Psychotherapy, Counselling and Health*, 3, 375–88.

Wachholz, S. and Stuhr, U. (1999) The concept of ideal types in psychoanalytic follow-up research. *Psychotherapy Research*, 9, 327–41.

Wade, P. and Bernstein, B. L. (1991) Cultural sensitivity training and counselors' race: effects on black female clients' perceptions and attrition. *Journal of Counseling Psychology*, 38, 9–15.

Waitman, A. and Conboy-Hill, S. (eds) (1992) *Psychotherapy and Mental Handicap*. London: Sage.

Walker, M. (ed.) (1995) *Morag – Myself or Mother Hen*. Buckingham: Open University Press.

Walker, M. (ed.) (1996) *Peta – A Feminist's Problem with Men*. Buckingham: Open University Press.

Wallace, A. F. C. (1958) Dreams and the wishes of the soul: a type of psychoanalytic theory among the seventeenth century Iroquois. *American Anthropologist*, 60, 234–48.

Waller, D. and Gilroy, A. (eds) (1992) *Art Therapy: A Handbook*. Buckingham: Open University Press.

Wallerstein, R. S. (1989) The psychotherapy research project of the Menninger Foundation: an overview. *Journal of Consulting and Cinical Psychology*, 57, 195–205.

Walls, G. B. (1980) Values and psychotherapy: a comment on 'Psychotherapy and Religious Values'. *Journal of Consulting and Clinical Psychology*, 48, 640–2.

Walter, T. (1996) A new model of grief: bereavement and biography. *Mortality*, 1, 7–25.

Wanigaratne, S. and Barker, C. (1995) Clients' preferences for styles of therapy. *British Journal of Clinical Psychology*, 34, 215–22.

Wanigaratne, S., Wallace, W., Pullin, J., Keaney, F. and Farmer, R. (1990) *Relapse Prevention for Addictive Behaviours: A Manual for Therapists*. Oxford: Blackwell.

Wapner, J. H., Klein, J. G., Friedlander, M. L. and Andrasik, F. J. (1986) Transferring psychotherapy clients: state of the art. *Professional Psychology: Research and Practice*, 17, 492–6.

Ward, C. A. (ed.) (1989) *Altered States of Consciousness and Mental Health: A Cross-cultural Perspective*. London: Sage.

Ward, D. E. (1984) Termination of individual counseling: concepts and strategies. *Journal of Counseling and Development*, 63, 21–5.

Ward, D. (1993) Empowerment and oppression. In J. Walmsley *et al.* (eds) *Health, Welfare and Practice: Reflecting on Roles and Relationships*. London: Sage.

Warnath, C. F. and Shelton, J. L. (1976) The ultimate disappointment: the burned-out counselor. *Personnel and Guidance Journal*, 55, 172–5.

Warner, M. S. (1998) A client-centered approach to therapeutic work with dissociated and fragile process. In L. S. Greenberg, J. C. Watson and G. Lietaer (eds) *Handbook of Experiential Psychotherapy*. New York: Guilford Press.

Waterhouse, R. (1993) 'Wild women don't have the blues': a feminist critique of 'person-centred' counselling and therapy. *Feminism and Psychology*, 3(1), 55–71.

Watkins, C. E. Jr and Campbell, V. L. (1990) *Testing in Counseling Practice.* Hillsdale, NJ: Lawrence Erlbaum.

Watkins, C. E. Jr and Schneider, L. J. (eds) (1991) *Research in Counseling.* Hillsdale, NJ: Lawrence Erlbaum.

Watson, G. (1940) Areas of agreement in psychotherapy. *American Journal of Orthopsychiatry,* 10, 698–709.

Watson, J. B. (1919) *Psychology from the Standpoint of a Behaviorist.* Philadelphia: J. B. Lippincott.

Watson, J. C., Goldman, R. and Vanaershcot, G. (1998a) Empathic: a postmodern way of being? In L. S. Greenberg, J. C. Watson and G. Lietaer (eds) *Handbook of Experiential Psychotherapy.* New York: Guilford Press.

Watson, J. C., Greenberg, L. S. and Lietaer, G. (1998b) The experiential paradigm unfolding: relationship and experiencing in therapy. In L. S. Greenberg, J. C. Watson and G. Lietaer (eds) *Handbook of Experiential Psychotherapy.* New York: Guilford Press.

Watson, N. (1984) The empirical status of Rogers's hypotheses of the necessary and sufficient conditions for effective psychotherapy. In R. F. Levant and J. M. Shlien (eds) *Client-centered Therapy and the Person-centered Approach: New Directions in Theory, Research and Practice.* New York: Praeger.

Watts, R. E. (1998) The remarkable parallel between Rogers' core conditions and Adler's social interest. *Journal of Individual Psychology,* 54, 4–9.

Webb, A. (2000) What makes it difficult for the supervisee to speak? In B. Lawton and C. Feltham (eds) *Taking Supervision Forward: Enquiries and Trends in Counselling and Psychotherapy.* London: Sage.

West, W. (1997) Integrating counselling, psychotherapy and healing: an inquiry into counsellors and psychotherapists whose work includes healing. *British Journal of Guidance and Counselling,* 25(3), 291–312.

Wexler, D. A. and Rice, L. N. (eds) (1974) *Innovations in Client-centered Therapy.* New York: Wiley.

Wexler, D. B. (1990) *Therapeutic Jurisprudence: The Law as Therapeutic Agent.* Durham, NC: Carolina Academic Press.

Wheeler, G. (1991) *Gestalt Reconsidered.* New York: Gardner Press.

Wheeler, S. (1996) *Training Counsellors: The Assessment of Competence.* London: Cassell.

Whiston, S. C. (2000) *Principles and Applications of Assessment in Counseling.* Belmont, CA: Brooks/Cole.

Whitaker, D. (1985) *Using Groups to Help People.* London: Tavistock/Routledge.

White, M. (1992) Deconstruction and therapy. In D. Epston and M. White (eds) *Experience, Contradiction, Narrative and Imagination.* Adelaide: Dulwich Centre Publications.

White, M. and Epston, D. (1990) *Narrative Means to Therapeutic Ends.* New York: Norton.

Whiteley, J. M. (1984) A historical perspective on the development of counseling psychology as a profession. In S. D. Brown and R. W. Lent (eds) *Handbook of Counseling Psychology.* New York: Wiley.

Whiteley, J. M., Sprinthall, N. A., Mosher, R. L. and Donaghy, R. T. (1967) Selection and evaluation of counselor effectiveness. *Journal of Counseling Psychology,* 14, 226–34.

Whitfield, G. (1988) Bioenergetics. In J. Rowan and W. Dryden (eds) *Innovative Therapy in Britain.* Milton Keynes: Open University Press.

Whitman, R. and Stock, D. (1958) The group focal conflict. *Psychiatry,* 21, 267–76.

Wigrem, J. (1994) Narrative completion in the treatment of trauma. *Psychotherapy,* 31, 415–23.

Wilbert, J. R. and Fulero, S. M. (1988) Impact of malpractice litigation on professional psychology: survey of practitioners. *Professional Psychology: Research and Practice,* 19(4), 379–82.

Wilkins, P. (1997) *Personal and Professional Development for Counsellors*. London: Sage.

Wilkinson, S. (ed.) (1996) *Feminist Social Psychologies: International Perspectives*. Buckingham: Open University Press.

Willi, J. (1999) *Ecological Psychotherapy: Developing by Shaping the Personal Niche*. Seattle: Hogrefe and Huber.

Willi, J., Frei, R. and Gunther, E. (2000) Psychotherapy of panic syndrome: focusing on ecological aspects of relationships. *American Journal of Psychotherapy*, 54, 226–42.

Williams, J. M. G. (1996) Memory processes in psychotherapy. In P. M. Salkovskis (ed.) *Frontiers of Cognitive Therapy*. New York: Guilford Press.

Wills, T. A. (1982) Nonspecific factors in helping relationships. In T. A. Wills (ed.) *Basic Processes in Helping Relationships*. New York: Academic Press.

Winnicott, D. W. (1958) *Collected Papers: Through Paediatrics to Psychoanalysis*. London: Hogarth.

Winnicott, D. W. (1964) *The Child, the Family and the Outside World*. Harmondsworth: Penguin.

Winnicott, D. W. (1965) *The Maturational Process and the Facilitating Environment*. London: Hogarth.

Winnicott, D. W. (1971) *Playing and Reality*. London: Hogarth.

Wise, E. A. (1988) Issues in psychotherapy with EAP clients. *Psychotherapy*, 25, 415–19.

Wittmer, J. and Lister, J. L. (1971) The Graduate Record Examination, 16PF questionnaire, and counseling effectiveness. *Counselor Education and Supervision*, 10, 293.

Wollheim, R. (1971) *Freud*. London: Fontana.

Wolpe, J. (1958) *Psychotherapy by Reciprocal Inhibition*. Stanford, CA: Stanford University Press.

Wolpe, J. (1978) Cognition and causation in human behavior and its therapy. *American Psychologist*, 33, 437–6.

Wood, E. C. and Wood, C. D. (1990) Referral issues in psychotherapy and psychoanalysis. *American Journal of Psychotherapy*, 44, 85–94.

Woods, K. M. and McNamara, J. R. (1980) Confidentiality: its effect on interviewee behavior. *Professional Psychology*, 11, 714–21.

Woody, R. H. (1989) *Business Success in Mental Health Practice: Modern Marketing, Management and Legal Strategies*. San Francisco: Jossey-Bass.

Wooley, S. C. (1994) The female therapist as outlaw. In P. Fallon, M. A. Katzman and S. C. Wooley (eds) *Feminist Perspectives on Eating Disorders*. New York: Guilford Press.

Woolfe, R. (1983) Counselling in a world of crisis: towards a sociology of counselling. *International Journal for the Advancement of Counselling*, 6, 167–76.

Woolfe, R., Strawbridge, S. and Dryden, W. (eds) (2002) *Handbook of Counselling Psychology*, 2nd edn. London: Sage.

Worell, J. (1981) New directions in counseling women. In E. Howell and M. Bayes (eds) *Women and Mental Health*. New York: Basic Books.

Worell, J. and Remer, P. (1992) *Feminist Perspectives in Therapy: An Empowerment Model for Women*. New York: Wiley.

Wosket, V. (1999) *The Therapeutic Use of Self: Counselling Practice, Research and Supervision*. London. Routledge.

Wyatt, G. (ed.) (2001) *Rogers' Therapeutic Conditions: Evolution, Theory and Practice. Volume 1: Congruence*. Ross-on-Wye: PCCS Books.

Wyrostok, N. (1995) The ritual as a psychotherapeutic intervention. *Psychotherapy*, 32, 397–404.

Yalom, I. D. (1975) *Theory and Practice of Group Psychotherapy*. New York: Basic Books.

Yalom, I. D. (1980) *Existential Psychotherapy*. New York: Basic Books.

Yalom, I. D. (1986) *Theory and Practice of Group Psychotherapy*, 3rd edn. New York: Basic Books.

Yalom, I. D. (1989) *Love's Executioner and Other Tales of Psychotherapy*. Harmondsworth: Penguin.

Yontef, G. M. (1995) Gestalt therapy. In A. S. Gurman and S. B. Messer (eds) *Essential Psychotherapies: Theory and Practice*. New York: Guilford Press.

Yontef, G. M. (1998) Dialogic Gestalt therapy. In L. S. Greenberg, J. C. Watson and G. Lietaer (eds) *Handbook of Experiential Psychotherapy*. New York: Guilford Press.

Yontef, G. M. and Simkin, J. S. (1989) Gestalt therapy. In R. J. Corsini and D. Wedding (eds) *Current Psychotherapies*, 4th edn. Itasca, IL: F. E. Peacock.

Young, H. S. (1988) Practising RET with Bible-Belt Christians. In W. Dryden and P. Trower (eds) *Developments in Rational-Emotive Therapy*. Milton Keynes: Open University Press.

Young, R. (1989) Helpful behaviors in the crisis center call. *Journal of Community Psychology*, 17, 70–7.

Young-Eisendrath, P. and Widermann, F. (1987) *Female Authority: Empowering Women through Psychotherapy*. New York: Guilford Press.

Zajonc, R. (1980) Feeling and thinking: preferences need no inferences. *American Psychologist*, 35, 151–75.

Zhu, S.-H. and Pierce, J. P. (1995) A new scheduling method for time-limited counseling. *Professional Psychology: Research and Practice*, 26, 624–5.

Zhu, S.-H., Tedeschi, G. J., Anderson, C. M. and Pierce, J. P. (1996) Telephone counseling for smoking cessation: what's in a call? *Journal of Counseling and Development*, 75, 93–102.

Zimmerman, M. A. (1995) Psychological empowerment: issues and illustrations. *American Journal of Community Psychology*, 23, 581–99.

Index

THE COUNSELLOR'S WORKBOOK
DEVELOPING A PERSONAL APPROACH

John McLeod

> This book provides a series of reflective learning tasks, linked to the best-selling Open University Press textbook, *An Introduction to Counselling*. It provides learning resources to support counsellors through key stages in training: building on life experience, engaging with theories and concepts, reflecting on cases, learning from critical issues in practice, and developing a professional identity. *The Counsellor's Workbook* draws upon narrative perspectives, in encouraging participants to construct a rich account of their counselling competencies, concepts, values and personal qualities. Learning tasks are cross-referenced to pages in *An Introduction to Counselling*, and other key sources.

The Counsellor's Workbook contributes to the process of becoming an effective counsellor by:

- Deepening and consolidating personal learning and development
- Facilitating the integration of theory, practice and personal experience
- Providing arenas for collaborative dialogue and exploration with fellow trainees

The Counsellor's Workbook is an invaluable resource for counselling students, tutors and trainers, and for experienced practitioners engaging in continuing professional development. It promotes an integrative approach to counselling, which emphasises the core relational and personal dimensions of all therapeutic work.

Contents:

Acknowledgements – How to use the workbook – Building on life experience: the foundations of a personal approach – Making sense: constructing a framework for understanding – Putting theory to use: thinking about cases – Reflecting on practice: challenges to therapeutic relationship – Developing a professional identity: putting it all together – Notes for tutors – Internet resources and further reading – References – Index.

(September 2004) c.200pp   0 335 21552 1 (Paperback) c. £22.99